Health Care Politics and Policy in America

Health Care Politics and Policy in America

THIRD EDITION

Kant Patel and Mark Rushefsky

M.E.Sharpe
Armonk, New York
London, England

To Kahlua
—K.P.

To my granddaughter Echo Nicol, the light of my life.
—M.E.R.

Library of Congress Cataloging-in-Publication Data

Patel, Kant, 1946–
    Health care politics and policy in America / Kant Patel and Mark Rushefsky.—3rd ed.
        p. cm.
    Includes bibliographical references and index.
    ISBN 0-7656-1478-2 (cloth : alk. paper) — ISBN 0-7656-1479-0 (pbk. : alk. paper)
      1. Medical policy—United States. 2. Medical care—Political aspects—United States.
    [DNLM: 1. Health Policy—United States. 2. Politics—United States. WA 540 AA1 P29h 2006]
    I. Rushefsky, Mark E., 1945– II. Title.

RA395.A3P285 2006
362.1′0973—dc22   2005024497

Politics is how society manages conflicts about values and interests. . . .
And no issues trigger battles over values and interests more quickly and
acutely than do the source and use of money in health reform proposals.
　　　　　　　　　　　　　　　　　　　　　—Lawrence D. Brown

Contents

List of Tables and Figures

Tables

Figures

Preface

We are gratified by the reception *Health Care Politics and Policy in America* has received. It has been well reviewed, it has sold well, and it has been adopted by many colleges and universities. The first edition was the first joint research project between Patel and Rushefsky. Since that time we have published several books on health care with M.E. Sharpe: *Politics, Power, and Policy Making: The Case of Health Care Reform in the 1990s*; *Health Care Policy in an Age of New Technologies*; and *The Politics of Public Health in the United States*. Patel began working on the first edition of the book while on a sabbatical in the spring of 1991. Rushefsky joined the project in 1994. It continues to be an interesting experience for both of us. We do not have the same kind of work habits. One of us (we won't tell you which one) is very meticulous and organized; the other is considerably more scattered and sloppy. This has sometimes led to noisy discussions and scampering to find things. This is the kind of book Felix and Oscar, the Odd Couple, might have written! One adjustment we did make was that the neat, meticulous one kept all the papers and files because the other misplaced his. That we remain close friends who share common interests in professional basketball (and computer games) helped the relationship. Patel, who is from Houston, roots for the Houston Rockets. Rushefsky, from New York, is a lifelong, avid, irrational Knicks fan.

Both of us have had a long involvement in health care, dating back to the 1970s. Rushefsky first became interested in health care when his wife, Cynthia, began teaching childbirth classes in rural Rocky Mount, Virginia. She trained some of the nurses and the wife of the administrator of the local rural hospital (about ten miles along winding mountain roads from where they lived), and that hospital maintained its maternity ward rather than close it. That was fortunate for the Rushefskys when their second child, Leah, was born shortly after midnight on Halloween. They just made it that ten miles to the hospital. Had that hospital not maintained its birthing facilities, they would have had to go another twenty-five miles to Roanoke. Given the speed with which Leah was born (so fast that she beat the doctor to the delivery room!), Rushefsky half-jokingly says she would have been born in Boones Mill (about halfway between Rocky Mount and Roanoke), which had no hospital. Updating from the first edition of this book, Leah is now married and has given Rushefsky and his wife their first grandchild, Echo Nichol, to whom they have dedicated this book. Echo was born prematurely, so the Rushefsky clan had a close encounter with the American health care system.

Patel's interest in health care was developed more conventionally, as an academic. He has a lifelong belief that access to good health care is a right. The two of us agree that the health care system has problems and that, before publication of the first edition of this book, there was no text that addressed those problems from a political perspective.

We have made some changes in this third edition of the book. All the chapters have been brought up to date. We look at the rise of managed care and its decline and resurgence. We discuss the new Medicare legislation. We look at the fiscal problems of the states and their impact on Medicaid. Both public programs face problematic futures. We discuss the increasing concern about malpractice, President Bush's stem cell policy, reproductive technologies, and the fascinating right-to-die case of Terri Schiavo. We examine the continued decline of employer-based health insurance and the movement toward a more consumer-driven health care. The twenty-first century will see considerable changes in the American health care system and we hope to have captured some of these tendencies.

Acknowledgments

As is typical of any book, this text is not the product of its authors only. We would like to thank Kant Patel's graduate assistant, Marquel Jacoway, for his work on the list of abbreviations and chronology and for checking and rechecking citations. Patel would also like to thank the Faculty Leave Committee at Southwest Missouri State University for the spring 1991 sabbatical that made the initial research for this project possible. We would also like to thank Patricia Kolb, vice president and editorial director at M.E. Sharpe, for her insightful judgment in continuing to support this project, as well as her assistant, Makiko Parsons. Thanks are also due to Angela Piliouras, production editor, and to her staff for the copyediting. Of course, any remaining errors are ours.

Kant Patel
Mark E. Rushefsky

List of Abbreviations

AAHP	American Association of Health Plans
AAPCC	Adjusted average per capita cost
AARP	American Association of Retired Persons
ACE	Accelerated compensable event
ADR	Alternate dispute resolution
AFDC	Aid to Families with Dependent Children
AFL-CIO	American Federation of Labor–Congress of Industrial Organizations
AHA	American Hospital Association
AHCA	American Health Care Association
AHCCCS	Arizona Health Care Cost Containment System
AHCPR	Agency for Health Care Policy and Research
AHCR	Agency for Health Care Research
AHIP	America's Health Insurance Plans
AHN	Artificial hydration and nutrition
AHPs	Accountable Health Plans
AHRQ	Agency for Healthcare Research and Quality
AI	Artificial insemination
AIDS	Acquired immunodeficiency syndrome
ALTCS	Arizona Long-Term Care System
AMA	American Medical Association
AMPAC	American Medical Political Action Committee
ANA	American Nurses Association
APHA	American Public Health Association
APN	Advanced Practice Nurse
ARTs	Assisted reproductive technologies
BBA	Balanced Budget Act
BCBSM	Blue Cross and Blue Shield of Minnesota
CalPERS	California Public Employees' Retirement System
CBO	Congressional Budget Office
CCHP	Consumer Choice Health Plan

CCMC	Committee on the Costs of Medical Care
CDC	Centers for Disease Control and Prevention
CDHC	Consumer-driven health care
CDF	Children's Defense Fund
CDRH	Center for Devices and Radiological Health (FDA)
CEAP	Clinical Effectiveness Assessment Program (American College of Physicians)
CHAMPUS	Civilian Health and Medical Program of the Uniformed Services
CHIP	Child Health Insurance Program
CMS	Centers for Medicare and Medicaid Services
CNM	Certified Nurse Midwife
CNS	Clinical Nurse Specialist
COBRA	Consolidated Omnibus Budget Reconciliation Act
CON	Certificate-of-need
CPI	Consumer price index
CPS	Current Population Survey
CRNA	Certified Registered Nurse Anesthetist
DATTA	Diagnostic and Therapeutic Technology Assessment Program
DCE	Designated compensable event
DDT	Dichlorodiphenyl Trichloreothane
DSH	Disproportionate Share Hospital
DHHS	Department of Health and Human Services
DNC	Democratic National Committee
DRGs	Diagnosis-related groups
EFM	Electronic fetal monitor
EKG	Electrocardiogram
EPSDT	Early and periodic screening, diagnosis, and treatment
ERISA	Employee Retirement Income Security Act
ESRD	End-stage renal disease
FDA	Food and Drug Administration
FDCF	Florida Department of Children and Families
FEHBP	Federal Employees Health Benefits Program
FELA	Federal Employees Liability Act
FERA	Federal Emergency Relief Administration
FFS	Fee-for-service
FPL	Federal Poverty Level
FSHCA	Federally Supported Health Centers Assistance Act
FTCA	Federal Tort Claims Act
FY	Fiscal year

GAO	General Accounting Office
GAO	Government Accountability Office
GATT	General Agreement on Tariffs and Trade
GDP	Gross domestic product
GIFT	Gamete intrafallopian transfer
HBC	Health Benefits Coalition
HCA	Hospital Corporation of America
HCCCCI	Health Care Cost and Coverage Crisis Index/Health Crisis Index
HCFA	Health Care Financing Administration
HEDIS	Health Plan Employer Data and Information Set
HHA	Home Health Agency
HHS	Health and Human Services, Department of
HI	Hospital insurance
HIAA	Health Insurance Association of America
HIPAA	Health Insurance Portability and Accountability Act
HIOs	Health insuring organizations
HIV	Human immunodeficiency virus
HMOs	Health maintenance organizations
HSAs	Health savings accounts
HSAs	Health systems agencies
HUGO	Human Genome Organization
ICU	Intensive care unit
IOGs	Illness outcome groups
IOM	Institute of Medicine
IPAs	Independent practice associations
IUI	Intrauterine insemination
IVF	In vitro fertilization
JCAH	Joint Commission on Accreditation of Hospitals
LPN	Licensed Practical Nurse
LTC	Long-term care
LVN	Licensed Vocational Nurse
MAA	Medical Assistance for the Aged
MAI	Medical adversity insurance
MCCA	Medicare Catastrophic Coverage Act
MCOs	Managed care organizations
Medi-Cal	California Medicaid program
MEG	Magnetoencephalography

MIC	Maternal and Infant Care
MICRA	Medical Injury Compensation Reform Act (California)
MMA	Medicare Modernization Act; also known as Medicare Prescription Drug Improvement and Modernization Act of 2003
MMIA	Medical Malpractice Immunity Act
MRI	Magnetic resonance imaging
MSA	Medical savings account
NAFTA	North American Free Trade Agreement
NAIC	National Association of Insurance Commissioners
NAMIC	National Association of Mutual Insurance Companies
NCHCT	National Center for Health Care Technology
NCHSR	National Center for Health Services Research
NCI	National Cancer Institute
NCQA	National Committee for Quality Assurance
NCSL	National Conference of State Legislatures
NFIB	National Federation of Independent Businesses
NHI	National health insurance
NICA	(Birth-Related) Neurological Injury Compensation Act (Florida and Virginia laws)
NIH	National Institutes of Health
NIOSH	National Institute for Occupational Safety and Health
NMEs	New molecular entities
NP	Nurse Practitioner
NPDB	National Practitioner Data Bank
NSF	National Science Foundation
OBRA	Omnibus Budget Reconciliation Act
OECD	Organization for Economic Cooperation and Development
OHP	Oregon Health Plan
OHTA	Office of Health Technology Assessment
OMAR	Office of Medical Application of Research
OMB	Office of Management and Budget
OSHA	Occupational Safety and Health Administration
OTA	Office of Technology Assessment
PAC	Political action committee
PBMs	Pharmaceutical benefit managers
PCCM	Primary care case management
PET	Position emission tomography
PGPs	Prepaid group plans
PHPs	Prepaid health plans

PMA	Premarket approval
POS	Point-of-service plan
PPOs	Preferred provider organizations
PPRC	Physician Payment Review Commission
PPS	Prospective Payment System
PROs	Peer Review Organizations
PSOs	Provider-sponsored organizations
PSROs	Professional Standards Review Organizations
PRWOA	Personal Responsibility and Work Opportunity Act
QMB	Qualified Medicare beneficiaries
QuIC	Quality Interagency Coordination Task Force
R&D	Research and development
RBRVS	Resource-based relative value scale
RVS	Relative value scale
RVU	Relative value unit
SCHIP	State Children's Health Insurance Program
S/HMOs	Social health maintenance organizations
SLMB	Specified low-income Medicare beneficiaries
SMI	Supplemental medical insurance
SSI	Supplemental Security Income
STIs	Sexually transmitted infections
TANF	Temporary Assistance to Needy Families
TEFRA	Tax Equity and Fiscal Responsibility Act
THCLA	Texas Health Care Liability Act
UCR	Usual, customary, and reasonable (fees payment system)
UHV	Universal health voucher
USPHS	U.S. Public Health Service
WHI	Women's Health Initiative
ZIFT	Zygote intrafallopian transfer

Chronology of Significant Events and Legislation in U.S. Health Care

1798   President John Adams signs into law an act providing for relief of sick and disabled seamen, which approved the establishment of the first Marine Hospital.

1799   The first Marine Hospital is established.

1847   The American Medical Association (AMA) is founded.

1863   The National Academy of Sciences is established to assist in caring for the Union Army.

1870   First Reorganization Act federalizes the Marine Hospital Service.

1872   The American Public Health Association (APHA) is founded. This organization is concerned with the social and economic aspects of health problems.

1878   The National Quarantine Act is signed into law. This legislation is designed to prevent entry into the country of persons with communicable diseases.

1899   The National Hospital Superintendent's Association is created. It later becomes the American Hospital Association (AHA).

1904   The Council on Medical Education is established by the AMA.

1908   Congress passes the Federal Employees' Liability Act, pre-empting state tort law, and designed to govern the liability claims brought by employees against railroads operating in interstate commerce.

1910   The Flexner Report is published, calling for the adoption of the German model of medicine, with scientifically based training, the strengthening of first-class medical schools, and the elimination of a great majority of inferior schools.

1912   The U.S. Public Health Service (USPHS) is formed from the Marine Hospital Service.

1921   The Sheppard-Towner Act is signed into law. It establishes the first federal grant-in-aid program for local child health clinics.

1928   The Sheppard-Towner Act is terminated.

1929   Blue Cross is established.

1930   The National Institutes of Health (NIH) is established for the purpose of discovering the causes, prevention, and cure of disease.

       President Herbert Hoover establishes the Committee on the Cost of Medical Care.

1934   The Federal Emergency Relief Administration (FERA) gives the first federal grants to local governments for public assistance to the poor, including financial support for health care.

1935   The Social Security Act of 1935 is signed into law. The act provides for unemployment compensation, old-age benefits, and other benefits.

1937   The National Cancer Act is passed by Congress, establishing the National Cancer Institute (NCI).

1939   The Murray-Wagner-Dingell Bill is introduced, proposing national health insurance.

1946   The National Hospital Survey and Construction Act (Hill-Burton Act) mandates the provision of federal funding to subsidize the construction of hospitals.

       The National Mental Health Act is signed into law, providing federal grants to states for research, prevention, diagnosis, and treatment of mental disorders.

1951   The Internal Revenue Service rules that employers' costs for health care insurance premiums are tax deductible.

1952   The nongovernmental Joint Commission on Accreditation of Hospitals (JCAH) is established.

       The Health Insurance Association of America (HIAA) is formed.

1960   The Kerr-Mills Act (Medical Assistance Act) is signed into law, providing federal matching payments to states for vendor payments.

1965   The Medicare and Medicaid programs are passed as amendments to the Social Security Act of 1935.

1966   The Comprehensive Health Planning Act is signed into law. This legislation is an attempt to implement health care facilities planning through the states.

1971   Ralph Nader's Health Research Group is founded.

Senator Edward Kennedy introduces the Health Security Act, which calls for a comprehensive program of free medical care.

1972   President Nixon, in response to Kennedy's plan, introduces the National Health Insurance Partnership Act.

The Professional Standards Review Organizations (PSROs) are created through the Social Security Amendments of 1972. The PSROs create a regulatory mechanism to encourage efficient and economical delivery of health care in the Medicare and Medicaid programs through peer review.

The Office of Technology Assessment (OTA) is established. This organization maintains, in part, a concern for medical technology assessment.

1973   The Health Maintenance Organization Act is signed into law. This legislation encouraged the development of health maintenance organizations (HMOs) in an attempt to induce competition in the health care market.

The U.S. Supreme Court legalizes abortion in *Roe v. Wade*.

1974   The Congressional Budget and Impoundment Control Act is signed into law.

The National Health Planning and Resource Development Act is signed into law. This legislation develops certificate-of-need (CON) requirements

The Employee Retirement Income Security Act (ERISA) of 1974 is signed into law. This legislation is concerned with protection of private employee benefits.

1975   The State of California passes the Medical Injury Compensation Reform Act, which places a cap of $250,000 on jury awards for noneconomic damages.

1976   The Quinlan case (concerning the right to die) is decided by the New Jersey Supreme Court.

1981   The Omnibus Budget Reconciliation Act (OBRA) of 1981 is passed. This legislation affects growth rates in Medicaid, reduces the number of those eligible for welfare, and changes Medicaid policy.

The Health Care Financing Administration (HCFA) grants waivers to states to pay for home health care.

1982   The Tax Equity and Fiscal Responsibility Act (TEFRA) of 1982 is signed into law, giving states discretion to require Medicaid beneficiaries to pay nominal fees for medical services.

1983   The Prospective Payment System (PPS), a mandate of the Deficit Reduction Act of 1982, begins. This system classifies illnesses into categories for reimbursement.

1984   The Deficit Reduction Act of 1984 requires Medicaid beneficiaries to assign to the states any rights they had to other health benefit programs.

1985   Congress creates the Physician Payment Review Commission (PPRC), which is charged with making recommendations regarding payment systems.

The Congress passed the Medical Malpractice Immunity Act (MMIA). The purpose of the law was to protect medical personnel from any liability arising out of performance of their official duties.

1986   The Omnibus Budget Reconciliation Act (OBRA) of 1986 gives the states the option to extend Medicaid coverage to pregnant women and infants who are members of households with incomes as high as 100 percent of the federal poverty level.

Congress passes the Health Care Quality Improvement Act. The act restricts the ability of an incompetent physician to move from state to state without disclosure or discovery of his or her previous incompetent or damaging performance.

1987   The Omnibus Budget Reconciliation Act of 1987 increases the income requirements of pregnant women and infants to 185 percent of the federal poverty level.

1988   The Medicare Catastrophic Coverage Act is passed.

The Pepper Commission Report is released, calling for coverage for long-term care and for universal coverage for those under the age of sixty-five.

The Omnibus Budget Reconciliation Act of 1989 requires provision of all Medicaid-allowed treatment to correct problems identified during early and periodic screening, diagnosis, and treatment (EPSDT).

The Medicare Catastrophic Coverage Act is repealed.

The Office of Health Technology Assessment (OHTA) is established. This office is responsible for advising the Health Care Financing Administration (HCFA) about technology as it is applied to Medicaid and Medicare programs.

The Agency for Health Care Policy and Research (AHCPR) develops guidelines on the appropriate treatment of common illnesses.

The U.S. Supreme Court, in *Webster v. Reproductive Health Services*, gives states the authority to regulate and thus restrict abortions in public clinics.

The Medicare Prospective Payment System is extended to physicians.

1990 The U.S. Supreme Court rules on the Cruzan (right-to-die) case.

On February 25, 1990, Terri Schiavo (a future right-to-die case) suffers a cardiac arrest, and her heart stops temporarily, causing brain damage.

1991 Harris Wofford wins special senatorial election in Pennsylvania, firmly placing health care on the policy agenda.

1992 Congress enacts the Prescription Drug Use Fee Act. The law requires the pharmaceutical industry to pay a user fee to finance hiring of additional review staff by the Food and Drug Administration.

1993 President Bill Clinton unveils his Health Security Act.

1994 Congress fails to pass any health reform bill.

November elections result in Republican control of Congress.

1995 It is reported that the Medicare Hospital Insurance Trust Fund will go bankrupt by the year 2002.

Republicans adopt a balanced budget target of 2002, calling for reductions in spending for Medicare and Medicaid.

President Clinton announces balanced budget target of 2005, with smaller reductions in Medicare and Medicaid.

President Clinton proposes federal regulation of private insurance.

Budget disputes between President Clinton and Congress result in two government shutdowns.

Congress passes the Federally Supported Health Centers Assistance Act (FSHCA). The law extended coverage under the Federal Tort Claims Act (FTCA) to community health centers that receive federal funding under a program sponsored by the Department of Health and Human Services.

1996   The federal welfare program is replaced, as Congress passes the Personal Responsibility and Work Opportunity Act.

Congress passes the Health Insurance Portability and Accountability Act.

Congress passes the Common Sense Liability Legal Reform Act, designed to restrict the amount of punitive damages that can be awarded in a civil action. President Clinton vetoes the bill.

Congress also gives mental health the same status as physical health.

States begin passing patients' rights bills, regulating health maintenance organizations.

1997   Congress passes the Balanced Budget Act, which calls for a budget surplus by 2002 and reforms Medicare, creating the Medicare+Choice program. It also extends the prospective payment system to nursing homes, home health care agencies, and hospice agencies.

The Balance Budget Act increases health insurance for children through the creation of the State Children's Health Insurance Program (SCHIP).

President Clinton signs into law the Volunteer Protection Act. The law protects America's volunteers from meritless, costly, and time-consuming lawsuits.

President Clinton establishes the Advisory Commission on Consumer Protection and Quality in Health Care Industry (also known as Quality Commission).

Texas passes patients' rights law allowing enterprise liability suits.

Columbia/HCA is charged with massive fraud, revamps hospital operations. Oxford Health Plans show significant financial losses.

Business and insurance companies lobby to thwart federal regulation of managed care plans.

1998   President Clinton proposes to extend Medicare to those aged 55–64 who are uninsured.

The federal government ends the fiscal year with the first surplus in almost three decades.

The Congressional Budget Office predicts a surplus of $1.6 trillion over the next decade.

The House passes a patients' rights bill. The Senate fails to act.

Federal investigators say the portability law passed by Congress in 1996 is not working.

The number of uninsured in United States exceeds 40 million people, almost 16 percent of the population.

Some HMOs drop out of the Medicare program, citing high costs and federal refusal to raise payments.

The House of Representatives votes to conduct impeachment inquiry against President Clinton.

2003   On December 8, President George W. Bush signs Medicare Prescription Drug Benefit program into law.

2003   On October 15, Terri Schiavo's feeding tube is removed under court order.

2003   The Florida legislature passes "Terri's Law," giving Governor Jeb Bush the power to issue a "one-time stay." Using this power, Governor Bush issues an executive order to reinstate the feeding tube in Terri Schiavo.

2004   Medicare drug discount card program begins.

2005   On March 21, Congress passes a narrowly crafted law, which is signed by President Bush and titled An Act of Relief of the Parents of Theresa Marie Schiavo. The law gives the U.S. District Court for the Middle District of Florida jurisdiction to hear and review Terri Schiavo's case.

On March 24, Judge George Greer issues a restraining order prohibiting the Florida Department of Children and Families (FDCF) from removing Terri Schiavo from the hospice or reinserting the feeding tube.

On March 31, Terri Schiavo passes away.

States such as Tennessee and Missouri make major cuts in their Medicaid programs.

2006   The Medicare prescription drug benefit begins.

Health Care Politics and Policy in America

1

Health Care Politics

Health care is the largest single industry in the country. Health policymaking in the United States involves a complex web of decisions made by various institutions and political actors across a broad spectrum of public and private sectors. These institutions and actors include federal, state, and local governments in the public sector. In the private sector they include health care providers such as hospitals and nursing homes; health care professionals; and health care purchasers such as insurance companies, industries, and consumers. In addition, a wide variety of interest groups influence and shape health care politics and policymaking.

These institutions and actors are involved throughout the policy cycle. The policy cycle includes getting problems to the government and agenda setting; policy formulation and legitimation; budgeting, implementation of, evaluation of, and decisions about policy continuation; and modifications and/or termination (Jones 1978; Rushefsky 2002). These institutions and actors interact at every stage of the policy cycle. No one institution or actor dominates any one stage of policy development. Each contributes to the process by providing input that often is designed to promote the institution's or the actor's own interests (L.D. Brown 1978).

Some of the problems in health care policymaking are rooted in this diversity of institutions and actors. Any decision designed to affect the health care system generates immediate and heated responses. Any attempt to regulate the health care system also produces pressures from opponents of regulation who favor market-oriented approaches to delivery of health care. Government regulations have often been thwarted by those being regulated as well as by actors in the system who oppose a strong government role (J.H.A. Brown 1978).

The development of a comprehensive and consistent health care policy is made difficult, if not impossible, by the shotgun approach followed by many policymakers, such as the president and Congress. For example, Congress deals with the most pressing problems one at a time and not in the framework of overall health care policy. Such an approach is often necessitated by the political realities of producing tangible results on a short-term basis for the purpose of reelection. Consequently, health care policy in the United States is in a constant state of fluidity. It lacks consistency and often encompasses a mishmash of programs involving conflicting values. It is not too surprising that the American health care system is often described as scandalous and wasteful (Dentzer 1990; Taylor 1990).

Policymakers' discretion is often limited by a wide variety of restraints imposed by the policy environment. Just as a policy environment can help facilitate policymaking, it can also hinder policy development by the number and types of constraints it imposes on policymakers. The constraints imposed by the policy environment make it difficult for the government to resolve issues in a new or innovative manner (Rosenbaum 1985). The health policy environment can be thought of as a total matrix of factors that influence and shape the health policy cycle. These factors include constitutional or legal requirements, institutional settings, shared understandings about the rules of the game, cultural values of a society, political ideology, economic resources, and technological innovations and their impact on the cost and delivery of health care services.

This chapter has two goals: to provide a detailed and systematic analysis of the health policy environment that shapes health care policymaking, and to examine the role played by key actors in the health care field. Chapter 2 provides a historical perspective on the development of health care policy in the United States. The remaining chapters discuss contemporary issues in health care: Medicaid and Medicare; the problems of the uninsured; women, minorities, and children; cost containment; medical liability and malpractice; health care technology; health care reform; and incrementalism. These policy issues are examined from the perspective of the conflicting values of access, quality, cost, regulation, market approaches, and generational conflicts involved in the distribution of health care resources.

The Health Policy Environment

Constitutional Environment

Over 200 years ago, the Founding Fathers established a constitutional system of government that had two purposes. First, it established a government with powers to act. But second, it attempted to prevent a tyranny of the majority. Having experienced the repressive measures of concentrated power under British rule, the Founding Fathers opted for a decentralized structure of government. The major features of the American system of government, discussed next, reflect these two conflicting objectives.

Separation of Powers, and Checks and Balances

The Constitution created a system that disperses political power and decision-making authority among various branches of government. The powers of the national government are divided among the legislative, executive, and judicial branches of government. This is known as the separation of powers. The powers of the three branches are not totally separated, however, and thus it is more accurate to describe this arrangement as three coequal branches of government sharing powers. The underlying principle behind such a sharing of powers was that it would lead to checks and balances. It is based on the assumption that other branches would check an attempt by one branch of government to assume too much power or abuse its powers. James Madison, one of the most influential delegates at the Constitutional Convention, argued in *The Federalist Papers* (No. 51) that "ambition must be made to counteract ambition" (Madison 1961a, 322).

Such a constitutional arrangement creates constant competition among these institutions for preeminence in various policy areas. It necessitates lengthy negotiations and compromises and bargaining in policymaking between the president and Congress. This makes it difficult to formulate a consistent and comprehensive set of policies. The result often is a government of deadlock and inaction. The problem becomes more pronounced during the periods of divided government, when different political parties control the White House and Congress. This includes divided control of the Congress itself. Between 1948 and 1992 we have experienced divided government 59 percent of the time (twenty-six out of forty-four years) and between 1969 and 1992, 83 percent of the time (twenty out of twenty-four years) (Stanley and Niemi 2001). During the first six years of the Reagan administration (1981–86), the control of Congress itself was divided, with Republicans in the majority in the Senate and Democrats in the majority in the House. Divided government was the norm during the George H.W. Bush administration (1988–92) and the Clinton administration (1993–2000). During the first term of the George W. Bush administration (2001–4), for about a year and a half, Democrats controlled the Senate and Republicans the House. For two and a half years, there was a unified government. In the elections of November 2004, President Bush was reelected and the Republicans retained control of both the House and the Senate. Thus, the unified government has continued in the second term of the Bush administration.

In the health policy area, this has necessitated a number of compromises between the president and Congress. For example, the Reagan administration proposed the consolidation of some thirty-five health programs into block grants. Congress authorized four block grants covering twenty-four programs accompanied by a 25 percent reduction in federal funding. Similarly, President Ronald Reagan proposed putting a cap on federal Medicaid dollars, but Congress refused (L.D. Brown 1984).

Some have argued that divided government may work better because it requires the president to reach out to members of the other party to create majority support for his programs. For example, Niskanen (2003) points to the fact that the Reagan tax laws of 1981 and 1986 were both approved by a House of Representatives controlled by the Democrats. He further argues that the rate of growth of real (inflation-adjusted) federal spending tends to be lower during periods of divided governments. Similarly, some of the policy successes of President Clinton, such as the North Atlantic Free Trade Agreement (NAFTA) and welfare reform, were the result of his success in getting support from Republicans in Congress (Galderisi, Herzberg, and McNamara

1996; Niskanen 2003). Others have tended to blame divided government for policy gridlock within Congress and between executive and legislatives branches of government (Galderisi, Herzberg, and McNamara 1996). However, Richard Conley (2003) points out that this argument does not withstand empirical scrutiny.

Even during periods of unified government (when the same party controls the White House and the Congress), one of which occurred for a brief period of time after the 1992 elections (1992–94), institutional jealousies and prerogatives made policymaking a problematic adventure (see chapter 9). However, this period of unified government lasted for only two years. The 1994 congressional elections again produced a divided government with the White House controlled by a Democrat (President Bill Clinton) and both houses of Congress controlled by Republicans (Schantz 2001). Given the fact that American political parties are not strictly ideologically driven and are more like a coalition of different interests, a unified government does not guarantee success for the president, as demonstrated by difficulties of the Carter administration and the first two years of the Clinton administration (Galderisi, Herzberg, and McNamara 1996).

Federalism

The Constitution also created a federal system of government in which governmental authority is dispersed and divided between the national and state governments. The controversy over whether power and authority should be more centralized in the national government or more decentralized in state and local governments has been a perennial question in American politics. In addition, both the national and the state governments have often delegated important functions to thousands of units of local government. As a result, it is difficult to find many governmental activities that do not, to some extent, involve all three levels of government. Thus, despite the increased role of the federal government in the health care field during the 1960s, overall authority over health policy remains divided and shared among the national, state, and local governments. This is especially true with respect to implementation of many health policies and programs. In fact, the Reagan administration's desire to decentralize authority led to an increased role for state governments in the implementation of health programs (Thompson 1986). In 1995, the Republican-controlled Congress proposed shifting more authority over social programs, including health care, to the states. This devolution of authority to states in the health policy area continued during the Clinton administration. The Bush administration has continued this trend by giving states more discretion, especially in the Medicaid program, by giving state government more flexibility to experiment with the program.

A federal system of government adds to the fragmentation of authority and thus increases complexity, jurisdictional competition, delays, duplication, finger pointing, and often the dodging of responsibilities by different levels of government in the health policy cycle. Attempts to reconcile many different geographical interests become problematic and tend to perpetuate a belief in organized chaos and flexible rules over central policymaking authority. The problem of regionalism and localism is accentuated by the need to satisfy the demands of a diverse and heterogeneous society. Thus, no single institution representing the nation as a whole defines the public interest and serves the public good. The result is a health care system made up of multiple "little governments" and "little empires" that pursue their own goals and interests. This in turn generates health policies that are vaguely defined and designed to serve "special publics" (Altenstetter 1974, 26–27).

Institutional Environment

The institutional environment consists of the rules, structures, and settings within which major institutions involved in policymaking and implementation operate. These include the legislative, executive, and judicial branches of government. Congress is the primary policymaking institution, while the executive is primarily responsible for implementing policies. The judiciary's principal responsibility is to resolve constitutional and legal conflicts. Since the beginning of the twentieth century, however, these areas of responsibility have become increasingly blurred, with all three branches of government sharing powers in the areas of policymaking, implementation, and adjudication.

Congress

Policymaking in Congress takes place in an environment of a decentralized and thus fragmented power structure where political power is dispersed among numerous committees and subcommittees in both chambers. This decentralization of power and authority in the committee structure has led some to describe Congress as a "kind of confederation of little legislatures" (Huitt 1970, 410). One of the consequences of this in health policymaking is competition among committees within and between the Senate and the House. The second consequence for health policymaking is bargaining and compromises. Thus, health policy formulation in Congress occurs in numerous subsystems with little coordination (L.D. Brown 1978). In the 104th Congress (1995–96), the Republican majority attempted to coordinate committee action under tight leadership control. House Speaker Newt Gingrich brought about more centralization of power in the House. He often stepped in and overruled committee chairmen on a range of significant legislation. This shift of power in the Speaker's office led to loss of autonomy of committee chairs at times. However, the ability of an individual to maintain discipline and exercise policy expertise is often found only in committees and subcommittees (Koszczuk 1995).

Senators and representatives are elected to represent their respective states and smaller congressional districts, which leads to an emphasis on pork-barrel politics to capture federal goods and services for their constituencies. This creates a tendency to promote state and local interests and less sensitivity to national interests and needs in health care policymaking.

The Executive

The Constitution assigns the president and the executive branch agencies (i.e., the bureaucracy) the role of implementing policies approved by Congress. During the 1960s, concerns about issues of access, quality, equity, and efficiency in the health care area led Congress to create many new programs, such as Medicare and Medicaid, to increase access. During the 1970s and 1980s, concerns over spiraling costs resulted in the creation of programs designed to contain rising health care costs through planning, peer review, regulation, and encouragement of the development of new health care delivery organizations such as health maintenance organizations (HMOs).

Congress routinely delegates the authority for making many decisions to bureaucratic agencies. For example, Congress created the Occupational Safety and Health Administration (OSHA) and gave it the authority to write regulations concerning workers' health, safety, and privacy in the workplace. In addition, Congress often passes laws that are vague, very broad, or both, leaving bureaucratic agencies a significant amount of discretionary power to fill in the details of the law. Congress uses its legislative oversight and budgetary powers to exercise control over bureaucratic agencies. Nevertheless, the fact remains that congressional delegation of authority and discretionary power enjoyed by bureaucratic agencies gives them a significant role in health policymaking and implementation.

As with Congress, power and authority in the bureaucracy is highly dispersed and fragmented. Various health policies are under the jurisdictions of many different federal agencies, which leads to overlapping jurisdictions, authority, and responsibilities. In addition, as we discussed earlier, in a federal system of government, state bureaucracies implement many federal programs either partially or totally. Such dispersal and fragmentation of authority creates competition and conflicts along both vertical and horizontal planes throughout the health policy cycle. Turf fighting over program implementation, authority, and resources becomes the name of the game. The health policy cycle operates in a dynamic environment of constantly changing alignments of bureaucratic agencies, congressional committees, policymakers, and various interest groups shaping and reshaping health policy.

The Judiciary

Courts and judges influence health policymaking and implementation through their interpretation of the Constitution and congressional laws. They make sure that implementation of laws meets constitutional standards and that administrative agencies discharge their assigned responsibilities. Federal courts are also responsible for enforcement of the Administrative Procedures Act, which governs administrative procedures in all federal agencies. In addition, individuals and groups who feel that the executive and legislative branches have failed to redress their grievances often resort to seeking help from the courts.

The federal courts, and the U.S. Supreme Court in particular, have come to play a significant role in policymaking in certain aspects of the health care field. The Supreme Court's 1973 decision in *Roe v. Wade*, legalizing abortion, was a major policy decision and a victory for groups supporting a woman's right to have an abortion. But a 1989 decision by the Supreme Court (*Webster v. Reproductive Health Services*), whereby the Supreme Court granted states authority to regulate and thus restrict abortions in public clinics, also suggests that the Court's position may change with changes in the composition of justices on the Court. Whether a more conservative Supreme Court in the future overturns *Roe v. Wade* remains to be seen given the reelection of George W. Bush and increased Republican majorities in both the House and the Senate as a result of 2004 elections.

The impact of health care technology on the treatment and delivery of health services and the ethical concerns raised by medical technology have drawn state and federal courts into such varied topics as organ transplants, stem cell research, health care surrogacy, quality of life, and the right to die with dignity, among others (see Patel and Rushefsky 2002).

Political Environment

The political environment includes a shared understanding among policymakers about how policy decisions should be made and the underlying values, political feasibility (public opinion), electoral cycles, influence of organized interest groups, and political ideologies. The political environment itself is influenced and shaped by the constitutional, legal, institutional, economic, and technological environment of a given policy area.

Consensus Building

We have already discussed how the constitutional and institutional environments create diffused and fragmented systems of authority and responsibility in the health policy cycle. This in turn creates a political environment that is conducive to constant bargaining and compromises among major institutions and key actors in the health policy field. Since no single institution or actor is in a position to dominate the process, coalition building becomes inevitable. It also injects logrolling (trading votes to secure favors) and pork-barrel politics (obtaining government projects for one's legislative district) into the policy adoption and implementation stages. One of the consequences of this is that the policymaking process is invariably driven toward consensus building among diverse and conflicting interests. This often results in contradictory policies or policies that contain conflicting values (Allison 1971). Thus, the policymaking process, instead of being a science of creating policy that solves a problem, becomes an art of creating a consensus that holds conflicting and diverse interests together in order to create majority support for that policy. The political logic of coalition building in order to create a consensus creates a situation in which any measure that is successful, be it congressional or presidential, will have been changed in ways its proponents did not foresee or desire (L.D. Brown 1978). Attempts at comprehensive change, as in the health care reform debate of the 1990s and other attempts at national health insurance, often fail. Thus, what change does come about is piecemeal and incremental, epitomized by Medicaid and Medicare.

Incrementalism

Policymakers also share decision-making values that favor incremental policymaking, that is, relatively small or incremental changes and modifications in existing policies. Thus, rather than consider all possible alternatives in a comprehensive manner, policymakers concentrate only on marginal values or relatively few alternatives that bring about marginal changes in existing policies (Lindblom 1959). Incrementalism is politically attractive to policymakers because small policy adjustments reduce the impact of negative and politically risky consequences. Nevertheless, incremental policymaking can also inhibit imagination, innovation, and fresh new approaches to the solution of problems (Rosenbaum 1985). Policymakers end up creating policies aimed at "satisfying" diverse interests, rather than problem solving. Herbert Simon (1957) first introduced the term "satisficing" to describe an outcome that is good enough. In other words, "satisficing" involves behavior that attempts to achieve some minimum level of a particular variable but does not strive to achieve its maximum possible value. He called this "bounded rationality."

Political Feasibility

Policymakers are also influenced and guided in their policy deliberations by political feasibility (Huitt 1970). This involves judgment about whether it is possible to enact a policy given the political realities. One of the major political realities that policymakers face is the potential public reaction to a proposed policy. All the major institutions and actors involved in policymaking are influenced by considerations of political feasibility. This is especially true of elected public officials. Members of Congress are more apt to support and vote for a policy that is likely to be popular with their constituents than a policy that may produce a strong negative reaction from their constituents. For example, members are more likely to support tax cuts over increased taxes. Throughout the book we have discussed how public opinion has shaped health care politics and policy.

Electoral Cycle

Policymakers are influenced in their deliberations by the electoral cycle and the necessity of reelection. Thus, policy decisions are viewed from the perspective of potential electoral consequences. This is all the more true near election time. The policymaking process is driven by the need to produce short-term tangible benefits.

The fact that the president, senators, and representatives not only have different constituencies to serve but different term lengths in office make electoral calculations a permanent fixture of the political environment. For example, during the 1980 presidential primary campaign, Senator Edward Kennedy (D-MA), who was challenging the incumbent, Jimmy Carter, for the Democratic Party's nomination for the presidency, advocated a plan for universal national health insurance. When his proposal proved to be popular with the general public, the Carter administration was forced to propose a scaled-down version of a health insurance plan. Carter went on to win the Democratic Party's nomination but lost the general election to Ronald Reagan. The issue of national health insurance also receded from prominence on the national policy agenda because of the Reagan administration's commitment to deregulation and decentralization in health care, as well as the economic realities of the federal budget deficit. Health care reform came back on the national agenda as a result of a special senatorial election in Pennsylvania in 1991 and the presidential campaign of 1992, in which the Democratic nominee, Bill Clinton, governor of Arkansas, made health care reform a cornerstone of his campaign. However, the Clinton administration failed in its effort at health care reform (Rushefsky and Patel 1998). The failure to overhaul the American health care system during the Clinton administration was followed by few incremental, stopgap measures, such as the Health Insurance Portability and Accountability Act (HIPAA) of 1996 and the State Children's Health Insurance Program (SCHIP), enacted in 1997.

The issue of health care reform reemerged during the presidential campaign of 2004 due to the rising costs of health care and the increasing numbers of uninsured Americans. Both candidates, incumbent George W. Bush, and the Democratic nominee, Senator John Kerry (D-MA), made health care a theme of their campaigns. The health care plans proposed by the two candidates differed in scope and philosophy. Bush's plan offered tax credits, that is, tax-deductible health savings accounts and new purchasing pools, to help individuals and small businesses buy insurance coverage. Kerry's plan proposed to build on the current public–private insurance system and included expansion of Medicaid and SCHIP to provide insurance coverage to more people and called for the government to reimburse employers who chose to participate as much as 75 percent of the cost of catastrophic cases (Connolly 2004).

Public Philosophy and Political Ideology

Political ideology is the set of political beliefs and values by which policy actors in all policy arenas operate (Klein 1984). Within the health care system it is possible to identify the ideology of the medical profession, health care administrators, planners, and policymakers. The term "public philosophy," in contrast, is a broader concept and can be defined as an outlook on public affairs shared by a wide coalition in a nation (Beer 1965). A public philosophy often may not be explicit, but the ideological debate on issues takes place within its confines.

The underlying principle in American public philosophy, resulting from constitutional guarantees of freedom of speech, expression, and petition, is that organized interests should have an important role in influencing public policies. The public philosophy in the United States was influenced greatly by the writing of John Locke, a seventeenth-century English philosopher. A central feature of Locke's argument is the belief that ultimate authority resides in the individual's inalienable right to seek his or her own self-preservation. According to Locke, people form a government to protect their natural right of self-preservation. For Locke, the right to self-preservation is closely associated with the right to acquire property. This Lockean idea pervades American political thought and institutions (Bayes 1982).

The clearest integration of this Lockean idea is found in James Madison's "Federalist 10." According to Madison, a faction constituted a number of citizens united by a common passion or interest adverse to the rights of other citizens or to the permanent and aggregate interests of the community. Madison argued that factions were evil and could lead to tyranny. Yet, elimination of the causes of factions was not a solution because it could also destroy liberty. Therefore, Madison advocated controlling the effects of factions. Since American society is composed of a large number of geographic, ethnic, racial, economic, and religious groups, the way to control the negative effects of factions, according to Madison, was to create a representative form of government. In such a representative government, public views can be refined and enlarged by passing them through the medium of a chosen body of citizens (the legislature) whose wisdom can help determine the true interest of the country. Madison also asserted that a large republic was less susceptible to tyranny than a small one because in a large republic many different interests will exist, making it difficult for any one interest regularly to dominate all other interests (Madison 1961b).

This in turn helped create a philosophy of liberalism, which argues that all interests should be able to penetrate the political arena. Theodore Lowi describes this philosophy as interest group liberalism (Lowi 1967). Such a political system is called a pluralistic system, which is characterized by many channels of access with various interest groups exercising countervailing veto power. This system is justified in terms of equality and the openness that guarantees political freedom, which in turn can be used to achieve social and economic freedoms (Wilsford 1991).

The decentralized governmental structure based on separation of powers, checks and balances, and federalism is designed to give interest groups access throughout the policy cycle. Thus, ironically, a Madisonian system designed to prevent a tyranny of the majority and control the mischiefs of factions (interest groups) also gives these factions many opportunities for devilment. To formulate health policy under such a system requires public officials and institutions to reconcile the conflicting interests of many organized groups. In theory, the role of the government becomes one of neutral arbitrator resolving conflicts among organized groups. The broad and diffused distribution of political influences across numerous and diverse interest groups blurs the distinction between public and private power (Truman 1951).

Private interests battle with one another and define themselves in terms of the public interest. But because all interest groups do not have equal resources, those with more economic resources have greater access to channels of influence and thus more opportunities for engaging in mischief. As McConnell has persuasively argued, small groups monopolize political power by successfully defining their own narrow interests as the general public interest (McConnell 1966). For example, for many years, the American Medical Association (AMA) based its opposition to national health insurance on the ground that socialized medicine would be against the general public interest because it would deprive patients of their freedom of choice and would lead to poor-quality medical care. In a pluralistic system based on the public philosophy of interest-group liberalism, private economic, regional, and constituency interests are justified as public interests by appealing to values of individualism, constitution, democracy, freedom, and equality, which make up an important part of American culture and belief systems. Private interests as well as public officials often justify their narrow parochial interests as public interest. The consensus created from compromises and bargaining among competing interests gets defined as the public interest. The role of the government, according to the pluralistic formulation, becomes one of protecting these diverse and competing interests by creating a consensus through the give-and-take of politics.

The framework of pluralism assumes that multiple elites rule specific areas of public policy as a "subgovernment" or an "iron triangle." The concepts of subgovernment or iron triangle presume a small circle of participants, such as a couple of congressional committees (a few legislators), executive agencies (a few bureaucrats), and interest groups who become semiautonomous in policymaking in a particular policy area (Mawhinney 2001). However, others have argued that while this scenario is true in explaining policymaking prior to the 1970s, these concepts of rigid subgovernment or iron triangle no longer capture the role of interest groups in policymaking (Heclo 1978). The interest group explosion of the 1970s has replaced the subgovernment or iron triangle model of policymaking with the issue networks model of policymaking. Issue networks are comprised of a large number of participants with variable degrees of mutual commitment or dependence on others in the environment (Heclo 1978). Interest groups form networks and alliances with other groups for the purpose of working together to act as policy advocacy groups to achieve mutual objectives. This idea of issue networks has become widely accepted as an empirical description of how policymaking takes place in the United States (Heaney 2004; Tichenor and Harris 2002/2003).

Reforming the present health care system becomes difficult because every reform proposal gets trapped in pluralistic processes designed to safeguard all existing professional and organizational interests. Ideological conflicts between those who want to protect the professional monopoly and autonomy of the medical profession and those who want more health care planning and regulation are contained within a pluralistic institutional framework that prevents either side from generating enough power to bring about significant reforms designed to integrate and coordinate health care (Alford 1975). Market reformers blame bureaucratic interference and cumbersome regulations for the problems of the health care system. They call for less regulation and more incentive-based reforms to increase and diversify health care facilities and delivery of services. The libertarian ideology of distributive justice is most evident in arguments for competitive market reforms. According to this ideology, increased reliance on market competition for allocative decisions would result in a more efficient allocation of resources than we now have. Republicans in general, and conservatives in particular, support this position. Bureaucratic reformers blame market competition for the defects of the present system and call for more regulation and planning. This argument is based on the egalitarian ideology, which emphasizes the just distribution of health care resources based on need. The concern is to provide equal access to decent-quality health care for everyone at a reasonable cost. Democrats in general, and liberals in particular, support this position (Berki 1983).

Thus the health care system exhibits a continuous conflict and strain between the values of efficiency, access, equality, rights, and freedom. This is reflected in the contradictions between people's expectations for equal access to decent-quality health care, the failure of the private sector to provide equal access, and the inability of the public sector to compensate completely for the inadequacies of the private sector.

Which health policies are pursued at a given point in time depends on which ideology is dominant at that time. During the 1960s and early 1970s, the dominance of egalitarian ideology resulted in bureaucratic reformers' success in creating health policies designed to increase access to health care and at the same time provide quality care at a reasonable cost through such policies as Medicare, Medicaid, health care planning, and regulation. The ascendancy of libertarian ideology during the 1970s, and particularly the 1980s, led to the creation of health policies—supported by market reformers—aimed at cost containment and economic efficiency. This was attempted through deregulation, cuts in federal funds, encouragement of development of alternative health delivery organizations such as HMOs, and the establishment of a Prospective Payment System (PPS) of hospital payment for Medicare patients through diagnosis-related groups (DRGs). These policies were designed to induce diversity and competition in the health care system through market incentives. It should be noted that that the PPS initiative itself was regulatory in nature.

Economic Environment

Decisions about health care policies are invariably intertwined with economics. Health care affects and is affected by the economic environment in a number of ways. The economic environment consists of a network of institutions, laws, and rules that deal with primary questions such as what goods and services to produce, how they should be produced, and for whom (Samuelson 1970). The economic point of view is also rooted in three fundamental assumptions: (1) resources are limited or scarce in relation to human wants, (2) resources have alternative uses, and (3) people have different wants and do not attach the same importance to them (Fuchs 1995). Because economic resources are limited and have alternative uses, decisions must be made with regard to how and for what purposes to use these resources. The concept of opportunity cost suggests that when deciding to use resources in a certain way, one loses the opportunity to obtain benefits of using resources in some other way.

The economic environment affects policy decisions in health care in a number of ways. At any given point in time, health policymakers are influenced in their decisions by the notion of economic feasibility. When an economy is growing at a healthy rate, making economic resources available, policymakers find it economically feasible to establish new programs. Such was the case during the 1960s and to an extent in the early 1970s, when a number of new programs designed to increase access to health care were created. But corresponding increases in health care costs, a slowed rate of economic growth, the massive federal budget deficits, and an executive branch dominated by a conservative political philosophy during the 1980s not only made it economically difficult to establish new health care programs but made it possible to cut expenditures on federal health programs (Sorkin 1986). If one accepts the assumptions of scarcity of resources and the existence of competing goals, then the question faced by health policymakers becomes how to bring about the optimum distribution of health care resources (Fuchs 1986). What is needed is not simply cost containment but a cost-effective health care system (Fuchs 1986). Former Secretary of Health, Education, and Welfare Joseph A. Califano, Jr., has argued that one of the major problems with the U.S. health care system is that it is less cost effective than health care systems in other industrialized countries (Califano 1988). In a constrained economic environment, health policymakers are confronted with making choices and establishing priorities that are not easy to make.

One of the major issues in health care is that of deciding how to value health. An environment of limited resources and constantly changing health care needs requires value judgments by policymakers about priorities (Mooney 1986). How much of society's resources should be devoted to health care? What priorities should be assigned to different groups competing for the same health care resources? Should more priority be given to the health care needs of the elderly or to those of infants and children? Should everyone be entitled to an organ transplant, regardless of cost or the ability to pay? In recent years, a constrained economic environment has increased concerns about values of cost effectiveness and efficiency. It has prompted some states to attempt health care rationing. This has generated significant controversy and public debate over the conflicting values of efficiency, access, and equality.

Technological Environment

Dramatic advances in health care technology in the past thirty years have revolutionized the nature and delivery of health services in the United States. The rapid pace with which new biomedical technologies are developed and the swiftness with which they are adopted have transformed many hospitals into very complex and resource-intensive institutions, and have changed the very nature of medical practice (Cohen and Cohodes 1982).

New health care technologies have been linked to the problems of cost and quality of health care in the United States (Fineberg and Hiatt 1979). Since every change in technology involves costs and benefits, the formulation of a good public policy depends on an accurate assessment of the relative magnitudes of costs and benefits. The nature of technological change can have profound effects on resource requirements (Fuchs 1986).

The technological revolution in biomedicine also raises questions about what medical technology should be developed and what is the proper and appropriate level of medical intervention to treat an illness. Since health care costs make up an increasing part of the government budget, the role of the government becomes crucial with respect to allocation of health care resources. Should health care technologies be available to all persons on an equal basis? If not, what criteria should be used to decide who gets scarce health resources and who does not? Should government be involved in technology assessment and play a role in encouraging or discouraging the development of particular technology through its funding? Should the government establish legal and ethical guidelines not only with respect to biomedical research but also regarding application of biomedical technology? We explore these questions in chapter 8.

Key Health Policy Actors

The key policy actors in the health care system include a variety of public and private institutions and groups such as health care providers, health care practitioners, health care purchasers, and health insurers. The remainder of this chapter examines the role of the key health policy actors.

Health Care Purchasers

In 2002, the total combined expenditures by the federal, state, and local governments to fund health care services were $713.4 billion. This represents 45.9 percent of the total national health care expenditures of $1,553.0 trillion during the same year (Heffler et al. 2004). This alone makes the federal, state, and local governments key actors in the health care system. Since health expenditures continue to climb and require an increasingly larger share of the budget, the role of all three levels of government in health care has also increased.

The Federal Government

Today the federal government is one of the major purchasers of health care. In 2002 the federal government spent $504.7 billion on health care, representing 32.5 percent of the total national health care expenditures (Heffler et al. 2004). The majority of federal health spending is for health services provided to low-income individuals and others eligible through Medicaid, people over sixty-five years of age through Medicare, military personnel and their dependents, veterans, federal civilian employees, and Native Americans (Hospital Insurance Association of America 1990). Of these, the major bulk of the expenditures is taken up by Medicare and Medicaid programs. Medicare accounted for 52.9 percent of the total federal spending for health care in 2002, with Medicaid accounting for another 29.2 percent (Heffler et al. 2004).

The three major branches of government play a crucial role in the health policy cycle. The primary policymaking responsibility lies with Congress. Most federal programs are implemented by numerous bureaucratic agencies in the executive branch of government. This makes the president and the bureaucracy important actors, especially during the implementation stage of the health policy cycle. In recent years the federal courts, especially the U.S. Supreme Court, have become major actors in the health policy cycle. The number, frequency, and complexity of legal, constitutional, and ethical issues is on the increase as a result of advances in medical technology. The federal courts are increasingly called on to resolve some of these conflicts.

The Department of Health and Human Services (DHHS) carries out congressional mandates in the health care and social services fields. The department has many agencies and centers. The department is headed by a secretary who is appointed by the president with Senate confirmation. He is responsible for administering federal health care programs and activities. He advises the president on health, welfare, and income security programs and policies of the federal government. The Office of the Secretary of HHS include Offices of the Surgeon General, Civil Rights, the General Counsel, the Inspector General, and Assistant Secretary for Public Health Emergency Preparedness (U.S. Government Manual 2004–5; "About HHS" n.d.).

The DHHS also includes many agencies and centers that perform important functions related to health and human services. The Administration on Aging is responsible for all issues involving the elderly. The Administration for Children and Families is responsible for all issues pertaining to children, youth, and families, including things such as child support enforcement, developmental disabilities, and family assistance, among others. The Agency for Health Research and Quality is responsible for supporting research related to improving the quality of health care, reducing health care costs, and addressing issues of patient safety and medical errors. The Agency for Toxic Substances and Disease Registry is responsible for prevention of exposure to toxic and hazardous substances. The Substance Abuse and Mental Health Services Administration is responsible for prevention and treatment of addictive and mental disorders. The Health Resources and Services Administration is responsible for making essential primary care services accessible to poor, uninsured, and geographically isolated persons. The Indian Health Service provides comprehensive health services for American Indians and Alaska Natives (U.S. Government Manual 2004–5; "About HHS" n.d.).

Some of the most important centers, institutes, and agencies within the DHHS include the Centers for Disease Control and Prevention (CDC), the Centers for Medicare and Medicaid Services (CMS), the National Institutes of Health (NIH), and the Food and Drug Administration (FDA). The CDC is charged with the responsibility for protecting the public's health, preventing and controlling diseases, and responding to public health emergencies. The CMS oversees the Medicare program, the federal portion of the Medicaid program, and the State Children's Health Insurance Program. The NIH supports biomedical and behavioral research through its various institutes. The Food and Drug Administration is responsible for ensuring the safety of food, drugs, biological products, and medical devices (U.S. Government Manual, 2004–5; "About HHS" n.d.).

State and Local Governments

Because of the federal system of government, state and local governments are important actors in the health care field. During 2002, state and local governments spent $208.7 billion on health care. This amounted to 13.4 percent of the total national health care expenditures. In 2002, Medicaid accounted for about 49.3 percent of the total state and local expenditures for health care (Heffler et al. 2004).

The public health programs of state health agencies and local health departments are primarily involved in four areas. These include personal health, environmental health, health resources, and laboratory services. In addition, they perform general administrative and service functions. A sizable part of state health agencies' expenditures goes for maternal and child health, mental health, communicable disease, and handicapped children (Hospital Insurance Association of America 1990). State governments have traditionally been involved in licensing and accreditation of health care providers, as well as insurance regulation. In recent years, state governments have also become involved in rate setting, negotiated or competitively bid fixed-price arrangements, and health care rationing to control health care costs. Some states have also been in the forefront of health care reform. We consider the role of the states more fully in chapters 6 and 9.

Industries

Large industries and firms are also major purchasers of health care. Many major industries and firms provide health insurance coverage to their employees as part of a benefit package. Today a majority of workers in the United States are employed by firms that offer health insurance (Hospital Insurance Association of America 1990). Factors that seem to have a bearing on whether employers provide health insurance benefits or not are employer size, employee job tenure, wage level, full-time work status, industry, and union membership (Mellow 1982). The health insurance coverage provided by employer group insurance plans also varies widely with respect to the scope of covered services, conditions of eligibility, and the share of employees' contribution to the plan (Chollet 1984).

Major industries and firms have become key actors in the health care system because of the cost they incur in providing health insurance for their workers. A survey of 3,000 employers conducted in 2003 by Mercer Human Resource Consulting, Inc., found that the average cost of health benefits (all medical and dental plans offered) for active employees increased from $5,646 per employee in 2002 to $6,215 in 2003. This represented an increase of 10.1 percent, in a year in which the general inflation barely cracked 2 percent ("Mercer's National Survey of Employer-Sponsored Health Plans 2003" 2004). Such dramatic increases in health care costs have made businesses more conscious of their costs and have led them to use a variety of cost-cutting measures, such as managed care and encouraging or requiring employees to enroll in prepaid group plans for health services. Employers are also passing an increasing share of insurance costs to their workers by increasing deductibles and copayments, which has forced many employees to forgo health insurance coverage altogether. The percentage of all workers receiving health insurance coverage through their employers dropped from 65 percent in 2001 to 61 percent in 2004. The amount workers contributed for family coverage increased from $1,788 in 2001 to $2,661 in 2004, while the average annual amount workers contributed for individual coverage increased from $360 to $558 during the same period (Colliver 2004).

Many employers continue to provide health insurance coverage to their employees after they retire. As businesses struggle to control rising health care costs, many companies are dropping health benefits for future retirees and are asking current retirees to pay more for their health insurance coverage. According to a survey of many of the largest employers conducted by the Kaiser Family Foundation and Hewitt Associates, 79 percent of employers reported that they had increased their retirees' contributions for premiums, 53 percent had increased copayments or coinsurance for prescription drugs, and 37 percent had raised deductibles for health care services. In addition, 20 percent raised out-of-pocket limits on retirees' obligations and 13 percent changed their plans to offer retirees access to group health benefits with retirees paying 100 percent of the costs ("Survey Finds Businesses and Retirees Hit with . . ." 2004).

Health Care Providers

The major health care providers include institutions such as hospitals, nursing homes, and pharmacies, as well as professionals such as physicians, nurses, and dentists. They are important actors in the health care system because they not only deliver health care services but also influence the way in which services are delivered and the type of services that are delivered. The major feature of the U.S. health care system is its entrepreneurial nature. Pharmacies and manufacturers of pharmaceutical and medical equipment and suppliers are private, profit-making enterprises. Similarly, many nursing homes are for-profit institutions. Most physicians are private practitioners.

Hospitals

According to a 2003 survey of U.S. hospitals by the American Hospital Association (AHA), there are a total of 5,764 registered hospitals with total staffed beds of 965,256. Registered hospitals are those that meet the AHA's criteria for registration as a hospital (American Hospital Association 2005). Of the total registered hospitals, 4,895 are community hospitals, of which 2,984 are nongovernmental not-for-profit hospitals, 790 are investor-owned for-profit hospitals, and 1,121 are state and local government hospitals. The remainder is made up of federal government hospitals, nonfederal psychiatric hospitals, nonfederal long-term care hospitals, and hospital units of institutions such as prison hospitals and college infirmaries (American Hospital Association 2005). Hospitals have become the primary setting for the delivery of health care services because most of the sophisticated medical technology and equipment are located there. Hospitals vary by purpose and ownership.

Many not-for-profit hospitals (those that are community run or church affiliated) provide short-term care. States run psychiatric hospitals. The federal government operates veterans' hospitals. There are also an increasing number of proprietary or profit-making hospitals. A recent study conducted by Dr. P.J. Devereaux and colleagues at McMaster University in Hamilton, Ontario, reviewed medical studies on hospital care in the United States covering 350,000 patients and hundreds of for-profit hospitals concluded that U.S. hospitals owned by investors with the aim of making money are less cost-efficient and have higher death rates compared to nonprofit hospitals ("Study: For-Profit Hospitals Bill Bigger" 2004). In addition, hospital ownership of HMOs is also growing. The number of hospital-owned HMO plans increased from forty-three in 1994 to eighty in 2000, representing an increase of 86 percent ("Hospital-Owned HMOs" 2001). This in turn raises the question of the role of corporate medicine in the United States. Court and Smith (1999) have provided a strong indictment of "corporate medicine" as practiced by HMOs. They argue that U.S. medicine has been taken over by a corporate marketplace that looks only for profits, a practice that endangers patients and leads to significant waste of health care resources.

Nursing Homes

In 2003, there were about 15,245 licensed nursing homes. Between 1994 and 2003, the number of licensed nursing homes in the United States remained largely unchanged—from 15,142 in 1994 to 15,245 in 2003. In 2003, the number of licensed nursing home beds was around 1.7 million, compared to 1.6 million in 1994 ("eManaged Care Trends Digest 2004" n.d.). A majority of nursing homes are proprietary, that is, operated for profit. A small number of voluntary or not-for-profit nursing homes are operated by charitable organizations, mainly religious (U.S. Census Bureau 2003) Nursing homes generally provide long-term care, and most of the people they serve are elderly. A sizable portion of their revenues comes from the government. Nursing homes are also heavily regulated by state and local governments.

Physicians

Physicians are key actors in the health care system, because they are the primary caregivers. They enjoy considerable professional autonomy. There are over 870,000 physicians in the United States (American Medical Association 2005). A majority of them are specialists who conduct their practices in a hospital setting. Over the years, the number of generalists or family doctors has declined considerably (Rosenthal 1993). Physicians play a pivotal role and occupy a unique position in the health care system. Since they not only diagnose an illness but also prescribe treatment, they control the supply of as well as the demand for health care services. In the process, they exert substantial influence over the pattern of health resources utilization in general and hospital resources in particular.

Physicians work in one or more of several specialties, such as family and general medicine, general pediatrics, obstetrics and gynecology, surgery, and anesthesiology, among others. There are over 180 specialties. They conduct their practices in private offices; hospitals; and federal, state, and local governments. Some work in outpatient care centers or educational services. An increasing number of physicians are partners or salaried employees of group practice or managed care organizations such as HMOs and preferred provider organizations (PPOs) (Bureau of Labor Statistics 2004–5a).

In addition, physician assistants held about 63,000 jobs in 2002. They work under the supervision of a physician and their duties are determined by the supervising physicians and by state law. Sometimes they may be the principal care providers in rural areas and inner-city clinics where a physician is present only a couple of days a week. They are formally trained to provide diagnostic, therapeutic, and preventive health care services, as delegated by a physician (Bureau of Labor Statistics, 2004–5b).

Nurses

Registered nurses (RNs) constitute the largest health care occupation, with 2.3 million jobs. Hospital nurses form the largest group of nurses. Most of them are staff nurses who provide bedside nursing care and carry out medical regimens. Office nurses care for outpatients in physicians' offices, clinics, and ambulatory surgical centers. Home health care nurses provide nursing services to patients at home while nursing care facility nurses work in long-term care facilities such as nursing homes. Public health nurses work in government and private agencies including clinics, schools, and community settings to improve the overall health of the community. Occupational health nurses (industrial nurses) provide nursing care at worksites (Bureau of Labor Statistics 2004–5c).

Licensed practical nurses (LPNs) or licensed vocational nurses (LVNs) provide care under the direction of physicians and registered nurses. In 2002, LPNs held about 702,000 jobs in the health care field, of whom about 28 percent worked in hospitals, 26 percent worked in nursing care facilities, and 12 percent in physicians' offices. The remaining LPNs worked in a variety of other settings, such as home health care services, community care facilities, educational institutions, and the like (Bureau of Labor Statistics 2004–5d).

Advanced practice nurses (APNs) are carving out a new role in health care delivery. The advanced practice nurse is an umbrella term given to a registered nurse who has met advanced educational and clinical requirements beyond the years of basic nursing education required of all RNs. Advance practice nurses can be classified under four types: nurse practitioner (NP), certified nurse midwife (CNM), clinical nurse specialist (CNS), and certified registered nurse anesthetist (CRNA). NPs are qualified to handle a wide range of basic health problems and most of them have specialties, such as adult, family, or pediatric care. CNMs provide well-woman gynecological and low-risk obstetrical care. CNSs are qualified to handle a wide range of physical and mental health problems and they provide primary care and psychotherapy. CRNAs administer more then 65 percent of all anesthetics given to patients each year ("Advance Practice Nursing" 1993).

According to the Bureau of Labor Statistics, registered nurses top the list of the ten occupations with the largest projected growth in the years 2002–12. The number of registered nurses is expected to grow to 2.9 million in 2012. After a steady decline from 1995 to 2000, enrollments in entry-level baccalaureate nursing programs have increased and many qualified applicants have been turned away due to insufficient faculty, classrooms, and clinical sites. President Bush, in his proposed 2005 budget, has requested $147 million for nursing development workforce programs, including the Nurse Reinvestment Act ("Registered Nurses Rank Number One in Job Growth" 2004).

Third-Party Payers

The U.S. health care system over the years has undergone dramatic changes. One of the fundamental changes that have occurred since the early 1930s is the method of payment for health care services. Before the rise of the modern health insurance system, the nature of financial transactions between patient and health care provider was largely a direct one-on-one transaction. Under this system the patient paid for health services directly to the health care provider out of his or her own pocket. The birth of the modern health insurance system came in 1929 with the establishment of the Blue Cross plans for hospital insurance. A third-party-payer system was created under which a consumer paid predetermined monthly premiums to an insurance company. In return, the insurance company agreed to pay the health care provider for a specified range of health services received by the consumer. The Blue Shield plans, initiated by physicians, followed, based on a similar concept. Over the years, the number of private health insurance companies increased. Between 1930 and 1950, health insurance companies not only continued to cover more and more people under such plans but also expanded the scope of coverage. In 1965 the federal government entered the picture by creating two major insurance programs—Medicare for the elderly and Medicaid for the poor.

In 2003, of the total 288.2 million U.S. population, 243.3 million Americans (84.4 percent of the population) were covered by health insurance, while 45 million (15.6 percent of the population) were without health insurance coverage. Of the 243.3 million persons covered by health insurance, 197.8 million (81.3 percent) were covered by private health insurance (U.S. Census Bureau 2004).

The number of uninsured increased from 43.6 million (15.2 percent) in 2002 to 45 million (15.6 percent) in 2003. The percentage and number of people covered by employment-based health insurance dropped from 175.3 million (61.3 percent) in 2002 to 174 million (60.4 percent) in 2003. The number and percentage of people covered by government health insurance programs increased from 73.6 million (25.7 percent) to 76.8 million (26.6 percent) in 2003 (U.S. Census Bureau 2004). It is important to note that percentages given by the type of insurance coverage are not mutually exclusive. People can be covered by more than one type of health insurance coverage during the year. Thus, the combined percentages may add up to more than one hundred.

Of the total national health care expenditures of $1.553 trillion in 2002, 40.4 percent was spent by private health insurance and other private funds. The federal government spent about 32.5 percent, and state and local governments spent another 13.4 percent. The remaining 13.7 percent was out-of-pocket expenses paid by the consumers (Heffler et al. 2004).

Cost increases and pressure from employers have led insurance companies to look for ways to cut costs as well as increase the premiums they charge. Many insurance companies have begun to develop managed care systems. The concept of managed care involves arrangements with selected providers such as HMOs and PPOs to furnish a comprehensive set of health care services to its members, formal programs for ongoing quality assurance and utilization review, explicit standards for selection of health care providers, and financial incentives for members to use providers and procedures covered by the plan (Lazenby and Letsch 1990). The role of health insurers is changing significantly (Freudenheim 1990a; Kerr 1993). This has led Robert M. Brandon, vice-president of Citizen Action, an advocacy group, to charge that health insurance companies are engaging in "cream-skimming and cherry-picking" that eliminate or penalize firms and employees that could put them at risk of high payments, rather than offering coverage to all at rates that pool the risk (Rich 1991).

Consumers

The public can exert influence on health care policies not only as purchasers of health care but also by the perceptions, attitudes, and values they bring to the health care system as consumers. In 2002, consumers spent $212.5 billion (15.8 percent) in out-of-pocket expenses for personal health care services out of a total of $1.3 trillion of personal health care expenditures (Heffler et al. 2004).

The public's perception of the U.S. health care system is negative. This was clearly reflected in various public opinion polls conducted during the 1980s and 1990s. A study examining the public's feeling about health care systems found that of the ten countries included in the study, the lowest degree of satisfaction with health care systems was in the United States and the highest was in Canada (Blendon et al. 1990). Surveys by the *Los Angeles Times* in March 1990, NBC in 1989, and Louis Harris & Associates in 1988 all showed that majorities of at least 61 percent of those polled supported establishing a Canadian-style comprehensive national health system. Despite escalating health care costs, the general public also shows a preference for more spending for health care, but they themselves do not want to pay the bill. They want the government to pay the cost of health care (Freudenheim 1990b). In 1987 a Harris poll asked a random sample of 1,250 Americans whether some limit should be set, say $5 million, on what we can afford to spend to save a life. Fifty-one percent of the respondents said that no limit should be set (Morin 1990). Surveys also show that Americans want more health care, not less. About half of all Americans believe that the United States spends too little on health care. Polls also suggest that the public does not believe the increased health care costs have been matched by similar increases in the quality of treatment (Morin 1990).

Those who are dissatisfied with the current system cite the high cost of care and lack of access—lack of availability of health care or health insurance—as the primary reasons for their dissatisfaction. While a majority of Americans express a preference for a Canadian-style national health system, many also think that a government-run system would adversely affect their freedom of choice and lower quality of care, and they express doubt that such a system would lower costs (Jajich-Toth and Roper 1990). Public dissatisfaction with the current health care system leads many people to support a change, but they are also ambivalent about the options that would change the system. This partly explains why President Clinton's health care reform efforts aimed at overhauling the U.S. health care system failed during the 1993–94 period. Public opinion initially showed strong support for the reform effort. However, by the summer of 1994, public support for such a major reform had fallen below 50 percent.

The U.S. public still continues to express concern over problems with the U.S. health care system. In a series of public opinion polls conduced by the Kaiser Family Foundation, the public expressed concern over several issues. In a poll conducted in January 2000, 54 percent favored building on the current system instead of switching to a system in which individuals would buy their own health insurance and would receive a tax credit or subsidy to help them with the cost of the plan. In a poll conducted in February 2003, a slight majority of 52 percent expressed a willingness to pay more (either higher insurance premiums or higher taxes) in order to increase the number of Americans who have health insurance. In a January 2004 poll, 48 percent agreed with the statement that access to health care should be a right. In a poll conducted in February 2004, 82 percent listed lowering the cost of health insurance and prescription drugs as very important, while another 77 percent supported increasing the number of Americans covered by health insurance. Seventy-five percent of the respondents indicated that helping families with the cost of long-term care for the elderly and disabled was very important, while another 70 percent stated that improving the quality of medical care was very important (Kaiser Health Poll Report 2004).

An examination of data from twenty-two national polls during the 2004 presidential campaign indicated that health care ranked as the fourth most important issue to voters in the 2004 presidential elections. The top health issues of concern to the voters were the costs of health care and prescription drugs, the uninsured, and Medicare. However, the economy, the war in Iraq, and the war on terrorism were ranked higher by the voters (Blendon et al. 2004).

Shifting perceptions and attitudes on the part of the public present interesting dilemmas and value conflicts for health policymakers. The public often wants change but is unsure and apprehensive about it. The public wants more spending on health care by the government but there is a limit as to how much more they are willing to pay. On their part, health policymakers concerned with the impact of escalating health care costs on the budget want to contain costs and at the same time provide access to quality care for all Americans.

Interest Groups

The role of interest groups in U.S. politics has been debated intensely from the time of the founding of the Republic. The philosophy of interest-group liberalism has accorded interest groups a dominant role in U.S. politics. Proponents have praised interest groups for advancing the cause of U.S. democracy by providing access for citizen participation in the political process. Opponents have argued that special interests are stealing the United States (Navarro 1984) and destroying democracy (Bennett and DiLorenzo 1985). Regardless of how one feels about interest groups, there is no denying the fact that they have become important political power brokers in U.S. politics (Smith 1972). Since the 1970s, American society has also witnessed a rise in the number of public interest groups, that is, citizens' lobbies, to counter the influence of special interest groups in American politics (Miller 1985). Public interest groups presumably champion the cause of the public interest or the common good, while special or private interest groups work to advance narrow causes for the benefit of their members (Mahood 1990).

Health care affects everyone in society. A wide variety of interests—health care providers, purchasers, third-party payers, suppliers, consumers—are affected by what happens within the field of health care. Thus it is not too surprising that the number and variety of groups involved in health care politics and policymaking is very large (Feldstein 1984; Ward 1979). For example, over 1,000 health-related groups are listed in the *Encyclopedia of Associations* (Hedblad 2003).

The universal nature of illness gives health care professionals such as physicians important psychological and political leverage. Given their unique position, they are able to influence developments in the health care field. The introduction of government-sponsored health insurance programs such as Medicare and Medicaid has also made hospitals and skilled nursing facilities important players. The technical nature of modern medicine gives drug and medical supply companies significant leverage in the health field. Similarly, insurance companies as third-party payers have also come to play an important role (Bayes 1982).

One of the major ways in which these groups try to influence the political process is through their political action committees (PACs). During the 2000 election cycle, 219 health PACs contributed over $22 million to federal candidates, with 58 percent of it going to Republicans and 42 percent going to Democrats ("Health PAC Contribution to Federal Candidates 1999–2000" n.d.). According to the data released by the Federal Election Commission on October 25, 2004, about 264 health PACs had contributed over $27 million to federal candidates, with 66 percent going to Republicans and 34 percent going to Democrats ("Health PAC Contributions to Federal Candidates 2004" n.d.).

While it is impossible to discuss all the interest groups involved in the health care field, some of the major groups should be mentioned. Many of them are professional or trade associations of key actors in the health care field.

American Medical Association

The American Medical Association is one of the largest and most influential health-related groups (Wilbur 1979). It is a professional association of physicians with a membership of about 297,000 (Hedblad 2003). It is the voice of organized medicine and as such acts as an umbrella organization of U.S. medicine. Its main functions include representing the interests of its members; providing scientific and socioeconomic information; keeping data on the profession; and developing and maintaining standards of professional education, training, and performance (Campion 1984).

The AMA has grassroots political power and is very active in lobbying Congress on health-related issues. It is very well financed. It has one of the largest political action committees. During the 2001–2 election cycle, the AMA made total campaign contributions of $2.4 million to federal candidates and was ranked fifth among the top twenty PAC contributors ("Top 20 PAC Contributors to Federal Candidates, 2001–2002" n.d.). According to the Federal Election Commission report filed on October 25, 2004, the AMA contributed around $1.8 million to federal candidates during the 2003–4 election cycle and ranked eighth among the top twenty PAC contributors ("Top 20 PAC Contributors to Federal Candidates, 2003–2004" n.d.).

The AMA has acted as a voice of free enterprise and fee-for-service independent medical practice in the health care field. Much of its effort has been directed toward protecting the economic interests of its members and opposing policies that threaten those interests or threaten their professional autonomy. For example, for a long time the AMA has successfully argued against a national health insurance program because of the fear of losing its professional autonomy and a decline in physicians' income. But the organization has articulated its opposition to national health insurance not on the ground of protecting self-interest but by using the rhetoric of defending free enterprise and patients' freedom to choose their own doctors. It has argued that adoption of national health insurance would lead to lower quality of health care and services. The AMA has not been above using scare tactics to achieve its objectives.

The AMA is not the only physician group that has attempted to influence the political process. PACs representing groups such as physician assistants, clinical urologists, orthopedic surgeons, and emergency physicians have also contributed funds to political campaigns ("Health Professionals: PAC Contributions to Federal Candidates" n.d.).

American Nurses Association

The American Nurses Association (ANA) is a professional organization that represents the country's 2.7 million RNs and acts as a voice for the nursing professions. Besides promoting advances in nursing professions by fostering high standards of nursing practice, the ANA also lobbies Congress and regulatory agencies on health care issues affecting nurses and the general public ("ANA's Statement of Purpose" n.d.). Through its legislative and political program, the ANA has taken positions on issues such as Medicare reform, patient rights, whistle-blower protection for health care workers, and access to health care. The association has advocated for an expanded role for RNs and APNs in the delivery of basic and primary health care ("ANA's Statement of Purpose" n.d.).

American Hospital Association

The National Hospital Superintendents' Association was created in 1899. The membership in this organization was limited to chief executive officers of hospitals. A few years after the organization's founding, its name was changed to the American Hospital Association (AHA). In 1917 it changed from an individual membership organization to an organization of institutions (Weeks and Berman 1985). Today, the AHA represents individuals and health care institutions including hospitals, health care systems, and pre- and post-acute health care delivery organizations. It has a membership of about 54,500 (Hedblad 2003). In addition to conducting research and education projects, it acts as the voice of hospitals and represents their interests in national health policy development. Its advocacy efforts have included lobbying executive and legislative branches of government ("About the AHA" n.d.).

America's Health Insurance Plans

America's Health Insurance Plans (AHIP) is the voice of U.S. health insurers. AHIP is the national association that represents nearly 1,300 member companies that provide health insurance coverage to more than 200 million Americans. The association represents the interests of its members on legislative and regulatory issues at the federal and state levels ("About AHIP" n.d.).

Among the health insurers, the major commercial insurers are Blue Cross and Blue Shield. The Blue Cross plans were developed by the hospitals through the AHA, while the Blue Shield plans were developed by physicians through the AMA. The Blue Cross and Blue Shield plans are the nation's largest family of health benefit companies. The Blue Cross Blue Shield provides coverage to more than 92 million people ("History of Blue Cross Blue Shield" n.d.).

American Health Care Association

The American Health Care Association (AHCA) is a nonprofit federation of affiliated state organizations representing more than 10,000 nonprofit and for-profit assisted living, nursing facility, developmentally disabled, and subacute care providers for elderly and disabled people . The organization represents the long-term care community to the government, business people, and the general public. It has focused its attention on issues of availability, quality, affordability, and fair payment in health care. The AHCA also maintains a liaison with government agencies, Congress, and other professional health care associations ("Profile of American Health Care Association" n.d.).

Other Groups

The increase in the number of people enrolled in managed care plans has also led to a dramatic increase in the number of managed care organizations (MCOs). MCOs vary significantly in their structures, financing mechanisms, and benefit packages. A broad range of health insurers, medical groups, hospitals, and health systems are considered managed care organizations. MCOs can take the form of an HMO, PPO, or point-of-service (POS) plan. Today, there are more than 1,620 managed care organizations, representing about 3,935 plan types (Harris 2003).

A number of groups represent hospital equipment suppliers and manufacturers of drugs and health care products and attempt to influence health care politics and policies. The increased cost of providing health care to employees has led many businesses and industries to form health coalitions to search for solutions to spiraling health care costs. Such coalitions are rapidly expanding in number (Meyerhoff and Crozier 1984). The many major health coalitions include the Alliance of Business for Cost Containment; the Coalition on Health Care Costs, Quality, and Access; the National Leadership Coalition for Health Care Reforms; and the Washington Business Group on Health. A consortium of business groups representing small companies, called the Partnership on Health Care and Employment, was formed to oppose legislative proposals requiring all employers to offer health insurance to its employees. It includes the Chamber of Commerce, the American Farm Bureau Federation, the National Restaurant Association, and about 350 corporations (Kosterlitz 1991).

The number of health-related public interest groups has also increased. One of the most active groups is Ralph Nader's Health Research Group, founded in 1971. Its main objectives include protecting consumers and increasing public awareness on a variety of health issues. It promotes research-based systemwide changes in health care policy and works to ban or relabel unsafe or ineffective drugs and medical devices. It also acts as an information resource for consumers about doctors disciplined by state medical boards, dispute resolution in Medicare HMOs, and hospital cesarean birth rates ("About Health Research Group" n.d.). Public interest groups typically rely on methods such as coalition forming, litigation, lobbying, testifying before congressional committees, and participation in regulatory proceedings to influence health care policies.

Conclusion

Health care politics and policies in the United States are shaped by a variety of factors. Health policy reflects a combination of initiatives taken by institutions and actors in the public and private sectors. The health policy cycle is influenced and shaped by the constitutional, institutional, political, economic, ideological, and technological environment within which it operates. The public philosophy of interest-group liberalism combined with constitutionally guaranteed freedom of speech, association, and petition allow a variety of interest groups to promote policies for private profit and to successfully defeat policies they perceive as harmful to their interests. Interest groups promote their narrow private interests using the rhetoric of the common good. The consensus created through compromise and bargaining between narrow private interests is often defined as the public interest. Such a policy process makes the establishment of a comprehensive national health policy highly improbable, if not impossible. The result is a series of health care programs and policies that often reflects conflicting values of access, equality, quality of care, and efficiency.

References

"About the AHA." n.d. Online at www.aha.org.
"About AHIP." n.d. Online at www.ahip.org.
"About HHS." n.d. Online at www.hhs.gov.
"About Health Research Group" n.d. Online at www.citizen.org.
"Advance Practice Nursing: A New Age in Health Care." 1993. American Nursing Association. Online at www.nursingworld.org/readroom/fsadvprc.htm.
Alford, Robert A. 1975. *Health Care Politics: Ideological and Interest Group Barriers to Reform*. Chicago: University of Chicago Press.
Allison, Graham. 1971. *The Essence of Decision*. Boston: Little, Brown.
Altenstetter, Christa. 1974. *Health Policy-Making and Administration in West Germany and the United States*. Beverly Hills, Calif.: Sage.
American Hospital Association. 2005. *AHA Hospital Statistics*. Chicago: Health Forum Publishing Company.
American Medical Association. 2005. *Physician Characteristics and Distribution in the US, 2005*. Chicago: AMA Press.

"ANA's Statement of Purpose." n.d. Online at www.ana.org.

Babcock, Charles R. 1993. "Health Care Fears Open Up the Pocketbooks." *Washington Post National Weekly Edition*, June 7–13.

Bayes, Jane H. 1982. *Ideologies and Interest-Group Politics*. Novato, Calif.: Chandler and Sharp.

Beer, S.H. 1965. *Modern British Politics*. London: Faber and Faber.

Bennett, James T., and Thomas J. DiLorenzo. 1985. *Destroying America: How Government Funds Partisan Politics*. Washington, D.C.: Cato Institute.

Berki, S.E. 1983. "Health Care Policy: Lessons from the Past and Issues of the Future." *Annals of the American Academy of Political and Social Science* 468 (July): 231–46.

Blendon, Robert J; Drew E. Altman; John M. Benson; and Mollyann Brodie. 2004. "Election 2004: Health Care in the 2004 Presidential Election." *New England Journal of Medicine* 351, no. 13 (September 23): 314–21.

Blendon, Robert J.; Robert Leitman; Ian Morrison; and Karen Donelan. 1990. "Satisfaction with Health Systems in Ten Nations." *Health Affairs* 9, no. 2 (Summer): 185–92.

Brown, J.H.A. 1978. *The Politics of Health Care*. Cambridge, Mass: Ballinger.

Brown, Lawrence D. 1978. "The Formulation of Federal Health Care Policy." *Bulletin of the New York Academy of Medicine* 54, no. 1 (January): 45–58.

———. 1984. *Health Policy in the Reagan Administration: A Critical Appraisal*. Washington, D.C.: Brookings Institution.

Bureau of Labor Statistics, U.S. Department of Labor. 2004–5a. *Occupational Outlook Handbook* Physicians and Surgeons. Online at bls.gov.oco/ocos074.htm.

———. 2004–5b. *Occupational Outlook Handbook*. Physician Assistants. Online at bls.gov.oco/ocos081.htm.

———. 2004–5c. *Occupational Outlook Handbook*. Registered Nurses. Online at bls.gov.oco/ocos083.htm.

———. 2004–5d. *Occupational Outlook Handbook*. Licensed Practical and Licensed Vocational Nurses. Online at bls.gov.oco/ocos102.htm

Burner, Sally T.; Daniel R. Waldo; and David R. McKusick. 1992. "National Health Expenditures Projections through 2030." *Health Care Financing Review* 14, no. 1 (Fall): 1–29.

Califano, Joseph A. 1988. "The Health-Care Chaos." *New York Times Magazine*, March 20.

Campion, Frank D. 1984. *The AMA and U.S. Health Policy Since 1940*. Chicago: University of Chicago Press.

Chollet, Deborah J. 1984. *Employer-Provided Health Benefits: Coverage, Provisions and Policy Issues*. Washington, D.C.: Employee Benefit Research Institute.

Cohen, Alan B., and Donald R. Cohodes. 1982. "Certificate of Need and Low Capital-Cost Medical Technology." *Milbank Memorial Fund Quarterly/Health and Society* 60, no. 2 (Spring): 307–28.

Colliver, Victoria. 2004. "In Critical Condition: Health Care in America. How the Health Care System Is Failing—and Why It Is Hard to Fix It." *San Francisco Chronicle*, October 11.

Conley, Richard S. 2003. *The Presidency, Congress, and Divided Government: A Postwar Assessment*. College Station: Texas A&M University Press.

Connolly, Ceci. 2004. "Health Plans Differ in Scope and Philosophy." *Washington Post*, October 22. Online at www.washingtonpost.com.

Court, Jamie, and Francis Smith. 1999. *Making a Killing: HMOs and the Threat to Your Health*. Monroe, Me.: Common Courage Press.

Dentzer, Susan. 1990. "America's Scandalous Health Care." *U.S. News and World Report*, March 12: 25–30.

"eManaged Care Trends Digest 2004" n.d. Online at www.managedcaredigest.com.

Feldstein, Paul J. 1984. "Health Associations and the Legislative Process." In *Health Politics and Policy*, ed. Theodore J. Litman and Leonard S. Robins, 223–42. New York: Wiley.

Fineberg, H.V., and H.H. Hiatt. 1979. "Evaluation of Medical Practices: The Case for Technology Assessment." *New England Journal of Medicine* 301, no. 20: 1086–91.

Freudenheim, Milt. 1990a. "Business and Health: Health Insurers Changing Roles." *New York Times*, January 16.

———. 1990b. "Business and Health: Most Want U.S. to Pay the Bill." *New York Times*, July 3.

Fuchs, Victor R. 1986. *The Health Economy*. Cambridge, Mass.: Harvard University Press.

———. 1995. *Who Shall Live? Health, Economics and Social Choice*. New York: Basic Books.

Galderisi, Peter; Roberta Q. Herzberg; and Peter McNamara, eds. 1996. *Divided Government: Change, Uncertainty, and the Constitutional Order*. New York: Rowman and Littlefield Publishers.

Harris, Phyllis. 2003. *The National Directory of Managed Care Organizations*. 4th edition. Allenwood, N.J.: Health Resource Publishing.

Health Insurance Association of America.1998. *Sourcebook of Health Insurance Data*. Washington, D.C.: Health Insurance Association of America.

"Health PAC Contributions to Federal Candidates 1999–2000." n.d. Center for Responsive Politics. Online at www.opensecrets.org.

"Health PAC Contributions to Federal Candidates 2004." n.d. Center for Responsive Politics. Online at www.opensecrets.org.

"Health Professionals: PAC Contributions to Federal Candidates." n.d. Center for Responsive Politics. Online at www.opensecrets.org.

Heaney, Michael T. 2004. "Issue Networks, Information, and Interest Group Alliances: The Case of Wisconsin Welfare Politics, 1993–99." *State Politics and Policy Quarterly* 4, no. 3 (Fall): 237–70.

Heclo, Hugh. 1978. "Issues Networks and the Executive Establishment." In *The New American Political System*, ed. Anthony King, 87–124. Washington, D.C.: American Enterprise Institute Press.

Hedblad, Alan. 2003. *Encyclopedia of Associations*. 40th edition. New York: Gale Research.

Heffler, Stephen; Sheila Smith; Sean Keehan; M. Kent Clemens; Mark Zezza; and Christopher Truffer. 2004. "Health Spending Projections Through 2013." *Health Affairs* (Web exclusive), February 11. Online at content.healthaffairs.org/cgi/reprint/hlthaff.w4.79v1.

"History of Blue Cross Blue Shield" n.d. Online at www.bcbs.com.

Hospital Insurance Association of America. 1990. *Source Book of Health Insurance Data*. Washington, D.C.: Hospital Insurance Association of America.

"Hospital-Owned HMOs." 2001. *eManaged Care Trends Digest*. Online at www.managedcaredigest.com.

Huitt, Ralph. 1970. "Political Feasibility." In *Policy Analysis in Political Science*, ed. Ira Sharkansky, pp. 399–412. Chicago: Markham.

Jajich-Toth, Cindy, and Burns W. Roper. 1990. "Americans' Views on Health Care: A Study in Contradictions." *Health Affairs* 9, no. 4 (Winter): 149–57.

Jones, Charles O. 1978. *An Introduction to the Study of Public Policy*. North Scituate, Mass: Duxbury Press.

Kaiser Health Poll Report. 2004. March–April Edition. Online at www.kff.org/healthpollreport/archive_April2004/1.cfm.

Kerr, Peter. 1993. "The Changing Definition of Health Insurers." *New York Times*, May 10.

Klein, Rudolf. 1984. "The Political Ideology vs. the Reality of Politics: The Case of Britain's Health Services in the 1980s." *Milbank Memorial Fund Quarterly/Health and Society* 62, no. 1 (Winter): 82–109.

Kosterlitz, Julie. 1991. "Softening Resistance." *National Journal* 23, no. 2 (January 12): 64–68.

Koszczuk, Jackie. 1995. "Gingrich Puts More Power into Speaker's Hands." *Congressional Quarterly Weekly Report* 53, no. 39 (October 7): 3049–51.

Lazenby, Helen C., and Suzanne W. Letsch. 1990. "National Health Expenditures, 1989." *Health Care Financing Review* 12, no. 2 (Winter): 1–26.

Levit, Katharine R.; Arthur L. Sensebig; Cathy A. Cowen; Helen C. Lazenby; Patricia A. McDonnell; Darleen K. Won; Lekha Sivarajan; Jean M. Stiller; Carolyn S. Donham; and Madie S. Stewart. 1994. "National Health Expenditures, 1993." *Health Care Financing Review* 16, no. 1 (Fall): 247–94.

Lindblom, Charles E. 1959. "The Science of Muddling Through." *Public Administration Review* 19 (Spring): 79–88.

Lowi, Theodore. 1967. "The Public Philosophy: Interest Group Liberalism." *American Political Science Review* 61, no. 1 (March): 5–24.

Madison, James. 1961a. "Federalist 51." In *The Federalist Papers*, ed. Clinton Rossiter pp. 320–325. New York: New American Library.

———. 1961b. "Federalist 10." In *The Federalist Papers*, ed. Clinton Rossiter, 77–84. New York: New American Library.

Mahood, H.R. 1990. *Interest Group Politics in America: A New Intensity*. Englewood Cliffs, N.J.: Prentice Hall.

Mawhinney, Hanne B. 2001. "Theoretical Approaches to Understanding Interest Groups." *Educational Policy* 15, no. 1 (January/March): 187–214.

McConnell, Grant. 1966. *Private Power and American Democracy*. New York: Knopf.

"Mercer's National Survey of Employer-Sponsored Health Plans 2003." 2004. Mercer Human Resource Consulting, Inc. Press Release. February 25. Online at www.mercerhr.com/knowledgecenter/reportsummary.jhtml?idContent=1051300.

Mellow, Wesley S. 1982. "Determinants of Health Insurance and Pension Coverage." *Monthly Labor Review* 105, no. 5 (May): 30–32.

Meyerhoff, Allen S., and David A. Crozier. 1984. "Health Care Coalitions: The Evolution of a Movement." *Health Affairs* 3, no. 1 (Spring): 120–27.

Miller, Stephen. 1985. *Special Interest Groups in American Politics*. New Brunswick, N.J.: Transaction.

Mooney, Gavin. 1986. *Economics, Medicine and Health Care*. Atlantic Highlands, N.J.: Humanities Press.

Morin, Richard. 1990. "Americans Want Health Care to Save Lives Whatever the Cost." *Washington Post National Weekly Edition*, February 5–11.

"National Health Care Expenditures Projections: 2003–2013." n.d. Centers for Medicare and Medicaid Services, Office of the Actuary. Online at www.cms.hhs.gov/statistics/nhe/projections-2003/proj2003.pdf.

Navarro, Peter. 1984. *The Policy Game: How Special Interests and Ideologues Are Stealing America*. New York: Wiley.

Niskanen, William A. 2003. "A Case for Divided Government." *Cato Policy Report* 25, no. 2 (March/April): 2.

Office of the Federal Register, National Archives and Records Administration.1990. *The United States Government Manual 1990/91*. Washington, D.C.: Government Printing Office.

Patel, Kant, and Mark Rushefsky. 2002. *Health Care Policy in an Age of New Technologies*. Armonk, N.Y.: M.E. Sharpe, Inc.

"Profile of American Health Care Association." n.d. Online at www.ahca.org.

"Registered Nurses Rank Number One in Job Growth." 2004. American Nurses Association Press Release, February 12.

Rich, Spencer. 1991. "Are Insurers Playing Favorites?" *Washington Post National Weekly Edition* (June 24–30): 37.

Rosenbaum, Walter A. 1985. *Environmental Politics and Policy*. Washington, D.C.: CQ Press.

Rosenthal, Elisabeth. 1993. "Medicine Suffers as Fewer Doctors Join Front Lines." *New York Times*, May 24.

Rushefsky, Mark. 2002. *Public Policy in the United States: At the Dawn of the Twenty-First Century*. Armonk, N.Y.: M.E. Sharpe, Inc.

Rushefsky, Mark, and Kant Patel. 1998. *Politics, Power and Policy Making: The Case of Health Care Reform in the 1990s*. Armonk, N.Y.: M.E. Sharpe, Inc.

Samuelson, Paul. 1970. *Economics*. New York: McGraw-Hill.

Schantz, Harvey L., ed. 2001. *Politics in an Era of Divided Government: Elections and Governance in the Second Clinton Administration*. New York: Routledge.

Silver, George A. 1998. "Health-Care Systems." Grolier Multimedia Encyclopedia.

Simon, Herbert A. 1957. *Models of Man: Social and Rational; Mathematical Essays on Rational Behavior in Society Setting*. New York: Wiley.

Smith, Judith G., ed. 1972. *Political Brokers: Money, Organizations, Power and People*. New York: Liveright.

Sorkin, Alan L. 1986. *Health Care and the Changing Economic Environment*. Lexington, Mass.: D.C. Heath.

Stanley, Harold W., and Richard G. Niemi. 2001. *Vital Statistics on American Politics, 2001–2002*. Washington, D.C.: CQ Press.

"Study: For-Profit Hospitals Bill Bigger." 2004. Online at CNN.Com.

"Survey Finds Businesses and Retirees Hit with Double-Digit Increases in Retiree Health Costs in 2004, with Higher Premium Likely in Future." 2004 News Release, December 14. The Henry J. Kaiser Family Foundation. Online at www.kff.org/medicare/med121404nr.cfm.

Taylor, Humphrey. 1990. "U.S. Health Care Built for Waste." *New York Times,* April 17.

Thompson, Frank J. 1986. "New Federalism and Health Care Policy: States and the Old Questions." *Journal of Health Politics, Policy and Law* 11, no. 4 (Tenth Anniversary Issue): 647–69.

Tichenor, Daniel J., and Richard A. Harris. 2002/2003. "Organized Interests and American Political Development." *Political Science Quarterly* 117, no. 4 (Winter): 587–612.

"Top 20 PAC Contributors to Federal Candidates, 2001–2002" n.d. Center for Responsive Politics. Online at www.opensecrets.org.

"Top 20 PAC Contributors to Federal Candidates, 2003–2004" n.d. Center for Responsive Politics. Online at www.opensecrets.org.

Truman, David B. 1951. *Governmental Process, Political Interests and Public Opinion*. New York: Knopf.

U.S. Census Bureau. n.d. "Health Insurance Coverage: 1995." Online at www.census.gov/hhes/hlthins/cover95/c95taba.html.

———. 2003. *Statistical Abstract of the United States, 2003*. Washington, D.C.: U.S. Government Printing Office.

———. 2004. *Income, Poverty, and Health Insurance Coverage in the United States: 2003*. Washington, D.C.: U.S. Government Printing Office.

U.S. Government Manual. 2004–5 edition. Online at www.gpoaccess.gov/gmanual/browse-gm-04-html.

Vladeck, Bruce C. 1980. *Unloving Care: The Nursing Home Tragedy*. New York: Basic Books.

Wagner, Lynn. 1990. "Health PACs Modest Donors—Study." *Modern Healthcare* 20, no. 38 (September 24): 4.

Ward, Paul D. 1979. "Health Lobbies: Vested Interests and Pressure Politics." In *Politics of Health*, ed. Douglas Carter and Philip R. Lee, 28–47. Huntington, N.Y.: Robert F. Krieger.

Weeks, Lewis E., and Howard J. Berman. 1985. *Shapers of American Health Care Policy: An Oral History*. Ann Arbor, Mich.: Health Administration Press.

Wilbur, Dwight L. 1979. "The AMA in Washington." In *Politics of Health*, ed. Douglas Carter and Philip R. Lee, 48–50. Huntington, N.Y.: Robert F. Krieger.

Wilsford, David. 1991. *Doctors and the State: The Politics of Health Care in France and the United States*. Durham, N.C.: Duke University Press.

2

Health Care Policy in the United States

There are substantial differences in the health care systems of various countries. They differ with respect to financing, delivery of health care, and the role of the government. Today there are three primary models of health care. In a mostly private health care system, workers and their dependents are covered through private insurance, even though the insurance is generally bought through employers. Government provides public insurance programs for those not covered by private insurance. Mostly private hospitals and doctors deliver health care. The United States is an example of such a system (Hacker 2002).

Other countries have a health care system that is mostly public. Health care is paid out of general taxation or through payroll taxes. It is provided by publicly owned hospitals and salaried doctors. Examples of countries with such a system include Great Britain, Sweden, and Italy. The third model of health care system is a hybrid model. In such a system, health care is mostly publicly financed, generally through payroll taxes, but is delivered by private hospitals and doctors. Germany, Japan, Canada, France, and Holland exhibit variants of this model. Most countries incorporate public and private elements in their health care systems ("A Survey of Health Care" 1991).

As mentioned, the U.S. health care system follows the model of the mostly private health care system. A majority of Americans are covered through private insurance, usually bought through their employers. The government provides public insurance programs to cover the health care needs of groups such as the poor, the disabled, the elderly, veterans, and children. Nevertheless, public insurance programs do not cover all uninsured Americans. Public programs do not cover a sizable number of individuals who cannot afford private health insurance for one reason or another.

The United States spends proportionately more money on health care than all other Western industrialized nations. Statistics compiled by the Organization for Economic Cooperation and Development (OECD) indicate that in 2002 total health care expenditures in the United States amounted to 14.6 percent of gross domestic product (GDP), compared to 10.9 percent for Germany, 9.7 percent for France, 9.6 percent for Canada, and 7.7 percent for Great Britain. Among the thirty member countries of the OECD, the United States ranked first in terms of percent of GDP devoted to health care expenditures. During the same year, the United States also spent more money per capita on health care than any other member country. In 2002, United States spent $5,267 per capita on health care, compared to $2,817 in Germany, $2,736 in France, $2,931 in Canada, and $2,160 in Great Britain ("OECD Health Data" 2004). U.S. per capita spending of $5,267 in 2002 was almost 140 percent above the OECD average of $2,144 ("Health Spending in Most OECD Countries Rises . . ." 2004).

Despite the fact that the United States spent more money per capita on health care, in 2001 it ranked lower than Germany, France, Canada, and Great Britain in male and female life expectancy. The United States also had higher infant mortality rates compared to Germany, France, Canada, and Great Britain ("OECD Health Data" 2004).

The U.S. health care system also has other problems. Health care costs continue to soar. The number of uninsured Americans continues to rise and is currently estimated to be around 45 million. By the early 1990s, many hospitals in large cities were reporting long waiting lines in emergency rooms, with many Medicaid patients leaving in frustration without receiving treatment (Baker, Stevens and Brook 1991; Bindman et al. 1991; Hilts 1991). The City Hospital Visiting Committee, in its annual report in 1991, described hospital care in New York City's municipal hospitals as the worst in recent memory (Belkin 1991). Rising malpractice insurance costs also forced many of the nation's community health centers to cut or eliminate services for low-income patients (Pear 1991). Law enforcement officials in several states were investigating private psychiatric hospital chains on charges that they had systematically misdiagnosed, mistreated, and abused patients to increase their profits from insurance claims (Kerr 1991).

As mentioned in chapter 1, a majority of Americans express very low satisfaction with the U.S. health care system and believe that increased health care expenditures have not been matched by similar increases in the quality of treatment. The U.S. health care system has been referred to as "broken" (The Health Care System Is Broken . . ." 1991), "sick" (Lewis 1991), "a disgrace" (Ehrenreich 1990), "wasteful" (Terris 1990), "built for waste" (Taylor 1990), and "scandalous" (Dentzer 1990). More recent literature has described the U.S. health care system as "unsystematic" (Budrys 2001), "overdosed" (Abramson 2004), in "critical condition" (Bartlett and Steele 2004), or in "financial crisis" (Clark and McEldowney 2001).

In this chapter we examine the historical development of health care policies in the United States. We discuss private- and public-sector policy initiatives and various factors that have shaped health care policy. The major emphasis is on the development of federal health care policies and how these policies have attempted to address the goals of equity, quality, and efficiency. The chapter also briefly explores the roles of state and local governments.

Health Care in the Nineteenth Century

The progress of medicine, or the "healing arts," was very slow in the 1700s and 1800s. Neither health care nor the biosciences received a great deal of popular support in the United States in the early 1800s. The biological sciences were not very popular with the general public. During the 1840s, a proposal for the establishment of a National Institute of Science, funded by the federal government, was rejected repeatedly by Congress. Finally, during the Civil War, the National Academy of Sciences was established in 1863 on the grounds of its usefulness to the Union armies (Hill 1976).

The American Medical Association (AMA) was formed in 1847. During the latter part of the nineteenth century, physicians and pharmacists were the sole dispensers of professionally recognized health services. Most physicians were trained through apprenticeships with practicing physicians. Physicians also established "diploma mills" to train several students at a time. Later, private and public schools set up medical schools to train physicians. Physicians made their living treating patients for fees and received very little money from the government. The same was true of pharmacists, who later developed drugstores to supplement their income from prescriptions. Thus, private practice and fee for service became firmly established in the early U.S. health care system (Anderson 1985).

During the nineteenth century, public health activities were devoted to preventing the spread of communicable diseases and were confined primarily to major cities until the Civil War. In response to epidemics, a city board or commission was appointed to establish regulations for the maintenance of a sanitary environment. Only after the Civil War did state boards of health become popular. By the end of the nineteenth century, boards of health had been established within the governments of most large cities and at the state level. Their functions were limited to enforcement of sanitary regulations and control of certain communicable diseases. The scope of the health departments did not expand until the turn of the century (Patel and Rushefsky 2004, Roemer 1986). Public health services were separated from the private practice of medicine, and public health officers were not allowed to practice medicine (Patel and Rushefsky 2004).

General hospitals, as we know them today, did not exist. Poorhouses and almshouses provided care for destitute persons. The origin of a hospital system in the United States is associated with the establishment of the first Marine Hospital in 1799 (Raffel 1980). Both the army and the navy had their own requirements for treating sickness, and they differed from those of the U.S. Marine Service. Between 1830 and 1860, marine hospitals proliferated. During the Civil War, the Marine Hospital System was very much neglected and the number of hospitals decreased. In 1869, Congress reviewed the Marine Hospital System and passed the first Reorganization Act in 1870. Under this law, the Marine Hospital Service was federalized and formally organized as a national agency with a central headquarters (U.S. Health Resources Administration 1976).

The building of mental hospitals also preceded the development of personal health services. Mental hospitals were and continue to be largely publicly owned and operated.

The last quarter of the nineteenth century saw a steady advance in medical science. Antiseptic surgery was highly developed by 1875. The science of microbiology was introduced, and techniques of vaccination were developed. The advent of anesthesia and antisepsis made general hospitals a relatively safe place for surgery. Mostly voluntary community boards and churches established the early general hospitals. The growing economy made it possible for hospitals to obtain capital funds from philanthropists and operating funds from paying patients. Voluntary hospitals, because of their charitable and nonprofit charters, were obligated to provide care for the poor. Physicians began to admit patients to hospitals for surgeries. Patients paid for hospital charges and physicians' fees. In return, hospitals provided physicians with their facilities to provide free care for the poor. In 1875 there were very few general hospitals in the country. Tremendous growth in number of hospitals occurred in the twentieth century. For example, by 2003, there were a total of 5,764 registered hospitals in the United States (American Hospital Association 2005).

The Transformation of American Medicine: 1900–1935

During the first decade of the twentieth century, the process of consolidation of medical education and the transformation of American medicine began to take shape. For a number of years, the AMA had been trying to force inferior medical schools to close in order to reduce the numbers of institutions competing for philanthropic support (Fox 1986). Reform of medical schools was the top priority of the AMA. The Council on Medical Education, established by the AMA in 1904, elevated and standardized requirements for medical education for physicians. In addition, in order to identify and pressure weaker institutions, the council began to grade medical schools and later extended its evaluation to include curriculum, facilities, faculty, and requirements for admissions (Starr 1982).

Philanthropic foundations often had power and influence, but they lacked authority. Their financial power was limited by their fear that legislatures that chartered them would restrict their power or tax them out of existence. Nevertheless, placing medical education on a more scientific basis had also become their top priority. Several foundations began to finance studies that recommended reorganization of medical education and medical care. The AMA Council invited an outside group, the Carnegie Foundation for the Advancement of Teaching, to investigate medical schools. Abraham Flexner, as a representative of the Carnegie Foundation, visited each of the medical schools in the country during 1909 and 1910. He saw a great discrepancy between medical science and medical education. His report, known as the Flexner Report, was published in 1910 and recommended adoption of the German model of medicine with scientifically based training, the strengthening of first-class medical schools, and the elimination of a great majority of inferior schools.

Following the Flexner Report, the process of consolidation of medical education proceeded at a rapid pace. By 1915, the number of medical schools had decreased from 131 to 95. Similarly, the number of graduates from medical schools dropped from 5,440 to 3,536. Mergers between class A and class B schools became common. The AMA Council became a national accrediting agency for medical schools, and many states came to accept its judgments regarding medical schools. The new system increased the homogeneity and cohesiveness of the medical profession (Starr 1982). By the 1940s the AMA had become a powerful political force and a major player in shaping U.S. health care policy (Campion 1984).

Another significant development during this period was the rise of the third-party payment system in U.S. medicine. Prior to the 1930s, medical insurance programs were nonexistent. During the Great Depression of the 1930s, the incomes of hospitals and physicians declined. Many people could not afford to pay hospitals or physicians for their medical services. Realizing that they could operate better with a steady income, hospitals began to sponsor prepayment plans, which came to be known as the Blue Cross plans. Similarly, prepayment plans for physicians' services in the hospital, especially surgery, also began to appear. Sponsored by state medical societies, they became known as Blue Shield plans. Both the Blue Cross and the Blue Shield plans were very successful. During the 1940s, the federal government encouraged the development of private, voluntary insurance plans. For example, Congress gave voluntary plans a financial boost by legislating that health insurance and pensions were fringe benefits and exempt from a wartime freeze on wages. Thus, employers could offer their workers health care fringe benefits by paying for part or all of the cost of their insurance premiums. A ruling by the Internal Revenue Service in 1951 that employers' costs for premiums were a tax-deductible expense made large-scale development of private health insurance viable.

The rise of third-party payment led to increases in visits to physicians and admissions to hospitals. The third-party payment system replaced the financing system based on one-on-one financial transactions between patient and physician. Third-party payers insulated health care consumers from the realities of health care costs, leading to overconsumption, a problem called "moral hazard" by economists. Physicians and hospitals prospered. Since insurance companies reimbursed hospitals for the charges and/or costs of hospital services received by the patient, third-party payments made hospitals financially secure and independent because they could count on a steady income. Physicians prospered because they were paid by voluntary health insurance according to generous fee schedules negotiated by the Blue Shield plans.

The Role of the Federal Government

The Beginnings: 1800s

During much of the nineteenth century, the role of the federal government in health care was limited to providing public health services. In 1798 President John Adams signed into law an act that provided for the relief of sick and disabled seamen. This led to the development of marine hospitals during the nineteenth century. The American Public Health Association (APHA), composed mainly of social workers, was founded in 1872. Its main concern was the social and economic aspects of health problems. Following the Civil War, Congress in 1878 passed a National Quarantine Act for the purpose of preventing entry into the country of persons with communicable diseases. The period from 1870 to 1910 witnessed the maturation of the government's public health services. Health boards and health departments became widespread features of local and state governments; their functions were limited to the enforcement of sanitary regulations and control of communicable diseases. The AMA, which earlier had supported an expanded federal role in health care, came to view increased public health activities as a threat to economic interests of the physicians. The AMA began to attack all proposals designed to extend the role of government in health care.

Limited Federal Role: 1900–1930

During the late nineteenth and the early part of the twentieth century, countries in Europe were establishing compulsory sickness insurance programs. Germany established the first national system of compulsory sickness insurance in 1883. Similar systems were established in Austria in 1888, Hungary in 1891, Norway in 1910, Britain in 1911, Russia in 1912, and the Netherlands in 1913. France and Italy required sickness insurance in only a few industries. Countries such as Sweden, Denmark, and Switzerland gave extensive state aid to voluntary funds and provided incentives for membership (Starr 1982).

The federal government in the United States, in contrast to happenings in Europe, took no action to subsidize voluntary funds or to make sickness insurance mandatory. This partly reflected existing political conditions and institutions in the United States, where, as a result of the influence of the public philosophy of classical liberalism, government was highly decentralized and played a very small role in regulation of the economy or in promoting social welfare.

Health insurance became a political issue in the United States on the eve of World War I. The progress of a workmen's compensation law between 1910 and 1913 encouraged reformers to believe that adoption of compulsory insurance against industrial accidents would lead to the adoption of compulsory sickness insurance. But the progressive reformers' hopes of strengthening government and adopting compulsory sickness insurance were soon dashed. Opposition from physicians and pharmaceutical and insurance companies defeated their reform proposals. In addition, both labor unions and business, fearing competition from government in social welfare programs, failed to support the reformers. By 1920, the movement for compulsory sickness insurance had faded from the political agenda.

Under pressure from the labor movement and children's advocates, Congress passed the Sheppard-Towner Act in 1921. It established the first federal grant-in-aid program for local child health clinics. But many local health departments refused to accept these grants because the AMA and local medical societies strongly opposed the program. Congress allowed the program to terminate in 1928 (Roemer 1984).

Thus, the federal government's role in health care remained very limited during the nineteenth and early twentieth centuries.

Expansion of Health Facilities and Services: 1930–1960

A number of significant developments took place in the health care field during the 1930s. One major development, as mentioned earlier, was the start of a third-party payment system with the establishment of the Blue Cross and Blue Shield insurance plans. This revolutionized health care financing and led to employer-based health insurance programs. A second development concerned advances in medical technology and the discovery of antibiotics. Antibiotics changed the focus of medical care from prevention of disease through inoculation and hygiene to cure of illnesses (Bernstein and Bernstein 1988). For the first time, sulfa drugs and penicillin gave physicians their true power to cure (Easterbrook 1987). The third development was the shift from local control of health and welfare issues to state and especially federal government control. Workmen's compensation, pensions, unemployment insurance, and certain medical services came to be perceived by the people as the responsibility of the federal government (Greifinger and Sidel 1978). This was because of the Great Depression and the economic problems of state and local governments. The problems facing the country were too large for any but federal solutions.

The establishment of the National Institutes of Health (NIH) in 1930, with a broad mandate for ascertaining the cause, prevention, and cure of disease, reflected the increased role of the federal government in health care in general and in public health services in particular. It also paved the way for public funding of biomedical research through the NIH and later through the National Science Foundation (NSF). In 1934, during the Great Depression, the Federal Emergency Relief Administration gave the first federal grants to local governments for public assistance to the poor, including financial support for medical care.

During the depression, there was also an increased demand for social insurance as differentiated from insurance against specific risks. Most Western countries had placed a higher priority on establishing health insurance programs as a natural outgrowth of insurance against industrial accidents. Old-age pensions and unemployment insurance programs received a lower priority in these countries. In the United States, with millions of people out of work as a result of the depression, unemployment insurance and old-age pensions received the higher priority. Thus the United States, rather than move in the direction of providing free medical care or reimbursement for its costs, as many Western European countries had done, attempted to supply more general social security benefits.

The Social Security Act of 1935 provided for unemployment compensation, old-age pensions, and other benefits. The early planning of the legislation had initially included health insurance as part of the package. However, the Roosevelt administration did not want to jeopardize the enactment of the entire law because of strong opposition to health insurance by the medical profession. Therefore, national health insurance was omitted from the final legislative proposal. The Social Security Act did extend the role of the federal government in health care by including provisions designed to strengthen public health services. These provisions called for federal matching grants-in-aid to states for maternal and infant care and diagnosis and treatment of crippled children. Federal grants were also made available for general public health purposes under the administration of the U.S. Public Health Service (USPHS), which had evolved in 1912 from the Marine Hospital Service.

In 1937 Congress passed the National Cancer Act. It established the National Cancer Institute (NCI) and set a national pattern for the federal support of biomedical research. The law authorized the NCI to conduct research in its own laboratories and to award grants to nongovernment scientists and institutions for training scientists and clinicians.

During 1935–36 the USPHS conducted a national health survey that revealed many untreated diseases in the population, especially in low-income groups. This led Senator Robert Wagner (D-NY), sponsor of the Social Security Act, to introduce an amendment to the act that would have provided federal grants to the states for the organization of health insurance plans covering workers and their dependents. The onset of World War II postponed any serious consideration of such a plan (Roemer 1986). Similar attempts to establish a health insurance program under the Truman administration were defeated during the 1940s. The medical profession had succeeded in defeating proposals for any national health insurance.

After the war, the Truman administration called for the expansion of hospitals, increased support for public health, maternal and child health services, and federal aid for medical research and education. The administration's aim was to expand the country's medical resources and facilities, reduce the financial burden for their use, and in the process expand access to medical care (Starr 1982). One major problem was that no new hospital construction took place during the depression or World War II, a period of some sixteen years.

In 1946 Congress passed the National Hospital Survey and Construction Act, also known as the Hill-Burton Act. This program provided federal funds to subsidize construction of hospitals in areas of bed shortages, mainly in rural counties. State public health agencies were made responsible for surveying the hospital bed supply in each state, and for developing a master plan for the construction of new hospitals. They were also assigned the task of inspecting and licensing all hospitals and related facilities.

Physicians welcomed Hill-Burton funds and actively sought them for construction of new hospitals for reasons of prestige, convenience, and service. Many physicians did not have privileges to treat their patients in the limited number of hospitals that were in existence. These physicians, faced with a limited supply of hospitals and beds and restricted access to them, supported the construction of new hospitals in the hope that they would enjoy the privilege of treating their patients in newly constructed hospitals. In addition, local pressure favoring nearby facilities, tax-favored bonds, and assured income from insurance companies and later from Medicare contributed to the proliferation of hospitals (Bernstein and Bernstein 1988).

As the number of hospitals increased, a nongovernmental Joint Commission on Accreditation of Hospitals was established in 1952. Between 1947 and 1966, the number of voluntary, not-for-profit hospitals increased from 2,584 to 3,426. During the same period, state and local government general hospitals increased from 785 to 1,453. The total number of hospitals (for-profit, state and local government, and voluntary not-for-profit) increased from 4,445 to 5,736. The rate of hospital admission per 1,000 population increased from 54 in 1935 to 129 in 1960 (Stevens 1989).

Congress, in 1946, also passed the National Mental Health Act. This law provided federal grants to states for research, prevention, diagnosis, and treatment of mental disorders. During the 1950s, there was also further expansion of public health services at the federal level. The NIH greatly expanded support of biomedical research. By the end of the 1950s, the role of the federal government in health care had increased significantly compared to its role in the early 1900s. There was a corresponding increase in the role of state and local governments in the field of public health services.

Increasing Access to Health Care: The 1960s

From the 1920s to the 1950s, efforts to establish a system of national health care or insurance for the entire population had failed because of charges from the medical profession and others that such plans would constitute "socialized medicine." The concept of socialized medicine went against the general public philosophy of classical liberalism, which advocates a limited role for government, and the specific philosophy of interest-group liberalism, wherein different interest groups exercise countervailing veto power over governmental policy decisions.

Faced with opposition to comprehensive change, advocates of a national system of health care or insurance changed their strategy and objectives and turned to an incremental strategy. They began to advocate increasing access to health care for the needy. Rather than push for universal coverage, under which the federal government would provide health insurance to all on a compulsory basis, they began to push for a limited system of health insurance for specific needy groups such as the elderly. The elderly were a perfect target group for providing help because of their greater medical need, inadequate financial resources, and the loss of employment-based group medical insurance upon retirement. Additionally, the elderly were deemed worthy and were not stigmatized as a failed group, as were welfare recipients (Schneider and Ingram 2004). The health care problems of the elderly would be faced by most of us; almost everyone grows old, after all. This new approach also accommodated the federal structure of government by emphasizing that such programs would be administered by state governments with the federal government providing financial aid to states.

The result was the passage of the Kerr-Mills Act (also known as the Medical Assistance Act) by Congress in 1960. The law provided federal matching payments to states for vendor (provider) payments and allowed states to include the medically needy (i.e., elderly, blind, and disabled persons with low income who were not on public assistance). The act also suggested the scope of services to be covered, such as hospitals, nursing homes, physicians, and other health services. It also required each state to plan for institutional and noninstitutional care as a condition of federal cost sharing. State participation in the program was optional, and states were left free to determine eligibility and the extent of services provided. Most important, the act established the concept of "medical indigency."

The Kerr-Mills program proved to be neither effective nor adequate (Bernstein and Bernstein 1988). It failed to provide significant relief for a substantial portion of the elderly population. An investigation by the Senate Subcommittee on the Health of the Elderly in 1963 revealed that only 1 percent of the nation's elderly received help under the program. The report also highlighted several other problems such as stringent eligibility rules and high administrative costs of state governments (U.S. Health Resources Administration 1976). Clearly, the issue of financing health care for the elderly had not been resolved and remained on the political agenda.

The Kennedy administration, on assuming office in 1961, was committed to increasing access to health care for millions of Americans. Having won a narrow victory in the 1960 presidential election, however, President Kennedy was not in a position to push for a universal insurance program. He faced a Congress that was not very amenable to his legislative proposals. He hoped that the 1962 congressional elections would produce a more receptive Congress. But he was able to keep the issue of health care needs of the elderly alive and on the political agenda (Fein 1986). On February 21, 1963, Kennedy delivered his "Special Message on Aiding Our Senior Citizens." The message contained thirty-nine legislative recommendations. The key proposal was Medicare to meet the medical needs of the elderly. It had two objectives. One was protection against the cost of serious illness. The other was to serve as a base of insurance protection on which supplementary private programs could be added (David 1985). The assassination of Kennedy in November 1963 left the task of carrying on the battle for Medicare to his successor, Lyndon Johnson.

Lyndon Johnson adopted most of John F. Kennedy's unfinished legislative proposals and incorporated them into the Great Society's War on Poverty program. After civil rights, Medicare was second in priority with the Johnson administration. Johnson saw Medicare as an essential part of his War on Poverty (David 1985). Johnson won a landslide victory in the 1964 presidential election, which allowed him to claim a public mandate for his programs. Equally important was the fact that Democrats also won major victories in congressional elections. The administration now had enough votes in the House and the Senate for the passage of its health care proposals.

Health insurance was at the top of the legislative agenda in 1965. The Johnson administration proposed hospital insurance for the elderly, financed through payroll taxes. Republicans offered a proposal for subsidized, voluntary insurance for the aged, including coverage for physicians' services financed through general revenues. The AMA opposed both plans and advocated expansion of the Kerr-Mills program of matching grants to the states for vendor payments for the needy. Both opponents and proponents used traditional concepts, symbols, and clichés in the debate. Opponents, especially the AMA and insurance companies, opposed the Johnson administration's proposal on the grounds that it was compulsory, it represented socialized medicine, it would reduce the quality of care, and it was "un-American." The proponents defended the plan as designed to help the needy by providing them with access to medical care and thus compatible with American ideals of equity and equality (Skidmore 1970).

Congress in 1965 passed the Medicare program for the elderly and the Medicaid program for the poor as amendments to the Social Security Act of 1935. This final product was a classic compromise between three competing proposals. It included a compulsory health insurance program for the elderly, financed through payroll taxes (Medicare Part A, the Johnson administration proposal), a voluntary insurance program for physicians' services subsidized through general revenues (Medicare Part B, the Republican proposal), and an expanded means-tested program administered by the states (Medicaid, the AMA proposal).

In addition to Medicare and Medicaid, a number of other health programs, such as Maternal and Infant Care (MIC), the Children Supplemental Feeding Program, and community health centers were created during the 1960s as part of Johnson's War on Poverty.

The principal objective of the Medicare and Medicaid programs was to provide equal access to health care for the elderly and the poor. Both programs dramatically increased access to health care (Darling 1986). Medicare helped alleviate substantial financially related barriers to equal access to health care that existed before the program's enactment (Long and Settle 1984). It greatly expanded financial access to acute care for the elderly and disabled (Aaron 1991).

In recent years, concerns over rising health care costs and efforts at cost containment have led to tradeoffs between cost containment and access to health care. This has created new problems and gaps in access to health care. The next section provides a brief overview of the federal government's efforts at health care cost containment. Chapter 6 provides a more detailed examination and evaluation of major policy initiatives undertaken by federal and state governments, as well as the private sector, to contain health care costs.

Efforts at Health Care Cost Containment: The 1970s to the 1980s

The 1970s represented a decade of transition in the U.S. health care system. Prior to this time, federal health care policy was shaped by a number of assumptions. One of the major assumptions was that the health care system suffered from too few health care facilities and services. The health care system needed more hospitals, physicians, technology, and biomedical research. Biomedical research was encouraged through federal funds for the National Institutes of Health, while new hospital construction was encouraged with federal funds provided through the Hill-Burton program. The second assumption was that one of the serious problems with the health care system was limited financial access to health care among disadvantaged citizens. The establishment of Medicare and Medicaid by the federal government was an effort to increase access to health care for the needy. The third assumption was that competitive markets and regulatory strategies do not work in the health care field (Brown 1986).

By the 1970s, these assumptions had come under increased scrutiny. As we discussed earlier in the chapter, the Hill-Burton program led to a significant expansion in the number of voluntary, not-for-profit, and state and local government hospitals. Policymakers came to recognize that the health care system was too large. This was in sharp contrast to the assumption before the 1960s that the health care system was too small. By the 1970s there was an increasing concern with the nation's sizable surplus of hospital beds and physicians. There was a realization that one of the reasons for increased health care costs was unconstrained diffusion of biomedical technology and an excess supply of hospitals and physicians, which encouraged excessive tests and treatments. Similarly, while Medicare and Medicaid had increased financial access to health care for the elderly and the needy, increased access had also led to increases in health care costs. From the beginning, outlays for Medicare and Medicaid greatly exceeded initial projections. When Medicare was established, the federal government had deliberately chosen to reimburse physicians in a generous manner to win their political support.

By the 1970s health care costs had risen dramatically. Total national health care expenditure increased from $27.1 billion in 1960 to $74.3 billion in 1970. During this same period, federal health care expenditures increased from $2.9 billion to $17.8 billion, while state and local governments' health care expenditures increased from $3.7 billion to $9.9 billion. Similar increases were evident in hospital care and physician services (Levit et al. 1994b). From 1966 to 1970, Medicare expenditures increased from $1.6 billion to $7.1 billion, while Medicaid expenditures increased from $1.3 billion to $5.3 billion. Increases in medical care inflation outstripped overall inflation (Levit et al. 1994b).

Policymakers' concerns began to shift from providing access and quality health care to containing rising health care costs. Ironically, there was an increased tolerance for government regulation of the health care system and at the same time encouragement of a competitive market strategy to contain health care costs. During the 1970s and 1980s, the federal government and the states undertook a number of regulatory and market-oriented policy initiatives in an effort to contain costs. These policy initiatives are examined in more detail in chapter 6, which discusses cost containment.

During its first two years in office, the Nixon administration proposed only moderate changes in the health care programs and proposed to hold the line on appropriations. In fact, President Nixon signed into law various acts designed to extend community mental health centers, migrant health centers, and programs designed to support training of health care personnel, among others.

Beginning in 1971, the Nixon administration sought to curtail health care programs. In his health message to Congress on February 18, 1971, Nixon argued that "costs have skyrocketed but values have not kept pace. We are investing more of our nation's resources in the health of our people but we are not getting full return on our

Table 2.1

Selected Health Care Expenditures, 1960–2005 (in billions of dollars)

	1960	1965	1970	1975	1980	1985	1990	1995	2000	2001	2002	2003[c]	2004[c]	2005[c]
National health expenditures	27.1	41.6	74.3	132.9	251.1	420.1	696.6	993.3	1,309.4	1,420.7	1,553.0	1,673.6	1,793.6	1,920.8
Federal health expenditures	2.9	4.8	17.8	36.4	72.0	123.6	195.8	326.1	416.0	460.3	504.7	535.2	569.1	605.0
State and local health expenditures	3.7	5.5	9.9	18.7	33.3	51.5	90.7	129.8	178.6	192.0	208.7	223.8	240.5	259.3
Medicare expenditures			7.7	15.7	37.5	70.4	112.1	185.3	225.1	246.5	267.1	280.9	296.2	309.5
Medicaid expenditures[a]			5.4	12.9	26.1	39.7	75.4	146.2	203.4	224.4	250.4	269.3	292.7	319.2
Hospital health care	9.3	14.0	28.0	52.4	102.7	167.9	256.5	347.0	413.2	444.3	486.5	518.1	551.7	585.8
Physician/clinical services[b]	5.3	8.2	13.6	23.3	45.2	74.0	140.5	201.9	290.3	315.1	339.5	362.8	386.8	412.0
Per capita amount (in hundreds of dollars)	143	204	348	592	1,067	1,699	2,738	3,697	4,670	5,021	5,440	5,808	6,167	6,547

Sources: Compiled from Levit et al. 1991, 1994a, 2000; Heffler et al. 2004; National Center for Health Statistics 2003.
[a]Medicaid figures combine federal, state, and local expenditures. Also includes Medicaid SCHIP Expansion beginning in 1998.
[b]Includes physician and clinical services.
[c]Figures for 2003, 2004, and 2005 are projections.

investment," (Nixon 1971). Nixon sought curtailment in federal categorical grant programs and vetoed legislation designed to renew and expand these programs. He also relied on the strategy of impounding funds already appropriated. A struggle between the executive branch headed by a Republican president and a Congress controlled by Democrats ensued. The Democratic Congress was able to override some of Nixon's vetoes, and the battle over impoundment of funds ended up in the federal courts. It also ultimately led Congress in 1974 to enact the Congressional Budget and Impoundment Control Act, which Nixon signed into law a few days before he resigned from the presidency in the aftermath of the Watergate scandal. Despite Nixon's conflicts with Congress, a number of cost-containment initiatives were begun during this time.

PSROs and HMOs

One of the factors often cited as responsible for increased health care costs was the overutilization of health care resources. The rising costs of Medicare and Medicaid created concern in Congress about the cost and quality of care provided in these programs. Congress created the Professional Standards Review Organizations (PSROs) through the Social Security Amendments Act of 1972. It created a regulatory mechanism to encourage efficient and economical delivery of health care in the Medicare and Medicaid programs through peer review. More than 200 local PSROs were created and staffed by local physicians to review and monitor care provided to Medicare and Medicaid patients by hospitals, skilled nursing homes, and extended-care facilities. The PSROs were given the authority to deny approval of payment to physicians who provided services to Medicare and Medicaid patients.

In 1971, Senator Edward Kennedy (D-MA) introduced the Health Security Act in Congress, which was backed by organized labor. The bill called for a comprehensive program of free medical care and would have replaced all public and private health plans in a single federally operated health insurance system. The act would have set a national budget, allocated funds to regions, and obligated private physicians and hospitals to keep within budget constraints.

Opponents immediately described the plan as socialized medicine, a pejorative term used to help polarize debate. In reality, it was not socialized medicine, because the plan did not involve nationalization of health care facilities such as hospitals and did not require doctors to work on salary.

Nixon was interested in seeking reelection in 1972. The president felt compelled to respond to Kennedy's political challenge by proposing the National Health Insurance Partnership Act, which consisted of two parts. The first part, Family Health Insurance Plan, was a federally financed plan to provide health insurance for all low-income families. The second part, the National Health Insurance Standards Act, would be financed by private funds, would set standards for employer health insurance programs, and would require coverage of employees. But this plan could not win the necessary support for passage, since up to 40 million persons would still lack coverage (Norris 1984).

Nixon was not interested in starting a national health insurance program. The administration wanted some kind of plan to control health care costs that would look uniquely Republican. Nixon hoped to promote market-oriented reforms designed to encourage competition in the health care market as a way of controlling costs. He was interested in developing a health strategy that would create a more efficient health care system, balance the supply of health care resources and demands, and at the same time assure equal access to health care.

The Nixon administration's key proposal was to provide federal funds for the development of health maintenance organizations (HMOs). In 1973, nearly three years after Nixon first sent his proposal to Congress, the Health Maintenance Organization Act was passed. It was a much more modest plan than originally conceived and reflected the necessity of bargaining and compromises between the president and Congress. For example, the first Senate bill had authorized $5.2 billion over three years for start-up costs. The version signed into law authorized $375 million over three years for projects more limited in scope (Falkson 1980; Norris 1984).

HMOs are a system in which enrollees pay a fixed fee (capitation) in advance, and in return they receive a comprehensive set of health services. The Nixon administration believed that HMOs would promote competition with traditional health care delivery systems by creating incentives for shifting health services utilization from more costly inpatient services such as hospitals and skilled nursing facilities to less costly outpatient services such as visits to doctors' offices. We consider HMOs and market reforms in later chapters.

Controlling Costs by Planning

The federal government during the late 1960s and the 1970s also emphasized health planning to contain rising health care costs. The rationale for planning was based on the argument that there was an abundance of health care facilities and services—too many hospitals, too many hospital beds, and too much medical equipment. Unnecessary expansion and duplication led to overutilization of health care resources. The Comprehensive Health Planning Act of 1966 was an attempt at health care facilities planning through the states. Comprehensive health planning agencies were to be established in every state and in local areas. Their principal focus was hospital planning. The law also established the goal of providing the highest level of health care attainable to every person. Thus the law attempted to synthesize the goal of cost containment with the goal of providing access and quality care to everyone.

In 1972 the federal government, through the section 1122 amendments to the Social Security Act, limited Medicare/Medicaid reimbursements to approved expansions. Congress in 1974 passed the National Health Planning and Resource Development Act. This law replaced the Comprehensive Health Planning Act and such other health planning programs as the regional medical programs and the Hill-Burton programs. The law required all states to adopt certificate-of-need laws by

1980. Certificate-of-need (CON) laws require hospitals to document community need to obtain approval for major capital expenditures for expansion of facilities and services. The law also established a network of health systems agencies at state and local levels to administer the certificate-of-need laws.

Despite these efforts, overall health care costs continued to soar. The Medicare and Medicaid programs were also experiencing dramatic increases in expenditures. A recession combined with inflation during 1974–75 made efforts at expansion in medical programs politically impossible. The movement for national health insurance was stalled despite the election of a heavily Democratic Congress in 1974. Having assumed the office of the presidency following Nixon's resignation, President Gerald Ford proposed a national health insurance plan in his first message to Congress in 1974. However, by 1976 the Ford administration had withdrawn the plan on the grounds that it would be inflationary.

Jimmy Carter, as a Democratic candidate for president in the 1976 election, also pledged his support for a comprehensive national health insurance program. His support during the Democratic primaries was a response to a political challenge by Senator Edward Kennedy, who was also seeking the party's nomination. Carter's continued support for a national health insurance program during the general election partly reflected his desire to win labor's support for his election.

Nevertheless, after assuming office in January 1977, Carter was hampered by budget constraints and was less anxious to push for a national health insurance program. From 1971 to 1974, under the Economic Stabilization Program, economywide wage and price controls were in effect. Hospital prices were subject to control under this program; however, this had a limited effect in controlling hospital costs. In 1977, the Carter administration proposed a series of all-payer revenue controls on hospitals, known as the hospital cost-containment proposal. The Carter administration argued that controlling hospital costs was necessary because traditional market forces would not keep those costs down. The proposal was strongly opposed by the medical industry in general and hospitals in particular. It also did not receive enthusiastic support in Congress. After three years of legislative battles, the proposal was defeated in favor of a promised voluntary effort by hospitals to contain costs.

During the 1980 Democratic primary season, Senator Kennedy again challenged Carter. The president promised a national health care program, but one that would be implemented only when the economy, reeling from energy shocks and high interest and inflation rates, stabilized. Thus, the second half of the 1970s represented a political stalemate in the health policy area. Opposing and conflicting interests prevented adoption of any systematic and comprehensive set of health policies (Starr 1982).

The Reagan Administration

After having campaigned on a platform of antiregulation and less government, Ronald Reagan became president in January 1981. Reagan sought to reduce expenditures for social programs, including health care. His "new federalism" proposal of 1982 attempted to decentralize authority and responsibility, giving state and local governments more discretion.

During the first two years of the Reagan administration, Congress enacted significant changes in federal health programs to restrain budget deficits, provide states with greater authority over health funding, and at the same time reduce federal funding for some health programs. Funding for health planning and health maintenance organizations was eventually eliminated. The PSRO program was renamed Peer Review Organizations (PROs) and its funding was reduced from $58 million in 1980 to $15 million in 1983. The Reagan administration also succeeded in replacing twenty-one categorical grant programs in the areas of prevention, mental health, maternal and child health care, and primary care into four block grants. Funding for Medicare and Medicaid was also reduced (Etheredge 1983).

The Reagan administration proposed a swap (the new federalism proposal) in which the federal government would assume full responsibility for funding Medicaid in return for state governments taking over responsibility for Aid to Families with Dependent Children (AFDC) and the food stamp program. Intense opposition from state governments caused the administration to drop this proposal from its legislative agenda.

The biggest innovation of the Reagan administration was the introduction in 1983 of the Prospective Payment System (PPS), mandated by the Deficit Reduction Act of 1982, for reimbursement to hospitals under the Medicare program in the hope of reducing Medicare costs and making hospitals more efficient. As discussed earlier, when Medicare was created, it provided for a generous reimbursement to hospitals based on a retrospective, reasonable cost basis for services provided to Medicare patients. Under the new system, illnesses are classified into one of 468 diagnosis-related groups (DRGs). Each category is assigned a treatment rate, and hospitals are reimbursed according to these rates. If hospitals spend more money on treatment, they have to absorb the additional costs. If they spend less money than the established rates, they can keep the overpayment as profit. The new system was phased in over a period of time and did not go into full effect until 1987.

By the mid-1980s it was also becoming clear that the Medicare program was unable to meet the health expenses of its beneficiaries. Their out-of-pocket expenses for services covered by Medicare were on the rise. In addition, the Medicare program did not provide coverage for certain basic services such as outpatient prescription drugs, custodial care, and most of the cost of nursing home care. The Reagan administration tried to address this problem of "medigap." In his 1986 State of the Union message, President Reagan unveiled his proposal for an expansion of Medicare. Congress passed his proposal in 1988 as the Medicare Catastrophic Coverage Act.

The law modified both program benefits and financing with changes to be phased in over a period of several years beginning in 1989. The act provided for coverage of outpatient prescription drugs such as home intravenously administered antibiotic and other FDA-approved drugs, as well as mammography screening for elderly and disabled beneficiaries. The act also expanded coverage of inpatient hospital days from ninety days to an unlimited number of days per year. Similarly, the act increased the number of days of coverage for skilled nursing facility, home health care, and hospice coverage. The act also reduced the amount of deductibles and coinsurance for certain coverage. The new benefits were to be financed entirely by the beneficiaries themselves through supplemental premiums. The act increased monthly premiums for Part B of Medicare and increased the tax liability of higher-income beneficiaries.

The Medicare Catastrophic Coverage Act was very unpopular, particularly among the affluent elderly. One reason for their opposition was the fact that they would shoulder most of the burden of financing the proposed changes through increases in their taxes. Many elderly did not like the idea of paying additional taxes to finance the new coverage. A second reason for the opposition was the fact that many of the elderly were satisfied with the supplemental private insurance coverage they had purchased to cover the gaps in the Medicare program. Another major criticism of the act was that while it made modest changes in Medicare nursing home benefits, it did not extend Medicare coverage to long-term nursing home care (Rice, Desmond, and Gable 1990). Long-term care is the type of care most likely to devastate the elderly financially (Rice and Gable 1986).

The George H.W. Bush Administration

George H.W. Bush was sworn in as president in January of 1989. In November of 1989 Congress repealed the Medicare Catastrophic Coverage Act due to significant protests against the act. This defeat of one of the most significant expansions in the Medicare program since its creation in 1965 seemed likely to make Congress less enthusiastic about reforms in Medicare or about undertaking any new initiatives with respect to long-term care (Rice, Desmond, and Gable 1990).

Despite all the efforts at cost containment, national health care expenditures increased from $251.1 billion in 1980 to $696.6 billion by 1990. The cost of Medicare and Medicaid jumped from $37.5 and $26.1 billion in 1980 to $112.1 and $75.4 billion respectively in 1990. Per capita expenditure on health care doubled from $1,067 in 1980 to $2,738 in 1990 (see Table 2.1).

Health care costs continued to skyrocket during the early 1990s. National health care expenditures as a percent of gross domestic product increased from 12.6 percent in 1990 to 13.6 percent in 1992. The per capita expenditures rose from $2,738 in 1990 to $3,094 in 1992 (see Table 2.2). During the 1960s and 1970s the medical price index was lower than the consumer price index. However, since 1985, the medical price index has been outpacing the total consumer price index. By 1990, the consumer price index stood at 130.7, while the medical price index was considerably higher at 162.8 (see Table 2.3)

Polls in the early 1990s indicated that a majority of Americans had a negative view of the U.S. health care system and were in favor of reforming the system. Health care reform emerged on the national policy agenda with the approaching presidential elections in November of 1992. President George H.W. Bush, in February 1992, announced new health care initiatives. He proposed a series of reforms, including tax credits of

Table 2.2

National Health Care Expenditures, Per Capita Expenditures, and National Health Expenditures as Percent of GDP, 1990–2005 (in billions of dollars)

	1990	1991	1992	1993	1994	1995	1996	1997	1998	1999	2000	2001	2002	2003[c]	2004[c]	2005[c]
National health expenditures	696.6	755.6	820.3	884.2	947.7	999.3	1,039.4	1,088.2	1,150.3	1,222.6	1,309.4	1,420.7	1,553.0	1,673.6	1,793.6	1,920.8
Federal health expenditures	195.8	224.7	254.3	280.6	301.2	326.1	347.3	363.0	368.4	386.4	416.0	460.3	504.7	535.2	569.1	605.0
State and local health expenditures	90.7	98.0	103.2	107.3	121.8	129.8	133.1	139.2	152.9	166.4	178.6	192.0	208.7	223.8	240.5	259.3
Medicare expenditures	112.1	123.3	138.3	154.2	166.9	185.3	199.4	211.3	210.2	213.5	225.1	246.5	267.1	280.9	296.2	309.5
Medicaid expenditures[b]	75.4	93.3	108.0	117.9	134.6	146.2	154.1	160.0	171.5	186.8	203.4	224.4	250.4	269.3	292.7	319.2
Hospital health care	256.5	282.3	306.0	326.6	335.7	347.0	359.4	370.2	378.5	393.5	413.2	444.3	486.5	518.1	551.7	585.8
Physician services	140.5	150.3	161.8	171.2	193.0	201.9	208.5	217.8	256.8	270.9	290.3	315.1	339.5	362.8	386.8	412.0
Per capita amount (in hundreds $)	2,738	2,882	3,094	3,299	3,501	3,637	3,772	3,912	4,179	4,402	4,670	5,021	5,440	5,808	6,167	6,547
National health expenditures as percent of GDP (%)	12.6	13.2	13.6	13.9	13.6	13.7	13.6	13.4	13.1	13.2	13.3	14.1	14.9	15.3	15.5	15.7

Sources: Levit et al. 1994, 2000; Heffler et al. 2004.

[a]Calculated from Table 2.1.

[b]Medicaid figures combine federal, state, and local expenditures.

[c]Figures for 2003, 2004, and 2005 are projections.

Table 2.3

Consumer Price Index, 1960–2002 (1982–84 = 100)

	All items	Medical price index
1960	29.6	22.3
1965	31.5	25.2
1970	38.8	34.0
1975	53.8	47.5
1980	82.4	74.9
1985	107.6	113.5
1990	130.7	162.8
1995	152.4	220.5
2000	172.2	260.8
2001	177.1	272.8
2002	179.9	286.6

Sources: U.S. Census Bureau 1996, 2003.

up to $3,750 per year for families with incomes of up to $70,000 and a voucher for the same amount for poor families. The estimated cost of the program, about $100 billion, was to be paid for by placing limits on Medicare and Medicaid programs. Under the plan, the self-employed would receive a tax deduction equal to the size of the premiums. Small businesses would receive tax inducements. There was also a proposal for mild insurance reform (Wines 1992).

The Bush initiative was clearly in response to the coming presidential election and to the promise of Bill Clinton, Arkansas governor and Democratic candidate, that he would offer a plan for comprehensive reform of the U.S. health care system. By October 1992, both President Bush and Governor Clinton (as Democratic nominee for president) had endorsed managed care as the centerpieces of their health care plans. The comprehensive reform of the U.S. health care system became one of the major campaign issues in the 1992 presidential election. During the campaign, Bill Clinton promised that, if elected, he would deliver a comprehensive reform package for the U.S. health care system that would provide universal coverage to all Americans. Bill Clinton won the presidency. However, he had managed to garner only 43 percent of the popular vote in a three-candidate race.

The Clinton Administration and Health Care Reforms

President Clinton's plan was presented to the nation in a speech before the joint session of Congress in September of 1993, and a bill was sent to Congress in October. The proposal, entitled the Health Security Act, was very comprehensive; it proposed a fundamental restructuring of the U.S. health care system. The bill provided universal coverage through an employer mandate. It also provided subsidies for poor persons and workers without insurance. The plan would provide a minimum benefits package covering a variety of services such as hospital, emergency, clinical preventive, mental health and substance abuse, family planning, pregnancy-related, hospice, home health care, extended care, outpatient laboratory, vision, hearing, and dental services, among others (White House Domestic Policy Council 1993). "The health care plan that is always there" became the slogan for the Clinton plan (Clymer 1993). The plan was based on the concept of managed competition. For more detailed analysis of the Clinton plan and competing plans, see chapter 9.

The initial reaction to the Clinton plan was positive. Deliberation over health care reform in Congress did not begin until 1994, an election year. Several competing plans emerged in Congress on both sides of the aisles. The competing plans ranged from a more radical proposal of a single-payer system to plans that proposed only minor changes to the system, designed to deal with specific concerns. As the debate over these competing plans intensified, none of the plans managed to attract majority support. The initial positive reaction to the Clinton plan turned more negative as the plan was criticized and attacked by a variety of interest groups and Republicans in Congress. Republican leaders had made a strategic decision not to support the Clinton plan and to make the Clinton administration's failure to reform the health care system a campaign issue in the 1994 congressional elections. It was classic election-year politics. As the debate continued, public support for the Clinton plan as well as support for fundamental reform of the U.S. health care system also declined. Opponents of comprehensive reforms argued that the U.S. health care system was not facing a crisis requiring major changes and that the problems of the health care system could be addressed through incremental reforms.

Ultimately, this was the view that prevailed, and by the late summer of 1994 President Clinton's Health Security Act was declared dead and buried. Several factors account for this failure. Some of the important reasons included the Clinton administration's miscalculation and mismanagement of the issue, attack from interest groups opposed to the plan, partisan politics, election-year politics, a decline in President Clinton's popularity, and declining public support for comprehensive reform (Fallows 1995; Morin 1994; Patel 2003, Patel and Rushefsky 1998; Starr 1995). Another window of opportunity for reform of the U.S. health care system had opened and closed without any comprehensive reforms (Brady and Buckley 1995; Brodie and Blendon 1995; Canaham-Clyne 1995; Jacobs and Shapiro 1995; Navarro 1995; Patel and Rushefsky 1998; Steinmo and Watts 1995; Thomas 1995).

Republicans used a three-pronged approach in the 1994 election campaign: develop a positive governing agenda, derail Clinton's agenda, and amass a large campaign war chest (Balz and Brownstein 1996). The Republican Party also came up with the Contract with America, a ten-point platform that included a balanced budget amendment, a line-item veto for the president, a crime bill, welfare reform, a family tax-cut plan, and parental rights in education. In addition, the Republican strategy of not cooperating with the president on the issue of comprehensive health care reform and then blaming President Clinton for its failure—on the basis that it was a bureaucratic, big-brother, big-government reform plan—paid handsome dividends in the 1994 congressional elections. The voters delivered the worst midterm repudiation that any president had received since Harry Truman in 1946. Republicans gained control of both the House and the Senate. The Republican victories extended to gubernatorial and state legislative races as well. A post-election survey conducted by President Clinton's pollster Stanley Greenberg identified the health care plan as the single item that directly linked Clinton with big government (Balz and Brownstein 1996). According to a survey of voters conducted on election day, President Clinton's failure to reform the health care system was a major reason Democrats suffered at the polls. Furthermore, polls also showed that the voters were strongly opposed to the comprehensive health care reform and instead favored incremental solution of the nation's health care problems (Iglehart 1995).

The Republicans came up with a budget plan and the Congress adopted a budget resolution for fiscal year (FY) 1996. It promised to balance the budget within seven years. It called for a $245 billion tax cut. It advocated reducing projected spending (growth rate) on Medicare by $270 billion and Medicaid spending by $182 billion over the next seven years. The Medicaid program was to be turned into a block grant and turned over to the states. The Democrats went on the offensive and portrayed themselves as the savior of the elderly and the poor (Medicare and the Medicaid) and argued that Republicans were willing to cut these programs to provide a tax cut for the wealthy. President Clinton refused to accept the Republican plan. He was determined not to cave into Republican demands. The stalemate between the president and the Republican Congress led to partial shutdown of government two times. This confrontation backfired on the Republicans, as they saw public support for the Contract with America decline sharply. No action was taken on the proposed reduction in spending for Medicare and Medicaid.

In 1996 legislation on the FY 1997 budget, the Republican leadership proposed block grants to replace the Medicaid and AFDC programs. They also wanted welfare reform. President Clinton had indicated that while he supported welfare reforms, he was strongly opposed to turning Medicaid into a block-grant program. Twice he vetoed legislation that tried to turn both Medicaid and the AFDC program into block grants. Finally, the Republicans dropped their proposal to turn Medicaid into a block grant. Once this was done, the welfare reform bill easily passed Congress, and President Clinton signed into law the bill known as the Personal Responsibility and Work Opportunity Act (PRWOA) of 1996. The new law included changes in welfare, supplemental security income, child support enforcement, and food stamp and social services. The main feature of the law is the Temporary Assistance to Needy Families (TANF) program, under which states are given a block grant to design their own welfare program. The Medicaid program was left virtually intact.

Despite the partisan acrimony that dominated the 104th Congress in 1995 and 1996 over the issue of a balanced budget amendment, Congress did succeed in passing some incremental reforms. One of the crowning achievements of the 104th Congress was the passage of the Health Insurance Portability and Accountability Act (HIPAA) of 1996, which President Clinton signed into law in August. Two of the major provisions of the bill include placing limits on insurance companies' authority to deny coverage or to impose preexisting condition exclusions, and guaranteeing portability of insurance coverage when a person leave his or her job voluntarily or involuntarily ("Kassebaum-Kennedy Health Insurance Bill Clears Congress" 1996).

President Clinton won an impressive reelection in 1996. The Republicans were able to retain their majorities in the House and the Senate with narrower margins. President Clinton and the Republican-controlled Congress managed to address another issue that had become an area of concern, the increased number of children who lacked health insurance coverage. The Balanced Budget Act of 1997 provided funds to expand health insurance coverage for children by creating the State Children's Health Insurance Program (SCHIP) as part of title XXI of the Social Security Act. Several states have taken advantage of this program and have expanded health insurance coverage to uninsured children in their states (Congressional Budget Office 1998). The SCHIP program is discussed in more detail in chapter 3 on Medicaid. The 1997 legislation also made significant changes in the Medicare program (see chapter 4).

The expansion of managed competition in the health care marketplace as a way to cut costs has led to dramatic increase in the enrollment of millions of Americans in health maintenance organizations and preferred provider organizations (PPOs). This in turn has raised concerns about managed care plans that deny or limit provision of health care services to their members in order to cut costs. Some legislators and consumer advocates have suggested the passage of a patients' bill of rights to protect patients against unfair, arbitrary, and capricious decisions by managed care plans. President Clinton proposed such a bill, which would have allowed patients to sue their managed care plans and/or managed care organizations such as HMOs and PPOs. The Republicans in Congress proposed their own version of a patients' bill of rights, which did not allow patients to sue their health care plans or provider organizations. The Congress, under the George W. Bush administration, has failed to enact a patients' bill of rights. What, if anything ultimately, will come out of this struggle in the form of congressional legislation remains to be seen.

The George W. Bush Administration

George W. Bush won the presidency in the election of 2000 by receiving 271 votes (270 needed to win) in the Electoral College, even though his opponent, the Democratic Party candidate Al Gore, received more than half a million more popular votes. Bush had articulated a conservative political agenda during his presidential campaign of 2000. One of the very first health issues he had to confront was the federal funding for stem cell research.

Stem Cell Policy

Embryonic stem cell research has generated a significant amount of controversy and heated discussion among its supporters and opponents, especially over the question of whether the federal government should fund such research. Supporters of stem cell research have argued that it could lead to discovery of cures for diseases such as Parkinson's, Alzheimer's, and diabetes. Such research, including therapeutic cloning, can help address problems of organ shortages and donor organ rejection. Supporters of stem cell research argue that such research is ethical because it promises to reduce human suffering and because thousands of frozen embryos are often discarded or destroyed at fertility clinics anyway. Opponents of stem cell research argue that such research is unethical and immoral because embryos are human and deserve the same full rights as humans, that embryos should not be used to serve an instrumental value, taking life to prevent the suffering of others is unjustified, and research with embryonic stem cells so far is not very promising (Patel and Rushefsky 2005).

Federal funding for embryonic stem cell research became a major issue in the 2000 presidential campaign. During the campaign, in order to attract the votes of Catholics and conservative evangelical Christians, George Bush indicated that he opposed federal funding for research that requires embryos to be destroyed or discarded. Upon assuming the presidency, Bush was confronted with the task of formulating a policy on the question of federal funding for stem cell research.

In August of 2001, President Bush, in his first televised address to the nation, announced his policy decision. He argued that as a result of private research, more than sixty genetically diverse stem cell lines were already in existence that were created from embryos that were already destroyed. He further argued that these stem cell lines had the ability to regenerate themselves indefinitely, creating more opportunity for research. Thus, he argued that he would allow federal funds to be used for research only on these existing stem cell lines where the life and death decision had already been made.

President Bush's policy decision was essentially a political one designed to satisfy competing political interests and ethical values and was not based on any sound ethical principles, even though he tried to portray his decision as highly ethical (Patel and Rushefsky 2005). The decision failed to satisfy either the supporters or opponents of stem cell research completely. As Eric Cohen has pointed out, President Bush's decision is analogous to the Missouri Compromise that permitted Missouri to enter the Union as a slave state and Maine as a free state. It sought to find a political compromise between competing interests and viewpoints (Cohen 2002). Furthermore, instead of more than sixty stem cell lines, in reality there are only about seventeen viable existing lines for researchers to work with because many of the other stem cell lines were damaged or lacked genetic diversity.

Given the fact that federal funding is limited to existing stem cells, embryonic stem cell research has turned into a state-by-state battle between proponents and opponents. Some states are moving ahead with stem cell research using only state funding. California voters in November 2004 approved a ballot initiative to spend $3 billion on stem cell research. States such as New Jersey, Wisconsin, and Illinois are budgeting public funds or considering ballot initiatives such as California's to prevent a "brain drain" of biomedical researchers to the West Coast. Social conservatives and anti-abortion activists in states such as Arkansas, Iowa, Louisiana, Michigan,

Nebraska, North Dakota, South Dakota, and Virginia have succeeded in imposing bans or limits on stem cell research (Kasindorf 2004).

The federal government exercises control only over stem cell research that it funds. There are no restrictions on stem cell research carried on in the private sector. Citing lack of leadership by the federal government, the National Academy of Sciences has proposed ethical guidelines to govern research with human embryonic stem cells. Major guidelines include the following: (1) laboratories doing such research should run proposed studies past a review board made up of community members and scientists; (2) women who donate eggs for embryonic stem cell research should not be paid; (3) no human embryo should be grown in a lab for more than fourteen days; and (4) human embryonic stem cells may not be transplanted into an early human embryo. However, experiments in which human embryonic stem cells are transplanted into animals to study development and treatment of diseases is permitted with tight regulations ("Stem-Cell Guidelines: Ethics of a New Science" 2005; Wade 2005).

In 2005, the Republican controlled House of Representatives passed a bill designed to expand federal funding for stem cell research beyond what President Bush's order allows. President Bush had vowed to veto any measure that would expand federal financing of stem cell research (Stolberg 2005; Tumulty 2005). The Senate failed to act on the bill

The war in Afghanistan, followed by the war in Iraq and the war on terrorism following the terrorist attack of September 11, 2001, put many health care issues on the back burner. However, escalating health care costs, especially the costs of prescription drugs, elevated the issue of health care back on the national agenda during the presidential election of 2004. Voters ranked health care as the fourth most important issue in deciding their vote for president in 2004. The top health care issues for the voters were the cost of health care and prescription drugs, prescription drug benefits for the elderly, the problem of the uninsured, and Medicare (Blendon et al. 2004; "Cost and Coverage are Top Health Care Issues in Election 2004" 2004.)

Cost of Prescription Drugs and the Pharmaceutical Industry

According to a comprehensive report on the nation's health issued by the federal government in December 2004, more than 44 percent of Americans take at least one prescription drug, while 16.5 percent take at least three (Pear 2004a; Schmid 2004). The use of antidepressant drugs among U.S. adults has also soared (Vedantam 2004). The report documented the growing use of medication in the last decade. Prescription drugs, which make up around one-tenth of the total U.S. medical bill, were the fastest growing expenditures (Schmid 2004).

Rapidly rising prescription drug costs, growing concern about the affordability of needed drugs, and the significantly high profits earned by drug manufacturers helped elevate this issue on the national policy agenda. In 1993, Americans spent $50.6 billions on prescription drugs. By 2002, the amount had increased to $162.4 billion—a more than three-fold increase. Expenditures for prescription drugs are projected to be

Table 2.4

Expenditures for Prescription Drugs and Percent Change from Previous Year, 1993–2010

	Amount of $ (in billions)	% Change from previous year
1993	50.6	
1994	55.2	9.1
1995	61.0	10.5
1996	68.9	13.0
1997	78.5	13.9
1998	87.3	11.2
1999	104.4	19.6
2000	121.5	16.4
2001	140.8	15.9
2002	162.4	15.3
2003	184.1	13.4
2004	207.9	12.9
2005	233.6	12.4
Projected:		
2006	261.8	12.1
2007	292.4	11.7
2008	325.3	11.3
2009	360.1	10.7
2010	396.7	10.2

Sources: Levit et al. 2000; Heffler et al. 2004.

around $396.7 billion by the year 2010 (see Table 2.4). Overall, although prescription drug spending is a relatively small proportion of total national health care spending (about 10.4 percent in 2002), it is one of the fastest growing components. Three factors have contributed to the increases in spending for prescription drugs. One factor is increased use. The number of prescriptions purchased increased from 2 billion in 1993 to 3.4 billion in 2003—an increase of 70 percent. A second factor is the proliferation of different kinds of drugs, with newer and higher-priced drugs replacing older ones. The FDA, on average, approves about thirty new drugs annually. The third factor is the almost 25 percent increase in manufacturers' prices for existing drugs. Retail prescription prices have increased an average of 7.4 percent a year from 1993 to 2003. This is double the average inflation rate of 2.5 percent (Kaiser Family Foundation 2004).

The significant increases in the cost of prescription drugs combined with significant profit margins earned by drug companies has put the drug industry in the limelight. There has been a dramatic increase in the literature that has questioned the honesty and motives of the drug companies. Maier (1997) has argued that drug companies have given millions of dollars in political contributions to curry favor with lawmakers to help them when they get into trouble with FDA regulators. Critics also charge that there is an incestuous relationship between drug companies, politicians, and federal regulatory agencies that breeds corruption. This perception has been reaffirmed by David Graham, a reviewer in the FDA's Office of Drug Safety, in his testimony before the Senate Finance Committee regarding the controversy surrounding the recall of Vioxx, an arthritis drug made by Merck. He testified that federal drug regulators are virtually incapable of protecting the United States from unsafe drugs and that federal regulators are far too likely to surrender to the demands of the drug makers (Harris 2004a).

The documents disclosed in lawsuits filed against Merck by users of Vioxx suggest that Merck executives and scientists had discussed the possible link between Vioxx and heart damage years before the company publicly admitted that the drug could cause harm and took it off the market (Harris 2004b). Merck used celebrity ice-skaters to promote the drug, with expenditures of $161 million. It was the most heavily advertised drug in 2000 (Hawthorne 2003). Soon after the recall of Vioxx came the news that some other painkiller drugs, such as Celebrex and Aleve, have been linked to increased risk of heart attack (O'Connor 2004). However, in February of 2005, a government expert panel voted to endorse continued marketing of the huge-selling painkillers Celebrex, Bextra, and Vioxx. According to disclosurers in medical journals and other public records, ten members of the expert panel who cast their vote in favor of continued marketing of these drugs had worked as consultants to the drug makers in recent years (Harris and Berenson 2005).

In light of the experience of Vioxx, it is clear that the United States needs a better system to detect harmful effects of drugs already on the market. The editors of the *Journal of the American Medical Association* have called for the establishment of a new watchdog agency that should be independent of the FDA and the drug industry. According to these editors, the nation's current system for tracking drugs is inadequate because drug makers are the ones who collect and evaluate most of the information on the side effects from their own products and then report it to the FDA. In addition, the system relies on voluntary reports from doctors, which leaves many adverse effects unreported (Grady 2004).

Part of the problem is that the FDA has, over the years, shifted its efforts by reducing its number of laboratories and its network of independent drug experts in favor of hiring more people to approve drugs. According to David Kessler, former commissioner of the FDA, the FDA has placed higher priority on new drug review over its field and postmarketing surveillance efforts (Harris 2004a). According to an internal survey of 400 FDA scientists, about two-thirds of them indicated that they are less than fully confident in the agency's monitoring of the safety of prescription drugs being sold ("Oversight is Lacking, F.D.A. Scientists Say" 2004). The public's confidence in the FDA is undermined by the revolving door between policymakers and the pharmaceutical industry, as exemplified recently by Billy Tauzin's taking on the position of president of the Pharmaceutical Research and Manufacturers of America, the pharmaceutical industry's top lobbyist group (Pear 2004b). Representative Tauzin had been the head of the House committee that regulates the pharmaceutical industry and author of the new prescription drug law before his retirement.

Greider (2003) provides an analysis of how the drug industry boosts sales, bilks consumers in the most lucrative drug market in the world, and puts consumers' health and budgets at their mercy. Goozner (2004) uses several case studies dealing with discovery, development, and commercialization of a number of significant drugs to dismantle the pharmaceutical industry's assertion that drug prices must be kept high in order to stimulate cutting-edge research. He further argues that almost all the important new drugs of the past twenty-five years have actually originated from research at taxpayer-funded universities and at the NIH and that, once the innovative work is over, the pharmaceutical companies have stepped in to reap the profits.

Jerry Avron, a Harvard Medical School researcher and clinician and chief of the division of pharmacoepidemiology and pharmacoeconomics at Brigham and Women's Hospital in Boston, argues that millions of dollars a year are wasted on prescription drugs that are excessively priced, poorly prescribed, or improperly taken. He presents an unflattering view of the pharmaceutical industry and argues that changes are necessary in the industry itself to eliminate pressure to prescribe the most heavily advertised and costly new drugs when old drugs are equally effective (Avron 2004). According to Abramson (2004), a former family practitioner who teaches at Harvard Medical School, Americans are overmedicated and overmedicalized as a result of the commercialization of health care.

Jerome Kassirer (2005), a former editor-in-chief of the *New England Journal of Medicine*, argues that the U.S. health care system has been turned into a commercial enterprise because of the drug industry's huge expenditures for courting doctors to use their products and for recruiting physicians to tout their drugs. He describes the financial connections that exist between the companies that make drugs and the doctors who prescribe them. Marcia Angell (2004), another former editor-in-chief of the *New England Journal of Medicine*, argues that prescription drugs are very expensive because the pharmaceutical industry is fraught with corruption. She argues that a huge portion of the revenue generated by big drug companies goes not into research and development (R&D) but into aggressive marketing campaigns to sell their products, while most of the actual R&D work is done by universities funded by the government. Drug companies are offering high-priced junkets to doctors as educational opportunities, which are in reality nothing more than bribes to get doctors to prescribe their drugs.

What is even more impressive is that many of the most recent criticisms of the pharmaceutical industry have come from industry insiders who know how drug companies work and are willing to speak out against some of their practices. These include people such as Peter Rost, a top marketing executive of a drug company, and Arthur Kuebel, a sales representative and ex-lobbyist who promoted drug products to doctors and left the business in disgust (Barry 2004). Drug companies can make more profit from investing in marginal improvements over existing therapies and spending money on advertisements with high markups on drug prices than from investing in riskier, ground-breaking drugs. Thus, it is not surprising that the FDA has classified only about 20 percent of the drugs developed over the last ten years as qualitative breakthroughs (Porter 2004).

In response to the widespread criticism of the government's handling of drug safety problems, the FDA announced in February 2005 that it will create a board made up of scientists drawn from the federal government to monitor drug safety and to advise it on drug complications and warn patients about unsafe drugs. The board will make its conclusions public on its Web page but it will have independent power to force withdrawal of drugs. It will act largely in an advisory capacity (Harris 2005; Kaufman 2005). However, critics are not convinced that a new drug safety panel will be enough to polish the tarnished reputation of the FDA (Gorman 2005).

Medicare Prescription Drug Benefit

The problem of the high cost of prescription drugs is more acute for many seniors, especially those with low income and/or with multiple health problems. They often must make a difficult choice between health care and other consumption needs. The problem is more dire for seniors on Medicare with low fixed incomes. Medicare did not provide coverage for prescription drugs. Seniors with very low income qualify for Medicaid. Many seniors purchase additional insurance to cover expenses that Medicare does not cover. Yet, about one-third of Medicare beneficiaries in 2003 did not have coverage for prescription drugs and prescription drug coverage is becoming increasingly more expensive to obtain (Fan, Sharpe, and Hong 2003).

The Bush administration saw a political opening. Democrats had for years talked about providing drug benefits to Medicare recipients but had failed to deliver. With the presidential election only a year away, Republicans saw an opportunity to take the issue of Medicare away from the Democrats by proposing and passing a Medicare prescription drug benefit program. On December 8, 2003, President Bush signed a $400 billion Medicare prescription drug benefit into law (Nather 2003). The program is set to begin in 2006. Under the program, Medicare recipients can join a prescription drug plan and pay about $35 in monthly premiums. After a deductible of $250, the plan will pay 75 percent of drug costs. The program also provides additional assistance to help low-income beneficiaries. Chapter 4 in this volume on Medicare provides a more detailed discussion of the Medicare prescription drug benefit program.

The Presidential Election of 2004

President Bush and Democratic nominee Senator John Kerry (D-MA) provided different approaches to dealing with the problems of health care. President Bush advocated tax credits to small businesses to set up Health Savings Accounts (HSAs), direct help to low-income families to purchase HSAs, and medical liability reforms, and opposed the importation of drugs from Canada and other countries to reduce the cost of prescription drugs. John Kerry promised to make health care affordable to everyone by cutting family health care premiums by $1,000 per year and extending health care coverage to most adults and children. He advocated allowing every American access to the Federal Employees Health Benefit Program (FEHBP)—the same plan that covers members of Congress. He also supported reimportation of drugs.

President Bush not only won reelection, but the Republican Party also picked up more seats in the Senate and the House in the November 2004 elections. Public opinion polls seem to suggest that the American public is willing to support a number of health care reform initiatives by the George W. Bush administration. More than 90 percent are in favor of requiring drug companies to publish the results of all clinical trials of their drugs and allowing small employers to pool their resources to buy health insurance for their employees. Eighty-three percent support expanding tax-free health savings accounts and 82 percent support legalizing the importation of brand-name drugs from Canada and other countries. Sixty-one percent support medical malpractice reform ("Bush Administration Can Expect High Level of Support . . ." 2004). How successful President Bush and his GOP allies in Congress will be in pushing for tort reforms designed to place a cap on medical malpractice awards remains to be seen. President Bush has nominated Michael O. Leavitt, a former governor of Utah, to be secretary of Health and Human Services to replace Tommy G. Thompson. He is expected to cut billions of dollars from the government's massive health programs for the elderly, poor, and disabled to pare the federal budget deficit.

The Role of State and Local Governments in Health Care

The topic of health care politics and policy in the United States is indivisible from the issues of American federalism (Peterson 2001). The distribution of authority and responsibility between different levels of government within a federal system is a topic of continuous debate. Health care policy has not been exempt from this debate (Rich and White 1996). Initially, the role of the federal government and of state and local governments was very limited. In the previous section we discussed how the federal government became increasingly involved in health care policy and how it plays a major role today with respect to access, quality, efficiency, and cost containment. This section briefly discusses the changing role of state and local governments in health care in our federal system.

During much of the nineteenth century, the role of state and local governments was confined to public health activities. The role of local governments in public health was stimulated by the great epidemics of the late eighteenth and early nineteenth centuries. Municipalities established health boards or health departments to deal with problems of sanitation, poor housing, and quarantine. For example, health departments were established in Baltimore in 1798, Charleston in 1815, Philadelphia in 1818, and Providence in 1832 (Hanlon and Picker 1974).

Similarly, the states' role in public health was initially limited to special committees or commissions to control communicable diseases. The first state health department was established in Louisiana in 1855. State governments also played a significant role in personal health care through the establishment of state mental hospitals (Lee and Estes 1983).

By the beginning of the twentieth century, state and local governments were active in the delivery of personal health services. During the first decade of the 1900s, state governments also began the regulation and licensure of hospitals. The New Deal dramatically expanded the role of the national government in social welfare through the New Deal program in the 1930s. But it was not until the end of World War II that detailed state regulations and licensure procedures for hospitals became more common (Rosenbloom 1983). The power and reach of the national government grew dramatically in the postwar period due to John F. Kennedy's New Frontier and Lyndon B. Johnson's Great Society programs—which included the Medicare and Medicaid programs enacted in 1960s. It also brought new resources, rules, and enforcement from the national government to state and local governments (Peterson 2001). This also ushered in a period of cooperative federalism (Grodzins 1966) with national, state, and local governments working together as partners. In this new partnership, the national government took the lead and state governments became avenues for innovations.

During the 1960s and 1970s, state governments took on many new functions; some of them fundamentally changed the traditional public health activities of subnational governments (Manning and Vladeck 1983). The federal health programs of the 1960s dramatically changed the functions of state and local governments in health care. There was increased federal support for the delivery of health care services by institutions that traditionally served the poor (i.e., public hospitals and local health departments). The establishment of the joint federal-state Medicaid program also increased revenues available to public hospitals and local health departments. Thus, by the 1980s, state and local governments were not only heavily involved in traditional public health activities such as health monitoring, sanitation, and disease control but were also key participants in the financing and delivery of personal health care services, particularly to the poor through Medicaid and other programs. The traditional public health focus on sanitation and communicable diseases also expanded to cover a broad range of protection against human-made environmental and occupational hazards to personal health (Altman and Morgan 1983).

State governments are heavily involved in the regulation and licensure of health care facilities, such as hospitals and nursing homes, and in licensing health care professionals such as physicians and nurses. They also regulate hospital costs and prices through hospital rate setting. Furthermore, they have become important purchasers of health care services, especially for the poor. Thus, state and local governments play an important role, not only in public health activities, but in health care financing, delivery, and regulation of services as well. This increased role is reflected in the fact that between 1979 and 1981 alone state and local government health expenditures increased by 35 percent (Rosenbloom 1983). State and local government health care expenditures jumped from 3.7 billion in 1960 to 33.3 billion in 1980 (see Table 2.1).

The new federalism policies of the Nixon administration and especially the Reagan administration created new challenges for state and local governments. The Reagan administration placed heavy emphasis on decentralization, increased sharing of responsibilities and authority, and more discretion for state and local governments in the implementation of health programs. The diminishing federal responsibility for health care in the early 1980s resulted in increased cost shifting from the federal to state and local governments.

To some, the Reagan administration's new federalism strategy was largely a means of cutting the federal budget rather than sharing responsibilities (Nathan et al. 1982). The increased discretion granted to state governments in the implementation of health policy raises the question of commitment, capacity, and progressivity of state governments. Conservatives have placed great emphasis on devolution of authority and financial responsibility back to the states, without much concern for adequate access to health care for all segments of the society (Thompson 1986). This concern is heightened by some evidence that state and local governments may be even more susceptible to the influence of special interests than the federal government. Thus, compared to the federal government, some have argued that state governments are less likely to make decisions in the public interest (Lee and Estes 1983).

Federal budget reductions designed to contain rising health care costs left many states unable to meet the financial burden of meeting the health care needs of the poor under the Medicaid program. More stringent Medicaid eligibility rules also left a sizable number of poor people with no access to health care under the Medicaid program. Thus, the Medicaid program is increasingly confronted with a tradeoff between cost containment and access to health care (Holahan and Cohen 1986). During the 1990s, state governments increasingly felt the burdens of rapidly rising costs in the Medicaid program. The Clinton administration, while sympathetic to state concerns, continued the devolution of authority to state governments started under the Reagan administration.

Many state governments have attempted innovative approaches to health care reform in general (Brown and Sparer 2001; Parmet 1993; Sparer 1998, 2004; Weil, Wiender and Holahan 1998) and Medicaid reform in particular (Daniels 1998; Davidson and Somers 1998) to deal with problems of rising health care costs and access to health care. The role of state governments is examined in more detail in chapters 3, 6, and 9, on Medicaid, health care cost containment, and reforming the system, respectively.

The United States Supreme Court, after several decades of silence, has also reentered the debate over federalism. The central message in the Court's new federalism decisions involving the Tenth Amendment, the Eleventh Amendment, and the Interstate Commerce Clause is that the federal government should think twice before imposing federal regulations on states.

All this raises a concern about the impact of new federalism initiatives on the issue of access to quality health care on the part of the elderly, the poor, and the uninsured. The liberals' vision of a national health insurance program is likely to remain illusive, confronted with the reality of enormous federal budget deficits and the antitax mood prevalent in the country.

Despite this, it should be noted that states have become major actors in health policy reform, from regulation to rationing, to innovative competitive strategies to cut health care costs, including the costs of prescription drugs. This has become all the more true with some of the changes and incremental reforms passed by Congress and signed into law by President Clinton during the 1990s in the area of welfare reform, health insurance reforms, and children's health insurance. This devolution of authority to state governments has given them more autonomy and more freedom to innovate, and subsequently state governments are likely to become even more important players in the future. State governments have already provided significant leadership in the area of expanding health insurance coverage to children and medical liability reforms. We consider these changes in later chapters.

Conclusion

The United States remains the only major Western industrialized nation without a national health insurance system. Health care policy in the United States results from a combination of decisions made and initiatives undertaken by various levels of government and the private sector. Though the role of federal, state, and local governments in health care policy has expanded significantly in the twentieth century, the U.S. health care system remains a mostly private system. Policymakers in the United States have mainly followed a middle road between a totally private health care system and a publicly financed national health care system.

The federal government's health policy initiatives have focused on concerns about values of access (equality), quality of care, and cost efficiency. The federal role in health care has gone through three distinct stages. The first stage was characterized by policies designed to increase access through expansion of health care facilities, services, and resources. The second stage was characterized by policies specifically designed to provide equal access and quality care to needy groups such as the elderly and the poor. The third stage was characterized by policies designed to contain rising health care costs.

Nevertheless, with respect to providing equal access to health care, federal policies have never displayed or practiced a broad commitment to ensuring that all Americans receive needed health care. Instead, the federal government has always followed an incremental approach by creating specific policies such as Medicare, Medicaid, and numerous categorical grant programs targeted at narrowly defined groups or problems (Darling 1986).

Medicare, Medicaid, SCHIP, Medicare prescription drug benefit programs, and other federal grant-in-aid programs have increased access to health care by removing some of the financial obstacles faced by needy groups. However, problems remain, and recent evidence suggests the emergence of new difficulties. The demise of the Medicare Catastrophic Coverage Act has left many poor elderly with significant gaps in their Medicare coverage because they cannot afford to buy supplemental private insurance. This problem is likely to grow as the number of elderly in the population increases. One of the biggest problems is Medicare's failure to provide coverage for long-term care. Similarly, a significant number of poor people are not covered under the Medicaid program. More and more people are falling through the cracks in the health care safety net, as reflected in the increased number of uninsured Americans and the decline in employer-based health insurance. Moreover, hospitals in many major cities are facing a crisis situation (Beck, Glick, Joseph, and Katel 1991; King 1990; Specter 1990).

Because government intervention in U.S. politics takes place within the context of the public philosophy of interest-group liberalism and cynicism about government regulation, governmental input has tended to occur at the margin rather than the core of the problem (Mechanic 1981). Powerful interest groups have been able to exercise veto power over proposed policies. For example, since the 1920s numerous attempts by the federal government to establish some form of national health insurance that would guarantee health care access to everyone have been defeated by powerful interests such as the AMA and insurance companies. Such groups have successfully defended and protected their narrow and selfish interests, even if they have done so in the name of protecting the public interest by appealing to the value of freedom to choose one's doctor and by raising the specter of "socialized medicine," which they argue would lower the quality of health care. In recent years the issue of national health insurance has been pushed back on the legislative agenda because of an economic environment characterized by huge federal budget deficits and a protracted recession.

Both liberals and conservatives have had difficulty in carrying out an ideologically faithful health care policy. Thus, for example, while the Nixon administration advocated a competitive market strategy and successfully pushed for federal support for the development of HMOs, it also had to accept increased federal government regulations in the form of peer review organizations. Similarly, the important innovation of the PPS for Medicare reimbursement under the Reagan administration relied on regulatory price-control mechanisms to encourage efficiency in the health care market. President George W. Bush created the largest expansion of the Medicare program with the drug prescription benefit program. President Clinton's efforts to overhaul the U.S. health care system through a national health insurance system failed to pass Congress. Both liberals and conservatives had to contend with powerful interest groups. For example, insurance companies, hospitals, and the medical profession have welcomed some regulatory relief, but they have not shown a great deal of enthusiasm for the conservative program of increased competition in the health care market (Starr 1982). Liberal efforts at major reforms to increase health care access have been successfully thwarted by these same interest groups.

The constitutional structure of separation of powers and checks and balances combined with the increased frequency of divided government have necessitated constant bargaining and compromises between the two houses of Congress and between the president and Congress. The federal structure of government has produced a continuous debate in health care policy over the proper distribution of authority and responsibility between the different levels of government. Different presidents have stressed different objectives in this regard. The Johnson administration in the 1960s placed more emphasis on increasing health care access by the federal government. In contrast, the Reagan administration in the 1980s emphasized deregulation and devolution of authority to state and local governments. The failure of the Clinton administration to secure the passage of a national health insurance system, escalating health care costs, and especially the dramatic increase in Medicaid costs to the states, have led many states to attempt reforms at the state level. The constantly changing political climate, public mood, and the desire to win election or reelection make short-term solutions to problems of health care appealing to many policymakers. Under such circumstances, a comprehensive and consistent set of policies directed at long-term solutions becomes difficult to attain.

Plan of the Book

We finish this chapter with a brief overview of the remainder of the book. Chapter 3 examines Medicaid. We explore Medicaid's structure and the coverage provided by the program, with an emphasis on its federal nature. We look at problems with Medicaid and latest developments in the program. We explore gaps in Medicaid coverage and attempts by states to control costs.

Chapter 4 looks at Medicare and the problem of long-term care. The chapter describes Medicare, the primary program of health care for the elderly and certain categories of the disabled. It looks at the cost and financing problems, recent changes, and gaps in the program. One of the gaps was the lack of prescription drug coverage. We have included a discussion of the new Medicare drug benefit program passed under the George W. Bush administration. The second major gap is long-term care, the subject of the second part of the chapter. We discuss the participants in the long-term-care industry and the financing of this difficult problem.

Chapter 5 has as its principal topics access and equity. In particular, we discuss two overlapping aspects. One is the uninsured. We look at the access aspect: the problem of those without adequate health insurance or with more. We seek answers to the question of why the numbers of uninsured have increased in recent years. We tie these answers to current pressures for health care reform. The second, related, part of the chapter looks at the equity aspect: disadvantaged groups in U.S. society. Here we specifically concentrate on minority groups, women, and low-income persons. There is some overlap between the low-income group and the other two groups, as there is between these groups and the uninsured.

Chapter 6 spotlights perhaps the major driving force behind change in the health care field, the ever-increasing costs of health care. We explore explanations for cost increases and attempts at cost containment. This chapter highlights efforts at the state and federal levels as well as by the private sector.

Chapter 7 examines the issue of medical liability and malpractice. We explore the origins and development of the concepts of negligence and liability, the pros and cons of the current tort system, and proposed alternatives and attempts at reform by the federal and state governments. The chapter ends with a discussion of the changing concept of liability with the advent of managed care and new alternative health care delivery organizations such as HMOs and PPOs.

The subject of chapter 8 is technology and health care. Technology is one of the factors that have been implicated in health care cost increases. Some commentators point to advances in health care technology in the United States as indicating the virtues of the system, while others suggest it is responsible for overuse of care. Technology also presents numerous ethical concerns. In this chapter we discuss the factors that have contributed to the growth of medical technology, the cost of medical technology, the issue of technology assessment, and the ethical dilemmas raised by high-tech medicine.

Chapter 9 explores attempts at comprehensive health care reform in the 1990s. We examine the health care reform proposal of President Clinton, competing proposals, and the politics surrounding the various reform proposals. We also discuss market-reform concepts as an integral part of health care reform.

Chapter 10 explores incremental reforms that have taken place following the failed attempt at comprehensive and fundamental reform of the U.S. health care system during 1993 and 1994. The chapter begins with a discussion and an analysis of the Republican proposals in 1995 and 1996, focusing on Medicare and Medicaid. It then discusses the proposals that did pass, such as portability of insurance, moderate federal regulation of managed care plans, and welfare reforms. The chapter ends with an examination of the 1997 balanced budget agreement, which included changes in Medicare and expansion of health insurance for children.

Chapter 11 summarizes the major issues and problems of the U.S. health care system discussed in the previous chapters. We also present our prognosis and recommendations for change.

References

Aaron, Henry J. 1991. *Serious and Unstable Condition: Financing America's Health Care.* Washington, D.C.: Brookings Institution.

Abramson, John. 2004. *Overdosed America: The Broken Promise of American Medicine.* New York: HarperCollins.

Altman, Drew E., and Douglas H. Morgan. 1983. "The Role of the State and Local Government in Health." *Health Affairs* 2, no. 4 (Winter): 7–31.

American Hospital Association. 2005. *AHA Hospital Statistics.* Chicago: Health Forum Publishing Company.

Anderson, Odin W. 1985. *Health Services in the United States: A Growth Enterprise Since 1875.* Ann Arbor, Mich.: Health Administration Press.

Angell, Marcia. 2004. *The Truth about the Drug Companies: How They Deceive Us and What to Do About it.* New York: Random House.

Avron, Jerry. 2004. *Powerful Medicine: The Benefits, Risks, and Costs of Prescription Drugs.* New York: Alfred A. Knopf.

Baker, David W.; Carl D. Stevens; and Robert H. Brook. 1991. "Patients Who Leave a Public Hospital Emergency Department without Being Seen by a Physician." *Journal of the American Medical Association* 266, no. 8 (August 28): 1085–90.

Balz, Dan, and Ronald J. Brownstein. 1996. *Storming the Gates: Protest Politics and the Republican Revival.* Boston: Little, Brown.

Barlett, Donald L., and James B. Steele. 2004. *Critical Condition: How Health Care in America Became Big Business—and Bad Medicine*. New York: Doubleday.

Barry, Patricia. 2004. "The Insiders." *AARP Bulletin* 45, no. 10 (November): 10–15.

Beck, Melinda; Daniel Glick; Nadine Joseph; and Peter Katel. 1991. "State of Emergency." *Newsweek*, October 14.

Belkin, Lisa. 1991. "Hospitals Sacked, A Report Asserts." *New York Times*, October 22.

Bernstein, Merton C., and Joan Broadshaug Bernstein. 1988. *Social Security: The System That Works*. New York: Basic Books.

Bindman, Andrew; Kevin Grumbach; Dennis Keane; Loren Rauch; and John M. Luce. 1991. "Consequences of Queuing for Care at a Public Hospital Emergency Department." *Journal of the American Medical Association* 266, no. 8 (August 28): 1091–96.

Blendon, Robert J; Drew E. Altman; John M. Benson; and Mollyann Brodie. 2004. "Health Care in the 2004 Presidential Election." *New England Journal of Medicine* 351, no. 13 (September): 1314–22.

Brady, David, and Kara M. Buckley. 1995. "Health Care Reform in the 103d Congress: A Predictable Failure." *Journal of Health Politics, Policy and Law* 20, no. 2 (Summer): 447–54.

Brodie, Mollyann, and Robert J. Blendon. 1995. "The Public's Contribution to Congressional Gridlock on Health Care Reform." *Journal of Health Politics, Policy and Law* 20, no. 2 (Summer): 403–10.

Brown, Lawrence D. 1986. "Introduction to a Decade of Transition." *Journal of Health Politics, Policy and Law* 11, no. 4: 569–83.

Brown, Lawrence D., and Michael S. Sparer. 2001. "Window Shopping: State Health Reform Politics in the 1990s." *Health Affairs* 20, no. 1 (January/February): 50–68.

Budrys, Grace. 2001. *Our Unsystematic Health Care System*. Lanham, Md.: Rowman & Littlefield Publishers.

"Bush Administration Can Expect High Level of Support for Several Potential Healthcare Reform Initiatives." 2004. *The Wall Street Journal* 3, no. 23 (November 30): 1–4.

Campion, Frank D. 1984. *The AMA and U.S. Health Policy since 1940*. Chicago: Chicago Review Press.

Canaham-Clyne, John P. 1995. "Clinton's Folly—The Health Care Debacle." *New Politics* 5, no. 2 (Winter): 27.

Clark, Cal, and Rene McEldowney, eds. 2001. *The Health Care Financial Crisis: Strategies for Overcoming an "Unholy Trinity."* Huntington, N.Y.: Nova Science Publishers.

Clymer, Adam. 1993. "Clinton Asks Backing for Sweeping Change in the Health System." *New York Times*, September 23.

Cohen, Eric. 2002. "Bush's Stem Cell Ruling: A Missouri Compromise." In *The Future Is Now: America Confronts the New Genetics*, ed. William Kristol and Eric Cohen, 316–18. Lanham, Md.: Rowman & Littlefield.

Congressional Budget Office. 1998. "Expanding Health Insurance Coverage for Children under Title XXI of the Social Security Act." February and August. Online at www.cbo.gov/ftpdocs/3xx/doc353/kids-hi.pdf.

"Cost and Coverage are Top Health Care Issues in Election 2004." 2004. *Wall Street Journal Online* 3, no. 21 (October): 1–5.

Daniels, Mark R., ed. 1998. *Medicaid Reform and the American States: Case Studies of Managed Care*. Westport, Conn.: Auburn House.

Darling, Helen. 1986. "The Role of the Federal Government in Assuring Access to Health Care." *Inquiry* 23, no. 1 (Fall): 286–95.

David, Sheri I. 1985. *With Dignity: The Search for Medicare and Medicaid*. Westport, Conn.: Greenwood Press.

Davidson, Stephen M., and Stephen A. Somers, eds. 1998. *Remaking Medicaid: Managed Care for the Public Good*. San Francisco: Jossey-Bass.

Dentzer, Susan. 1990. "America's Scandalous Health Care." *U.S. News and World Report*, March 12.

Easterbrook, Gregg. 1987. "The Revolution in Medicine." *Newsweek*, January 26.

Ehrenreich, Barbara. 1990. "Our Health-Care Disgrace." *Time*, December 10.

Etheredge, Lynn. 1983. "Reagan, Congress and Health Spending." *Health Affairs* 2, no. 1 (Spring): 14–24.

Falkson, Joseph L. 1980. *HMOs and the Politics of Health Service Reform*. Chicago: American Hospital Association.

Fallows, James. 1995. "A Triumph of Misinformation," *Atlantic Monthly* 275, no. 1 (January): 26–37.

Fan, Jessie X.; Deanna L. Sharpe; and Goog-Soog Hong. 2003. "Health Care and Prescription Drug Spending by Seniors." *Monthly Labor Review Online* 126, no. 3 (March).

Fein, Rashi. 1986. *Medical Care, Medical Costs: The Search for a Health Insurance Policy*. Cambridge, Mass.: Harvard University Press.

Fox, Daniel M. 1986. *Health Policies, Health Politics: The British and American Experience: 1911–1965*. Princeton, N.J.: Princeton University Press.

Goozner, Merrill. 2004. *The $800 Million Pill: The Truth Behind the Cost of New Drugs*. Berkeley: University of California Press.

Gorman, Christine. 2005. "Can the FDA Heal Itself?" *Time*, February 28.

Grady, Denise. 2004. "Medical Journal Calls for a New Drug Watchdog." *New York Times*, November 23.

Greider, Katharine. 2003. *The Big Fix: How the Pharmaceutical Industry Rips Off American Consumers*. New York: Public Affairs.

Greifinger, Robert B., and Victor William Sidel. 1978. "Three Centuries of Medical Care." In *Medical Care in the United States*, ed. Eric F. Oatman, 12–26. New York: H.W. Wilson Company.

Grodzins, Morton. 1966. *The American System: A New View of Government in the United States*. Chicago: Rand McNally.

Hacker, Jacob S. 2002. *The Divided Welfare State: The Battle Over Public and Private Social Benefits in the United States*. Cambridge, Mass.: Cambridge University Press.

Hanlon, John T., and George E. Picker. 1974. *Public Health: Administration and Practice*. St. Louis, Mo.: C.V. Mosby.

Harris, Gardiner. 2004a. "F.D.A. Failing in Drug Safety, Official Asserts." *New York Times*, November 19.

———. 2004b. "At F.D.A., Strong Drug Ties and Less Monitoring." *New York Times*, December 6.

———. 2005. "F.D.A. to Create Advisory Board on Drug Safety." *New York Times*, February 16. Online at nytimes.com.

Harris, Gardiner, and Alex Berenson. 2005. "10 Voters on Panel Backing Pain Pills Had Industry Ties." *New York Times*, February 25. Online at nytimes.com.

Hawthorne, Fran. 2003. *The Merck Druggernaut: The Inside Story of a Pharmaceutical Giant*. Hoboken, N.J.: Wiley.

"The Health Care System Is Broken and Here Is How To Fix It." *New York Times*, July 22.

"Health Spending in Most OECD Countries Rises, with the U.S. Outstripping all Others." 2004. OECD Press Release. March 6. Online at www.oecd.org.

Heffler, Stephen et al. 2004. "Health Spending Projections Through 2013." *Health Affairs Web Exclusive* (February 11): W4-79–93. Online at content.healthaffairs.org/cgi/reprint/hlthaff.w4.79v1.

Hill, Lister. 1976. "Health in America: A Personal Perspective." In *Health in America: 1776–1976*, pp. 3–15. ed. U.S. Department of Health, Education, and Welfare, Washington, D.C.: Government Printing Office.

Hilts, Philip J. 1991. "Many Leave Emergency Room Needing Care." *New York Times*, August 27.

Holahan, John F., and Joel W. Cohen. 1986. *Medicaid: The Trade-Off between Cost-Containment and Access to Care.* Washington, D.C.: Urban Institute Press.

Iglehart, John K. 1995. "Health Policy Report: Republicans and the New Politics of Health Care." *New England Journal of Medicine* 332, no. 14 (April 6): 972–75.

Jacobs, Lawrence R., and Robert Y. Shapiro. 1995. "Don't Blame the Public for Failed Health Care Reform." *Journal of Health Politics, Policy and Law* 20, no. 2 (Summer): 411–23.

Joseph, Nadine, and Katel, Peter. 1991. "State of Emergency." *Newsweek,* October 14.

Kaiser Family Foundation. 2004. "Prescription Drug Trends." Fact-Sheet #3057-03. Online at www.kff.org.

"Kassebaum-Kennedy Health Insurance Bill Clears Congress." 1996. Washington, D.C.: Families USA, August. Online at www.epn.org/families/Kafeka.html.

Kasindorf, Martin. 2004. "States Play Catch-up on Stem Cells." *USA Today,* December 17.

Kassirer, Jerome P. 2005. *On the Take: How America's Complicity With Big Business Can Endanger Your Health.* New York: Oxford University Press.

Kaufman, Marc. 2005. "FDA Plans New Board to Monitor Drug Safety." *Washington Post,* February 16. Online at washingtonpost.com.

Kerr, Peter. 1991. "Chains of Mental Hospitals Faces Inquiry in Four States." *New York Times,* October 22.

King, Peter. 1990. "The City as a Patient." *Newsweek,* February 19.

Lee, Philip R., and Carroll L. Estes. 1983. "New Federalism and Health Policy." *Annals of the American Academy of Political and Social Science* 468 (July): 88–102.

Levit, Katharine R., et al. 1991. "National Health Expenditures, 1990." *Health Care Financing Review* 13, no. 1 (Fall): 29–54.

———. 1994a. "National Health Care Spending Trends, 1960–1993." *Health Affairs* 13, no. 5 (Winter): 14–31.

———. 1994b. "National Health Expenditures, 1993." *Health Care Financing Review* 16, no. 1 (Fall): 247–94.

———. 2000. "Health Spending in 1998: Signals of Change." *Health Affairs* 19, no. 1 (January–February): 124–32.

Lewis, Anthony. 1991. "A Sick System." *New York Times,* June 3.

Long, Stephen H., and Russell F. Settle. 1984. "Medicare and the Disadvantaged Elderly: Objectives and Outcomes." *Milbank Memorial Fund Quarterly/Health and Society* 62, no. 4 (Fall): 609–56.

Maier, Timothy W. 1997. "Pharmaceuticals: What Do They Buy." *Insight on the News* 13, no. 25 (July 7): 14–15.

Manning, Bayless, and Bruce Vladeck. 1983. "The Role of State and Local Government in Health." *Health Affairs* 2, no. 4 (Winter): 134–40.

Mechanic, David. 1981. "Some Dilemmas in Health Care Policy." *Milbank Memorial Fund Quarterly/Health and Society* 59, no. 1 (Winter): 1–14.

Morin, Richard. 1994. "A Health Care Reform Post-Mortem." *Washington Post National Weekly Edition,* September 12–18.

Nathan, Richard P. et al. 1982. "Initial Effects of the Fiscal Year 1982 Reductions in Federal Domestic Spending." In *Reductions in U.S. Domestic Spending: How They Affect State and Local Governments,* ed. John W. Ellwood, 315–49. New Brunswick, N.J.: Transaction.

Nather, David. 2003. "GOP Hones 'Can Do' Pitch to Party Base, Swing Voters." *Congressional Quarterly Weekly* 61, no. 48 (December 13): 3062–64.

National Center for Health Statistics, U.S. Department of Health and Human Services. 2003. *Health, United States, 2003: With Chartbook on Trends in the Health of Americans.* Washington, D.C.: U.S. Government Printing Office.

Navarro, Vicente. 1995. "Why Congress Did Not Enact Health Care Reform." *Journal of Health Politics, Policy and Law* 20, no. 2 (Summer): 455–62.

Nixon, Richard M. 1971. "Message to Congress." *Weekly Compilation of Presidential Documents*. Washington, D.C.: Office of the Federal Register, February 18.

Norris, Jonas. 1984. *Searching for a Cure: National Health Policy Considered*. New York: PICA Press.

O'Connor, Anahad. 2004. "Vioxx. Celebrex. Now Aleve. What's a Patient to Think?" *New York Times*, December 29.

"OECD Health Data." 2004. Available online at www.oecd.org.

"Oversight Is Lacking, F.D.A. Scientists Say." 2004. *New York Times*, December 16.

Parmet, Wendy E. 1993. "Regulation and Federalism: Legal Impediments to State Health Care Reform." *American Journal of Law and Medicine* 19, no. 1–2: 121–45.

Patel, Kant. 2003. "Presidential Rhetoric and the Strategy of Going Public: President Clinton and the Health Care Reform." *Journal of Health and Social Policy* 18, no. 2: 21–42.

Patel, Kant, and Mark Rushefsky. 1998. "Health Policy Community and Health Care Reform in the United States." *Health: An Interdisciplinary Journal for the Social Study of Health, Illness and Medicine* 2, no. 4 (October): 459–84.

———. 2004. *The Politics of Public Health in the United States*. New York: M.E. Sharpe.

———. 2005. "President Bush and Stem Cell Policy: The Politics of Policy Making." *White House Studies Journal* 5, no.1 (Special issue): 37–52.

Pear, Robert. 1991. "Health Clinics Cut Services as Cost of Insurance Soars." *New York Times*, August 21.

———. 2004a. "Americans Relying More on Prescription Drugs, Report Says." *New York Times*, December 3.

———. 2004b. "House's Author of Drug Benefit Joins Lobbyists." *New York Times*, December 16.

Peterson, Mark A. 2001. "Editor's Note: Health Politics and Policy in a Federal System." *Journal of Health Politics, Policy and Law* 26, no. 6 (December): 1217–22.

Porter, Eduardo. 2004. "Do New Drugs Always Have to Cost So Much?" *New York Times*, November 14.

Raffel, Marshall W. 1980. *The U.S. Health System: Origins and Functions*. New York: Wiley.

Rice, Thomas; Katherine Desmond; and Jon Gable. 1990. "The Medicare Catastrophic Coverage Act: A Post-Mortem." *Health Affairs* 9, no. 3 (Fall): 75–87.

Rice, Thomas, and Jon Gable. 1986. "Protecting the Elderly Against High Health Care Costs." *Health Affairs* 5, no. 3 (Fall): 5–21.

Rich, Robert F., and William D. White, eds. 1996. *Health Policy, Federalism, and the American States*. Washington, D.C.: Urban Institute Press.

Roemer, Milton I. 1984. "The Politics of Public Health in the United States." In *Health Politics and Policy*, ed. Theodore J. Litman and Leonard S. Robins, 261–73. New York: Wiley.

———. 1986. *An Introduction to the U.S. Health Care System*, 2d ed. New York: Springer.

Rosenbloom, David. 1983. "New Ways to Keep Old Promises in Health Care." *Health Affairs* 2, no. 4 (Winter): 41–53.

Schmid, Randolph E. 2004. "40 Percent in U.S. Use Prescription Drugs." *Washington Post*, December 2.

Schneider, Ann L., and Helen M. Ingram. 2004. *Deserving and Entitled: Social Constructions and Public Policy*. New York: State University of New York Press.

Shapiro, Joseph P. 1991. "How States Cook the Books." *U.S. News and World Report*, July 29.

Skidmore, Max J. 1970. *Medicare and the American Rhetoric of Reconciliation*. University, AL: University of Alabama Press.

Sparer, Michael S. 1998. "Devolution of Power: An Interim Report Card." *Health Affairs* 17, no. 3 (May/June): 7–17.

———. 2004. "States and the Politics of Incrementalism: Health Policy in Wisconsin During the 1990s." *Journal of Health Politics, Policy and Law* 29, no. 2 (April): 269–92.

Specter, Michael. 1990. "Putting Michigan Hospitals on the Critical List." *Washington Post National Weekly Edition*, June 4–10.

Starr, Paul. 1982. *The Social Transformation of American Medicine*. New York: Basic Books.

———. 1995. "What Happened to Health Care Reform?" *American Prospect*, no. 20 (Winter): 20–31.

Steinmo, Sven, and Jon Watts. 1995. "It's the Institutions, Stupid! Why Comprehensive National Health Insurance Always Fails in America." *Journal of Health Politics, Policy and Law* 20, no. 2 (Summer): 329–72.

"Stem-Cell Guidelines: Ethics of a New Science." 2005. *Time*, May 9.

Stevens, Rosemary. 1989. *In Sickness and in Wealth: American Hospitals in the Twentieth Century*. New York: Basic Books.

Stolberg, Sheryl G. 2005. "In Rare Threat, Bush Vows to Veto of Stem Cell Bill." *New York Times*, May 21.

"A Survey of Health Care: Surgery Needed." 1991. *Economist* (July 6): 4–5.

"Tauzin to Head Pharmaceutical Lobbying Group." 2004. *Washington Post*, December 15. Online at www.washingtonpost.com.

Taylor, Humphrey. 1990 "U.S. Health Care: Built for Waste." *New York Times*, April 17.

Terris, Milton. 1990. "A Wasteful System That Doesn't Work." *Progressive* 54, no. 10 (October): 14–16.

Thomas, W. John. 1995. "Clinton Health Care Reform Plan: A Failed Dramatic Presentation." *Stanford Law and Policy Review* 7, no. 1: 83–104.

Thompson, Frank J. 1986. "New Federalism and Health Care Policy: States and the Old Questions." *Journal of Health Politics, Policy and Law* 11, no. 4 (Tenth Anniversary Issue): 647–69.

Tumulty, Karen. 2005. "Stem Cells: Why Bush's Ban Could Be Reversed." *Time*, May 23: 26–30.

U.S. Census Bureau. 1996. *Statistical Abstract of the United States, 1996*. Washington, D.C.: Government Printing Office.

———. 2003. *Statistical Abstract of the United States, 2003*. Washington, D.C.: Government Printing Office.

U.S. Health Resources Administration. 1976. *Health in America: 1776–1976*. Rockville, Md.: U.S. Department of Health, Education, and Welfare.

Vedantam, Shankar. 2004. "Antidepressant Use by U.S. Adults Soars." *Washington Post*, December 3.

Wade, Nicholas. 2005. "Group of Scientists Draft Rules on Ethics for Stem Cell Research." *New York Times*, April 27. Online at nytimes.com.

Weil, Alan; Joshua M. Wiedner; and John Holahan. 1998. "Assessing the New Federalism and State Health Policy." *Health Affairs* 17, no. 6 (November/December): 162–64.

White House Domestic Policy Council. 1993. *The President's Health Security Act: The Clinton Blueprint*. New York: Times Books.

Wines, Michael. 1992. "Bush Announces Health Plan, Filling Gap in Re-Election Bid." *New York Times*, September 23.

3

Medicaid

Health Care for the Poor

The establishment of Medicare and Medicaid in 1965 was the result of a lengthy debate during the early part of the twentieth century over the role of the federal government in financing health care. The debate among policymakers focused on two competing models. One was a universal coverage model, under which the federal government would provide health insurance to all people on a compulsory basis financed by taxes on earnings. The second model envisioned a more limited role for the federal government. This model would limit the federal government's role in providing assistance to needy groups in society. In the past, most federal health care laws had followed the second model (Ginsburg 1988). The political environment—structure and processes—made such an incremental approach feasible.

In the 1930s, President Herbert Hoover established the Committee on the Costs of Medical Care (CCMC). This committee's assessment of U.S. health care specifically focused on challenges facing low-income Americans in obtaining health care. Prior to the passage of Medicaid in 1965, a hodgepodge of poorly funded federal programs existed for the poor (Goldfield 2003). The 1950 amendments to the Social Security Act authorized matching grants to the states for direct vendor (provider) payments for treatment of individuals on public assistance. During the late 1950s, the debate focused on the problem of hospital costs faced by the aged. The cost of hospital care doubled in the 1950s. Support increased for addressing the problem of hospital costs of the elderly because the aged were presumed to be both needy and deserving (Starr 1982). In 1960, Congress passed the Kerr-Mills Act, creating the Medical Assistance for the Aged (MAA) program. This act expanded federal matching funds to the states for vendor payments, and, more importantly, it allowed states to include the "medically needy"—that is, elderly, blind, and disabled persons with low incomes who were not on public assistance. However, many states moved very slowly or failed to move at all to take advantage of the Kerr-Mills Act.

The Democratic Party's sweep of the 1964 elections guaranteed further action with respect to the role of the federal government in health care. Lyndon Johnson was elected to the presidency with an overwhelming popular vote. The Democrats gained a two-to-one majority in the House of Representatives. This made it possible for Congress in 1965 to create the Medicare and Medicaid programs. Both were in the forefront of Lyndon Johnson's Great Society programs designed to help the poor and the disadvantaged (Davis and Reynolds 1977). Medicare was established as a program for the elderly, Medicaid as a program for the poor. The final shape of both programs represented compromises among competing models and approaches. The Democratic plan for a compulsory hospital insurance program, financed through payroll taxes under Social Security, became Part A of Medicare. The Republican-supported plan of a government-subsidized, voluntary insurance program financed through general revenues to cover physicians' bills became Part B of Medicare. The AMA opposed both plans and pushed a plan of its own to expand the Kerr-Mills program to the needy. An expanded means-tested program for the poor administered by the states became the Medicaid program.

The generally accepted political explanation for the creation of Medicaid is that the program was created almost as an afterthought to Medicare (Grannemann and Pauly 1983). Medicaid was intended to "pick up the pieces" left over by Medicare. It was designed to cover deductibles and coinsurance for indigent Medicare patients. The program was intended to pay for services not covered, or covered only inadequately, by Medicare (i.e., outpatient and nursing home care), and to pay the cost of medical care of indigent persons other than the elderly (Brown 1984).

Although Medicare and Medicaid were adopted at the same time, there are fundamental differences between the two. The Medicare program has enjoyed public popularity and legitimacy because it is tied to Social Security, a program that is contributory in nature (i.e., through Social Security taxes paid by workers). In contrast, from the beginning, Medicaid has been burdened by the stigma of being a public assistance (i.e., welfare) program. Medicare has uniform national standards for eligibility and benefits. In sharp contrast, Medicaid lets states decide on eligibility and benefit standards. Another major difference is that physician reimbursement under Medicaid is much lower than under Medicare or private insurance; consequently, very few physicians participate in the Medicaid program (Starr 1982). In addition, Medicare is financed and administered solely by the federal government, while Medicaid is financed by both the federal and the state governments on a matching basis and is administered by the state governments.

Program Objective and Structure

Medicaid was established to increase the access of the poor to health care by providing them with financial assistance to meet their medical needs. Although federal law created the program, the intent was to encourage state governments to set up a "unified system of health care" for certain low-income individuals (Schneider 1988). The federal government encouraged state participation and compliance with the program in several ways. The federal government provided matching funds to encourage states to expand their existing medical assistance programs. Today, the federal Medicaid matching ratio varies from a minimum of 50 percent to a maximum of 83 percent. Second, state governments were given the responsibility for establishing program requirements. Finally, states were given the option of making the administration of the program a local as opposed to a state responsibility.

Thus the Medicaid program was created as a partnership between different levels of government to improve access and quality of health care for the poor. The national government establishes broad program guidelines, promotes and monitors program development, and provides financial assistance through matching grants. State governments are given significant control over important aspects of the scope and structure of the program. For example, state governments enjoy discretionary authority for establishing eligibility standards, the nature and scope of benefits provided, and mechanisms used to reimburse health care providers.

Medicaid is an excellent example of how the federal structure of government shapes the dynamics of policymaking and implementation. On the one hand, the federal structure, with its multiple governments, shared authority, political autonomy, and constitutional ambiguities, has allowed states to act as laboratories for innovation and experimentation in the Medicaid program. On the other hand, the same federal structure of government produces overlapping jurisdictions and wastefulness, and encourages the promotion of narrow and parochial interests that make it difficult to solve serious problems. It allows one level of government to pass the buck to another level by playing the federalism game.

Medicaid: Eligibility and Coverage, Services and Benefits

Eligibility and Coverage

Medicaid provides medical assistance to poor persons who fit into one of the designated groups. The program's main target groups are children and mothers who receive Aid to Families with Dependent Children (AFDC), the elderly poor over the age of sixty-five, and disabled or blind persons who qualify for the Supplemental Security Income (SSI) program—a federal program for the aged, blind, and disabled. The Personal Responsibility and Work Opportunity Reconciliation Act (PRWORA) of 1996 replaced the AFDC program with the Temporary Assistance for Needy Families (TANF) program. The federal government sets the income limits for the SSI program. Thus, state Medicaid programs are required to include all "categorically needy" persons—those who meet the requirements for the AFDC program that were in effect in their state on July 16, 1996, or, at the option of the state: children under the age of six whose family income is at or below 133 percent of the federal poverty level (FPL); pregnant women whose family income is at or below 133 percent of the FPL; Supplemental Security Income recipients in most states; all children born after September 1998 who are under age nineteen, in families whose income is at or below FPL; and some other special protected groups and certain Medicare beneficiaries.

States also have an option to provide Medicaid coverage for other "categorically needy" groups, such as infants up to the age of one and pregnant women not covered under the mandatory rules whose family income is no more than 185 percent of the FPL; children under the age of twenty-one who meet the AFDC income and resource requirements that were in effect in their state on July 17, 1996; institutionalized individuals eligible under a "special income level"; and individuals who would be eligible if institutionalized, but who are receiving care under home and community-based service waivers (Centers for Medicare and Medicaid Services 2003).

States may elect to provide coverage to people who are not required to be covered by federal law. State governments can receive federal matching funds for providing coverage to these optional groups. Such optional groups include the "medically needy." Benefit and eligibility provisions for Medicaid for "medically needy" persons do not have to be as extensive as for the categorically needy and may be very restrictive. However, if a state elects to have a "medically needy" program, the federal government requires that certain groups be included. Children under age nineteen and pregnant women who are medically needy must be covered, and prenatal and delivery care as well as ambulatory care for children must be provided. As of August 2002, thirty-six states had opted to have a "medically needy" program (Centers for Medicare and Medicaid Services 2003).

Services and Benefits

A state's Medicaid program must offer medical assistance for certain basic services to most categorically needy persons. These services include inpatient and outpatient hospital services; physician services; nursing facility services for persons under the age of twenty-one; rural health clinic services; pediatric and family nurse practitioner services; nurse-midwife services; federally qualified health-center services; prenatal care; vaccines for children; family planning services and supplies; home health care for persons eligible for skilled-nursing services; laboratory and X-ray services; and early and periodic screening, diagnostic, and treatment (EPSDT) services for children under age twenty-one (Centers for Medicare and Medicaid Services 2003).

States can also receive federal matching funds if they elect to provide other optional services such as diagnostic and clinic services, intermediate care facilities for the mentally retarded, prescribed drugs and prosthetic devices, optometrist services and eyeglasses, transportation services, rehabilitation and physical therapy services, home and community-based care for certain persons with chronic impairment, and nursing care services for children under age twenty-one (Centers for Medicare and Medicaid Services 2003).

States are permitted to restrict the amount of services per beneficiary. For example, a state may limit the number of days in hospitals or number of visits to physicians per year that it would cover. States also enjoy significant discretion with respect to the method of payment to health care providers. Medicaid operates as a vendor payment program. States can pay health care providers directly on a fee-for-service basis, or states can pay for Medicaid services through a variety of prepayment arrangements such as health maintenance organizations (HMOs). Each state enjoys broad discretion in determining the payment methodology and payment rates for services. The expectation is that state payment rates should be sufficient enough to enlist enough providers to make services available to the general population within that geographic area. Providers participating in Medicaid must accept Medicaid payment rates as payment in full. State governments are also required to make additional payments to qualified hospitals that provide inpatient services to a disproportionate number of Medicaid beneficiaries; these hospitals are known as disproportionate share hospitals (DSHs). The federal share of payments to DSHs has varied over time (Centers for Medicare and Medicaid Services 2003).

Originally, Medicaid was viewed as a limited entitlement program for the poor. Over time, the scope of the program has expanded considerably. Congress imposed various federal mandates requiring states to expand Medicaid coverage to women and children during the 1980s and 1990s. Today, Medicaid is the most heterogeneous insurance program in the country, with a diverse group of beneficiaries such as children, people with disabilities, and the elderly. The program provides a diverse range of services such as maternity care, prescription drugs, and nursing home care. Finally, a variety of institutions such as public hospitals, children's hospitals, community health centers, and public clinics depend on the Medicaid program for their survival (Mann and Westmoreland 2004).

Major Trends in the Medicaid Program

Program Costs

As the data in Table 3.1 document, the Medicaid program has experienced dramatic increases in overall program cost from the beginning. Total Medicaid expenditures increased from $5.3 billion in 1970 to $250.4 billion in 2002. The total program expenditures are projected to rise to $319.2 billion by 2005. In the early years of the program, the primary reason for increases in program cost was the growth in the number of eligible recipients. Spending for Medicaid increased at a much slower rate during the early 1980s due to the recession, the reduction in federal matching rates, and the programmatic changes introduced in the Omnibus Budget Reconciliation Act (OBRA) of 1981 (Holahan and Cohen 1986). As a result of new federal mandates imposed by Congress between 1984 and 1990 that expanded Medicaid coverage, the annual growth rate increased again. As Table 3.2 shows, Medicaid expenditures increased from $59.2 billion in 1989 to $71.7 billion in 1990, an increase of 21.3 percent. Even more dramatic was the increase that came during 1991 when the total program cost jumped to $89.6 billion. This represented an increase of 24.9 percent. Factors that contributed to this dramatic increase were the expansions in Medicaid eligibility and a slowdown in the economy. Both factors caused additional individuals to qualify for coverage (Letsch et al. 1992).

Table 3.1

Medicaid Expenditures and Percent Change from Previous Year, 1970–2005
(in billions of dollars)

	Total[a]	Percent change from previous year[b]	Federal	Percent change from from previous year[c]	State/ local	Percent change from previous year[d]
1970	5.3		2.9		2.4	
1975	13.6	31.3	7.6	32.4	6.0	30.0
1980	24.8	16.5	13.7	16.1	11.1	17.0
1985	39.7	12.1	21.9	12.0	17.8	12.1
1990	71.7	16.1	40.7	17.2	31.1	14.9
1991	89.6	24.9	54.3	33.4	35.3	13.5
1992	101.6	13.4	65.4	20.4	36.2	2.5
1993	114.6	12.8	73.5	12.4	41.1	13.5
1994	123.3	7.6	77.7	5.7	45.6	11.0
1995	131.4	6.6	82.0	5.5	49.4	8.3
1996	139.7	6.6	87.4	6.6	52.3	5.9
1997	160.0	14.5	95.0	8.7	65.0	24.3
1998	170.6	6.6	100.3	5.6	70.3	8.2
1999	186.7	9.4	108.4	8.1	78.3	11.4
2000	202.7	8.6	118.4	9.2	84.3	7.7
2001	224.2	10.6	132.0	11.5	92.2	9.4
2002	250.4	11.7	147.5	11.7	102.9	11.6
2003[e]	269.3	7.5	158.3	7.3	111.0	7.9
2004[e]	292.7	8.7	171.9	8.6	120.8	8.8
2005[e]	319.2	9.1	187.4	9.0	131.8	9.1

Sources: For the years 1970 and 1975, Gibson and Waldo 1981. For the years 1980, 1985, and 1990, Letsch et al. 1992. For the years 1991–96, Levit et al. 1997, 2000, 2002. For the years 2001–5, Heffler et al. 2004.
[a]Totals calculated from columns 4 and 6.
[b]Calculated from column 2.
[c]Calculated from column 4.
[d]Calculated from column 6.
[e]Numbers for 2003, 2004, and 2005 are estimates.

The federal cost of the Medicaid program alone increased from $2.9 billion in 1970 to $13.7 billion in 1980 and $40.7 billion in 1990. Federal spending by 2002 had increased it to $147.5 billion. The federal expenditures are projected to rise to $187.4 billion by 2005 (see Table 3.1).

State governments have also experienced significant increases in their program costs. The combined cost of state and local governments for Medicaid increased from $2.4 billion in 1970 to $11.1 billion in 1980, $31.1 billion in 1990, and $84.3 billion in 2000. By 2002, state and local governments were spending $102.9 billion. Total state and local expenditures are projected to be around $131.8 billion by 2005 (see Table 3.1). Needless to say, program costs, eligibility standards, and benefit levels vary significantly among the states. The amount of optional services (those beyond the ones mandated by the federal government) and the mix of services provided by the state governments also vary a great deal. "The maze of eligibility rules is enough to make anyone sick" (Specter 1991).

Overall, three factors have contributed to the steady growth in program expenditures. First, since Medicaid is an "entitlement" program, individuals who meet eligibility criteria are automatically covered. Thus, program costs increase any time the size of the population in need increases. Second, Medicaid, like other health insurance systems, pays health care providers and not the recipients who receive treatment. Thus, overall health care costs directly influence Medicaid expenditures. During the 1970s and 1980s, the cost of medical care increased annually by an average of 8.5 percent. Some of the increases in the Medicaid expenditures are attributable to general medical cost inflation (Schneider 1988). Throughout the 1990s, medical costs increased at a much higher rate than the overall consumer price index (see Table 2.3). Third, the creation of the State Children's Health Insurance Program (SCHIP) in 1997 provided health insurance coverage to millions of children, adding to the cost of the Medicaid program.

Total Medicaid expenditures increased by only single digits during 1994, 1995, and 1996, compared to the double-digit growth rates in the early 1990s. Similarly, during the same years, the growth rate in the federal and state/local costs of the Medicaid program also experienced considerable decline. There are a number of factors that might help explain this decline. One possible explanation is that there was a decline in AFDC rolls due to an improved economy and state efforts to reduce welfare rolls. Second, during this time, the growth in the coverage for children and pregnant women also declined. Third, the growth in the number of blind and disabled Medicaid recipients also declined. Fourth, the rapid growth in Medicaid managed care might also explain the decline in program growth rate. Another possible explanation is the drop in average annual medical price inflation during the mid-1990s (Holahan and Liska 1997).

Medicaid program expenditures increased again following the creation of SCHIP. Under the program, the federal government began to provide matching funds to assist states in providing health insurance coverage for uninsured children (Rosenbaum et al. 1998). Between 1998 and 2002, total Medicaid expenditures increased from $170.6 billion to $250.4 billion (see Table 3.2). The SCHIP program and its impact are discussed in greater detail later in this chapter.

Despite the dramatic increases in spending for Medicaid, the program fails to insure millions of poor people who are ineligible to receive Medicaid because they do not fall into one of the eligible categories. It is not surprising that Medicaid is often called a monster (Samuelson 1991). Since its creation, the Medicaid program has occupied center stage in the debate over the proper role of the federal and state governments in meeting the health care needs of the poor. Since states enjoy significant discretion in setting eligibility and benefit standards, it is not surprising that there is considerable variation in how much individual states spend

Table 3.2

Total Medicaid Expenditures and Number of Beneficiaries, 1966–2004

	Total expenditures (in billions of dollars)	Number of beneficiaries (in millions)
1966	1.3	—
1967	3.0	—
1968	3.4	—
1969	4.0	—
1970	5.3	—
1971	6.4	—
1972	8.0	17.6
1973	9.1	19.6
1974	10.6	21.5
1975	13.6	22.0
1976	14.5	22.8
1977	16.6	22.8
1978	18.5	22.0
1979	21.2	21.5
1980	24.8	21.6
1981	28.9	21.9
1982	30.6	21.6
1983	33.6	21.5
1984	36.0	21.6
1985	39.7	21.8
1986	42.9	22.5
1987	48.2	23.1
1988	52.1	22.9
1989	59.2	23.5
1990	71.7	25.2
1991	89.6	27.9
1992	101.6	31.1
1993	114.6	33.4
1994	123.3	35.0
1995	131.4	36.2
1996	139.7	36.1
1997	160.0	34.9
1998	170.6	40.0
1999	186.7	42.9
2000	202.7	44.5
2001	224.2	48.4
2002	250.4	51.4
2003*	269.3	53.3
2004*	292.7	54.6

Sources: Compiled from Levit et al. 1991, 1997, 2000, 2002; Centers for Medicare and Medicaid Services 1997, 191; 2001, 299; 2003; Heffler et al. 2004.
    *Numbers for 2003 and 2004 are estimates.

on the Medicaid program. Why do some states spend four times as much as other states to provide health care to the disadvantaged groups and what factors explain this variation?

Kousser (2002) analyzes the impact of political and socioeconomic factors to explain state spending decisions. The early literature (Key 1949; Lockard 1959) tended to attribute great significance to political factors, especially political party structure, in influencing states' spending on social services. However, during the 1960s, several scholars (Dawson and Robinson 1963; Dye 1966; Hofferbert 1966) argued that the socioeconomic and demographic factors in individual states influenced the level of spending on social services and party structure and party control had little effect. Most such studies failed to differentiate between the portion of state expenditures that is mandated by the federal government and that which is authorized by state policymakers themselves. Kousser (2002), in his analysis, focuses only on states' discretionary spending on Medicaid from 1980 to 1993, a variable that truly reflects the decisions of state policymakers. He concludes that political party control strongly influences levels of state spending for Medicaid. States with Democratic-controlled legislatures tend to fund their Medicaid programs more generously than those controlled by Republicans. While economic conditions do affect states' optional spending levels, they have a much weaker impact than party control.

Program Beneficiaries

The Medicaid program serves a varied group of individuals—the elderly, people with disabilities, low-income families with children, poor adults and children. The elderly and people with disabilities who reside in nursing homes constitute the major portion of Medicaid expenditures. The various groups who are beneficiaries of the Medicaid program have different political characteristics. For example, the elderly in their sixties and early seventies have the highest voting rates among all age groups. In sharp contrast, those receiving AFDC (until 1996) and TANF (since 1996) generally have below-average educations, low incomes, and lower rates of voting. They also carry the stigma of being "welfare recipients." Children are at a special disadvantage in getting policymakers to pay attention to their needs because they are not political participants. The advancement of children's interests depends on policymakers' own goals, interest groups that speak on their behalf, and the altruism of voters. Since the mid-1990s, people with disabilities have become more active in interest groups. Also, Medicaid eligibility standards for low-income groups are transitory, while for other groups, such as the elderly, they are permanent and fixed, making it easier to politically mobilize the elderly compared to low-income beneficiaries (Kronebusch 1997).

Policymakers are more likely to respond to the needs of those groups that are politically mobilized and have high levels of political participation. Thus, Democrats, who draw support from blue-collar workers and people having lower incomes and less formal education, are more likely to support higher expenditures for social programs compared to Republicans, who draw their support more from upper-income groups and people with higher levels of education who work in managerial and professional occupations. Similarly, when it comes to program cutbacks, those groups who are difficult to mobilize and have low participation rates might see their benefits cut more than other groups. Economic factors may also influence spending. "Welfare recipients" are expected to work, while there are no such general expectations about children. Furthermore, programs for children are viewed as investments with long-term payoffs (Kronebusch 1997). Medicaid spending may reflect a variety of these factors.

Medicaid has experienced a steady growth in the number of beneficiaries. Those receiving Medicaid nationwide increased from 17.6 million in 1972 to 25.2 million in 1990. By 2002, the number had grown to 51.4 million people. By 2004, the estimated number of beneficiaries was expected to be 54.6 million (see Table 3.2). It is important to note that the number of recipients has fluctuated over time. In the early years of the program's history, the number of recipients increased because eligibility for Medicaid increased. Paul Ginsburg cites four main reasons for this: states increased their need standards for AFDC, making more people eligible for Medicaid; the number of female-headed households (i.e., those categorically eligible for AFDC) increased as this demographic trend continued during the 1980s; organizations mounted public information campaigns to increase awareness and participation in the program; and additional states initiated Medicaid programs (Ginsburg 1988).

The number of beneficiaries declined slightly and/or remained steady during the early 1980s but began to rise again beginning in the mid-1980s and continued to rise during the 1990s (see Table 3.2). The decline in the number of recipients can be attributed to the fact that from 1980 to 1984, eligibility for Medicaid was either directly or indirectly limited as a result of budget cuts by the Reagan administration. Medicaid coverage for poor and near-poor people declined from 53 percent in 1980 to 46 percent in 1985. Factors contributing to this decline included failure to update state income standards, changes in Medicaid eligibility policy, and federal and state changes in AFDC eligibility policy. The 1981 Omnibus Budget Reconciliation Act established new limits on both income and resources for AFDC and Medicaid eligibility. It also limited cash assistance and Medicaid for certain groups of potential beneficiaries (Davis et al. 1990).

By 1985, however, this downward trend in the number of Medicaid beneficiaries was reversed, and the number of recipients began to increase. This was largely caused by new federal mandates imposed by Congress between 1984 and 1990. Most of these mandates significantly expanded Medicaid eligibility for women and children. Between 1989 and 1991, the number of recipients increased by 4.4 million, with a significant portion of the increase attributable to federal mandates. For example, about one-half of the three million additional recipients qualifying for Medicaid between 1990 and 1991 were eligible because of mandated program expansions. The major beneficiaries of the mandated program expansions were children (Letsch et al. 1992). The creation of SCHIP in 1997 expanded the number of beneficiaries, as more children were provided health insurance coverage through the Medicaid program in many states. The changes introduced in the Medicaid program during the 1980s and 1990s are discussed in more detail later in this chapter.

Changes in the Composition of Medicaid Beneficiaries

Over the years, the composition of the Medicaid clientele has changed. This in turn has affected patterns of Medicaid expenditures and enrollments. Between 1975 and 2002, the percentage of low-income aged beneficiaries declined from 16.4 percent to 9.5 percent. During the same time period the percentage of children and disabled people increased. In 1975, disabled persons accounted for 11.2 percent of the total Medicaid population; in 2002, they accounted for 16.1 percent. Similarly, the proportion of children in the Medicaid program increased from 43.6 percent of total beneficiaries in 1975 to 48.6 percent in 2002. (see Table 3.3).

In 1975, disabled persons accounted for 25.7 percent of Medicaid payments; in 1999, they accounted for 42.9 percent of the payments. In 1975, elderly beneficiaries accounted for 35.6 percent of total Medicaid payments; in 1999, they accounted for 27.7 percent of total payments. In 1975, adults accounted for 16.8 percent of Medicaid payments; in 1999, they accounted for 9.6 percent. Children accounted for 17.8 percent of total Medicaid payments in 1975 and 15.7 percent of payments in 1999 (Centers for Medicare and Medicaid Services 2001). Today, children constitute the largest and fastest-growing component of the Medicaid population.

The elderly and the disabled are the most costly beneficiaries covered by the program. The elderly averaged about $11,268 per beneficiary, the disabled averaged about $9,832 per beneficiary, and adults averaged about $2,104 per beneficiary in 1999. In contrast, children averaged only about $1,282 per beneficiary. The average for all recipients in 1999 was $3,819 (Centers for Medicare and Medicaid Services 2001).

There has also been a shift in the nature of the program. This shift has been away from an acute-care program for the disabled, poor adults, and children toward a long-term-care program for the elderly and chronically ill. In view of this shift toward long-term care, it is not surprising that elderly, blind, and disabled people are consuming a major share of Medicaid resources (Holahan and Cohen 1986). As the data in Table 3.4 reveal, Medicaid's share of total nursing home care expenditures increased from $0.9 billion (out of total expenditures of $4.2 billion) in 1970 to $50.9 billion (out of total expenditures of $103.2 billion) in 2002. Medicaid accounted for 21.4 percent of total nursing home care expenditures in 1970. By 2002, Medicaid accounted for almost 50 percent of total nursing home care expenditures. By the 1970s, Medicaid had become the major purchaser in the nursing home market. In fact, by 1980, Medicaid spending on nursing home care had surpassed all other public sources combined and also slightly exceeded out-of-pocket payments for nursing home care. Today, Medicaid has become the main financier for more than half of all U.S. nursing home patient days (Grogan and Patashnik 2003a).

The Omnibus Budget Reconciliation Act of 1980 included the Boren Amendment, which linked Medicaid's nursing home payment policy with minimum federal and state quality-of-care standards. State Medicaid officials had opposed the Boren Amendment because, they argued, it would cause states to spend too much on nursing home

Table 3.3

Number of Medicaid Persons Served by Eligibility Group, FYs 1975–2004

	Total served	Children (in millions)	Per-centage	Adults (in millions)	Per-centage	Aged (in millions)	Per-centage	Disabled (in millions)	Per-centage	Other	Per-centage
1975	22.0	9.6	43.6	4.5	20.6	3.6	16.4	2.5	11.2	2.5	8.2
1976	22.8	9.9	43.5	4.8	20.9	3.6	15.8	2.7	11.7	2.7	8.1
1977	22.8	9.6	42.3	4.8	21.0	3.6	15.9	2.8	12.3	2.9	8.6
1978	22.0	9.3	42.7	4.6	21.1	3.4	15.4	2.7	12.4	2.7	8.4
1979	21.5	9.1	42.3	4.6	21.2	3.4	15.6	2.7	12.8	2.7	8.0
1980	21.6	9.3	43.2	4.9	22.6	3.4	15.9	2.9	13.5	2.9	4.8
1981	21.9	9.6	43.6	5.2	23.6	3.4	15.3	3.0	14.0	3.0	3.5
1982	21.6	9.6	44.3	5.4	24.8	3.2	15.0	2.9	13.4	2.9	2.6
1983	21.5	9.5	44.2	5.6	25.9	3.4	15.6	2.9	13.6	2.9	0.6
1984	21.6	9.6	44.8	5.6	25.9	3.2	15.0	2.9	13.5	2.9	0.8
1985	21.8	9.7	44.7	5.5	25.3	3.0	14.0	3.0	13.8	3.0	2.1
1986	22.5	10.0	44.5	5.6	25.1	3.1	13.9	3.2	14.1	3.2	2.3
1987	23.1	10.1	44.0	5.6	24.2	3.2	14.0	3.4	14.6	3.4	3.2
1988	22.9	10.0	43.8	5.5	24.0	3.2	13.8	3.5	15.2	3.5	3.1
1989	23.5	10.3	43.9	5.7	24.3	3.1	13.3	3.6	15.3	3.6	3.2

Year											
1990	25.2	11.2	44.4	6.0	23.8	3.2	12.7	3.7	14.7	3.7	4.4
1991	27.9	12.8	46.0	6.7	24.0	3.3	11.9	4.0	14.4	4.0	3.7
1992	31.1	15.2	48.8	7.0	22.6	3.7	12.0	4.5	14.4	4.5	2.2
1993	33.4	16.3	48.7	7.5	22.4	3.9	11.6	5.0	15.0	5.0	2.3
1994	35.0	17.1	49.1	7.6	21.6	4.0	11.5	5.4	15.6	5.4	2.2
1995	36.2	17.1	47.3	7.6	21.0	4.1	11.4	5.8	16.1	5.8	4.2
1996	36.1	16.7	46.3	7.1	19.7	4.3	11.9	6.2	17.2	1.7	4.7
1997	34.9	15.8	45.3	6.8	19.5	3.9	11.2	6.1	17.5	2.2	6.3
1998	40.0	18.9	47.3	7.9	19.8	3.9	9.8	6.6	16.5	2.6	6.5
1999	42.9	21.3	50.0	9.7	22.6	4.5	10.5	7.3	17.0	NA	NA
2000	44.5	22.0	49.4	10.4	23.4	4.6	10.3	7.5	16.9	NA	NA
2001	48.4	23.7	49.0	12.0	24.8	4.8	9.9	8.0	16.5	NA	NA
2002	51.4	25.0	48.6	13.2	25.7	4.9	9.5	8.3	16.1	NA	NA
2003*	53.3	25.9	48.6	13.8	25.9	5.0	9.4	8.6	16.1	NA	NA
2004*	54.6	26.6	48.7	14.2	26.0	5.1	9.2	8.8	16.1	NA	NA

Sources: Compiled from Centers for Medicare and Medicaid Services 1997, 191; 2001, 299; 2003.

Notes: Percentages and raw numbers may not add up to 100 or total number due to rounding. Increase in number of enrollees after 1997 reflects SCHIP expansion; NA = Not Applicable. In 1997, the other Title XIX category was dropped and the enrollees therein were subsumed in the remaining categories. Also, in 1998, Medicaid beneficiaries were redefined to include enrollees on behalf of whom capitation payment is made; *Numbers for 2003 and 2004 are estimates

Table 3.4

Medicaid's Share of Total Nursing Home Care Expenditures, 1970–2002

	Total nursing care expenditures (in billions of dollars)	Medicaid share (in billions of dollars)	Medicaid share (percent)
1970	4.2	0.9	21.4
1980	17.6	8.8	50.0
1990	50.9	23.1	45.4
1991	57.2	27.5	48.0
1992	62.3	30.2	48.5
1993	66.3	32.4	48.9
1994	70.9	34.3	48.4
1995	75.2	35.5	47.2
1996	78.5	37.5	47.8
1997	85.1	39.6	46.5
1998	89.1	40.1	45.0
1999	89.6	41.8	46.7
2000	93.8	44.6	47.5
2001	99.1	46.8	47.3
2002	103.2	50.9	49.3

Sources: Levit et al. 1997; Centers for Medicare and Medicaid Services 2002.

care. The Balanced Budget Act of 1997 repealed the Boren Amendment and gave states more flexibility to set payment for nursing home care (Grabowski et al. 2004). States have used three methods for nursing home care. Under a retrospective method, Medicaid payment is determined after the services are provided based on costs incurred by the facility. Under a prospective method, rates are set in advance of care regardless of actual costs to the facility. A combination method uses both retrospective and prospective methods. Did the state governments use the added flexibility to control nursing home costs? A comprehensive survey of state nursing home payment policies during 1999–2002 suggests that aggregate inflation-adjusted Medicaid payment rates rose steadily and that there was no sizable increase in the adoption of other cost-cutting policies by state governments (Grabowski et al. 2004).

The Medicaid Program during the Reagan and Bush Years: 1980–1992

Two significant developments occurred in the Medicaid program during the 1980s. First, the Reagan administration introduced major changes in the early 1980s designed to decentralize Medicaid. State governments were given more autonomy and more flexibility to enable them to attempt innovative approaches to providing health care for the poor while also containing rising Medicaid costs. Second, beginning in 1984–85, Democrats in Congress succeeded in imposing various mandates on the states designed to expand Medicaid coverage.

Reagan's New Federalism and the Decentralization of the Medicaid Program: 1981–1984

One of the major goals of the Reagan administration was to restructure the role of the federal, state, and local governments through the concept of "new federalism." New federalism was designed to decrease the role of the federal government and increase the role of the state governments in domestic policy areas. The Reagan administration tried to restrict the open-ended matching feature of the Medicaid program by proposing to limit the growth rate of the federal government's annual contribution to Medicaid to 5 percent. Congress did not support this proposal.

The most important spending and policy shift affecting health care for the poor was incorporated in the Omnibus Budget Reconciliation Act of 1981 (OBRA-81). This legislation contained three major changes affecting Medicaid. First, the federal contribution to Medicaid was directly reduced by 3 percent in 1982, 4 percent in 1983, and 4.5 percent in 1984. Second, changes in federal welfare eligibility policy reduced welfare rolls and thereby the number of eligible Medicaid recipients. Third, the law contained many fundamental policy changes with far-reaching implications for Medicaid itself (Altman 1983). For example, although Medicaid had historically followed Medicare's reasonable-cost reimbursement principle, the act allowed states to pay health care providers (hospitals, nursing homes) on a basis other than reasonable cost. In addition, OBRA-81 restricted "categorically needy" coverage and states were also given new discretion to restrict coverage under "medically needy" programs (Grogan and Patashnik 2003b).

OBRA-81 also authorized formal retreat from the principle of free choice about provider eligibility. The act gave states wide discretion, on approval from the secretary of health and human services (HHS), to limit Medicaid recipients' freedom to choose their doctors or hospitals. Other provisions made it easier to use new kinds of health care providers, particularly HMOs. The law also granted states wide discretion in deciding whom they would cover under Medicaid. It also authorized a provision allowing payment, through waiver from the secretary of HHS, for a wide range of home and community services that states could cover as an alternative to nursing home care. OBRA-81 also allowed the states to buy laboratory services and medical devices via competitive bidding.

The Tax Equity and Fiscal Responsibility Act (TEFRA) of 1982 created new financing initiatives that allowed shifting costs to beneficiaries and third parties by granting the states discretion to require Medicaid beneficiaries to pay nominal fees for medical services.

In 1982, President Ronald Reagan, as part of his new federalism, suggested a swap of programs between the federal and the state governments. He proposed that the federal government take over full responsibility for Medicaid in return for state governments taking over food stamp and AFDC programs (Gross 1982). Reactions to the proposal were mixed. State governors liked the idea of the federal government's assuming full responsibility for the Medicaid program, but they wanted to defer action on the AFDC-food stamp portion of the swap (Jordan 1982). The reaction on Capitol Hill ranged from tepid to frigid. The majority of Democrats were hostile to the plan (Barnett 1982). New York City's Democratic mayor, Ed Koch, termed the Reagan plan "a con job, a snare and a delusion, a steal by the feds" (Magnuson 1982). Because of the controversy surrounding the proposal, the plan was dropped and never submitted to Congress.

The Deficit Reduction Act of 1984 required Medicaid beneficiaries to assign to the states any rights they had to other health benefit programs. This allowed the states to collect from such programs any available payments for medical care for the covered beneficiaries.

President Reagan's new federalism initiatives posed a different challenge to the health policies established over the prior fifty years (Lee and Estes 1983). The new federalism's emphasis on decentralization, with its focus on state- and local-level decision making, raised some fundamental questions. Could the state governments contain dramatically rising costs and provide access and quality care to the poor? How states responded to this challenge would shape the future course of Medicaid policy, in particular, and health care policy, in general.

Congressional Expansion of the Medicaid Program: 1984–1990

By 1984, the 1981 Reagan initiative to prune the AFDC rosters was beginning to be challenged, and Congress began to ease eligibility standards. Since 1984, many incremental extensions of the Medicaid program have been aimed primarily at covering more low-income pregnant women, infants, and children. Thus, for example, under the Deficit Reduction Act of 1984 Congress required states to broaden their Medicaid coverage to include more low-income women during their first pregnancy, pregnant women in two-parent families in which the principal breadwinner was unemployed, and poor children up to the age of five in two-parent families.

The impetus for further expansion came from a 1985 Institute of Medicine report, which showed that every $1 spent on prenatal care saved $3.38 on care needed by low-birth-weight babies. The Consolidated Omnibus Budget Reconciliation Act of 1985 (COBRA) required coverage of all remaining pregnant women meeting AFDC financial standards (Grogan and Patashnik 2003b). The Omnibus Budget Reconciliation Act of 1986 gave states the option to extend Medicaid coverage to pregnant women and to infants up to the age of one year who were members of households with incomes of as much as 100 percent of the federal poverty level (Grogan and Patashnik 2003b).

The Omnibus Budget Reconciliation Act of 1987 required states to provide coverage to all children up to age seven born after September 30, 1983, who met AFDC eligibility standards. States were also given the option to cover all children up to age eight born after September 30, 1983, with a family income of up to 100 percent of the federal poverty level (Grogan and Patashnik 2003b).

In 1988, Congress passed the Medicare Catastrophic Coverage Act (MCCA), under which states were given the option of allowing Medicaid coverage to all pregnant women and infants with family income of up to 185 percent of the federal poverty level (Grogan and Patashnik 2003b). The law also helped avoid impoverishing the spouses of patients who receive Medicaid-financed nursing home care. The "spousal impoverishment" benefit—one of the few provisions that survived the repeal of MCCA in 1989—substantially raised the amount of income that spouses could retain before handing the balance over to Medicaid to help defray the cost of a patient's nursing home care. The federal law allowed states to let "at-home" spouses retain as much as $66,480 of the couple's combined assets and as much as $1,662 in monthly income (Kosterlitz 1991).

The Omnibus Budget Reconciliation Act of 1989 required coverage of pregnant women and infants under age one with incomes of under 100 percent of the federal poverty level (Grogan and Patashnik 2003b). It also mandated provision of all Medicaid-allowed treatments to correct problems identified during early and periodic screening, diagnosis, and treatment, even if the treatment was otherwise not covered under the state Medicaid plan. The act also required periodic screening under EPSDT if medical problems were suspected.

The Budget and Reconciliation Act of 1990 required Medicaid coverage of children under age eighteen if the family income was below 100 percent of the federal poverty line (Grogan and Patashnik 2003b).

President Reagan's new federalism initiatives posed a new challenge to the health policies established over the previous fifty years (Lee and Estes 1983). The Reagan administration was willing to grant states more discretion when such discretion promised cost reductions (Lee and Estes 1983; Thompson 1986).

Federal Government's Response to State Taxes on Hospitals and Health Care Providers

The incremental expansion in Medicaid coverage for pregnant women, infants, and children between 1984 and 1990, and the "spousal impoverishment" benefit of 1988 led to a significant increase in the number of Medicaid recipients. The total number of recipients increased from 21.6 million in 1984 to 27.9 million in 1991. This expansion in coverage and the increased number of recipients, combined with the 1990–91 recession, forced many states into a situation of fiscal crisis. According to a national survey conducted in 1991 by the National Association of Budget Officers and the National Governors' Association, the recession and Medicaid expansion mandates from the federal government forced more than half of all states to cut spending or increase revenues to avoid deficits in fiscal year 1991. Twenty-eight states faced total revenue shortfalls totaling $9.6 billion in 1991. Thirty-two states reported that their Medicaid spending would exceed their projections for the year (Wagner 1991). According to a report by the General Accounting Office, this expansion of Medicaid through federal mandates helped improved health coverage (General Accounting Office 1991).

In response to federally mandated program expansions and increasing program costs, state governments came to rely on a very controversial and growing practice known as "bootstrapping," also called "FTF" for "Fool the Feds." The practice involved states ordering doctors and other health care providers to hike up their fees so that the cost could be passed on to Washington.

Prior to 1985, the Health Care Financing Administration (HCFA) had allowed states to finance their share of Medicaid training expenditures through donation to the program by hospitals and other providers. However, states were not allowed to count such donations as part of the state-matching fund for the Medicaid program. In November of 1985, HCFA reversed this position and began to allow states to count private and public donations from hospitals and other providers as part of their matching funds.

State governments wasted very little time in trying to take advantage of the new rule. Thirty-seven states passed laws that charged doctors, hospitals, and other Medicaid providers an extra tax. The money then was returned to hospitals in the form of higher Medicaid reimbursements. Since the federal government reimbursed anywhere from 50 to 83 percent of state Medicaid costs, the more a state charged, the more it got back. If hospitals were unwilling to play along with the "voluntary donation" scheme, the states could pull the same trick by charging "provider taxes." The state levied a uniform tax on all hospitals, doctors, and other health care providers. The tax revenues were routed back to the providers of Medicaid services in the form of higher Medicaid reimbursements (Shapiro 1991; Tucker 1991). According to Richard Kusserow, inspector general of HHS, such provider taxes and donation programs might "change the very nature of the whole federal-state partnership" (Tucker 1991). By 1990 all but six states had a donation or provider tax program.

Concerned over this development, the Bush administration in September of 1991 proposed new rules intended to eliminate what it described as a "scam" used by the states to extract $3 billion to $5 billion a year from the federal government. Under the proposed rule, the federal government would not match spending by states for Medicaid if the state's money came from donations or special taxes paid by hospitals and nursing homes. The administration claimed that this practice of raising federal money by counting donations and taxes as part of a state's Medicaid share was a major reason for the explosion of the federal government's Medicaid costs. A statement issued on behalf of the National Governors' Association warned that if the proposed rules were adopted they could lead to the closing of hospitals, and women and children would lose eligibility for Medicaid (Pear 1991a). After strong opposition from state officials, a deal was struck in which states could continue the program if every hospital was taxed by the method.

The new rules imposed several important restrictions. First, health care-related taxes eligible for federal matching funds had to be broad based and uniformly imposed, and had to include all members of a class, such as all inpatient hospitals, all physicians, or all HMOs and other prepaid entities. Second, those taxes could not make up more than 25 percent of a state's share of Medicaid. Finally, the taxes could not contain a "hold harmless" provision, which guaranteed that health care providers would have the tax they paid returned to them (Hudson 1992). Based on the above rules, Congress in 1991 passed a law, the Medicaid Voluntary Contribution and Provider-Specific Tax Amendments of 1991, that closed the "provider taxes" loophole. With few exceptions, the law eliminated federal matching payments for provider donations. Second, it held out the possibility of federal matching for provider-specific taxes only if they were uniform, broad based, and did not exempt providers from the cost of the tax.

The law also capped the revenue from such taxes for purposes of state matching at 25 percent of state Medicaid spending. Finally, the law prohibited states from guaranteeing that DHS payments would exceed the tax payment for each hospital (Thompson 1998). But the story did not end with the 1991 law. According to the rules published by the Health Care Financing Administration in August 1993, the provider taxes had to be broad based and uniform. In addition, states had to drop "hold harmless" clauses. The HCFA has since disallowed millions of dollars worth of claims made by many states ("HCFA, States Spar—Again—Over Medicaid Provider Taxes" 1995; Morgan 1995).

Lawsuits over State Medicaid Reimbursements

The 1981 OBRA eliminated altogether the federal requirement for reasonable-cost reimbursement. As we discussed earlier, under this act, states were required to pay only the "reasonable and adequate" rates needed to meet the costs of "efficiently and economically operated facilities." This was also known as the Boren Amendment, named after Senator David Boren (D-OK). States had to consider only the special needs of institutions serving a disproportionate number of poor persons and to assure "reasonable access" to services and "adequate quality."

State governments facing budget problems began to change their rate-setting formulas to reduce reimbursements to hospitals and nursing homes. This in turn led hospitals and nursing homes to file lawsuits against states to force them to increase Medicaid payments to levels that more closely reflect what it costs to treat patients. Not only did the number of Medicaid lawsuits increase, but the legal and political complexities involved in such lawsuits also increased (Durda 1991). In February 1990, a federal judge ordered the state of Pennsylvania to increase its reimbursements to Temple University Hospital, the state's largest provider of health care to the poor. The judge declared that Pennsylvania's Medicaid rates were arbitrary and that the rate-setting formula used by the state was simply a mechanism to keep the total medical assistance cost within the welfare department budget (Pear 1990). In a decision handed down in June 1990, the U.S. Supreme Court upheld the right of hospitals and other providers to sue the states for higher Medicaid payments (Pear 1990).

According to a American Hospital Association survey, hospitals, on average, receive 78 cents for every $1 it costs to care for Medicaid patients. Judges in several cases reached similar conclusions. In many states, judges have ruled that Medicaid payments to health care providers do not meet the standards of "reasonable and adequate" compensation under the law. Judges in several states have also concluded that states often base their payments simply on budget considerations. Federal and state spending increased by several billion dollars a year as a result of court judgments, settlements, and rate increases granted by states in anticipation of lawsuits (Pear 1991b). As mentioned previously, the Balanced Budget Act of 1997 repealed the Boren Amendment. This gave states more flexibility to set payment levels for nursing home care (Grabowski et al. 2004).

Despite the Reagan administration's efforts to control the cost of Medicaid, total Medicaid expenditures increased from $24.8 billion in 1980 to $33.6 billion in 1983. With the expansion of Medicaid coverage under the federal mandates from 1984 to 1990, the total cost of the Medicaid program increased from $36.0 billion to $71.7 billion during that period. By 2002, Medicaid expenditures had risen to $250.4 billion and were estimated to be around $292.7 billion by 2004 (see Table 3.2).

Further Devolution of the Medicaid Program during the Clinton Administration: 1992–1998

The failure of President Clinton's effort to reform the U.S. health care system through the Health Security Act of 1993 and the resulting Republican control of Congress in the 1994 elections unleashed two forces on the Medicaid program—a push for policy devolution to the states, and a continued desire to expand health care coverage for the uninsured. The 104th Congress, under the leadership of the Republican Party, tried to bolster the role of the states in providing health care to the poor by transforming the Medicaid program into a block grant as part of the Balanced Budget Act of 1996. President Clinton vetoed the measure, and other similar attempts by Republicans to turn Medicaid into a block grant met with the same results. President Clinton argued that the Republican proposal would lead to huge cuts in spending for Medicaid, Medicare, education, and the environment. He further argued that the Medicaid program was the cornerstone for support of senior citizens living in nursing homes. Thus, Medicaid was no longer viewed as only a safety net for the economically disadvantaged (Grogan and Patashnik 2003b).

During the 1990s, there was substantial Medicaid-related activity in three areas: (1) further devolution of the Medicaid program through the increased use of waivers, allowing states to experiment with such methods as managed care; (2) welfare reform; (3) the creation of SCHIP.

Use of Waivers

President Clinton pursued his own vision of Medicaid devolution (Thompson 1998). The Clinton administration allowed states more flexibility on Medicaid funds and supported states' efforts at innovation and experimentation. For example, President Clinton ordered the federal government to make it easier for states to use Medicaid funds to introduce new health care programs for the poor. The administration also eased paperwork requirements related to states' requests for waivers in two ways. First, the Department of Health and Human Services was no longer allowed to make numerous requests for information and clarifications on a state's waiver application. Second, the Health Care Financing Administration was ordered to develop a list of state programs already approved for waiver. The purpose of this was to allow other states seeking to start similar programs to adopt them immediately, without having to go through the paperwork themselves (Friedman 1993).

Upon assuming office in 1992, the Clinton administration began to provide states with waivers to experiment with their Medicaid programs. The HCFA, relying upon the demonstration authority embedded in Section 1115 of the Social Security Act, approved dramatic changes in the Medicaid programs of many states. Prior to this, in the absence of a special waiver from the federal government, states were restricted to running their Medicaid programs under a traditional fee-for-service delivery system. Three major restrictions were imposed on the states. First, under the freedom-of-choice requirement, states were required to allow Medicaid beneficiaries to seek services from the provider of their choice. Second, states were required to offer the same benefit package to all mandatory Medicaid eligibility groups under the comparability requirement. Finally, every managed care program must be established on a statewide basis. Medicaid managed care is discussed in more detail later in this chapter.

Two main options available to states for gaining immunity from these requirements were to either establish voluntary managed care programs or seek waivers from the federal government (Guyer 1998). There are two basic types of waivers available. The 1915(b) waiver gives states the right to waive the freedom-of-choice, comparability, and statewide requirements. Under this waiver, states are not required to give Medicaid beneficiaries a choice of providers, even though they still must offer beneficiaries some choice of health plans. However, states cannot use the 1915(b) waiver to expand coverage to new populations, to change the Medicaid benefit package, to restrict access to family planning providers, or to restrict access to federally qualified health centers (Guyer 1998).

States that want more flexibility than is allowed under a 1915(b) waiver can apply for a Section 1115 research-and-demonstration waiver. This waiver gives states freedom from many of the Medicaid program's federal requirements. Like a 1915(b) waiver, a 1115 waiver allows a state waiver from freedom-of-choice, comparability, and statewide requirements. Furthermore, states under a 1115 waiver can contract with managed care plans that do not meet all the federal criteria, and may be allowed to limit voluntary disenrollment to a single period each year. Under a 1115 waiver, a state must test an innovative approach in administering the Medicaid program and must allow the federal government to monitor and evaluate its activities. States are prohibited from altering the medical assistance given to pregnant women and children, from imposing copayments on Medicaid-eligible individuals, and from waiving spousal impoverishment protections for institutionalized persons, among other prohibitions. The Clinton administration demonstrated even more flexibility by granting waivers to states whose proposals included the modest goal of advancing health care reform initiative. Thus, a 1115 waiver can be used to establish a statewide demonstration program or to run a small-scale reform project (Guyer 1998).

Welfare Reform

The Personal Responsibility and Work Opportunity Reconciliation Act of 1996 repealed the Aid to Families with Dependent Children (AFDC) program and replaced it with Temporary Assistance for Needy Families (TANF). This is a block-grant program to the states. The Medicaid program itself remained intact; however, its traditional ties to the welfare program were severed. Thus, as welfare rolls are reduced and as individuals and families lose their eligibility, they may continue to be eligible for the Medicaid program. The key issue faced by the states is how to reach the growing number of low-income parents and, even more important, children who will continue to be eligible for Medicaid but not for TANF. These parents and children used to be tracked through the welfare offices (Fubini 1997). With welfare reform, the number of uninsured children was expected to rise. The *Wall Street Journal* predicted that welfare reform was likely to increase the percentage of uninsured children from 20 percent in 1997 to 30 percent by the year 2002 (Grahan 1997). Reform advocates argued that uninsured children were a logical group for whom to expand Medicaid coverage because children are relatively inexpensive to insure and they can benefit a great deal from coverage. Congress responded to this concern by creating the SCHIP program in 1997.

State Children's Health Insurance Program

The Balanced Budget Act of 1997 provided about $40 billion in federal funds over the 1998–2007 period to expand health insurance coverage for children by creating the State Children's Health Insurance Program (SCHIP) as part of title XXI of the Social Security Act. The formula for allocating federal SCHIP funds among states depends on estimates of the number of uninsured and low-income children in each state. To qualify for SCHIP funds, a state must submit a plan to HCFA detailing how it intends to expand coverage for children. States have the freedom to use their SCHIP funds to expand Medicaid to cover children by raising their Medicaid income-eligibility standards, to develop or expand other insurance programs for children, or to provide services directly (Congressional Budget Office 1997). SCHIP is discussed in more detail later in this chapter.

Thus, during the 1980s and 1990s, policymakers enacted major expansions in Medicaid coverage, offering new health benefits to poor women and children along with other groups. Some saw Medicaid expansion as a road to achieving universal health insurance coverage. Medicaid was increasingly cast not as a safety net program for the poor but as a broad-based social welfare entitlement for all Americans, including middle-class citizens (Grogan and Patashnik 2003b).

The Medicaid Program and the State Governments: Innovations and Experimentation, from the 1980s to the 1990s

The decentralization of the Medicaid program under the Reagan, Bush, and Clinton administrations, on the one hand, and significant expansion of the program through federal mandates between 1984 and 1990, on the other, raises a fundamental question: Can state governments contain the rising cost of the Medicaid program and still provide increased access and high-quality care to the poor? How states respond to this challenge will shape the future course of Medicaid policy. In the rest of this chapter we analyze how state governments have responded to the Medicaid program's decentralization and expansion during the 1980s and the 1990s.

By the early 1980s, health care cost containment had emerged as a major issue for state and local governments. Confronted with more discretionary authority and the need to reduce Medicaid expenditures, state governments responded to new federal initiatives of the 1980s and 1990s in a variety of ways (Patel 1996). The story of Medicaid reform varies from state to state (Daniels 1998). The discussion that follows focuses on some of the major responses of state governments.

Cutbacks in Eligibility, Benefits, and Coverage

During the 1980s, in response to federal cuts in matching funds, many states turned to strategies such as placing limits on income eligibility standards, reducing coverage of optional groups, and reducing the amount of services covered in an attempt to reduce state expenditures under Medicaid.

States selected options that were easy to implement and promised the quickest savings. Some states attempted Medicaid cuts by reducing the number of people on the program, reducing benefits for those covered, or both (Altman and Morgan 1983). These are attractive options for state governments because state agencies are the ones that make such decisions, and they have the machinery to calculate the amount of savings that can be generated. Nevertheless, these cost-saving methods are most likely to affect low-income patients adversely (Altman 1983) .

In a nationwide survey, the Intergovernmental Health Policy Project at George Washington University found that in 1981 alone more than thirty states reduced Medicaid benefits or limited Medicaid eligibility. By January 1982, twenty-four states had restricted use of medical services by placing limits on the number of visits to doctors, emergency rooms, and outpatient facilities. Eleven states had placed limits on the number of hospital days covered under Medicaid, while another eight states had eliminated certain optional services (Altman 1983). Many states used a combination of stringent income criteria and limited optional service coverage to constrain enrollments and outlays.

By 1982, most of the states had made only small increases in AFDC benefit levels, or none at all, thereby allowing inflation to raise earnings of employed welfare recipients above the eligibility ceiling. People between the ages of eighteen and twenty-one were declared ineligible for AFDC in several states. Some states, such as California and Washington, reduced patients' medically needy coverage by increasing the amount that recipients must "spend down" before Medicaid eligibility begins. Thus, by 1982 most states had reduced eligibility (Bovbjerg and Holahan 1982). The number of total Medicaid recipients declined from 22 million in 1981 to 21.6 million in 1982. Reduction in Medicaid eligibility is an area where one of the goals of OBRA was realized by the early 1980s (Holahan and Cohen 1986).

Similarly, states were active in reducing service coverage. States such as Illinois, Massachusetts, Michigan, Missouri, and Rhode Island placed limits or increased existing limits on hospital days, eliminating weekend admissions, reducing the coverage of preoperative days, and ending payment for inpatient surgery when the service could be provided on an outpatient basis. California, Connecticut, Illinois, New Jersey, and North Carolina directly limited physician visits to "lock in" overutilizing patients or to "lock out" providers found to provide too many services or poor-quality care. Several states also added controls on the number of nursing home days (in either skilled nursing or intermediate-care facilities) they will pay for. Several states extended limits on drug coverage. Other states placed limits on optional services such as dentists, chiropractors, and optometrists, or eliminated coverage for such services completely (Johnson 1983).

As we discussed earlier in the chapter, federal mandates imposed between 1984 and 1990 designed to expand coverage to women and children dramatically increased the number of Medicaid beneficiaries. The result is that despite state governments' attempts to reduce program cost and enrollments, both increased dramatically in the late 1980s and early 1990s. While federal mandates have helped increase access to the health care system, especially for poor women and children, they have also significantly increased program costs at both the federal and state levels of governments. Again, we were faced with the conflicting values of access versus cost.

Increased Use of Copayments for Medicaid Services

During the 1980s, use of copayments became common in many states. Several states required copayments for many Medicaid services (Johnson 1983). The assumption here is that copayments force the beneficiary to ask whether the care is really worth paying for and thus make him or her more cost conscious. Some view copayments as an ideal mechanism for eliminating services not highly valued by Medicaid recipients. Others fear that even small copayments will result in drastic reductions in the use of health care services by the poor. Some early studies have suggested that copayments do indeed reduce expenditures on medical services. More importantly, the effects of copayments, at least with income-related upper limits, did not vary significantly with the family income of those participating in these studies. Thus, supporters of use of the copayment approach argue that the fear of reduced use of health services by the poor because of copayments is unfounded (Newhouse et al. 1981). However, it should be noted that states that have received 1915(b) and 1115 waivers are now significantly restricted in their use of copayments.

Competitive Bidding: Contractual and Prudent Buyer Arrangements

Another approach—a competitive strategy—used by the states is to attempt a fundamental reform in their approach to Medicaid. This involves replacing a fee-for-service system with negotiated or competitively bid fixed-price arrangements for Medicaid services. The 1981 OBRA also greatly expanded state authority by allowing states to purchase in bulk durable medical equipment, lab tests, and X-ray services. Some states are using bulk purchase arrangements for goods such as eyeglasses, hearing aids, and laboratory services. The objective is to buy from the lowest bidder, rather than to reimburse every retail seller at his or her price.

California Medicaid Program—Medi-Cal

For example, California relies on negotiated fixed-price arrangements. Selective contracting of hospitals by the California Medicaid program (Medi-Cal) was established in 1983. During that year the state negotiated all-inclusive per diem rates on an individual basis with eligible hospitals. Once the rate was determined, hospitals had to absorb costs that exceeded the negotiated level. Medi-Cal patients are required to go to a contracting hospital, and contracting facilities must treat patients coming to them. Contracting applied to more than half of California's hospitals and more than 75 percent of its Medicaid hospitalizations (Holahan 1988).

The Arizona Health Care Cost Containment System—AHCCCS

The Arizona Health Care Cost Containment System (AHCCCS), implemented in 1982, relies on provider bidding for the delivery of health care to the indigent. Prior to AHCCCS, Arizona did not participate in Medicaid. The Arizona Medicaid program puts out various types of care for per capita bids, and counties as well as private-sector providers compete for prepaid contracts. In such a prepaid, capitated system of health care, financial risk bearing is shifted, partially from the consumer and totally from the third-party insurer, to the provider. According to proponents, such a system internalizes economic incentives (Vogel 1984). Competitive bidding is also becoming increasingly popular for health care services such as clinical laboratory services, home health care, and mental health care (McCombs and Christianson 1987). Originally, the AHCCCS program did not cover nursing home care. However, in 1989, the Arizona Long-Term Care System (ALTCS) was incorporated into AHCCCS. ALTCS provides a full range of acute home-based and community-based and nursing home services to persons eligible for Medicaid who are at risk of institutionalization.

An analysis of the Arizona system in 1985 revealed that, overall, a lower proportion of the poor were enrolled in AHCCCS in 1984 than in county programs in 1982. Access to care increased for AHCCCS enrollees in 1984 compared to county patients in 1982. Nevertheless, the study also discovered significant undercoverage of the medically indigent and the medically needy. The study concluded that AHCCCS may be a viable alternative to conventional Medicaid programs, but poor persons who were financially ineligible for AHCCCS were experiencing decreased opportunities for health services (Freeman and Kirkman-Liff 1985). Thus it remains to be seen whether a competitive bidding approach helps contain costs without sacrificing access or quality of care.

The Tennessee Medicaid Experiment—TennCare

In the mid-1990s, Tennessee made history when it replaced its traditional Medicaid program by implementing TennCare. Under this program it extended coverage to uninsured and uninsurable adults and children. The program provides a wide range of medical services that include inpatient and outpatient hospital care, physician services, prescription drugs, laboratory and X-ray services, medical supplies, home health care, and hospice care, among others. All beneficiaries are served by capitated managed care organizations (MCOs) that are HMOs. Approximately 25 percent of the Tennessee population is enrolled in TennCare (Larson and Williams 2003).

Rationing of Medicaid Services

The state of Oregon implemented an innovative approach to address problems of cost and access in its Medicaid program. In 1987, the state decided to stop financing most organ transplants for Medicaid patients, and to use the money instead for prenatal care for pregnant women. In 1990, the state produced a more revolutionary Medicaid plan. As we discussed earlier, a large number of poor people do not have access to Medicaid because they do not meet eligibility criteria. The state proposed that under its plan, Medicaid would cover all poor people in the state but may not cover all medical services. In other words, the plan proposed a tradeoff—increased access in return for reduced benefits. The state ranked most medical services as more or less economically worthwhile to treat under the plan. If money ran out before all services were covered, the lowest-priority services would not be covered. In March 1993, the HCFA under the Clinton administration granted the state of Oregon a waiver from federal statutes to implement such a program. The state plan is called Oregon Health Plan (OHP). Critics charged that the plan targets the poor—mainly women and children, who make up most of the Medicaid population (Kosterlitz 1990). They also argued that such a meat-ax approach to health care would inevitably lead to gross misallocation of resources (Schwartz and Aaron 1985, 1990).

Use of Medicaid Waivers for Home- and Community-Based Services

Section 2176 of OBRA-81 allowed states to seek waivers from the Department of Health and Human Services for a variety of home- and community-based services provided to certain individuals—the elderly, the physically disabled, the developmentally disabled, and the mentally ill—who would otherwise require nursing home care. States that have approval from HHS can receive matching funds. The objective of section 2176 was to encourage a move away from the use of more expensive treatment in nursing homes and other long-term-care facilities and toward less expensive home- and community-based services when appropriate. The traditional purpose of the waiver process has been to allow HHS to conduct demonstrations on alternative delivery and financing schemes. The waiver provisions of the OBRA-81 were based on early successes of demonstration projects in this area.

Such waiver programs have become popular with many states and have grown rapidly since their creation in 1981. By 1985, forty-two states were providing a broad range of health and social services under seventy-five waiver programs. The number of beneficiaries had increased steadily under such waiver programs. For example, the number of aged and/or physically disabled beneficiaries increased from 6,389 in 1981 to 45,934 in 1984. Similarly, the number of developmentally disabled and chronically mentally ill beneficiaries increased from 10,000 to 21,823 during the same period (Laudicina and Burwell 1988). This trend continued in the 1990s due to political pressure on long-term-care policymakers to expand home and community-based services under Medicaid. The number of Medicaid home and community-based programs, the number of participants, and inflation-adjusted spending has continued to grow. Between 1992 and 2001, seventy-six new waivers were added. During the 1990s, there was a 285 percent increase in waiver participants (Kitchener et al. 2005). The impact of rising Medicaid costs has further fueled state Medicaid activities ("Financial Pressures Fuel More State . . ." 2004). Given the budget deficits reported by most states in 2003, it is not too surprising that some states are beginning to restrict access to waivers through spending caps and waiting lists (Kitchener et al. 2005). Thus, the political popularity of waiver programs does not mean that all states find them cost effective. Waivers do provide states with a way to secure additional federal funding for services that otherwise would have to be funded entirely through state revenues (Laudicina and Burwell 1988).

New Approaches to Reimbursing Providers

Payments to Physicians

States have generally enjoyed significant discretion over Medicaid payments to physicians. The Medicaid program has traditionally paid physicians much less than Medicare or private insurers. For example, under the Medicaid program, states are mandated to pay physicians "usual, customary, and reasonable" fees (UCR payment system). The Medicaid statute, however, never imposed any specific method of payment on the states except that the fee should be high enough to assure reasonable access to care for Medicaid beneficiaries.

Through waivers, states can pay physicians a set fee or capitation payment rather than a fee-for-service payment. States also can establish case management programs linking patients to solo or group practice physicians or to an HMO (Kern, Windham, and Griswold, 1986). States may, under a waiver program, enroll Medicaid patients in an HMO and restrict their use of other providers.

Several state Medicaid programs imposed significant limits or ceilings on physician payment. Some states turned to the use of fee schedules. The average Medicaid payment for a visit to a physician is estimated to be only 65 percent of the average charge for visits of other patients. Medicare pays about 84 percent on the average. The result is that many physicians do not accept Medicaid patients; the willingness to accept them varies with the level of Medicaid payments (Sloan, Mitchell, and Cromwell 1978). This raises questions about access of Medicaid recipients to physicians. When Medicaid cuts have to be made, state programs often attempt to impose further restrictions on physicians' fees. Such efforts are often misguided. In general, physicians' fees constitute a very small percentage of total Medicaid spending. Thus, trying to save money by limiting payments to physicians may not be the best way to reduce program costs. In fact, reduced physician participation may drive many beneficiaries to substitute services at a greater cost to Medicaid.

Because of the very low physician rate paid by many states, a large number of physicians refuse to treat Medicaid patients (Ginsburg 1988). Thus, physician participation rates in Medicaid vary significantly across the country. In recent years, to increase physician participation in the Medicaid program, several states increased physician payment rates. For example, California's Medicaid program—Medi-Cal—which is the country's largest program, has one of the lowest rates of physician participation. Despite the fact that California, in August 2000, raised physician Medi-Cal payments from an average of 57 percent to 65.2 percent of fees paid by other patients, physician participation rates in the state Medicaid program did not reveal any significant increase (Bindman, Yoon, and Grumbach 2003). Between 1998 and 2003, physicians' fees increased by an average of 27.4 percent nationwide. Yet, in most states, Medicaid reimbursement rates still remained below Medicare reimbursement rates. Thus, despite the fee increase, the physician participation rate in the Medicaid program, as measured by a national average, increased only slightly, from 61 percent in 1997 to 62 percent in 2001 ("Medicaid Physician Fees Rise Sharply . . ." 2004). Despite small gains, the relative attractiveness of Medicaid patients to physicians has not improved much over a longer term (Zuckerman, McFeeters, and Cunningham, 2004).

Payments to Hospitals

In contrast to physician payment, Medicaid has generally been required to pay hospitals on the same basis as Medicare, which is using a "reasonable cost" reimbursement method. With the 1972 amendments to the Social Security Act, however, there has been a gradual trend toward paying less than the actual cost. The amendments allowed states, with approval from HHS, to use alternate (to Medicare) payment methods for Medicaid.

OBRA-81 gave states more flexibility to develop and implement new Medicaid hospital payment methods as long as those payments were reasonable and adequate to meet the costs of "efficiently and economically operated facilities." The only requirements were that payment levels take into consideration the circumstances of hospitals serving a disproportionate number of low-income persons and that payments be sufficient to ensure Medicaid patients reasonable access to adequate-quality services (Bovbjerg and Holahan 1982) .

Faced with reduced revenues and increased health care costs, state governments have tried various strategies to contain costs. By 1982, seventeen states had legislation requiring the disclosure, review (such as HSAs and certificate-of-need [CON]), or regulation of hospital rates or budgets. States such as California converted their hospital payment approach to selective contracting on the basis of price negotiated for services provided.

One major alternative payment method used by state governments is rate setting. Many states have adopted some form of hospital rate review or prospective reimbursement system. In some states, rate setting applies only to Medicaid, while in others the rate applies to all payers (Grannemann and Pauley 1983). Rate-setting programs fall into three broad strategies to control Medicaid costs: multiple-payer rate setting, Medicaid-only prospective payment, and selective contracting (Holahan 1988).

The state rate-setting strategy emerged, in the mid-1970s, in several eastern industrial states as a regulatory device in response to Medicaid's financial crisis. Limited prospective payment schemes for Medicaid reimbursement were adopted in Kentucky, Missouri, Alabama, Georgia, Mississippi, and North Carolina (Crozier 1982).

State rate-setting programs have produced mixed results. Proponents have argued that some mandatory prospective rate-setting programs have been successful in reducing hospital expenditures per patient day, per admission, and per capita (Coelen and Sullivan 1981). Other studies have also demonstrated that states have achieved modest success in containing Medicaid payments to hospitals under different rate-setting strategies—multiple-payer rate setting, Medicaid-only rate setting, and selective contracting—with some being more effective than others (Holahan 1988). States that use all-payer rate setting are able to force down hospital prices for all payers. In states where the payment systems apply only to Medicaid, savings appear to be temporary and may not be sustained over a long period (Davis et al. 1990).

Medicaid Managed Care in the 1990s

In response to problems of cost and access, state governments have increasingly turned to managed care systems in the Medicaid program. Many state governments have also moved in the direction of "privatization" of their Medicaid programs. States and the federal government continue to fund the program jointly, but the day-to-day control of health plans for the poor is being turned over to MCOs or private insurers. Many states require Medicaid recipients to enroll in some form of MCO. Case managers or primary-care physicians are assigned to watch Medicaid patients' health.

They act as gatekeepers to control and coordinate the delivery of health services in a cost-conscious manner. The emphasis is on low-cost preventive care, outpatient services, and less reliance on emergency hospital care and costly specialists as a way of reducing costs (Anders 1993).

OBRA-81 gave states more flexibility to design managed care plans. In addition, HCFA allowed states to experiment with innovative approaches to Medicaid through research and demonstration projects. In most instances, states must obtain a waiver of federal statutory requirements from HCFA. Most states rapidly began to develop managed care programs. According to a study by the General Accounting Office, Medicaid-managed care enrollment more than doubled between 1987 and 1992 and included about 3.6 million beneficiaries nationwide, representing about 12 percent of the total Medicaid population as of June 1992. Thirty-six states were operating one or more mandatory managed care programs for Medicaid beneficiaries in February 1993 (General Accounting Office 1993). Today, all states except Alaska, Mississippi, and Wyoming have Medicaid managed care programs in place.

As discussed earlier in the chapter, the use of managed care for the Medicaid program was given a significant boost during the Clinton administration by HCFA's announcement of new rules pertaining to the Medicaid program that made it easier for the states to gain 1915(b) and 1115 waivers from the federal government.

States participating in managed care share a common approach but employ a variety of models. State governments in their Medicaid managed care programs use two main organizational approaches. One is a risk-based capitation approach under which states contract with MCOs. They could be private HMOs or prepaid health plans (PHPs). States ask MCOs to take either full risk for a comprehensive list of Medicaid benefits or partial risk for a subset of services. The second organizational approach utilized by states is that of primary care case management (PCCM) in which the program recruits primary care providers to act as gatekeepers in return for a per recipient case management payment. Under this approach, providers are still reimbursed according to fee-for-service (FFS) (Grogan 1997).

As Grogan (1997) points out, both approaches utilize key elements of "managed care," such as gatekeeper mechanisms, and create financial incentives to change provider behavior. However, there are some major differences between these two approaches. First, the PCCM approach leaves the existing health care delivery system mainly intact. In contrast, the risk-based approach dramatically changes the way traditional Medicaid providers do business. Second, the PCCM approach does not include the notion of competition and PCCM program providers do not compete for Medicaid recipients, while in the risked-based capitation approach health plans compete for Medicaid enrollees. Third, under PCCM, recipients must select a primary care provider but can generally switch providers at any time. In a risk-based program, recipients must first select an MCO and then a primary care provider within that organization (Grogan 1997).

The end result is that there are a variety of MCOs utilized by states (Guyer 1998).

Some state plans utilize HMOs. HMOs can be public or private entities authorized by state law that are either federally qualified or meet a state plan's definition of HMO. While states have considerable flexibility to define HMOs as they wish, their definition must require HMOs to give Medicaid enrollees the same access to services as other plan participants and to protect Medicaid enrollees from losses if the HMO becomes insolvent. Most HMOs are risk-based programs that agree to provide beneficiaries with a substantial portion of the Medicaid benefit package they are entitled to in exchange for a capitated payment. If the payment falls short, the HMO suffers a loss. By the same token, if the plan can reduce the cost of services provided to less than the capitated payment, it makes a profit. HMOs can also contract with state Medicaid agencies on a partial-risk or nonrisk basis. In a partial-risk plan, HMOs can suffer losses if actual costs exceed capitated payment but they are responsible for providing a less than comprehensive set of services. Under a nonrisk plan, if the cost of providing services is larger than expected, the state can adjust the size of its capitated payment to the plan (Guyer 1998).

Some states utilize what are called health insuring organizations (HIOs). HIOs assume the risk of loss if the payment is inadequate to cover beneficiaries' health care expenses. However, unlike HMOs, HIOs generally do not deliver care. Since 1995, Congress has held HIOs to the same regulatory standards as HMOs, if they offer a full-risk comprehensive set of services. However, if they do not offer a comprehensive set of services, they face fewer federal regulatory requirements (Guyer 1998).

Another delivery model utilized by states is called prepaid health plans. These plans fall into two categories. One type of PHP provides services on a nonrisk basis or provides less than comprehensive range of services on a risk basis. The second type of PHP, often referred to as a "grandfathered" PHP, is statutorily defined, and is allowed to engage in comprehensive risk contracting without having to meet the same regulatory standards as an HMO or a regular PHP (Guyer 1998). The PHPs can be inpatient health plans or ambulatory health plans.

Some states use PCCMs. These are not plans or separate organizations. They are programs under which Medicaid beneficiaries select a primary care provider. Generally, a primary care provider contracts directly with a state Medicaid agency and is paid on a fee-for-service basis to provide primary care services directly to the assigned beneficiaries. In some states, such as California, PCCM providers operate on a partial capitation basis, while in other states PCCM providers are at risk for outpatient services only (Guyer 1998). In addition, there are programs that provide all-inclusive care for the elderly. Also, there are Medicaid-only MCOs and commercial MCOs.

There are several explanations of why state governments are using their increased discretion to encourage or require Medicaid beneficiaries to enroll in managed care. One primary reason is the belief that moving beneficiaries into managed care will significantly help reduce program costs. A second is the belief that managed care will provide beneficiaries better access to high-quality care. A third reason is that managed care fits into the general trend toward privatization and contracting out in the health care sector (Sparer 1998).

Table 3.5

Medicaid Managed Care Enrollment—National Trends, 1991–2003

	Total Medicaid population (in thousands)	Fee-for-service (FFS) population (in thousands)	Managed care population (in thousands)	Percentage managed care population	Percentage change from previous year
1991	28,280,000	25,583,603	2,696,397		
1992	30.926,390	27,291,874	3,634,516	11.8	34.8
1993	33,430,051	28,621,100	4,808,951	14.4	32.3
1994	33,634,000	25,839.750	7,794,250	23.2	62.1
1995*	33,373,000	23,573,000	9,800,000	29.4	25.7
1996	33,241,147	19,911,028	13,330,119	40.1	36.0
1997	32,092,380	16,746,878	15,345,502	47.8	15.1
1998	30,896,635	14,322,639	16,573,996	53.6	8.0
1999	31,940,188	14,183,585	17,756,603	55.6	7.1
2000	33,690,364	14,904,227	18,786,137	55.8	5.8
2001	36,562,567	15,788,754	20,773,813	56.8	10.6
2002	40,147,539	17,029,871	23,117,668	57.6	11.3
2003	42,740,719	17,477,846	25,262,873	59.1	9.3

Sources: Health Care Financing Administration, Medicaid Managed Care Page, online at hcfa.gov/medicaid/trends97.htm; "Managed Care Trends," Centers for Medicare and Medicaid Services, online at www.cms.hhs.gov/medicaid/managedcare/trends03.pdf.
   *Numbers are approximates.

Table 3.6

National Summary of Medicaid Managed Care Enrollment by Plan Type, June 30, 2003

	Number of plans	Number of enrollees (in thousands)	Percentage of total enrollment
Health Insuring Organization	5	531,349	1.6
Commercial Managed Care Organizations	164	9,920,954	29.0
Medicaid-Only Managed Care Organizations	120	6.848,585	20.0
Primary Care Case Management	42	6,142,646	18.0
Prepaid Inpatient Health Plan	109	7,468,909	21.9
Prepaid Ambulatory Health Plan	27	2,999,392	8.8
Program of All-Inclusive Care for the Elderly	22	5,670	0.2
Other	22	190,216	.5
Total	511	34,107,721	100.0

Source: "National Breakout of Managed Care Entities and Enrollment as of June 30, 2003," online at www.cms.hhs.gov/medicaid/managedcare/plansum03.pdf.
   Note: This table provides duplicated figures by plan type. The total number of enrollees includes 8,844,848 individuals who were enrolled in more than one managed care plan. It also includes individuals who were enrolled in state health care reform programs that expanded eligibility beyond traditional Medicaid eligibility standards.

The 1990s have witnessed an unprecedented increase in the number of Medicaid patients enrolled in managed care programs. Table 3.5 provides nationwide data on Medicaid managed care enrollment. In 1992, only 11.8 percent of Medicaid beneficiaries were enrolled in managed care plans. The number of Medicaid managed care enrollees had reached 47.8 percent in 1997. By 2003, 59.1 percent of the total Medicaid population was enrolled in managed care plans.

With respect to different organizational models, commercial MCOs, Medicaid-only MCOs, PCCMs, and prepaid inpatient health plans appear to be the ones enrolling most Medicaid beneficiaries (see Table 3.6). In June 2003, there were 164 commercial MCOs enrolling about 29 percent of the Medicaid managed care population in the states. Another 21.9 percent of the Medicaid managed care population was enrolled in 109 prepaid inpatient health plans. Also 20 percent were enrolled in 120 Medicaid-only MCOs. PCCM programs had enrolled another 18 percent of the Medicaid population through forty-two plans. Almost 89 percent of the Medicaid managed care population was enrolled in one of the four major organizational models we have described, while about 11 percent belonged to other organizational forms.

Table 3.7 provides data on Medicaid managed care enrollment on a state-by-state basis as of June 2003. A quick glance at the data suggests significant variations in Medicaid managed care enrollment among fifty states and U.S. territories. It ranges from zero percent of the Medicaid population enrolled in managed care plans in states such as Alaska, Mississippi, and Wyoming to 100 percent of Medicaid patients enrolled in managed care plans in states such as Tennessee. In a large majority of the states, 50 percent or more of the Medicaid beneficiaries were enrolled in managed care plans. Thus, it is clear that the Clinton administration's grant of 1915(b) and 1115 waivers to states and the decentralization of the Medicaid program encouraged states to move in the direction of managed care as one of the cost-saving measures.

The results of managed care experiments by state governments in containing Medicaid costs have been mixed. Some of the studies have found that managed care can save money. One study examined twenty-five managed care programs and found that per-member costs were 5 to 15 percent lower than in conventional Medicaid programs (Anders 1993). Many other studies of managed care plans have demonstrated that such plans have largely failed to improve recipients' access (Anderson and Fox 1987; Freund et al. 1989; Kotelchuk 1992). A General Accounting Office study concluded that "managed care plans have had mixed results in improving access to care, assuring the quality of services, and saving money" (General Accounting Office 1993). More recent studies have also raised doubts about Medicaid managed care's ability to save significant amounts of money for state and local governments. In state governments' earlier estimates, the savings expected to be gained due to managed care were about 15 percent, relative to fee-for-service care. However, most states today anticipate savings to be in the range of 5 to 10 percent. One reason is that despite the dramatic growth in Medicaid managed care enrollment in this decade, very few states are enrolling the elderly or the disabled, who are the most expensive Medicaid beneficiaries (Holahan et al. 1998).

Table 3.7

Medicaid Managed Care Enrollment by States, June 30, 2003 (in thousands)

State or area	Medicaid enrollment	Managed care enrollment	Percentage enrolled in managed care
Alabama	760,527	404,797	53.23
Alaska	95,335	0	0.00
Arizona	901,655	808,506	89.67
Arkansas	557,074	374,067	67.15
California	6,272,109	3,258,787	51.96
Colorado	330,499	262,263	79.35
Connecticut	405,064	294,331	72.66
Delaware	121,676	86,709	71.26
Florida	2,214,058	1,354,025	61.16
Georgia	1,448,645	1,212,639	83.71
Hawaii	179,522	141,399	78.76
Idaho	156,935	101,257	64.25
Illinois	1,580,944	137,682	8.71
Indiana	707,168	502,401	71.04
Iowa	266,737	243,954	91.46
Kansas	246,186	141,119	57.32
Kentucky	663,002	611,878	92.29
Louisiana	861,846	505,434	58.65
Maine	249,738	148,151	59.32
Maryland	681,096	466,688	68.52
Massachusetts	915,114	572,835	62.60
Michigan	1,322,261	1,314,810	99.44
Minnesota	552,779	362,349	65.55
Mississippi	720,304	0	0.00
Missouri	950,694	425,161	44.72
Montana	80,378	55,372	68.89
Nebraska	197,378	142,377	72.13
Nevada	164,033	74,923	45.68
New Hampshire	91,262	13,407	14.69
New Jersey	782,309	525,864	67.22
New Mexico	404,497	261,015	64.53
New York	3,645,834	1,914,794	52.52
North Carolina	1,074,616	749,152	69.71
North Dakota	53,806	35,515	66.01
Ohio	1,515,712	436,146	28.77
Oklahoma	498,031	338,859	68.04
Oregon	425,627	330,874	77.74
Pennsylvania	1,492,095	1,192,031	79.89
Rhode Island	178,543	119,257	66.79
South Carolina	862,175	71,195	8.26
South Dakota	93,208	90,733	97.34
Tennessee	1,304,794	1,304,794	100.00
Texas	2,559,248	1,065,945	41.65
Utah	187,823	162,364	86.45
Vermont	131,051	85,751	65.43
Virginia	583,999	262,961	45.03
Washington	1,059,865	854,861	80.66

(continued)

West Virginia	296,220	151,515	51.15
Wisconsin	739,431	349,246	47.23
Wyoming	56,209	0	00.0
District of Columbia	128,185	85,370	66.60
Puerto Rico	957,298	857,310	89.56
Virgin Islands	16,125	0	00.0
Total	42,740,719	25,262,873	59.11

Source: "Medicaid Managed Care Enrollment as of June 30, 2003," Centers for Medicare and Medicaid Services, online at www.cms.hhs.gov/Medicaid/managedcare/mcsten03.pdf.

Michael Sparer has provided five excellent explanations of why expected savings from the Medicaid managed care programs are likely to be more modest than earlier projections. First, many Medicaid initiatives by the states have focused on welfare mothers and their children, who are the least expensive part of the Medicaid population. Second, most states are paying high capitation rates to build up managed care capacity. Third, the technology of risk adjustment is not very advanced. Fourth, the start-up cost for new Medicaid initiatives by the states is often very high. Finally, the extent of managed care savings depends on the fee-for-service expenditure patterns in a particular state. States that already have an inexpensive fee-for-service program are not likely to realize a great deal of savings (Sparer 1998). The Medicaid managed care and cost savings may vary from state to state. Thomas Oliver, in his study of Medicaid managed care in Maryland, concluded that the assumption that managed care would deliver significant savings has failed to materialize. In fact, some of the major health plans in the state did not participate in the program because of what they perceived to be heavy government regulations of managed care programs (Oliver 1998). Overall, researchers have concluded that there is very little evidence to suggest that managed care plans can produce significant savings (Hurley and Zuckerman 2002). One of the important reasons why Medicaid managed care may fail to generate substantial savings is that up to this point the main focus has been on enrolling nondisabled children and their parents while the elderly and disabled are often excluded from managed care enrollment. For example, in the state of New York, nondisabled children and their parents account for only about 20 percent of Medicaid program spending while the elderly and disabled represent about 70 percent of the total Medicaid costs in the state. This means that managed care would have to gain significant savings from its low-expenditure base to affect overall spending (Haslanger and Tallon 2004). Whether managed care plans have had a substantial effect on Medicaid cost reduction or not may remain the subject of much discussion and debate.

Managed care programs are also plagued with other problems. In states that do not monitor HMO behavior, such plans may offer impressive marketing but poor care. Such HMOs are often referred to as "Medicaid mills." Some HMOs snap up the healthiest patients, leaving traditional Medicaid to deal with sicker people. In addition, paperwork is always a problem because many Medicaid recipients go on and off program rolls as their income and family status change (Anders 1993). The expansion of

Medicaid managed care may also decrease access to specialists since specialists are less likely to accept new Medicaid managed care patients compared to Medicaid fee-for-service patients (Backus et al. 2001).

The rapid transformation of Medicaid programs in all states presents important challenges to the policymakers. The increased devolution of Medicaid policymaking to the states raises the question of whether states' health bureaucracies have the capacity to design and implement cost-effective health care delivery systems to meet the needs of the vulnerable populations. The potential of Medicaid managed care to improve access, quality of care, and save money is matched by many of the pitfalls and challenges it presents (Daniels 1998; Davidson and Somers 1998).

In fact, courts are increasingly becoming involved in issues related to quality of care provided by MCOs. For example, the 2000 case of *Frew v. Gilbert* in a Texas federal district court drew attention to the issue of quality of care in Medicaid managed care programs. The district court judge in his opinion criticized the state of Texas for its failure to provide adequate health care to impoverished children through its Medicaid program and recited a laundry list of problems with Texas's early periodic screening, diagnostic, and treatment program. The judge in particular emphasized the deficiencies in the care provided by MCOs and indicated that well-child checkups given in Medicaid HMOs were grossly inadequate (Mello 2002). However, this case was more an aberration because other plaintiffs have found it difficult to successfully sue a Medicaid or Medicare HMO due to the fact that beneficiaries are often frail, elderly, ill, poorly educated, non-English speaking, and have low income. Often the time and effort involved in pursuing a court action acts as a discouragement. Another barrier is the Eleventh Amendment's restriction on suits against state governments (Mello 2002). It is also unclear whether Medicaid HMOs are state actors that can be sued for deprivation of constitutional due process because the federal courts, including the U.S. Supreme Court, have taken contrary and often confusing positions (Mello 2002).

State Governments, Medicaid, and Children's Insurance Program

As we discussed earlier in the chapter, the failure of attempts at comprehensive reform of the U.S. health care system after the 1993–94 period led advocates of reforms to push for incremental changes. In the past, Medicare and Medicaid programs had targeted specific groups of Americans for protection. Following this model, the advocates of reforms argued that the next logical group that needed government protection was uninsured persons. The Health Insurance Portability and Accounting Act of 1996 provided some protection to uninsured adult Americans by placing limits on insurance companies' ability to deny coverage for preexisting conditions and by allowing portability of insurance from one job to the next. The next logical group to target was the large number of children who lacked any health insurance (Flint 1997). The result was the creation of the State Children's Health Insurance Program as part of title XXI of the Social Security Act under the 1997 Balanced Budget Act.

Under the program, the federal government provides matching funds to assist states in providing health insurance coverage for uninsured children (Rosenbaum et al. 1998). At the time SCHIP was being debated, approximately 11.3 million children were without any health insurance coverage (Edmunds and Teitelbaum 2000). SCHIP was adopted to address the gap in health insurance coverage for low-income children who were not poor enough to qualify for Medicaid (Cunningham and Kirby 2004). Within three years of the establishment of SCHIP, all states had implemented the program and, by 2002, enrollment has surpassed 3.6 million (Rosenbaum and Budetti 2003). As a result of SCHIP, the percentage of publicly insured children who fell in the 100–200 percent range of the poverty group increased from 1997 to 2001, and the uninsurance rates declined (Cunningham and Kirby 2004).

State governments have several options for the use of SCHIP funds (Children's Defense Fund 1997; Congressional Budget Office 1997). One option states have is to use the funds to expand the Medicaid program to cover more children (Weil 1997). In such a case, states build on existing institutional structures and make very few program modifications. Many advocates favor this approach because Medicaid already provides a comprehensive benefit package for children. Opponents argue that some low-income families may not apply for coverage because of the perceived stigma associated with the Medicaid program. Medicaid expansion may also expose state government to financial risks.

A second option for states is to fund an alternative new insurance program, separate from Medicaid, with the SCHIP funds. Such an approach is more attractive to states that already had such a program in place funded by state and local governments. For example, California, Colorado, Florida, Massachusetts, Minnesota, New York, Pennsylvania, Tennessee, and Washington had already developed their own children's health insurance programs. This also gives them the advantage of not having to satisfy all the federal requirements of the Medicaid program, such as the mandatory benefits and limits on cost sharing. Since such a program is not an individual entitlement, program outlays can be capped.

The third option available to states is to use a combination of the first two approaches. Table 3.8 provides data on SCHIP options used by the states, the dates programs were implemented, and the upper-eligibility levels set by the state governments, As can be seen from the table, sixteen states have elected to expand their Medicaid programs, fifteen states have created separate programs, while the remaining nineteen states use combinations of both. By the end of 1999, all states except Hawaii and Washington had implemented SCHIPs. Hawaii and Washington implemented the program in 2000. There is also a considerable variation in upper eligibility established by different states. In 1999, upper eligibility in Arkansas and Tennessee was set at 100 percent of the federal poverty level; the upper eligibility level in New Jersey was set at 350 percent of the poverty level; and the states of Connecticut, Missouri, New Hampshire, and Vermont had set the upper eligibility at 300 percent of the federal poverty level.

Table 3.8

State Children's Health Insurance Program 1999: Program Type, Implementation Date, and Upper Eligibility (as percent of federal poverty level)

State/Area	Type of SCHIP	Date implemented	Upper eligibility (%)
Alabama	Combination	02/01/98	200
Alaska	Medicaid	03/01/99	200
Arizona	Separate	11/01/98	200
Arkansas	Medicaid	10/01/98	100
California	Combination	03/01/98	250
Colorado	Separate	04/22/98	185
Connecticut	Combination	07/01/98	300
Delaware	Separate	02/01/99	200
Florida	Combination	04/01/98	200
Georgia	Separate	11/01/98	200
Hawaii	Medicaid	07/01/00	200
Idaho	Medicaid	10/01/97	150
Illinois	Combination	01/05/98	185
Indiana	Combination	10/01/97	200
Iowa	Combination	07/01/98	200
Kansas	Separate	01/01/99	200
Kentucky	Combination	07/01/98	200
Louisiana	Medicaid	11/01/98	150
Maine	Combination	07/01/98	185
Maryland	Medicaid	07/01/98	200
Massachusetts	Combination	10/01/97	200
Michigan	Combination	05/01/98	200
Minnesota	Medicaid	10/01/98	280
Mississippi	Combination	07/01/98	200
Missouri	Medicaid	09/01/98	300
Montana	Separate	01/01/99	150
Nebraska	Medicaid	05/01/98	185
Nevada	Separate	10/01/98	200
New Hampshire	Combination	05/01/98	300
New Jersey	Combination	03/01/98	350
New Mexico	Medicaid	03/31/99	235
New York	Combination	04/15/98	192
North Carolina	Separate	10/01/98	200
North Dakota	Combination	10/01/98	140
Ohio	Medicaid	01/01/98	200
Oklahoma	Medicaid	12/01/97	185
Oregon	Separate	07/01/98	170
Pennsylvania	Separate	05/28/98	200
Rhode Island	Medicaid	10/01/97	250
South Carolina	Medicaid	10/01/97	150
South Dakota	Combination	07/01/98	200
Tennessee	Medicaid	10/01/97	100
Texas	Combination	07/01/98	200
Utah	Separate	08/03/98	200
Vermont	Separate	10/01/98	300
Virginia	Separate	10/22/98	185

(continued)

Washington	Separate	02/01/00	250
West Virginia	Combination	07/01/98	150
Wisconsin	Medicaid	04/01/99	185
Wyoming	Separate	12/01/99	133
American Samoa	Medicaid	04/01/99	NA
District of Columbia	Medicaid	10/01/98	200
Puerto Rico	Medicaid	01/01/98	200

Source: Centers for Medicare and Medicaid Services, online at www.cms.hhs.gov/schip/enrollment/fy99-00.pdf.

As can be expected, the number of children covered by SCHIP varies from state to state. Table 3.9 provides data for total enrollment in SCHIP from 1999 to 2003. As can be seen, the total enrollment in SCHIP increased in all states from 1999 to 2003. Some states experienced dramatic increases. For example, in California enrollment in SCHIP increased from 222,351 in 1999 to 955,152 in 2003. Total enrollment in Georgia increased from 47,581 in 1999 to 251,711 in 2003.

Preliminary Assessment of SCHIP

Early studies have concluded that SCHIP has been very successful on several fronts. It is clear that SCHIP has helped provide health insurance coverage to a significant number of poor children as reflected in the increased enrollment and the decline in the number of uninsured children in the states. Table 3.10 presents data on percentage of uninsured children by states. The percentages listed are averages of three years' percentages, not percentages of the average number. The data provide the percentage of uninsured children before and after the implementation of the SCHIP.

In all but four states, the three-year average for 2001, 2002, and 2003 of uninsured children at or below 200 percent of the federal poverty level without health insurance is lower compared to the three-year average for 1995, 1996, and 1997. The only exceptions are Hawaii, Illinois, and Pennsylvania, which recorded a slight increase, while the average for Wisconsin remained the same. Some states reported dramatic decreases in percentages of low-income uninsured children. The reported number of health insurance enrollment increases and/or decreases in low-income children under SCHIP often varies among different studies because of different methodologies used.

A 2000 study by the Children's Defense Fund (Edmunds and Tietelbaum 2000), ranked states by the progress they made in increasing insurance coverage by SCHIP enrollment alone and SCHIP and Medicaid enrollment combined. According to this study, Alaska, Massachusetts, Maryland, New York, and Louisiana ranked among the top five in increasing insurance coverage using combined SCHIP and Medicaid enrollment, while the bottom five states were Montana, Tennessee, Wisconsin, Michigan, and Oregon. Using SCHIP enrollment alone, the top five states in increasing enrollment were Alaska, New York, Massachusetts, Missouri, and Maine, while the bottom five states were Montana, Tennessee, Texas, North Dakota, and Arkansas.

Table 3.9

State Children's Health Insurance Program: Total Enrollment by States for FYs 1999–2003 (in thousands)

State/Area	FY1999	FY2000	FY2001	FY2002	FY2003
Alabama	38,980	37,587	68,179	83,359	78,554
Alaska	8,033	13,413	21,831	22,306	22,934
Arizona	26,807	60,803	86,863	92,673	90,468
Arkansas	913	1,892	2,884	1,912	NA
California	222,351	477,615	697,306	861,445	955,152
Colorado	24,116	34,889	45,773	51,826	74,144
Connecticut	9,912	18,804	18,632	20,500	20,971
Delaware	2,433	4,474	5,567	9,719	9,903
Florida	154,594	227,463	298,705	368,180	443,177
Georgia	47,581	120,626	182,762	221,005	251,711
Hawaii	0	2,256	7,137	8,474	12,022
Idaho	8,482	12,449	16,896	16,895	16,877
Illinois	42,699	62,507	83,510	68,032	135,609
Indiana	31,246	44,373	56,986	66,225	73,762
Iowa	9,795	19,958	23,270	34,506	37,060
Kansas	14,443	26,306	34,279	40,838	45,662
Kentucky	18,579	55,593	68,273	93,941	94,053
Louisiana	21,580	49,995	69,579	87,675	104,908
Maine	13,657	22,742	27,003	22,586	29,474
Maryland	18,072	93,081	109,983	125,180	130,161
Massachusetts	67,852	113,034	108,308	119,732	128,790
Michigan	26,652	37,148	76,181	71,882	77,467
Minnesota	21	24	49	49	48
Mississippi	13,218	20,451	52,436	64,805	75,010
Missouri	49,529	73,825	106,954	150,533	150,954
Montana	1,019	8,317	13,518	13,875	13,084
Nebraska	9,713	11,400	13,933	16,227	45,490
Nevada	7,802	15,946	28,026	37,878	47,183
New Hampshire	4,554	4,272	5,982	8,138	9,893
New Jersey	75,652	89,034	99,847	117,053	119,272
New Mexico	4,500	6,106	10,347	19,940	18,841
New York	521,301	769,457	872,949	807,145	795,111
North Carolina	57,300	103,567	99,995	120,378	150,444
North Dakota	266	2,573	3,404	4,463	4,953
Ohio	83,688	111,436	162,446	183,034	207,854
Oklahoma	40,196	57,719	38,858	84,490	91,914
Oregon	27,285	37,067	41,468	42,976	44,752
Pennsylvania	81,758	119,710	141,163	148,689	160,015
Rhode Island	7,288	11,539	17,398	19,515	24,505
South Carolina	45,737	59,853	66,183	66,591	90,764
South Dakota	3,191	5,888	9,043	11,233	12,288
Tennessee	9,732	14,861	8,615	10,216	NA
Texas	50,878	130,519	501,167	727,459	726,428
Utah	13,040	25,294	34,655	33,808	37,766
Vermont	2,055	4,081	5,352	6,162	6,467
Virginia	16,895	37,681	73,102	67,974	83,716
Washington	0	2,616	7,621	8,754	9,571
West Virginia	7,957	21,659	33,144	35,949	35,320
Wisconsin	12,949	47,140	57,183	59,850	68,641
Wyoming	0	2,547	4,652	5,059	5,241
District of Columbia	3,029	2,264	2,807	5,060	5,875

Source: Centers for Medicare and Medicaid Services, online at www.cms.hhs.gov/schip/enrollment/schip03rev2.pdf.

Table 3.10

Low-Income Uninsured Children by State: Three-Year Averages—1995, 1996, 1997 and 2001, 2002, 2003

	Three-year averages for 1995, 1996, 1997			Three-year averages for 2001, 2002, 2003		
	Total children under 19 all income levels (in thousands)	At or below 200% of poverty (percent)	At or below 200% of poverty without health insurance (percent)	Total children under 19 all income levels (in thousands)	At or below 200% of poverty (percent)	At or below 200% of poverty without health insurance (percent)
Alabama	1,181	47.8	10.6	1,170	42.9	6.5
Alaska	225	29.0	8.1	201	31.8	5.4
Arizona	1,385	53.7	20.3	1,575	43.4	11.7
Arkansas	774	56.7	16.7	716	51.6	7.0
California	9,591	48.1	12.7	10,109	41.2	8.8
Colorado	1,069	30.5	8.8	1,210	32.4	8.6
Connecticut	916	31.7	6.4	885	25.6	4.7
Delaware	198	38.4	9.6	208	29.2	4.5
Florida	3,483	46.8	12.7	4,102	41.6	10.2
Georgia	2,107	46.2	11.8	2,374	38.5	8.3
Hawaii	315	42.4	4.1	326	35.0	4.2
Idaho	363	46.2	10.2	391	43.5	8.7
Illinois	3,437	38.4	6.4	3,363	35.8	7.0
Indiana	1,536	32.1	7.8	1,627	34.5	6.4
Iowa	847	37.5	7.1	757	30.8	4.4
Kansas	754	38.4	7.0	715	32.5	4.9
Kentucky	1,051	45.3	10.7	1,039	43.8	7.7
Louisiana	1,210	52.6	15.6	1,260	48.7	9.3
Maine	292	39.1	9.9	288	37.5	3.6
Maryland	1,370	31.0	6.6	1,464	23.2	4.1
Massachusetts	1,532	33.9	5.1	1,520	29.3	3.1
Michigan	2,746	35.6	5.2	2,614	34.5	4.2
Minnesota	1,409	32.7	3.7	1,276	24.2	3.5
Mississippi	825	58.3	8.0	1,467	32.8	3.2

(continued)

Table 3.10 (continued)

	Three-year averages for 1995, 1996, 1997			Three-year averages for 2001, 2002, 2003		
	Total children under 19 all income levels (in thousands)	At or below 200% of poverty (percent)	At or below 200% of poverty without health insurance (percent)	Total children under 19 all income levels (in thousands)	At or below 200% of poverty (percent)	At or below 200% of poverty without health insurance (percent)
Montana	254	50.6	13.2	230	45.4	9.2
Nebraska	487	37.3	4.6	463	31.2	3.8
Nevada	438	36.9	12.8	605	39.6	11.5
New Hampshire	315	27.7	4.9	315	22.1	2.4
New Jersey	2,044	28.4	8.6	2,160	26.0	6.0
New Mexico	628	59.3	17.7	520	53.2	10.4
New York	5,009	45.3	9.5	4,828	40.5	5.6
North Carolina	1,812	41.9	10.9	2,158	43.6	8.2
North Dakota	182	35.8	8.2	149	37.2	5.5
Ohio	3,166	36.9	6.4	2,958	33.3	5.1
Oklahoma	934	48.0	15.3	918	46.2	10.0
Oregon	861	41.3	9.2	882	38.9	7.5
Pennsylvania	3,127	36.7	5.5	2,969	33.9	6.1
Rhode Island	227	34.5	6.4	257	31.2	3.0
South Carolina	1,060	47.5	13.2	1,071	40.5	5.6
South Dakota	199	41.1	5.9	201	33.0	4.4
Tennessee	1,566	49.6	10.5	1,461	42.1	5.6
Texas	5,893	49.8	17.6	6,467	48.5	15.1
Utah	724	37.5	7.1	788	34.5	6.1
Vermont	163	37.6	3.2	141	30.9	2.2
Virginia	1,637	38.9	6.7	1,884	28.5	5.0
Washington	1,562	35.0	6.4	1,598	35.5	5.4
West Virginia	382	51.5	6.8	415	49.4	5.4
Wisconsin	1,496	31.7	3.5	1,395	31.5	3.5
Wyoming	147	42.3	9.8	127	36.3	7.3
District of Columbia	127	57.3	9.1	115	52.9	6.1

Source: U.S. Census Bureau, "Low Income Uninsured Children by State," online at www.census.gov/hhes/hlthins/lowinckid.html.

Note: Percentages listed are averages over the three years' percentages, not the percentage of the average number (calculated as "number" divided by "total children"). Results may differ slightly, based on the method used.

Thus, SCHIP has been successful in reducing the number of uninsured children (Coles 2003; Dick et al. 2004; Kronebusch and Elbel 2004a, b; "Report Gives SCHIP Good Marks. . ." 2003; Selden, Hudson, and Banthin 2004). SCHIPs administered as Medicaid expansions have been more successful than either separate SCHIP plans or combination plans in enrolling children (Kronebusch and Elbel 2004a).

The SCHIP program has also been credited with producing considerable cost savings over the long term. A study found that Minnesota saved about $60 million in uncompensated care over five years through its MinnesotaCare program—a combined SCHIP and Medicaid program. The state of New York found that simplifying the enrollment process reduced the administrative costs of Medicaid and SCHIP and saved the state $112 per form (Park and Oliver 2004).

Despite these successes, SCHIP suffers from some shortcomings and faces numerous challenges. The incremental nature of SCHIP, combined with the layering of SCHIP on top of existing programs, has often created problems of coordination and equity. Inequities are produced across states by the fact that those states that had already expanded Medicaid coverage to children could not receive the higher SCHIP matching rates for those children. Also, SCHIP has substituted for private insurance coverage to some extent. In addition, some SCHIP eligible children are still uninsured. Finally, as of June 2003, seven states were using SCHIP funds to cover adults, which introduced trade-offs (Kenney and Chang 2004). Waiting periods and premiums, combined with stringent welfare reforms introduced in several states, have often acted as barriers to enrollment (Kronebusch and Elbel 2004a, b).

The success of SCHIP was endangered by budget problems faced by state governments in 2003 and 2004. In 2003, states from California to New York were facing budget crises due to faltering state revenue collections and the weakness of the national economic recovery. SCHIP has not been immune to budget cuts. The "SCHIP dip" provision in the original legislation that reduced federal matching funds during fiscal years 2002 through 2004 made matters worse for states. In August 2003, Congress passed the "SCHIP fix," which allowed states to use $2.7 billion in unspent SCHIP money that was scheduled to revert back to the federal treasury (Park and Oliver 2004). Two annual surveys of fifty states released by the Kaiser Commission on Medicaid and the Uninsured showed that between April 2003 and July 2004, twenty-three states took actions that made it more difficult to secure and retain health coverage for children and families. The actions included freezing enrollment for varying periods, more stringent enrollment and retention procedures, and premium hikes (Ross and Cox 2004; Smith et al. 2004). The result is that in many states the rate of SCHIP enrollment growth has slowed while some states have experienced enrollment declines (Park and Oliver 2004).

Medicaid: Middle-Class Entitlement?

During the late 1980s, Medicaid came under attack on the grounds that the affluent elderly were misusing the program. Critics of the program charged that it was increasingly used to provide expensive benefits, that is, nursing home care, for the middle-class and affluent elderly. The "spousal impoverishment" benefit expanded Medicaid's role for the middle class. Many families began to see Medicaid as middle-class entitlement, as a way to preserve the family's life savings and property in the event that one or both parents require high-cost nursing home care (Baker 1992).

The middle-class and affluent elderly were increasingly utilizing ways not sanctioned by the government to retain family wealth and at the same time take advantage of Medicaid benefits. Numerous techniques for sheltering assets or transferring them to family members as a prelude to getting Medicaid to pay the bills for nursing home care were employed. These included maneuvers such as opening joint bank accounts, holding property in joint tenancy, investing in irrevocable and nontransferable annuities, and paying family members for services such as shopping and providing transportation. An army of lawyers and financial advisors were counseling affluent Americans on how to shuffle, shed, or shelter an elderly family member's assets to qualify for Medicaid nursing home benefits. Such maneuvers, often called "Medicaid estate planning," were legal but ran counter to the intent of the law.

By 1996, Medicaid was paying about 47.8 percent of the nation's $78.5 billion nursing home bill. By 2002, Medicaid was paying 49.3 percent of the nation's total nursing home care expenditures of $103.2 billion (see Table 3.4).

The state of Virginia tried to close some of these loopholes and gaps in the Medicaid program. The state's General Assembly rejected a proposed tax on hospitals, nursing homes, and doctors. Nevertheless, one of the measures approved would allow state Medicaid officials to recover up to $92,000 in assets transferred within four years of a patient's becoming eligible for Medicaid by going after the heir or recipient. Federal law bars transfer within two and one-half years of eligibility and allows states to extend that period (Baker 1992).

A few states tried to find ways to allow more of the affluent elderly to benefit from the Medicaid program. Some states devised experiments that allowed these elderly to hang on to more of their assets and be entitled to Medicaid benefits provided that they bought long-term-care insurance. Under such experimental plans, elderly participants were required to contribute to the cost of their care in a more rational way, by pooling risks. Such a plan, supporters argued, would save states money. The more middle-class people who bought long-term-care insurance, the fewer would "spend down" their savings and end up on Medicaid at public expense (Kosterlitz 1991).

The federal government tried to address this problem in the Health Insurance Portability and Accountability Act of 1996 by making it a federal crime, under certain circumstances, to transfer assets to qualify for Medicaid coverage for nursing homes or other long-term care. Section 217 of the law stated that anyone who knowingly and willfully disposed of assets (including any transfer in trust) in order to become eligible for medical assistance will be guilty of misdemeanor if convicted and subject to fines up to $10,000 or imprisonment of up to one year or both (Donner 1997). It also would lead to imposition of a period of ineligibility for such a person. This law squarely targeted the middle-class elderly ("Congress Says Some Medicaid Planning Is a Federal

Crime" 1996). The law was often referred to as "Granny Goes to Jail" (Caplin 1998). However, this provision of the law had become so unpopular and controversial that the Balanced Budget Act of 1997 replaced Section 217 with Section 4734 (Donner 1997). Under the new provisions, as amended, criminal penalties are now imposed on anyone who knowingly and willfully counsels and assists an individual to dispose of assets in order to become eligible for medical assistance. Thus, the amended provision makes attorneys and others who advise the middle-class elderly on Medicaid estate planning the direct targets (Institute of Continuing Legal Education 1997).

Many argue that Section 4734 is no panacea because its scope is still open to interpretation. Opponents have also attacked it as an unconstitutional infringement on the First Amendment freedom of speech guarantees on the ground that it is unconstitutional to prevent an attorney from providing counsel to a client about legal activities. Furthermore, they argue that transferring assets is legal, provided the individual does not apply for Medicaid during the period of ineligibility triggered by the transfer (Donner 1997).

Congress is again considering a crackdown on financial planning strategies used by middle-class families to shift the cost of nursing home care for the elderly to the federal government. Charles E. Grassley, the chairman of the Senate Finance Committee, has denounced the practice as "legal shenanigans" and vowed to help stop turning Medicaid into an asset protection program. Closing the loopholes could save Medicaid $1 billion to $2 billion over five years. However, whatever attempt to close these loopholes President Bush supports, it is likely to generate a strong political backlash (Alonso-Zaldivar 2005). In an effort to pare Medicaid, addressing the problem of long-term care has become the major focus (Gross 2005).

Meanwhile, states and counties have began to crack down on people who make themselves appear poor in order to have the government pay for their nursing home care. They are proposing regulations to make it even harder for nursing home residents to shelter assets and use trusts and other estate-planning techniques to avoid gift taxes (Higgins 2003). Several states are also trying to fight the problem by encouraging middle-aged and older individuals to invest in alternative long-term-care insurance. Currently, only about 10 percent of the elderly and an even smaller percentage of middle-aged adults have long-term care insurance. However, the number of people buying such insurance is increasing. By 2002, half the states were offering some type of tax incentive for people who buy long-term-care insurance ("Promise of Coverage" 2004). There does not appear to be an easy legislative solution or resolution regarding Medicaid estate planning.

Republicans and Democrats have pursued very different strategies with different political agendas. Republicans, since the early 1980s, have followed a long-term strategy aimed at dramatically changing entitlements in the United States. Significant budget cuts in federal grant-in-aid programs during the Reagan administration and Republican attempts to turn Medicaid into a block grant program reflected this strategy. On the other hand, Democrats have attempted to broaden the Medicaid program to expand health care coverage to additional groups. President Clinton in his budget battle with Republicans in Congress during the 1990s, portrayed Medicaid as essential for protecting the elderly from large nursing home expenses and suggested that Medicaid was not just a safety net program designed to protect the poor but a broad-based entitlement that protected all Americans. Thus, the politics of Medicaid had turned into a "campaign mode" of legislative politics in the context of partisan mobilization (Smith 2002).

The Current Fiscal Crisis of Medicaid

State governments all across the country are facing budget shortfalls and Medicaid spending, as a percentage of state spending, is taking up a larger and larger share of the state budgets. A report released by the National Association of State Budget Officers in October of 2004 indicated that, for the first time, state Medicaid spending may grow larger than state spending on K–12 education. In 2003, Medicaid spending totaled 21.4 percent of all state spending (including federal funds), while K–12 spending accounted for 21.7 percent. The state budget officers' projections for fiscal year 2004 spending showed that, in over twenty states, the percentage of state spending on Medicaid may surpass spending on K–12 education. It is no surprise that Medicaid is referred to as the 800-pound gorilla of state budgets (Richard 2004).

According to the Kaiser Commission on Medicaid and the Uninsured, Medicaid spending growth of 9.5 percent outpaced state tax revenue growth of 3.4 percent in 2004. Faced with budget shortfalls, state governments may limit public insurance coverage that could lead to the loss of gains made in providing health insurance coverage to children and low-income families (Ross and Cox 2004; Smith et al. 2004). In fact, all fifty states implemented Medicaid cost control strategies and planed to implement new strategies in 2005. State governments have primarily relied on four cost-control strategies: controlling drug costs, reducing or freezing provider payments, reducing eligibility and benefits, and imposing new provider taxes to maximize federal matching dollars. According to the Center on Budget and Policy Priorities, up to 1.7 million people could lose Medicaid coverage under proposals either finalized or under consideration by state legislatures (American Hospital Association 2003; Collins, Bussard, and Combes 2003). Further, pressure to cut Medicaid spending is likely to come from the federal government. By 2004, the federal government had a deficit of $413 billion. Programs like Medicaid and Medicare are likely to be targeted to meet the Bush administration's commitment to cut the federal deficit in half over the next five years (Kaiser Commission on Medicaid and the Uninsured 2005). If federal contributions are limited, states will have to decide whether to increase their own funds or make cuts in the Medicaid program. Several states have already shown that they are likely to cut Medicaid programs.

Before the 2004 budgets went into effect, thirty-seven states had enacted emergency spending cuts of $14.5 billion during FY 2003, including cuts in Medicaid spending. In California, faced with a deficit of $38 billion, the state had stopped making Medicaid reimbursements. Pennsylvania had reduced Medicaid spending by

$250 billion. Eligibility changes in Tennessee and Oregon were likely to lead to hundreds of thousands losing their insurance coverage (Collins, Bussard, and Combes 2003; Sloane 2003). In Texas, budget cuts included slashing eligibility for SCHIP, which trimmed program enrollment by 29 percent (Thrall 2004).

States that in the 1980s and 1990s had adopted innovative approaches, including managed care and expanding coverage under the Medicaid program, have experienced major problems. Under federal waivers, the state of Oregon had expanded Medicaid coverage to all poor people in the state, in return for the rationing of medical services in 1993. The program was considered a success because it helped decrease the percentage of uninsured. It also helped reduce uncompensated care in hospitals, the use of hospital emergency services, and cost shifting (Leichter 1999). However, the program was experiencing cost problems by 1996 (Firshein 1996). The methodology the state used to arrive at a prioritized list of services to be covered under the Medicaid program and cost estimates of the program were called "guesstimates" and "pseudoscience" by critics (Astrue 1994). In November 2002, Oregon voters resoundingly defeated a ballot initiative that would have created a state-financed health system guaranteeing universal coverage for all, financed through steep tax increases ("States, Alone, Can't Cure Ills" 2002). In response to budget pressures, Oregon implemented significant benefit reductions and increased premiums and cost sharing in Oregon Health Plan Standard, Oregon's program for poor parents and other adults. It also eliminated the "medically needy" program. Since its implementation, enrollment in the program has dropped by over half, to about 50,000 enrollees (LeCouteur et al. 2004).

California experienced similar financial problems with its Medi-Cal Medicaid program. When the fiscal year ended in June of 2003, the State Department of Health Services ran out of money and health care institutions were preparing for defaults on Medi-Cal payments. It required the passage of a $727 million emergency bill and a $1 billion loan to ensure that institutional health care providers would get paid by Medi-Cal (Beckley 2003). In 2004, Governor Arnold Schwarzenegger proposed reductions in fees to doctors and other medical providers under the Medi-Cal program (Broder 2004).

The Arizona Health Care Cost Containment System (AHCCCS) program was started in 1982 as an alternative to the traditional Medicaid program. Before AHCCCS, Arizona was the only state not participating in Medicaid. Quality and access studies of AHCCCS have revealed mixed results. Some studies have shown that the program is doing worse than a traditional Medicaid program (McCall 1997). In 1997, two Arizona HMOs quit the Medicaid business, a move that forced 17,000 members to switch to a new health plan. The two health plans cited financial difficulties as the reason—they were not making any money serving the indigent ("Health Plans Back Out of Ariz. Medicaid" 1997).

The TennCare program in Tennessee has been plagued by management, operational, and financial problems. Enrollees have experienced many changes in how their care is managed as well as who provides the care (Larson and Williams 2003).

For a decade, TennCare had been one of the most expansive Medicaid programs, covering 23 percent of the state's population. Due to rapidly rising costs in 2004, Tennessee Governor Phil Bredesen won approval of cost-saving measures from the state legislature and sought waivers from the Bush administration from federal Medicaid rules that would let the state impose benefit cuts starting in January 2005 (Welch and Appleby 2004). However, faced with court challenges by health care advocacy groups, the governor, on November 10, 2004, announced that the state would dissolve the TennCare program unless advocacy groups backed off court challenges ("Tenn. Gov. Seeks to End Supplemental Medicaid Plan" 2004). The TennCare program at the time of its inauguration was hailed as a model for the nation. Today, the TennCare plan is once again being held up as a model—this time of failure (Lyman 2004).

Faced with a projected budget gap of $4 billion in the fiscal year beginning on April 1, 2005, Governor George Pataki of New York proposed nearly $1 billion in spending cuts for health care and Medicaid to the state legislature. One of the most significant proposed benefit reductions is the elimination of mental health services for adult enrollees in Family Health Plus, a program for the working poor. He has also proposed cuts in reimbursement rates for hospitals and nursing homes (A. Baker 2005).

The examples discussed above illustrate just the tip of the iceberg. In 2005, all fifty states are expected to propose cuts in Medicaid programs in their states. Fearful of the federal government shifting more Medicaid costs to the states, the nation's governors are launching a bipartisan lobbying effort to preserve states' Medicaid allotment (Belluck 2004).

The Medicaid program has been described as the "workhorse" of the U.S. health care system because whenever policymakers want to provide health insurance to new population groups, they turn to Medicaid (Weil 2003). However, Medicaid has also been described as the "Pac Man" of the state budgets because it crowds out other state spending (McDonough 2003). Some have attributed the fiscal crisis of Medicaid to state overspending in general, and generous and excessive spending on Medicaid. However, others have argued that the real causes of the Medicaid fiscal crisis are a combination of tax cuts adopted by state governments in the 1990s, a growing weakness in state tax structures, and state requirements of balanced budgets. They argue that it is not the spending growth in Medicaid but a real decline in state revenues that has generated the fiscal crisis. According to this argument, the Medicaid program is not the bogeyman that it is made out to be (Miller 2003). Others have argued that Medicaid gets very little respect because, like Cinderella, the program has ended up in the wrong household—state governments. While state governments may not be the "evil stepmother," the reality is that the financial condition of state governments is linked to that of the U.S. economy, and health sector spending tends to be countercyclical. This means that health sector spending rises fastest when the economy experiences a downturn. Such was the case during recessions of the mid-1970s, the early 1990s, the late 1980s/early 1990s, and the early 2000s (McDonough 2003).

Medicaid Reform

Over the years, a variety of proposals have been floated to reform the Medicaid program. In the past, reform proposals have included ideas such as returning Medicaid to its original purpose by making poverty the sole criterion for Medicaid eligibility; changing the federal funding formula; federalizing Medicaid; dividing Medicaid into two programs—one program dealing with acute care and the other dealing with long-term care; and merging Medicaid and Medicare in part or in whole and using the market share created by the merged programs to achieve greater economies of scale (de Alteriis 1992).

Today, as state governments try to tackle the problem of rising Medicaid costs, they are looking for ways to reform the Medicaid program. Governor Jeb Bush of Florida has recently proposed a radical restructuring of Florida's Medicaid program designed to provide incentives for better services by giving program beneficiaries more choices to rein in the rate of growth in spending. Under the plan, each beneficiary would be assigned a premium that they could use to purchase coverage for basic and catastrophic care. Premiums would be adjusted for risk, so a person with a severe health condition would pay higher premiums. The beneficiary could choose among HMOs, insurers, or a community-based network of physicians and hospitals. Patients who followed the medical plan laid out by their physicians with respect to medication, vaccination of their children, stopping smoking, and so forth, would earn extra money that would be deposited in their flexible-spending accounts. They could use this money for medical services not covered under the basic plan. The plan will require approval by the state legislature and a waiver from the Department of Health and Human Services ("Medicaid Rx" 2005). Other states are considering a variety of reforms.

Similarly, as the national government's expenditures for Medicaid have risen over the years, the Bush administration is reportedly considering widespread changes in the Medicaid system that include giving states fixed sums of money or block grants, instead of basing federal Medicaid payments on actual costs and enrollment (A. Baker 2005). In early 2003, the Bush administration tried a similar proposal in order to save money in the long run. However, that proposal backfired, as states and consumer advocates argued that it would create further hardship for the poor and jeopardize state finances (Fong and Tieman 2004; Pear 2005). Despite increased Republican majorities in both the House and the Senate after the 2004 elections, Bush's proposal may face stiff opposition from state governors. While most governors are attracted to the idea of devolution—giving state governments more authority and flexibility in administering social safety net programs—many of them also worry that a shift in authority and responsibilities from federal to state governments will come without any guarantee of long-term federal support. They fear that the end result would be many unfunded federal mandates that would put them in the politically risky position of making painful decisions about raising taxes or cutting benefits (Starr and Dunham 2003). State governors have urged the Bush administration and Congress not to cut the federal-state health care programs for the poor by promising to come up with innovative ways to cut costs (Tanner 2005).

Medicaid was the biggest target for cuts in President Bush's proposed $2.57 trillion budget for 2006. The Bush budget proposed $60 billion in Medicaid cuts. However, the cuts would be partly offset by $15 billion in new spending on home care for the elderly and disabled instead of nursing home care. Savings are expected to come from the overhaul of the Medicaid program, cracking down on some accounting methods states used to increase their share of federal dollars, tying payments for drugs to average sale prices rather than wholesale prices, and by tightening the rules overseeing asset giveaways by seniors who want to qualify for Medicaid ("Bush Budget Plan Focuses on Tax Cuts and Defense" 2005). The House approved a steep cut in Medicaid program but the Senate voted to strip the budget of Medicaid cuts and to instead create a one-year commission to recommend changes to the program (Pear and Stolberg 2005, Stolberg 2005a). The compromise version of the 2006 federal budget of $2.56 trillion approved by the House and the Senate in April of 2005 included the trimming of Medicaid by only $10 billion over five years. The White House, as part of the compromise, also agreed to create a bipartisan commission to study and make recommendations on the Medicaid program (Stolberg 2005b). According to an announcement by the secretary of health and human services, he will appoint fifteen voting members and fifteen nonvoting members to the commission. Republican and Democratic lawmakers were invited to designate four nonvoting members each. However, Democratic leaders in the House and the Senate have refused to participate in such a commission, arguing that they will not accept a nonvoting, advisory role (Freking 2005).

Bill Richardson, Democratic governor of New Mexico, has argued that many of Bush's proposals are recycled ideas. He has suggested that instead of turning federal Medicaid funds into block grants, the federal government should block-grant states. Under his proposal, states would be prohibited by law from spending more than a fixed amount on health care, with the federal government paying the rest. The result would be that, instead of shifting all risks of unexpected costs to states, it will shift such risks and costs to the federal government (Richardson 2005).

The future of Medicaid remains clouded. Regardless of what shape Medicaid reform takes, one thing is certain: Medicaid will continue to occupy a vital role in the U.S. health care system because the program is essential to cover those priced out of the private insurance market (Mann and Westmoreland 2004).

Conclusion

Medicaid policy has, in a sense, come full circle. The Reagan administration, in the early 1980s, used the conservative rhetoric of decentralization as a way of giving states more discretionary authority and reducing Medicaid enrollment. In the process, the administration also attempted to reduce the federal costs of the program and pass along some of its financial burden to the states. The Democrats in Congress during the mid-1980s used the liberal rhetoric of equal access and quality of care to expand the Medicaid program incrementally through the use of federal mandates. The 1990s again witnessed significant decentralization of the Medicaid program under the Clinton administration.

The decentralization of the Medicaid program by the Reagan administration in the early 1980s gave state governments greater flexibility to experiment with new approaches in delivering health care to the poor. The subsequent program expansion through congressional mandates significantly increased the number of recipients, as well as program costs. Concerned with the dramatically rising cost of a program that is consuming an ever-larger portion of state budgets, state governments have used the Medicaid program in innovative ways to respond to the access and health care financing issues. Some have experimented with service delivery, payment reforms, and outreach programs. These approaches have included the rationing of Medicaid services, the increased use of Medicaid waivers for home or community-based services, fixed-price arrangements with health care providers, hospital rate setting, and the bulk-rate purchase of equipment and services. More emphasis has also been placed on case management and managed care. Many states have established new programs designed to provide preventive and primary care. States are trying innovative ways to expand coverage and at the same time control rising costs (Coughlin 1994).

The results of these experiments have been mixed. While a few have been successful in containing specific costs, the overall cost of the program continues to rise both at the federal and the state levels. Rationing in the Medicaid program leads to concerns about reduced access and limited choices. The same concerns arise in managed care programs. Reduction in payments to physicians has often made them more reluctant to accept Medicaid patients. Hospital rate-setting programs, especially those confined to the Medicaid program, in general have not been very successful.

Increased micromanagement of the Medicaid program by the federal government through congressional mandates in the late 1980s created additional problems for states. State governments' ability to fund the program was severely tested. Growing caseloads, declining revenues, and balanced-budget requirements compounded the problem. Hospitals and other health care providers began to sue states over reimbursement rates. In a majority of cases, states lost. The crisis of escalating Medicaid costs is not likely to be resolved until the problems of long-term care, reimbursement levels, and the uninsured are addressed in one form or another.

State governments alone are not likely to solve the problems of Medicaid and its cost because of fundamental impediments in the federal system. As Deborah Stone has argued, state governments lack sufficient autonomy from the federal government in the area of health care financing. Nor do they have sufficient power over private insurers, doctors, and hospitals. Federal law governing Medicaid limits the options available to state governments. The problem is too big and too complex for state-based solutions (Stone 1992).

Medicaid policy reflects the dictum that the more things change, the more they stay the same. The Medicaid policy process is driven to a significant extent by the forces of federalism that often produce policies geared toward short-term, patchwork answers, rather than long-term solutions. All the new state experiments and innovations have failed to produce any consensus on how best to contain costs. These experiments have offered many different models of cost containment, but none that is satisfactory to all parties. It is clear that the program cannot continue on its current course, given stagnant or declining resources, on the one hand, and pressure to provide coverage to more people, on the other. Additional ad hoc, stopgap fixes are likely to produce more dissatisfaction with the program among policymakers, health care providers, program administrators, and advocacy groups. The Medicaid program, in many ways, represents the best and the worst of American politics. It reflects the best of the American tradition of helping the poor and disadvantaged groups who cannot help themselves. It also reflects the worst of American politics— that of an incremental, patchwork approach to policymaking—influenced by the vagaries of electoral and economic cycles that often produce irrational and incomprehensible public policy.

References

Alonso-Zaldivar, Ricardo. 2005. "Senate Takes on Medicaid Loopholes." *Los Angeles Times*, June 30.

Altman, Drew E. 1983. "Health Care for the Poor." *Annals of the American Academy of Political and Social Sciences* 468 (July): 103–21.

Altman, Drew E., and Douglas H. Morgan. 1983. "The Role of the State and Local Government in Health." *Health Affairs* 2, no. 4 (Winter): 7–31.

American Hospital Association. 2003. "The Medicaid Dilemma: Shrinking Budget, Difficult Choices." *TrendWatch* 5, no. 2: 1–10.

Anders, George. 1993. "Many States Embrace Managed Care System for Medicaid Patients." *Wall Street Journal*, June 11.

Anderson, Maren D., and Peter D. Fox. 1987. "Lessons Learned from Medicaid Managed Care Approaches." *Health Affairs* 6, no. 1 (Spring): 71–88.

Astrue, Michael J. 1994. "Pseudoscience and the Law: The Case of the Oregon Medicaid Rationing Experiment." *Issues in Law and Medicine* 9, no. 4 (Spring): 375–86.

Backus, Lisa; Dennis Osmond; Kevin Brumbach; Karen Vranizan; Lucy Phuong; and Andrew Bindman. 2001. "Specialists and Primary Care Physicians' Participation in Medicaid Managed Care." *Journal of General Internal Medicine* 16, no. 12 (December): 815–21.

Baker, Al. 2005. "Pataki Aides Sketch $1 Billion in Proposed Cuts in Health Care and Medicaid Spending." *New York Times*, January 18.

Baker, Donald P. 1992. "Squeezing Through the Loophole in the Medicaid Law." *Washington Post National Weekly Edition*, March 2–8.

Barnett, David L. 1982. "Reagan's Bold New Blueprint." *U.S. News and World Report*, February 8.

Beckley, Elizabeth T. 2003. "Crisis State." *Modern Physician* 7, no. 8 (August): 5.

Belluck, Oam. 2004. "Governors Unite in Medicaid Fight." *New York Times*, December 26.

Bindman, Andrew B; Jean Yoon; and Kevin Grumbach. 2003. "Trends in Physician Participation in Medicaid: The California Experience." *Journal of Ambulatory Care Management* 26, no. 4 (October–December): 334–43.

Bovbjerg, Randall R., Esq., and John Holahan. 1982. *Medicaid in the Reagan Era: Federal Policy and State Choices*. Washington, D.C.: Urban Institute.

Broder, John M. 2004. "Schwarzenegger Budget Denies Some Health Care." *New York Times*, January 18.

Brown, Richard E. 1984. "Medicare and Medicaid: Band-Aids for the Old and Poor." In *Reforming Medicine: Lessons of the Last Quarter Century*, ed. Victor W. Sidel and Ruth Sidel, 50–76. New York: Pantheon.

"Bush Budget Plan Focuses on Tax Cuts and Defense." 2005. *Los Angeles Times*, February 8. Online at www.latimes.com.

Caplin, Joan. 1998. "Law's Demise Means New Options." *Money* 27, no. 13 (special issue): 109.

Centers for Medicare and Medicaid Services. 1997. *Health Care Financing Review. Medicare and Medicaid: Statistical Supplement, 1997*. Washington, D.C.: U.S. Government Printing Office.

————. 2001. *Health Care Financing Review. Medicare and Medicaid: Statistical Supplement, 2001*. Washington, D.C.: U.S. Government Printing Office.

————. 2002. "Nursing Home Care Expenditures Aggregate and Per Capita Amounts and Percent Distribution, by Sources of Funds: Selected Calendar Years 1980–2002." Online at www.cms.hhs.gov/statistics/nhe/historical/t7.asp.

————. 2003. "Medicaid: A Brief Summary." (November). Online at www.cms.hhs.gov.

Children's Defense Fund. 1997. *States Should Consider Building on Medicaid*. December 3: 1–4. Online at www.childrensdefense.org.

Coelen, Craig, and Daniel Sullivan. 1981. "An Analysis of the Effects of Prospective Reimbursement Programs on Hospital Expenditures." *Health Care Financing Review* 1, no. 3 (Winter): 62–73.

Coles, Adrienne. 2003. "SCHIP: Meeting the Health Care Needs of Children." *NEA Today* 21, no. 5 (February): 19.

Collins, Molly; Paula A. Bussard; and John R. Combes. 2003. "The Worsening Medicaid Fiscal Crisis." *Journal of Ambulatory Care Management* 26, no. 4 (October–December): 349–54.

"Congress Says Some Medicaid Planning Is a Federal Crime." 1996. *Elder Law Issues* 4, no. 7 (August 19). Online at www.elder-law.com.

Congressional Budget Office. 1997. *Expanding Health Insurance Coverage for Children under Title XXI of the Social Security Act*. Washington, D.C.: Congressional Budget Office.

Coughlin, Teresa A. 1994. *Medicaid Since 1980: Costs, Coverage, and the Shifting Alliance between the Federal Government and the States*. Washington, D.C.: Urban Institute.

Crozier, David A. 1982. "State Rate Setting: A Status Report." *Health Affairs* 1, no. 2 (Summer): 66–83.

Cunningham, Peter, and James Kirby. 2004. "Children's Health Coverage: A Quarter-Century of Change." *Health Affairs* 23, no. 5 (September–October): 27–38.

Daniels, Mark R., ed. 1998. *Medicaid Reform and the American States: Case Studies on the Politics of Managed Care*. Westport, Conn.: Auburn House.

Davidson, Stephen M., and Stephen A. Somers, eds. 1998. *Remaking Medicaid: Managed Care for the Public Good*. San Francisco: Jossey-Bass.

Davis, Karen; Gerard F. Anderson; Diane Rowland; and Earl P. Steinberg. 1990. *Health Care Cost Containment*. Baltimore, Md.: Johns Hopkins University Press.

Davis, Karen, and Roger Reynolds. 1977. *The Impact of Medicare and Medicaid on Access to Medical Care*. Washington, D.C.: Brookings Institution.

Dawson, R.E., and J. Robinson. 1963. "Interparty Competition, Economic Variables, and Welfare Policies in the American States." *Journal of Politics* 25, no. 1 (February): 265–89.

De Alteriis, Martin. 1992. "Medicaid's Role Moves Toward Universal Health Care." *Policy Studies Review* 11, no. 3–4 (Autumn–Winter): 203–21.

Dick, Andrew W; Cindy Brach; R. Andrew Allison; Elizabeth Shenkman; Laura P. Shone; Peter G. Szilagyi; Jonathan D. Klein; and Eugene M. Lewit. 2004. "SCHIP's Impact in Three States: How Do the Most Vulnerable Children Fare?" *Health Affairs* 23, no. 5 (September–October): 63–65.

Donner, Terry A. 1997. "Medicaid Estate Planning: Still Not Resolved." *Nursing Homes Long Term Care Management* 46, no. 10 (November–December): 21–23.

Durda, David. 1991. "Number of Medicaid Lawsuits Belies Complexities Involved in Such Filings." *Modern Health Care* 21, no. 8 (February 25): 31–32.

Dye, Thomas. R. 1966. *Politics, Economics, and the Public Policy Outcomes in the American States.* Chicago: Rand McNally.

Edmunds, Margo, and Martha Teitelbaum. 2000. "All Over the Map: A Progress Report on the State Children's Health Insurance Program (CHIP)." Washington, D.C.: Children's Defense Fund.

"Financial Pressures Fuel More States' Medicaid Waiver Activity." 2004. *Mental Health Weekly* 14, no. 40 (October 18): 1, 3.

Firshein, Janet. 1996. "Oregon Rationing Experiment Faces Hard Times." *Lancet* 347, no. 9008 (April 20): 1110.

Flint, Samuel S. 1997. "Insuring Children: The Next Steps." *Health Affairs* 16, no. 4 (July/August): 79–81.

Fong, Tony, and Jeff Tieman. 2004. "Politics Front and Center." *Modern Healthcare* 34, no. 2 (Janaury 12): 26–28.

Freeman, Howard E., and Bradford L. Kirkman-Liff. 1985. "Health Care Under AHCCCS: An Examination of Arizona's Alternative to Medicaid." *Health Services Research* 20, no. 3 (August): 245–66.

Freking, Kevin. 2005. "Dem Lawmakers Refuse Medicaid Commission." Associated Press, May 26. Online at news.yahoo.com.

Freund, Deborah A.; Louis F. Rossiter; and Peter D. Fox. 1989. "Evaluation of the Medicaid Competition Demonstrations." *Health Care Financing Review* 11 (Winter): 81–97.

Friedman, Thomas L. 1993. "Clinton Allowing States Flexibility on Medicaid Funds." *New York Times*, February 2.

Fubini, Sylvia. 1997. "Medicaid Under Welfare Reform." *Health Care Trends* 1, no. 2 (February): 1–2, 15.

General Accounting Office. 1991. *Medicaid Expansions.* Washington, D.C.: Government Printing Office.

———. 1993. *Medicaid: States Turn to Managed Care to Improve Access and Control Costs.* Gaithersburg, Md.: General Accounting Office.

Gibson, Robert M., and Daniel R. Waldo. 1981. "National Health Expenditures, 1980." *Health Care Financing Review* 3, no. 1 (September): 45–46.

Ginsburg, Paul B. 1988. "Public Insurance Programs: Medicare and Medicaid." In *Health Care in America: The Political Economy of Hospitals and Health Insurance*, ed. H.E. Frech III, 179–215. San Francisco: Pacific Research Institute for Public Policy.

Goldfield, Norbert. 2003. "The Crisis Confronting Medicaid." *Journal of Ambulatory Care Management* 26, no. 4 (October–December): 277–84.

Grabowski, David C.; Zhanlian Feng; Orna Intrator; and Vincent Mor. 2004. "Recent Trends in State Nursing Home Payment Policies." *Health Affairs*, Web exclusive W4 (January–June): 363–73.

Grahan, Ellen. 1997. "When Terrible Twos Become Terrible Teens." *Wall Street Journal*, Eastern Edition, 229, issue 25 (February 5): B1.

Grannemann, Thomas W., and Mark V. Pauly. 1983. *Controlling Medicaid Costs: Federalism, Competition, and Choice.* Washington, D.C.: American Enterprise Institute for Public Policy Research.

Grogan, Colleen M. 1997. "The Medicaid Managed Care Policy Consensus for Welfare Recipients: A Reflection of Traditional Welfare Concern." *Journal of Health Politics, Policy and Law* 22, no. 3 (June): 815–38.

Grogan, Colleen M., and Eric M. Patashnik. 2003a. "Universalism within Targeting: Nursing Home Care, the Middle Class, and the Politics of the Medicaid Program." *Social Service Review* 71, no. 1 (March): 51–71.

————. 2003b. "Between Welfare Medicine and Mainstream Entitlement: Medicaid at the Political Crossroads." *Journal of Health Politics, Policy and Law* 28, no. 5 (October): 821–38.

Gross, George. 1982. "Reagan's 'Bold' Aid Reform." *Nation's Cities Weekly* 5, no. 5 (February 1): 1, 8.

Gross, Jane. 2005. "In Effort to Pare Medicaid, Long-Term Care Is Focus." *New York Times*, June 27.

Guyer, Jocelyn. 1998. "States' Options for Implementing Medicaid Managed Care." Princeton, N.J.: Center for Health Care Strategies. Online at www.chcs.org.

Haslanger, Kathryn., and James R. Tallon. 2004. "Medicaid Managed Care: There Is More for States to Do." *Managed Care Quarterly* 12, no. 1 (Winter): 1–4.

"HCFA, States Spar—Again—Over Medicaid Provider Taxes." 1995. *State Health Notes* 16, no. 200 (March 20): 1–3.

Health Care Financing Administration. 1997. "Children's Insurance Program: State Plans." Online at www.hcfa.gov.

"Health Plans Back Out of Ariz. Medicaid" 1997. *Hospitals and Health Networks* 71, no. 11 (June 5): 56.

Heffler, Stephen; Sheila Smith; Sean Keehan; M. Kent Clemens; Mark Zezza; and Christopher Truffer. 2004. "Health Spending Projections Through 2013." *Health Affairs Web Exclusive* (February 11): W4-79–W4-93. Online at content.healthaffairs.org/cgi/reprint/hlthaff.w4.79v1.

Higgins, Michelle. 2003. "Getting Poor on Purpose." *Wall Street Journal*–Eastern Edition, 241, no. 38 (February 25): D1.

Hofferbert, R.I. 1966. "The Relations Between Public Policy and Some Structural and Environmental Variables."*American Political Science Review* 60, no. 1 (March): 73–82.

Holahan, John. 1988. "The Impact of Alternative Hospital Payment Systems on Medicaid Costs." *Inquiry* 25, no. 4 (Winter): 519–20.

Holahan, John F., and Joel W. Cohen. 1986. *Medicaid: The Trade-Off between Cost-Containment and Access to Care.* Washington, D.C.: Urban Institute Press.

Holahan, John F., and David Liska. 1997. "The Slowdown in Medicaid Spending Growth: Will It Continue?" *Health Affairs* 16, no. 2 (March/April): 157–63.

Holahan, John; Stephen Zuckerman; Allison Evans; and Suresh Rangarajan. 1998. "Medicaid Managed Care in Thirteen States." *Health Affairs* 17, no. 3 (May/June): 43–63.

Hudson, Terese. 1992. "States Scramble for Solutions Under New Medicaid Law." *Hospitals* 66, no. 11 (June 5): 52–56.

Hurley, Robert, and Stephen Zuckerman. 2002. "Medicaid Managed Care: State Flexibility in Action." Discussion Papers. Washington, D.C.: Urban Institute Press. Online at www.urban.org/uploadedpdf/310449.pdf.

Institute of Continuing Legal Education. 1997. "Balanced Budget Act Targets Medicaid Planning Advice." Online at www.icle.org.

Johnson, Kathryn. 1983. "Major Surgery for Ailing Medicaid Program." *U.S. News and World Report*, October 17.

Jordan, Fred. 1982. "Governors OK Alternative Plan on Federalism." *Nation's Cities Weekly* 5, no. 5 (March 1): 1, 9.

Kaiser Commission on Medicaid and the Uninsured. 2005. *Medicaid: Issues in Restructuring Federal Financing.* January. Online at www.kff.org/about/kcmu.cfm.

Kenney, Genevieve, and Debbie I. Chang. 2004. "The State Children's Health Insurance Program: Successes, Shortcomings, and Challenges." *Health Affairs* 23, no. 5 (September–October): 51–62.

Kern, Rosemary G., and Susan R. Windham, with Paula Griswold. 1986. *Medicaid and Other Experiments in State Health Policy.* Washington, D.C.: American Enterprise Institute for Public Policy Research.

Key, V.O. 1949. *Southern Politics.* New York: Knopf.

Kitchener, Martin; Terence Ng; Nancy Miller; and Charlene Harrington. 2005. "Medicaid Home and Community-Based Services: National Program Trends." *Health Affairs* 24, no. 1 (January–February): 206–12.

Kosterlitz, Julie. 1990. "Rationing Health Care." *National Journal* 22, no. 26 (June 30): 1590–95.

———. 1991. "Middle-Class Medicaid." *National Journal* 23, no. 45 (November 9): 2731–38.

Kotelchuck, Ronda. 1992. "Medicaid Managed Care: A Mixed Review." *Health/PAC Bulletin* 22, no. 3 (Fall): 4–11.

Kousser, Thad. 2002. "The Politics of Discretionary Spending, 1980–1993." *Journal of Health Politics, Policy, and Law* 27, no. 4 (August): 639–71.

Kronebusch, Karl. 1997. "Medicaid and the Politics of Groups: Recipients, Providers, and Policy Making." *Journal of Health Politics, Policy and Law* 22, no. 3 (June): 839–78.

Kronebusch, Karl, and Brian Elbel. 2004a. "Enrolling Children in Public Insurance: SCHIP, Medicaid, and State Implementation." *Journal of Health Politics, Policy and Law* 29, no. 3 (June): 451–89.

———. 2004b. "Simplifying Children's Medicaid and SCHIP: What Helps? What Hurts? What's Next for the States?" *Health Affairs* 23, no. 3 (May–June): 233–46.

Larson, Celia, and Jannie Williams. 2003. "Sociological Context of TennCare: A Public Health Perspective." *Journal of Ambulatory Care Manager* 26, no. 4 (October–December): 315–21.

Laudicina, Susan S., and Brian Burwell. 1988. "Profile of Medicaid Home and Community-Based Care Waivers, 1985: Findings of a National Survey." *Journal of Health Politics, Policy and Law* 13, no. 3 (Fall): 525–46.

LeCouteur, Gene; Michael Perry, Samantha Artiga; and David Rousseau. 2004. *The Impact of Medicaid Reductions in Oregon: Focus Group Insights.* Kaiser Commission on Medicaid and the Uninsured. Online at www.kff.org/medicaid/7233.cfm.

Lee, Philip R., and Carroll L. Estes. 1983. "New Federalism and Health Policy." *Annals of the American Academy of Political and Social Science* 468 (July): 88–102.

Leichter, Howard M. 1999. "Oregon's Bold Experiment: Whatever Happened to Rationing?" *Journal of Health Politics, Policy, and Law* 24, no. 1 (February): 147–59.

Letsch, Suzanne W.; Helen C. Lazenby; Katharine R. Levit; and Cathy A. Cowan. 1992. "National Health Expenditures, 1991." *Health Care Financing Review* 14, no. 2 (Winter): 1–30.

Levit, Katharine R.; Helen C. Lazenby; Cathy A. Cowan; and Suzanne W. Letsch. 1991. "National Health Expenditures, 1990." *Health Care Financing Review* 13, no. 1 (Fall): 29–54.

Levit, Katharine R.; Arthur L. Sensebig; Cathy A. Cowen; Helen C. Lazenby; Patricia A. McDonnell; Darleen K. Won; Lekha Sivarajan; Jean M. Stiller; Carolyn S. Donham; and Madie S. Stewart. 1994. "National Health Expenditures, 1993." *Health Care Financing Review* 16, no. 1 (Fall): 247–94.

Levit, Katharine R.; Helen C. Lazenby; Bradley R. Braden; Cathy A. Cowan; Arthur R. Sensenig; Patricia A. McDonnell; Jean S. Stiller; Darleen K. Won; Anne B. Martin; Lekha Sivarajan; Carolyn S. Donham; Anna M. Long; and Madie W. Stewart. 1997. "National Health Expenditures, 1996." *Health Care Financing Review* 19, no. 1 (Fall): 161–200.

Levit, Katharine R; Cathy Cowan; Helen Lazenby; Arthur Sensenig; Patricia McDonnell; Jean Stiller; Ann Martin; and the Health Accounts Team. 2000. "Health Spending in 1998: Signals of Change." *Health Affairs* 19, no. 1 (January–February): 124–32.

Levit, Katharine R.; Cynthia Smith; Cathy Cowan; Helen Lazenby; and Anne Martin. 2002. "Inflation Spurs Health Spending in 2000." *Health Affairs* 21, no. 1 (January–February): 172–81.

Lockard, Duane. 1959. *New England State Politics.* Princeton, N.J.: Princeton University Press.

Lyman, Rick. 2004. "Once a Model, A Health Plan is Endangered." *New York Times*, November 20.

Magnuson, Ed. 1982. "New Federalism or Feudalism?" *Time*, February 8.

Mann, Cindy, and Tim Westmoreland. 2004. "Attending to Medicaid." *Journal of Law, Medicine & Ethics* 32, no. 3 (Fall): 416–25.

McCall, Nelda. 1997. "Lessons from Arizona's Medicaid Managed Care Program." *Health Affairs* 16, no. 4 (July–August): 194–99.

McCombs, Jeffrey S., and Jon B. Christianson. 1987. "Applying Competitive Bidding to Health Care." *Journal of Health Politics, Policy and Law* 12, no. 4 (Winter): 703–21.

McDonough, John E. 2003. "The Clouded Future of Medicaid." *Journal of Ambulatory Care Management* 26, no. 4 (October–December): 369–72.

"Medicaid Physician Fees Rise Sharply but Still Trail Medicare in Most States." 2004. *Modern Health Care* 34, no. 38 (September 20): 30.

"Medicaid Rx." 2005. *Wall Street Journal.* February 2, A14.

Mello, Michelle M. 2002. "Policing Medicaid and Medicare Managed Care: The Role of Courts and Administrative Agencies." *Journal of Health Politics, Policy and Law* 27, no. 3 (June): 465–94.

Miller, Michael. 2003. "The Policy and Political Context of Defending Medicaid." *Journal of Ambulatory Care Management* 26, no. 4 (October–December): 307–14.

Morgan, Dan. 1995. "Medicaid Bills Come Home to Roost." *Washington Post National Weekly Edition*, February 6–12.

Newhouse, Joseph P., et al. 1981. "Some Interim Results from a Controlled Trial of Cost Sharing in Health Insurance." *New England Journal of Medicine* 305, no. 25 (December): 1501–7.

Oliver, Thomas R. 1998. "The Collision of Economics and Politics in Medicaid Managed Care: Reflections on the Course of Reform in Maryland." *Milbank Quarterly* 76, no. 1 (March): 59–101.

Park, Hy Gia, and Leah Oliver. 2004. "Is SCHIP Shipshape?" *State Legislatures* 30, no. 5 (May): 16–19.

Patel, Kant. 1996. "Medicaid: Perspectives from the States." *Journal of Health and Social Policy* 7, no. 3: 1–20.

Pear, Robert. 1990. "Ruling May Lead to Big Rise in States' Medicaid Costs." *New York Times*, July 5.

———. 1991a. "U.S. Moves to Curb Medicaid Payments for Many States." *New York Times*, September 11.

———. 1991b. "Suits Force U.S. and States to Pay More for Medicaid." *New York Times*, October 29.

———. 2005. "Bush Nominee Wants States to Get Medicaid Flexibility." *New York Times*, January 19.

Pear, Robert, and Sheryl Stolberg. 2005. "Medicaid Panel Is Said to Be a Key to a Deal on Budget." *New York Times*, April 27. Online at nytimes.com.

"Promise of Coverage: Long-Term Care—The Ticking Time Bomb." 2004. *Governing Magazine* (February): 50.

"Report Gives SCHIP Good Marks for Covering Uninsured Children." 2003. *Congress Daily*, April 8: 13.

Richard, Alan. 2004. "Medicaid Threatens K-12 Share of State Budgets." *Education Week* 24, no. 8 (October 20): 20.

Richardson, Bill. 2005. "The Wrong Prescription for Medicaid." *Washington Post*, Janaury 22. Online at washingtonpost.com.

Rosenbaum, Sarah H., and Peter Budetti. 2003. "Low-Income Children and Health Insurance: Old News and New Realities." *Pediatrics* supplement 2, no. 112 (December): 551–53.

Rosenbaum, Sarah H.; Kay Johnson; Colleen Sonosky; Anne Markus; and Chris DeGraw. 1998. "The Children's Hour: The State Children's Health Insurance Program." *Health Affairs* 17, no. 1 (January/February): 75–89.

Ross, Donna C., and Laura Cox. 2004. *Beneath the Surface: Barriers Threaten to Slow Progress on Expanding Health Coverage of Children and Families: 50 State Update on Eligibility,*

Enrollment, Renewal and Cost-Sharing Practices in Medicaid and SCHIP. Washington, D.C.: Henry J. Kaiser Family Foundation.

Samuelson, Robert J. 1991. "Medicaid Monster." *Washington Post National Weekly Edition,* May 12–16.

Schneider, Saundra K. 1988. "Intergovernmental Influences on Medicaid Program Expenditures." *Public Administration Review* 48, no. 4 (July/August): 756–63.

Schwartz, William B., and Henry J. Aaron. 1985. *Health Care Costs: The Social Tradeoffs.* Washington, D.C.: Brookings Institution.

———. 1990. "The Achilles Heel of Health Care Rationing." *New York Times,* July 9.

Selden, Thomas N.; Julie L. Hudson; and Jessica S. Banthin. 2004. "Tracking Changes in Eligibility and Coverage Among Children, 1996–2002." *Health Affairs* 23, no. 5 (September–October): 39–50.

Shapiro, Joseph P. 1991. "How States Cook the Books." *U.S. News and World Report* (July 29): 24–25.

Sloan, Frank A.; Janet Mitchell; and Jerry Cromwell. 1978. "Physician Participation in State Medicaid Programs." *Journal of Human Resources* 13 (Supplement): 211–45.

Sloane, Todd. 2003. "Medicaid Mayhem." *Modern Healthcare* 33, no. 27 (July 7): 21.

Smith, David G. 2002. *Entitlement Politics: Medicare and Medicaid, 1995–2001.* New York: Aldine de Gruyter.

Smith, Vernon; Rekha Ramesh; Kathleen Gifford; Eileen Ellis; Robin Rudowitz; and Molly O'Malley. 2004. *The Continuing Medicaid Budget Challenge: State Medicaid Spending Growth and Cost Containment in Fiscal Years 2004 and 2005: Results from a 5-State Survey.* Washington, D.C.: Henry J. Kaiser Family Foundation.

Sparer, Michael S. 1998. "Devolution of Power: An Interim Report Card." *Health Affairs* 17, no. 3 (May/June): 7–16.

Specter, Michael. 1991. "Medicaid's Crazy Quilt of Care." *Washington Post National Weekly Edition,* August 26–September 1.

Starr, Alexandra, and Richard S. Dunham. 2003. "Can Bush Really Finish Off the Great Society?" *Business Week,* no. 3841 (July 14): 47.

Starr, Paul. 1982. *The Social Transformation of American Medicine.* New York: Basic Books.

"States, Alone, Can't Cure Ills." 2002. *USA Today,* November 7.

Stolberg, Sheryl. 2005a. "Congress Passes Budget with Cuts in Medicaid and in Taxes." *New York Times,* April 29. Online at nytimes.com.

———. 2005b. "In Blow to Bush, Senators Reject Cuts to Medicaid." *New York Times,* March 18. Online at nytimes.com.

Stone, Deborah A. 1992. "Why States Can't Solve Health Care Crisis." *American Prospect,* no. 9 (Spring): 51–60.

Tanner, Robert. 2005. "States Press Bush, Congress on Medicaid." *Washington Post,* January 19. Online at washingtonpost.com.

"Tenn. Gov. Seeks to End Supplemental Medicaid Plan." 2004. *CongressDaily,* November 10.

Thompson, Frank J. 1986. "New Federalism and Health Care Policy: States and the Old Questions." *Journal of Health Politics, Policy and Law* 11, no. 4 (Tenth Anniversary Issue): 647–69.

———. 1998. "The Faces of Devolution." In *Medicaid and Devolution: A View from the States,* ed. Frank J. Thompson, 15–55. Washington, D.C.: Brookings Institution.

Thrall, Hudson. 2004. "Mega Medicaid Cuts." *Hospital and Health Networks* 78, no. 9 (September): 20–22.

Tucker, William. 1991. "A Leak in Medicaid." *Forbes* 148, no. 1 (July 8): 46–48.

Vogel, Ronald J. 1984. "An Analysis of Structural Incentives in the Arizona Health Care Cost-Containment System." *Health Care Financing Review* 5, no. 4 (Summer): 13–32.

Wagner, Lynn. 1989. "Access for All People." *Modern Healthcare* 19, no. 30 (July 28): 28.

————. 1991. "28 States Face Potential Deficits." *Modern Healthcare* 21, no. 1 (January 7): 2.

Weil, Alan. 1997. "The New Children's Health Insurance Program: Should States Expand Medicaid?" Series A, no. A-13, October. Washington, D.C.: Urban Institute.

————. 2003. "There Is Something About Medicaid." *Health Affairs* 22, no. 1 (January–February): 13–30.

Welch, William M, and Julie Appleby. 2004. "States Watching Tennessee's Health Care Plan for the Poor." *USA Today*, July 6.

Zuckerman, Stephen; Joshua McFeeters; and Peter Cunningham. 2004. "Changes in Medicaid Physician Fees, 1998–2003: Implications for Physician Participation." *Health Affairs*, Web Exclusive, W4 (January–June): 374–84.

4

Medicare

Health Care for the Elderly and Disabled

*Much of the current debate is about Medicare's future mistakes what
Medicare is and what it is designed to achieve. Medicare isn't just a
trust fund. Medicare isn't just a certain kind of health care system,
called fee for service. And Medicare is a lot more than just another
number in the federal budget debate. Medicare is designed, at
bottom, for two purposes. First, Medicare helps assure that older
Americans and those with disabilities have access to the same
standard of quality health care services as most Americans. Second,
Medicare is an essential part of economic security. It is an insurance
system that protects beneficiaries and their families from the
high and unpredictable costs of health care services*
—John C. Rother (n.d.)

Medicare is the largest public-sector health care program in the United States, in
terms of both dollars and numbers of people covered. It began as an alternative to
national health insurance and remains one of the most popular government programs.
Despite its popularity, it has often been a target for those seeking to curtail government spending. Further, significant changes in the course of the forty-year history of
the program provide lessons for the possible expansion of government provision of
health care services. The 1990s, especially the late 1990s, saw a significant transformation in Medicare. In the early 2000s legislation both expanded Medicare benefits
and threatened the very nature of the program itself. Cost and coverage problems
remain an issue, as does the lack of coverage for long-term care.

In this chapter, we closely examine Medicare. We begin by looking at its origin
and structure. We then look at some of the changes and problems with the program
and how those problems have been addressed. We close this portion of the chapter by
examining proposed solutions. We next turn to the problem of long-term care and

how that has been addressed in the United States. We look at some solutions to those problems and make some final conclusions about Medicare.

The Origins of Medicare

As mentioned in chapter 2, national health insurance (NHI) was first considered in the early twentieth century, during Woodrow Wilson's administration. But the onset of World War I, the linkage between NHI and Germany (which was the first to adopt NHI), and opposition to national health insurance on the part of the AMA killed the program. During the development of what eventually became the Social Security Act of 1935, policy formulators (the Committee for Economic Security) considered and rejected the idea of adding a national health insurance provision. They believed, based on responses to the mere mention of national health insurance, that including national health insurance would sink the entire Social Security bill (Marmor 2000; Oberlander 2003, Starr 1982). Beginning in 1939, bills for national health insurance were introduced in Congress (e.g., the Murray-Wagner-Dingell legislation). Marmor (2000, 7) points out that, though the Democrats had a numerical majority, they did not have a "programmatic majority" to enact the legislation. That is, there was insufficient unity within the majority Democratic Party, a problem that was repeated in 1994 (see chapter 9). The 1948 Democratic national platform called for national health insurance. Despite Truman's victory in that election, the Murray-Wagner-Dingell proposal died, never coming out of committee in Congress.

Advocates of national health insurance then tried an alternative strategy. The new strategy was incremental in nature, focusing on a group or groups that had reasonably high status but could not afford health insurance. The ideal group was the elderly. Marmor (2000, 15) describes the politics behind the new strategy:

> The concentration on the burdens of the aged was a ploy for sympathy. The disavowal of aims to change fundamentally the American medical system was a sop to AMA fears, and the exclusion of physician services benefits was a response to past AMA hysteria. The focus on the financial burdens of receiving hospital care took as given the existing structure of the private medical care world, and stressed the issue of spreading the costs of using available services within that world. The organization of health care, with its inefficiencies and resistance to cost-reduction, was a fundamental but politically sensitive problem which consensus-minded reformers wanted to avoid when they opted for 60 days of hospitalization insurance for the aged in 1951 as a promising "small" beginning.

The above quote contains several important points. It shows the attempt to accommodate potential opposition, primarily the medical profession. It did this in several ways. This incremental strategy excluded coverage of physician services (though Medicare as enacted did include such coverage but treated it differently from hospital care). It limited the number of hospital days covered, the "small beginning," a feature that remains an integral part of Medicare. Finally, it left the structure of American medicine alone. That structure was the private practice of physicians and the fee-for-service system.[1] Some of these features would eventually be changed in the 1980s and 1990s.

But they were at least partly responsible for some of the problems that Medicare has faced. A final note: the attempt at political accommodation was also a feature of the Clinton administration's Health Security Act. In any event, the finance committees in Congress held hearings on Medicare from 1958 to 1965 (Marmor 2000).

In 1960 Congress passed the Kerr-Mills bill, which provided federal assistance (50–80 percent) to states to help with hospital care for the aged poor. In other words, Kerr-Mills was a welfare program, with all the accompanying problems and stigma of means-tested (income-based) programs. By 1963, many states had not enacted programs to use Kerr-Mills (Starr 1982).

John F. Kennedy's campaign platform in 1960 included health insurance for the aged. Attempts were made to push a narrow program for the elderly from the beginning of the Kennedy administration. The conservative coalition (Republicans and southern Democrats) that had long opposed liberal legislation was able to delay enactment of the program, but the great electoral victory of Lyndon Johnson in 1964 accompanied by a large liberal Democratic majority in Congress allowed passage of a number of programs, part of the Johnson administration's Great Society. For our purposes, the important bill was Medicare, passed in 1965.

The law (title 18 [XVIII] amendments to the 1935 Social Security Act) was broader than envisioned under the incrementalist strategy following the Truman administration. It included physician services and covered a large section of the aged population, not just those who were poor but those covered by Social Security. Thus it embodied a social insurance concept, where subscribers made contributions, rather than assistance to the poor, which required means testing. Medicare would cover a large portion of the population, and virtually all would contribute and benefit.[2]

Program Objectives and Structure

Objectives

The original design or theory of the program has been aptly stated by Thompson: "If Washington paid mainstream rates to providers for delivering medical care to the elderly, they would receive increased amounts of needed care" (1981, 155).

The problem facing the elderly was that, for several reasons, they could not afford health insurance. First, health insurance was available to individuals and families largely through the workplace. As retirees, the elderly were (in most cases) no longer eligible to receive health insurance benefits. Second, because retirees were no longer part of a larger group through their jobs, they would not be able to gain the benefits of group insurance. Individual insurance rates are considerably higher than group rates. Finally, the elderly were (and are) more at risk of needing medical care (more likely to experience periods of illness, especially extended illness) and expensive care than those of working age. The combination of these three factors meant that few private health insurance companies would offer a policy to retirees, and those that were offered were prohibitively expensive. In 1963, only about 54 percent of the elderly (sixty-five years and older) had hospital insurance (calculated from U.S. Bureau of the Census 1966).

Medicare resolved many of these problems. In 1995, 99.7 percent of those sixty-five or older were covered by insurance. By comparison, nearly 10 percent of those under eighteen had no health insurance (U.S. Bureau of the Census 1997). Medicare had achieved its primary goal of providing health insurance for the elderly. Whether it was adequate is another story.

Structure

Medicare is open to those over sixty-five years of age, those disabled and receiving Social Security cash benefits, and those suffering from end-stage renal disease (ESRD, or kidney failure) (Petrie 1992).

The program has four parts, though the fourth part does not take effect until 2006 (see below). The hospital insurance (HI, or Part A) program covers inpatient hospital expenses for specified periods. Recipients are covered for up to ninety days for a benefit period and have a lifetime reserve of sixty hospital days. Payment is made for room and board in semiprivate rooms and for such hospital services as nursing and pharmaceuticals. Part A also pays for hospice services, home health care, and limited skilled nursing care (Kaiser Family Foundation 2004). Table 4.1 lists the services covered under Part A.

The second portion of Medicare is the supplemental medical insurance program (SMI, or Part B). This is a voluntary program, though most Medicare recipients subscribe to it. SMI covers a wide range of physician and outpatient services, including diagnostic and surgical procedures and radiology. It also covers ambulance services, medical supplies, clinical services, and blood transfusions. Table 4.2 lists the services covered under Part B.

The third portion of Medicare, Part C, focuses on managed care. Under the Balanced Budget Act (BBA) of 1997, the program was entitled "Medicare+Choice." Under the 2003 Medicare Modernization Act (MMA), it is known as "Medicare Advantage." It is through this program that Medicare recipients enroll in managed care programs such as health maintenance organizations (HMOs).

The final, and newest, part of Medicare is Part D. Under the MMA, Medicare recipients will, beginning in January 2006, be eligible for drug coverage. We will discuss this legislation in more detail below.

As important as what is covered is what is not covered. In two major areas, Medicare coverage is extremely limited: in catastrophic coverage, that is, coverage of hospital stays that exceed the specified limits, and in long-term-care coverage. We will address these issues later in this chapter.

Financing Medicare

Medicare is financed through a combination of subscriber and tax payments. The hospital insurance and supplemental medical insurance programs are financed differently. We begin with the hospital program.

The bulk of funds for the hospital insurance trust fund comes from the payroll tax (1.45 percent), a part of the Social Security tax that employees and employers pay

Table 4.1

Medicare Part A: Hospital-Insurance Covered Services for 2005

Services	Benefit	Medicare pays	Recipient pays
Hospitalization: Semi-private room and board, general nursing, and other hospital services and supplies.	First 60 days 61st-90th day 91st-150th day[a] Beyond 150th day	All but $912 All but $228 a day All but $456 a day Nothing	$912 $228 per day $456 per day All costs
Skilled nursing facility: Semi-private room and board, general nursing, skilled nursing, and rehabilitative services and other services and supplies[b]	First 20 days Additional 80 days Beyond 100 days	100% of approved amount All by $114 a day Nothing	Nothing Up to $114 a day All costs
Home health care: Part-time or intermittent skilled care, home health aide services, durable medical equipment and other supplies, and other services	Unlimited as long as recipient meets Medicare conditions	100% of approved amount; 80% of approved amount for durable equipment	Nothing for services; 20% of approved amount for durable equipment
Hospice care	For as long as doctor certifies need	All but limited costs for outpatient drugs and inpatient respite care	Limited costs for outpatient drugs and inpatient respite care
Blood	Unlimited if medically necessary	All but first 3 pints per calendar year	First 3 pints[c]

Source: www.medicare.gov.

[a]This 60-reserve-day benefit may be used only once in a lifetime.

[b]Neither Medicare nor private Medigap insurance will pay for most nursing home care.

[c]Blood paid for or replaced under Part B of Medicare during the calendar year will not have to be paid for or replaced under Part A.

(1.45 percent each).[3] In addition, there are copayments when Medicare recipients use hospital services. There is a one-time deductible (paid before Medicare starts paying) equal to the average cost of one day in the hospital. For 2004, that amount was $876 for each benefit period (Kaiser Family Foundation 2004); the 2005 figure is $912 (Centers for Medicare and Medicaid Services 2004b) Medicare then pays for the entire cost of hospitalization for the next fifty-nine days. If the hospitalization lasts longer than sixty days, there is a copayment equal to one-quarter of a hospital day ($219 as of 2004, $228 for 2005) for days sixty-one through ninety. Each Medicare

Table 4.2

Medicare Part B: Medical-Insurance Covered Services for 2005

Services	Benefit	Medicare pays	Recipient pays
Medical Expenses: Doctors' services, inpatient and outpatient medical and surgical services and supplies, physical and speech therapy, diagnostic tests, durable medical equipment, and other services	Unlimited if medically necessary	80% of approved amount (after $110 deductible); 50% of approved charges for most outpatient mental services	$110 deductible* plus 20% of approved amount and limited charges above approved amount
Clinical Laboratory Services: Blood tests, urinalysis, and more	Unlimited if medically necessary	100% of approved amount; 80% of approved amount for durable medical equipment	Nothing for services; 20% of approved amount for durable medical equipment
Home Health Care: Part-time or intermittent skilled care, home health aide services, durable medical equipment and other supplies, and other services	Unlimited as long as recipient meets Medicare conditions	100% of approved amount; 80% of approved amount for durable equipment	Nothing for services; 20% of approved amount for durable equipment
Outpatient Hospital Treatment: Services for the diagnosis or treatment of illness or injury	Unlimited if medically necessary	Medicare payment to hospital based on hospital cost	20% of billed amount (after $110 deductible)
Blood	Unlimited if medically necessary	80% of approved amount (after $110 deductible and starting with 4th pint)	First 3 pints plus 20% of approved amount for additional pints (after $110 deductible)

Source: www.medicare.gov. 2005 Part B monthly premium: $78.20 (higher if recipient enrolls late).

*Once recipient has had $110 of expenses covered services in 2005, the Part B deductible does not apply to any further covered services received for the rest of the year.

recipient has a reserve equal to sixty hospital days, which can be used past day ninety. The copayment is then half of the inpatient hospital deductible ($438 as of 2004; $456 in 2005) per day (Centers for Medicare and Medicaid Services 2004b). Under Part A, Medicare also pays for hospice and home health care with very limited

Table 4.3

Medicare Beneficiary Cost-Sharing Liability, Selected Years
(as a percent of costs)

	1977	1985	1995	1999
Total	18.0	7.0	37.0	16.8
Hospital insurance	17.6	8.3	17.6	8.3
Supplemental medical insurance	14.0	7.6	23.4	26.7

Sources: "Medicare and Medicaid Statistical Supplement, 1997," 53; "Medicare and Medicaid Statistical Supplement, 2001," Table 19.

deductibles. Approved home health care services do not have a deductible and there is a 20 percent copayment for durable medical equipment, such as oxygen and wheelchairs. Those eligible for skilled nursing home services do not have to pay a deductible for the first twenty days. For the next eighty days, the deductible is $109.50 per day (as of 2004, $114 in 2005) (Centers for Medicare and Medicaid 2004b).

The supplemental insurance program, or Part B, is financed through a combination of general federal revenues and Medicare subscriber premiums. Premiums and tax contributions were approximately equal in 1971; since that time, tax contributions have dwarfed premiums. The federal government pays 75 percent of the costs and premiums cover the remaining 25 percent (Kaiser Family Foundation 2004). That is why, even given the cost increases in Part B copayments, SMI remains a bargain. One can see this in the beneficiary cost-sharing liability percentages (see Table 4.3).

Virtually all Medicare recipients (almost 98 percent) are enrolled in the supplemental insurance program (Part B). The 2004 premium (the amount paid each month) is $66.60 and is deducted from Social Security checks (Kaiser Family Foundation 2004). The Centers for Medicare and Medicaid Services (CMS) announced a 17 percent increase in Part B premiums in 2004, raising the monthly premiums to $78.20 for 2005 ("Those Soaring Medicare Premiums" 2004). This is the largest yearly increase in Part B premiums in the program's history. There is also a $100 deductible as of 2004. This is scheduled to increase to $110 in 2005 and then increase by the percentage increase in Medicare expenditures. There is a 20 percent copayment for Part B services, with Medicare paying 80 percent of of those services. Physician charges as determined under the physician fee scale phased in beginning in 1992. Physicians elect each year whether to accept full assignment, that is, whether to accept the Medicare fee schedule (participating). If the physician does accept the fee schedule, Medicare is billed by the physician and the recipient pays the balance (what is known as balance billing). Physicians do not have to accept full assignment. They can charge up to 115 percent of the Medicare fee schedule.

An example may help explain the fee schedule. Assume that you are a Medicare recipient who needs to visit a doctor for a Medicare-approved service. Your doctor would normally charge $200, given the services provided. According to the Medicare physician fee schedule, the visit is worth $142. Medicare then will pay 80 percent of the $142, or $113.60. Now it gets complicated. Consider these two cases: In case 1, the physician accepts full assignment, or the $142. He or she then sends in the paperwork to Medicare and receives a reimbursement of $113.60. You, the Medicare patient, pay the balance, or $28.40, to the doctor. Now take case 2: The physician does not accept full assignment. He or she can charge up to 115 percent of the $142, or $163.30. The physician bills the patient for the entire amount. The patient pays the doctor and files for reimbursement from Medicare. The Medicare recipient receives $113.60 from Medicare and has to pay the physician $49.70. From the standpoint of the recipient, using a physician who does not accept full assignment would cost an additional $21.30, an increase in the copayment of 75 percent. It obviously pays the Medicare recipient to use physicians who accept assignment.

Over time, Medicare cost sharing has become a higher proportion of the elderly's income (Moon 1996). Perhaps the best way to see this is to look at the percentage of Social Security income that will be spent on Medicare. In 2006, when the new Medicare drug law takes effect, recipients will have to pay an estimated 37 percent of Social Security income for the various cost-sharing features of Medicare. This is projected to increase to about 40 percent five years later and to almost 50 percent a decade after that (Welch 2004). Of course, an alleviating factor is that benefits will have also increased.

Supplementing Medicare

Because of the substantial and growing cost-sharing provisions (premiums, deductibles, and copayments) and coverage gaps, many Medicare recipients have looked for ways to supplement their Medicare plans. As of 2001, almost 90 percent of the elderly population had some kind of health coverage in addition to Medicare (Kaiser Family Foundation 2004). Of these, 34 percent were covered through a current or former employer, 23 percent owned individual coverage (e.g., a Medigap policy), 12 percent were also Medicaid beneficiaries (dual eligibles), and 18 percent participated in HMOs (Kaiser Family Foundation 2004).

Medicaid Buy-In

For Medicare beneficiaries who are also eligible for Medicaid (i.e., low-income individuals), there is state buy-in coverage. In 2000, some 6.8 million people (about 18 percent of Medicare recipients) were partially or fully eligible for both programs (Hudman 2004). States pay the premium under Part B and any cost sharing. What is covered under Medicare is paid for by Medicare and what is covered under Medicaid (such as prescription drugs or long-term care) is paid for by Medicaid. About a third of those eligible for the state buy-in either are disabled or suffer from kidney failure (end-stage renal disease) (Kaiser Commission on

Medicaid and the Uninsured 2004). Seventy percent of the dual eligibles have incomes less than $10,000 (2000 data), and are disproportionately female and minority (Hispanic and African American). They are also more likely to be in poorer health and more likely to be in some kind of institutional care, such as nursing homes, than nondual Medicare enrollees. Spending on them is much higher than for nondual Medicare and Medicaid recipients (Kaiser Commission on Medicaid and the Uninsured 2004).

There are three groups of Medicare beneficiaries who qualify for the Medicaid buy-in. One group are those who are either categorically (eligible for programs such as Supplemental Security Income) or medically needy. Additionally, there are two low-income groups that also qualify for the buy-in: those whose income is below the poverty line with limited assets (qualified Medicare beneficiaries, or QMBs) and those whose income are just over the poverty line (120 percent of the poverty) with limited assets (specified low-income Medicare beneficiaries, or SLMBs). QMBs are limited to help with paying for Part B premiums and cost sharing while SLMBs are limited to help with Part B premiums (Merrell, Colby, and Hogan 1997).

The state buy-ins will change somewhat beginning in 2006, when the Medicare Modernization Act prescription benefit takes affect. The law requires that states pay for their Medicaid/Medicare beneficiaries (see below).

Medigap

Another solution is private supplemental medical insurance, so-called medigap policies. Such policies are provided by insurance companies or group organizations such as the American Association of Retired Persons (AARP). In 2001, over 8 million people purchased medigap policies (Kaiser Family Foundation 2004). Medigap policies raise the average cost of health care because policyholders pay the full cost of that insurance, which includes administrative and advertising costs plus profits for insurance (Moon 1996). Such policies, as might be expected, are expensive.

There are ten standardized medigap policies, labeled A through J. Table 4.4 shows the different policies and their benefits. The more expensive plans cover drug benefits, and some have very high deductibles. Additionally, a relatively new feature of Medicare law is Medicare Select. Such medigap plans are a variant of managed care concepts. In this case, enrollees are limited to a list of doctors and hospitals who will provide services. According to CMS, such policies, which are offered in a limited number of states, are cheaper than nonselect medigap policies. In essence, a recipient choosing one of the select plans will be in a closed-panel HMO. Some of the medigap policies will change in 2006 as the Medicare Modernization Act takes effect (Centers for Medicare and Medicaid Services 2004a).

HMOs pay not only for Medicare benefits and the financial gaps (deductibles, etc.) but can also provide additional benefits, such as prescription drug coverage. By 2001, about 18 percent of Medicare beneficiaries were enrolled in HMOs (Kaiser Family Foundation 2003).

Table 4.4

Types of Medigap Policies: Medigap Plans A through J (basic benefits)*

	Plan A	Plan B	Plan C	Plan D	Plan E	Plan F[a]	Plan G	Plan H	Plan I	Plan J[a]
Basic	Basic									
Skilled Nursing Coinsurance			Skilled Nursing Coinsurance	Skilled Nursing Coinsurance	Skilled Nursing Coinsurance	Skilled Nursing Coinsurance	Skilled Nursing Coinsurance	Skilled Nursing Coinsurance	Skilled Nursing Coinsurance	Skilled Nursing Coinsurance
Medicare Part A Deductible		Medicare Part A Deductible	Medicare Part A Deductible	Medicare Part A Deductible	Medicare Part A Deductible	Medicare Part A Deductible	Medicare Part A Deductible	Medicare Part A Deductible	Medicare Part A Deductible	Medicare Part A Deductible
Medicare Part B Deductible			Medicare Deductible		Part B	Medicare Deductible			Part B	Medicare Deductible
Medicare Part B Excess Charge (100%)						Medicare Part B Excess Charge (100%)	Medicare Part B Excess Charge (100%)		Medicare Part B Excess Charge (100%)	Medicare Part B Excess Charge (100%)
Foreign Travel Emergency			Foreign Travel Emergency	Foreign Travel Emergency	Foreign Travel Emergency	Foreign Travel Emergency	Foreign Travel Emergency	Foreign Travel Emergency	Foreign Travel Emergency	Foreign Travel Emergency
At-Home Recovery				At-Home Recovery			At-Home Recovery		At-Home Recovery	At-Home Recovery
Basic Drug Benefit ($1,250 Limit)								Basic Drug Benefit ($1,250 Limit)	Basic Drug Benefit ($1,250 Limit)	Basic Drug Benefit ($1,250 Limit)
Preventive Care[b]					Preventive Care[b]					Preventive Care[b]

Source: Centers for Medicare and Medicaid Services (2004a, 13).

* All plans offer a basic benefit that covers Part A coinsurance and cost of 365 extra lifetime hospital days; Part B coinsurance or deductible; and first three pints of blood each year.

[a] Plan F and J also have a high-deductible option.

[b] Medigap policies cover some preventive care that isn't covered by Medicare.

Employment Retiree Benefits

A third way that beneficiaries can supplement Medicare coverage is through their former employers. A number of those companies that insure their workers also insure their retirees. As of 2001, some 34 percent of Medicare enrollees were in employer retirement plans (Kaiser Family Foundation 2004).

However, there has been a major drop in such coverage. Large employers, the ones most likely to cover workers and retirees, significantly decreased their coverage of retirees, from 66 percent in 1998 to just 38 percent five years later. This is part of a larger trend of reducing employer coverage, largely due to the cost problems. We will take this issue up in chapter 5.

Medicare, Balanced Budgets, and Managed Care

The search for ways to reduce the costs of Medicare, particularly future costs, has led policymakers and others to look toward a fourth way to supplement Medicare coverage. Managed care has emerged as perhaps the most important policy solution for reducing Medicare costs.

In the 1980s, Medicare began enrolling recipients in managed care organizations (MCOs) such as HMOs as a means of restraining cost increases while maintaining quality of care for recipients. In addition, it was hoped that Medicare recipients would gain access to the same range of services as other patients while restraining costs (Brown et al. 1993). The plans often offered important additional services that Medicare did not offer, such as prescription drugs. The plans also did not originally charge for their services and allowed Medicare beneficiaries to avoid the high costs of medigap policies (Freudenheim 1997). In 1961, four years before the enactment of Medicare and Medicaid, the elderly paid, on average, about 11 percent of their after-tax income on health care; in 1994, that number had risen to 18 percent. Much of this was due to increases in the premiums for medigap policies, which in some cases increased by more than 40 percent by 1996 (Dallek 1996).

A major move toward Medicare managed care and greater choice came in 1997 (see Marmor 2000; Oberlander 2003; Palazzolo 1999; Rushefsky and Patel 1998). To understand what happened, we need to go back to 1995. The Republicans gained control of Congress following the 1994 off-year elections. Their policy agenda, most of which was stated in the Contract with America, was to balance the federal budget and to cut taxes. Doing so required significant budget cuts. Medicare (and Medicaid) were targeted for significant cuts. The FY 1996 budget that Congress passed called for $270 billion in savings over a seven-year period (Marmor 2000; Rushefsky and Patel 1998).

Here we have an interesting play of semantics and politics. The Republican proposal called for cuts in projected spending increases. It did not call for actual reductions in Medicare spending, at least on the surface. Managed care and HMOs would be one way to reduce spending increases, by making the system more efficient; at least so claimed the Republicans (Rushefsky and Patel 1998).

Table 4.5

Medicare Expenditures, 1970–2005 (in billions of dollars)

1970	7.7	1996	199.4
1975	15.7	1997	211.3
1980	37.5	1998	210.2
1985	70.4	1999	213.5
1990	112.1	2000	225.1
1991	123.3	2001	225.1
1992	138.3	2002	267.1
1993	154.2	2003	280.9
1994	166.9	2004	296.2
1995	185.3	2005	309.5

Source: See Table 2.1.

Democrats, especially President Clinton, saw the proposed cuts as real, not just a slower increase in spending. The reasoning here was twofold. First, as the population ages, Medicare enrollment will increase. By definition, then, Medicare spending will have to increase, even if spending per beneficiary is kept constant or decreases. And Medicare spending per beneficiary was, in fact, decreasing.

The bill that Republicans wanted would have capped Medicare spending. That is, Medicare would have had a ceiling or limit on spending that could not be breached. Given the uncertainties of spending on health care, particularly for seniors, this would have had an enormous impact on the program. Further, Republicans wanted automatic cuts if the ceiling were breached (Oberlander 2003). As Oberlander (2003) points out, these two features would have meant the end of the entitlement to Medicare. Versions of these ideas were resurrected in the 2003 legislation discussed below. President Clinton vetoed budget bills containing the Medicare cuts. Congress refused to increase the debt limit and the federal government experienced two partial shutdowns. Eventually, the Republicans caved in, and Clinton's presidency experienced new life.

But in a sense, the Republicans won two years later. Congress, still controlled by Republicans, and President Clinton agreed on a bill to balance the budget with the Balanced Budget Act (BBA) of 1997 (Kahn and Kuttner 1999; Palazzolo 1999). The BBA contained changes that significantly affected Medicare. First, the BBA provided for additional cuts in provider reimbursements. Second, the bill extended prospective payment to nursing homes, hospice agencies, and home health care agencies. The impact of these two provisions resulted in a considerable slowdown in Medicare expenditures (see Table 4.5). For the only time in its history, Medicare expenditures in one year (1998) were lower than in the previous year (1997). Indeed, the changes were so strict that the outcry led to their being loosened several years later (Oberlander 2003). But from our standpoint, the most important change was the establishment of the Medicare+Choice program.

The appeal of managed care was twofold. First, it presented the possibility of controlling costs, something that has been a problem for Medicare from its origins. Secondly, it offered beneficiaries services, such as prescription drug coverage, that they could not get under regular Medicare. At least in the beginning, managed care enrollees would not have to pay anything additional for the benefits. Medicare would cover the costs and save money. Everyone would win.

But enrollment was not increasing sufficiently. One reason might be because there was insufficient choice among types of plans. Prior to the BBA of 1997, the choice was between traditional Medicare and HMOs. The BBA of 1997 expanded choice through the Medicare+Choice program.

Under the BBA, Medicare recipients had a choice of seven different types of plans (see Table 4.6). Recipients would now be able to have a selection of plans that would rival that of private employer-based plans. The Medicare+Choice program (Part C) undermined traditional or regular Medicare. It attempted to fragment the Medicare community. The idea that everybody had the same plan, an idea that underlay the consensus about Medicare (Oberlander 2003), would be eliminated. The proponents of choice hoped to wean beneficiaries away from Medicare, modernize Medicare, and move Medicare to more efficient health care plans. The plans were to be competitive, based on price and quality (Newman and Langwell 1999).

The intent of the BBA is most striking when one considers the last two plans listed in Table 4.6. The first of these is medical savings accounts (MSAs). This was an experiment, though proponents wanted an expanded version, limited to some 700,000 beneficiaries. Recipients would be able to put funds in a tax-free savings account and use that money for much of their health care expenses. Medicare would then act as a catastrophic insurance policy. MSAs would fragment Medicare even more than just mere choice. The concept reemerged under a slightly different name in the 2003 legislation.

The last plan is the privately contracted fee-for-service plan. This is similar to the British system in that citizens can see doctors for services outside of Medicare, but pay for them on their own. Again, this would change the nature of Medicare.

The program did not work out as planned, which laid the groundwork for the 2003 legislation. Newman and Langwell (1999) predicted that the enrollment growth estimated for the new program, and based on increases in HMO enrollments in previous years, might not actually occur. Their reasoning was that while there were cost savings for Medicare HMO beneficiaries and Medicare itself, expanding the availability of choice would encourage the growth of such plans to areas where Medicare reimbursements were lower and would encourage sicker Medicare recipients to join. They suggested that, under the new program, plans might withdraw from the Medicare market.

As subsequent data showed, the program did not work as planned. For one thing, enrollment in managed care plans declined in 2000 and 2001. HMOs withdrew from some areas, leaving recipients without any similar health plan. In 2001, nearly one million recipients lost their health care plan (Gold 2001). Further, plans that remained became less generous to their beneficiaries. More of them were requiring premiums and fewer were covering prescription drugs (Gold 2001; see also Biles, Dallek and Nicholas 2004).

Table 4.6

Choice of Plans under Medicare+Choice

Plan	Definition
Fee-for-Service	The beneficiary can visit any doctor. Medicare pays a set fee for each service. Most beneficiaries, however, purchase private supplemental insurance to pay for uncovered costs.
Health Maintenance Organization (HMO)	The beneficiary can use only the doctors and health facilities on a limited list, but often receives extra benefits. A gatekeeper oversees the patient's total care and makes referrals to specialists. Medicare pays the HMO a set fee in advance to cover all patient services for a period of time.
Point-of-Service	In this special kind of HMO, the beneficiary can visit doctors outside the network but must pay an additional cost.
Preferred Provider Organization (PPO)	The beneficiary can visit any doctor in the health care network without a referral, or see doctors outside the network at an additional cost. Medicare pays a set fee in advance to cover all patient services for a period of time.
Provider-Sponsored Organization (PSO)	These new health plans will be created, owned, and operated by doctors and hospitals. They will resemble managed care plans, in which Medicare pays the health plan a monthly fee for each recipient.
Medical Savings Account (MSA)	Medicare provides catastrophic insurance coverage and advances a portion of the high deductible. At the end of the year, the beneficiary may keep any unused Medicare money.
Privately Contracted Fee-for-Service	The beneficiary may visit any doctor or purchase any health plan but pays extra for uncovered or expensive services.

Source: Reprinted with permission from *National Journal,* August 16, 1997. Copyright 2005 by *National Journal.* All rights reserved.

One of the more interesting aspects of the debate over Medicare+Choice and the withdrawal of plans, one that also affected the 2003 legislation, had to do with payments to plans by Medicare. The Health Care Financing Administration (HCFA, now the Centers for Medicare and Medicaid Services, or CMS) reasoned that HMOs would be able to save money serving their clientele. So the reimbursement rate for HMOs was set at 95 percent of the average spending on Medicare beneficiaries (adjusted average per capita cost, or AAPCC). Paradoxically, both HCFA and HMOs claimed that they were losing money on the deal. The HCFA's claim was based on HMOs' enrolling healthier segments of the Medicare population, whose costs would be less than average. The HMOs' claim was based on recipients making more use, particularly of the prescription drug benefit, than anticipated.

A four-year evaluation found that risk plans (where the plan would not get more money from HCFA if their costs increased) tended to enroll healthier-than-average Medicare recipients. Those enrolled in risk plans had 20 percent lower Medicare reimbursements than those not so enrolled. Further, they were less likely to be disabled or have chronic health problems than those enrolled in risk plans. Such a pattern of enrollment, called favorable selection, has often been charged to HMOs. The evaluation study estimates that given favorable selection, costs to Medicare were actually 5.7 percent higher than with the fee-for-service system (Brown et al. 1993; see also Biles, Dallek and Nicholas 2004; Congressional Budget Office 1997; Oberlander 1997).

On the other hand, HMOs do tend to reduce the length of hospital stays over the fee-for-service system, though they do not reduce the number of admissions. For other services, HMOs tend to reduce the intensity of services (the number of services provided) from 10 to 20 percent (Congressional Budget Office 1997). The effects are greatest for those who are chronically ill (Oberlander 1997). Quality of care for HMO Medicare recipients was about equal to that of fee-for-service Medicare recipients (Brown et al. 1993).

One question that could be asked is how satisfied Medicare recipients are with managed care plans. A study by Nelson (1997) found that most Medicare HMO enrollees were satisfied with their access to care, such as being admitted to a hospital, seeing a specialist, making an appointment, or receiving desired home health care. Most were able to select their primary care physician and had received enough information to obtain care. Those more likely to report access problems were from "vulnerable subgroups" (151–52), such as the nonelderly disabled, those whose health was less than good, the oldest beneficiaries, and those with functional disabilities. African Americans seemed less satisfied with their HMOs than whites. Even so, most of these groups said they would recommend the plan to others with health problems. Adequacy of home health care services appears more likely under Medicare fee-for-service than under managed care.

A more recent study by Tudor, Riley, and Ingber (1998) compared Medicare HMO enrollees with Medicare nonenrollees. The study found that HMO enrollees were more likely to receive preventive services (such as flu shots) than were nonenrollees. HMO enrollees were more satisfied with their cost of care and with receiving care at a single location than were nonenrollees. Otherwise, there seemed to be about the same level of satisfaction between the two groups. Nonenrollees were more likely to express satisfaction with the doctor-patient relationship than were HMO enrollees.

In general, Tudor et al. found that Medicare beneficiaries, regardless of whether they were enrolled in an HMO, seemed satisfied with their care. They even noted that enrollee satisfaction had increased, though they also noted that those who were highly dissatisfied with their HMO simply disenrolled and were not part of the analysis.

Riley, Ingber, and Tudor (1997) also looked at those who had disenrolled from their HMOs. They noted that the disenrollment provisions provided a kind of a safety valve for those who were extremely dissatisfied with their plan. They also pointed out that disenrollment has declined. Those who disenrolled were older and less healthy than those who stayed, but many of those who disenrolled switched plans (sometimes because the beneficiaries moved). The authors also observed that those who enrolled with a preexisting chronic condition (such as cancer) were much more likely to disenroll than those who developed the condition after enrolling.

Disabled Medicare enrollees had about the same level of satisfaction with HMOs as elderly HMO enrollees, though the former group faced somewhat higher levels of access problems than did the latter group, particularly concerning specialists and home health care services (Gold et al. 1997).

Regardless of the lack of success of the Medicare+Choice program, particularly with regards to health maintenance organizations, the Balanced Budget Act of 1997 was one of the most significant policy developments in the history of Medicare. Alternative plans such as those included in Medicare+Choice reappear in the 2003 Medicare Modernization Act (see below).

The Disaster of the Medicare Catastrophic Coverage Act

One of the more interesting episodes in the history of Medicare (and U.S. health care policy in general) revolves around the Medicare Catastrophic Coverage Act (MCCA) of 1988. The notion of catastrophic coverage is that there may be medical expenses that can cause financial hardship or ruin to a family. Preventing financial ruin is one of the purposes of health insurance in the first place, certainly of the Medicare program. Such catastrophic expenses might include diseases such as cancer or AIDS that progress over a lengthy period of time and thus are very costly. Long-term care (to be considered in detail below) can also deplete the life savings of the average family in a couple of years.

As we have seen, Medicare, historically, did not cover everything. There is extremely limited long-term-care coverage, there was no coverage of prescription drugs outside of hospitals (until 2006, with the new Medicare legislation to be discussed below), and there are limits on hospital and physician services. Medigap policies were developed by the private sector to cover some of the holes in Medicare coverage. HMOs can also provide additional services. Nevertheless, there were (and are) Medicare recipients who cannot afford medigap policies (low-income and disabled recipients) and whose copayments would wreak hardship on families.

With this as background, the road toward the Medicare Catastrophic Coverage Act began in January 1986 with President Reagan's State of the Union address. The president discussed the problem of catastrophic expenses and suggested that coverage should be broadened for all sectors of the population, not just the elderly. Reagan also suggested that any solution should rely on the private sector (Schur, Berk, and Mohr 1990) .

The president set up a commission headed by Otis Bowen, then secretary of the Department of Health and Human Services (HHS). The commission was supposed to look at both long-term and acute-care problems. Indeed, testimony before the Bowen Commission emphasized the problems of long-term care; however, the commission decided to focus on acute care for Medicare recipients as the easiest step that could be taken (Moon 1996).

The commission's original idea was to add a cap or limit of $2,000 on yearly expenses paid by Medicare beneficiaries. Once the limit had been reached, Medicare would pay Part A and B deductibles and coinsurance. The cost to the beneficiary would be $59 a month added to Part B premiums. The cost of this proposed expansion was $2 billion. Congress accepted the administration proposal as a framework for change. As is typical of congressional-presidential relations, this was seen as an opening bid by a Republican administration. The Democrats would try to expand benefits but keep the self-financing provisions (Moon 1996).

MCCA was passed in June 1988 with significant changes from the Bowen proposal. It eliminated limitations on hospital benefits including coinsurance, with the exception of a yearly deductible. It increased limits on stays in skilled nursing facilities. It increased provisions for home health care. It provided for a limit on Part B services (to $1,370 for 1990 and with adjustments to the cap in subsequent years). It provided for coverage of outpatient prescription drugs, with a deductible and coinsurance dropping to 20 percent by 1993 (Moon 1996).

The act also included a self-financing provision. A surtax was assessed on Medicare beneficiaries in a progressive manner. That is, low-income recipients would pay $22.50 (if their tax liability was $150), with the highest surtax limited to $800 for an individual with income greater than $35,000 or $1,600 for a couple with incomes greater than $70,000 a year. The law also required that the surtax be paid beginning in 1989, though benefits would not begin until 1990 (Moon 1996).[4]

At first glance, there should have been considerable support for the new law. Groups representing the aging population, especially the AARP, were enthusiastic advocates of the legislation. But there was opposition. The drug industry opposed the legislation, fearing the imposition of cost controls (a stance it also took in regard to health care reform in 1993–94, though the industry supported the 2003 legislation that did pass). The National Committee to Protect Social Security and Medicare was against the financing package because it would require beneficiaries to pay for all the new benefits, rather than rely on a combination of taxes and beneficiary contributions (Moon 1996).

It was also true that MCCA had redistributive implications. As we have seen, those least likely to have supplemental medical insurance (medigap policies) were at the low end of the income scale. They would have benefited more by the law than those at the high end. The progressive nature of the financing enhanced the redistributive effect (Moon 1996).

Additionally, Medicare beneficiaries did not understand the law, despite the considerable publicity that surrounded its enactment. A telephone survey of Medicare recipients documented this problem. For example, only 19 percent of the respondents knew that Medicare did not cover the costs of an extended nursing home stay. Few knew about the financing details or about the drug benefit. Once respondents were briefed about the new law, many were opposed. Indeed, those opposed held that opinion more strongly than those who favored it. The elderly were concerned about all costs, such as the deductibles for prescription medication. They also seemed satisfied with their medigap policies (Rice, Desmond, and Gable 1990).

From the standpoint of wealthier Medicare recipients, MCCA did not appear to be much of a bargain. They were more likely to have private insurance that already gave them what MCCA would do, plus they were asked to make a larger contribution to the program. Thus they did not see themselves as benefiting, but as having to pay for the expansion nevertheless.

Apart from the opposition of the two groups mentioned above that financed mail campaigns against the law, it appeared that the new premiums would build up faster than anticipated, yet the costs of some benefits (particularly the drug benefit) had been underestimated. Town meetings held by Congress in the summer of 1989 demonstrated the discontent. Given all this, Congress repealed the law in November 1989, about eighteen months after it had been passed (Moon 1996).

Controlling Costs

From the beginning, a chief concern about the Medicare program was cost. Several dimensions of costs play a role. One that has been discussed earlier was costs to the Medicare beneficiary. Here we can look at the copayments and deductible that recipients have to make under Parts A and B and premiums under Part B (and the new Parts C and D). We have also looked, to a certain extent, at the problem of cost through HMOs and medigap policies.

The other major dimension of cost control is costs to the federal government. As Medicare became more expensive for a variety of reasons, federal administrators and policymakers sought ways to curb those costs. Some of this could be done by raising premiums and deductibles for Medicare recipients. But by far the largest target of cost control was providers: physicians, hospitals, and so forth. From the beginning, the politics of Medicare revolved around the issue of provider payment, beginning with hospitals and then expanding to doctors (see Feder 1977; Thompson 1981). In addition, the size of the Medicare program made it a tempting target for those seeking either to cut government spending and/or reduce the budget deficit. Medicare played a key role in the 1995–97 budget debates, a debate that ultimately led to significant changes in the program.

Consider, first, the increase in expenditures and enrollments in Medicare (see Tables 4.5 and 4.7). Medicare expenditures in 1970 were about $7.7 billion, about 43.3 percent of federal health expenditures and 10.4 percent of total personal health expenditures. In 1995, Medicare expenditures were $185.3 billion, representing almost 58 percent of federal personal health care expenditures and almost 19 percent of total personal health care expenditures. By 2002, Medicare expenditures were $267.1 billion, representing almost 53 percent of federal health expenditures and 17.2 percent of total personal health expenditures (Heffler et al. 2004). One could argue that because Medicare began only in 1965, it would surely make large increases starting from such a small base. Nevertheless, doing similar calculations for 1980 to 1995 showed how much quicker Medicare was growing than the overall health sector. Overall personal health care expenditures increased by about 136 percent, federal expenditures

Table 4.7

Medicare Enrollees, Selected Years, 1975–2004 (in millions of enrollees)

	Total enrollees	Aged	Disabled
1975	24.9	22.7	2.2
1980	28.4	25.5	3.0
1985	31.1	28.1	2.9
1990	34.3	31.0	3.3
1995	37.6	33.2	4.4
2000	39.7	34.3	5.4
2001	40.1	34.5	5.6
2002	40.7	34.7	6.0
2003	41.1	35.0	6.1
2004	41.7	35.3	6.4

Source: Centers for Medicare and Medicaid Services (2003b).

increased by about 353 percent, but Medicare expenditures during the same period increased by about 394 percent. Considering the concern about overall increases in health care, such rapid increases in Medicare could not help but raise alarms.

One of the reasons for the increase in program expenditures was the increase in the number of Medicare beneficiaries (see Table 4.7). When the program began operation, in 1966, there were a little over 19 million enrollees. By 1970, that number had increased to over 20 million people. The 1972 amendments to the Social Security Act added the disabled and those suffering from end-stage renal disease (kidney failure). By 1995, there were approximately 37.6 million Medicare enrollees, 4.4 million of whom were disabled. That represents an increase of about 83 percent in total recipients. By 2002, the number of Medicare recipients had increased to 40.7 million people, including 6 million disabled (Centers for Medicare and Medicaid Services 2003b). This represents an increase of about 8 percent since 1995.

Another reason is the growing generosity of Medicare in the sense that cost sharing on the part of Medicare recipients has become relatively smaller. In 1977, cost sharing amounted to about 18 percent of total expenditures. By 1983, the number had decreased to 17.6 percent. By 1995, that figure had decreased to about 14 percent (calculated from Health Care Financing Administration, "Medicare and Medicaid Statistical Supplement, 1995," 54). Other reasons include increases caused by general inflation, health care inflation over and above general inflation, and changes in the technology of health care.

When policymakers began to seriously consider imposing cost-control measures on Medicare they focused first on hospitals. As is true for overall national health care expenditures, hospitals accounted for the largest single portion of Medicare expenditures. In 2002, hospital inpatient services were about $102 billion, approximately 50 percent of total Medicare payments. By contrast, physician services accounted for about $61 billion, approximately 26 percent of total Medicare payments (calculated from Centers for Medicare and Medicaid Services 2003a).

When Medicare began, it contained the usual compromise provision "that the federal insurance program would not interfere in the practice of medicine or the structure of the medical care industry" (J. Feder 1977, 1). But it was inevitable that the federal government would have to take steps as the program became relatively more expensive. One way to understand that inevitability is to consider the theory of imbalanced political interests and its application to Medicare (Marmor, Wittman, and Heagy 1983).

At the beginning of the program, Medicare amounted to a relatively small percentage of federal expenditures. In FY 1970, five years after Medicare was established, Medicare expenditures amounted to about 4 percent of federal expenditures. Hospitals and physicians were faced with concentrated benefits and costs of payment and regulatory policies. The program was too small in the early years for the federal government to pay much concern. Ten years later, however, Medicare had increased to about 6.4 percent, and by 1997 an estimated 11.9 percent of federal expenditures (calculated from U.S. Bureau of the Census 1997). As Medicare spending continued to increase faster than overall spending, the federal government developed its own set of interests in cost containment that would counterbalance provider interests.[5] Additionally, there was, and is, the continual concern that the hospital trust fund will eventually become insolvent. In the early 1980s, the federal government looked at hospital cost containment in Medicare. During the latter part of the decade it turned to physician payments. Eventually, other providers, such as nursing homes and home health care agencies, were covered by prospective payment.

Prospective Payment System and Cost Containment

The strain on the federal health budget (mentioned above) laid the political foundation for federal regulation of hospital costs (Steinwald and Sloan 1981). Proponents of regulation claimed that it could reduce waste and inefficiency without sacrificing quality of care. (Joskow 1981)

The Omnibus Budget Reconciliation Act of 1981 made minor changes in the Medicare program. It tightened limits on Medicare reimbursement to generate cost savings. The Tax Equity and Fiscal Responsibility Act (TEFRA) of 1982 established a limit on the rate of increase over time in Medicare hospital payment rates, incorporated a case-mix index based on diagnosis-related groupings (DRGs), and provided incentive payments to hospitals defined as efficient. The law also directed the Department of Health and Human Services to design a prospective payment plan for the Medicare program. The TEFRA system was replaced in 1983 by the Prospective Payment System (PPS) for Medicare reimbursement to hospitals.

The PPS for Medicare reimbursement was modeled after a New Jersey program.[6] Faced with health care cost increases, inadequate care for the poor, pressure on the state Medicaid budget, and rising hospital charges, New Jersey adopted in 1978 a prospective reimbursement mechanism for all payers based on 467 DRGs. Implementation of PPS in New Jersey was phased in between 1980 and 1982. The Health Care Financing Administration (HCFA) in the Department of Health and Human

Services had been supporting research, development, demonstration, and evaluation in cost control since the early 1970s, and the New Jersey DRG system was one of its demonstration projects. The adoption by the federal government in 1983 of a prospective payment mechanism based on DRGs for Medicare reimbursement to hospitals was a natural outgrowth of the New Jersey experiment (Morone and Dunham 1986).

The rationale behind replacing the retrospective payment system was that under that system hospitals had no incentive to economize in their use of health care resources in treating Medicare patients. If anything, such a system encouraged overutilization of health resources because hospitals were assured that they would be reimbursed for all reasonable costs incurred. PPS was based on the assumption that given built-in incentives hospitals would be forced to consider cost factors in treatment and would be encouraged to be economically more efficient. Thus, inefficient hospitals would be forced to close. An economically more efficient hospital sector would help contain increases in hospital costs. PPS was viewed as a method of influencing hospital activities, creating cost-containment constraints, and introducing incentives into hospital payments (Shaffer 1983). The cost-control incentive was the primary purpose in establishing PPS.

Under PPS, hospitals are paid according to a schedule of preestablished rates linked to 468 DRGs. All major categories of diagnosis are classified into 492 categories. Each category is assigned a treatment rate, and hospitals are reimbursed according to these rates. There are economic incentives in the form of rewards and punishments built into the system. If a hospital spends more money than the preestablished rate for a particular diagnostic treatment, the hospital must absorb the additional cost. If the hospital spends less money than the preestablished rate, it is still paid the preestablished rate, and it can keep the overpayment as profit. The Health Care Financing Administration was assigned the responsibility for establishing the DRG payment schedule. To safeguard against reduction in quality of care as a result of PPS, Congress assigned to Peer Review Organizations (PROs) the responsibility for monitoring the quality and appropriateness of care for Medicare patients. If a PRO finds inappropriate or substandard care, the hospital may be denied Medicare payment. If a pattern of inappropriate or substandard care is discovered, the hospital Medicare provider agreement may be terminated.

The shift in the Medicare payment method to hospitals from a retrospective reimbursement system to a prospective payment system based on DRGs was one of the most far-reaching change in the Medicare program since its inception (Vladeck 1984). The changeover to PPS was the first major change in Medicare expected to revolutionize the economics of U.S. health care (Dolnec and Dougherty 1985). DRGs changed the incentive structure facing providers (hospitals in this case) using a regulatory approach. Managed care, on the other hand, changed the incentives structure using a market or private-sector approach.

The implementation of PPS slowed the growth rate of hospital costs, largely through reduced hospital admissions. Concerns about cost shifting to third-party payers have not materialized, and there is no evidence to support the fear that Medicare patients were being denied beneficial care. Hospitals (and doctors) have accepted PPS, and it has become an accepted, if not liked, part of Medicare.

Controlling Physician Costs

As we have seen, the Prospective Payment System focused on hospitals, but it also had an indirect effect on doctors. Hospitals are the structure or framework, but doctors decide medical or surgical treatment. The PPS, by creating a ceiling on hospital reimbursements, caused hospitals to pressure doctors so as to limit hospital expenditures. But physicians had independent effects on Medicare expenditures and government budgets.

General revenues make up a significant portion of Part B expenditures. After the 1972 Social Security amendments, increases in premiums were limited by increases in Social Security beneficiary payments. Thus, whereas in 1972 beneficiary premiums almost equaled general revenue contributions, by 1995 beneficiary premiums accounted for a little over 27.4 percent of Part B program payments.[7] With hospital expenses easing a bit, attention naturally turned to expenditures on the next biggest item, physicians. By 1995, such expenses accounted for 21.7 percent of total Medicare spending (Levit, Lazenby, and Stewart 1996).

In some ways, though Medicare based payments on usual and customary fees, the process was administratively complex and created inequities in physician income and dissatisfaction among physicians. In 1984, Congress froze Medicare physician reimbursements and then limited balance billing (the amount doctors could charge above Medicare). Further, there were significant increases in Medicare beneficiary cost sharing above increases in Social Security benefits. A final factor leading to change was the passage and implementation of the Prospective Payment System for hospitals. As Oliver points out, PPS "demonstrated that health cost containment was both technically feasible and politically feasible" (Oliver 1993, 120).

Although the Reagan administration did not consider a physician payment schedule program, Congress acted. It froze physician fees in Medicare and ordered the Office of Technology Assessment to evaluate different payment schemes. In 1985, Congress created the Physician Payment Review Commission (PPRC), through an omnibus budget reconciliation act, and ordered it to make recommendations regarding a payment system. It simultaneously ordered the Department of Health and Human Services to develop a fee schedule, based on a resource-based relative value scale (RBRVS). Such a scale was adopted in 1989, again through an omnibus budget reconciliation act. The HFCA began implementing the fee schedule in 1992 and it was fully implemented in 1996 (Moon 1996).

A relative value scale (RVS) compares the complexity and time of services offered (Moon 1996). Thus a simple office visit would have a lower RVS than a coronary bypass operation. The fee schedule also contains adjustments for geography, and there is a conversion factor that translates the results into dollar amounts.

Additionally, volume standards help in establishing growth rates in physician payments (Moon 1996).

The impact of the fee schedule varied, depending on the kind of service. Fees for office and hospital visits were generally increased; fees for surgery were significantly reduced. It is no wonder that physicians and their associations were unhappy with the fee schedules. Political pressure by interest groups, Congress, and the Bush administration led the HCFA to liberalize the fee schedule (Oliver 1993). In 1998, the HCFA began using a single conversion factor for all physician services, effectively raising the conversion factor for primary care and nonsurgical care and lowering it for surgical services ("Victory" 1997). The 1997 balanced budget called for changes in the fee schedule components to be fully implemented by 2002 (Physician Payment Review Commission 1997). By FY 2004, physician spending was down to 17.4 percent of total Medicare spending (Centers for Medicare and Medicaid Services 2004c).

The figures through 2002 (Table 4.5) show the impact of cost controls, especially the Balanced Budget Amendment of 1997. Consider the 1998–2002 period by comparison. Overall health expenditures increased by about 35 percent and federal health expenditures increased by about 37 percent. Medicare expenditures, on the other hand, grew by only about 27 percent during the same time period.

The Problem of Long-Term Care

> Although the impetus behind the nation's quest for health care reform is public dissatisfaction over glaring deficiencies in America's acute-care health system—primarily excessive cost and the inability of millions of Americans to get health insurance—the way the nation provides for the financing and delivery of long-term care (LTC) may be even more badly in need of reform. Strong considerations, both public policy and moral, argue for addressing health care for the uninsured first, before long-term care. Yet no other part of the health care system generates as much passionate discontent as does long-term care. (Weiner and Illston 1994, 17)

As we saw in the discussion of the Medicare Catastrophic Coverage Act, one of the important gaps in Medicare pertains to long-term care. We begin this section by looking at some of the data concerning long-term care.

A first point is the significant increase in expenditures on nursing homes. In 1970, about $4.2 billion was spent on nursing homes. By 1995, that figure had risen to $77.9 billion, an increase of 1,754 percent (calculated from Levit et al. 1996). In 2002, nursing home expenditures rose to $103.2 billion, an increase of over 32 percent (calculated from Heffler et al. 2004).

Second, Medicare (and most private medical insurance) focuses on short-term or acute care. It provides limited coverage for skilled nursing care, and then only after a hospital episode on physician orders. The bulk of spending on nursing homes is from Medicaid and out-of-pocket expenditures. Out of the $103.2 billion spent on nursing homes nationally in 2002, Medicare accounted for only about 12 percent (O'Brien and Elias 2004).

Consider 2002 data. Out of $252 billion spent by Medicare through Parts A and B, nursing home care accounted for $14.7 billion, a little over 14 percent of nursing home care (calculated from Centers for Medicare and Medicaid Services 2003a). Medicaid paid about 50 percent of nursing home care ($51.6 billion). Private health insurance paid for only 7 percent of nursing home care ($7.2 billion), while out-of-pocket payments were 26 percent of such costs ($26.8 billion) (calculated from O'Brien and Elias 2004). We should note here some of the changes in proportions of Medicare, Medicaid and private insurance coverage since 1995. In 1995, Medicare paid for 9.4 percent of nursing home expenses, Medicaid for 46.5 percent, and private insurance 3.3 percent. Out-of-pocket nursing home expenses covered 36.7 percent of nursing home expenses (Patel and Rushefsky 1999).

Having looked at expenditure data, we can look at the population likely to need long-term care.

> Nearly 10 million Americans need long-term services and supports to assist them in life's daily activities. Tasks that most people take for granted—getting dressed, getting to the bathroom, walking, shopping, preparing meals—are often impossible or difficult for people with disabling physical or mental conditions to accomplish on their own. For some people, these needs are lifetime needs. Children born with severe physical impairments, developmental disabilities, or a degenerative disease often need care throughout their lives. Teenagers and adults who incur traumatic injuries, such as spinal cord injuries, may need care for decades. The elderly also often need some long-term care services due to decreasing mobility and cognitive functioning that often comes with aging, with needs ranging from simple assistance with bathing and dressing and meal preparation, to more extensive services for those who are disabled by a serious illness, such as a stroke or Alzheimer's disease. In 2000, there were an estimated 9.5 million people with long-term care needs in the U.S., including 6 million elderly and 3.5 million nonelderly. (O'Brien and Elias 2004, 1)

The number of elderly (those sixty-five and over) is growing rapidly, and the segment of the elderly population growing the fastest is eighty-five and older. Thus there are projections that the need for long-term-care services, especially nursing homes, will double over the next twenty to thirty years. The projection is that the nursing home population will increase to 3.6 million people in 2018, while those needing home health care will increase to 7.4 million (Weiner and Illston 1994).

Interestingly, it appears that disabilities among the elderly are declining while they are increasing in the under sixty-five group (Cutler 2001). One reason is that AIDS has become more of a chronic than an acute disease; thus survival times of those suffering from AIDS, especially given the advent of new medical therapies, have increased (Vladeck, Miller, and Clauser 1993). As the baby-boom generation ages, long-term-care needs will increase, though estimates of the dimensions of the problem vary.

The nursing home industry was born of two actions by the federal government. One, in 1950, was an amendment to the Social Security Act prohibiting payments to residents living in institutional settings such as boardinghouses that did not provide health care. The other major development was the establishment of Medicaid. Though Medicaid does not pick up all the nursing home bill, it does pay for the medically indigent in nursing homes. These two developments created a situation in which long-term care became synonymous with nursing homes.

Long-term care can be delivered outside nursing homes, either home- or community-based. Much care for the elderly is given by relatives or friends and volunteers. This is free care and does not figure into the estimates of long-term care expenditures. The value of this free care greatly exceeds spending on more formal long-term care (Anderson and Knickman 2001; Tilly, Goldenson and Kasten 2001). Fifty-seven percent of the elderly needing some type of long-term care receive it from unpaid caregivers and another 36 percent receive both paid and unpaid services (Tilly, Goldenson, and Kasten 2001).

Despite the relatively small number of the elderly in nursing homes, the threat of a nursing home stay is that it can wipe out lifetime savings. In 1988, nursing homes cost an average of $25,000 a year. By 1995, that figure rose to $41,000 a year (Weiner and Stevenson 1998). In 1999, the figure was over $46,600, and for 2002, over $50,000 a year (1999 figure calculated from Health and Human Services 2003, Table 124; 2002 figure calculated from MetLife 2002, 6). By 2004, nursing home costs approached, in some cases, $70,000 ("Nursing Home Cost Hits $70,000 Per Year" 2004). Eligibility for Medicaid requires spending down one's savings. Many who start out in nursing homes as privately paying patients end up as Medicaid recipients. Further, the middle class has increasingly seen Medicaid as a middle-class entitlement, a way to protect life savings. Thus, families transfer funds from the elderly person to other members of the family so that the elderly person can become eligible for Medicaid. While Congress has tightened the rules (states and the HCFA can look at transfers up to three years prior to placement in a nursing home), the problem remains (Fein 1994).

Long-term care thus presents several problems at different levels. At the level of the individual, the problem is financial: being able to afford long-term care, or in some cases being able to arrange it. From the standpoint of government, the problem is the ever-increasing costs of long-term care. From a societal standpoint, the problem is the increasing demand for long-term care in the twenty-first century.

Home and Informal Care

As we have seen above, much care for the elderly is given in the home by relatives, that is, unpaid informal assistance. This includes meals, transportation, and home health care. Only a small minority of the elderly at any one time live in a nursing home. Relatives (mainly spouses and children) caring for the elderly need help and understanding as they deal with work and home conflicts (Tilly, Goldenson, and Kasten 2001).

One way that these informal caregivers, the overwhelming majority of whom are women, can be assisted is by employers (both public and private) in the workplace. They can provide options for their employees that will help them assist their disabled

Table 4.8

Medicare Home Health Care Enrollees and Costs, 1974–1999

	Number of persons served (in thousands)	Total Medicare payments (in thousands of dollars)	Medicare payments per person served ($)	Medicare payments per enrollee ($)
1974	392.7	147,499	3,606	
1980	957.4	770.703	767	26
1985	1,588.6	2,124,312	1,285	66
1990	1,967.1	5,031,248	2,469	142
1995	3,469.4	21,591,139	6,045	616
1999	2,719.7	11,370,780	4,069	344

Source: "Medicare and Medicaid Statistical Supplement" 1997 and 2001.

relatives. Such programs could reduce the chances of institutionalization of the disabled elderly by about a third (General Accounting Office 1994). Such policies are generally not available through small businesses, and there is considerable variation among employers. "Elder care" is also available to public-sector employees at all levels of government. While the options are available, however, they are not widely encouraged or promoted (General Accounting Office 1994). The potential cost of such programs is a limiting factor. A more recent General Accounting Office (GAO, now Government Accountability Office) report (2001) on financing of long-term care made no mention of employee elderly care benefits. A search of the Employee Benefits Research Institute (EBRI) Web site conducted by the authors also found no mention of such programs.

An alternative to informal home care and nursing homes (institutionalization) is the use of home health care agencies. Under Part A, Medicare will pay for services if the enrollee is "under the care of a physician, confined to home, and need[s] skilled nursing services on an intermittent basis" (Moon 1996, 79; see also Centers for Medicare and Medicaid Services 2004a, 27) Since 1989, Medicare has, after a Supreme Court decision, relaxed eligibility requirements for home health care. The result has been a massive increase in use of services and increased costs. Medicare will pay 100 percent of home health care visits and 80 percent of durable equipment costs (Centers for Medicare and Medicaid Services 2004a). Table 4.8 presents the data on use and costs. As can be seen from the table, there was a massive increase in use and an even larger increase in costs. The liberalization of the home health care benefit led to an increase in the number of home health care agencies, particularly by proprietary (for-profit) agencies (General Accounting Office 1997). The Government Accountability Office has found, in a series of reports, that overpayments (even under the new system, see below) have been made, that service complaints have not been adequately handled, and oversight by state and federal agencies has been weak (see, for example, Government Accountability Office 2002, 2004a).

The major change that occurred in regard to home health care agencies came in the Balanced Budget Act of 1997. It called for a prospective payment system, similar to what already existed for hospital and physician services, for nursing homes, home health care agencies, and hospice services. The effect of the BBA can be seen in Table 4.8, with the significant decrease in both enrollees and costs.

A related issue concerns *hospices*. A hospice is a service that provides specialized care for people who are near death. Hospices can provide counseling to both the patient and the family, as well as drugs, medical supplies, and a variety of services. Hospice services can be delivered in hospitals, or nursing homes, or at home. To be eligible for Medicare reimbursement, the patient must be diagnosed as within six months of dying. Hospice services are also one of the fastest-growing components of Medicare, costing about $6.3 billion in FY 2004 (Centers for Medicare and Medicaid Services n.d.).

Long-Term-Care Policy Alternatives

One policy alternative increasingly investigated is long-term-care (LTC) insurance. LTC is an indemnity type policy. It pays a certain amount ($100–$200) per day that the recipient is in a facility, usually with some limits on how long the policyholder will be covered (Congressional Budget Office 2004). Insurance could be sold to the elderly, say when they become sixty-five years old, or to younger people where they work so that a reserve fund could be established.

The long-term-care insurance market is relatively new and still small. The product was almost nonexistent before 1986; by 1998, some 5.8 million policies had been sold (Tilly, Goldenson, and Kasten 2001). Janet Shikles, of the General Accounting Office, testified before Congress that the long-term-care insurance market looked like the "medigap" insurance market prior to congressional reforms. "Early Medigap policies varied greatly in value and coverage. State regulation was inconsistent, with sales and market abuses a recurring problem" (Shikles 1991, 2).

The problem Shikles identified is that policies vary as to what is covered, whether prior hospitalization is necessary, inflation adjustments for coverage, amount of premiums, increases in premiums, and length of time the policy is in effect. A study by the Brookings Institution found that only wealthier people are likely to buy long-term-care insurance and that such insurance would reduce total nursing home care costs by 7 to 20 percent in the next century (Rice, Thomas, and Weissert 1989). Reinforcing this view is the expense of long-term care insurance, which varies by age and coverage. There are four basic types of long-term insurance plans (Tilly, Goldenson, and Kasten 2001). The first is the base plan, which simply pays a stated sum per day. The second is a nonforfeiture plan, which provides some protection in the event the policyholder decides to drop the policy. The third provides protection against inflation, and the fourth combines the inflation and nonforfeiture plans. The base plan for a person age forty in 1997 cost $274 a year. The combined plan cost that same person $770 a year. For a sixty-five-year-old, the same plans cost, respectively, $1,007 and

$2,305. Finally, for a seventy-nine-year-old, the yearly premiums are, respectively, $4,100 and $7,022 (Tilly, Goldenson, and Kasten 2001).

There are two reasons for the high premiums. First, unlike regular health insurance, long-term-care insurance is sold to individuals rather than to groups (even though it may be available through an employer), and thus administrative costs are high. The population that buys it is limited generally to those sixty-five and older, the group most likely to need the insurance. Thus, the insurance is sold to high-risk individuals (Weiner and Illston 1994).

Thus, while private long-term-care insurance has the potential for alleviating some of the cost problems, the long-term-care issue has not been fully dealt with. It is not yet a mature policy and requires considerable standardization.

There are several possible solutions to the problem of financing long-term care. One proposal is to combine long-term-care insurance with Medicaid. Individuals could buy the policy and then turn to Medicaid when funds run out. Such policies would be more affordable than solely private LTC insurance policies. Medicaid (state and federal governments) saves as well because it does not have to pay for long-term care until the private insurance runs out (Perin 1994).

Another possibility, recommended by the Forum for State Health Policy Leadership, is that the long-term-care system try to accommodate the desire of consumers (patients) to have home-based health services and to be independent, and should place greater reliance on private funding sources than on Medicaid (Fox-Grage 1997; Weiner and Stevenson 1998).

If LTC insurance is increasingly the wave of the future (and given state and federal efforts to limit Medicaid expenditures, particularly their impact on state budgets; see chapter 3), there is another policy alternative that would make long-term care insurance less expensive: tax credits. Tax credits have become an increasingly prominent policy tool in both health care and other policy areas (for a discussion of tax credits and health care reform, see chapter 10). Thirty-eight states offer such tax credits, many more generous than the federal government offers (calculated from AARP 2003).

President George W. Bush has proposed a tax deduction for the purchasing of LTC insurance. The proposal would allow both individual premiums and any employer contributions to be deducted. Further, the administration proposed allowing an addition personal exemption on an individual's income tax for those taking care of an elderly relative (Park 2004). While this appears to be an interesting idea, there are also problems. The tax deduction is most likely to help those at the higher income brackets because the deduction is most valuable at those higher levels. For those who do not pay federal income tax or whose highest marginal tax bracket is low (10 or 15 percent), there would be no benefit. Thus, those who most likely need the help are the least likely to get it from this plan (Park 2004). Further, in the event of a tax reform that simplifies the system, tax credits such as this one might be eliminated.

Feder, Komisar, and Niefeld (2000) argue that while the logic of long-term insurance for meeting the needs of the elderly is strong, the reality is that there are questions about the adequacy of coverage and that tax subsidies raise equity issues. Their preferred solution, therefore, is expanded public support:

> Expanded social insurance is an alternative to public support for private insurance. For example, Medicare could be expanded to include long-term care, entitling all Americans, regardless of income, to some insurance protection should they become greatly impaired. However, investment of resources to sustain the social insurance we have (Medicare and Social Security), let alone the social insurance we might have, is subject to considerable debate. Despite the nation's current prosperity and underlying wealth [they are writing in 2000], our willingness to redistribute resources to reflect the aging of the population seems to be in question. (Feder, Komisar, and Niefeld 2000, 53)

Under current economic and political conditions, expansion of Medicare for increased support of long-term care is improbable.

Prescriptions and Change

As previously noted, Medicare, when it was adopted and throughout most of its existence, had some important gaps. We have already discussed cost sharing and liability and long-term care. The other major gap was in prescription medications. Medicare pays for such medications while the Medicare recipient is in a hospital or a skilled-nursing home. It did not, traditionally, pay for outpatient prescription drugs. The 1988 Medicare Catastrophic Coverage Act did, as we have seen, provide for the addition of such a benefit. But because of the politics surrounding it (see Marmor 2000; Oberlander 2003), the law was repealed the next year. In 2003 a new law was enacted that provided a prescription drug benefit, plus much more. The politics surrounding that new law and the policy implications of what that law has done represent the greatest change in Medicare since the 1997 Balanced Budget Act and possibly since the origin of Medicare itself (see Oliver, Lee, and Lipton 2004; Rushefsky 2004).

The Need for Prescription Drug Coverage

Before we look at the history of drug coverage proposals and the 2003 proposals in particular, we should examine why such an addition to Medicare was necessary. Much of the biomedical revolution in the late twentieth and early twenty-first centuries was in the area of pharmaceuticals. One measure of the revolution in the use of pharmaceuticals can be seen in national health expenditure data (see Table 2.4). As can be seen, overall spending on prescription medications rose fairly rapidly during all the years shown in Table 2.4, but especially in the 1999–2003 period. For 2002, spending on prescription medications accounted for 11 percent of all national health care expenditures, but also represented16 percent of the *increase* in expenditures in 2002 (Levit et al. 2004). Further, one set of projections suggests that spending on prescription medications will increase from $162.4 billion in 2002 (10.5 percent of total spending) to $519.8 billion in 2013 (15.8 percent of total spending) (calculated from Heffler et al. 2004).

One reason this is important is that the elderly population (sixty-five plus) makes higher use of prescription medications because they are more likely to have chronic conditions that require such use. Xu's (2003) analysis finds that the nonelderly are more likely to rate their health as good or excellent than the elderly. The elderly are also more likely to have chronic conditions such as cancer, asthma, arthritis, and so forth than the nonelderly (HIV/AIDS is the one area where the younger group has a higher incidence of chronic conditions). Of course, spending on prescription medications is not uniformly distributed among the elderly; average spending is misleading. Those with fewer or no chronic conditions will spend considerably less than those who have chronic or more serious conditions (Steinberg et al. 2000). This spending pattern is supported in a study by Thomas, Ritter, and Walleck (2001). They found that those with high prescription drug use accounted for a significant and growing proportion of total health care spending. In 1997, those spending more than $3,000 a year on prescription medications accounted for 20 percent of total health care spending; by 2000, they accounted for 42 percent. Putting it in a slightly different manner, those spending more than $6,000 a year on prescription medications made up 1.7 percent of the elderly population but accounted for 10.5 percent of total health care spending (Thomas, Ritter, and Walleck 2001). Another reason for projected increases in prescription spending by the elderly is demographic. There will be more of them as the baby boomer generation begins to retire.

Further, studies have shown that those who have no insurance or poor insurance coverage for prescription medications are less likely to use them or adhere to the prescribed regimen than those who do (Mojtabai and Olfson 2003). Seniors with chronic illnesses, such as diabetes and hypertension, who have no prescription drug coverage are more likely to skip using their medications than similar seniors who do have such coverage (Newman 2004).

Of course, many seniors do have prescription drug coverage of some sort (see Table 4.9 which reflects 2003 data), but coverage differs greatly from plan to plan and such coverage has been also affected by the 2003 legislation, as discussed below. A couple of points need to be made about Table 4.9. First, it shows the breakdown for Medicare beneficiaries who are not institutionalized (e.g., not in nursing homes), about 33 million people. Second, even though the majority of beneficiaries have some kind of prescription medication coverage, the coverage may be limited. Finally, the largest category, retirees who have employer-sponsored plans, is shrinking. In 1996, the percentage of those sixty-five to sixty-nine years old with employer-sponsored plans was 45.5 percent, with 40.1 percent having drug coverage. By 2000, the numbers had shrunk to 39.4 percent and 35.4 percent, respectively (Cooper and How 2004;1 Stuart et al. 2003). This represents a decline, over five years, of 13.4 percent for health insurance coverage and 11.7 percent for drug coverage.

Additionally, those without prescription drug coverage spend more out of pocket than those who do have such coverage. Table 4.10 presents the data for 2002: the average total payments and average out-of-pocket payments for prescription medications, by plan and by beneficiary. Several things stand out from this table.

Table 4.9

Sources of Prescription Drug Coverage, 2003

Type of plan	Percentage of Medicare beneficiaries
Employer-sponsored	34
Medicare HMO	17
Medicaid	11
Medigap	10
Other public	6
No coverage	22

Source: Patricia Newman, "The New Medicare Prescription Drug Benefit: An Overview." The Henry J. Kaiser Family Foundation, February 2004. This information was printed with permission of the Henry J. Kaiser Family Foundation. The Kaiser Family Foundation, based in Menlo Park, California, is a nonprofit, independent national health care philanthropy and is not associated with Kaiser Permanente or Kaiser Industries.

Table 4.10

Average Spending on Prescription Drugs by Medicare Beneficiary and by Source of Coverage, 2002

	Total spending	Average out-of-pocket
All beneficiaries	$2,322	$999
Medicaid	$2,864	$510
Employer/retiree	$2,775	$880
Other	$2,513	$761
Medigap/MC+	$2,091	$1,094
No coverage	$1,356	$1,356

Source: Kaiser Family Foundation 2003.

First, those with the highest average spending levels are either covered by Medicaid or by employer-retiree plans. Second, those without any coverage spend the least. Third, those without coverage spend the most money out–of pocket.

Another aspect of the history and debate over a Medicare prescription drug benefit is the cost of the drugs themselves, particularly to seniors. Families USA (2003) argued that the growth in spending for prescription drugs (overall, not just for seniors) is a function of three factors: the very rapidly rising cost of the drugs, greater utilization of prescription medications, and greater use of newer and more expensive medications. Their study of the fifty most prescribed drugs used by seniors showed they increased much faster than the overall inflation rate. According to their study, the annual average wholesale cost for these top fifty drugs rose from $960 in January 1996 to $1,439 by January 2003. Their 2004 study (Families USA 2004a) examined the top thirty drugs used by seniors. It found that during the January 2003–January 2004 period, the price of those thirty drugs rose by 6.5 percent, compared to 1.5 percent for inflation (measured by the consumer price index, or CPI). This is a rate 4.3 times faster than inflation.

The Road to Change

The Clinton administration made two efforts to include prescription drug coverage within Medicare. The first came in the context of the Clinton proposal for national health insurance, the Health Security Act. The proposal called for it to be included as part of Part B and to raise the Part B premium by $11 a month. It included a $250 deductible, with a coinsurance above the deductible of 20 percent, and a cap on coinsurance of $1,000 (Oliver, Lee, and Lipton 2004). The failure of the Clinton plan (or any other) to be passed during this period (1993–94) meant that the proposed benefit was still missing.

Near the end of the Clinton administration and as the 2000 elections approached, there was renewed activity over the benefit. The new Clinton proposal was considerably different from the 1993 version. Of course, the politics had changed and now the benefit was a stand-alone proposal, rather than part of a more encompassing one. The proposal would have created a Part D (Part C was the Medicare+Choice program created in the 1997 BBA). It called for a $24-a-month premium for 2002 (which was when the benefit would begin), rising to $44 a month six years later. There was no deductible and beneficiaries were to pay half of their drug costs, up to a a maximum of $2,500. After the first $5,000 of costs, the beneficiary would pay the full amount. There would have been assistance for low-income beneficiaries and the benefit would have been administered by regional pharmacy benefit management (PBM) companies. The cost was estimated at $118 billion over a ten-year period (Oliver, Lee, and Lipton 2004). The inclusion of private pharmacy benefit plans was due to the advent of managed care. Such plans were used by large employers or managed care organizations, with the idea that this would lead to efficiencies and cost savings (Medicare Watch 1999).

Some important perspectives on the Clinton proposal crop up in the 2003 legislation. The Medicare Watch (1999) analysis suggests that the pharmaceutical industry was not very supportive of the proposal. While the new benefit would have likely increased the use of their products (the intent of the program), it might also, as discussed earlier, have led to price controls.

There was also concern about how the proposal would affect employer-retiree plans. The fear was that such a new proposal would lead employers to drop such coverage, putting more pressure on Medicare. The Clinton proposal contained subsidies for employers to continue such coverage (Medicare Watch 1999). Medigap plans would have had to be restructured because some of them contained a prescription drug package (Medicare Watch 1999).

Medicare HMOs would have benefited from the new plan. Because the original or regular Medicare program would have had the new benefit, payments to HMOs would have increased. Therefore, they could have offered a more generous program and attracted more beneficiaries.

The Heritage Foundation (a conservative think tank) found much to dislike in the Clinton proposals. Frogue and Moffit (2000) described four specific problems with the proposal. First, beneficiaries with very expensive medication needs would still have faced serious costs, given the $5,000 ceiling on benefits. A second problem was that those at the lower end of the wage scale would have been paying for benefits for wealthy retired people. A third problem was that the proposal would have provided incentives for employers to drop their retired-employee health care system. Fourth, Frogue and Moffit thought that the actual cost of the program for seniors would be higher than estimated. Fifth, the Clinton plan called for only one regional pharmacy benefit management company that would offer plans. This would limit the competition that Heritage and others thought crucial to modernizing Medicare.

For Frogue and Moffit, the problems with Medicare were twofold. One was the solvency of the trust fund. According to them, the trust was going to run out of money soon. More importantly, the Clinton plan left the bureaucratic structure in place.

> Perhaps even more seriously, Medicare is evolving from a health insurance program for future retirees into a bureaucratic leviathan that undermines the personal liberty and privacy of patients and the professional independence and integrity of physicians. The program's highly centralized regulatory structure is evolving rapidly into a massive system of bureaucratic control over virtually every aspect of the financing and delivery of health services to America's retirees. (Frogue and Moffit 2000, 3)

Republicans began offering their version of a plan and presidential politics became involved. The Republican plan was based on subsidizing private insurance companies that would then offer drug benefits to Medicare recipients (Pear 2000). Both Vice President Al Gore and Texas Governor George W. Bush offered plans during the 2000 presidential campaign. The Gore plan was essentially the Clinton plan. Gore's plan would allow Medicare to negotiate prices with the pharmaceutical companies (Serafini 2000).

The Bush plan was a more modest one that relied on the states for the first four years of the program to offer a benefit to their seniors. The plan included payments to the states and subsidies for low-income recipients. States would participate in the program on a voluntary basis. The more permanent program would be based on private plans offering the benefit and subsidies for low-income seniors. Federal spending would be capped at $6,000 per beneficiary ("The Bush Prescription Drug Plan" 2000). The idea was that competition among the plans would be able to control costs. Further, the goal of the Bush plan was to move more Medicare recipients into HMOs (Dao 2000). Serafini (2000, 2980) described the goals of the Bush plan as follows:

> Overall, Bush has focused on making Medicare less of a one-size-fits-all program. He wants to strengthen Medicare by providing more choice and more private-sector alternatives. In particular, he supports the idea of seniors opening medical savings accounts— tax-free accounts from which they can pay their health care bills. And, after they spent a certain amount of money in any one year, a catastrophic health insurance policy would kick in.

Bush offered a version of his plan after assuming the presidency. Sitting in the background was the Bipartisan Commission on the Future of Medicare that favored a premium-support plan (Toner 2001). Premium-support plans would give Medicare recipients a certain amount of money from which to purchase a health care plan on their own. Other terms for these types of plans are vouchers and defined-contribution plans. Such a change would dramatically alter the nature of Medicare. Proposals by congressional Democrats envisioned a more expansive plan, costing about double the Bush plan ($300 plus billion) over a ten-year period (Pear 2001a).

In July 2001 President Bush presented his Medicare proposal. It included a discount card transitional program and changing Medicare to be more like private insurance plans (i.e., HMOs) (Kaisernetwork.org 2001). The principles of the plan, similar to what was finally passed, were:

- The private sector should play a major role in delivering drug benefits and managing drug costs, but the federal government must provide substantial subsidies for all beneficiaries.
- Elderly people should be able to choose the company that, under the administration's plan for an overhaul, would manage their pharmacy benefits. No company should have a monopoly; there should be at least two "pharmacy benefit managers" in each region.
- The federal government should set an overall limit on the out-of-pocket pharmaceutical expenses of Medicare beneficiaries.
- People content with their existing Medicare coverage could keep it. The government would pay employers to continue drug coverage as part of retiree health benefits.
- The government should, for the first time, make payments to H.M.O.'s to cover the cost of providing drug benefits. Congress should make other changes to reverse the exodus of H.M.O.'s from Medicare. (Pear 2001b)

The push for a prescription benefit took a back seat after the September 11, 2001, terrorist attacks against the United States. Democrats and Republicans disagreed on the specifics and the focus turned to the response to the terrorist attacks and the war on terrorism (Welch 2001). Additionally, HMOs continued dropping their participation in Medicare, claiming that their reimbursements were too low (see, for example, Pear 2001c). Many HMOs that stayed in the program either eliminated the prescription drug benefit or severely restricted it (Kaisernetwork.org 2002).

In 2002, Bush offered a new version of his plan, including discount cards, assistance to states that offer help to their low-income seniors, and a modest plan directed at low-income seniors. The plan would cost an estimated $77 billion over ten years and cover about three million Medicare recipients. Another $190 billion would be used to reform Medicare (B. Feder 2002). That started a concern about whether there was sufficient money in the Bush plan for the prescription drug benefit. Both congressional Democrats and Republicans argued that it was not nearly enough. Numbers between $300 and $700 billion were bandied about as more appropriate ("In 'Rare' Agreement" 2002). In 2002, congressional Republicans offered a bill that would cost an estimated $350 billion over ten years, would employ discount cards during the transitional period, cover low-income seniors, and provide coverage for very high costs for others. The plan would rely on private insurance companies ("GOP to Unveil Drug-Benefit Plan" 2002). Democrats offered a more generous bill (Pear 2002). Throughout 2002 and 2003, Bush continued to push for the legislation (see, for example, Guggenheim 2002). A House Republican bill contained increased payments to a variety of providers ("House GOP Unveils Final Version" 2002).

Apart from differences in the costs and generosity of the House Republican and Democratic proposals ($350 billion for the Republican proposal, $800 billion for the Democratic proposal), how the benefits would be delivered indicated philosophical differences about the role of government in general and Medicare in particular. The Democrats preferred that the benefit be part of Medicare, similar to Part B. Republicans wanted the benefits to be delivered by private insurance companies, on the grounds that they were more efficient than government programs and competition would help control costs (Toner 2002). While the House succeeded in passing a Republican bill, the Senate, controlled by Democrats, was not able to pass the legislation (Hook 2002; Oliver, Lee, and Lipton 2004).

A Bill Becomes a Law

That set the stage for action in 2003. Fueled by the war on terrorism and the coming war with Iraq, Republicans regained control of the Senate that they had lost in 2001 (thanks to the defection of Vermont Senator Jim Jeffords). With control of both houses of Congress and the presidency in Republican hands, it was inevitable that a Republican version of a Medicare prescription drug benefit would pass. Republican control of the House, though not large, was firm. Republican control of the Senate was much smaller. Also, given the rules of the Senate, where minorities have a greater ability to thwart a small majority, the House and Senate would pass somewhat different legislation. And it would take a fair amount of finagling to produce the final bill. The Bush administration position was that it wanted a bill before 2004 and was willing to approve almost anything (Oliver, Lee, and Lipton 2004). One important aspect of the Bush proposal was that only those who opted for the private plan would be offered a drug benefit. Both Republicans and Democrats opposed this position and it was not in the final legislation (Oliver, Lee, and Lipton 2004).

Both the House and Senate versions were passed in June 2003. Because the two versions were different, a conference committee was necessary to reconcile differences. Negotiations took some four months and required considerable compromises. Oliver, Lee, and Lipton (2004, 34) note that "sweeteners" were placed in the bill to help it assuage different groups. These included some provision for obtaining benefits while staying in regular Medicare. Various interest groups also made out well, including providers, drug companies, and employers (Oliver, Lee, and Lipton 2004).

In order to gain passage, at least three unusual maneuvers were necessary. The first had to do with how the conference committee operated. Members of both houses are appointed to the committee by the respective house leaders from both parties. The normal "Congress makes a law" view of how things are done is that there would be negotiations among the members. However, Republicans, who controlled Congress, held their own set of negotiations with almost no Democratic input. Then the resultant compromise was presented to the entire conference committee, with majority Republican control, and approved by the committee (Cohen, Victor, and Baumann 2004). One of the strongest supporters of the original Senate bill was Edward Kennedy (D-MA). After the compromise he found that the changes were so significant that he could no longer support it.

One could see the differences in the titles of the three bills. The Senate bill was entitled the "Prescription Drug and Medicare Improvement Act of 2003." The House bill was entitled the "Medicare Prescription Drug and Modernization Act of 2003." The bill produced by the conference committee, the final version, was entitled the "Medicare Prescription Drug, Improvement, and Modernization Act of 2003" (Health Policy Alternatives, Inc. 2003).

As one example of the change from the House and Senate bills to the conference bill, consider the status of dual eligibles, low-income seniors who were also eligible for Medicaid. Under the Senate bill, those dual eligibles receiving coverage under a Medicaid program would not be eligible for the Medicare Part D coverage. Under the House bill, dual eligibles could enroll in Part D coverage. State obligations to provide drug coverage would be gradually eliminated and states could require dual eligibles to enroll in Part D. Under the conference bill, states would no longer be reimbursed for drugs covered under Part D (the states would have to transfer funds into Part D [Caplan and Housman 2004]). In essence, dual eligibles would only be able to get coverage under Part D (Health Policy Alternatives, Inc. 2003).

A second intriguing manipulation concerned the vote in the House on the conference bill. Normally floor votes in the House take fifteen minutes, according to House rules. However, the leadership did not have sufficient votes to pass the bill during that fifteen-minute period. In a virtually unprecedented maneuver, they kept voting open for three hours, searching for votes (Cohen, Victor, and Baumann 2004).

A third and related element was how the leadership apparently got one of their votes. Nick Smith's (R-MI) son was campaigning for office to replace the retiring congressman. Smith asserted that he changed his "no" vote to "yes" after threats and promises of campaign assistance by Tom DeLay (R-TX) (see Green 2005) for his son seeking to replace him. Smith later said that it did not happen, but there is every reason to believe he was offered a bribe on the floor of the House (Center for American Progress 2004; Chait 2004).[8]

The fourth event was related to the estimated costs of the prescription benefit. When Governor Bush began proposing a prescription benefit, the costs were quite modest. As president, Bush's proposal was in the $170 billion range. After he agreed to sign a proposal, his one condition was that it not cost more than $400 billion over a ten-year period, and those were the estimates used in considering the bill. However, an actuary for the Centers for Medicare and Medicaid Services (CMS) estimated that the bill might cost as much as $540 billion over the ten-year period. The importance of this estimate is that conservative Republicans were unhappy about the original $400 billion estimate. The extra $140 billion in estimated costs might have resulted in more Republican votes against the bill. Tom Scully, then the administrator of CMS, ordered the actuary not to submit his estimate to Congress and threatened to fire him if he did (Center for American Progress 2004). So Congress considered the bill with the smaller estimate.

A last example of manipulation took place after the legislation was passed and signed. The administration was concerned about criticism of the new law and also wanted credit for having passed a prescription benefit. It hired a lobbyist to promote the law through advertising using public funds. Part of the campaign included a video story sent to local television stations that was used as if it were actual news (i.e., appearing to be a reporter). According to the Government Accountability Office, this was illegal (Chait 2004).

What Is in the Law

The Interim Phase: Discount Cards

The Medicare Prescription Drug, Improvement, and Modernization Act of 2003 (or Medicare Modernization Act, abbreviated as MMA) is a complex piece of legislation. The first portion of the new law is the discount card program. This is one program, as mentioned above, that President Bush has strongly supported (Stevenson 2004). Seniors will select from an array of discount cards approved by the CMS and offered by pharmaceutical companies, pharmacies, and health plans. This portion of the law began on June 1, 2004, and lasted through January 2006, when the full prescription plan will be in force. The cards cost about $30 a year and there is a $600 subsidy each year for low-income seniors.

The discount card program has already raised some questions and issues. First, the program promised a 10 to15 percent (or more) discount. But will seniors really save? Increases in pharmaceutical prices diminished some of the discount ("Drugmakers Benefit Most" 2004). Further, it appears that seniors who either import drugs from Canada or have access to Veterans Affairs benefits will do better than using the cards (MacKeen 2004).

But there are a couple of other features of the transitional discount card program that will reappear in the permanent program beginning in 2006. First, seniors have an enrollment period during which they select their card. Once enrolled, they cannot change cards until the next open enrollment period (2005). This makes a certain amount of sense and is an integral part of choice-based plans, such as the Federal Employees Health Benefits Program (FEHPB), the California Public Employees' Retirement System (CalPERS), and any kind of defined-contribution or premium-support proposal, going back to Alain Enthoven's Consumer-Choice Health Plan, which he is still advocating (Enthoven 1980, 2003). Health plans need to have some stability in their membership. However, the companies offering the cards can change the prices of the drugs offered or even what drugs are offered on a weekly basis. Consumers can only pick one card. Therefore, they might enroll in a discount card plan that offers needed medications, only to find out later that the medications are not offered anymore.

The second feature of the cards that will also affect the 2006 plan is the amount of choice available. Seniors are directed to the Medicare Web site, Medicare.org, and then asked what medications they use. The site then displays the choices. We decided to explore the issue of choice in 2004. One of the coauthors uses two medications, one for sinus problems and one for cholesterol. In our area there were more than thirty choices. Too much choice is not necessarily good. Further, there were issues related to the accuracy of the data on the Web site and prices were also subject to change.

The impact and popularity of the discount program is mixed. A summer 2004 survey found that most seniors felt that the discount cards did not save them sufficient money and were confusing to use (Kaiser Family Foundation/Harvard School of Public Health 2004). According to the survey, 9 percent had already signed up, another 17 percent were planning on signing up, and 60 percent had no plans to sign up. Even then, the numbers are a bit misleading. For example, in September 2004, Medicare announced that it was sending discount cards (that is, automatically enrolling them) to some 1.8 million low-income Medicare beneficiaries (O'Dell 2004).

One complaint about the discount card program, ironically, is that there may be too much choice. That is, seniors may be faced with so many choices of discount card plans that they will be unable to make a choice at all or make poor choices (Pear and Toner 2004; see also Schwartz 2003; Solomon 2004). According to a December 2004 Government Accountability Office report (2004b), there have been considerable difficulties with the Medicare hotline established under the new law. The GAO report found that the hotline operators gave correct responses to only 69 percent of their test inquiries. The operators, who work for private companies, were not sufficiently well trained, nor were the scripts they were using pretested for their effectiveness.

The New Drug Benefit (Part D)

The second part of the Medicare legislation is the drug benefit itself, the new Part D. This will be available to seniors on a "voluntary" basis. Voluntary is used advisedly, because those who do not meet the exceptions (for example, being part of an employee-retirement program that offers a prescription drug benefit at least as good as the Medicare one) and not enrolled by January 2006 face a 1 percent penalty for each month they do not enroll if they choose to do so later.

Seniors will have some choices to make even before they get to choose a plan. To receive the Part D benefits, seniors will either have to join a preferred provider organization (PPO) or HMO and get all their health care, including prescription drugs, from them. Alternatively, seniors could stay with Medicare but enroll in a private insurance plan that only offers a prescription drug benefit. No such plans existed at the time of the law's enactment, though the plans did make their appearance in the months leading up to implementation of the program. The third alternative, of course, is not to enroll in Part D. As indicated above, some will already have a plan through a former employer. Others may just not join a plan. This is a bit of a modification from the Bush plan that would have required all seniors who wanted the prescription benefit to join an HMO or PPO.

Seniors will pay a monthly premium and a deductible. Then, in a complex architecture, benefits rise and fall and rise again depending on the level of spending on the part of the individual. For example, there is the famous "doughnut hole," between $2,250 and $5,100, where the seniors would pay all the costs. These various levels are indexed and will continuously rise over the years (Altman 2004). The reason for the complex structure was to try to keep the costs of the program within the $400 billion cap that President Bush insisted upon (even though the administration knew that it would cost much more than that). Subsidies are available for low-income seniors. Whether seniors will be better or worse off under the new program than they are now depends upon what their circumstances are. Those who have particularly high prescription drug expenses and low-income families are likely to experience genuine benefits (Altman 2004; Serafini 2004a).

Seniors will have a choice of at least two plans, and formularies must include at least two drugs from each category. In January 2005, an advisory panel issued a recommendation for the formulary that contained 146 categories of drugs (Pear 2005a). In the event that no plans are available in a particular area, Medicare itself will provide the benefit, the "fallback" provision (Oliver, Lee, and Lipton 2004). Medicare+Choice has been transformed into Medicare Advantage (Part C). PPOs are included and all plans must offer a drug benefit.

One interesting part of the new drug benefit, because of the politics involved, concerns dual enrollees and the states. Under the new law, the states have to pay Medicare for the prescription drug costs of covering those enrolled in both Medicare and Medicaid. Some states have calculated that they will be paying for a federal service and will pay more than they spent on the benefit for their enrollees. As a result, some states have decided not to make the payments. For example, Texas Governor Rick Perry, President Bush's Republican successor, vetoed legislation in 2005 that would have appropriated money for that purpose (Pear 2005b; see also Smith, Gifford, and Kramer 2005). The possible confrontation between the two levels of government should be interesting to watch in future years.

Subsidies for the Favored

Another part of the legislation involves subsidies and other favors. One set of favors concerns provider reimbursement. Historically, the federal government has tried restraining the costs of Medicare by focusing on payments to providers. Doctors and hospitals are on fee schedules that have been the subject of negotiations over the years. Most of the time, the federal government has reduced payments to providers.

For example, the 1997 Balanced Budget Act significantly reduced payments to providers. This has created a problem where physicians are becoming more reluctant to accept Medicare patients. The 2003 Medicare law includes increases, rather than the proposed decreases, in payments to providers (Altman 2004).

A second related feature is centered around health plans, such as PPOs and HMOs. Recall that in the late 1990s and early 2000s, some HMOs exited the Medicare field, claiming that they were losing money on Medicare recipients. The new legislation provides for additional payments to those plans, some $14 billion. As Oliver, Lee, and Lipton (2004) point out, this means that these health care plans would be getting more per Medicare enrollee than Medicare on average would normally spend.

Third, employers who offer health care benefits for their retirees would also get subsidies. The subsidy amounts to about $81 billion and is intended to provide an incentive for employers to maintain their coverage. Interestingly, employers who reduce their coverage would still get the subsidy (Antos and Calfee 2004).

If there is an overall winner in the legislation, it is the pharmaceutical industry. As noted previously, the pharmaceutical industry had historically opposed the addition of a drug benefit for fear that it would lead to price controls. The MMA alleviates all its fears. Under the law, Medicare cannot negotiate drug prices. The states do engage in such negotiation under Medicaid, as does the Department of Veterans Affairs, but Medicare cannot. It will be up to the private plans to engage in the negotiations. Further, the legislation bans the reimportation of drugs from other countries. Under the law, the Food and Drug Administration will explore drug importation from Canada (Oliver, Lee, and Lipton 2004). Chapter 6 includes a discussion of drug reimportation.

Transforming Medicare Via the MMA

There are also some important provisions to the MMA that are very troubling, especially for those who strongly support Medicare. Marmor (2004) refers to various provisions of MMA as "the darker side." Park et al. (2003, 1) refer to the legislation as "troubling." Oberlander (2003) views the process leading to the MMA as the end of the consensus about what Medicare was supposed to be. These provisions seemed designed to accomplish President Bush's purpose of transforming Medicare into something else. What are these provisions?

Some have already been mentioned. The subsidies to private plans are one example (Park et al. 2003). Park et al. note that, for various reasons, private plans are already paid at higher rates than Medicare pays. The additional subsidy would mean that "private plans [are] being paid approximately 25 percent more than Medicare fee-for-service pays for comparable services to comparable benefits" (Park et al. 2003, 2). This would put Medicare at a competitive disadvantage and provide an incentive for people to move from traditional Medicare to private plans. The penalty for those eligible but not choosing to participate in Part D is another example of this. That, after all, was one of the goals of President Bush's initial offering.

Is that such a bad thing? After all, advocates of private plans, such as the president and the Heritage Institute, tout the virtues of the private sector and private plans. Government programs, they argue, are inherently inefficient.

One quick reply is that if private plans are so efficient and provide competition to Medicare, they would be more attractive to Medicare recipients and would not need additional subsidies. Further, there is the experience, mentioned above, of private plans leaving the Medicare+Choice program. Nor have private plans done a particularly good job of controlling costs. The Federal Employees Health Benefits Program and CalPERS have experienced double-digit increases in their premiums.

Another element of MMA is the premium-support program. This was a policy favored by a majority of members of the National Bipartisan Commission on the Future of Medicare and is very much related, historically, to the Consumer-Choice Health Plan. Under the MMA, six demonstration projects will be undertaken beginning in 2010 (Park et al. 2003). Under the law, recipients in the six areas will have a choice of an array of plans, including traditional Medicare. The catch here is that Medicare will establish an average benchmark cost for plans in the area. If the cost of the plan chosen is more than the average, then the recipient would have to pay the difference between the plan's costs and the average cost (Park et al. 2003).

This provision creates the market-type conditions that managed competition advocates, such as Enthoven, laud, and can be seen in FEHBP and CalPERS. But the provision would again undermine Medicare and help lead the transition to a different form, characterized by the dominance of private plans. The reason for this is the same reason that there has been a problem with Medicare+Choice. Healthier recipients are more likely to choose a private plan and sicker recipients more likely to remain with Medicare. If that is the case, then the average costs for Medicare are likely to increase much more than for the private plans. This is another way, as Park et al. (2003) point out, that the game is rigged toward the private sector. Indeed, they write:

> In short, while the idea of introducing more competition into Medicare through the expanded use of private plans has been promoted as a "reform" that can restrain rising Medicare costs, the reality is that the legislation *increases* Medicare costs by overpaying private plans in order to induce more beneficiaries to enroll in them. Examination of the details of the legislation indicates that the ideological goal of privatizing more of Medicare trumped the stated goal of using "competition" to restrain the rate of growth in Medicare costs. (Park et al. 2003, 5)

The advocacy group Families USA argues that relying on private plans is not a good idea for several reasons (Families USA 2004b). The experience with HMOs and Medicare+Choice shows that private plans cost Medicare money rather than saving it money. Families USA also points out that private plans have not been very reliable, with a number of them pulling out of the market. Further, recipients in private plans have experienced increasing out-of-pocket costs, especially for those in poorer health (i.e., those more likely to need health care services). Over the 1999–2002 period, healthier patients saw their out-of-pocket costs increase by 71 percent, while sicker patients saw their out-of-pocket costs increase by 116 percent, more than 60 percent higher than the healthier group. Families USA also said that recipients in private plans tend to be more dissatisfied with their plan than those in traditional Medicare. Finally, the group points out that private plans tend not to offer plans in rural areas. These findings are supported by empirical data, comparing Medicare beneficiaries with those under age sixty-five with private insurance. Medicare recipients are more pleased with the program and find it more stable (Davis et al. 2002). One problem that arises with premium-support proposals is a similar one that has arisen with the transitional discount cards and the prescription drug benefit: the question of choice. Sicker seniors will have a more difficult time making good choices than healthier ones (Biles, Dallek, and Nicholas 2004).

A third disconcerting element is the provision for health savings accounts (HSAs). The 1997 Balanced Budget Act called for an experiment with medical savings accounts (MSAs) limited to 700,000 participants. In 2003, this concept became transformed into HSAs. The HSA is another market-type policy that would transform not only Medicare, but the entire health care system (Park et al. 2003). Under this program, participants would put money into a tax-free account, similar to an individual retirement account. That money would then be used for medical expenses (and at that time would also be tax free). This provides an incentive to save for medical expenses on one's own rather than having insurance coverage. The amount of the account is limited and, for very high expenses, individuals or families would have to buy catastrophic policies (with very high deductibles).

There is a sense in which premium-support and HSA policies are very attractive. Perhaps the most attractive feature is that it limits government expenses. If we went to a full premium-support system, as advocated by the National Bipartisan Commission, then Medicare expenditures would be limited to the premium, regardless of the use or need for services. If we went to an HSA system, then the federal government's expenses are limited to the tax savings, again regardless of the use or need for services. Park et al. (2003) point out that these types of accounts are more likely to be used by healthier and wealthier people, leaving sicker and poorer people with their regular health insurance, resulting in increasing costs for them. We will have more to say about HSAs in chapter 10.

A fourth element is what happens to those with dual enrollment. Dual eligibles are those Medicare recipients whose income is sufficiently low that state Medicaid programs act as medigap policies. Dual eligibles have prescription drug coverage under Medicaid. However, the MMA would end this coverage. Medicaid would still be available as a "wraparound" (Park and Greenstein 2003, 1) policy except for the prescription drug coverage. Dual eligibles would have to get their coverage through the new Medicare program. That means that they would be subject to at least some of the cost-sharing provisions of the MMA (beyond low-income subsidies) and are therefore likely to find themselves worse off. For example, Park et al. (2003) point out that for those just above the poverty line, they will have copayments that are estimated to increase by 10 percent a year though their income, generally a fixed income (i.e.,

Social Security), will increase by only 2–3 percent a year. Further, because the private plans will set their own formularies, medications that were paid for by Medicaid may not be covered by the plan. The beneficiary would have to, if she or he wanted to or had to continue with that medication, pay for it entirely out of pocket, and none of the costs of the out-of-plan medication would count as part of the deductible or copayments. Medigap-type policies to cover the extra out-of-pocket costs will be very limited, available only through the company whose plan is picked. If the recipient's income is low enough, then state plans could provide some assistance (Marmor 2004).

It should also be pointed out at this time again that Medicare is prohibited from negotiating costs with pharmaceutical companies. The private plans, however, can, and very likely will, engage in some type of negotiation. This also stacks the deck against traditional Medicare.

One other portion of the law is perhaps the most disturbing. This is the part that deals with cost containment, or to put it another way, Medicare's long-term financial future (Caplan and Housman 2004). Certainly one of the factors driving policy in Medicare is the cost issue. Despite its relatively good record, Medicare expenditures continue to increase at a substantial rate and thus have an impact on the federal budget. There is also concern for the fiscal viability of the Medicare trust fund (see, for example, Serafini 2004b). Budget and fiscal issues have been a driving force in policy for Medicare (see Oberlander 2003). The focus on cost containment is thus understandable.

Under the MMA, if the projection of general revenue funding for Medicare exceeds 45 percent twice within seven years, the president must submit legislation to reduce the level to under that percentage (Caplan and Housman 2004). This is perhaps the most explosive part of the bill. With new medications and increasing use of outpatient stays, the portion of Medicare financed by general revenue will climb. The MMA itself contributes to the problem in several ways. First, the prescription drug benefit will increase the costs of the program. Secondly, rather than reduce payments to providers, the MMA increases payments. Thus, it is inevitable that the 45-percent level will be surpassed and significant changes will have to be made, though it is not clear what the nature of those changes would be. This "insolvency" standard was created entirely by the conference committee; it does not appear in either the House or Senate versions of the bill (Marmor 2004). Marmor (2004) states that the response to this new insolvency crisis is likely to be some combination of hikes in premiums (for Part B, and presumably for Part D) and benefit cuts. This would make Medicare less attractive to recipients and private plans more attractive.

Further Concerns

When the Medicare prescription program begins, with enrollments in 2005 and implementation in 2006, administrative or bureaucratic issues may present some problems. There will likely be difficulties in dealing with people who have disabilities, who have trouble speaking English, and for those with limited reading skills (Lamb 2004).

There are particular concerns for those Medicare recipients living in nursing homes (see Pear 2004). The experience with the discount cards in 2004 is not encouraging. About ten million people might be able to benefit from the discount cards, but, as of November 2004, only a little more than half had signed up. Even that number is a bit misleading, because health care plans have been automatically enrolling their subscribers in plans (Lamb 2004). One analysis of the new prescription benefit plan suggests that as many as nineteen million people would experience savings when the plan is implemented in 2006. Another ten million would find no advantage or might even pay more (see Mays et al. 2004; Sherman 2004).

There are three other areas of concern about the prescription drug benefit. First, there is the possibility that employers who provide health benefits, particularly prescription drug benefits, to their retirees, might drop the coverage, given the new benefit. As mentioned above, the MMA does contain some incentives for employers to maintain such coverage. According to an analysis by Families USA (2004c), both those retirees with employer-sponsored plans (about thirteen million people) and Medicaid dual eligibles (another 6.4 million people) could lose their coverage and be worse off. For example, there will be limitations on which drugs a subscriber can purchase under a given plan. There are much fewer restrictions under Medicaid. Further, as with the discount cards, plans can change their formularies (drugs covered under the plan) as well as raise costs of the drugs. Retiree plans are much more comprehensive than the new Medicare plan. Further, because of the subsidies given to companies offering health insurance to their retirees, some companies have begun to tell their former workers that if they choose to go with the new Medicare Part D program, they will be disenrolled entirely from the health care plan (Freudenheim and Pear 2005).

A second concern is skepticism about the new benefit on the part of Medicare beneficiaries. A survey during the summer of 2004 documents this (Kaiser Family Foundation/Harvard School of Public Health 2004). Nearly 50 percent of those surveyed had an unfavorable view of the new law as compared to a little more than a fourth of respondents who had a favorable view. This varied by party identification. Democrats and Independents had a much less favorable view of the law than did Republicans. Three reasons stood out for this unfavorable impression. First was the feeling that recipients would not save money from the benefit. Second, recipients found the new law confusing. Third, recipients saw the law as largely favoring health plans and drug companies. Another question found that comprehension about the law was quite limited among recipients.

The final concern has to do with continued large increases in prescription drug prices. Such prices continue to increase at a rapid rate, much higher than the rate of inflation. For the year ending September 2004, such prices rose on average by 7.4 percent, compared to overall inflation, which rose by 2.3 percent (see Tesoriero 2004; see also Families USA 2004a). The law has a set of premiums, deductibles, and gaps (the so-called "doughnut hole") that will cost subscribers. The new law limits the ability to negotiate lower prices on the part of Medicare.

Given President Bush's reelection in 2004 and the strengthened Republican majorities in Congress, the law will be implemented in 2006. However, the implementers have their work cut out for them if the new law is to be a success in filling this historic gap in Medicare.

One of the implementation issues is the role of private pharmacy benefit management (PBM) plans (Atlas 2004). There has been considerable experience with them in the private sector, managing drug benefits for employer health plans. They have much less experience working with government programs and working with seniors in various programs. One important aspect of the PBMs' role in the new Medicare program is that they will negotiate with pharmaceutical companies and with pharmacies for discounts for their members (Atlas 2004). Their private-sector experience will likely help in this area. There is some concern about their role in the new law:

> PBMs will be given considerable power to define which drugs will have what level of coverage and to negotiate price deals with drug makers. Their leverage over formularies and pricing in the commercial sector has already led to PBMs being accused of bias and self-dealing. The Medicare law, together with market dynamics, will have some influence on formulary design and pricing practices. Whether the protections are sufficient is today more a matter of speculation—and perhaps of one's political leanings—than of objective analysis. (Atlas 2004, W4-514)

Biles, Dallek, and Nicholas (2004) also suggest that there are major issues or challenges facing the new law, particularly the use of private plans. Based on the experience with Medicare+Choice, they see six major challenges, some of which we have already discussed: complexity of plan choices; efforts by plans to avoid costly enrollees; instability of providers, plans, and benefits; the lock-in feature (subscribers can change plans only once annually during specified periods); geographic inequality in benefits and plan choices (i.e., few if any plans in rural areas); and increased Medicare spending.

There is clearly much work to be done in the implementation phase if the new drug benefit is to be a success.

The Tenuous Future of Medicare

Financial considerations have been an important part of the politics and policy deliberations surrounding Medicare since the program began. One such problem, already mentioned, is the sheer size of the program combined with its rapid growth and its impact on the federal budget. Another aspect is that the increase in the size of Medicare beneficiary population (especially when the massive baby boom generation begins to retire) places increased pressure on Medicare. This is most clearly seen in estimates as to the future solvency of the Hospital Insurance (Part A) Trust Fund (see Table 4.11). The trust fund and budget impacts of Medicare came together in the politics of balanced budgets in the 1990s. These issues also will play a role in the future of Medicare in the twenty-first century.

Table 4.11

Trust Fund Predictions, 1995–2004

Date of report	Date of predicted bankruptcy
1995	2002
1996	2001
1997	2001
1998	2008
1999	2015
2000	2025
2001	2029
2002	2030
2003	2026
2004	2012

Source: Social Security and Medicare Trustees (various years).

On the one hand, there have been enhancements of Medicare benefits. The Medicare Modernization Act, however controversial, represents the major, but not the only example. For those joining Medicare after January 1, 2005, there will be new preventive benefits, such as physical exams and screening for diabetes, elevated blood pressure, and hearing and vision losses (Rainey 2004).

On the other hand, there are continual warnings that the financial future of Medicare is bleak. The Congressional Budget Office (CBO) issued a report in 2003 projecting significant increases in Medicare spending (Congressional Budget Office 2003; see also Abate 2004). The CBO said that demographic issues (retirement of the baby-boom generation, greater longevity in retirement), plus the increasing costs of medical care, are the pressures driving up costs. Enhanced technology and changes in program design also add to cost pressures. Using a middle-range set of assumptions, CBO projected that Medicare costs will increase from 2.4 percent of gross domestic product in 2004 to 8.3 percent by the year 2050. Even under the most optimistic set of assumptions, Medicare costs are projected to grow to 4.9 percent of gross domestic product by 2050 (Congressional Budget Office 2004). These costs also put pressure on overall federal spending and on government deficits. Any attempt to reduce or limit federal deficits will undoubtedly turn to Medicare (and Medicaid).

The Medicare trustees presented an equally gloomy future for Medicare spending (Social Security and Medicare Board of Trustees 2004). The trustees projected shortfalls in both Parts A and B. In particular, they pointed to the MMA as a major reason why there would be problems.

The CBO report looked at a series of possibilities for slowing program cost growths. The three sets investigated were: reducing the number of people receiving benefits, reducing the costs to government, and reducing costs per beneficiary. The first set of possibilities include raising the eligibility age to seventy. This would, of course, mean that a number of people who would ordinarily be covered after they turned sixty-five would not be covered. They would have to find other sources of insurance, a difficult task for seniors.

The second set of suggestions, reducing government's costs, could be done in several different ways. For example, the CBO report said that the recipient portion of supplemental medical insurance (Part B) could be increased from the current 25 percent. This would be done by increasing premiums. Other cost-sharing elements (i.e., deductibles and copayments) could also be increased.

Another way to decrease costs would be to reduce provider reimbursements. This has historically been the way Congress and administrators have sought to control costs. The best, but not the only, example of this was the Balanced Budget Act of 1997. The Medicare Modernization Act of 2003 reversed this trend, by providing for increased payments for providers and health plans. Ironically, however, pressure to reduce federal deficits has led Congress to once again consider lowering provider reimbursements ("Congress in February to Consider Medicare Payment Reduction" 2004; see also Lueck 2004).

The CBO report also suggests the possibility of using strategies such as increased use of private plans and more emphasis on disease management as ways of reducing costs per beneficiary.

Not all researchers are quite as alarmed as the authors of these reports. Haase (2004) points out that long-range projections are notoriously inaccurate. He also notes that the aging of the population is only a small factor in increased medical costs. Increased utilization of services and medical price inflation are more important factors. These two factors affect all costs, not just Medicare.

Conclusion

> The challenges posed by rising costs today combined with the future burdens that will arise from an aging population will require that changes be made in Medicare. But we should not begin this process of reassessment under the mistaken claim that the program is a failure. (Moon n.d.)

Medicare remains a popular program among the population at large. But problems remain in both the long and the short term. First, the cost of Medicare and the increases in those costs affect both recipients and the federal government. Second, as the baby boom generation begins retiring in 2010–11, additional pressures will be placed on the program. Additionally, Medicare has significant gaps in its coverage, particularly in long-term care. Even with the new prescription drug benefit, financial pressure on beneficiaries will remain. One estimate is that retirees will need about $108,000 to pay for medical costs not covered by Medicare if they live to be eighty and $300,000 if they live to be ninety-five (Bowman 2005).

The past three decades have seen significant change in the structure of Medicare. The 1980s saw the imposition of fee schedules for hospitals and physicians, and the beginning of Medicare managed care. The Balanced Budget Act of 1997 brought more potentially fundamental restructuring of Medicare. It extended fee schedules to other providers (e.g., home health care agencies) and instituted the Medicare+Choice program, which increased the types of plans beneficiaries could choose, even giving some (the wealthier ones) an opportunity to effectively drop out of the program. The 2003 Medicare Modernization Act created even more changes and challenges. It provided a prescription drug benefit, however limited it might be, and revamped the managed care program (Medicare Advantage). At the same time, it increased the fiscal pressure through the new benefit and provisions that create new threats (the 45-percent cap on general revenue funding).

The consensus that had existed from the beginning of the program about what Medicare would be is dissolving. Oberlander (1997, 2003) argues that the politics of Medicare up to 1994 led to a consensus, first that Medicare would be a public program, one that was operated by the federal government. The other element of the consensus was that the politics of Medicare was bipartisan, supported by Republicans and Democrats. The politics of Medicare subsequent to the November 1994 elections saw the unraveling of the consensus. Medicare was depicted by some as a failure, a throwback to the 1960s Great Society programs, and a problem of intergenerational equity (younger people paying for older people). Medicare+Choice was the result, with its medical savings accounts and private fee-for-service provisions. This has been supplanted by the MMA.

One simple example will show the changing nature of Medicare. From its beginning until the mid-1990s, Medicare was the equivalent of a universal national health insurance program for the elderly. All seniors were eligible and all had the same benefits, regardless of residence (unlike Medicaid). The MMA changed this by making it more of (though not nearly entirely) a means- or income-tested program, more like Medicaid or welfare. This is done by giving subsidies and more generous benefits to low-income recipients and by having higher Part B premiums for higher-income seniors (Moon 2004; Pauly 2004).

The Balanced Budget Act of 1997 had, for a while, protected the fiscal future of Medicare. This was combined with a vibrant economy in the late 1990s and the brief reappearance of federal budget surpluses during the Clinton administration. But the new legislation and the reappearance of substantial budget deficits in the twenty-first century have placed Medicare in a more precarious financial position.

A variety of proposals have been suggested that would affect Medicare in the twenty-first century. One proposal would be to increase the hospital insurance trust fund tax from 2.9 percent (half paid by employee, half by employer) to perhaps 4.5 percent. Other possibilities include raising the eligibility age from sixty-five to sixty-seven (which would also save money, though it would run counter to proposals to expand Medicare to those below sixty-five) and means-testing Part B premiums (higher premiums for wealthier beneficiaries) more completely (see the discussion in Pauly 2004; Moon 2004).

Other proposals could change the nature of the program. The halting move toward managed care, now with increased incentives and choices as a result of the BBA and its enhancement as the new Medicare Advantage program, has always promised a limitation on use and therefore cost savings. But managed care has proved to be a mixed blessing. The BBA reduced payments to HMOs at the same time that HMOs were beginning to raise their fees to Medicare subscribers. The MMA raised payments to managed care organizations in the hope of making them more attractive both to the organizations and Medicare recipients. But the increased payments would reduce future cost savings.

A more radical proposal is to rely on vouchers. This would be a premium-support or defined-benefit program. This was one of the recommendations of the National Bipartisan Commission on the Future of Medicare (1999) established by the 1997 BBA (though not adopted formally by the commission) (see Marmor 2000; Oberlander 2003). Under such a program, recipients would be able to purchase any plan they chose. This would hopefully bring competition and consumer choice into Medicare, eliminating the program as we know it.

Another proposal, based on European experience, is to use price controls through limits on spending (program controls), using such policy instruments as "fee schedules, volume controls, and spending caps" (Marmor and Oberlander 1998, 62; White 1995). For example, some have suggested that Medicare be allowed to negotiate with pharmaceutical companies to help reduce cost pressures, something not allowed under the MMA (see, for example, "Medicare Caveat" 2004). While the international experience does indicate the efficacy of program controls, in the political environment of turn-of-the-century America, a move toward regulatory controls seems unlikely. Further, the managed care revolution (discussed in chapters 9 and 10) points in the opposite direction.

Long-term care is an area that public policy has yet to come to grips with. The long-term-care insurance market has expanded, but not especially rapidly. Medicare can be expanded in a variety of ways to cover long-term-care needs. To the extent that public programs cover long-term care, Medicaid, with all its faults, remains the primary program (see chapter 3).

The twenty-first-century Medicare program is being built around the ideas found in the Balanced Budget and Medicare Modernization Acts. We live in a brave and scary new world.

Notes

1. For a thorough discussion of how health policy promised not to interfere with the practice of medicine, see Krause (1977).

2. This social insurance strategy, as described in Medicare, was a continuation of that initially incorporated into Social Security. The idea was that the program would be so popular, and everyone would have such an interest in it, that it would survive attack. That politically astute strategy seems to have worked well for both programs, though, as we discuss later in conjunction with the Balanced Budget Act of 1997 and the Medicare Modernization Act of 2003, the consensus surrounding Medicare has unraveled.

3. The Medicare Hospital Insurance tax is listed separately from the FICA tax on pay stubs.

4. The reason for the delay in benefits was to build up a reserve to begin paying for them.

The precedent for this is the original Social Security Act of 1935. Payments into the trust fund began in 1936, but the first Social Security checks did not begin until 1940.

5. Marmor's theory would work best under a system of national health insurance. This is undoubtedly one reason providers have long opposed such programs in the United States.

6. For a detailed discussion and analysis of the all-payer DRG system in New Jersey, see *Bulletin of the New York Academy of Medicine* 62, no. 6 (July/August 1986). The entire issue is devoted to the discussion of New Jersey's DRG system.

7. Calculated from Moon (1996, 38) and "Medicare and Medicaid Statistical Supplement, 1997" (1998, 28 and 37).

8. In the August 2004 primaries, Smith's son Brad lost the election (Noah 2004).

References

AARP. 2003. "States Offering Tax Incentives for Long-Term Care Insurance, 2002." AARP's Public Policy Institute. Online at www.aarp.org/bulletin/longterm/Articles/a2003-06-23-taxincentives-.html.

Abate, Tom. 2004. "Medicare Faces Cost Crisis." *San Francisco Chronicle*, November 7.

Altman, Drew E. 2004. "The New Medicare Prescription-Drug Legislation." *New England Journal of Medicine* 350, no. 1 (January 1): 9010.

Anderson, Gerard, and James R. Knickman. 2001. "Changing the Chronic Care System to Meet People's Needs." *Health Affairs* 20, no. 6 (November/December): 146–60.

Antos, Joseph, and John E. Calfee. 2004. "Of Sausage-Making and Medicare." *Health Policy Outlook* (January–February). Washington, D.C.: American Enterprise Institute for Public Policy Research. Online at www.aei.org.

Atlas, Robert F. 2004. "The Role of PBMs in Implementing the Medicare Prescription Drug Benefit." *Health Affairs* (October 28): W4-504–W4-515.

Biles, Brian; Geraldine Dallek; and Lauren Hersch Nicholas. 2004. "Medicare Advantage: Déjà Vu All Over Again?" *Health Affairs* (December 15): W4-586–W4-597. Online at www.healthaffairs.org.

Board of Trustees, Federal Old-Age and Survivors Insurance and Disability Trust Funds. 1997. "1997 Annual Report of the Board of Trustees of the Federal Old-Age Insurance and Disability Trust Funds." Washington, D.C.: Department of Health and Human Services.

Bowman, Lee. 2005. "Older Americans Fear Health Costs." *Detroit News*, June 29.

Brown, Randall S.; Dolores G. Clement; Jerold W. Hill; Sheldon M. Retchin; and Jeanette W. Bergeron. 1993. "Do Health Maintenance Organizations Work for Medicare?" *Health Care Financing Review* 15, no. 1 (Fall): 7–23.

"The Bush Prescription Drug Plan." 2000. *New York Times,* September 11.

Caplan, Craig, and Lori Housman. 2004. "Redefining Medicare's Long-Term Financial Health: A Closer Look at the 'Medicare Funding Warning' in the Trustee's Report." Washington, D.C.: AARP Public Policy Institute Issue Brief #67 (June).

Center for American Progress. 2004. "Administration Threatened Truth-Teller on Medicare Bill," March 12. Online at americanprogress.org.

Centers for Medicare and Medicaid Services. n.d. "2003 Data Compendium." Online at www.cms.hhs.gov/researchers/pubs/datacompendium/current/.

———. 2003a. "Medicare Benefit Payments by Type of Benefit." Washington, D.C.: Centers for Medicare and Medicaid Services. Online at www.cms.hhs.gov/researchers/pubs/datacompendium/current/.

———. 2003b. "Medicare Enrollees." Washington, D.C.: Centers for Medicare and Medicaid Services. Online at www.cms.hhs.gov/researchers/pubs/datacompendium/current/.

———. 2004a. *Your Medicare Benefits.* Washington, D.C.: Centers for Medicare and Medicaid Services.

———. 2004b. "What are the Medicare Premium and Coinsurance Rates for 2005?" Washington, D.C.: Centers for Medicare and Medicaid Services. Online at questions.medicare.gov/

cgi-bin/medicare.cfg/php/enduser/std_adp.php?p_faqid=1560&p_created=1095443945.
————. 2004c. "2004 CMS Statistics." Washington, D.C.: Centers for Medicare and Medicaid Services.
Chait, Jonathan. 2004. "Power from the People: The Case Against George W. Bush, Part II." *The New Republic* 231, no. 4,671 (July 26): 15–19.
Cohen, Richard E.; Kirk Victor; and David Baumann. 2004. "The State of Congress." *National Journal* 36, no. 2 (January 10): 82–105.
"Congress in February to Consider Medicare Payment Reduction" 2004. Kaisernetwork.org (November 15).
Congressional Budget Office. 1997. *Predicting How Changes in Medicare's Payment Rates Would Affect Risk Sector Enrollment and Costs.* Washington, D.C.: Congressional Budget Office, U.S. Congress.
————. 2003. "Long-Term Budget Outlook." Washington, D.C.: Congressional Budget Office (December). Online at www.cbo.gov.
————. 2004. "Financing Long-Term Care for the Elderly." Washington, D.C.: Congressional Budget Office (December). Online at www.cbo.gov.
Cooper, Barbara S., and Sabrina How. 2004. "Medicare's Future: Current Picture, Trends, and Medicare Prescription Drug Improvement & Modernization Act of 2003; Selected Charts." The Commonwealth Fund (February 24). Online at www.cmwf.org.
Cutler, David M. 2001. "Declining Disability among the Aging." *Health Affairs* 20, no. 6 (November/December): 11–27.
Dallek, Geraldine. 1996. *The Crushing Costs of Medicare Supplemental Policies.* Washington, D.C.: Families USA.
Dao, James. 2000. "On the Streets of Baltimore, the Word on Medicare is 'Expand,' Not 'Overhaul.'" *New York Times,* September 8.
Davis, Karen; Cathy Schoen; Michelle Doty; and Katie Tenney. 2002. "Medicare Versus Private Insurance: Rhetoric and Reality." *Health Affairs* (October 9): W311–W324. Web exclusive. Online at www.healthaffairs.org.
Dolnec, D.A., and C.J. Dougherty. 1985. "DRGs: The Counterrevolution in Financing Health Care." *Hastings Center Report* 15, no. 3 (June): 19–29.
"Drugmakers Benefit Most." 2004. Editorial. *USA Today,* July 11.
Enthoven, Alain C. 1980. *Health Plan: The Only Practical Solution to the Soaring Cost of Medicare Care.* Reading, MA.: Addison-Wesley.
————. 2003. "Employer-Based Health Insurance is Failing: Now What?" *Health Affairs* (May 28): W3-237–W3-249.
Families USA. 2003. "Out-of-Bounds: Rising Prescription Drug Prices for Seniors." Washington, D.C.: Families USA. Online at www.familiesusa.org.
————. 2004a. "Sticker Shock: Rising Prescription Drug Prices for Seniors." Washington, D.C.: Families USA. Online at www.familiesusa.org.
————. 2004b. "Private Plans: A Bad Choice for Medicare." Washington, D.C.: Families USA. Online at www.familiesusa.org.
————. 2004c. "Approximately Half of Americans in Medicare Are at Risk of Losing Coverage When the New Law is Implemented." Washington, D.C.: Families USA. Online at www.familiesusa.org.
Feder, Barbara. 2002. "Prescription Plan Wouldn't Cover All." *San Jose Mercury News,* January 30.
Feder, Judith M. 1977. *Medicare: The Politics of Federal Hospital Insurance.* Lexington, Mass.: D.C. Heath.
Feder, Judith M.; Harriet L. Komisar; and Marlene Niefeld. 2000. "Long-Term Care in the United States: An Overview." *Health Affairs* 19, no. 3 (May/June): 40–56.
Fein, Esther B. 1994. "Elderly Transfer Assets to Qualify for Medicaid." *New York Times,* September 25.
Fox-Grage, Wendy. 1997. *The Task Force Report: Long-Term Care Reform in the States.* Washington, D.C.: National Conference of State Legislatures.

Freudenheim, Milt. 1997. "Medicare H.M.O.'s to Trim Benefits for the Elderly." *New York Times*, December 2.

Freudenheim, Milt, and Robert Pear. 2005. "New Medicare Plan Presents a Drug Benefit Conundrum." *New York Times*, November 4.

Frogue, James, and Robert E. Moffit. 2000. "A Closer Look at Clinton's Medicare Proposal." *AEI Backgrounder*, #1346. Washington, D.C.: American Enterprise Institute.

General Accounting Office. 1994. "Long-term Care: Private Sector Elder Care Could Yield Multiple Benefits." Washington, D.C.: U.S. General Accounting Office.

———. 1997. "Medicare Home Health Agencies: Certification Process Ineffective in Excluding Problem Agencies." Washington, D.C.: U.S. General Accounting Office.

———. 2001. "Global Health: U.S. Agency for International Development Fights AIDS in Africa, but Better Data Needed to Measure Impact," GAO-01-449, March 23. Washington, D.C.: U.S. General Accounting Office.

Gold, Marsha. 2001. "Medicare+Choice: An Interim Report Card." *Health Affairs* 20, no. 4 (July/August): 120–38.

Gold, Marsha; Lyle Nelson; Randall Brown; Anne Ciemnecki; Anna Aizer; and Elizabeth Docteur. 1997. "Disabled Medicare Beneficiaries in HMOs." *Health Affairs* 16, no. 5 (September/October): 149–62.

"GOP to Unveil Drug-Benefit Plan." 2002. Associated Press, May 1.

Government Accountability Office. 2002. "Medicare Home Health Agencies: Weaknesses in Federal and State Oversight Mask Potential Quality Issues." Washington, D.C.: Government Accountability Office.

———. 2004a. "Medicare Home Health: Payments to Most Freestanding Home Health Agencies More Than Covered Their Costs." Washington, D.C.: U.S. Government Accountability Office.

———. 2004b. "Accuracy of Responses from the 1-800-MEDICARE Help Line Should Be Improved." Washington, D.C.: U.S. Government Accountability Office.

Green, Joshua. 2005. "The Hammer Falls." *Rolling Stone* (June 2): 35–39.

Guggenheim, Ken. 2002. "Bush Pushes for Medicare Changes." Associated Press, May 18.

Haase, Leif Wellington. 2004. "The Debate over Medicare Costs: A Primer." New York: The Century Foundation. (September 24).

Health Care Financing Administration. 1995. *Medicare and Medicaid Statistical Supplement, 1995.* Washington, D.C.: U.S. Department of Health and Human Services.

Health and Human Services. 2003. *Health United States 2003.* Washington, D.C.: Department of Health and Human Services. Online at www.cdc.gov/nchs/hus.htm.

Health Policy Alternatives, Inc. 2003. "A Side-by Side Comparison of the Prescription Drug Coverage Provisions of S. 1 and H.R. 1, and the Conference Report." Prepared for the Henry J. Kaiser Family Foundation (November 26). Online at www.kff.org.

Heffler, Stephen; Shelia Smith; Sean Keehan; M. Kent Clemens; Mark Zezza; and Christopher Truffer. 2004. "Health Spending Projections Through 2013." *Health Affairs* (February 11): W4-79–W4-93 (Web exclusive).

Hook, Janet. 2002. "Senior Drug Plans Killed." *Los Angeles Times*, July 24.

"House GOP Unveils Final Version of Medicare Package." 2002. Kaisernetwork.org, June 18.

Hudman, Julie. 2004. "The Basics of Medicaid." New York: Kaiser Commission on Medicaid and the Uninsured. Online at www.kaiseredu.org.

"In 'Rare Agreement,' Republicans, Democrats Say Bush's Proposed Allocation for Medicare Drug Benefit Not Enough." 2002. Kaisernetwork.org, February 26.

Joskow, Paul L. 1981. "Alternative Regulatory Mechanism for Controlling Hospital Costs." In *A New Approach to the Economics of Health Care*, ed. Mancur Olson, 219–57. Washington, D.C.: American Enterprise Institute for Public Policy Research.

Kaiser Commission on Medicaid and the Uninsured. 2004. "Dual Eligibles: Medicaid's Role in Filling Medicare's Gaps." Washington, D.C.: Kaiser Commission on Medicaid and the Uninsured, March.

Kaiser Family Foundation. 2003. "Medicare and Prescription Drug Spending Chartpack." Washington, D.C.: Kaiser Family Foundation. Online at www.kff.org.

————. 2004. *Medicare at a Glance Fact Sheet.* Online at www.kff.org.

Kaiser Family Foundation/Harvard School of Public Health. 2004. "Views of the New Medicare Drug Law: A Survey of People on Medicare." Menlo Park, Calif.: Henry J. Kaiser Foundation.

Kaisernetwork.org. 2001. "Bush Lays out Proposals for Medicare Reform, Prescription Drug Plan." July 13. Online at kaisernetwork.org.

————. 2002. "Many M+C Plans Dropping Prescription Drug Benefits or Charging More." Online at kaisernetwork.org.

Krause, Elliott A. 1977. *Power and Illness: The Political Sociology of Health and Medical Care.* New York: Elsevier.

Lamb, Gregory M. 2004. "Will Red Tape Seal Up Drug-Benefit Plans?" *The Christian Science Monitor,* November 17.

Levit, Katharine R.; Helen C. Lazenby; and Madie W. Stewart. 1996. "DataView: National Health Expenditures, 1995." *Health Care Financing Review* 18, no. 1 (Fall): 175–214.

Levit, Katharine, et al. 2004. "Health Spending Rebound Continues in 2002." *Health Affairs* 23, no. 1 (January/February): 147–59.

LTC America. 2005. "Medicare 2005." Melville, N.Y.: LTC America. Online at www.ltcamerica .com/Medicare%202005.htm.

Lueck, Sarah. 2004. "U.S. Health Plans Catch Fiscal Hawks' Eyes." *Wall Street Journal,* December 3.

MacKeen, Dawn. 2004. "Report: Medicare Cards Little Help." *Newsday,* July 15.

Marmor, Theodore. 2000. *The Politics of Medicare,* 2nd ed. Chicago: Aldine.

————. 2004. "The Medicare 'Reform' Legislation of 2003." A presentation based in large part on an essay published December 7, 2003 in *The Boston Globe,* by Ted Marmor and a colleague at Yale, Jacob Hacker.

Marmor, Theodore, and Jonathan Oberlander. 1998. "Rethinking Medicare Reform." *Health Affairs* 17, no. 1 (January/February): 52–68.

Marmor, Theodore R.; Donald A. Wittman; and Thomas C. Heagy. 1983. "The Politics of Medical Inflation." In *Political Analysis and American Medical Care,* ed. Theodore R. Marmor, 61–75. Cambridge, England: Cambridge University Press.

Mays, Jim; Monica Brener; Tricia Neuman; Juliette Kubanski; and Gary Claxton. 2004. "Estimates of Medicare Beneficiaries' Out-of-Pocket Drug Spending in 2006: Modeling the MMA." Prepared by Actuarial Research Corporation and the Henry J. Kaiser Family Foundation. Online at www.kff.org.

McCormack, Lauren A.; Peter D. Fox; and Marcia L. Graham. 1996. "Medigap Reform Legislation of 1990: Have the Objectives Been Met?" *Health Care Financing Review* 18, no. 1 (Fall): 157–74.

"Medicare Caveat." 2004. *The Boston Globe,* December 8.

"Medicare and Medicaid Statistical Supplement, 1997." 1998. *Health Care Financing Review.* Washington, D.C.: Government Printing Office.

"Medicare and Medicaid Statistical Supplement, 2001." 2002. *Health Care Financing Review.* Online at www.cms.hhs.gov/Review/Supp.

MedicareWatch. 1999. "President Clinton's Medicare Drug Benefit: Issues and Choices." Washington, D.C.: The Century Foundation (September).

Merrell, Katie; David C. Colby; and Christopher Hogan. 1997. "Medicare Beneficiaries Covered by Medicaid Buy-In Agreements." *Health Affairs* 16, no. 1 (January/February): 175–84.

MetLife Mature Market Institute. 2002. "MetLife Market Survey on Nursing Home and Home Health Care Costs 2002." Westport, Conn.: MetLife Mature Market Institute.

Mojtabai, Ramin, and Mark Olfson. 2003. "Medication Costs, Adherence, and Health Outcomes among Medicare Beneficiaries." *Health Affairs* 22, no. 4 (July/August): 220–29.

Moon, Marilyn. n.d. "Ensuring a Future for Medicare." Online at www.aarp.org/monthly/medicare3/viewmm.htm.

————. 1996. *Medicare Now and in the Future,* 2nd ed. Washington, D.C.: Urban Affairs Press.

————. 2004. "Medicare Means-Testing: A Skeptical View." *Health Affairs* (December 8): W4-558–W4-560. Online at www. healthaffairs.org.

Morone, James A., and Andrew B. Dunham. 1986. "Slouching toward National Health Insurance: The Unanticipated Politics of DRGs." *Bulletin of the New York Academy of Medicine* 62, no. 6 (July/August): 646–62.

National Bipartisan Commission on the Future of Medicare. 1999. "Building a Better Medicare for Today and Tomorrow." Online at: medicare.commission.gov/medicare/.

Nelson, Lyle. 1997. "Access to Care in Medicare HMOs, 1996." *Health Affairs* 16, no. 2 (March/April): 148–56.

Newman, Patricia. 2004. "The New Medicare Prescription Drug Benefit: An Overview." Powerpoint presentation. Kaiser Family Foundation (February).

Newman, Patricia, and Kathryn M. Langwell. 1999. "Medicare's Choice Explosion? Implications for Beneficiaries." *Health Affairs* 18, no. 1 (January/February): 150–60.

Noah, Timothy. 2004. "Brad Unbound." Online at slate.com.

"Nursing Home Cost Hits $70,000 Per Year." 2004. Santa Monica, CA.: Consumeraffairs.com. Online at consumeraffairs.com/news04/nursing_home_costs.html.

Oberlander, Jonathan B. 1997. "Managed Care and Medicare Reform." *Journal of Health Care Politics, Policy and Law* 22, no. 2 (April): 595–631.

———. 2003. *The Political Life of Medicare*. Chicago: University of Chicago Press.

O'Brien, Ellen, and Risa Elias. 2004. "Medicaid and Long-Term Care." Washington, D.C.: Kaiser Commission on Medicaid and the Uninsured.

O'Dell, Kathleen. 2004. "Medicare to Mail Drug Cards to Low-Income Seniors." *Springfield News-Leader,* September 23.

Oliver, Thomas R. 1993. "Analysis, Advice and Congressional Leadership: The Physician Payment Review Commission and the Politics of Medicare." *Journal of Health Politics, Policy and Law* 18, no. 1 (Spring): 113–74.

Oliver, Thomas R.; Philip R. Lee; and Helene L. Lipton. 2004. "A Political History of Medicare and Prescription Drug Coverage." Paper presented at the annual meeting of the American Political Science Association, September 2–5, Chicago.

Olson, Mancur, ed. 1981. *A New Approach to the Economics of Health Care*. Washington, D.C.: American Enterprise Institute for Public Policy Research.

Palazzolo, Daniel J. 1999. *Done Deal? The Politics of the 1997 Budget Agreement*. New York: Chatham House Publishers.

Park, Edwin. 2004. "Administration's Proposed Deduction for Long-Term Care Insurance Premiums Likely to be Ineffective and Costly, and of Primary Benefit to Higher-Income Individuals." Washington, D.C.: Center for Budget and Policy Priorities (February 18).

Park, Edwin, and Robert Greenstein. 2003. "Medicare Agreement Would Make Substantial Numbers of Seniors and People with Disabilities Worse Off than Under Current Law." Washington, D.C.: Center on Budget and Policy Priorities (November 21).

Park, Edwin; Melanie Nathanson; Robert Greenstein; and John Springer. 2003. "The Troubling Medicare Legislation." Washington, D.C.: Center on Budget and Policy Priorities (December 8).

Patel, Kant, and Mark E. Rushefsky. 1999. *Health Care Politics and Policy in America*, 2nd ed. Armonk, N.Y.: M.E. Sharpe.

Pauly, Mark V. 2004. "Means-Testing in Medicare." *Health Affairs* (December 8): W4-546–W4-557. Online at www.healthaffairs.org.

Pear, Robert. 2000. "Drug Benefits for Medicare Are Proposed by Democrats." *New York Times,* May 11.

———. 2001a. "Democrats Double Bush's Proposal on Prescription Drugs." *New York Times,* March 21.

———. 2001b. "Bush Drug Plan Calls for Discount Cards." *New York Times,* July 11.

———. 2001c. " H.M.O.'s Plan to Drop Medicare, Calling Fees Too Low." *New York Times,* September 21.

———. 2002. "Drug Plans For Elderly Are Unveiled By 2 Parties." *New York Times,* May 1.

———. 2004. "Medicare Law Said to Trouble Nursing Homes." *New York Times,* December 5.

————. 2005a. "Advisory Panel Lists Drugs It Wants New Law to Cover." *New York Times,* January 4.

————. 2005b. "States Rejecting Demand to Pay for Medicare Cost." *New York Times,* July 4.

Pear, Robert, and Robin Toner. 2004. "Partisan Arguing and Fine Print Seen as Hindering Medicare Law." *New York Times,* October 11.

Perin, Joshua. 1994. "Long-Term Care Insurance: Partnership Model Offers an Option." *State Health Notes* 15, no. 193 (November 28): 4–5.

Petrie, John T. 1992. "Overview of the Medicare Program." *Health Care Financing Review,* 1992 Annual Supplement, 1–14.

Physician Payment Review Commission. 1997. "A New Law Changes Practice Expense." *PPRC Update* no. 24 (August).

Quinn, Jane Bryant. 1997. "Medicare for Boomers." *Newsweek* 130, no. 15 (October 13): 55.

————. 1998. "Reinventing Medicare." *Newsweek* 132, no. 13 (September 28): 88.

Rainey, Richard. 2004. "Medicare Adds Preventive Benefits." *Los Angeles Times,* November 10.

Rice, Thomas; Katherine Desmond; and Jon Gable. 1990. "The Medicare Catastrophic Coverage Act: A Post-Mortem." *Health Affairs* 9, no. 3 (Fall): 75–87.

Rice, Thomas; Kathleen Thomas; and William Weissert. 1989. *The Impact of Owning Private Long-Term Care Insurance Policies on Out-of-Pocket Costs.* Washington, D.C.: American Association of Retired Persons.

Riley, Gerald F.; Melvin J. Ingber; and Cynthia G. Tudor. 1997. "Disenrollment of Medicare Beneficiaries from HMOs." *Health Affairs* 15, no. 5 (September/October): 117–24.

Rother, John C. n.d. "A Medicare in the 21st Century." Online at www.aarp.org/monthly/medicare3/viewjr.htm.

Rushefsky, Mark E. 2004. "Ending Medicare as We Know It?" Paper presented at the annual meeting of the American Political Science Association, September 2–5, Chicago.

Rushefsky, Mark E., and Kant Patel. 1998. *Power and Policy Making: The Case of Health Care Reform in the 1990s.* Armonk, NY: M.E. Sharpe.

Scanlon, William J. 2001. "Long-Term Care: Baby Boom Generation Increases Challenge of Financing Needed Services." Washington, D.C.: U.S. General Accounting Office. Testimony before the U.S. Senate Finance Committee (March 27).

Schoenman, Julie A.; Kevin J. Hayes; and C. Michael Cheng. 2001. "Medicare Physician Payment Changes: Impact on Physicians and Beneficiaries." *Health Affairs* 20, no. 2 (March/April): 263–73.

Schur, Claudia L.; Marc L. Berk; and Penny Mohr. 1990. "Understanding the Cost of a Catastrophic Drug Benefit." *Health Affairs* 9, no. 3 (Fall): 88–100.

Schwartz, Barry. 2003. *The Paradox of Choice: Why More is Less.* New York: HarperCollins.

Serafini, Marilyn Werber. 1997. "Brave New World." *National Journal* 29, no. 33 (August 16): 1636–39.

————. 2000. "Medicare Reforms May Be Too Expensive." *National Journal* 23, no. 39 (September 23): 2980–81.

————. 2004a. "Tough Sell." *National Journal* 36, no. 1 (January 3): 20–25.

————. 2004b. "The Real Medicare Crisis Ahead." *National Journal* 36, no. 23 (June 5): 1792–93.

Shaffer, Franklin A. 1983. "DRGs: History and Overview." *Nursing and Health Care* 4, no. 7 (September), 388–89.

Sherman, Mark. 2004. "Benefits Said to Vary in Medicare Plan." *Boston Globe,* November 23.

Shikles, Janet L. 1991. "Long-Term Care Insurance: Risk to Consumers Should Be Reduced." Washington, D.C.: General Accounting Office.

Smith, Vernon; Kathleen Gifford; and Sandy Kramer. 2005. "Implications of the Medicare Modernization Act for States." Menlo Park, Calif.: Henry J. Kaiser Foundation.

Social Security and Medicare Board of Trustees. 2004. "Status of the Social Security and Medicare Programs: A Summary of the 2004 Annual Reports." Washington, D.C.: Department of Health and Human Services. Online at www.ssa.gov/OACT/TRSUM/trsummary.html.

Solomon, John. 2004. "Memo Warned about Medicare Cards." *Washington Post,* October 15.
Starr, Paul. 1982. *The Social Transformation of American Medicine.* New York: Basic Books.
Steinberg, Earl P. et al. 2000. "Beyond Survey Data: A Claims-Based Analysis of Drug Use and Spending by the Elderly." *Health Affairs* 19, no. 2 (March/April): 198–211.
Steinwald, Bruce and Frank A. Sloan. 1981. "Regulatory Approaches to Hospital Cost Containment: A Synthesis of the Empirical Evidence." In *A New Approach to the Economics of Health Care,* ed. Mancur Olson, 273–308. Washington, D.C.: American Enterprise Institute for Public Policy.
Stevenson, Richard W. 2004. "Bush Lauds New Prescription Discount Cards." *New York Times,* June 14.
Stuart, Bruce et al. 2003. "Employer-Sponsored Health Insurance and Prescription Drug Coverage for New Retirees: Dramatic Declines in Five Years." *Health Affairs* (July 23): W3-334–W3-341.
Tesoriero, Heather Won. 2004. "Torrid Drug-Price Increases Pause." *Wall Street Journal,* December 6.
Thomas, Cindy Parks; Grant Ritter; and Stanley S. Walleck. 2001. "Growth in Prescription Drug Spending Among Insured Elders." *Health Affairs* 20, no. 5 (September/October): 265–77.
Thompson, Frank J. 1981. *Health Policy and the Bureaucracy: Politics and Implementation.* Cambridge, Mass.: MIT Press.
"Those Soaring Medicare Premiums." 2004. *New York Times,* September 17.
Tilly, Jane; Susan Goldenson; and Jessica Kasten. 2001. *Long-Term Care: Consumers, Providers, and Financing; A Chartbook.* Washington, D.C.: The Urban Institute.
Toner, Robin. 2001. "Major Battle Looms Over Medicare." *New York Times,* February 11.
———. 2002. "The Nation: The Prescription Drug Debate." *New York Times,* June 23.
Tudor, Cynthia G.; Gerald Riley; and Melvin J. Ingber. 1998. "Satisfaction with Care: Do Medicare HMOs Make a Difference?" *Health Affairs* 17, no. 2 (March/April): 165–76.
U.S. Bureau of the Census. 1966. *Statistical Abstract of the United States, 1966.* Washington, D.C.: U.S. Government Printing Office.
———. 1997. *Statistical Abstract of the United States, 1997.* Washington, D.C.: U.S. Government Printing Office.
———. 2003. *Statistical Abstract of the United States, 2003.* Washington, D.C.: U.S. Government Printing Office.
Vladeck, Bruce C. 1984. "Comment on Hospital Reimbursement under Medicare." *Milbank Memorial Fund Quarterly/Health and Society* 62, no. 2 (Spring): 269–78.
Vladeck, Bruce C.; Nancy A. Miller; and Steven B. Clauser. 1993. "The Changing Face of Long-Term Care." *Health Care Financing Review* 14, no. 4 (Summer): 5–23.
"Victory: Family Physicians Make Gains in Medicare Fee Schedule." 1997. *AAFD Directors' Newsletter* (November 13). Online at www.aafp.org/dn;/971113dl/2.html.
Weiner, Joshua M., and Laurel Hixon Illston. 1994. "How to Share the Burden: Long-Term Care Reform in the 1990s." *Brookings Review* 12, no. 2 (Spring): 16–21.
Weiner, Joshua M., and David G. Stevenson. 1998. "State Policy on Long-Term Care for the Elderly." *Health Affairs* 17, no. 3 (May/June): 81–100.
Welch, William M. 2001. "Attacks Prompt Lawmakers to Reorder Their Priorities." *USA Today,* September 17.
———. 2004. "Medical Costs Eat at Social Security." *USA Today,* September 13.
White, Joseph. 1995. *Competing Solutions: American Health Care Proposals and International Experience.* Washington, D.C.: Brookings Institution.
Xu, K. Tom. 2003. "Financial Disparities in Prescription Drug Use Between Elderly and Nonelderly Americans." *Health Affairs* 22, no. 5 (September/October): 210–21.

5

Health Care and the Disadvantaged

Falling through the Cracks

By 1970, health care policy in the United States had reached its maturity. Medicare and Medicaid were passed in 1965; private insurance covered most of working America. But health care costs went up dramatically beginning in the mid-1960s, and portions of the population were left out of the system. Two of the major problems of the health care system are cost increases and access. We consider the problem of cost increases in the next chapter. This chapter focuses on the problem of access and the disadvantaged.

We concentrate on issues of access to the health care system, the problem of the uninsured and the underinsured, low-income groups, and minorities and women. To some extent, these problems overlap. While a good portion of the uninsured are low-income people, some are not. While minorities in general have lower incomes than whites, not all the problems of minorities and health care result from lower incomes. Rural areas have access problems to health care in the same way that inner cities do: lack of providers. We spell out these interrelationships as we go along.

Perhaps the underlying issue in looking at the disadvantaged and health care is equality and equity. We begin this chapter by considering this issue.

Equality and Equity

Equality and equity do not mean the same things. Equality means that we should treat people who are in the same situation the same way or treat people who are in different situations differently. That is, we should not discriminate against someone on account of race, religion, age, sex, ethnic group, and so forth. One reality of the health care system, to be discussed later in the chapter, is that there is discrimination based on income or at least based on health insurance. Those with private insurance plans, especially very generous ones, tend to get better service than those on public plans (such as Medicaid); those without health insurance tend to get the worst care (Berk and Schur 1998). Some have argued that the United States has a two-tiered health care system, one for most of us and another for the poor. In Krause's words,

> we have, combining the doctors and the office and hospital settings, a two-class medical care system. On the one hand, few practitioners and a few public settings for the poor in either the ghetto or rural areas; on the other hand, many practitioners and voluntary non-profit hospitals for the middle class and the upper class in the suburbs. (Krause 1977)

This leads us to the notion of equity, an extension of the concept of equality. Equity is related to another concept, social justice. Both ideas suggest that, given that some are disadvantaged in the health care system, there should be an extra effort made to help overcome those disadvantages. This is, in a sense, the idea behind Medicaid (and to a lesser extent, Medicare). Medicaid recipients pay a minimal amount in copayments, if anything, for their health care. Instead, their health care is subsidized by the larger community (taxpayers) and to some extent by providers and their patients (in the sense that Medicaid reimbursements are lower than for privately insured patients and costs are shifted to privately insured patients). Compensatory education programs such as Head Start, where we devote more resources to children from impoverished backgrounds, are another example.

There are a number of philosophical concepts that support extending access to heath care services to those who do not have it. Daniels, Light, and Caplan (1996) argue that the appropriate philosophical ground is *fairness*. To the authors, fairness is related to social justice and equal opportunity, or what they call fair equal opportunity. This concept, not especially well defined in our opinion, sees health care as instrumental in that it allows people to function normally. The lack of health care services, according to their reasoning, shortens peoples' lives or makes it more difficult for them to function normally and therefore to live on a level playing field with other people. They write:

> A commitment to fair equality of opportunity thus recognizes that we should not allow people's prospects in life to be governed by correctable, morally arbitrary, or irrelevant differences between them, including those that result from disease and disability. . . . By designing a health care system that keeps *all* people as close as possible to normal functioning, given reasonable resource constraints, we can in one important way fulfill our moral and legal obligations to protect equality of opportunity. (Daniels, Light, and Caplan 1996, 22; emphasis in original)

Notice at the end of the quote the reference to resource constraints. Their view of fairness is balanced by a concern for liberty, social productivity, and efficiency (Daniels, Light, and Caplan 1996).

The bulk of their book develops ten benchmarks of fairness to evaluate health care policy and then applies those benchmarks to the current system, the Clinton proposals in 1993 and 1994, and managed care. Their benchmarks include universal access, equitable financing, value for money, public accountability, comparability, and degree of consumer choice. The evaluation by Daniels, Light, and Caplan of the 1993–94 proposals (see chapter 9) gives the highest evaluation to the single-payer plan, lower marks to the Clinton proposal, and lowest marks to a market-oriented plan. Daniels, Light, and Caplan also conclude that the trend toward managed care and system integration would move the United States further away from fairness than any of the proposals considered in the 1993–94 period.

Baird (1998) uses the concept of justice, in this case gender justice, to evaluate the U.S. health care system. The gender justice framework is summarized by Baird as follows:

> the framework of gender justice includes the principles of self-determination, which is composed of the criteria of self-development, recognition and democratic freedom; equality of gendered consequences; and diversity. (Baird 1998, 114)

Self-development refers to the ability of a policy to help people develop their capabilities. Recognition is accepting women's needs and experiences as legitimate, and respecting women. Democratic freedom refers to participating or determining actions that affect one's life. Equality of gendered consequences asks whether public policies, even those that are seemingly neutral, promote equality. Diversity recognizes differences between men and women, but also differences among women (minority versus white).

Others argue for the concept of a *right to health care*. Cust (1997) contends that there is a moral right to health care, what he calls a *just minimum*. He writes that the moral right to health care is based on the fact that it can mean the difference between living and dying, and that it also affects a person's quality of life. The notion of rights, he continues, asserts an obligation to fulfill those rights. However, Cust, like Daniels, Light, and Caplan, notes that the right is not unlimited because of resource constraints and the ever-increasing demand for heath care. Thus, he balances the moral right to health care with the notion of a just minimum.

One aspect of this underlying issue is whether health care is a right, in the same way that there is a right to education (a state mandate). In most industrialized countries, health care is indeed considered a right. The United States and South Africa are the only industrialized countries without national health care systems.[1] And as we shall see, one of the problems to be discussed is the increasing number of people without health insurance.

Watson (1994) argues that, at least for minorities, civil rights is at the base of health care inequities. He points to significant noneconomic barriers that lead to less access to health care and thus poorer health care for minorities. Thus, he advocates new civil rights legislation that would forbid discriminatory practices, including unintentional ones, "if they are not necessary to the provision of health care and if their goals cannot be substantially accomplished through less discriminatory alternatives" (Watson 1994, 132).

A human rights approach to health care, with similarities to the ideas discussed above, also provides justification for expanding access to health insurance and health care services. Chapman (1994) defines human rights as those rights people inherently have because they are human. Human rights exist within the context of a community (see the discussion of community below) and are given high, though not absolute, priority. Chapman writes that these rights are "regarded as essential to the adequate functioning of the human being within the context of community and (society) accepts responsibility for its promotion and protection" (Chapman 1994, 5). Thus there is the obligation on the part of society to fulfill those rights, though again there are limits to how much those rights, like some of the others we have discussed above, are fulfilled. Like Daniels, Light, and Caplan, Chapman holds that health care as a human right would be limited to those services that would allow a person to function in society and to achieve his or her potential. Chapman goes further when she states that:

> The litmus test in this model of human rights is the extent to which the rights of the most vulnerable and disadvantaged individuals and groups are assured by these arrangements. A human rights standard assumes a special obligation or bias in favor of the needs and rights of the poor, the disadvantaged, the powerless, and those at the periphery of society. (Chapman 1994, 7)

Aday (1993b) argues that we should not base our health care system on a right to health care, which is within the individualistic, liberal tradition of American politics (see chapter 1). Instead, we should employ the notion of the common good, that it is in the best interest of the community, of society, not just the individual, that all its members have access to health care.[2] Kari, Boyte, and Jennings (1994) argue that health care should be seen as a civic question, where all participate in policy deliberations and emphasis should be placed on preventing disease and promoting health.

Stone (1993) contends that in recent years, and for good financial reasons, the private insurance market has moved away from notions of community embodied in the civics and communitarian approach of Kari, Boyte, and Jennings. Insurance was originally intended as a means to spread the risk of individual misfortune among the larger community. Private insurers have increasingly sought to fragment the market, however, searching for those who are good health risks and placing more of the burden of financing care on those who are poor risks. This undermines the idea of community.

The debates over national health insurance, Medicare, Medicaid, and health care reform are, in a sense, marked by notions of community. Do we help those who are vulnerable or disadvantaged, or is everyone on his or her own? The implications of the two choices are not trivial.

Jecker (1993), likewise, suggests that the link between employment and health insurance itself creates injustices, an argument that Enthoven (2003) makes in a different context. Jecker argues that there is discrimination in the distribution of jobs, focusing on gender-based discrimination, and that this creates discrepancies in the availability of health insurance. We consider the problems of women and the health care system later in this chapter. As one example, consider that women are less likely to be employed in jobs that offer health insurance than men are.[3]

Thus, access to health care raises important ethical issues. What we must do now is document that the problems indeed do exist.

Uninsured and Underinsured

As noted, most people in the United States with health insurance have it through their jobs. In 2003, about 84.4 percent of the population were covered by health insurance, about the same percentage as in 1994 (see Table 5.1). Of that 84.4 percent in 2003, about 26.6 percent were insured by public programs. Comparing the 2003 numbers with 1994, we see that dependence on private insurance has gone down. Private insurance is generally linked to employment. Table 5.1 indicates that 68.6 percent of the population had employer-based insurance in 2003, compared to 70.3 percent in 1994. For those under sixty-five, coverage by employer-sponsored insurance in 2003 was 61.9 percent, a decline from 66 percent in 2000. This is partly, though not entirely, a function of the recession in 2001 and the slow job recovery for several years after that (Hoffman, Carbaugh, and Cook 2004; see also Holahan and Ghosh 2004).

Table 5.1 also presents data about the number and percentage of uninsured persons. Note that the percentage of persons without insurance increased from 1999 to 2003. For 2003, the number of uninsured persons was almost forty-five million. These numbers give an incomplete picture of the uninsurance problem. The data are, in a sense, a snapshot, a picture of those without insurance. A number of people experience spells of uninsurance during the year. One estimate is that about one-third of the population was without health insurance at some point during the period from 1996 to 1999, representing about 84.4 million people (Short and Graefe 2003).

The question to be raised is, why has health insurance coverage decreased?[4] This is an important question, given two facts. One is that much health insurance coverage, as noted earlier, is linked to jobs. This is the uniqueness of health care in the United States, a combination of public and private coverage, what Hacker (2002) calls the "divided welfare state." Second, such coverage decreased in the 1990s, even as job expansion was impressive. Job growth in the 2000s has been slower, with the first years of the recovery being exceptionally slow. Coverage has continued to decline.

One way of looking at this is to consider employment-based insurance for children. In 1988, about 73.6 percent of children were covered under private insurance, most of that through a parent's employer. By 2003, that number had declined to 65.9 percent (Bureau of the Census 2004a). It should be noted that the number of children without any coverage has remained stable because of expansions in Medicaid, though a number of Medicaid-eligible children are not covered. The numbers show that the unique basis of medical insurance in the United States is declining (Gould 2004). Why?

Table 5.1

Sources of Health Insurance Coverage, 1994–2003

	Percent of population insured by all sources	Percent of total insured by employer	Percent of population insured by public insurance*	Percent of population with nongroup insurance	Percent of population without health insurance	Number of people uninsured (in millions)*
2003	84.4	68.6	26.6	8.2	15.6	45.0
2002	84.8	69.6	25.7	8.3	15.2	43.6
2001	85.4	70.9	25.3	8.3	14.6	41.2
2000	85.8	71.9	24.7	7.8	14.2	39.8
1999	85.7	72.1	24.3	9.3	14.3	42.6
1998	83.7	70.2	24.3	8.2	16.3	44.3
1997	83.9	70.1	24.8	8.7	16.1	43.5
1996	84.4	70.2	25.9	9.0	15.6	41.7
1995	84.6	70.3	28.7	9.2	15.4	40.6
1994	84.8	70.3	29.3	9.4	15.3	39.7

Source: Bureau of the Census, "Health Insurance Coverage" [from 1994–2002]; Bureau of the Census 2004a, b.
Note: Public insurance includes Medicare, Medicaid, and military. Some people have coverage under more than one type of insurance (i.e., Medicare and Medicaid, or Medicare plus retiree insurance).
*Estimates of the number of uninsured were lowered in 1999.

The answer lies partly in the restructuring of the American economy. Insurance coverage is linked to size and type of firm (Claxton et al. 2004). The largest firms, those with 200 or more employees, are much more likely to offer health insurance to their employees than smaller firms. During the period from 1996 to 2004, an average of 99 percent of such firms offered the health insurance benefit in good times and bad. During the same period, 59 to 63 percent of firms with less than 200 employers offered health insurance. Further, the percentages varied depending on economic conditions. For example, 68 percent of such firms offered health insurance in 2000 and 2001; by 2004 the number was down to 63 percent. Barely half of the smallest firms offered health insurance in 2004. Much of the growth in jobs since the mid-1990s has been in smaller businesses, exactly those that are less likely to offer health insurance.

Why is there so much more insurance coverage in larger as opposed to smaller firms? While there is probably more turnover in smaller firms, the size factor is most important. The idea behind insurance is to spread or pool the risk over a large population. Insurance companies view each individual firm or individual buyer as a self-contained unit, instead of pooling all those covered under the insurance company's policies. Therefore, smaller firms have more difficulty in negotiating favorable rates for their employees than do larger companies. Their costs per employee are higher than in larger firms. Further, when faced with rising health insurance costs, small firms are more likely to drop the benefit entirely rather than turn to managed care or self-insurance (General Accounting Office 1997a; see also Gabel and Pickreign 2004).

Despite the more generous benefits in larger firms, erosion of insurance within these larger firms has also become noticeable. More than one-quarter of those uninsured were in families with at least one worker in a larger firm (500 or more employees) in 2001. Such firms also accounted for 32 percent of uninsured workers in 2001, up from 25 percent in 1987 (Glied, Lambrew, and Little 2003).

Another reason there has been erosion in employer-based health insurance has to do with the sectors of the economy that are growing and shrinking. Manufacturing firms and unionized firms (with much overlapping) are more likely to offer insurance than service-based or agricultural firms (Holahan and Ghosh 2004). For example, 96 percent of unionized firms offer health insurance to their employees compared to 61 percent of nonunion firms (Claxton et al. 2004). The service sector has experienced considerable growth, while the manufacturing sector and unionization have shrunk (Thorpe 1997).

Consider the following numbers. In 1970, some 20.7 million workers were in the manufacturing sector; by 1996, that number had declined to 20.5 million, a decrease of about 1.1 percent. In 2003, the number had shrunk still further to 16.9 million. By contrast, 20.4 million workers were in the service sector in 1970; by 1996, that number had increased to a little over 45 million workers, an increase of over 120 percent. By 2003, the number had increased to almost 74 million people. Another way of looking at this is to compare the relative shares of manufacturing and service workers. In 1970, the share of workers in manufacturing was 26.4 percent; in 1996, that share had declined to 16.2 percent; in 2003 it was 12.3 percent The share of workers in the service sector in 1970 was 25.9 percent, a little less than the manufacturing share. But by 1996, the service-sector share of jobs had increased to 35.6 percent. In 2003, the number had increased to 53.7 percent (calculated from Bureau of the Census 1997, 2004c). Thus, if there is less likelihood that the service sector will offer health insurance than the manufacturing sector, it is understandable why fewer workers have health insurance.

Wal-Mart, the largest employer in the United States, is a good example of these tendencies and problems. It has been criticized for failing to provide health care benefits for many of its employees. Most of those not receiving insurance were the lower-level and less-well paid workers. Almost half of the children of Wal-Mart employees are either in Medicaid programs or remain uninsured (Abelson 2005). Indeed, a study commissioned by the company found that the presence of Wal-Mart stores in a community tended to depress wages for its employees and as well as for other workers in the communities and to increase spending on Medicaid ("Wal-Mart Conference" 2005).

A related problem concerns younger retirees, those between fifty-five and sixty-five. Many such retirees once maintained their health care plans with their former companies. Larger firms (and unionized firms) are more likely to offer health insurance to their retired workers than smaller and nonunionized firms. However, even the larger firms are less likely to cover retirees. In 1988, 66 percent of large firms (200 or more workers) offered such a benefit. By 1999 the number was down to 40 percent. In 2004, the number was 36 percent (Claxton et al. 2004).

There are three other components to our understanding of the growth of the uninsured population. First is the growth in part-time or temporary workers. They are also unlikely to have health insurance, even if they work in firms that offer it to their full-time employees (Thorpe 1997). Second, a number of uninsured workers are covered as dependents under their spouses' health insurance. To the extent that this is the case, then the fact that not all firms offer health insurance is not quite as much of a problem. In 2003, 81.5 million workers had health insurance and another 77.8 million people had insurance as dependents of other workers (Fronstin 2004). Some of these 77.8 million are workers in jobs that offer health insurance. On the other hand, this amounts to a subsidy from firms that offer health insurance to firms that do not. Additionally, because of the changing job structure situation, sectors that provide dependent coverage are also shrinking, so it is not just those with insurance-covered jobs but the dependents in non-insurance-covered jobs who are losing coverage.

Another part of the explanation for the uninsurance problem is that Medicaid, the health care program for the poor, covers only 40 percent of those with low incomes, defined for our purposes as families with incomes less than $15,000 (calculated from Fronstin 2004, Figure 13). As we explained in chapter 3, Medicaid eligibility is set by states, and Medicaid is a costly program for them, even though the federal government picks up over half the costs. Medicaid increases, combined with other budget pressures, including spending on crime and education, tight fiscal circumstances, and resistance to tax increases, led to efforts to constrain spending (see chapters 3 and 10). Despite expansion of Medicaid coverage for children and the establishment of the State Children's Health Insurance Program (SCHIP) (chapter 3), many children in low-income families (about 20 percent) remain uninsured (Kaiser Commission on Medicaid and the Uninsured 2004a).

But there is a more fundamental reason for people's being uninsured: health insurance is expensive, an issue we discuss in the next chapter. This is one of the reasons, discussed earlier, that smaller firms are less likely to offer health insurance than larger firms. This is the issue that confronts larger companies such as General Motors and Wal-Mart. If it is difficult for small firms to afford insurance because of the small pool of workers, then it is even more difficult for individuals to afford it. Such plans are not only costly in terms of premiums but are likely to have significant cost-sharing provisions.

One last aspect remains. The section heading refers to the uninsured and the underinsured. The underinsured are those who have health insurance but whose insurance is inadequate for their present or future needs. This refers especially to those who may have illnesses such as AIDS (acquired immunodeficiency syndrome) or multiple sclerosis, chronic diseases that are potentially expensive to cover.

Profiling the Uninsured

The obvious picture of the uninsured is that they are poor. Insurance coverage is linked to income: those with lower incomes are less likely to be insured than those with higher incomes (Bureau of the Census 2004b). In terms of income, in 2003, over 36 percent of those with incomes below the poverty line were uninsured, and 30 percent of those with incomes between 100 and 199 percent of the poverty line were uninsured. By contrast, only 6 percent of those with incomes greater than 400 percent of the poverty line were uninsured (Hoffman, Carbaugh, and Cook 2004). Most of the increase in uninsurance in the period from 2000 to 2003 was among those with lower levels of income, less than 200 percent of the poverty line (Hoffman, Carbaugh, and Cook 2004). Among age groups, the youngest adults, ages nineteen to thirty-four, saw the greatest increase in being uninsured (Hoffman, Carbaugh, and Cook 2004).

A sizable number of uninsured people were in households where there were workers, and this was affected by whether family income was above or below 200 percent of the poverty line and whether there were one or two full-time workers, or whether the primary worker worked part-time. Only 41 percent of families with two full-time workers and incomes below 200 percent of the poverty line had employer-based health insurance compared to 87 percent of those with higher income. Similarly, the uninsurance rate was 30 percent for the former group compared to 6 percent for the latter group (Collins et al. 2004; Hoffman, Carbaugh, and Cook 2004). Part-time workers had very high uninsurance or noncoverage rates, 31 percent as compared to 18 percent for families with one full-time worker and 9 percent for families with two full-time workers (Hoffman, Carbaugh, and Cook 2004). Almost half of the uninsured worked in small firms or are self-employed (Hoffman, Carbaugh, and Cook

2004). Younger adults were more likely to be uninsured than other age groups. Minorities and foreign-born people (especially noncitizens) had high uninsurance rates (Hoffman, Carbaugh, and Cook 2004).

Consequences of Uninsurance or Underinsurance

There is a simple and easy, though not pleasant, answer to the question of the consequences of inadequate or no insurance. That answer is that such people are at higher risk of disease and death and are less likely to receive the services they need than are those who have insurance. This section documents that claim.

The uninsured are less likely than the insured to have a regular physician (see Committee on the Consequences of Uninsurance 2002; Kaiser Commission on Medicaid and the Uninsured 2004b). Uninsured people suffering from acute diseases are less likely, about a third less likely, to see a physician than those with acute illnesses who have health insurance (Hafner-Eaton 1993). The same is true for those suffering from chronic diseases, and the uninsured are also less likely to seek preventive care (Kaiser Commission on Medicaid and the Uninsured 2004b).

Because those lacking insurance also do not have a regular private physician they often use emergency rooms, particularly in public hospitals, as their primary source of care (Baker, Stevens, and Brook 1994) or they resort to some sort of self-care (Vuckovic 2000). The uninsured and the underinsured are also less likely to make use of early screening, preventive, or laboratory services (Broyles, Narine, and Brandt 2002; Fairbrother et al. 2003). Many who need care do not get it because they cannot afford it and are also likely to label their health condition as poor or fair (Hoffman et al. 2001). One result of delaying needed physician visits is that Medicaid patients and those without insurance are more likely to be hospitalized for conditions that could be avoided or treated outside hospitals than those with private insurance. Uninsured hospital patients are more likely to enter hospitals sicker and have shorter stays and fewer procedures performed on them than privately insured patients. They also have a higher death rate than insured patients (Committee on the Consequences of Uninsurance 2002).

Perhaps the most important impact is on children. Children whose families lack health insurance are less likely to see a physician than children in families with insurance (Children's Defense Fund 1998). Typical and treatable maladies of childhood, such as ear and throat infections, may go untreated and worsen (Quintana, Goldmann, and Homer, 1997).

Further, barriers other than lack of insurance may hinder needed physician visits. These include cost-sharing provisions, lack of transportation, and lack of child care (Stoddard, St. Peter, and Newacheck 1994). The General Accounting Office (now the Government Accountability Office) expressed the problem this way:

> But having health insurance is no guarantee that children will get appropriate, high-quality care. Some children live in families that do not understand the need for preventive care

or do not know how to seek high-quality care. Some live in neighborhoods that have few health care providers, where they have to travel further and wait longer for care. Some live in families in which most of the members do not speak English or defer getting care because they have had difficulty getting care previously. Some children have health insurance that does not cover some of the services they need the most—such as dental care or physical therapy for the developmentally disabled. . . . Such barriers can reduce the likelihood that even insured children will get the care they need. (General Accounting Office 1997b)

Lack of insurance may affect the most helpless of people, newly born babies. Uninsured women are less likely to receive prenatal care than are privately insured women (Oberg et al. 1990). Uninsured (and Medicaid-insured) babies are likely to be discharged from hospitals sooner than privately insured babies. This is the case even though uninsured or Medicaid-insured babies experience more serious health problems than privately insured babies (Braverman et al. 1991).

The presence of health insurance also has an impact on the diagnosis of breast cancer. Women who have no health insurance or are covered by Medicaid are more likely to have breast cancer diagnosed later in the progression of the disease and are more likely to die as a result than women with breast cancer who have private health insurance (Ayanian et al. 1993). More generally, cancer patients lacking health insurance are more likely to get inferior care than those with health insurance (Thorpe and Howard 2003).

Those without health insurance also perceive themselves as less healthy than those with insurance. Death rates may be higher for those who lack health insurance than for those with it. This may be because of both lack of access to medical care and lower quality of care when it is received (Committee on the Consequences of Uninsurance 2002).

A 2003 study found that those in the fifty-five to sixty-four age group (near-retired, but not yet eligible for Medicare) were less likely to be able to make use of advances in medical technology. The result is higher incidences of morbidity (sickness) and mortality (death) (Glied and Little 2003).

Further, the lack of health insurance coverage results in low-income families having to make difficult choices in how to allocate their budgets. The competing demands of housing, food, clothing, and so forth, lead lower-income families to forego purchasing health insurance (Long 2003).

Uninsurance and underinsurance have impacts beyond those of the individual. Because uninsured people are more likely to use expensive emergency rooms than to use a regular physician, the cost of that care is shifted to others. Indeed, hospitals in particular engage in considerable cost shifting, given service to the uninsured and the low reimbursement rates for Medicaid patients. Those with private insurance are charged more (and pay higher premiums) because of such cost shifting. Because of the Medicare hospital Prospective Payment System (PPS), discussed in chapter 4, shifting costs to Medicare patients is virtually impossible. Given this cost shifting, portions of the community pay for uninsured care, but not on an explicit basis. Further, the use of underwriting creates a situation where those who most need the help are least likely to get it. That runs against the grain of the purpose of insurance.

Further, use of emergency rooms and trauma centers by uninsured patients places a heavy demand on those facilities (Stern et al. 1991). Because of uncompensated care, hospitals and trauma centers face financial problems. A further insight into the problem is that a number of uninsured people using emergency rooms are pregnancy- and childbirth-related cases and often do not get needed prenatal care (Zollinger, Saywell, and Chu 1991). The managed care revolution, discussed in chapter 10, may exacerbate some of these tendencies. Indeed, in the 1990s, while the number of uninsured people increased, fewer hospitals provided uncompensated care, and those that did provide it, especially public hospitals, faced significant financial pressures (Cunningham and Tu 1997; see also Atkinson, Helms, and Needleman 1997; and Mann et al. 1997).

There are responses to being uninsured or inadequately insured. One is financial difficulty, and one way of handling such financial catastrophe is bankruptcy, much of it related to credit card debt. It appears that medical expenses are one cause of bankruptcy filings (see Himmelstein et al. 2005; Kilborn 1997). Legislation that passed in 2005 will make it more difficult for people with large medical bills to use bankruptcy to emerge from their debt (Appleby 2005).

What do underinsured people do to compensate for their potential financial risk? They face high premiums, coinsurance, and deductibles; stringent screening for pre-existing conditions; exclusions of specific conditions; and limitations on maximum insurance benefits. Kinney and Steinmetz (1994) argue that they form essentially an "insurance underground." These authors studied people who suffered from multiple sclerosis in Indiana and found various coping strategies. These included staying in jobs so as not to lose insurance coverage ("job lock") and avoiding filing claims that would call attention to their condition. The result is even more inadequate insurance coverage and access to care, and aggravation of the chronic health problem (Reed and Tu 2002).

Another response to lack of adequate insurance is that more families are becoming caregivers, sometimes for their elderly parents (see chapter 4 on Medicare) but often for a child or spouse (Fisher 1998).

Insurance and the Idea of Community

This brings us back to the issue of equity. Most health insurance provisions are put in place regardless of income. Consider a company that offers a health insurance plan covering dependents. The premiums are $350 a month for family coverage and there are cost-sharing provisions. All employees are offered the same plan. The general manager of the company makes $215,000 a year (before taxes) and the janitor makes $20,000 (before taxes). Both have to pay the $350 monthly premium. The premium is only 2.8 percent of the general manager's income, but is 21 percent of the janitor's income. Now extend this example to those who try to buy health insurance as individuals rather than as part of a group. Typically, premiums for individual policies are not as high as family group policies but are also not as generous. Cost-sharing provisions tend to be larger for individual policies (Kaiser Family Foundation 2004a; Pollack and Kronebusch 2004).

There is another way in which ethical issues play a role in the uninsurance and underinsurance problem. This is the problem of changes in insurance company policies. To simplify, health insurance policies can take two forms. On the one hand is community rating. This exists when everybody in the insurance pool pays the same premiums (though there may be differences based on age and other such factors, a practice known as risk adjustment). That way, the risk of using the insurance (needing health care) is spread over a larger population. Larger firms are more likely to have community rating than smaller firms. Because the pool of employees is larger, there is a larger group of workers over which to spread the risk. Smaller firms, with fewer workers, have a smaller group over which to spread the risk. Insurance companies could handle the problem by treating all those it insures as the community, so it would not matter whether the firm was large or small, or the policy was for an individual or a group. Note that pooling risk for individual policies by definition cannot be done.

There has been an increasing tendency for insurance companies to write policies based on experience rating. Under experience rating, the premiums are adjusted based on the likely risk of needing health care. A person with a chronic heart problem, for example, is more likely to need health care than one in good health with no chronic problems. Automobile insurance is written on this basis. Premiums are higher for those in the highest-risk groups. This includes those who have been in accidents and those in groups most likely to have accidents. For example, young single males have the highest auto insurance premiums of any group.

Such a practice makes sense from the standpoint of the insurance company, as well as policyholders in low-risk groups. Those more likely to need the service should pay more. Having community rating in auto insurance would mean higher rates for those in the low-risk groups and lower rates for those in the high-risk groups.

But health care and health insurance are not automobile insurance. People in good health can do more, can realize more of their potential, than those in poor health. Health care is instrumental in the sense that it enables one to do other things. If there is a systematic bias through experience rating, then it carries over into other areas.

Stone brings the debate of community versus experience rating out into the open, looking at its philosophical underpinnings:

> Actuarial fairness—each person paying for his own risk—is more than an idea about distributive justice. It is a method of organizing mutual aid by fragmenting communities into ever-smaller, more homogeneous groups and a method that leads ultimately to the destruction of mutual aid. This fragmentation must be accomplished by fostering in people a sense of their differences, rather than their commonalities, and their responsibility for themselves only, rather than their interdependence. Moreover, insurance necessarily operates on the logic of actuarial fairness when it, in turn, is organized as a competitive market. (Stone 1993)

Such a view is incorporated in President George W. Bush's "ownership society" perspective. Each person would buy his or her own health insurance using money put away in tax-deferred health savings accounts (Vieth 2004; see also chapter 10).

The important idea here is that the insurance practice of experience rating breaks down the idea of community. The community argument would support at a minimum insurance reform and at a maximum national health insurance. In-between policies might include tax subsidies and employer mandates.

There is another insurance practice, very much related to experience rating, that leads to some people being uninsured and others being underinsured. This is the practice of insurance underwriting. Underwriting occurs when an insurance company refuses to insure workers in an entire firm (a practice known as "redlining") or individuals with preexisting conditions. Examples of redlined firms include "those characterized by an older work force (over age fifty-five) or high employee turnover, those engaged in seasonal work or exposed to hazardous working conditions, those lacking an employer-employee relationship, and those 'known to present frequent claims submissions'" (Zellers, McLaughlin, and Frick 1992, 174–75). Those with preexisting conditions, such as cancer, diabetes, or AIDS, and those with conditions that are likely to result in costly claims in the future, may be denied insurance either permanently or during a specified time. In addition, limits may be placed on payments to such individuals. An alternative practice is to raise all the premiums for the groups significantly, sometimes to prohibitive levels. It is not just insurance companies that engage in this practice. Employers that self-insure, and thus do not come under state regulation as do insurance companies, can also deny claims. Another thing companies can do is simply fire workers with high health care costs. This is apparently happening with workers with disabilities as firms seek to limit their health care costs (see Pereira 2003).

There is a law, the Consolidated Omnibus Budget Reconciliation Act (COBRA), passed in 1986, that allows workers who lose their jobs to maintain their health insurance for up to eighteen months after they lost their job (Kreidler, n.d). While this does provide for some workers and their families, the insurance is expensive. Under COBRA, the displaced worker pays both the employee's and the employer's share of the costs, including any increases that might occur over the eighteen-month period. The costs are substantial. For 2003, employer-covered workers paid on average $508 a year in premiums for health insurance, while the employer paid $3,383. For family coverage, the numbers were $2,412 for the workers and $6,656 for the employer (Kaiser Family Foundation 2003). So the worker with family coverage who lost his or her job would be paying $9,068, more than three-and-a-half times what he or she previously paid, but without the job to pay for it.

Even those who are insured may be underinsured. Kinney and Steinmetz (1994, 637) provide a definition and estimate of underinsurance, based on the 1990 Pepper Commission report: "those at risk of spending more than 10 percent of their annual income for health care in the event of serious illness."

A Closer Look: The Poor, Minorities, and Women

In this section, we consider the health care problems of the disadvantaged, focusing on the poor, minorities, and women. To some extent, the material in this section overlaps with that in the previous section on the uninsured and the underinsured. But as we have noted, a sizable portion of the uninsured are not poor and do work. There are thus other problems that need to be addressed.

Pollack and Kronebusch (2004, 206) identify four factors or dimensions that make some groups likely to be uninsured (or underinsured) and therefore suffer the consequences that we have discussed above. These factors are: "needs that hinder access to insurance, general economic disadvantage, discrimination, and impaired and proxy decisionmaking."

Minorities and Low-Income Groups

In general, minorities and low-income groups do not have the same access to health care, or do not compare on the same level on health statistics as those who are white and/or wealthier. This is not a new phenomenon, as Byrd and Clayton (2003) make clear in their historical discussion of disparities in health care. In drawing this portrait of low-income and minority groups, we should point out that this is a statistical portrait. It applies in general to the groups discussed.

In looking at the health status of minority and low-income groups, we should note several important features. First, minority groups tend to have lower educational achievement, higher unemployment rates, higher crime rates, lower incomes and therefore higher poverty rates, higher proportions of female-headed families, and higher proportions of out-of-wedlock births. All of this seems to be correlated with health status. One of the confusing aspects of these data is that they are very much related to income. That is, many of these characteristics may be a result of poverty (socioeconomic class) rather than ethnicity (race) (Committee on the Consequences of Uninsurance 2002).[5]

One issue related to low-income groups suggests that their poorer health status is largely attributable to "risky" behaviors that they engage in, such as smoking, drinking, being overweight, and not exercising. In a sense, this is an argument that can be labeled "blaming the victim" (Ryan 1971; see also the discussion in Levy and Meltzer 2004). That is, this hypothesis suggests that higher mortality rates are due to actions taken (or not taken) by each person. A study reported in the June 3, 1998, issue of *JAMA* found that even considering such behaviors, low-income groups had higher mortality rates than higher income groups. Changing the behaviors would certainly help some, but mortality differences would remain (Lantz, House, and Chen 1998).

McBride argues that health care policy toward blacks went through three stages. The first stage was engagement (mid-1960s to late 1970s), where health care services and financing were increased to the black community and discrimination was lessened. The second phase, submersion, from the late 1970s to the mid-1980s, saw a cutback in social programs. For example, as a result of the 1981 Omnibus Budget and Reconciliation Act, the working poor were taken off AFDC and Medicaid rolls. The third phase, crisis recognition, began in the mid-1980s. This is a recognition that there is a problem, particularly in the large urban cities. But McBride points out that this last phase has not yet resulted in changed policies. Thus the health care problems of minorities and low-income groups remain (McBride 1993). Indeed, a study of Chicago, Houston, and Los Angeles noted "the progressive deterioration in the delivery of health care to the poor and the indigent since the beginnings of the 1980s" (Ginzberg 1994).

The issue of the health of minorities, especially African Americans, became part of the debate over Social Security reform in 2005. President George W. Bush (Manjoo 2005; Wallsten and Simon 2005) and others (see, for example, Tanner [2001] of the Cato Institute) have argued that Social Security in its current form disadvantages African Americans because their life spans are shorter than whites, thus they do not reap as much of the benefit.

This is a statement that is true on the face of it, but misleading. The reason is that African Americans have poorer health status than whites. They suffer from higher mortality rates due to homicide, AIDS (see below), and infant mortality. However, the life expectancy of African Americans at sixty-five is about the same as whites. The problem then is one of health care disparities, which were not addressed by President Bush (see Krugman 2005; Rockeymore 2005).

Minorities are more likely to be uninsured than the white population. For non-Hispanic whites, the uninsurance rate was 11.1 percent in 2003. The rate for African Americans was 19.5 percent, for Asians 18.7 percent, and for Hispanics 32.7 percent (Bureau of the Census 2004b; see also Pollack and Kronebusch 2004). We should thus expect the consequences of uninsurance to be higher among minorities than among the majority white population.

Age-adjusted death rates are higher for minorities than for whites. Death rates due to a variety of factors, including diabetes, cardiovascular disease, cancer, infant mortality, and substance abuse, are higher among minorities than for whites (Agency for Health Care Research and Quality 2003; Committee on the Consequences of Uninsurance 2002; Hogue, Hargraves, and Collins 2000). Minorities tend to have less access to prenatal care and to give birth at earlier ages (National Center for Health Statistics 2004). This tends to result in higher rates of premature and low-weight births (Agency for Health Care Research and Quality 2003). The low-birth-weight problem shows little change. There is, additionally, much variation within the Latino population. Puerto Rican women had the highest rate of low-weight births, while women from Mexico and Central and South America had low-weight birth rates close to the white rate (Millman 1993). Low-weight births in turn are associated with other problems (not just health) in later years. Infant mortality is higher among minorities. Further, children from minority and/or low-income families are less likely to receive all the necessary vaccinations (Agency for Health Care Research and Quality 2003).

Why do disadvantaged women not get full prenatal care? One reason is financial barriers. Minority and low-income women are less likely to have health insurance than the general population (Agency for Health Care Research and Quality 2003, Garner et al. 1996). Clarke et al. (1995) find that minority women are somewhat less likely to receive prenatal care than white women, are more likely to begin such care in the third trimester of pregnancy, and are more likely to receive inadequate care. With a few exceptions, those living in rural areas are less likely to receive adequate services than those living in metropolitan areas. African Americans comprised about 13 percent of the population and accounted for over 19 percent of the uninsured in 2002. Latinos comprise about 14 percent of the population, and almost 34 percent of the uninsured in 2002 (Kates and Leggoe 2005a; National Center for Health Statistics 2004). Even though Medicaid has been expanded in recent years (since 1986) to cover more prenatal care, many states have not taken the appropriate action. Further, even if all the states covered the entire poverty population of expectant mothers (100 percent of those under the poverty line), those just over the poverty line would still be excluded. It should be noted again that even with expansions in the late 1980s and early 1990s, Medicaid covered less than half of those under the federal poverty line, as we discussed in chapter 3.

Even if financial barriers did not exist, there are not enough doctors willing to work in low-income areas or with high-risk mothers. In 2001, only 62 percent of physicians accepted new Medicaid patients, and only 54 percent of primary care physicians did so (Zuckerman et al. 2004). Thus the services, even if affordable, might not be available.

Minorities also fare worse than the overall population in terms of chronic illnesses. The following quote, which dates to 1991, remains an adequate depiction of the situation:

> In general, Blacks are diagnosed and/or seek treatment later than Whites for many chronic diseases, and this may have significant implications for the efficacy of treatment and for survivorship for many chronic diseases. What is more, once under medical management or therapy, the treatment received by Blacks may be less aggressive than that received by Whites. (U.S. Department of Health and Human Services 1991)

For example, studies show that minority women are less likely to get screenings such as mammography and pap smears than whites (Agency for Health Care Research and Quality 2003). Minority women with breast cancer are less likely to receive surgery and more likely to receive no treatment than whites. A study of bladder cancer victims showed that African Americans were less likely to receive treatment than whites at similar stages of disease (Agency for Health Care Research and Quality 2003, U.S. Department of Health and Human Services 1991).

Another health problem of minorities, though it may not appear that way, is homicide rates. Homicide rates of African American males are 687 percent higher than those of white males (using 2002 numbers). They are also higher for Latinos, though the difference is not as great (National Center for Health Statistics 2004).

AIDS is another health problem that affects ethnicity differently. While a majority of AIDS victims are whites, the relative proportion of AIDS victims is disproportionately much higher among African Americans and Latinos. The white proportion is 7.2 cases per 100,000, versus 26.6 per 100,000 for Latinos and 75.2 per 100,000 for African Americans. To put it another way, whites are 69 percent of the population but accounted for 28 percent of new AIDS diagnoses in 2003, versus Latinos, who make up 14 percent of the population and accounted for 20 percent of new AIDS diagnoses, and African Americans, who make up 13 percent of the population but accounted for 49 percent of new AIDS diagnoses (Kates and Leggoe 2005a, b).

African American women are especially hard hit (see Auerbach 2004; Clemetson 2004; and Fears 2005). This became a bit of an issue during the 2004 vice presidential debates between Vice President Dick Cheney and his Democratic challenger, Senator John Edwards of North Carolina. The moderator of the debate, Gwen Ifill, an African American woman, asked the two candidates what the federal government should do to help stem the increase in AIDS among African American women. Neither candidate had an answer, nor even appeared to be familiar with the problem (Auerbach 2004).

But the numbers are indeed daunting. Recall the figures above about new AIDS diagnoses in 2003. African Americans accounted for 49 percent of new AIDS diagnoses. African American women accounted for more than one-third of that number, compared to white women, who made up 14 percent of new diagnoses among whites. African American women accounted for 67 percent of new AIDS diagnoses among women in 2003, compared to white women, who accounted for 15 percent, and Latin American women (Latinas), who accounted for 16 percent (Kates and Leggoe 2005a, b). Further, "AIDS is the fourth-leading cause of death among women in this country between the ages of 25 and 44, and is the *leading* cause of death among African American women ages 25 to 34" (Auerbach 2004, emphasis in original).

The data also show that African American women are more likely than either white women or Latinas to have acquired the virus through heterosexual sex. In urban centers, 32 percent of African American men who have had sex with other men are infected with the virus (Kates and Leggoe 2005a). Drug-related transmissions (i.e., intravenous drug users) are also another major path of HIV infection, though this is more significant for white women than for African American women. Auerbach (2004) summarizes the factors responsible for this epidemic:

> The experience of women and girls in the HIV-AIDS epidemic in the United States and around the world highlights how social arrangements, cultural norms, laws, policies and institutions contribute to the unequal status of women in society and to the spread of disease. Together they undermine the capacity of women and girls to exercise power over their own lives and to control the circumstances that increase their vulnerability to HIV infection, particularly in the context of sexual relationships. For African American women, gender inequalities are exacerbated by persistent racism.

The use of health services for minorities increased beginning in the 1960s with the advent of Medicaid. Nevertheless, such utilization remains below that of whites.

Further, minorities are less likely to have a private physician and more likely to seek primary care in hospital emergency rooms (Hogue and Hargraves 2000). Cutbacks in Medicaid during the 1980s led to a decreased use of services among minorities, but many cutbacks were reversed in the 1990s with the advent of the State Children's Health Insurance Program discussed in chapter 3. The economic problems of the recession in 2001, the slow recovery from the recession, and the fiscal distress experienced by the states, combined with continued Medicaid cost increases, led many states to enact cost-control measures that adversely impacted minorities and low-income families. This largely affected adults . A little more than one-third of states allow parents with incomes at the poverty level to receive Medicaid. In many cases, families with an adult making the minimum wage are not eligible for Medicaid (Ross and Cox 2004). Estimates are that just over 40 percent of the population below the poverty line is covered by Medicaid (calculated from Bureau of the Census 2003, 2004c). A little more than 19 percent of children in families below the poverty line lack health insurance (Bureau of the Census 2004b). Miller and Curties note that even programs such as Medicare, where essentially all who are sixty-five or older have insurance coverage, have not reduced disparities between blacks and whites in the use of health services (Miller and Curties 1993).

Ginzberg (1994) argues that much of the problem of access to health care is not just the result of lack of insurance but has a supply dimension: the expansiveness of the state Medicaid program and the availability of institutions, largely public, that treat charity cases. He also notes that the number of physicians is much lower in impoverished neighborhoods than in wealthier areas.

Americans of Latino descent appear to have the lowest level of health insurance coverage of any ethnic group, including blacks (Bureau of the Census 2004b). Further, there are differences in health insurance coverage within the Latino population, with Puerto Ricans and Cubans having considerably higher levels of coverage than other Latinos (Agency for Health Care Research and Quality 2003). Latinos also suffer from high rates of chronic diseases, such as cancer, diabetes, and AIDS (Agency for Health Care Research and Quality 2003; Kates and Leggoe 2005b).

There are several factors that explain these disparities in health experience, such as coverage and access, among racial and ethnic groups (Smedley, Stith, and Nelson 2003). One set of factors are at the patient level. These include refusal to accept services because of cultural differences between patient and provider. These appear to be minor factors in explaining disparities.

A second set of factors are at the level of the health care system. These include language barriers (especially among Latinos), time pressures facing physicians, and the geographical distribution of available services (i.e., physician and pharmaceutical). Interestingly, the managed care revolution, with its attempts at controlling the cost of health care, likely presents greater barriers to minorities, by displacing community-based systems (Smedley, Stith, and Nelson 2003).

The final set of factors are at the level of the care process, that is, the provider. There might be provider bias toward minorities or their behavior combined with clinical uncertainty in evaluating symptoms (Smedley, Stith, and Nelson 2003). All three sets of factors combine in some fashion to increase health care disparities.

Women

> Research has shown that many diseases and conditions, including heart disease, smoking, and lung cancer, affect women and men very differently. There are also several diseases, such as breast cancer and osteoporosis, that primarily affect women, and another range of conditions, including pregnancy, menopause, and certain reproductive-related cancers, that only affect women. Sex-based differences have been identified on several levels, including treatment efficacy, medication side effects, prevention strategies, and disease etiology. (Kaiser Family Foundation 2004b)

> [T]he issues of women's health cannot be understood only in biological terms, as simply the ills of the female of the species. Women and men are different, but we are also similar —and we both are divided by the social relations of class and race/ethnicity. To begin to understand how our social constitution affects our health, we must ask, repeatedly, what is different and what is similar across the social divides of gender, color, and class. We cannot assume that biology alone will provide the answers we need; instead, we must reframe the issues in the context of the social shaping of our human lives—as both biological creatures and historical actors. Otherwise, we will continue to mistake—as many before us have done—what is for what must be, and leave unchallenged the social forces that continue to create vast inequalities in health. (Krieger and Fee 1996, 27)

To a degree, women's health issues overlap those of minorities (race/ethnicity) and low-income groups (class). To the extent that women's income, especially in families headed by women, is low, then all the health problems associated with low income show up here. For example, issues surrounding prenatal care, while obviously a concern for women, are generally associated with low income. If programs aimed at low-income people are cut, as was done in the early 1980s and is again being done in the 2000s, then women will be affected.

On the other hand, there are certain issues that are unique to women, though of concern to men as well. Reproductive issues, such as abortion and family planning, are among the most controversial issues in health care or any policy field. In general, the availability of abortion, while not completely eliminated, has been reduced beginning in the late 1970s. Some of this has come about because of legislative changes, such as the Hyde amendment forbidding the use of federal Medicaid funds for abortion and similar action by some states. Some is a result of court decisions that have allowed restrictions, such as waiting periods. Another element has been the strong right-to-life movement, which has picketed abortion clinics. Medical schools are less frequently teaching abortion procedures. The election of the strong prolife George W. Bush administration in 2000 and 2004 enhances this trend. The possibility that President Bush may be able to name perhaps as many as three new Supreme Court justices, as well as numerous lower federal court justices, makes the future availability of abortion more tenuous.

Women are also less well protected by health insurance, both public and private. Fewer working women (39.4 percent) have employer-based health insurance than men (51.5 percent) (Fronstin 2004; see also Salganicoff et al. 2002). Baird (1998) notes that married men have higher rates of employer-provided insurance than married women. She also notes that divorce has a devastating effect on private health insurance for unemployed women. Women's employment careers tend to be intermittent (i.e., women may take time off for childbearing, or they may make job changes because their husbands move), and women are more often in lower-paying jobs that are less likely to offer health insurance. Medicaid coverage is sporadic. Fewer than half those eligible are covered, and doctors do not have to accept Medicaid patients. Women are less likely than men to have supplemental Medicare health insurance and are less likely to have their illnesses covered under Medicare (U.S. Department of Health and Human Services 1991), though this has begun to change somewhat with benefits being added to Medicare. Further, because women, on the average, live longer than men, issues of long-term care and chronic illnesses are critical (Salganicoff et al. 2002).

The above paragraph probably understates the problem. First, the percentage of workers covered by employer-based health insurance has declined. Further, there is a growing trend toward using part-time or temporary workers, also unlikely to have health insurance benefits.

There have been changes in the workforce participation of women and in the family structure, where there are two-worker families or where the family is headed by a female. Adjustments to these changes have been slow (the Family Leave Act is one recent adjustment). Muller's (1990, 73) words, written in 1990, still depict the problems facing women and health insurance coverage:

> Independent coverage, benefit content and duplication, and cost sharing are issues that affect women differently in different family situations. Employers have expanded their use of peripheral or contingent workers who have few or no benefit entitlements, drawing on a largely female labor supply. It is not feasible to count on workplace arrangements as the social instrument for protecting individuals against health care costs.

There is another important concern. There is some tendency for both private insurance and Medicare to reimburse at a lower rate for procedures unique to women. A study of gender-specific procedures by Goff et al. (1997a, b) found that Medicare relative value units (RVUs) were 50 percent higher for male-specific procedures than for a similar set of female-specific procedures. Furthermore, private insurance tends to use the RVU scale, and so whatever bias is found with the Medicare scale is replicated in the private sector. One more example: the male-impotency drug Viagra was immediately covered by many insurance plans, but prescription contraceptives for women were covered much more slowly by employer-based health insurance plans ("Gender Bias at Work" 1998; see also Kaiser Family Foundation 2004b).

The health care system treats women differently from men. Medicare tends to cover the kinds of diseases more predominant among men (i.e., heart attacks) better than the chronic diseases more prevalent among women. Men receive more preventive services than women. Women also tend to see a number of specialists, and so their care is often fragmented (Salganicoff et al. 2002). Two observers label women's health care as a "patchwork quilt with gaps" (Clancy and Massion 1992).

Further, as Hafner-Eaton (1993) points out, women are likely to have unnecessary surgeries, such as caesarean births, radical mastectomies, and hysterectomies. Despite this, much of the health research carried on in the United States uses the male as the model. Hafner-Eaton (1993, 843) writes:

> Government notwithstanding, the National Institutes of Health, as recently as 1990, allocated a mere 13.5% of biomedical research funds to women's health. The remainder of funds went to research on men's health or research affecting both. . . . Women's different hormonal balance from men's means that pharmaceuticals used to treat jointly shared conditions might not work, or, worse yet, could be seriously injurious if used as tested safely on men. The use of the male body and its reactions as the norm has detrimental consequences for women and many times for their children as well.

This bias in research has been somewhat alleviated. Since 1991, the U.S. Public Health Service and other federal agencies began to devote more resources to research on women (Mawrick 1992). In some cases, women have engaged in interest group activity to lobby for more medical research on women's issues. Perhaps the most prominent of these efforts focused on breast cancer.

The result of the lobbying was the Women's Health Initiative (WHI) within the National Institutes of Health (NIH) (see National Institutes of Health n.d.). The focus of the research, a fifteen-year study, is on colorectal and breast cancer, heart disease, and osteoporosis.

A related area in women's health that needs further funding is lung cancer. Lung cancer affects more women than breast cancer and has been rising fairly consistently since the 1960s. The survival rate for lung cancer (14 percent) is much lower than that for breast cancer (67 percent). Federally allocated funds for breast cancer research are about six times higher than those for lung cancer research (Brody 1998).

There is also some evidence to suggest that women are not nearly as disadvantaged by the health care system and in research as suggested above (Kadar 1994). Women seek care more frequently than men. The care received by women is at least as good as men's, and there is some tendency for women to receive more diagnostic tests than men. There is a gender difference in cardiac bypass procedures, largely because men who need the procedure tend to be younger (and thus to have fewer additional medical problems) and to have larger arteries (making the operation easier) than women.

Kadar (1994) points out that much innovative medical technology, such as ultrasound, was originally developed for women. He notes that women have a branch of medicine devoted strictly to them (gynecology) whereas men do not (urology probably being the closest).

It was mentioned earlier that only a small fraction of NIH medical research was conducted on women. Kadar (1994) observes that much medical research uses both men and women as subjects. The heightened awareness of breast cancer (the second leading cause of cancer deaths among women, with lung cancer the leading cause) has led to more substantial funding for prevention activities directed toward women. The Centers for Disease Control and Prevention (CDC) allocated $210 million in fiscal year 2004 for early detection. By comparison, prostate cancer, which is the most prevalent form of cancer in men, second only to skin cancer, was allotted $15.5 million in the same fiscal year. This is one-thirteenth the level of CDC funding for breast cancer prevention (National Center for Chronic Disease Prevention and Health Promotion n.d.).

Finally, Kadar (1994) mentions that, at the beginning of the twentieth century, men had a slightly longer life expectancy than women. By the second half of the twentieth century, the life expectancy of women was about 10 percent higher than for men. One of the reasons for the change is that childbirth has become safer. A second reason is that many infectious diseases have been virtually eliminated, and those that remain affect men more than women. Life expectancy, both from birth and from age sixty-five, remains higher for women than for men (National Center for Health Statistics 2004).

Granting Kadar's argument would mean that specific gender problems in health care are drastically overstated. To the extent that women are subject to the forces of ethnicity and class, however, the health of women remains an important concern.

Solutions to the Problems of Uninsurance and Underinsurance

The simple but difficult solution to the problem of lack of health insurance (or lack of adequate health insurance) would be a national health insurance (NHI) system. As we explored in chapter 2, the twentieth century is marked by failures to enact NHI (see Starr 1982). Mayes (2005) refers to this as "the elusive quest." From the early 1900s to the Clinton Health Security Act in the mid-1990s, all attempts fell short. What remains is what we have always done: resort to incremental change.

One possible solution to the problem of those without health insurance or those who are underinsured is to expand Medicaid. Medicaid has proven, in some respects, to be a flexible and generous program. The expansion could serve particularly low-income parents whose children are often on Medicaid while they are not (Dubay and Kenney 2004). Etheridge and Moore (2003) have a much more ambitious view in mind. The new program they propose would be need based, rather than category based; have national, rather than state, eligibility standards that would include low-income parents, low-income elderly, and the disabled; and allow those at high risk of substantial medical costs to buy into Medicaid. Etheridge and Moore argue that Medicaid has already been transformed into something different from what it was when enacted in 1965. Their proposal would extend the trend.

The major roadblock to such an expansion of Medicaid is the costs associated with such a change. As we explained in chapter 3, Medicaid's costs continue to increase, though largely because of population increases, which place stress on state and federal budgets (see Rowland and Tallon 2003). Both governors and the federal government (the George W. Bush administration) are looking for ways to restrain costs (see Pear 2005; Robinson 2005). Under such conditions, expansion of Medicaid is unlikely.

A companion proposal would expand Medicare (see, for example, Hacker 2001), essentially creating a "Part C" that would cover those not insured. It would have the same advantage as mentioned above concerning Medicaid: the structure is already in place. It would add two further advantages. First, Medicare is entirely a federal government program, so the fiscal impact on and program differences between states would not be a problem. Second, provider reimbursement is higher for Medicare than for Medicaid. Thus access to services would be greater. President Bill Clinton proposed expanding Medicare to early retirees (55-64) who did not have health insurance and allowing them to "buy in" to the program. But the proposal stood little chance of passage.

Hacker's proposal is a bit different, though it includes the "buy-in" feature. The proposal would, through a series of incremental steps, move toward more universal coverage. The plan has three components. Those lacking either employer-sponsored or Medicare coverage would buy into the program, with premiums based on income. Employers would either have to offer a plan with at least the same benefits as Medicare or pay into a fund. This is what is known as a "play-or-pay" provision, and is essentially an employer mandate. Tax benefits for employer plans would continue. The third element is an individual mandate, requiring all people to show that they have health insurance, similar to auto insurance requirements.

Given budgetary pressures that mounted during the early years of the twenty-first century, the political will to undertake such a program does not seem readily apparent. Combine this with the ever-increasing costs of the new Medicare drug benefit (see chapter 4) and this looks even less politically promising, however creative and innovative the plan is.

Another proposal, more typical of conservative and Republican proposals as opposed to the more liberal and Democratic Medicaid and Medicare proposals discussed above, would make use of tax credits and tax deductions. Presidents Nixon and George H.W. Bush offered variations of these proposals. Tax credits would be available to the poor, and deductions to middle-income families (including the self-employed). Such tax incentives would be provided to both individuals and employers. One proposal would offer individuals a $1,000 tax credit and families a $3,000 tax credit (Connolly 2005). This would help alleviate the cost of health insurance, but would be substantially less than the cost of nongroup health insurance. A related and more reform-minded proposal would make use of tax-sheltered health savings accounts and high-deductible (i.e., "catastrophic") insurance policies (see Alonso-Zaldivar 2005). We consider such plans in chapter 10.

One problem that would have to be faced with the tax deduction/credit approach is that health care and, concomitantly, insurance premiums would rise faster than the deduction or credit, even if they were indexed to cost-of-living changes (Pear 1992). Another problem with the proposal is that it does not guarantee coverage. Further, to make any appreciable impact on reducing the number of uninsured, the tax credit would have to be much larger than is typically proposed (see Reschovsky and Hadley 2004).

An example of such a tax-credit-based bill was the plan offered by the conservative Heritage Foundation. Butler (1991) argues that the major problem of the health care system, at least as concerns the problem of the uninsured, is the tax code. The tax code allows employers to treat health insurance as a business expense eligible for a tax deduction. This leads to three major problems, two of which are relevant to the uninsurance problem.

The first problem is that the system is inequitable. Assume that health insurance as a fringe benefit is part of the total employee compensation package. If this is so, then the cost of the health insurance if given as salary would be taxed at the highest marginal tax rate. Because high-wage workers are taxed at higher marginal rates than low-wage workers, the benefit would be highest for the high-wage workers. For those who must pay their own health insurance, the inequity is greater because they have only a limited tax deduction and thus must pay more from after-tax dollars (Butler 1991).

The second problem mentioned by Butler is "job lock," in which people keep their jobs for fear of losing health insurance coverage. By tying health insurance to employment, the tax code creates strong bonds between worker and job, a problem presumably dealt with by the Kassebaum-Kennedy bill. The final problem created by the tax code, though it is not directly related to the uninsurance problem, is that it creates inflationary pressures by severing the link between paying for the service and receiving it (Butler 1991).

The Heritage Foundation plan would eliminate the employer tax deduction for health care and replace it with a refundable tax credit for individuals. The tax credit would be available even to those who do not itemize their tax returns. If the health care tax credit were greater than the individual's tax obligation, the difference would be refunded to that individual. The credit would be geared toward the portion of family income spent on health care (insurance and out-of-pocket costs). If a family spent 10 percent of its income on health care, it would be eligible for a 20 percent tax credit (Butler 1991).

One interesting part of the proposal is the "health care social contract." Under the contract, all families would be required to join a health plan with a minimum package of benefits. Though Butler does not use the term, this plan is an individual mandate, rather than an employer mandate. The federal government would be part of the contract by guaranteeing the fiscal viability of the individual mandate, either through tax credits or through access to Medicaid and/or Medicare (Butler 1991).

The plan has important advantages. It severs the tie between work and health insurance (see Enthoven 2003). Employers would no longer have to worry about the increasing costs of health care and workers would not be tied to a job just because of the health insurance benefit. A second advantage is that it is equitable because it focuses on percentage of income regardless of size of income and would provide more help for those who need it more, such as low-income workers and those with chronic health problems. A third advantage is that the program would reduce the costs of Medicaid for both federal and state governments, thus reducing the strain on federal and state budgets or enabling the provision of somewhat more generous programs (Butler 1991).

Like all policy proposals, this one has its disadvantages as well. One is the equity consideration. The argument that Butler makes that the current tax deduction system is inequitable because those with higher incomes would pay at a higher tax rate than those with lower incomes is an assumption. The numbers, on the face of it, are correct. Consider the following:

Let us assume two families filing with the heads of household filing joint income taxes, one with a taxable income of $30,000 a year and the other with a taxable income of $90,000 a year. The families are the same size, and the primary workers for the two families work for the same company and get the same health insurance package from the employer. The employer contribution to both families' health insurance is the same, say $3,000 a year. If the tax deduction were removed and the employer kept the total compensation package the same, the workers would each receive, in theory, an additional $3,000 in salary. This would increase their taxable incomes to $33,000 and $93,000, respectively. The tax for the lower-income family would increase by $450, an increase of about 12 percent (using 2003 tax rates) in tax obligations and a marginal tax rate of 15 percent. The tax for the higher-income family would increase by $840, an increase of about 5.2 percent in tax obligations and a marginal tax rate of about 28 percent. Thus the equity consideration, if it is a consideration at all, would apply only to those whose income was too low to pay federal income taxes. Otherwise, the current system, as Butler explains it, actually favors lower-income families as long as they pay income taxes, if one looks at the actual increase in tax obligations versus marginal tax rates. So, in that sense, Butler is partially correct.

But he is incorrect in two other senses. First, workers get the health insurance but not the money. This is a "let-us-assume" proposition rather than the real world. That is, the employers under such a system might retain some of the $3,000 of health insurance costs rather than give it all to the employee. Second, consider how the tax credit system would work. Let us take our families from the above example, the $30,000 income family and the $90,000 income family. Under the new system, both pay the same percentage of their income on health care. For the first family that amounts to $3,000; for the second family it amounts to $9,000. These are the same in percentage terms, but the impacts on the two families are much different, given the original sizes of their incomes. Both would be eligible for a 20 percent tax credit, but that would amount to $600 for the lower-income family (a cut of 13.3 percent in tax obligation). For the upper-income family, the 20 percent tax credit would amount to $1,800 (a tax cut of 8.9 percent in tax obligation). While the percentage decrease of tax obligation would be lower for the higher-income family, thus seeming to be equitable, the tax credit would be three times as large as for the low-income family. It would be proportional at best.

A final problem with the tax credit plan is that while it may guarantee insurance coverage, it does not deal with the other problems discussed: risk rating and so forth. It also does not guarantee access to health care in inner cities and rural areas, a topic to be discussed below. The proposal is worth considering as perhaps one component of health reform.

Some analysts have looked for a compromise or consensus plan for expanding health insurance coverage. Davis and Schoen (2003) argue that there are areas of agreement, mainly over (1) the existence of the problem, (2) what groups in particular lack health insurance, and (3) the health consequences of not being insured. There are, however, substantial areas of disagreement about proposed solutions.

> The major disagreement is over the role of private insurance in covering the uninsured, whether public programs should be expanded to additional groups, and the commitment of adequate budgetary resources required to assist those who are unable to afford the full cost of health coverage. There is also the question of whether to focus simply on expanding coverage or to reform the delivery of health care services at the same time, and whether to focus expansion on the uninsured or to replace existing coverage with a new system of insurance for all. (Davis and Schoen 2003, W3-199)

Their plan contains a number of elements. The major part is the creation of what they call the Congressional Health Plan. This element would provide for choice of plans in the Federal Health Employees Benefits Program. Members of Congress would join the plan and it would be open to small businesses, those uninsured for six months and lacking group coverage, and those who are self-employed. The federal government would subsidize some of the costs to take account of adverse selection (that is, those who are most likely to use health services would sign up for the plan).

A second element is an individual mandate. A third element is refundable tax credits. Medicare would be expanded to cover more of the disabled, those near the retirement age without coverage, and dependents of Medicare beneficiaries. Medicaid and SCHIP would be expanded to include more people.

The plan would also include an employer mandate of the play-or-pay type. Dependents would be covered up to the age of twenty-three (it is generally twenty-one at this time). The plan could also be phased in, with the congressional health plan coming first. The plan could also be phased in by expanding over time, rather than right away, the number of people covered.

A similar plan was offered by Kahn and Pollack (2001). It is intriguing, not so much for the details of the proposal, but because of who is making it. At the time, Kahn was the president of the Health Insurance Association of America (HIAA), one of the major opponents of the Clinton Health Security Act of 1993. Pollack is the executive director of Families USA, an advocacy group that has long promoted more comprehensive coverage. Thus, the proposal comes from what they called "strange bedfellows" (Kahn and Pollack 2001, 40).

The Kahn and Pollack proposal has four principles or guidelines for extending health insurance coverage: maintain current coverage levels, build on existing structures, make best use of public funds, and focus on those in greatest need (2001, 42–43). The proposal, which they call a "second choice" (46) calls for three levels of coverage. The first level would be that Medicaid would be required to cover everybody within 133 percent of the poverty line. The second portion would be to use Medicaid or SCHIP to cover those up to 200 percent of the poverty line. The third part is a nonrefundable employer tax credit to help pay for low-income workers.

Meyer and Silow-Caroll (2003) argue for making use of the employment-based system because it has considerable public support. To improve access to insurance, there would be a mix of employer-based coverage, enhanced public programs (i.e., Medicaid), back-up insurance pools, and insurance-premium subsidies. Much of the population would be enrolled in some type of "insurance pool" (W3-416), either through one of the public programs or regional exchanges. This would create a number of very large purchasers who would be able to negotiate for lower prices. In many respects, this is related to the managed competition concept embodied in the Clinton Health Security Act.

Another alternative would be to expand the community health center program (Sardell 1988). Community health centers (originally called neighborhood health centers) were created during the 1960s as part of President Lyndon Johnson's War on Poverty. These centers offer comprehensive health services to those in impoverished inner-city neighborhoods and rural areas at minimal or no cost to clients (Davis and Schoen 1978; Starr 1982). By 1991, there were some 550 such centers. Evaluations of community health centers have been very positive (Davis and Schoen 1978). In 1991, the Advisory Council on Social Security recommended the addition of 250 more community health centers (Pear 1991). The community health center approach was embraced by President George W. Bush in his 2005 State of the Union message (Connolly 2005). As of 2004, there were some 1,000 community health centers around the country (National Association of Community Health Centers 2004); Bush would like to double that number.

There are two problems with such proposals. One is cost. Many community health centers face deficits (see McAlearney 2002). Community health centers also appear to be better at providing primary care for their uninsured clientele than more specialized care (Gusmano, Fairbrother, and Park 2002). A second, and probably more important issue, is ideological. Community health centers would put government in the business of more directly providing health services than Medicare or Medicaid.

Conclusion

In this chapter we have considered one of the major problems of the U.S. health care system, that of the disadvantaged. The uniquely American mix of public and private insurance programs, a post–World War II development, covers about 85 percent of the population but leaves over 40 million people without any insurance at all. Especially in the case of private insurance, it also leaves a portion of the population underinsured and vulnerable to catastrophic medical expenses.

One important consideration in the debate about expanding coverage is what the costs would be. The United States has been and is facing considerable health cost pressures, a topic we address in the next chapter. Certainly if we went to universal health insurance coverage, and access to services was less of a problem as well, there would be additional costs. But how much? While there is no way to know for sure, there have been analyses that suggest that the incremental costs may not be all that much. Hadley and Holahan (2003) estimate that the additional costs (remembering that even people and families without health insurance obtain care when absolutely necessary) is in the range of about $40 to $69 billion dollars per year. That seems like a lot of money. But our total health care bill in 2003 was over $1.6 trillion dollars (Heffler et al. 2005). The incremental costs are fairly small (3 to 6 percent).

Incremental reforms, the kind that generally characterize public policy in the United States, have begun to address some of these problems. The SCHIP program focuses on children. The Health Insurance Portability and Accountability Act addresses the "job lock" issue.

Medicaid, Medicare, or both, could be expanded to cover those without insurance, many of whom work. Using the tax system, through either subsidies to employers or tax credits for individuals or families, would also help. Insurance reforms, such as mandating community rating, would also be useful, though there are dangers in doing some of these things individually. A federal or state program of universal coverage, involving either employer or individual mandates, would likely be the simplest, though not necessarily the most politically feasible, way to deal with the problem.

Even were some or all of these policies undertaken, and they have been in some states, the problems of the disadvantaged would remain. Having insurance coverage is important. We know from a considerable body of evidence that those without health insurance have more health problems and receive less and poorer-quality service than those with health insurance. But if the providers are not in the geographical area, such as inner cities or rural areas, having insurance by itself is insufficient.

We also know that poverty, ethnicity, and gender play important and intermixing roles in health outcomes. We know that blacks and Latinos on the average have poorer health outcomes than whites. We know that minority women and their babies have poorer health outcomes: more troubling pregnancies, low birth weights, and so forth. Women are disadvantaged by a medical system that seems to take the white male as the model for research and insurance coverage.

These issues, which involve equality and equity, do not lend themselves to easy solutions. Perhaps the most viable solution is the community health center program, where providers are located in underserved areas. But the likelihood of the expansion of such programs is constrained by costs and ideology. In the absence of a comprehensive transformation of the U.S. health care system, it is likely that the problems of the disadvantaged will remain.

Notes

1. For a discussion of health care in the United States and other countries, see Graig (1999) and White (1995).

2. Aday (1993b) briefly discusses the liberal, individual rights tradition and the communitarian tradition that underlies the notion of the common good. See also Aday (1993a).

3. For critiques of Jecker's argument, see Ruttenberg (1993) and Rochefort (1993).

4. For a discussion of what is known and not known about the issue of uninsurance, largely from an economics standpoint, see McLaughlin (2004).

5. For a discussion of the class versus race issue, see Wilson (1978, 1987).

References

Abelson, Reed. 2005. "Wal-Mart's Health Care Struggle Is Corporate America's, Too." *New York Times* (October 29).

Aday, Lu Ann. 1993a. *At Risk in America: The Health and Health Care Needs of Vulnerable Populations in the United States*. San Francisco: Jossey-Bass.

————. 1993b. "Equity, Accessibility, and Ethical Issues: Is the U.S. Health Care Reform Debate Asking the Right Questions?" *American Behavioral Scientist* 36, no. 6 (July/August): 724–40.

Agency for Health Care Research and Quality. 2003. "National Healthcare Disparities Report." Washington, D.C.: U.S. Department of Health and Human Services.

Alonso-Zaldivar, Ricardo. 2005. "Healthcare Overhaul Is Quietly Underway." *Los Angeles Times,* January 31.

Appleby, Julie. 2005. "Medical Costs Prove a Burden Even for Some with Insurance." *USA Today* (April 29).

Atkinson, Graham; W. David Helms; and Jack Needleman. 1997. "State Trends in Hospital Uncompensated Care." *Health Affairs* 16, no. 4 (July/August): 233–41.

Auerbach, Judith D. 2004. "The Overlooked Victims of AIDS." *Washington Post,* October 14.

Ayanian, John Z.; Betsy A. Kohler; Toshi Abe; and Arnold M. Epstein. 1993. "The Relation between Health Insurance Coverage and Clinical Outcomes among Women with Breast Cancer." *New England Journal of Medicine* 329, no. 5 (July 29): 326–31.

Baird, Karen L. 1998. *Gender Justice and the Health Care System*. New York: Garland Publishing.

Baker, David W.; Carl D. Stevens; and Robert H. Brook. 1994. "Regular Source of Ambulatory Care and Medical Care Utilization by Patients Presenting to a Public Hospital Emergency Department." *Journal of the American Medical Association* 271, no. 24 (June 22): 1909–12.

Berk, Marc L., and Claudia L. Schur. 1998. "Access to Care: How Much Difference Does Medicaid Make?" *Health Affairs* 17, no. 3 (May/June): 169–80.

Braverman, Paula A.; Susan Egerter; Trude Bennett; and Jonathan Showstack. 1991. "Differences in Hospital Resource Allocation among Sick Newborns According to Insurance Coverage." *Journal of the American Medical Association* 266, no. 23 (December 18): 3300–3308.

Brody, Jane. 1998. "A Fatal Shift in Cancer's Gender Gap." *New York Times,* May 12.

Brown, Lawrence D., and Michael S. Sparer. 2003. "Poor Program's Progress: The Unanticipated Politics of Medicaid Policy." *Health Affairs* 22, no. 1 (January/February): 31–44.

Broyles, Robert W.; Lutchmie Narine; and Edward N. Brandt, Jr. 2002. "The Temporarily and Chronically Uninsured: Does Their Use of Primary Care Differ?" *Journal of Health Care for the Poor and Underserved* 13, no. 1 (February): 95–111.

Bureau of the Census. 1997. *Statistical Abstract of the United States 1997*. Washington, D.C.: U.S. Department of Commerce, Economics and Statistics Administration.

————. 2003. "Poverty in the United States 2002." Washington, D.C.: U.S. Department of Commerce, Economics and Statistics Administration.

————. 2004a. "Historical Health Insurance Tables." Washington, D.C.: U.S. Department of Commerce, Economics and Statistics Administration. Online at www.census.gov/hhes/www/hlthins/hlthins.html.

————. 2004b. "Income, Poverty, and Health Insurance Coverage in the United States: 2003." Washington, D.C.: U.S. Department of Commerce, Economics and Statistics Administration.

———. 2004c. *Statistical Abstract of the United States 2004*. Washington, D.C.: U.S. Department of Commerce, Economics and Statistics Administration.

Butler, Stuart M. 1991. "A Tax Reform Strategy to Deal with the Uninsured." *Journal of the American Medical Association* 265, no. 19 (May 15): 2541–43.

Byrd, W. Michael; and Linda A. Clayton. 2003. "Racial and Ethnic Disparities in Healthcare: A Background and History." In *Unequal Treatment*, ed. Brian D. Smedley, Adrienne Y. Stith, and Alan R. Nelson, 455–527. Washington, D.C.: National Academies Press.

Chapman, Audry R. 1994. "Introduction." In *Health Care Reform: A Human Rights Approach*, ed. Audrey R. Chapman, 1–32. Washington, D.C.: Georgetown University Press.

Children's Defense Fund. 1998. *The State of America's Children*. Washington, D.C.: Children's Defense Fund.

Clancy, Carolyn M., and Charlea T. Massion. 1992. "American Women's Health Care: A Patchwork Quilt with Gaps." *Journal of the American Medical Association* 268, no. 14 (October 24): 1918–20.

Clarke, Leslie L.; Christine A. Bono; Michael K. Miller; and Susan C. Malone. 1995. "Prenatal Care Use in Nonmetropolitan and Metropolitan America: Racial/Ethnic Differences." *Journal of Health Care for the Poor and Underserved* 6, no. 4 (November): 410–33.

Claxton, Gary; Isadora Gil; Ben Finder; and Erin Holve. 2004. "Employer Health Benefits 2004 Annual Survey." Menlo Park, Calif.: Henry J. Kaiser Family Foundation, and Chicago, Ill.: Health Research and Educational Trust.

Clemetson, Lynette. 2004. "Links Between Prison and AIDS Affecting Blacks Inside and Out." *New York Times*, August 6.

Collins, Sara R.; Karen Davis; Michelle Doty; and Alice Ho. 2004. "Wages, Benefits, and Workers' Health." New York: The Commonwealth Fund.

Committee on the Consequences of Uninsurance, Institute of Medicine. 2002. *Care Without Coverage: Too Little, Too Late*. Washington, D.C.: National Academy Press.

———. 2003. *Hidden Costs, Value Lost: Uninsurance in America*. Washington, D.C.: National Academy Press.

Connolly, Ceci. 2005. "Bush Plans to Broaden Health Care." *Washington Post*, February 4.

Cunningham, Peter J., and Ha T. Tu. 1997. "A Changing Picture of Uncompensated Care." *Health Affairs* 16, no. 4 (July/August): 167–75.

Cust, Kenneth F.T. 1997. *A Just Minimum of Health Care*. New York: University Press of America.

Daniels, Norman; Donald W. Light; and Ronald L. Caplan. 1996. *Benchmarks of Fairness for Health Care Reform*. New York: Oxford University Press.

Davis, Karen, and Cathy Schoen. 1978. *Health and the War on Poverty: A Ten-Year Proposal*. Washington, D.C.: Brookings Institution.

———. 2003. "Creating Consensus on Coverage Choices." *Health Affairs* (April 23): W3-199–W3-211. Online at healthaffairs.org.

Dubay, Lisa, and Genevieve Kenney. 2004. "Addressing Coverage Caps for Low-Income Parents." *Health Affairs* 23, no. 2 (March/April): 225–34.

Enthoven, Alain C. 2003. "Employment-Based Health Insurance is Failing: Now What?" *Health Affairs* (May 23): W3-237–W3-249. Online at healthaffairs.org.

Etheridge, Lynn, and Judith Moore. 2003. "A New Medicaid Program." *Health Affairs* (August 27): W3-426–W3-439. Online at healthaffairs.org.

Fairbrother, Gerry; Michael K. Gusmano; Heidi L. Park; and Roberta Scheinmann. 2003. "Care for the Uninsured in General Internists' Private Offices." *Health Affairs* 22, no. 6 (November/December): 217–24.

Fears, Darryl. 2005. "U.S. HIV Cases Soar Among Black Women." *Washington Post*, February 7.

Fisher, Ian. 1998. "Families Providing Complex Medicare, Tubes and All." *New York Times*, June 7.

Fronstin, Paul. 2004. "Sources of Health Insurance and Characteristics of the Uninsured: Analysis of the March 2004 Current Population Survey." Washington, D.C.: Employee Benefit Research Institute.

Gabel, Jon R., and Jeremy D. Pickreign. 2004. "Risky Business: When Mom and Pop Buy Health Insurance for Their Employees." New York: The Commonwealth Fund.

Garner, M.O.; S.P. Cliver; S.F. McNeal; and R.L. Goldenberg. 1996. "Ethnicity and Sources of Prenatal Care; Findings from a National Survey." *Birth* 23, no. 2: 84–87.

"Gender Bias at Work with Viagra, Physicians Say." 1998. *Springfield News-Leader*, May 13.

General Accounting Office. 1997a. *Employment-Based Health Insurance: Costs Increase and Family Coverage Decreases.* Washington, D.C.: General Accounting Office.
———. 1997b. *Health Insurance: Coverage Leads to Increased Health Care Access for Children.* Washington, D.C.: General Accounting Office.
Ginzberg, Eli. 1994. "Improving Health Care for the Poor." *Journal of the American Medical Association* 271, no. 6 (February): 464–65.
Glied, Sherry, and Sarah E. Little. 2003. "The Uninsured and the Benefits of Medical Progress." *Health Affairs* 22, no. 4 (July/August): 210–19.
Glied, Sherry; Jeanne W. Lambrew; and Sarah Little. 2003. "The Growing Share of Uninsured Workers Employed by Large Firms." New York: The Commonwealth Fund.
Goff, Barbara A.; H.G. Muntz; and J.M. Cain. 1997a. "Is Adam Worth More than Eve? The Financial Impact of Gender Bias in the Federal Reimbursement of Gynecological Procedures." *Gynecological Oncology* 64, no. 3 (March): 372–77.
———. 1997b. "Comparison of 1997 Medicare Relative Value Units for Gender-Specific Procedures: Is Adam Still Worth More than Eve?" *Gynecological Oncology* 66, no. 2 (August): 313–19.
Gould, Elise. 2004. "The Chronic Problem of Declining Health Coverage." EPI Issue Brief #202 (September 16). Washington, D.C.: Economic Policy Institute.
Graig, Laurene A. 1999. *Health of Nations: An International Perspective on U.S. Health Care Reform.* Washington, D.C.: CQ Press.
Gusmano, Michael K.; Gerry Fairbrother; and Heidi Park." 2002. "Exploring the Limits of the Safety Net: Community Health Centers and Care for the Uninsured." *Health Affairs* 21, no. 6 (November/December): 188–94.
Hacker, Jacob S. 2001. "Medicare Plus: Increasing Health Coverage by Expanding Medicare." In *Covering America: Real Remedies for the Uninsured; Volume I: Proposal Summaries,* ed. Elliot K. Wicks, 73–100. Washington, D.C.: Economic and Social Research Institute.
———. 2002. *The Divided Welfare State: The Battle over Public and Private Social Benefits in the United States.* New York: Cambridge University Press.
Hadley, Jack, and John Holahan. 2003. "Covering the Uninsured: How Much Would It Cost?" *Health Affairs* (June 4): W3-250–W3-265.
Hafner-Eaton, Chris. 1993. "Physician Utilization Disparities between the Uninsured and Insured: Comparisons of the Chronically Ill, Acutely Ill, and Well Nonelderly Populations." *Journal of the American Medical Association* 269, no. 6 (February 10): 787–82.
Heffler, Stephen et al. 2005. "U.S. Health Spending Projections for 2004–2014." *Health Affairs* (February 23): W5-74–W5-85. Online at healthaffairs.org.
Himmelstein, David U.; Elizabeth Warren; Deborah Thorne; and Steffie Woolhandler. 2005. "Illness and Injury as Contributors to Bankruptcy." *Health Affairs* (February 2): W5-63–W5-73. Online at healthaffairs.org.
Hoffman, Catherine; Alicia Carbaugh; and Allison Cook. 2004. "Health Insurance Coverage in America: 2003 Data Update." Washington, D.C.: Kaiser Commission on Medicaid and the Uninsured.
Hoffman, Catherine; Cathy Schoen; Diane Rowland; and Karen Davis. 2001. "Gaps in Health Coverage Among Working-Age Americans and the Consequences." *Journal of Health Care for the Poor and the Underserved* 12, no. 3 (August): 272–89.
Hogue, Carol J.R., and Martha A. Hargraves. 2000. "The Commonwealth Fund Minority Health Survey of 1994." In *Minority Health in America,* ed. Carol J.R. Hogue, Martha A. Hargraves, and Karen Scott Collins, 1–18. Baltimore, Md.: Johns Hopkins University Press.
Hogue, Carol J.R.; Martha A. Hargraves; and Karen Scott Collins, eds. 2000. *Minority Health in America: Findings and Policy Implications from the Commonwealth Fund Minority Health Survey.* Baltimore, Md.: Johns Hopkins University Press.
Holahan, John, and Arunabh Ghosh. 2004. "The Economic Downturn and Changes in Health Insurance Coverage, 2000–2003. " Washington, D.C.: Kaiser Commission on Medicaid and the Uninsured.
Jecker, Nancy S. 1993. "Can an Employer-Based Health Insurance System Be Just?" *Journal of Health Care Politics, Policy and Law* 18, no. 3 (Fall): 657–73.
Kadar, Andrew G. 1994. "The Sex-Bias Myth in Medicine." *Atlantic Monthly* 274, no. 2 (August): 66–70.

Kahn, Charles N. III, and Ronald F. Pollack. 2001. "Building a Consensus for Expanding Health Coverage." *Health Affairs* 20, no. 1 (January/February): 40–48.

Kaiser Commission on Medicaid and the Uninsured. 2004a. "Health Coverage for Low-Income Children." Washington, D.C.: Kaiser Commission on Medicaid and the Uninsured.

———. 2004b. "The Uninsured and Their Access to Care." Washington, D.C.: Kaiser Commission on Medicaid and the Uninsured.

Kaiser Family Foundation. 2003. "Employer Health Benefits: 2003 Summary of Findings." Menlo Park, Calif.: Kaiser Family Foundation.

———. 2004a. "Update on Individual Health Insurance." Menlo Park, Calif.: Kaiser Family Foundation.

———. 2004b. "Health Care & the 2004 Elections: Women's Health Policy." Menlo Park, Calif.: Kaiser Family Foundation.

Kari, Nancy; Harry C. Boyte; and Bruce Jennings. 1994 "Health as a Civic Question." Prepared for the American Civic Forum Madison, Wisc. Online at www.cpn.org/topics/health/healthquestion.html

Kates, Jennifer, and Alyssa Wilson Leggoe. 2005a. "African Americans and HIV/AIDS." Menlo Park, Calif.: Henry J. Kaiser Family Foundation.

———. 2005b. "Latinos and HIV/AIDS." Menlo Park, Calif.: Henry J. Kaiser Family Foundation.

Kilborn, Peter T. 1997. "Illness Is Turning into Financial Catastrophe for More of the Uninsured." *New York Times,* August 1.

Kinney, Eleanor D., and Suzanne K. Steinmetz. 1994. "Notes from the Insurance Underground: How the Chronically Ill Cope." *Journal of Health Politics, Policy and Law* 19, no. 3 (Fall): 637–41.

Krause, Elliott A. 1977. *Power and Illness: The Political Sociology of Health and Medical Care.* New York: Elsevier.

Kreidler, Mike. n.d. "Your Rights Under the U.S. COBRA Law." Olympia, Wash.: Office of the Insurance Commissioner. Online at www.insurance.wa.gov/factsheets/factsheet_detailprint.asp?FctShtRcdNum=14.

Krieger, Nancy, and Elizabeth Fee. 1996. "Man-Made Medicine and Women's Health." In *Man-Made Medicine,* ed. Kary L. Moss, 17–35. Durham, N.C.: Duke University Press.

Krugman, Paul 2005. "Little Black Lies." *New York Times,* January 28.

Lantz, Paul M.; J.S. House; and J. Chen. 1998. "Socioeconomic Factors, Health Behaviors, and Mortality." *Journal of the American Medical Association* 279, no. 21 (June): 1703–8.

Levy, Helen, and David Meltzer. 2004. "What Do We Really Know About Whether Health Insurance Affects Health?" In *Health Policy and the Uninsured,* ed. Catherine G. McLaughlin, 179–204. Washington, D.C.: Urban Institute Press.

Long, Sharon K. 2003. "Hardship Among the Uninsured: Choosing Among Food, Housing and Health Insurance." *New Federalism* Series B, no. B-54. Washington, D.C.: The Urban Institute.

Manjoo, Farhad. 2005. "Does Social Security Shortchange Blacks?" *Salon* (February 4). Online at salon.com.

Mann, Joyce M.; Glenn A. Melnick; Anil Bamezai; and Jack Zwanziger. 1997. "A Profile of Uncompensated Care, 1983–1995." *Health Affairs* 16, no. 4 (July/August): 223–32.

Mawrick, Charles. 1992. "Women's Health Action Plan Sees First Anniversary." *Journal of the American Medical Association* 268, no. 14 (October 14): 1816–18.

Mayes, Rick. 2005. *Universal Coverage: The Elusive Quest for National Health Insurance.* Ann Arbor: University of Michigan Press.

McAlearney, John S. 2002. "The Financial Performance of Community Health Centers: 1996–1999." *Health Affairs* 21, no. 2 (March/April): 219–25.

McBride, David. 1993. "Black America: From Community Health Care to Crisis Medicine." *Journal of Health Politics, Policy and Law* 18, no. 2 (Summer): 319–37.

McLaughlin, Catherine G., ed. 2004. *Health Policy and the Uninsured.* Washington, D.C.: Urban Institute Press.

Meyer, Jack A., and Sharon Silow-Carroll. 2003. "Building on the Job-Based Health Care System: What Would It Take?" *Health Affairs* (August 27): W3-415–W3-425. Online at healthaffairs.org.

Miller, Velvet G., and Janis L. Curties. 1993. "Health Care Reform and Race-Specific Policies." *Journal of Health Politics, Policy and Law* 18, no. 3 (Fall): 747–53.

Millman, Michael, ed. 1993. *Access to Health Care in America.* Washington, D.C.: National Academy Press.

Moss, Kary L., ed. 1996. *Man-Made Medicine: Women's Health, Public Policy, and Reform.* Durham, N.C.: Duke University Press.

Muller, Charlotte. 1990. *Health Care and Gender.* New York: Russell Sage Foundation.

National Association of Community Health Centers. 2004. "America's Health Centers." Bethesda, Md.: National Association of Community Health Centers. Online at www.nachc.com/research/Files/IntrotoHealthCenters8.04.pdf.

National Center for Chronic Disease Prevention and Health Promotion. n.d. "Cancer Prevention and Control." Washington, D.C.: Centers for Disease Control and Prevention, U.S. Department of Health and Human Services. Online at www.cdc.gov/cancer/ataglan.htm.

National Center for Health Statistics. 2004. "Health, United States. 2004." Hyattsville, Md.: Centers for Disease Control and Prevention, U.S. Department of Health and Human Services.

National Institutes of Health. n.d. "WHI Background and Overview." Washington, D.C.: U.S. Department of Health and Human Services. Online at www.nhlbi.nih.gov/whi/factsht.htm.

Oberg, Charles; Betty Lia-Hoagberg; Ellen Hodkinson; Catherine Skovholt; and Renee Vanman. 1990. "Prenatal Care Comparisons among Privately Insured, Uninsured, and Medicaid-Enrolled Women." *Public Health Reports* 105, no. 5 (September/October): 533–35.

Pear, Robert. 1991. "Panel Offers Health Plan to Bush on Uninsured." *New York Times,* December 20.

———. 1992. "President Leaves Many Areas Gray." *New York Times,* February 7.

———. 2005. "Governors Prepare to Fight Medicaid Cuts." *New York Times,* February 27.

Pereira, Joseph. 2003. "To Save on Health-Care Costs, Firms Fire Disabled Workers." *Wall Street Journal,* July 14.

Pollack, Harold, and Karl Kronebusch. 2004. "Health Insurance and Vulnerable Populations." In *Health Policy and the Uninsured,* ed. Catherine G. McLaughlin, 205–55. Washington, D.C.: Urban Institute Press.

Quintana, J.M.; D. Goldmann; and C. Homer. 1997. "Social Disparities in the Use of Diagnostic Tests for Children with Gastroenteritis." *International Journal of Quality of Health Care* 9, no. 6 (December): 419–25.

Reed, Marie C., and Ha T. Tu. 2002. "Triple Jeopardy, Chronically Ill and Uninsured in America." Washington, D.C.: Center for Studying Health System Change. Online at www.hschange.org.

Reschovsky, James D., and Jack Hadley. 2004. "The Effects of Tax Credits for Nongroup Insurance on Health Spending by the Uninsured." *Health Affairs* (February 25): W4-113–W4-127. Online at healthaffairs.org.

Robinson, Clay. 2005. "Rising Health Costs Could Bankrupt State, Perry Says." *Houston Chronicle,* February 15.

Rochefort, David A. 1993 "Commentary—The Pragmatic Appeal of Employment-Based Health Care Reform." *Journal of Health Care Politics, Policy and Law* 18, no. 3 (Fall): 683–93.

Rockeymore, Maya. 2005. "The Twilight Zone: Black History, Bush Style." *Black Commentator,* February 11. Online at www.blackcommentator.com/125/125_twilight_zone.html.

Ross, Donna Cohen, and Laura Cox. 2004. "Beneath the Surface: Barriers Threaten to Slow Progress on Expanding Health Coverage of Children and Families." Washington, D.C.: Kaiser Commission on Medicaid and the Uninsured.

Rowland, Diana, and Alina Salganicoff. 1994. "Commentary: Lessons from Medicaid—Improving Access to Office-Cased Physician Care for the Low-Income Population." *American Journal of Public Health* 84, no. 4 (April): 550–52.

Rowland, Diana, and James R. Tallon, Jr. 2003. "Medicaid: Lessons from a Decade." *Health Affairs* 22, no. 1 (January/February): 138–43.

Ruttenberg, Joan E. 1993 "Commentary—Revisiting the Employment-Insurance Link." *Journal of Health Care Politics, Policy and Law* 18, no. 3 (Fall): 675–81.

Ryan, William F. 1971. *Blaming the Victim.* New York: Pantheon Books.

Salganicoff, Alina; J. Zoe Beckerman; Roberta Wyn; and Victoria D. Ojeda. 2002. "Women's Health in the United States: Health Coverage and Access to Care." Menlo Park, Calif.: Henry J. Kaiser Family Foundation.

Sardell, Alice. 1988. *The U.S. Experiment in Social Medicine: The Community Health Center Program, 1965–1986.* Pittsburgh: University of Pittsburgh Press.

Short, Pamela Farley, and Deborah R. Graefe. 2003. "Battery-Powered Heath Insurance? Stability in Coverage of the Uninsured." *Health Affairs* 22, no. 6 (November/December): 244–55.

Smedley, Brian D.; Adrienne Y. Stith; and Alan R. Nelson, eds. 2003. *Unequal Treatment: Confronting Racial and Ethnic Disparities in Health Care*. Washington, D.C.: National Academies Press.

Smith, Vernon; Kathleen Gifford; Eileen Ellis; Robin Rudowitz; and Molly O'Malley. 2004. "The Continuing Medicaid Budget Challenge: State Medicaid Spending Growth and Cost Containment in Fiscal Years 2004 and 2005; Results from a 50-State Survey." Washington, D.C.: Kaiser Commission on Medicaid and the Uninsured.

Starr, Paul. 1982. *The Social Transformation of American Medicine*. New York: Basic Books.

Stern, Robert S.; Joel E. Weissman; and Arnold M. Epstein. 1991. "The Emergency Department as a Pathway for Admission for Poor and High-Cost Patients." *Journal of the American Medical Association* 266, no. 16 (October 23): 2238–46.

Stoddard, Jeffrey J.; Robert F. St. Peter; and Paul W. Newacheck. 1994. "Health Insurance Status and Ambulatory Care for Children." *New England Journal of Medicine* 330, no. 20 (May 19): 1421–25.

Stone, Deborah A. 1993. "The Struggle for the Soul of Health Insurance." *Journal of Health Politics, Policy and Law* 18, no. 2 (Summer): 287–317.

Tanner, Michael. 2001. "Disparate Impact: Social Security and African Americans." Washington, D.C.: Cato Institute. Briefing Paper #61 (February 5).

Thorpe, Kenneth E. 1997. *The Rising Number of Uninsured Workers: An Approaching Crisis in Health Care Financing*. Washington, D.C.: National Coalition on Health Care. Online at: www.americashealth.org/emerge.uninsured.html.

Thorpe, Kenneth E., and David Howard. 2003. "Health Insurance and Spending Among Cancer Patients." *Health Affairs* (April 9): W3-189–W3-198. Online at healthaffairs.org.

U.S. Department of Health and Human Services. 1991. *Health Status of Minorities and Low-Income Groups*, 3rd ed. Washington, D.C.: U.S. Government Printing Office.

Vieth, Warren 2004. "Bush Makes His Pitch for 'Ownership Society.'" *Los Angeles Times* (September 5).

Vuckovic, Nancy. 2000. "Self-Care Among the Uninsured: 'You Do What You Can Do.'" *Health Affairs* 19, no. 4 (July/August): 197–99.

Wallsten, Peter, and Richard Simon. 2005. "Bush Shifts Focus to Race in Debate on Social Security." *Los Angeles Times*, January 26.

"Wal-Mart Conference on Wal-Mart Draws Critics of Pay, Benefits." 2005. Bloomberg News (November 4). Online at http://www.bloomberg.com/apps/news?pid=10000103&sid =aFfX5fJN_6bI&refer=us

Watson, Sidney Dean. 1994. "Minority Access and Health Reform: A Civil Right to Health Care." *Journal of Law, Medicine and Ethics* 22, no. 2 (Summer): 127–37.

White, Joseph. 1995. *Competing Solutions: American Health Care Proposals and International Experience*. Washington, D.C.: Brookings Institution.

Wilson, William J. 1978. *The Declining Significance of Race: Blacks and Changing American Institutions*. Chicago: University of Chicago Press.

———. 1987. *The Truly Disadvantaged: The Inner City, the Underclass, and Public Policy*. Chicago: University of Chicago Press.

Zellers, Wendy K.; Catherine G. McLaughlin; and Kevin D. Frick. 1992. "Small-Business Health Insurance: Only Healthy Need Apply." *Health Affairs* 11, no. 1 (Spring): 174–75.

Zollinger, Terrel W.; Robert M. Saywell, Jr.; and David K.W. Chu. 1991. "Uncompensated Hospital Care for Pregnancy and Childbirth Cases." *American Journal of Public Health* 81, no. 8 (August): 1017–22.

Zuckerman, Stephen; Joshua McFeeters; Peter Cunningham; and Len Nichols. 2004. "Changes in Medicaid Physician Fees, 1998–2003: Implications for Physician Participation." *Health Affairs* (June 23): W4-374–W4-384. Online at healthaffairs.org.

6

Health Care Cost Containment

The 1960s saw a dramatic expansion in social programs. Civil rights, women's rights, educational opportunities, and improved housing and health care for citizens were the battle cries of a social revolution as the federal government attempted to expand individual opportunities. In the health field, health care came to be viewed as a right, rather than a privilege. Providing access to decent health care became the primary goal of the federal government. STILL AN ISSUE

In 1965, the federal government established Medicare and Medicaid to provide increased access to health care for the elderly and the poor. These programs were dramatically successful in increasing access to health care for large numbers of people (Davis and Schoen 1978). The creation and implementation of such programs was made possible by a healthy economy. Additionally, the Comprehensive Health Planning Act and Public Health Services Amendments of 1966 (PL 89-749) established the goal of providing the highest level of health care attainable to every person.

By the late 1960s and early 1970s, the focus began to shift from providing access to concern about rising health care costs. The cost of health care in the United States had been rising faster than the general growth rate of the economy. Health care expenditures accounted for an increased share of the national income (Evans 1986). As shown in Table 6.1, national health care expenditures increased from $27.1 billion in 1960 to $74.3 billion in 1970 and to $251.1 billion in 1980. In 1990, national health care expenditures jumped to $696.6 billion and had reached $1,804.7 billion by 2004. Spending for health care amounted to 12.2 percent of the gross domestic product (GDP) in 1990, more than double the figure of 5.1 percent in 1960, and had reached 15.4 percent of GDP by 2004. National health care expenditures were projected to reach 18.7 percent of GDP by 2014 (Heffler et al. 2005).

Another way of looking at the explosion in health care costs is to examine the third column in Table 6.1, which shows the percentage increase in health care expenditures from the previous period. Average annual percent growth remained in double digits from 1960 to 1990. It was only during the 1990s that the average annual growth dipped into single digits. In fact, from 1991 to 1996, average annual percent growth

Table 6.1

National Health Care Expenditures, 1960–2004

	National health care expenditures ($ billions)	As percentage of GDP	Average annual percent growth from previous year shown
1960	27.1	5.1	10.6
1970	74.3	7.1	12.9
1980	251.1	8.9	11.0
1990	696.6	12.2	9.6
1995	993.3	13.6	4.4
2000	1,309.4	13.3	6.4
2001	1,420.7	14.1	8.5
2002	1,553.0	14.9	9.3
2003	1,678.9	14.9	9.3
2004*	1,804.7	15.4	7.5

Sources: Levit et al. 1991, 1994b, 1997, 2000, 2003; Heffler et al., 2004, 2005; Smith et al. 2005.
  *estimated

declined every year. It declined from 9.6 percent in 1991 to 4.4 percent in 1995, and has remained at single-digit increases through 2004.

Hospital and physician care accounted for a little more than half of all health care expenditures in 2003 (down about two percentage points since 1996). Private sources (private insurance and out-of-pocket expenses) accounted for about 49 percent of the total national health expenditures. Public health spending of $721.6 billion in 2003 accounted for 45.6 percent of all national health care expenditures (see Table 6.2).

While physician and hospital services are the bulk of health care spending, pre-scription medications are the fastest growing component. In 1993, such spending was 5.8 percent of total health spending; by 2004, it was an estimated 11.1 percent. The projection is that spending on prescription medications will amount to 14.5 percent by 2014 (calculated from Heffler et al. 2005). Spending on medications has equaled or exceeded 10 percent for most of the 1990s and 2000s (through 2004) (Heffler et al. 2005). Because of the intense interest in these rising costs, we will consider efforts to control prescription drug costs later in the chapter.

Another way to think about the problem, one which combines this chapter's focus on health care costs with chapter 4's focus on access, is to consider the "health crisis index" (Sager and Socolar 2005). This index is similar to the "misery index" that became prominent during the late 1970s and early 1980s, which combined interest rates with the unemployment rate (see Rushefsky 2002).

The health crisis index combines the health spending share of GDP with the per-centage of unemployed. Figure 6.1 shows several important trends. The first is from 1987 to 1993, which indicates a steep rise, about 3.4 percent per year (calculated from Sager and Socolar 2005). The second trend is from 1992 through 2000. While

Table 6.2

National Health Care Expenditures by Sources of Funds and Types of Expenditures, 2003 (in billions of dollars)

	Total	Out of pocket	Private insurance	Medi- care	State/ federal Medicaid	Other public
Total national health care expenditures	1,678.9	230.5 (13.3%)	600.6 (35.8%)	283.1 (16.9%)	268.6 (16%)	213.9 (12.8%)
Hospital care	515.9	16.3 (3.2%)	177.4 (34.4%)	156.4 (30.3%)	87.5 (16%)	56.8 (11%)
Physician services	369.7	37.6 (10.2%)	183.6 (49.7%)	73.8 (20%)	26.4 (7.1%)	22.8 (6.2%)
Dental services	74.3	32.9 (44.3%)	36.5 (49.1%)	0.1 (0.1%)	4.2 (5.6%)	0.6 (0.8%)
Home health care	40.0	6.6 (16.5%)	7.3 (18.3%)	12.9 (32.3%)	9.9 (24.8%)	2.1 (5.3%)
Prescription drugs	179.2	53.2 (29.7%)	82.9 (42.3%)	2.8 (1.6%)	33.9 (18.9%)	6.4 (3.6%)
Nursing homes	110.8	30.9 (27.9%)	8.5 (7.7%)	13.7 (12.4%)	51 (46.0%)	2.5 (2.3%)

Source: Smith et al. 2005.

Figure 6.1 shows some ups and downs, the end of this period clearly shows declines in the health crisis index. This is a function of several factors, including the managed care revolution (see later in this chapter and chapter 9), restraints on Medicare spending through the Balanced Budget Act of 1997 (see chapter 4), and a declining unemployment rate (and therefore increased coverage).

The third trend apparent in Figure 6.1 is the 2000 to 2003 period. The index rises again, at an average annual rate of 2.1 percent. This is attributable to increases in spending and increases in the uninsured rate (calculated from Sager and Socolar 2005).

One possible relationship does not seem to hold. Overall price inflation, as measured by the consumer price index (CPI), has gone in pretty much the opposite direction from health expenditures. Inflation stayed level or dropped for much of the 2000s, while health care expenditures increased (Kaiser Family Foundation n.d.).

Health care spending increases affect all sectors of society. We addressed health care spending issues for the major public programs, Medicaid and Medicare, in chapters 3 and 4. Employers and employees also face health care cost issues. Compared to changes in inflation and workers' earnings, health insurance premiums have soared, with the exception of the brief period around 1996 (see Figure 6.2). This creates problems for both employers and employees. Employers are facing ever-increasing costs (which hurt their international competitiveness) and seek ways to reduce costs,

Figure 6.1   **Health Crisis Index, 1987–2003**

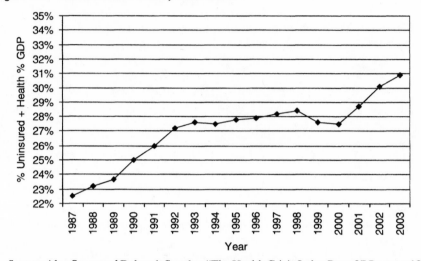

Source: Alan Sager and Deborah Socolar, "The Health Crisis Index Rose 37 Percent, 1987–2003." Boston, MA: Health Reform Program, Boston University School of Public Health, March 2005. www.healthreformprogram.org. Used with permission.

Figure 6.2   **Increases in Employer Health Premiums Compared to Inflation and Worker Earnings: 1988–2004**

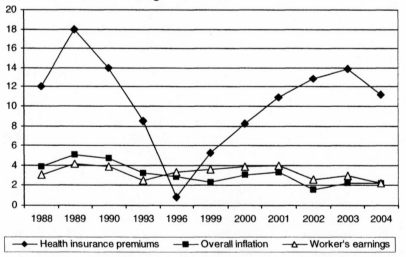

Source: Kaiser Family Foundation (n.d.), "Trends and Indicators in the Changing Health Care Marketplace," #7301. The Henry J. Kaiser Foundation, April 2005. This information was reprinted with permission of the Henry J. Kaiser Family Foundation. The Kaiser Foundation, based in Menlo, California, is a nonprofit, independent national health care philanthropy and is not associated with Kaiser Permanente or Kaiser Industries.

either through more efficient health plans for their employees, shifting costs to their employees (which is increasingly being done), or reducing the number of people covered. As we saw in the previous chapter, employer-sponsored health care has declined. Employees are faced with ever-increasing premiums that outstrip increases in their wages.

We will examine some strategies to control costs later, but one point should be made now: the premium increases do not seem to distinguish between conventional insurance plans and the managed care/competition plans. For the 1996–2004 period, average annual plan increases for all types of plans were 8.5 percent. Conventional plans saw increases of 8 percent, while health maintenance organizations (HMOs) and preferred provider organizations (PPOs) saw increases of 8.4 to 8.5 percent. Only point of service (POS) providers saw somewhat smaller increases, 7.7 percent (Kaiser Family Foundation n.d.).

A related point is that two of the heralded large public employer plans, the Federal Employees Health Benefits Program (FEHBP) and the California Public Employees Retirement System (CalPERS), saw annual premium increases about the same, or in some years, higher, than for all employer-sponsored plans (Kaiser Family Foundation, n.d.). The reason for pointing this out is that both plans, which are forms of managed competition and defined benefit/premium support plans, have been touted as models for the transformation of the U.S. health care system. The data strongly suggest that those two plans have not yet found the answer to the problem.

Three other aspects of health care costs need to be mentioned. The first is the concentration of costs. The sickest 1 percent of the population accounted for a little over 22 percent of all health care spending, the sickest 5 percent of the population accounted for over 48 percent of spending, and the sickest 50 percent of the population accounted for almost 97 percent of all spending (Kaiser Family Foundation n.d.). These percentages have been fairly stable over the years (Berk and Monheit 2001).

The second aspect is related, in a sense, to the first. Similar to the concentration of costs among the population, there is a concentration of costs among medical conditions. Thorpe, Florence, and Joski (2004) estimate that the top fifteen conditions accounted for about 56 percent of the increases in spending over a thirteen-year period and the five top conditions accounted for about 31 percent of the increases. The five top conditions are "heart disease, <u>mental disorders,</u> pulmonary disorders, cancer and <u>trauma</u>" (Thorpe, Florence, and Joski 2004, W4-441). Depending on the condition, the increases attributable to each of the fifteen conditions result from some combination of a larger population, an increase in treating the condition, or an increase in the cost per case. *mental disorders + trauma 2 big ones that affect military + veterans*

Finally, we can examine U.S. health care spending in a comparative perspective. The United States spends relatively more on health care than any other country. In 2000, the United States spent 13 percent of GDP on health care compared to an average of 8 percent in the OECD (the Organization for Economic Cooperation and Development) (Anderson et al. 2003). The next highest spenders are Germany and Switzerland at 10.6 percent and 10.7 percent, respectively. No other country spends more than 10 percent of GDP. Anderson et al. (2003) argue that relatively uncontrolled prices for health care in the United States result in the major reason for the differences.

Despite spending so much money on health care, some have argued that the health status of Americans trails that of other industrialized countries. Comparing the most highly industrialized countries, the United States ranks twelfth overall and at the bottom on the important indicators of low birth rate and neonatal and infant mortality (see Kawachi 2005). A recent survey of adults with recent health care problems in six countries found that "The United States often stands out with high medical errors and inefficient care and has the worst performance for access/cost barriers and financial burdens" (Schoen et al. 2005). certainly the attitude for military + their families

There are many causes for such dramatic increases in health care costs. To some, increased costs are the result of increased public expectations about the health care system, advances in health care technology and their success, and the prevailing sentiment that health care is a right (McGregor 1981). Others see health care cost increases in fee for service, a medical arms race among hospitals, insurance companies and third-party payers, and the purchasers of health care, such as the federal government and industries that, for a long time, ignored the cost problem (Latham 1983). Still others argue that virtually all the medical care price inflation of recent years can be accounted for by general inflation, the labor intensity of health industries, the behavior of wage rates during inflation, and the pattern of labor-productivity changes (Virts and Wilson 1984).

Nor is the problem a new one. The Committee on the Costs of Medical Care (CCMC) was formed in the late 1920s because of the high costs of hospital care at a time when health insurance had not yet come into existence (see Ross 2002; Starr 1982).

If there is any agreement among policymakers, health care practitioners, researchers, and health care consumers and purchasers, it is that health care costs too much. The federal government is one of the largest purchasers of health care. Federal health care expenditures constitute a significant and growing portion of the federal budget, and the tax burden is large. The new Medicare Modernization Act (2003), discussed in chapter 4, places increasing pressure on policymakers because of the additional costs created by the new drug benefit. Accordingly, federal policymakers and bureaucrats face great pressure to contain health care costs (Mechanic 1981). States are facing ever-increasing Medicaid costs and private employers are looking for ways to alleviate their growing health care costs. Those with insurance, private or public, are also facing increasing costs. The question for policymakers has become one of how to contain costs and still maintain quality medical service (Jones 1982). The focus in the health care policy debate has shifted from "Should we contain costs?" to "How should we contain costs?" (Grumbach and Bodenheimer 1990, 120)

The debate over how to contain rising health care costs centers on two broad approaches or strategies.[1] One strategy relies on government regulation, while the other relies on increasing competition in the health care market (see, for example, Enthoven and Singer 1997; Etheredge 1997; Evans 1997; Moran 1997; Rice 1997; and Zatkin

1997). During the decades of the 1970s, the 1980s, and the 1990s, the federal government tried both regulatory and competitive strategies to contain health costs. Similarly, state governments and the private sector have undertaken many initiatives in an attempt to contain rising health care costs. In the 2000s, policymakers once again turned to competitive or marketlike approaches.

This chapter has three purposes. First, it provides a brief theoretical rationale of regulatory and market strategies. Second, it examines the regulatory and market strategies used by the federal government to contain rising health care costs. Third, it analyzes state government and private-sector innovations and initiatives to contain health care costs.

Theoretical Framework: Government Regulation and Market Competition

The Regulatory Strategy

One of the most important assumptions of the regulatory strategy is that the health care market suffers from too many shortcomings. The seminal work in this field is an article published by the economist Kenneth Arrow (1963; see also Relman 2005; Stone 2002, 2005. For a retrospective discussion of Arrow's article, see the October 2001 issue of *Journal of Health Politics, Policy and Law*). Government regulation can therefore help improve the performance of the market. Thus, one motivation for economic regulation of the system is the premise that the system suffers from serious market failures, including information disparities between providers and consumers of health services (called information asymmetries) and an insurance system (third-party financing) that masks the costs of health services (Arrow 1963). This in turn produces excessive expenditures, inefficiency, and maldistribution of labor power and resources. A related market failure is that the health care system has a severe equity problem (differential access to services and financing) (see Morone and Jacobs [2005] and chapter 5). Thus the government must play a role, under this assumption, in providing greater access to the health care market for those who cannot afford it (McClure 1981). The second assumption of the regulatory strategy is that the health care market is different from other economic markets (Relman 2005). In health care, physicians control both supply and demand because the physician is both the patient's consultant on what services are needed and the provider of these services. Physicians are not trained to think in terms of aggregate costs. Physicians not only influence cost decisions regarding individual patients but also influence the growth and expansion of health care institutions, thus affecting hospital costs. In addition, the third-party-payment system, based on private health insurance and government payment, tends to remove the patient from the effects of health care costs, a perspective that colors some of the policy proposals of the twenty-first century (see chapter 10).

Another important potential difference between medical care and other goods and services is the absence of consumer information about appropriate price and quality levels (Arrow 1963; Pauly 1978). The role of information in facilitating choices about health care goods and services is crucial (Varner and Christy 1986). Some have argued that the medical market is on the verge of remedying the information deficit and that the determination of whether medical care is different from other goods and services is ultimately a political question (Pauly 1978).

The third assumption of the regulatory strategy is that public regulation promotes important values of political accountability, public access to information, and public participation (Weiner 1982). The regulatory process is characterized by a high degree of formal due process. The requirements of public notices, public meetings, adversary procedures, formal recordkeeping, and limits on appeals help inform consumers by providing access to information and extending to them an opportunity to participate in the policymaking process.

Thus, government regulation of the health care system is justified on many grounds: as a way of improving the workings of the health care market, providing equity, and promoting crucial public values with the hope that it will help contain health care costs. Some advocates of a regulatory strategy argue that a pure market in health care is unattainable and thus regulation is the second-best choice (Altman and Weiner 1978). Others argue for a more tightly regulated health care system as the best policy (Vladeck 1981, 1984).

Critics of the regulatory strategy charge that examples of past regulatory failures suggest that government regulation does not work (see, for example, Breyer 1979). These critics argue that too many fundamental structural and incentive problems are stacked against good regulatory performance (McClure 1981)[2] and that comprehensive regulation will raise, not lower, the true cost of medical care (Goodman 1980), thus contributing to health care cost inflation (Durenberger 1982). Regulation is not cost effective; it produces inefficiency and prevents technological innovations. Regulation often produces a cartel-like situation resulting in a monopoly on prices because regulatory agencies become captured by the regulated industry (Noll 1975). To the critics of a regulatory strategy the answer is competitive market strategy. "Competition" and market reform are the buzzwords for many health policymakers and health care providers (see, for example, Cannon and Tanner 2005; Herzlinger 1997).

The Market Strategy

New, alternative mechanisms of health care delivery must be found that will provide health care consumers with multiple choices having cost consequences. Creating conditions for fair market competition will produce competition in the market, which will help contain health care costs (Enthoven 1980; Cannon and Tanner 2005). New incentives should be created. To make businesses more conscious of health care costs, tax laws should be altered to place a ceiling on the total amount of health insurance premiums that employers can deduct as a business expense. To make consumers more conscious of health care costs, insurance plans should rely on coinsurance and deductibles (Enthoven 1978a, b). What is needed, some have argued, is to combine markets with a minimal but necessary amount of government regulation. This combination is known as managed competition (Enthoven 1988; Frech and Ginsburg 1988). Examples of programs or policies that rely on combining market-oriented competitive strategy with some government regulations include the Medicare Prospective Payment System (PPS), also known as diagnosis-related groups (DRGs), and the use of organizations such as HMOs and PPOs to provide managed care on a precapitated basis to enrollees.

Some pro-competition advocates, such as Clark Havighurst (1982), have argued that one of the most effective and least intrusive methods for assuring fair competition is enforcement of antitrust laws. Antitrust principles are based on the assumptions that competition promotes efficiency and innovation and encourages diversity through decentralization, and that competitive markets are more stable than noncompetitive markets because the former adjust continuously to market conditions. These assumptions, in turn, are based on social values of individual initiative, individual freedom of choice, and the dangers of big business and big government (Pollard 1981). This does not mean that a competitive market would be unregulated; any competitive market requires monitoring and intervention from time to time to assure that competition is fair and open. According to antitrust enforcement advocates, given the potential for exercise of monopoly power by physicians, hospitals, and other health care providers, policing health care markets must be an integral part of reforms designed to enhance competition (Pollard 1981).

In summary, advocates of the competitive strategy argue that improving structural mechanisms and changing incentives through introduction of competition in the health care market will result in better economic performance and reduced health care costs.

Critics of the competitive strategy are skeptical of the results of market competition. To some, the prospects of a competitive strategy are promising but uncertain technically and politically (McClure 1983). Others argue that markets in health care are usually pseudo-markets dominated by one side of the transaction (Evans 1983), and that the supporters of competition may be grossly overemphasizing the beneficial results (Ginzberg 1982). It would take more than the stimulus from increased consumer cost sharing or reduced tax subsidies to produce competitive behavior on the part of health care providers (Gabel and Monheit 1983). Opponents of an antitrust enforcement strategy argue that professional autonomy and self-regulation produce significant social benefits. In addition, physicians are likely to oppose antitrust enforcement because a free market could be worse for physicians' economic well-being than government regulation. Physicians often reap substantial economic benefits from regulations they control and from the government programs that pay the bills (Starr 1980).

The Role of the Federal Government in Cost Containment

Over the years, the federal government has followed a middle road between the harsh realities of a private health care marketplace and a nationally planned and regulated health care system through a comprehensive national health insurance system. Thus, while the federal government has used both regulatory and competitive strategies in an effort to contain health care costs, the major efforts have been in the regulatory field. One of the regulatory strategies used by the federal government has been health care planning.

Health Care Planning and Cost Containment

During the late 1960s and early 1970s, the federal government responded to the concerns of rising health care costs by adopting various regulatory mechanisms. Health planning emerged as one of the major methods for controlling health care costs. While the federal government had always engaged in some planning, not until the late 1960s and early 1970s did health care planning become a dominant theme. Planning relies on a regulatory strategy and uses centralized decision making to guide the allocation of resources and ensure access to services.

The rationale for health care planning is based on the argument of excess capacity in the health care system in general, and in the hospital industry in particular, as a significant contributor to rising health care costs. The argument is that there are too many hospitals, beds, and medical equipment. This not only creates unnecessary expansion and duplication of expensive resources but also leads to overutilization of medical facilities (Goodman 1980). Supply creates its own demand, following Roemer's argument that "a bed built is a bed filled is a bed billed" (Roemer 1961) This excess capacity, expansion, and duplication were encouraged by factors such as the third-party-payment system, the inability of the market to induce inefficient hospitals to reduce the number of beds or go out of business altogether, and competition among hospitals for prestige and physicians (Havighurst 1973).

While early approaches to planning were aimed at ensuring high-quality health care for everyone,[3] health planning in the 1960s and 1970s focused explicitly on the problem of rising costs. One of the significant regulatory developments in the area of health care planning was certificate-of-need (CON) legislation. By 1973, twenty-three states had adopted such laws. The federal government got into the act with the passage of the 1972 amendments to the Social Security Act of 1935. This created the section 1122 program, which called for review of hospital expansion proposals when Medicare funding might be involved.

Two years later, the federal government assumed control of the entire CON process. The National Health Planning and Resource Development Act of 1974 (PL 93-641) provided an institutional framework for health care planning. It replaced three previous federal programs: Comprehensive Health Planning, the Regional Medical Program, and the Hill-Burton Hospital Construction Program (Kennedy and Baruch 1980–81). The law required all states to adopt CON laws by 1980. The law also established a network of state and local health planning agencies to shape local health systems based on national priorities. More than 200 local health systems agencies (HSAs) were established, each responsible for governing a specific area, to administer the CON laws. State health planning development agencies roughly paralleled the roles and responsibilities of local HSAs. The law provided for the representation of consumer and provider interests in the HSAs. Federal efforts at creating CON legislation ended during the Reagan administration, which was opposed to federal intervention.

CON laws require hospitals to document community need to obtain approval for major capital expenditures for expansion of physical plants, equipment, and services. The primary purpose of these laws was to prevent unnecessary investment in facilities and services. The laws were also designed to prevent the entry of new providers in the health care market unless a clear need was demonstrated.

Did the CON laws and the HSAs help contain overall growth in hospital costs in particular and health care costs in general? The available empirical evidence overwhelmingly points to the failure of health care planning to control health care costs. Research findings show little evidence that CON constrained investment or had any significant effect on the total level of investment (Gelman 1982; see also Salkever and Bice 1976). CON laws may have changed the composition of investment, but they may, in fact, have led to increased overall hospital costs (Salkever and Bice 1979). There was some evidence that programs that focused on hospital beds alone may have had more success than those dealing with review of expansion of facilities, equipment, and services. Nevertheless, the effects of these narrowly focused programs were very weak. The investment in anticipation of regulation, rather than the effect of the CON laws, explain some initial decline in investment after adoption of the CON programs.

What accounts for the failure of CON laws and HSAs? There are many explanations. One possible explanation is the capture theory of regulation (see, for example, Laffont and Tirole 1991; McConnell 1970). This is the theory that regulatory agencies may adopt policies similar to the ones desired by the regulated industry, resulting in a cartel or monopoly situation. This occurs when a regulated industry subverts or captures the regulatory agency through politically inspired appointments, lucrative employment prospects in the industry for cooperative regulators, regulated industry's ability to outspend the regulatory agency, and industry's influence with the elected officials who control a regulatory agency's appropriations. The fact that the American Hospital Association supported CON laws—and a fairly close correlation exists between the attitudes of the hospital industry and the regulators—may lend some legitimacy to this argument, even though it would be difficult to prove (Goodman 1980; Havighurst 1973).

A second explanation is that, despite consumer representation in the HSAs, provider interests have many more advantages in terms of information, expertise, and legal counsel (Bicknell and Walsh 1976; Salkever and Bice 1979). In addition, consistent political participation by consumers in the form of attending public hearings was difficult to achieve because it required time, effort, and money (Marmor and Morone 1979). Representatives of the health care providers dominated most public meetings (Lewin and Associates 1975). It has also been argued that pluralist interest-group representation, as occurred within HSAs, leads to bargaining, log-rolling, and collusive competition among narrowly defined special interests in which the interest of the general public is not well served (Vladeck 1977).

A third explanation for the failure of the CON laws and HSAs lies in the lack of public support. A nationwide public opinion poll in 1978 revealed that the public had very little confidence in, and recognition of, HSAs and had little support for hospital cost-containment strategies and their consequences. There was also little support for the goals and consequences of cost-containment strategies among groups traditionally underrepresented in health planning activities (Mick and Thompson 1984).

Within less than a decade, health planning, as established under the National Health Planning and Resource Development Act of 1974, was dismantled by the Reagan administration. Congress reduced health planning funding from $167 million in 1980 to $58 million in 1983 (Etheredge 1983). Most of the states eliminated local HSAs, though some states maintain CON programs (the authors' home state of Missouri is one example).

Professional Standards Review and Cost Containment

One of the factors often cited as responsible for rising health care costs is overutilization of health care resources. The rise in health care costs since the enactment of Medicare and Medicaid programs in the mid-1960s created concern in Congress about the cost and quality of these programs, concerns that are still present forty years after those two programs were created. The Social Security Amendments of 1972 established the Professional Standards Review Organization (PSRO) program. The PSRO program was designed as a peer-review mechanism to promote effective yet efficient and economical delivery of health care services for government-financed programs such as Medicare and Medicaid. Under the law, more than 200 local PSROs were created and staffed by local physicians to review and monitor care provided to Medicare and Medicaid patients by hospitals, extended-care facilities, and skilled nursing homes. The PSROs were responsible for determining whether the care provided was medically necessary, of professional quality, and delivered in an appropriate health care facility. They also had the authority to deny approval of payment for services to physicians who provide care to Medicaid and Medicare patients. Two of the stated goals of the program were to eliminate unnecessary medical treatment and to eliminate unnecessary institutionalization. Thus, the PSRO program was created as a regulatory mechanism for reducing the cost of federal health care programs.

Did the PSRO program succeed in achieving cost reductions? The majority of evidence suggests that it did not. A 1981 study by the Congressional Budget Office concluded that the cost of the program exceeded its benefits. Although the program slightly reduced Medicare utilization overall, it consumed more resources than it saved. It had very little impact on the federal budget (Congressional Budget Office 1981).

Many explanations are offered for this. One is that PSROs controlled by local physicians had no incentives to reduce utilization because such reduction would lead to reduced federal payments to the locality. Second, the program suffered from potential conflict between quality-enhancing and cost-reducing goals, a persistent problem (Ginzberg 1977). Third, the PSRO program could be used to advance the cartel objectives of health care providers (Goodman 1980). Doctor-policing laws such as PSRO or hospital peer review committees aimed at self-policing are generally ineffective because of a reluctance to speak out against colleagues, concern over libel lawsuits, and problems of due process safeguards (see Cassidy 1984; Rosenberg 1984; Varlova 1984).

The Reagan administration came to office in 1981 strongly supporting the elimination of federal regulatory programs. The PSRO program was on the administration's target list, but it failed to eliminate the program because of opposition in Congress. Federal funding for the PSRO program was cut from $58 million in 1980 to $15 million in 1983 (Etheredge 1983). Congress, through the Tax Equity and Fiscal Responsibility Act of 1982 (PL 97-248), renamed the program Peer Review Organizations (PROs). Today, PROs are responsible for reviewing the appropriateness and quality of health care provided to Medicare beneficiaries. The Medicare program has relied on the PROs to safeguard against inadequate medical treatment for individual patients. In 1987 the scope of the program was expanded beyond hospital-based care to include review of outpatient care.

While utilization review from a public standpoint remains weak, the private sector has moved in this direction. Indeed, one of the newer health care reform concepts, to be discussed in chapters 9 and 10, is managed care. Though the term was not used originally, managed care is a fundamental part of the health maintenance strategy.

Health Maintenance Organizations, Managed Care, and Cost Containment

The CON, HSA, and PSRO programs were examples of behavioral regulations. These programs were designed to scrutinize decisions about utilization, expansion, and acquisition of health care resources by providers. They were based on the assumption that changing behavior and cutting waste could contain health care costs (Brown 1986). They were not very successful.

During the early 1970s, the federal government also tried a competitive market strategy to contain health care costs through prepaid group plans (PGPs), commonly known as HMOs. The concept of PGPs was not new. Such plans had existed in the health care system without any federal assistance since the 1920s. During the early 1970s, the number of HMOs grew as a result of favorable market conditions and the rhetorical support provided by the Nixon administration. According to one estimate, the number of HMOs increased from 41 in 1970 to 133 in 1973 (McNeil and Schlenker 1975).

Dr. Paul M. Ellwood, Jr., a key health advisor to President Richard Nixon, is credited with bringing the competitive market strategy in the form of HMOs to the attention of national health policymakers (Falkson 1980). In 1970 the Nixon administration asked Congress to create a new HMO option for Medicare recipients. In 1971 the administration began to use discretionary funds to plan the development of about a hundred HMOs around the country and asked Congress to create a special HMO development plan. The Department of Health, Education, and Welfare (now the Department of Health and Human Services) argued that there could be as many as 1,700 HMOs within a few years, with perhaps as many as forty million people enrolled (U.S. Department of Health, Education, and Welfare 1971). After long debate, Congress passed the Health Maintenance Organization Act (PL 93-222) of 1973.

The federal government assumed the role of venture capitalist (Iglehart 1980). It encouraged the development of HMOs in an attempt to induce competition in the health care market with the hope of containing health costs. This market strategy was designed to eliminate, or at least reduce, centralized health care bureaucracy and replace it with decentralized market building. This was to be accomplished through the use of federal funds to support efforts in developing new health care organizations and alternative means of health care delivery. It promised pluralism, choice, efficiency, and reorganization through competition, markets, and incentives (Ellwood 1971; Havighurst 1970). The expectation was that HMOs would contain costs by (1) creating incentives for channeling health service utilization from costly inpatient settings (hospitals, skilled nursing homes, etc.) to less costly outpatient settings (visits to doctors' offices), (2) promoting competition with traditional health care delivery systems, and (3) exercising market power by obtaining preferential prices from various health care providers (Falkson 1980–81).

An HMO is a prepaid medical practice delivering a comprehensive set of health care services to enrollees for a fixed fee (capitation) paid in advance. The Health Maintenance Organization Act of 1973 provided for an expenditure of $375 million over five years. Most of these funds were used to encourage development of HMOs by providing start-up costs. The law offered federally qualified HMOs three basic benefits: (1) money for development of HMOs; (2) overriding of certain restrictive state laws; and (3) a mandate to employers, covered by the Fair Labor Standards Act of 1938, that employ twenty-five or more employees to offer HMO coverage as an alternative to whatever other health plans they provide. This was designed to provide health care consumers with at least a dual choice in health plans. In return, to qualify for federal funds, HMOs were to deliver a comprehensive package of benefits to a broadly representative population on an equitable basis with consumer participation. This was to be done at the same price as or a lower price than traditional forms of health insurance (Rosoff 1975).

The original legislation so heavily burdened HMOs with special services (comprehensive benefits, open enrollment, dual choice, and limits on copayments) and pricing requirements (same premiums to be charged to all enrollees, that is, "community rate" as opposed to "experience rate") (Rosoff 1975) that very few developers applied for federal support. By 1975, only five HMOs had qualified for federal support. Between 1974 and 1976, the growth in the number of federally supported HMOs was very slow.

To remedy this problem the HMO amendments of 1976 and 1978 deregulated service and pricing requirements, including a reduction in service requirements and the elimination of open enrollment with the exception of large and established programs. In 1981 the federal government stopped providing new grants to HMOs. Since then, the federal government has focused its attention on the promotion of competition in general, incentives designed to increase private-sector involvement in HMO development, and risk contracts to HMOs that agree to enroll Medicare beneficiaries. We discussed the experience with Medicaid managed care in chapter 3 and Medicare managed care in chapter 4. The health maintenance strategy has morphed or been transformed into the managed care strategy and is discussed in chapter 9.

Prospective Payment System and Cost Containment

With the enactment of Medicaid and Medicare in the mid-1960s, the federal government became a major purchaser of health services in the health care market. Part of the increase in overall health care costs is attributed to dramatic increases in the cost of these programs. Federal spending for these programs has almost doubled every five years. By 1980, spending had reached about $61.2 billion, and it constituted about 27.8 percent of total national health spending—financing health care for about fifty million people (Levit et al. 1994a). At the same time, hospital costs were also rising dramatically. The cost of hospital care had increased from $28 billion in 1970 to $102.7 billion in 1980 (Levit et al 1994a). From 1977 to 1982, Medicare hospital expenditures grew at an average annual rate of 18 percent compared to a 14.6 percent increase in overall hospital spending (Gibson et al. 1984).

The burden on the federal health budget created the political environment for federal regulation of hospital costs (see Marmor, Wittman, and Heagy 1983; Steinwald and Sloan 1981). Advocates of regulation argued that cost controls on hospitals would limit waste and inefficiency without sacrificing quality of care.

President Carter, in response to rising hospital costs, proposed hospital cost containment legislation (HR 6575) designed to constrain the rate of increase in hospital costs and to limit the rate of increase in hospital revenues. The hospital industry strongly opposed such a measure and proposed a voluntary plan to control costs on its own. The controversy surrounding both plans led to their demise in 1979.

As mentioned earlier, President Ronald Reagan came to office in 1981 with the expressed intention of eliminating federal regulatory health care programs in favor of a market-oriented, competitive strategy to contain health care costs. Federal funding was cut for health planning programs, and the PSRO program was renamed PRO and given reduced funding. Budget cuts were made in Medicaid and Medicare, and new federal grants for HMO start-up were eliminated.

Minor changes were made in Medicare by the Omnibus Budget Reconciliation Act of 1981. This included tightening Medicare reimbursement payments. The 1982 Tax Equity and Fiscal Responsibility Act (TEFRA) limited the increase in Medicare hospital payment rates, created an early basis for prospective payment based on a case-mix index, and called for incentive payments to hospitals defined as efficient. TEFRA required that the Department of Health and Human Services (HHS) design a prospective payment plan for the Medicare program. That new system, implemented in 1983, was the Prospective Payment System (PPS) for Medicare reimbursement to hospitals. The PPS for Medicare reimbursement was based on the New Jersey diagnosis-related groups (DRGs) program.[4] This is an example of the federal government embracing a program originally implemented at the state level.[5]

Under PPS, hospitals are paid according to a schedule of preestablished rates linked to 468 DRGs. All major diagnoses are classified into 468 categories, with each category assigned a treatment rate. Hospitals are reimbursed according to these rates. There are economic incentives in the form of rewards and punishments built into the system. If a hospital spends more money than the preestablished rate for a particular diagnostic treatment, the hospital must absorb the additional cost. If the hospital spends less money than the preestablished rate, it is still paid the preestablished rate and can keep the overpayment as profit. The Health Care Financing Administration (now the Centers of Medicare and Medicaid Services) within HHS was assigned the responsibility of establishing the DRG payment schedule. To safeguard against reduction in quality of care as a result of PPS, Congress assigned PROs the responsibility of monitoring the quality and appropriateness of care for Medicare patients. If a PRO finds inappropriate or substandard care, the hospital may be denied Medicare payment. If a pattern of inappropriate or substandard care is discovered, the hospital Medicare provider agreement may be terminated.

There are three major kinds of hospital regulations: facilities and service regulation, utilization review, and rate and revenue regulations (Sloan 1982a). The first two were used by the federal government in programs such as CON, HSAs, and PSROs. The DRGs, under the PPS, involved rate and revenue regulations, commonly referred to as price regulation. Price regulation typically involves a regulatory agency that establishes a minimum, maximum, or range of prices an individual or an institution can charge for particular goods or services (Meir 1985). The rationale behind replacing the retrospective payment system was that under that system, hospitals had no incentive to economize in their use of health care resources in treating Medicare patients. If anything, such a system tended to encourage overutilization of health resources, since hospitals were assured that they would be reimbursed for all reasonable costs incurred. PPS was based on the assumption that given built-in incentives, hospitals would be forced to consider cost factors in treatment and would be encouraged to be economically more efficient. Thus, inefficient hospitals would be forced to close. An economically more efficient hospital sector would help contain increases in hospital costs. PPS was viewed as a method of influencing hospital activities, creating cost-containment constraints, and introducing incentives into hospital payments (Shaffer 1983). The cost-control incentive was the primary purpose in establishing the PPS (Quade 1989). As we saw in chapter 4, additional Medicare prospective payment mechanisms were imposed on physicians in 1989 and on nursing homes, home health care agencies, and hospice agencies in 1997 (the latter as a result of the 1997 Balanced Budget Act).

Evaluating the Prospective Payment System

How well has the prospective payment system constrained hospital cost increases? The initial years of PPS showed some reduction in the growth rate of hospital costs. Hospital expenditures increased more slowly in the first three years of PPS implementation as compared to the three previous years. Indeed, those increases declined each year from 1983 to 1987.[6] Cost reductions have largely resulted from reduced admissions. Occupancy rates fell, and length of hospital stay was reduced. There does not appear to have been any cost shifting, nor has the quality of care for Medicare patients declined (Sloan, Morrisey, and Valvono 1988; see also Medicare Payment Advisory Commission 2004).

Between 1984 and 1991, PPS payment per caseload rose at an annual rate of 6.4 percent (2.5 percent faster than the CPI). Between 1991 and 1995, PPS payment per case had decelerated to 4.2 percent per year. PPS cost per case actually declined in 1994 and again in 1995 (Guterman 1998). Medicare payments per hospital discharge were flat from 1996 to 2000 and then began a steep rise in 2001 and 2002 (Medicare Payment Advisory Commission 2004).The most recent data indicate that over the past several years the hospital industry has managed to improve the balance of revenue and expenses in the face of strong pressure from private payers. Hospital inpatient margins were negative in 1991 (–2.4 percent), reached a peak in 1997 (16.7 percent), and have declined significantly through 2002 (4.7 percent). The overall margin (including most institutional care) declined from 10.3 percent in 1996 (the first year for which such data were collected) to 1.7 percent in 2002 (Medicare Payment Advisory Commission 2004). Cost shifting to outpatient care has occurred.

PPS has proven successful in reining in cost increases for nursing homes, home health care agencies, and hospices after the 1997 BBA. In 1998, nursing home expenditures went up by 6.8 percent and expenditures on home health care agencies rose by 13.1 percent. The next year nursing home expenditures increased by 0.5 percent and home health care expenditures *decreased* by 3.7 percent. While expenditures on these two programs increased in subsequent years, the increases were smaller than prior to the 1997 legislation (Office of the Actuary 2004). McCall et al. (2001) suggest that there was a significant decline in the use of home health care services after the passage of the BBA. Part of this was due to the decline in the number of such agencies (see Dean 1998).

There have been criticisms of the payment system. Some suggest that hospitals seek ways to limit the impact of the new hospital regulations (see, for example, Lave 1984). Because price regulation is a tax on hospital behavior, it not only affects price but also hospital output and quality and quantity of services. Hospitals respond by attempting to reduce the use of affected services or resources by modifying their practices and products (Cook et al. 1983). Hospitals modify the cost of regulation by seeking an area unaffected by the regulation, that is, the "unregulated margin." Organizations respond to regulation through institutional, managerial, and technical changes (Parsons 1956). Hospitals altered services, influenced practices, and changed the products offered to decrease the impact of regulation at the expense of Medicare patients. They also changed the mix of services offered in the inpatient Medicare market and expanded the surgical market because surgical DRGs are more profitable than medical DRGs. Often, services were cut (Gay, Kronenfeld, and Baker 1989).

State Governments and Cost Containment

During the 1960s and 1970s, there was rapid growth in state and local governments' public health programs. They took on many new functions in the health care field by expanding their role beyond the traditional public health activities (Sun Valley Forum 1983). Their traditional role focused largely on problems of sanitation and communicable disease. During the 1960s and 1970s, state and local governments' role expanded to include a broad range of environmental concerns: air and water pollution, radiation control, hazardous waste, and occupational health and safety, as well as the delivery of medical services, particularly to the poor (as a result of the federal Medicaid program).

This expanded role also led to dramatic increases in health care expenditures of state governments. Their total health care expenditures increased from $9.9 billion in 1970 to $33.2 billion in 1980. Medicaid expenditures accounted for $11.4 billion in 1980 (Lazenby and Letsch 1990).

By the early 1980s, health care cost containment had emerged as a major issue for state and local governments. A number of factors contributed to this. One was the general taxpayer revolt in many states that followed the passage of Proposition 13 in California. The second factor was a national recession, which left state and local governments with reduced resources. Third, and perhaps most important, was the sharp cutback in federal aid that occurred during the first term of the Reagan administration. The consolidation of many categorical health grants into block grants substantially reduced available federal money. The federal Medicaid contribution was reduced 3 percent in 1982, 4 percent in 1983, and 4.5 percent in 1984. The administration showed considerable interest in granting states more discretion when such discretion seemed to promise cost reductions (for a detailed discussion of the evolution of health policy and its implications for federalism, see Thompson 1981).

Faced with reduced revenues and increased health care costs, state governments attempted a number of different strategies to contain cost increases (Leeds 1996). By 1982, seventeen states had legislation requiring the disclosure, review (such as HSAs and CON), or regulation of hospital rates or budgets. By the 2000s, states were faced with severe budget issues and looked to health cost containment as a way to alleviate their problems.

The Rise and Demise of State Rate-Setting Programs

One major strategy used by the state governments during the 1970s and 1980s was rate setting. The rate-setting strategy was developed with the encouragement of the federal government through legislation and support from several administrations. This strategy emerged in the mid-1970s as the regulatory instrument of choice in several eastern industrial states as a response to Medicaid's financial crisis. By the 1980s hospital rate-setting programs were no longer confined to traditionally proregulatory states in the industrial Northeast. Limited prospective payment schemes for Medicaid reimbursement were adopted in Kentucky, Missouri, Alabama, Georgia, Mississippi, and North Carolina (Crozier 1982). Some states introduced mandatory rate-setting programs, while others solicited voluntary compliance with the results of the review process or operated as disclosure programs. There was a considerable amount of diversity in these programs. Some related to revenues, others to costs. Most programs were revenue based and were concerned with the total financial needs of the hospital. The cost-based programs were used for establishing reasonable payment rates for hospitals (Esposito et al. 1982). During the 1980s more than thirty states established some form of rate-setting program.

Proponents of regulation saw state rate setting as an approach most likely to win political support and argued that hospital expenditures exceed corresponding benefits. Therefore, American society in general, and government in particular, can no longer afford to finance the excess. In contrast, proponents of medical marketplace competition argued that the imposition of rate setting tends to remove flexibility and interest in innovation from the hospitals affected. State rate regulations involve a complex set of issues such as which providers to regulate, how the rate-setting body should be organized, and how it should set rates (Cohen 1975).

State rate-setting programs have produced varying results. Proponents argued that some mandatory prospective rate-setting programs were successful in reducing hospital expenditures per patient day, per admission, and per capita (Coelen and Sullivan 1981). Opponents argued that in many states, rate-setting programs have failed to produce the promised results, and the positive impact of state rate-setting programs has been overstated (Mitchell 1982). The failure of some state rate-setting programs was attributed to the fact that regulators often lack the necessary skills in the complex field of financial regulation and have fewer resources than the hospital industry. For example, the State Rate-Setting Commission in Massachusetts had only a few professionally trained people in a bureau that sets rates for 140 acute-care hospitals in the state. The staff of virtually every major hospital was larger than the state's (Rosenbloom 1983). In sum, state rate-setting programs did not provide a "quick fix" for the rapid rise in spending for hospital care (Sloan 1982b).

Beginning with Wisconsin in 1986, states that had been in the forefront of rate-setting strategy began to abandon it. By the mid-1990s, state rate-setting programs nearly disappeared because most states that had established rate-setting programs during the 1970s and 1980s had begun to deregulate and abandon them. John McDonough (1997) provides four reasons for the demise of the rate-setting program. One reason was that during the early 1990s, the growth in the number of HMOs directly collided with state rate-setting programs. All mandatory systems had to decide up front whether to require HMOs to pay state-regulated hospital charges or to permit negotiated rates of payment lower than approved charges paid by Blue Cross, commercial carriers, and other public payers. When public officials had to choose whether to bring HMOs under the rate-setting scheme or to let all plans compete on the same basis, deregulation won out. A second reason was that statutes and regulations dealing with rate setting were complex and often incomprehensible. The confusion created suspicion that rate setting was subject to excessive gaming by powerful players (i.e., teaching and urban hospitals). A third reason was the changing interest-group landscape. Again, the steady growth of managed care was a key element in this. Furthermore, the American Hospital Association (AHA), which had supported rate setting in the 1970s, dropped its support in the 1980s. Fourth was the fact that states that deregulated their rate-setting programs had experienced political change in the form of shifting from Democratic to Republican or independent control.

The most successful state rate-setting program, and one of the very few remaining, is in Maryland. It is unique because it operates with the support of the Maryland Hospital Association. The four factors that have allowed Maryland to keep its rate-setting program on track are: the ability to prevent HMOs from engaging in competitive discounting, flexibility provided to regulators to adapt to changing environment, the maintenance of a Medicare waiver that has placed regulatory opponents on the defensive, and the maintenance of Democratic control in the executive and legislative branches (McDonough 1997). The result has been dramatic. Hospital rate increases have been lower in Maryland than in any other state (SEIU Local 503 2005). Apart from the support of the Maryland Hospital Association, another reason for the program's success was that it covers all sources of payment and thus prevents cost shifting. At the same time, the program is flexible enough to account for inflation and to cover losses for charitable or uncompensated care (Rich 1992).

Health Care Rationing

Some states have attempted Medicaid cuts by reducing the number of people on the program, reducing benefits for those who are covered, or both. The George W. Bush administration encouraged the states to cut their Medicaid costs, because such actions would also reduce federal Medicaid spending (Lueck 2005).

Tennessee and Missouri led the way in 2005, with Tennessee cutting some 300,000 people from Medicaid, cutting payments to managed care organizations, and reducing benefits, and Missouri passing legislation that cuts some 100,000 people from the rolls and reduces benefits for others (see Goodwin 2005 and Wadhwani 2005; see also chapter 3). A new theme is being heard in the health care field. It implies that there are limits to what we can expect and afford in the way of health care. It is based on the notion that health care costs are rising disproportionately compared to the small or marginal gains in overall national health. Therefore, we must establish priorities in health services and become more rational in our health care spending.

Advocates of this new school of thought argue that health care costs are out of control and that regulatory controls on spending or competitive approaches based on economic incentives are doomed to fail. Regulatory approaches are, it is asserted, based on the faulty assumption that medical care produces health, and more care produces more health. The only realistic solution, therefore, is the rationing of health care resources. If the United States is serious about containing health care costs, society will have to forgo some medical benefits, and patients should not expect to receive all the care they want regardless of the costs (Aaron and Schwartz 1984, 1990). Proponents argue that health care rationing already exists in the actions of insurance companies, legislatures, hospitals, physicians, and individual premium payers, and we need to get on with the public business of determining how health care rationing should be carried out ethically (Menzel 1990). Observers call the existing de facto rationing "silent rationing," "under-the-table rationing," "rationing by finance," or "rationing by wallet" (Mechanic 1997).

All countries engage in some form of rationing (see Patel and Rushefsky 2002, chapter 6). In the United States, the major example of rationing is in organ transplantation. There are many more people who need new lungs, kidneys, hearts, and so forth, than there are available organs. There are both state and federal laws governing the process of deciding who will receive the organs (see President's Council on Bioethics 2003). These include the Uniform Anatomical Gift Act of 1968 and the Organ Transplantation Act of 1984.[7]

Rationing can be explicit or implicit. *Implicit rationing* refers to discretionary decisions made by professionals, managers, and other health care personnel within the established budgetary guidelines. *Explicit rationing* refers to decisions made by an administrative authority regarding the amount of resources and types of resources to be made available, eligible populations, and specific rules for allocation. Explicit rationing is effected through constraining levels of available technology, locations of facilities and programs, expenditure levels, and the like (Mechanic 1997). The effort in the Medicaid program to establish treatment priorities represents one of the most explicit forms of rationing in the United States (Mechanic 1997).

In Oregon, health care rationing moved beyond the talking point and took action to change the way in which health care programs were structured (see chapter 3). The state provoked a national debate in 1987 when it decided to stop financing most organ transplants for Medicaid patients and use the money instead for prenatal care for pregnant women. In 1990 it produced a revolutionary Medicaid plan. Rather than offer a minority of the poor a comparatively full package of services, the state proposed to give all its poor access to health care but with a reduced level of services. The state ranked most medical conditions as least or most economically worthwhile to treat under the plan. If money ran out before all services were covered, the lowest-priority services would not be covered. Faced with intense criticisms of the listed priorities, in 1991 Oregon health officials overhauled the ranking and produced a new list. The George H.W. Bush administration turned down Oregon's request for a Medicaid waiver, necessary to implement rationing, partly on the grounds that it might conflict with the Americans with Disabilities Act. The Clinton administration, however, did issue the waiver in 1993 and the program began operation in 1994 (Guglielmo 2004). Despite the state's best efforts, Oregon had to resort to the more common means of rationing: reducing Medicaid rolls (from 90,000 to 54,000) (Guglielmo 2004). No other state has sought to engage in the kind of explicit rationing and public discussion based on the Oregon model (Yegian 2004).

David Mechanic provides five reasons to be skeptical about explicit rationing. One reason is that once bureaucratic decisions have been made and put in place (i.e., once explicit standards are established), they are resistant to change because constituencies develop to preserve the status quo. Developing explicit standards is difficult and often impossible. It is not a science. Second, medical care involves a process of discovery and negotiation between a patient and a health care provider, not simply application of technical means. Third, patients have different experiences, needs, tastes, preferences, and values. Two patients in comparable medical situations may require different treatments. Fourth, explicit rationing will result in inflexibility in responding to the contingencies of people's real lives. Fifth, explicit rationing will be susceptible to political manipulation. Once decisions are removed from a dialogue between patient and doctor to the public arena, they become subject to political, social, moral, and legal turf battles (Mechanic 1997).

States have also resorted to moving Medicaid recipients into managed care organizations as a way to save money (see chapter 3; Draper, Hurley, and Short 2004). The experience has not been entirely successful, given the continued increase in Medicaid expenditures. Medicaid provider reimbursements are already quite low. But the important point is that managed care is a form of rationing, even if we do not explicitly discuss it (see chapter 9).

Evaluating Public Cost Containment Programs

As we have seen, both the federal and state governments are searching for ways to reduce their health care costs. How successful have they been? At one level, the answer is clearly not very successful. Overall health care costs continue to rise, as do costs for the two major public-sector programs, Medicare and Medicaid. There have been some individual successes, such as Maryland's rate-regulation program. And when the federal government wants to restrain costs, it can do so, at least for a short period of time. The 1997 Balanced Budget Act showed this was possible, largely through reductions in provider reimbursements.

On the other hand, there is some evidence that the health care sector will respond to real and possible pressure for change (Altman and Levitt 2003). Consider Figure 6.3. It shows the annual change in private health care spending from 1961 to about 2000. There are lots of ups and downs, and they are related to actions or proposed actions by the federal government. The enactment of Medicare and Medicaid in 1965 led to a step rise in spending. The wage-and-price-control program instituted by President Nixon in 1971 (in response to what was then considered high inflation) led to a drastic decline in the increase. When the Nixon administration was ready to lift the controls in 1974, there was some thought given to leaving them on for hospitals. The hospital industry promised to control prices and we can see what happened beginning in 1975. A similar sequence of events occurred in the late 1970s. The Carter administration strongly considered controls over hospital pricing and uniform accounting for hospitals. The industry promised that, through its voluntary efforts, it would restrain increases. The next decline came in the early and mid-1990s, with the Clinton Health Security Act proposal and the advent of managed care. The Clinton proposal failed, but managed care did seem to restrain spending increases, for a while. But as we moved to the late 1990s, the managed care revolution faltered and costs started increasing again. Figure 6.3 indicates that the Balanced Budget Act of 1997 brought about another change, as spending increases dipped at the end of the twentieth century.

Bodenheimer (2003) points out that while private spending increases show a wave-like, up-and-down appearance over time (as in Figure 6.3), Medicare spending shows consistent declines on a per capita basis. So, public-sector actions, if there is a political will to withstand the pain of cuts/restraints and the pressure of affected interests, can be effective.

The Private Sector and Cost Containment

The dramatic rise in health care costs also has had significant consequences for the private sector. During the 1980s, many corporations spent 25 percent of their gross revenues to provide medical coverage for their employees. According to a national survey of 1,955 employers conducted by Foster Higgins & Company of New York, an average company spent 21.6 percent more in 1990 to provide doctor and hospital care to its employees than in 1989. During the 1989–90 period, the cost to employers of providing employee health care benefits rose 46.3 percent (Swoboda 1991). This led the business community to search for solutions to contain health care costs. Many businesses participate in freestanding health policy groups or health coalitions. Business reformers pushed the concept of managed care (Kosterlitz 1991). The term implies a stepped-up coordination and oversight of employee use of medical care for eliminating unnecessary care typically found in insurance plans. In managed care programs, companies limit the medical care of their employees to doctors and hospitals that agree to provide care for a set price (Swoboda 1990). Health maintenance organizations embody the concept of managed care.

During the late 1970s, the business community was not very concerned about rising health care costs and was not very interested in acting to control them (Sapolsky et al. 1981). Since the early 1980s, however, faced with a dramatic rise in costs, the private sector has begun to look for solutions to the problem. As a major purchaser of health care services, business has become conscious of its capability and responsibility for controlling health care costs. The private sector has become concerned because

Figure 6.3   **Annual Change in Private Health Spending Per Capita, 1961–2001**

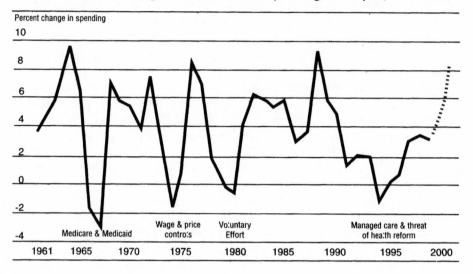

Source: Altman and Levitt 2003 (p. W84).

soaring costs are having negative effects on profit margins and international competitiveness (Iglehart 1982; Zakaria 2005). The government has fostered the emergence
of private-sector initiatives through legislative changes that alter incentives by providing technical assistance and/or financial support, and by demonstrating feasible
options in its own cost-containment strategy as a major purchaser of health services
(Tell, Falik, and Fox 1984).

The cost-containment initiatives undertaken by the private sector fall into four
major strategies: cost sharing, direct action, managed care, and wellness programs.[8]

Cost Sharing

One category consists of greater employee cost sharing for health services. The patient shares in the direct cost of health care services for his or her own coverage or
that of dependents. Cost sharing can include deductibles, coinsurance, or copayments.
A deductible is the fixed amount that must be paid by the patient before the insurance
benefits begin. Coinsurance is the percentage contribution patients pay once the deductible is exceeded. Copayments are generally a fixed contribution, rather than a
percentage contribution, toward each unit of service. This strategy helps reduce the
cost to the employers by shifting part of the cost to the patient. It is based on the belief
that when patients are made to share a higher cost for treatment (negative incentive),
they will reduce health service utilization. Some studies have demonstrated that cost
sharing in the form of deductibles or coinsurance reduces the use of health care services (Lee and Tollen 2002; Newhouse et al. 1981; Robinson 2002). Others have

argued that increased cost shifting is not in the best interest of the workers, that some of the cost savings are illusory, and that other savings are likely to be one-time savings (Davis et al. 1990). Whatever the case, more and more employers are seeking to reduce costs through cost sharing.

For example, medium- and large-size companies, those most likely to provide health insurance for their workers and workers' dependents, are less likely to pay the full premium for the health insurance benefit. In 2000, 29 percent of such companies paid the full premium for their workers; by 2004, that percentage had decreased to 17 percent, a decline of over 40 percent in just four years. The comparable percentages for family coverage are 11 percent (in 2000) and 6 percent (in 2004), a decline of over 45 percent (Freudenheim 2005).

Cost-sharing requirements are increasing for all types of plans. During the 1988–93 period, the average deductible for conventional plans increased 9 to 10 percent a year. Over the 2000–2004 period, the average deductible for individual coverage in conventional plans increased by almost 67 percent; for family coverage, the increase was a little over 48 percent. Even for PPO and POS plans, the increases were substantial, 64 and 300 percent respectively (calculated from Exhibit 4.4, section 4, in Kaiser Family Foundation n.d.). Increases in cost sharing are also occurring through changes in covered benefits and less coverage of active workers, dependents, and retirees. A 2004 survey of large employers (200 or more workers) found substantial interest in increasing cost sharing. Eighty-three percent said they were very likely or somewhat likely to increase employee cost sharing. Fifty-five percent said they were very likely or somewhat likely to increase how much employees pay for prescription drugs, while 51 percent were considering increasing deductibles and co-payments (Kaiser Family Foundation and Health Research and Education Trust 2004).

Perhaps the ultimate in cost sharing is a disturbing new trend. Companies have begun to eliminate certain coverage. This has taken two forms. In one, companies that self-insure, rather than use a third-party health insurer, have cut or drastically reduced benefits for employees with diseases that are very expensive. In some cases, employers have been releasing disabled workers. A 2002 survey found that 51 percent of survey companies fired employees who were placed on long-term disability (Pereira 2003). Companies have looked at cutting family and retiree coverage (see, for example, Saranow 2005). In 1988, 66 percent of large firms offered health insurance to their retirees. by 2003, that number had dropped to 38 percent (Neuman 2004). The worker or former worker is left to use his or her own resources, or to rely on public-sector programs.

Direct Action

A second category of initiatives is designed to reduce health service utilization, especially the use of hospital services, through direct action. Here, initiatives include requiring a second opinion for surgery, doing a preadmission review (often prospective) of all nonemergency hospital admissions, making a more careful review of medical claims, providing coverage of certain services and procedures on an outpatient basis only, and providing incentives to shift care to an outpatient setting.

HMOs, PPOs, and Managed Care

The third set of initiatives consists of encouraging or requiring employees to use HMOs or PPOs for health care services. A PPO either restricts beneficiaries to a list of providers such as hospitals and physicians or provides financial incentives for beneficiaries to obtain their care from the list of preferred providers. Providers are generally selected on the basis of lower price or lower expected utilization.

PPOs differ from traditional health insurance plans in two ways. In PPOs, the insurer takes an active role in negotiating payment rates or selecting providers, and the providers are on notice to comply with aggressive utilization review procedures.

PPOs also differ from HMOs. PPO providers are paid on a fee-for-service basis and thus are not at financial risk for services they provide, nor do they have incentives to reduce utilization. Under PPOs, beneficiaries can use providers outside the PPO plan, which is not the case with HMOs. Unlike HMOs, PPOs do not generally practice in a common location or in group practices (Davis et al. 1990). PPOs are mainly sponsored by health care providers such as hospitals and physicians and by insurance companies.

Prepaid group practice plans such as HMOs and PPOs are based on the concept of managed care to contain costs. Allen Buchanan (1998) has outlined five cost-containment (or rationing) techniques that are commonly identified with the concept of managed care. One technique for cost containment is payment limits. An example of such a technique is the use of DRGs by the federal government to reimburse hospitals for Medicare patient fees. A second technique is a requirement of preauthorization for medical services such as surgeries. A third technique is the use of primary care physicians as "gatekeepers" to control access to specialists. A fourth technique is "de-skilling" (i.e., using less trained providers to provide certain services). A fifth technique is to provide financial incentives to physicians to limit utilization of care. Managed care is a fancy name for rationing.

In recent years the managed care market has gone through significant changes. In 1988, 73 percent of workers with employer-sponsored health insurance were enrolled in conventional, fee-for-service health care plans, 16 percent in HMOs, and 11 percent in PPOs. By 1996, only 27 percent of employees were enrolled in conventional plans, 31 percent in HMOs, 28 percent in PPOs, and 14 percent in POS plans. By 2004, the trend away from conventional plans, seen in the 1996 data, was full blown. Only 5 percent of employees were in conventional plans, 25 percent in HMOs, 55 percent in PPOs, and 15 percent in POS plans (Kaiser Family Foundation n.d.). As the data indicate, the major changes are moving away from conventional plans and moving to looser forms of managed care plans, even within the HMO market (Draper et al. 2002).

The Impact of HMOs and Managed Care on Costs

Has HMO and managed care development helped to contain health care costs? The success of a competitive health strategy depends on the creation of health care delivery systems that are more efficient than the traditional system, and that are able to compete on price, benefits, access, style of medical care, and the existence of sufficient numbers of such systems throughout the country (Moran 1981). A review of the literature on HMO performance by Miller and Luft (2002) suggests that HMOs, the type of managed care plan most likely to control costs, has not been very successful at doing so.

One way that HMOs try to restrain costs is by lowering utilization. Miller and Luft found mixed results here, with some studies showing lower use of ambulatory services by HMO members over conventional plans, but the overall evidence is weak. The same appears to be true for hospital admissions and hospital length-of-stays. They write (Miller and Luft 2002, 80–81):

> Recent evidence indicates that, overall, the trade off [of quality and access for cost control] has not been as severe as some had feared—HMOs have led to lower costs, and while access and satisfaction seem to have suffered, quality of care has been comparable for all types of enrollees combined. At the same time, most (but not all) HMOs have not accomplished what their proponents had promised: changing clinical practice processes and improving quality of care relative to the existing system, while containing costs for both purchasers and consumers.

On the other hand, there is some evidence to suggest that managed care organizations have not succeeded any better than traditional or indemnity plans in controlling costs. According to the Kaiser Family Foundation 2004 business survey, individual coverage plan costs were highest for conventional plans, at $3,820 per year, with the lowest being HMOs at $3,458. For family coverage, the highest cost plan was PPOs at $10,217; HMOs were the lowest at $9,504. Conventional family coverage plans cost $9,602 (Kaiser Family Foundation n.d.). There are differences, but they are not great.

Another way of looking at this is to consider changes in employer health plan premiums over time. In the 1996–2004 period, premiums increased by an average of 8.5 percent per year overall. Conventional plans saw an average annual increase of 8.0 percent, HMOs 8.4 percent, PPOs 8.5 percent, and POS plans 7.7 percent (Kaiser Family Foundation n.d.). Again, there are some differences, but the superiority of managed-care-type plans over conventional plans in controlling costs is minimal at best.

Wellness Programs

The fourth set of initiatives consists of employee wellness programs. Larger employers are increasingly promoting programs designed to encourage healthier lifestyles and behavior. The emphasis is on preventive care to reduce the need for health care services. The assumption here is that prevention will lead to healthier workers and therefore reduced health care costs. The focus is on such lifestyle issues as smoking and obesity, as well as disease management related to chronic diseases (see Fleming 2005). One survey found that only 10 percent of U.S. companies utilize wellness programs ("Only 1 in 10 Firms Are Serious About Wellness" 2004).

Such employee wellness programs tend to penalize workers with unhealthy lifestyles by reducing their health care benefits. Some health care experts express concern over such meddling by employers because some of the health care problems of workers may be related to hereditary, environmental, or socioeconomic factors over which they have very little control. Some firms have also begun to consider lifestyles in hiring and firing decisions. This led the American Civil Liberties Union to charge that some employers are overstepping their bounds. It argued that if employers are allowed to refuse to hire workers, or to fire them, because of something they do in their private lives, workers will not have any private lives left (American Civil Liberties Union 1998; Miller and Bradburn 1991).

Other Private-Sector Initiatives

In addition to the four major strategies discussed above, industries and firms are beginning to rely on other initiatives to contain rising health care costs. A number of organizations have moved toward self-insurance. Rather than contract out with private insurance companies, these companies try to reduce their health costs through administrative savings. One important feature of self-insurance is that such plans are not covered under the federal Employee Retirement Income Security Act (ERISA) and are therefore not regulated by the states. This allows employer flexibility in maintaining or cutting coverage, though it also means less protections for workers (Gabel, Jensen, and Hawkins 2003). This was part of the debate over federal patients' bill of rights legislation (see chapter 7).

Some large businesses have begun to offer general medical services at in-house medical clinics, staffed by their own doctors or provided by contract medical firms as a cheaper alternative to constantly rising insurance rates (Fuhrmans 2005). Besides saving on drugs and tests, companies can save money by avoiding unnecessary hospitalization through careful monitoring of individual workers' health. A large company can also negotiate low fees with contracted medical firms. In addition to the cost savings, one of the most attractive features of such initiatives is the convenience it offers.

Private Insurers

Private insurers are also undertaking cost-control initiatives. Some of them are moving away from spreading the cost of health insurance equally across all groups and are increasingly charging different rates for different people. Young and healthy employees are charged less at the expense of older and less healthy workers. Blue Cross and Blue Shield of Minnesota (BCBSM) became the first national insurer to link health care reimbursement directly to patient outcomes. The plan, which went into effect in January 1991, used a new system of risk classification called illness outcome groups (IOGs) to classify illnesses by their expected rate of adverse outcomes. Other initiatives include trying to reduce administrative costs and working with other carriers (especially among the Blue Cross/Blue Shield group) to develop a network of low-cost providers (see BlueCross BlueShield of Kansas City n.d.).

The Private Sector and Health Care Cost Containment

Sources of data on trends in health spending vary considerably in their completeness and consistency. The growth rate of private-sector health care spending during the 1990s slowed significantly as did the rate of growth of employers' health care costs, which reflects slower growth in premium costs per enrollee. The growth in employers' premiums or costs fell from double-digit rates early in the decade to 2 percent or less in 1995 and 1996. The growth rate of private-sector spending for health insurance fell steadily between 1990 and 1994, reaching 2.5 percent in 1994 and staying at that level in 1995. In 1990, it was 14 percent (Congressional Budget Office 1997).

In the latter part of the twentieth century and the early years of the twenty-first century, spending and premiums rose dramatically, although they declined a bit by 2004. Private-sector health insurance premiums rose by an average of 11.6 percent during this period (2000–2004) (calculated from California HealthCare Foundation 2005, 17). Efforts to control costs on the part of the private sector seem no more successful than public efforts.

A Strategy for Controlling Costs

Controlling health care costs is never going to be easy, nor like the "Global War on Terror," is there an end in sight. But there are some promising strategies. One such strategy has been offered by Karen Davis (2005), president of the Commonwealth Fund. She suggests ten steps that look at the supply side of health, which, she argues, have been successfully implemented in other countries.

The first step is better management of people with chronic conditions. One of several examples she provides is that better management of people with diabetes could reduce hospitalizations. The second step is to note that there is strong regional variation in how medical conditions are treated. Reducing the variations could save considerable funds. It would require better record keeping and sharing of data about such things as provider charges and patient outcomes.

Third, Davis suggests that there is overuse of medical procedures. More education for both providers and patients would help. The fourth step is very intriguing: Davis recommends that insurers and public programs stop reimbursing providers for medical errors, what she calls "co-morbidity adjustments." This could save billions of dollars and also signal the need to providers to be more careful.

The fifth step is a simple one, which we have briefly mentioned in this chapter and in chapter 4: negotiate prices for pharmaceuticals. Davis recommends allowing Medicare to negotiate prices. Sixth is to reduce administrative costs by standardizing insurance procedures. She writes:

> Private insurance companies have "overhead" of about 12 to 15 percent of revenues. Simplifying and standardizing private insurance could reduce administrative expenses. Hospitals, physicians, and other health care providers incur major administrative expenses as a result of variations across insurers and public programs in terms of benefits covered, payment regulations, conditions of provider participation, and coverage policies. Standardizing products and promoting common practices across all private and public insurers could save hospital and physician administrative costs. (Davis 2005)

The seventh recommendation, which follows from some of the earlier ones, is to make use of evidence-based medicine in making medical decisions. The eighth step is to make sure that every person has a regular provider who will be responsible for the care of the patient. This is known as primary care management and Davis cites studies indicating savings from such programs.

The ninth step, again related to some of the earlier recommendations, is to reduce duplication of tests and paperwork. The last recommendation is to implement information technology that would help avoid duplication and errors and assist continuity of care.

Davis notes that the changes would save money while at the same time reducing provider income and possibly reducing jobs. This statement suggests one of the major problems of reform in the health care field: every dollar spent on health care is a dollar of revenue or income for someone. Nevertheless, Davis suggests that the savings from these changes could be used to improve the system: cover the uninsured, pay for new information technology, expand screening programs, and so forth. Perhaps some combination of demand and supply controls might be the way to go.

Conclusion

This chapter has examined various regulatory and competitive strategies by the federal and state governments and the private sector to contain health care costs. Federal strategies aimed at health planning and peer reviews have proven to be failures. There is some evidence that the competitive strategy of HMOs has lowered costs to enrollees and reduced their hospitalization rates. However, the impact of Medicare managed care on containment of overall health care costs has been very limited, though perhaps the new Medicare Advantage program will have more success. The changeover from a retrospective payment to a prospective payment system for Medicare reimbursements to hospitals, through the DRGs, has reduced the average length of hospital stays and has slowed the growth rate in hospital costs for the initial years of PPS. Medicare costs have continued to climb upward, however, and PPS has had limited impact on overall health care costs. The growth rate in the Medicare program has not shown any decline or slowdown. While the overall growth rate for all national health care expenditures slowed considerably in the mid- to late-1990s, more recent data have shown higher increases.

State efforts in cost containment have had a limited impact on overall health care costs. State rate-setting programs have shown mixed results. States' attempts to replace the fee-for-service system with a negotiated or competitively bid fixed-price arrangement for Medicaid services, as in California and Arizona, have shown some success in reducing costs. There is no denying the fact that state governments' push in the direction of Medicaid managed care has paid some dividends, as reflected in savings materialized and a slowed growth rate in spending for the Medicaid program. Ever-increasing Medicaid costs have led states to cut back their programs, but the impact of such changes is that fewer people will be covered.

Private-sector innovations have also resulted in some health care cost containment. However, cost shifting, utilization reviews, and increased reliance on HMOs and PPOs present a potential concern about access and equity. Wellness programs are increasing but are still not widespread among all industries.

Overall, a combination of regulatory and competitive strategies has produced some success in slowing the growth rate of health care spending. A number of factors are likely to influence the future direction of health care spending.

First, government efforts to formulate health policies directed toward cost containment must be made in a political environment. Just as in any other public policy area, the interplay between various interest groups and partisan conflicts leads to the formulation of policies built on compromises, bargaining, and consensus building, which fail to produce the desired results.

Second, the value of cost containment inevitably comes into conflict with the cherished values of access and high-quality care in American culture. Almost all government programs aimed at cost containment have also attempted to ensure access and quality of care. Public opposition is likely to be high in any program that attempts to reduce access or lower the quality of services or the number of services provided. Furthermore, many health care providers are likely to oppose rationing of health services.

Third, demographic changes are likely to create further pressures for more, not less, spending. When the baby boom generation begins to reach retirement age between the years 2010 and 2015, there is going to be a dramatic increase in the number of elderly people in our society. This is going to accelerate demand for health care resources.

Finally, technological advances in medicine are likely to continue at a rapid pace. Medical technology is very expensive, and it is one of the major contributors to increases in health care costs. We, as a society, have come to value medical technology regardless of the cost and regardless of the benefits it brings. Advances in medical technology have helped prolong life, and in some instances have eased pain and suffering, but they cannot cure many major illnesses. Nevertheless, the general public clings to the glimmer of hope offered by medical technology, and society's notions of health, life span, and life itself have changed. Until we as a society learn to resolve these value conflicts, future prospects for health care cost containment remain tenuous.

Notes

1. This is an old debate. See, for example, Dahl and Lindblom (1953), Friedman (1962), Hayek (1950), and Lindblom (1977).

2. McClure (1981) outlines a series of structural and incentive problems such as diffused consumer interests versus concentrated political interests, political problems, and technical content problems. For a theoretical argument against government regulation analogous to the concept of market failure, see Wolf (1979).

3. The major example of the early planning effort was the Hospital Survey and Construction Act of 1946, better known as the Hill-Burton Act.

4. For a detailed discussion and analysis of the all-payer DRG system in New Jersey, see *Bulletin of the New York Academy of Medicine* 62, no. 6.

5. For an excellent analysis of the political process through which the DRG system was initiated first in New Jersey and then at the federal level, see Morone and Dunham (1986).

6. Authors' calculations, based on various issues of the *Statistical Abstract of the United States*.

7. The PBS documentary "Who Plays God," which was aired in 1996, discusses issues surrounding organ transplantation.

8. Much of the discussion that follows is derived from Davis et al. (1990), Sullivan (1984), and Tell, Falik, and Fox (1984).

References

Aaron, Henry J., and William B. Schwartz. 1984. *The Painful Prescription: Rationing Hospital Care*. Washington, D.C.: Brookings Institution.

———. 1990. "Rationing Health Care: The Choice before Us." *Science* 247, no. 4941 (January 26): 418–22.

Altman, Drew E., and Larry Levitt. 2003. "The Sad History of Health Care Cost Containment as Told in One Chart." *Health Affairs* (October 25): W83–W84.

Altman, Stuart H., and Sanford L. Weiner. 1978. "Regulation As a Second Best Choice." In *Competition in the Health Care Sector: Past, Present, and Future,* Bureau of Economics, U.S. Federal Trade Commission, 421–27. Washington, D.C.: Government Printing Office.

American Civil Liberties Union. 1998. "Legislative Briefing Kit: Lifestyle Discrimination in the Workplace." Washington, D.C.: American Civil Liberties Union. Online at www.aclu.org/WorkplaceRights/WorkplaceRights.cfm?ID=9080&c=34.

Anderson, Gerard F.; Uwe E. Reinhardt; Peter S. Huskey; and Varduhl Petrosyan. 2003. "It's the Prices, Stupid: Why the United States is So Different From Other Countries." *Health Affairs* 22, no. 3 (May/June): 89–105.

Arrow, Kenneth J. 1963. "Uncertainty and the Welfare Economics of Medical Care." *American Economic Review* LIII, no. 5 (December): 851–83.

Berk, Marc L., and Alan C. Monheit. 2001. "The Concentration of Health Care Expenditures, Revisited." *Health Affairs* 20, no. 2 (March/April): 9–18.

Berki, S.E. 1983. "Health Care Policy: Lessons from the Past and Issues of the Future." *Annals of the American Academy of Political and Social Science* 468 (July): 231–46.

Bicknell, William J., and Diana C. Walsh. 1976. "Critical Experiences in Organizing and Administering a State Certificate-of-Need Program." *Public Health Reports* 91 (January/February): 29–45.

BlueCross Blue Shield of Kansas City. n.d. "Rising Healthcare Costs: What is BCBSKC Doing?" Online at www.bcbskc.com/eprise/main/Public/Content/About_BCBSKC/News/Healthcare_Cost_Campaign/HCcosts2.html.

Bodenheimer, Thomas. 2003. "The Not-So-Sad History of Medicare Cost Containment as Told in One Chart." *Health Affairs* (October 25): W88–W90. Online at healthaffairs.org.

Breyer, S. 1979. "Analyzing Regulatory Failure: Mismatches, Less Restrictive Alternatives and Reform." *Harvard Law Review* 92, no. 1: 549–609.

Brown, Lawrence D. 1986. "Introduction to a Decade of Transition." *Journal of Health Politics, Policy and Law* 11, no. 4 (Winter): 569–83.

Buchanan, Allen. 1998. "Managed Care: Rationing without Justice, but Not Unjustly." *Journal of Health Politics, Policy and Law* 23, no. 4 (Winter): 617–34.

California HealthCare Foundation. 2005. "Health Care Costs 101: A Snapshot." Oakland, Calif.: California HealthCare Foundation.

Cannon, Michael F.; and Michael D. Tanner. 2005. *Healthy Competition: What's Holding Back Health Care and How to Free It*. Washington, D.C.: Cato Institute.

Cassidy, Robert. 1984. "Can You Really Speak Your Mind in Peer Review?" *Medical Economics* 61 (January 23): 246–62.

Coelen, Craig, and Daniel Sullivan. 1981. "An Analysis of the Effects of Prospective Reimbursement Programs on Hospital Expenditures." *Health Care Financing Review* 1, no. 3 (Winter): 62–73.

Cohen, Harold. 1975. "State Rate Regulation." In *Controls on Health Care*, ed. Institute of Medicine, 123–35. Washington, D.C.: National Academy of Sciences.

Congressional Budget Office. 1981. *The Impact of PSROs on Health-Care Costs: Update of CBO's 1979 Evaluation*. Washington, D.C.: U.S. Government Printing Office.

———. 1997. *Trends in Spending by the Private Sector*. Washington, D.C.: Congressional Budget Office, U.S. Congress.

Cook, Karen; Steven M. Shortell; Douglas A. Conrad; and Michael A. Morrisey. 1983. "A Theory of Organization Response to Regulation: The Case of Hospitals." *Academy of Management Review* 8, no. 2: 193–205.

Crozier, David A. 1982. "State Rate Setting: A Status Report." *Health Affairs* 1, no. 2 (Summer): 66–83.

Dahl, Robert A., and Charles E. Lindblom. 1953. *Politics, Economics and Planning*. New York: Harper and Row.

Davis, Karen. 2005. "Taking a Walk on the Supply Side: 10 Steps to Control Health Care Costs." New York: Commonwealth Fund. Online at www.cmwf.org.

Davis, Karen; Gerard F. Anderson; Diane Rowland; and Earl P. Steinberg. 1990. *Health Care Cost Containment*. Baltimore, Md.: Johns Hopkins University Press.

Davis, Karen, and Cathy Schoen. 1978. *Health and the War on Poverty: A Ten-Year Proposal*. Washington, D.C.: Brookings Institution.

Dean, Lia. 1998. "Home Health Rules Squeeze the Sickest." *St. Louis Post-Dispatch*, August 2.

Draper, Debra A.; Robert E. Hurley; and Ashley C. Short. 2004. "Medicaid Managed Care: The Last Bastion of the HMO?" *Health Affairs* 23, no. 2 (March/April): 155–67.

Draper, Debra A.; Robert E. Hurley; Cara S. Lesser; and Bradley C. Strunk. 2002. "The Changing Face of Managed Care." *Health Affairs* 21, no. 1 (January/February): 11–23.

Durenberger, David F. 1982. "The Politics of Health." In *Competition in the Marketplace: Health Care in the 1980s*, ed. James R. Gay and Barbara J. Sax Jacobs, 4. New York: Spectrum Publications.

Ellwood, Paul M., Jr. 1971. "Health Maintenance Strategy." *Medical Care* 9 (May/June): 291–98.

———. 1975. "Alternative to Regulation: Improving the Market." In *Controls on Health Care*, Institute of Medicine, 49–72. Washington, D.C.: National Academy of Sciences.

Enthoven, Alain C. 1978a. "Consumer Choice Health Plans" (first of two parts). *New England Journal of Medicine* 298 (March 23): 650–58.

———. 1978b. "Consumer Choice Health Plans" (second of two parts). *New England Journal of Medicine* 298 (March 30): 709–20.

———. 1980. *Health Plan: The Only Practical Solution to the Soaring Cost of Medicare Care*. Reading, Mass.: Addison-Wesley.

———. 1988. "Managed Competition of Alternate Delivery System." *Journal of Health Politics, Policy and Law* 13, no. 2 (Summer): 305–21.

Enthoven, Alain C., and Sara J. Singer. 1997. "Markets and Collective Action in Regulating Managed Care." *Health Affairs* 16, no. 6 (November/December): 26–32.

Esposito, Alfonso et al. 1982. "Abstracts of State Legislated Hospital Cost-Containment Programs." *Health Care Financing Review* 4, no. 2 (December): 129–58.

Etheredge, Lynn. 1983. "Reagan, Congress and Health Spending." *Health Affairs* 2, no. 1 (Spring): 14–24.

———. 1997. "Promarket Regulation: An SEC-FASB Model." *Health Affairs* 16, no. 6 (November/December): 22–25.

Evans, Robert G. 1983. "Incomplete Vertical Integration in the Health Care Industry: Pseudomarkets and Pseudopolicies." *Annals of the American Academy of Political and Social Science* 468 (July): 60–87.

———. 1986. "Finding the Levers, Finding the Courage: Lessons from Cost Containment in North America." *Journal of Health Politics, Policy and Law* 11, no. 4 (Winter): 585–615.

———. 1997. "Going for the Gold: The Redistributive Agenda behind Market-Based Health Care Reform." *Journal of Health Politics, Policy and Law* 22, no. 2 (Summer): 427–66.

Falkson, Joseph L. 1980. *HMOs and the Politics of Health Service Reform*. Chicago: American Hospital Association and Robert J. Brady.

———. 1980–81. "Market Reform, Health Systems, and HMOs." *Policy Studies Journal* 9, no. 2: 213–20.

Fleming, Sibley. 2005. "Wellness Programs Lighten Health Costs." *American City & County* 120, no. 3 (March): 8–10.

Frech, H.E., III, and Paul B. Ginsburg. 1988. "Competition Among Health Insurers, Revisited." *Journal of Health Politics, Policy and Law* 13, no. 2 (Summer): 279–91.

Freudenheim, Milt. 2005. "Fewer Employers Totally Covering Health Premiums." *New York Times,* March 23.

Friedman, Milton (with the assistance of Rose D. Friedman). 1962. *Capitalism and Freedom*. Chicago: University of Chicago Press.

Fuhrmans, Vanessa. 2005. "One Cure for High Health Costs: In-House Clinics at Companies." *Wall Street Journal,* February 11.

Gable, Jon R.; Gail A. Jensen; and Samantha Hawkins. 2003. "Self-Insurance in Times of Growing and Retreating Managed Care." *Health Affairs* 22, no. 2 (March/April): 202–10.

Gabel, Jon R., and Alan C. Monheit. 1983. "Will Competition Plans Change Insurer-Provider Relationships?" *Milbank Memorial Fund Quarterly/Health and Society* 61, no. 4 (Fall): 614–40.

Gay, E. Greer; Jennie J. Kronenfeld; and Samuel L. Baker. 1989."An Appraisal of Organizational Response to Fiscally Constraining Regulation: The Case of Hospitals and DRGs." *Journal of Health and Social Behavior* 30, no. 1 (March): 41–55.

Gelman, Judith. 1982. *Competition and Health Planning. An Issue Paper*. Bureau of Economics, U.S. Federal Trade Commission. Washington, D.C.: Government Printing Office.

Gibson, Robert M.; Katharine R. Levit; Helen Lazenby; and Daniel R. Waldo. 1984. "National Health Expenditures, 1983." *Health Care Financing Review* 6, no. 2 (Winter): 1–29.

Ginzberg, Eli. 1977. *The Limits of Health Reform: The Search for Realism*. New York: Basic Books.

———. 1982. "Procompetition in Health Care: Policy or Fantasy?" *Milbank Memorial Fund Quarterly/Health and Society* 60, no. 3 (Summer): 386–98.

Goodman, John C. 1980. *The Regulation of Medical Care: Is the Price Too High?* San Francisco: Cato Institute.

Goodwin, James. 2005. "State Senate Votes to End Medicaid System." *Springfield News-Leader,* March 16.

Grumbach, Kevin, and Thomas Bodenheimer. 1990. "Reins or Fences: A Physician's View of Cost Containment." *Health Affairs* 9, no. 4 (Winter): 120–26.

Guglielmo, Wayne J. 2004. "Why Oregon's Rationing Plan is Gasping for Air." *Medical Economics,* April 19. Online at www.memag.com/memag/article/articleDetail.jsp?id=127172 &pageID=1.

Guterman, Stuart. 1998. "The Balanced Budget Act of 1997: Will Hospitals Take a Hit on Their PPS Margins? *Health Affairs* 17, no. 1 (January/February): 159–66.

Havighurst, Clark C. 1970. "Health Maintenance Organizations and the Market for Health Services." *Law and Contemporary Problems* 35, no. 1 (Autumn): 716–95.

———. 1973. "Regulation of Health Facilities and Services by 'Certificate of Need.'" *Virginia Law Review* 59, no. 7 (October): 1143–1233.

———. 1982. *Deregulating the Health Care Industry: Planning for Competition*. Cambridge, Mass.: Ballinger Publishing Company.

Hayek, Friedrich A. 1950. *The Road to Serfdom*. Chicago: University of Chicago Press.

Heffler, Stephen, et al. 2004. "Health Spending Projections Through 2013." *Health Affairs,* February 11. Web exclusive online at healthaffairs.org.

———. 2005. "Health Spending Projections Through 2014." *Health Affairs,* February 23: W5-74– W5-85. Web exclusive online at healthaffairs.org.

Herzlinger, Regina. 1997. *Market Drive Health Care: Who Wins, Who Loses in the Transformation of America's largest Service Industry.* Cambridge, Mass.: Perseus Books.

Iglehart, John K. 1980. "The Federal Government as Venture Capitalist: How Does It Fare?" *Milbank Memorial Fund Quarterly/Health and Society* 59, no. 4 (Fall): 656–66.

———. 1982. "Health Care and American Business." *New England Journal of Medicine* 306, no. 20: 120–24.

Jones, James R. 1982. "Cost Pressures and Health Policy Reforms." *Health Affairs* 1, no. 3 (Summer): 39–47.

Kaiser Family Foundation. n.d. "Trends and Indicators in the Changing Health Care Marketplace." Menlo Park, Calif.: Kaiser Family Foundation. Online at www.kff.org/insurance/7031/index.cfm.

Kaiser Family Foundation and Health Research and Education Trust. 2004. "Employer Health Benefits: Annual Survey 2004." Menlo Park, Calif.: Kaiser Family Foundation.

Kawachi, Ichiro. 2005. "Why the United States Is Not Number One in Health." In *Healthy, Wealthy, & Fair,* ed. James A. Morone and Lawrence R. Jacobs, 19–35. New York: Oxford University Press.

Kennedy, Louanne, and Bernard M. Baruch. 1980–81. "Health Planning in an Age of Austerity." *Policy Studies Journal* 9, no. 2 (Special #1): 232–41.

Kosterlitz, Julie. 1991. "Softening Resistance." *National Journal* 23, no. 2 (January 12): 64–68.

Laffont, Jean-Jacques, and Jean Tirole. 1991. "The Politics of Government Decision-Making: A Theory of Regulatory Capture." *Quarterly Journal of Economics* 106, no. 4 (November): 1089–1127.

Latham, Bryan W. 1983. *Health Care Costs: There Are Solutions.* New York: American Management Association.

Lave, Judith R. 1984. "Hospital Reimbursement under Medicare." *Milbank Memorial Fund Quarterly/Health and Society* 62, no. 2 (Spring): 251–78.

Lazenby, Helen C., and Suzanne W. Letsch. 1990. "National Health Expenditures, 1989." *Health Care Financing Review* 12, no. 2 (Winter): 1–26.

Lee, Jason S., and Laura Tollen. 2002. "How Low Can You Go? The Impact of Reduced Benefits and Increased Cost Sharing." *Health Affairs,* June 19: W229–W241. Online at healthaffairs.org.

Leeds, Helen. 1996. *Health Care Cost Containment in the States: Strategies from the 1990s.* Washington, D.C.: Intergovernmental Health Policy Project.

Levit, Katharine R., et al. 1991. "National Health Expenditures, 1990." *Health Care Financing Review* 13, no. 1 (Fall): 29–54.

———. 1994a. "National Health Expenditures, 1993." *Health Care Financing Review* 16, no. 1 (Fall): 247–94.

———. 1994b. "National Health Care Spending Trends, 1960–1993." *Health Affairs* 13, no. 5 (Winter): 14–31.

———. 1997. "National Health Expenditures, 1996." *Health Care Financing Review* 19, no. 1 (Fall): 161–200.

———. 2000. "Health Spending in 1998: Signals of Change." *Health Affairs* 19, no. 1 (January–February): 124–32.

———. 2003. "Trends in U.S. Health Care Spending, 2001." *Health Affairs* 22, no. 1 (January/February): 154–64.

Lewin and Associates, Inc. 1975. *Evaluation of the Efficiency and Effectiveness of the Section 1122 Review Process.* Springfield, Va.: National Technical Information Service.

Lindblom, Charles E. 1977. *Politics and Markets: The World's Political Economic System.* New York: Basic Books.

Lueck, Sarah. 2005. "White House Encourages States to Trim Medicaid." *Wall Street Journal,* March 17.

Marmor, Theodore, and James Morone. 1979. "HSAs and the Representation of Consumer Interests: Conceptual Issues and Litigation Problems." *Health Law Project Library Bulletin* 4 (April): 117–28.

Marmor, Theodore R.; Donald A. Wittman; and Thomas C. Heagy. 1983. "The Politics of Medical Inflation." In *Political Analysis and American Medical Care,* ed. Theodore R. Marmor, 71–75. Cambridge, U.K.: Cambridge University Press.

McCall, Nelda; Harriet L. Komisar; Andrew Petersons; and Stanley Moore. 2001. "Medicare Home Health Before and After the BBA." *Health Affairs* 20, no. 3 (May/June): 189–98.

McClure, Walter. 1981. "Structural and Incentive Problems in Economic Regulation of Medical Care." *Milbank Memorial Quarterly/Health and Society* 59, no. 2 (Spring): 107–44.

———. 1983. "The Competitive Strategy for Medical Care." *Annals of the American Academy of Political and Social Science* 469 (July): 30–47.

McConnell, Grant. 1970. *Private Power & American Democracy.* New York: Vintage Books.

McDonough, John E. 1997. "Tracking the Demise of State Hospital Rate Setting." *Health Affairs* 16, no. 1 (January/February): 142–49.

McGregor, Maurice. 1981. "Hospital Costs: Can They Be Cut?" *Milbank Memorial Fund Quarterly/Health and Society* 59, no. 1 (Winter): 89–98.

McNeil, Richard, Jr., and Robert E. Schlenker. 1975. "HMOs, Competition and Government." *Milbank Memorial Fund Quarterly/Health and Society* 53, no. 1 (Spring): 195–224.

Mechanic, David. 1981. "Some Dilemmas in Health Care Policy." *Milbank Memorial Fund Quarterly/Health and Society* 59, no. 1 (Winter): 1–14.

———. 1997. "Muddling Through Elegantly: Finding the Proper Balance in Rationing." *Health Affairs* 16, no. 5 (September/October): 83–92.

Medicare Payment Advisory Commission. 2004. *A Data Book: Healthcare Spending and the Medicare Program.* Washington, D.C.: Medicare Payment Advisory Commission. Online at www.medpac.gov/publications.

Meir, Kenneth J. 1985. *Regulation: Politics, Bureaucracy and Economics.* New York: St. Martin's Press.

Menzel, Paul T. 1990. *Strong Medicine: The Ethical Rationing of Health Care.* New York: Oxford University Press.

Mick, Stephen S., and John D. Thompson. 1984. "Public Attitude toward Health Planning under the Health Systems Agencies." *Journal of Health Politics, Policy and Law* 9, no. 4 (Winter): 783–800.

Miller, Annetta, and Elizabeth Bradburn. 1991. "Shape Up—or Else." *Newsweek* (July 1): 42–43.

Miller, Robert H., and Harold S. Luft. 2002. "HMO Plan Performance Update: Analysis of the Literature, 1997–2001." *Health Affairs* 21, no. 4 (July/August): 63–86.

Mitchell, Samuel A. 1982. "Issues, Evidence, and the Policymaker's Dilemma." *Health Affairs* 1, no. 3 (Summer): 84–98.

Moran, Donald W. 1981. "HMOs, Competition, and the Politics of Minimum Benefits." *Milbank Memorial Fund Quarterly/Health and Society* 59, no. 2 (Spring): 190–208.

———. 1997. "Federal Regulation of Managed Care: An Impulse in Search of a Theory?" *Health Affairs* 16, no. 6 (November/December): 7–21.

Morone, James A., and Andrew B. Dunham. 1986. "Slouching toward National Health Insurance: The Unanticipated Politics of DRGs." *Bulletin of the New York Academy of Medicine* 62, no. 6 (July/August): 646–62.

Morone, James A., and Lawrence R. Jacobs, eds. 2005. *Healthy, Wealthy, & Fair: Health Care and the Good Society.* New York: Oxford University Press.

Neuman, Patricia. 2004. "The State of Retiree Health Benefits: Historical Trends and Future Uncertainties." Testimony before the Special Committee on Aging, United States Senate, 108th Congress, 2nd session (May 17). Online at kff.org/medicare/loader.cfm?url=/commonspot/security/getfile.cfm&PageID=36242.

Newhouse, Joseph P., et al. 1981. "Some Interim Results from a Controlled Trial of Cost Sharing in Health Insurance." *New England Journal of Medicine* 305, no. 25 (December): 1501–7.

Noll, Roger G. 1975. "The Consequences of Public Utility Regulation of Hospitals." In *Controls on Health Care,* ed. Institute of Medicine, 32–48. Washington, D.C.: National Academy of Sciences.

Office of the Actuary. 2004. "Health Care Expenditures Projections: 2003–2013." Washington, D.C.: Centers for Medicare and Medicaid Services. Online at www.cms.hhs.gov/statistics/nhe.

"Only 1 in 10 Firms Are Serious About Wellness." 2004. *Business and Management Practices: Industrial Safety and Hygiene News* 38, no. 1: 10.

Parsons, Talcott E. 1956. "Suggestions for a Sociological Approach to a Theory of Organizations." *Administrative Science Quarterly* 1: 63–85.

Patel, Kant, and Mark E. Rushefsky. 2002. *Health Care Policy in an Age of New Technologies.* Armonk, N.Y.: M.E. Sharpe.

Pauly, Mark V. 1978. "Is Medical Care Different?" In *Competition in the Health Care Sector: Past, Present and Future,* ed. Bureau of Economics, U.S. Federal Trade Commission, 19–48. Washington, D.C.: Government Printing Office.

Pereira, Joseph. 2003. "To Save on Health-Care Costs, Firms Fire Disabled Workers." *Wall Street Journal,* July 14.

Pollard, Michael R. 1981. "The Essential Role of Antitrust in a Competitive Market for Health Services." *Milbank Memorial Fund Quarterly/Health and Society* 59, no. 2 (Spring): 256–68.
President's Council on Bioethics. 2003. "Organ Transplantation: Ethical Dilemmas and Policy Choices." Staff background paper. Washington, D.C.: Executive Office of the President. Online at www.bioethics.gov/background/org_transplant.html.
Quade, E.S. 1989. *Analysis for Public Decisions,* 3rd ed. New York: Elsevier.
Relman, Arnold S. 2005. "The Health of Nations." *The New Republic* 232, no. 4,703 (March 7): 23–30.
Rice, Thomas. 1997. "Can Markets Give Us the Health System We Want?" *Journal of Health Politics, Policy and Law* 22, no. 2 (1997): 383–426.
Rich, Spencer. 1992. "How One State Holds Down Costs in its Hospitals." *Washington Post National Weekly Edition* (December 21–27): 33–34.
Robinson, James. 2002. "Renewed Emphasis on Consumer Cost Sharing in Health Insurance Benefit Design." *Health Affairs,* March 20: W1439–W154. Online at healthaffairs.org.
Roemer, Milton I. 1961. "Hospitals Utilization and the Supply of Physicians." *Journal of the American Medical Association* 178, no. 1 (December): 933–89.
Rosenberg, Charlotte L. 1984. "Why Doctor-Policing Laws Don't Work." *Medical Economics* 61 (March 5): 84–96.
Rosenbloom, David. 1983. "New Ways to Keep Old Promises in Health Care." *Health Affairs* 2, no. 4 (Winter): 41–53.
Rosoff, Arnold J. 1975. "Phase Two of the Federal HMO Development Program: New Directions after a Shaky Start." *American Journal of Law and Medicine* 1, no. 2 (Fall): 209–43.
Ross, James S. 2002. "The Committee on the Costs of Medical Care and the History of Health Insurance in the United States." *Einstein Quarterly Journal of Biological Medicine* 19: 129–34.
Rushefsky, Mark E. 2002. *Public Policy in the United States: At the Dawn of the Twenty-First Century.* Armonk, N.Y.: M.E. Sharpe.
Sager, Alan, and Deborah Socolar. 2005. "The Health Crisis Index Rose 37 Percent, 1987–2003." Boston, Mass.: Health Reform Program, Boston University School of Public Health. Online at www.healthreformprogram.org.
Salkever, David S., and Thomas W. Bice. 1976. "The Impact of Certificate of Need Controls on Hospital Investment." *Milbank Memorial Fund Quarterly/Health and Society* 54, no. 1 (Spring): 185–214.
———. 1979. *Hospital Certificate-of-Need Controls: Impact on Investment, Costs and Use.* Washington, D.C.: American Enterprise Institute for Public Policy Research.
Sapolsky, Harvey M.; Drew Altman; Richard Greene; and Judith D. Moore. 1981. "Corporate Attitude toward Health Care Costs." *Milbank Memorial Fund Quarterly/Health and Society* 59, no. 4 (Fall): 561–85.
Saranow, Jennifer. 2005. "As Health Care Costs Rise, Some Big Employers Move to Cut Dependents' Coverage." *Wall Street Journal,* March 3.
Schoen, Cathy et al. 2005. "Taking the Pulse of Health Care Systems: Experiences of Patients with Health Problems in Six Countries." *Health Affairs* (November 3): W5-509–W5-525. Online at healthaffairs.org.
SEIU Local 503. 2005. "Senator Gary George Gives Warm Welcome to Maryland Hospital Rate Regulators." Online at www.seiu503.org/action/healthcare/marylandrates.cfm.
Shaffer, Franklin A. 1983. "DRGs: History and Overview." *Nursing and Health Care* 4, no. 7 (September): 388–89.
Sloan, Frank A. 1982a. "Government and the Regulation of Hospital Care." *Journal of American Economic Review* 72 (May): 196–201.
———. 1982b. "Reviews: An Economist." *Health Affairs* 1, no. 3 (Summer): 113–18.
Sloan, Frank A.; Michael A. Morrisey; and Joseph Valvona. 1988. "Effects of the Medicare Prospective Payment System on Hospital Costs Containment: An Early Appraisal." *Milbank Memorial Fund Quarterly/Health and Society* 66, no. 2 (Spring): 191–220.
Smith, Cynthia, et al. 2005. "Health Spending Growth Slows in 2003." *Health Affairs* 24, no. 1 (January/February): 185–194.
Starr, Paul. 1980. "Changing the Balance of Power in American Medicine." *Milbank Memorial Fund Quarterly/Health and Society* 58, no. 1 (Winter): 166–72.
———. 1982. *The Social Transformation of American Medicine.* New York: Basic Books.

Steinwald, Bruce, and Frank A. Sloan. 1981. "Regulatory Approaches to Hospital Cost Containment: A Synthesis of the Empirical Evidence." In *A New Approach to the Economics of Health Care,* ed. Mancur Olson, 273–308. Washington, D.C.: American Enterprise Institute for Public Policy.

Stone, Deborah. 2002. *Policy Paradox: The Art of Political Decision Making,* revised ed. New York: W.W. Norton.

———. 2005. "How Market Ideology Guarantees Racial Inequality." In *Wealthy, Healthy, & Fair,* ed. James A. Morone and Lawrence R. Jacobs, 65–89. New York: Oxford University Press.

Sullivan, Sean. 1984. *Managing Health Care Costs: Private Sector Innovations.* Washington, D.C.: American Enterprise for Public Policy Research.

Sun Valley Forum on National Health, Harrison Conference Center. 1983. "The Role of State and Local Government in Health." *Health Affairs* 2, no. 4 (Winter): 134–39.

Swoboda, Frank. 1990. "A Surgical Strike Against Corporate Health Care Costs: Firms Try Managed Plans to Remedy Soaring Expenses." *Washington Post National Weekly Edition* (February 19–25): 20.

———. 1991. "The Mercury Rises for Health Care Costs." *Washington Post National Weekly Edition* (February 4–10): 21.

Tell, Eileen J.; Marilyn Falik; and Peter D. Fox. 1984. "Private-Sector Health Care Initiatives: A Comparative Perspective from Four Communities." *Milbank Memorial Fund Quarterly/Health and Society* 62, no. 3 (Summer): 357–79.

Thompson, Frank J. 1981. *Health Policy and the Bureaucracy: Politics and Implementation.* Cambridge, Mass.: MIT Press.

Thorpe, Kenneth E.; Curtis S. Florence; and Peter Joski. 2004. "Which Medical Conditions Account for the Rise in Health Care Spending? *Health Affairs* (August 25): W4-437–W4-445. Online at healthaffairs.org.

U.S. Department of Health, Education, and Welfare. 1971. *Toward a Comprehensive Health Policy for the 1970s: A White Paper.* Washington, D.C.: U. S. Government Printing Office.

Varlova, John. 1984. "A $2.2 Million Lesson in the Perils of Peer Review." *Medical Economics* 61 (December 24): 56–61.

Varner, Theresa, and Jack Christy. 1986. "Consumer Information Needs in a Competitive Health Care Environment." *Health Care Financing Review* (Annual Supplement): 99–104.

Virts, John R., and George W. Wilson. 1984. "Inflation and Health Care Prices." *Health Affairs* 3, no. 1 (Spring): 88–100.

Vladeck, Bruce C. 1977. "Interest Group Representation and the HSAs: Health Planning and Political Theory." *American Journal of Public Health* 67, no. 1 (January): 23–29.

———. 1981. "The Market vs. Regulation: The Case for Regulation." *Milbank Memorial Fund Quarterly/Health and Society* 59, no. 2 (Spring): 209–23.

———. 1984. "Variation Data and the Regulatory Rationale." *Health Affairs* 3, no. 2 (Summer): 102–9.

Wadhwani, Anita. 2005. "Court Ruling Clears Way to Ax TennCare Rolls." *Memphis Tennessean,* April 13.

Weiner, Stephen M. 1982. "On Public Values and Private Regulation: Some Reflections on Cost Containment Strategies." *Milbank Memorial Fund Quarterly/Health and Society* 59, no. 2 (Spring): 269–96.

Wolf, Charles, Jr. 1979. "A Theory of Non-Market Failures." *Public Interest* 55 (Spring): 114–23.

Yegian, Jill Matthews. 2004. "Conference Summary: Setting Priorities in Medical Care Through Benefit Design and Medical Management." *Health Affairs* (May 19): W4-300–W4-304. Online at healthaffairs.org.

Zakaria, Fareed. 2005. "How We Drive Our Jobs Away." *Newsweek* CXLV, no. 16 (April 18): 43.

Zatkin, Steve. 1997. "A Health Plan's View of Government Regulation." *Health Affairs* 16, no. 6 (November/December): 33–35.

7

Medical Malpractice and Medical Liability

Medical Errors, Medical Injury, and Patient Safety

After an analysis of a representative cross-section of medical records from hospitals in New York in 1984, the Harvard Medical Practice Study concluded that adverse events (negligent or otherwise) occurred in 3.7 percent of hospital stays during the time period of the study. Of those stays, 27.6 percent were caused by negligence. This amounted to about 1 percent of all hospital stays. However, the number of claims filed was eight times lower than the number of events caused by negligence (Harvard Medical Practice Study 1990). Researchers from the University of Chicago who measured the frequency of medical errors in patient care in three surgical units also found that only a small number of patients whose health was seriously affected by discovered errors took steps to suggest that they were dissatisfied with their care (Andrews 1993). In other words, very few patients who become victims of an adverse medical event ever file a claim. According to another study, nearly 1 percent of all hospital patients in the United States suffer harm because of substandard care. Of those who suffer harm, 25 percent die and another 6 percent suffer permanent disability, which translates to about 84,000 patient deaths and 20,000 permanent disabilities (White 1994).

According to the Institute of Medicine's (2000) report *To Err Is Human*, as many as 98,000 people die in hospitals each year as a result of medical errors that could have been prevented. In addition, thousands more are injured because of mistakes made in doctors' offices, nursing homes, and outpatient clinics because of a complex system of care that is designed for efficiency and not necessarily patient safety (Lieberman 2004). The Institute of Medicine (IOM) defines medical error as the failure to complete a planned action as intended or the use of a wrong plan to achieve a given goal. According to the IOM report, medical errors typically include things such as wrong or delayed diagnosis, an adverse drug event (prescribing the wrong drug, inaccurate dosage, etc.), improper transfusion, surgical injuries (including wrong site surgery), restraint-related injuries or deaths, falls, burns, and mistaken medical identities. Aside from the cost in human life, the report also argued that preventable medical errors cost between $17 billion and $29 billion per year in hospitals nationwide. Medical errors also lead to reduced trust in the nation's health care system, and loss of morale among health care professionals.

A variety of factors have been cited as contributing to medical errors. These include the fragmented and decentralized nature of the U.S. health care system, the lack of emphasis on prevention of medical errors in the process by which health professionals are licensed and accredited, the lack of computerized patient medical records, a medical liability system that works as an impediment to discovery of medical errors, and extended work hours of doctors.

For example, two studies funded by the National Institute for Occupational Safety and Health (NIOSH) and the Agency for Healthcare Research and Quality (AHRQ) found that the rate of serious medical errors committed by first-year doctors in training (interns) in two intensive care units (ICUs) at a Boston hospital fell significantly when traditional thirty-hour-in-a-row extended work shifts were eliminated and when the interns' continuous work schedules were replaced with an intervention work schedule that limited their work shifts to sixteen hours. One of the studies found that interns made 35.9 percent more serious medical errors during the traditional thirty-hour work schedule than during the intervention schedule (Landrigan et al. 2004). The second study found that eliminating extended work shifts in an ICU significantly decreased attention failures during night work hours (Lockley et al. 2004).

One of the main conclusions of the IOM (2000) report is that a majority of medical errors are not due to negligence on the part of individual or group health care professionals but rather are caused by faulty systems, processes, and conditions that lead health care professionals to make mistakes. The report made a series of recommendations to reduce the problem of medical errors, such as a national effort to create leadership, research tools, and protocols to enhance patient safety; creating both mandatory and voluntary systems for reporting medical errors; raising standards of expectations and performance through professional groups and oversight organizations; and implementation of safe practices at the health care delivery level.

Soon after the release of the IOM report, the Clinton administration issued an executive order instructing government agencies that oversee health care programs to implement proven techniques for reducing medical errors. The Clinton administration also created a task force to find strategies for reducing medical errors. Congress additionally held many public hearings on patient safety during 2000. This has led to the patient safety movement. Its goal is to create a safe environment in which information is shared and analyzed without fear of individual recrimination (Sage 2003).

Today, many state governments and many private-sector actors are taking actions to reduce medical errors. At present, about twenty states have implemented mandatory reporting systems to improve patient safety. However, state medical boards in the past have been very reluctant to penalize physicians who make medical mistakes, let alone make the mistakes public. Furthermore, many physicians who find themselves in trouble in one state simply move and restart their careers in another state because many malpractice cases are never reported to a national repository for doctor discipline records known as the National Practitioner Data Bank. Hospitals and medical boards are never penalized for their failure to report to the data bank (Thompson 2005a, b). In response to the growing demand for public access to such information, some twenty-eight states now make information on physician mistakes public. In 2001, the Federation of State Medical Boards opened a "DocInfo" database that lists all disciplinary actions taken by individual state medical boards. Consumers can access the information for a fee (Gearon 2001).

In the private sector, many organizations have taken steps to reduce medical errors and improve patient safety (Findlay 2000). One area of reform argues for a national computerized information system (Aspden et al. 2004). Executives of some leading companies, such as General Motors and General Electric, have created a Leapfrog Group that encourages all employers to make safe medicine a top priority of the health insurance they provide. The group began a voluntary campaign in 2001 to encourage hospitals to adopt computer drug-ordering systems to reduce medical errors. Unfortunately, of the 1,200 hospitals targeted by the group in 2003, only 38 hospitals have complied with its standards for electronic drug ordering because of resistance on the part of doctors who see it as questioning their judgment (Lieberman 2004). Consumers also sometimes resist new technologies such as computerized/ digitized patient medical records due to fear of infringement of their privacy (Lieberman 2004). The United States trails other English-speaking countries in the use of electronic medical records and electronic prescribing ("U.S. Trails Other Countries . . ." 2001).

The problem of medical errors has received considerable attention, as reflected in publications of several books, such as Banja's (2005) *Medical Errors and Medical Narcissism*, Wachter and Shojania's (2004) *Internal Bleeding*, Gibson and Singh's (2003) *Wall of Silence*, and Rosenthal and Sutcliffe's (2002) *Medical Error: What Do We Know? What Do We Do?* However, meaningful reforms designed to reduce medical errors are often difficult to achieve because of politics ("Politics Keeps Real Remedies Off Radar" 2004). Despite the publicity and efforts designed to reduce preventable medical errors, the general public still fears that they will become victims of such errors. A nationwide survey of over 2,000 people sponsored by the Kaiser Family Foundation, the AHRQ, and the Harvard School of Public Health found that about half of Americans still worry about the safety of their medical care. Thirty-four percent of respondents said that either they or a family member had direct experience with a medical error, with 21 percent reporting that a medical error had resulted in serious health consequences. More than half (55 percent) of the respondents indicated that they were dissatisfied with health care in the United States. Only 28 percent of the respondents reported that the physician or other health care provider informed them of the medical error. Ninety-two percent felt that serious medical errors should be reported on a routine basis, and 88 percent said that physicians should be required to tell a patient if a medical error resulted in serious harm. Perhaps the most surprising finding of the survey was that, of those patients who had experienced serious health consequences due to medical error, only 14 percent had filed a medical malpractice lawsuit (Kaiser Family Foundation, Agency for Healthcare Research and Quality, and Harvard School of Public Health 2004). If medical errors are as widespread as many of the recent reports and publications suggest, compensating patients who have suffered as a result of medical errors is important, whether it is done through tort litigation or some other mechanism (Sage 2004).

The Origins of Medical Malpractice

The problem of medical malpractice can be traced historically from the Code of Hammurabi, established by the King of Babylon around 2200 B.C.E., to its acknowledgment, revision, and refinement by Egyptians, Greeks, and Romans; and through its doctrinal development in fourteenth-century England (Schmidt, Heckert, and Mercer 1991). The Hammurabi Code replaced the practice of personal violence against medical practitioners that was prevalent at the time through the establishment of a synonymous system of retribution. Thus, for example, if a doctor treated a patient with a knife and the patient died, the doctor's hand was cut off (Gadd 1965). A similar notion of "an eye for an eye" was also advocated by the Mosaic Code of the Israelites. The limited size of their population and the need to preserve optimum manpower ultimately led to revision of the code by the eleventh century. The concept of an "eye for an eye" was replaced by the idea of monetary compensation for damages. The compensation was to be equal to the difference in value of the injured person before and after the incident if he were a slave being sold for six years of service (Blackman and Bailey 1990, American College of Legal Medicine 1988). In Greece, Hippocrates, the "father of medicine," around 460 B.C.E. promulgated an oath governing the conduct of physicians and surgeons. Part of the oath called on the physician to follow a regimen for the benefit of the patients (Gordon 1970). The Justinian Code, written between 529 C.E. and 564 C.E., made an attempt to control medical practitioners. It called for an examination to test the physicians' professional competency, a limitation on the number of physicians, as well as penalties for malpractice (Wetch 1977).

As the legal and court systems evolved in England over the eleventh and twelfth centuries from "blood feuds" or "clan retribution" and lynching to a system involving a grand jury, a "petit jury," and trial by juries to resolve disputes, it also led to the accumulation of a large body of recorded decisions by the courts in both civil and criminal trials. This body of decisions and the custom of applying these previous decisions to new cases came to be known as the "common law." The actual practice of following the precedent also came to be known as "stare decisis." This was the same body of common law that was ultimately brought to the American colonies, and it became the basis for the American legal system (Wood 1993).

Development of the Common Law in England

Some of the early medical malpractice cases in England were brought against medical practitioners in the form of criminal proceedings. A case raising allegations of medical malpractice and the issue of professional liability involving a physician occurred around 1290. However, at that time there was no distinction made between those practicing legitimate medicine and those practicing quackery (*Britton: Homicide* 1864). "Witch doctors," "medicine men," and so on, practiced their craft through potions, magic spells, and appeals to supernatural beings, along with legitimate medicine. Ultimately, codes were developed to protect the members of the community from inept and careless practitioners. However, it was not until the year 1511 that England provided for the licensure of physicians under which examinations were administered by the bishop of the diocese in which the physician wished to practice. Later on, the Royal College of Physicians was granted a charter for the self-regulation of the medical profession. The British Parliament confirmed the charter in 1522, paving the way for self-regulation by the medical profession (Shindell 1965).

As the courts tried to find legal theories and remedies, the concept of "negligence" began to enter into judicial decisions. Soon after, the concepts of "duty" and "standard of care" came to be recognized as well. The term "tort" derives from the Latin word *tortus,* which means crooked or twisted. This term later came to be associated with a "body of law" that redressed wrongs other than breach of contract. Thus, tort actions are designed to protect individuals from being harmed. Those who considered themselves to be wronged and wanted to gain access to the court were required to file a writ. Two writs served as a basis for tort action. "Trespass" related to all forcible, direct, and immediate injuries, whether to person or to property, and "trespass on the case" was designed to afford a remedy for wrongful conduct resulting in injuries that were not forcible or direct. This paved the way for the theory of tort law. This notion of "trespass," or direct injury, and "trespass on a case," or indirect injury, was ultimately replaced by notions of "intentional tort" and "unintentional tort," or negligence (Wood 1993).

Initially, the concept of negligence under English common law was applied only in terms of "the nonfeasance," or the failure to perform within the contractual context. Negligence as carelessness in the performance of an affirmative act that caused harm was not considered. Physicians were basically regarded as members of a public calling who had a duty to serve all comers, and their liability was defined accordingly (Wood 1993). The rise of commercialism led to a changed role of the physician, and the legal premise for liability focused on the contract itself. Under this new understanding, the physician's undertaking came to be regarded as the true foundation on which to base an action. It was an actionable wrong if a physician undertook to provide medical services for a fee and failed to do what was promised. It was an actionable wrong, not because the law obligated the physician to provide a service, but because the physician had agreed to assume the obligation toward the patient; that is, because of a breach of contract (Wood 1993).

Things changed dramatically in 1374 when a medical malpractice case helped set a major precedent. The case was heard in the court of the King's Bench in England with Chief Justice John Cavendish presiding. The case involved a London surgeon named John Swanlond, who treated the crushed and mangled hand of Agnes of Stratton. The patient's hand was severely deformed, and she and her husband sued Dr. Swanlond for misfeasance (poor performance) under a breach of contract theory. According to the medical records, Dr. Swanlond guaranteed to competently cure the wound for reasonable payment. He later denied making such a statement. The suit charged that Dr. Swanlond had so negligently conducted his cure that the patient's hand was impaired and it was maimed by her injury (Spiegel and Kavaler 1997). The standards of the Hippocratic Oath were applied and the judge ruled that if the surgeon performed well, exercised the limits of his abilities, and acted with due diligence, he should not be held culpable. The court did not limit the scope of its consideration to whether the surgeon had performed his services under the contract. The court went a step further and scrutinized the quality of services rendered based upon a physician's assumed duty under the contract, as well as the legal duty imposed on him to exercise some degree of care in the treatment of his patients. This decision established the precedent for applying the negligence concept under a contract theory to cases of misfeasance (poor performance) by a medical practitioner (Wood 1993). While the physician in this case was held not liable, the court established a precedent that if a patient is harmed as a result of the physician's negligence, the physician would be held liable and the law will provide a remedy. This laid the foundation for the contemporary standards of the "ordinary reasonable/prudent physicians," (Spiegel and Kavaler 1997). In 1553, an edict, the *Constitutio Criminalis*, by King Charles V, allowed judges to call expert witnesses to testify in medico-legal cases (Spiegel and Kavaler 1997).

The blurred lines of distinction between action in contract and tort following the 1374 ruling continued to create a dilemma for the court for many years to come. Finally, in 1615, Sir Edward Coke, known as the "father of the common law" decided a case that established the foundation in English common law for allowing an action against a physician for negligence to be brought under a theory other than contract. He ruled that the law gives the party sufficient remedy to recover for default of performance or for negligence in the performance. The negligence cases can stand alone, without a primary action in trespass and outside the contract (Wood 1993).

Medical Malpractice and Liability in the United States

The Nineteenth Century

U.S. laws in the area of medical liability were derived from the common law established in England (De Ville 1990). Thus, the development of the concept of negligence as the major standard of civil liability in tort closely followed the British experience. The first recorded malpractice suit in the United States took place in Connecticut in 1794 in *Cross v. Guthrie*. A Connecticut physician, Dr. Cross, had performed a mastectomy on one of Mrs. Guthrie's breasts and she died three hours later. Her husband sued the surgeon, alleging negligence and claiming £1,000 in damages for "his cost, expenses, and deprivation of the service and company of his wife" (Spiegel and Kavaler 1997, 288–89). It was argued that the physician had broken and violated his undertaking and promise to the plaintiff to perform the operation skillfully and safely. It further argued that the physician's "professional performance was unskilled, ignorant and cruel, contrary to all the well known rules and principles in practice in such cases" (Gordon 1970). The court agreed with the plaintiff and awarded him 40 pounds for the loss of his wife's companionship.

In early U.S. history, medical malpractice lawsuits were rare (Jost 2003). Between 1800 and 1835, medical malpractice was almost unknown in the United States, and between 1812 and 1835, *The New England Journal of Medicine and Survey* and its successor, *The Boston Medical and Surgical Journal*, reported only three malpractice cases. However, between 1835 and 1865, medical malpractice suits began to deluge the courts and the *Boston Medical and Surgical Journal* reported forty-five cases. Thus, it can be argued that the first medical malpractice crisis began in the 1830s (Spiegel and Kavaler 1997). Factors that contributed to this crisis were cultural changes, growing urbanization, and religious and philosophical views stressing human perfectibility that weakened inhibitions against lawsuits. Also, medical progress played a part. For example, by the 1830s, doctors had developed techniques that allowed them to save rather than amputate limbs and that allowed patients and juries to judge imperfect results against the prevailing standards (Jost 2003). By 1853, *The Western Journal of Medical and Physical Sciences* lamented the fact that malpractice suits occurred in every month of the year. Over a period of time prior to the Civil War, a variety of state courts rendered decisions that established the fundamental principles of medical malpractice in the United States. Analyzing the case law, C.R. Burns (1969) classified twenty-one pre-Civil War appellate court decisions between 1845 and 1861 into five groupings:

1. with respect to physician's education and knowledge, the courts established the rule that a medical practitioner was legally responsible for what he said he was able to do;
2. the courts also established the idea that the level of skill expected of a medical practitioner was ordinary skill and not extraordinary skill;
3. the courts ascertained that physicians' contracts required them to use reasonable and ordinary care in the application of their knowledge and skill;
4. whenever there was reasonable ground for diagnostic doubts and difference of opinion about treatment, if the physician exercised his best judgment, he was not liable for errors of judgment or mistakes;
5. legally, physicians were not required to guarantee or ensure a cure.

By the mid-1800s, various courts in the United States had delineated standards of professional conduct for tort action. Negligence as a separate and distinct basis of tort liability was recognized in the United States around 1825 (Wood 1993).

One troubling problem dealt with regular versus irregular physicians. Regular or orthodox physicians received their training at medical schools that were often linked to a university. Irregular physicians included American Indian doctors, root doctors, and homeopaths who secured their medical education in a variety of ways. In the early 1800s, most state medical licensure laws were often weak or nonexistent. By 1830, medical societies had been established in many of the states, and they advocated examination and licensing of physicians. State legislatures responded by passing licensing laws that were statewide in coverage but varied widely from one state to the next (Derbyshire 1969). The American Medical Association, founded in 1846, advocated reforms in medical education but made little progress. The early promise of the medical malpractice laws to protect the public was not fulfilled. In fact, between 1820 and 1870, licensing requirements deteriorated. From 1873, beginning in Texas, state boards of medical examiners were established, and by 1895 nearly all states had such entities. All states developed procedures for the examination and licensure of physicians (Derbyshire 1969). Flexner, in 1910, called state boards "instruments through which the reconstruction of medical education will be largely effected" (Flexner 1910). Today, states, through their medical practice laws, not only decide who may practice in a state but also define the conditions under which a physician may practice.

Physicians' experience with malpractice between 1865 and 1900 followed a course set earlier in the century and became a prelude to the twentieth century. Physicians were encouraged when malpractice rates abated somewhat during the 1860s. By the end of the decade the problem of medical malpractice was no longer perceived as urgent. However, by 1872 patients were suing doctors with renewed energy. Even though appellate court decisions are an ambiguous measure of trial court litigation rates, the fact remained that state appellate courts handled an increasing number of cases in each of the decades: twenty-five cases in 1860–70, forty-five in 1870–80, forty-seven in 1880–90, seventy-seven in 1890–1900, and 116 in 1900–1910 (Smith 1941; Weigel 1974).

Between 1865 and 1900, damage awards also climbed slowly, and appellate courts refused to overturn or reduce the gradually increasing malpractice judgments. Doctors ceased to blame their fellow physicians for their medical malpractice woes and began to argue that the poor and laboring classes were their main tormentors and that greed, status, and class resentment led them to sue physicians for medical malpractice. It was further argued that physicians and corporations were often regarded as fair game by the penniless clients of desperate lawyers. Physicians felt that working-class juries were susceptible to lawyers who constantly drew contrasts between the poor laboring man, on the one hand, and the rich doctor on the other. Physicians also denounced the increased use of contingency fees by lawyers representing poor patients (De Ville 1990). While it is true that class resentment existed against physicians, much of the antagonism against doctors was due more to their demand for social status and prestige for their learned profession than to their wealth. In early America, Jacksonians were repelled by the quasi-aristocratic views espoused by physicians. Physicians' average incomes still placed most of them only in the middle class (De Ville 1990).

Physicians began to realize the problems of risking their reputations, legal fees, and court costs involved in fighting every case in court. This inspired the concept of group defense organizations. Legal defense associations sponsored by local medical societies very quickly became popular in many states. Organized physicians also became a potent political force, and many medical societies began to look for legislative remedies for malpractice lawsuits. However, most of their efforts were not very successful (De Ville 1990).

Courts accepted a variety of substitutes for the term "ordinary" in the description of physicians' responsibilities. Appellate courts were in general agreement that terms such as "average skill," "fair knowledge and skill," "adequate care," and "reasonable skill" were valid synonyms for "ordinary." Furthermore, the courts also ruled that a physician could not be held liable for malpractice if a patient contributed in any way to his or her injury. However, some appellate judges fashioned an exception to the strict doctrine of contributory negligence: It was possible to hold a physician responsible for damages caused by his negligence even if the patient may have aggravated the injury. Courts also, over a period of time, ratified the locality principle. According to this principle, a physician's standard of skill should be judged by local circumstances (De Ville 1990).

The Twentieth Century

By the beginning of the twentieth century, medical education had improved, medical societies were able to blunt the effects of intraprofessional competition, and licensure requirements were present in all states. However, medical malpractice suits continued, partly due to rapidly advancing medical technology. Advances in surgical techniques fostered more malpractice lawsuits because, by the "golden age of surgery" in the 1920s, expectations of successful surgery were so high that when these expectations were not met, malpractice lawsuits followed (Jost 2003). Medical discoveries in bacteriological science, nutritional advances, and pharmacological advances improved and routinized more treatments. It was during the 1930s and 1940s that scientists invented the miracle sulfonamide drugs and penicillin. Surgery had become common by the first half of the twentieth century. Discoveries in immunology, heredity, molecular biology, and chemistry, as well as the development of diagnostics and therapeutic technologies since the 1940s, dramatically improved modern medicine. Technology raised demands and expectations, which in turn led to higher dissatisfaction when treatments failed (De Ville 1990). The 1960s brought about a change in the relatively stable medical malpractice climate due to liberalization of laws and the availability of experts to testify in courts. While litigation increased, claim frequency against individual physicians remained relatively low (Sage 2004). For example, as of 1960, there were only about 1.3 malpractice lawsuits per one hundred physicians. By 2003, there were fifteen lawsuits per one hundred physicians (Jost 2003).

The Medical Malpractice Crisis of the 1970s

During the 1950s, the medical malpractice insurance market was very stable. By the 1960s, the severity (financial exposure associated with each claim) of claims had become much higher and more variable, making it difficult for insurers to price coverage accurately. As a result, by the early 1970s medical malpractice insurance coverage had become a tough business for commercial insurers (Sage 2004).

The medical malpractice insurance system in the United States underwent a "crisis" in the decades of the 1970s and 1980s (Sloan, Bovbjerg, and Githens 1991). The crisis of the 1970s was a crisis of availability, while the crisis of the 1980s was one of affordability (Jost 2003).

From 1974 to 1975, malpractice insurance premiums increased over 300 percent (Danzon 1990), and physicians in some states could not find coverage at any price. By the mid-1970s, the malpractice insurance market was considered to be experiencing a crisis (Danzon 1985; Sloan, Bovbjerg, and Githens 1991; Robinson 1991). The frequency of malpractice claims (per one hundred physicians) increased at about 10 percent a year during the 1970s and 1980s, with sharp increases in the early 1970s and the early 1980s and slower growth in the second halves of both decades (Danzon 1991). Not only did the frequency of claims increase but so did the severity of claims. Due to an unexpected surge in claims, many medical malpractice insurance companies either announced large hikes in premiums or withdrew from some state markets altogether, making it difficult to for physicians to get coverage. Large numbers of physicians were left without any insurance coverage (Jost 2003; Sage 2004). Medical groups created their own insurance companies (often called bedpan mutuals) to provide insurance coverage to doctors who were left without any. By the 1980s, 50 to 60 percent of U.S. physicians were covered by such physician mutual insurance companies (Jost 2003). To protest the situation, physicians organized strikes and demanded relief from state legislatures against malpractice lawsuits. California responded by passing the Medical Injury Compensation Reform Act (MICRA) in 1975 that placed a cap of $250,000 on jury awards for noneconomic damages (Studdert, Yang, and Mello 2004).

The Medical Malpractice Crisis of the 1980s

The medical malpractice crisis of the 1980s was characterized more by an upswing in insurance prices than the unavailability of coverage. The number of claims more than doubled, from 7.9 per one hundred physicians in 1976 to 17.8 in 1985, while the average payouts for successful claims increased from $17,600 to $70,200 during the same time frame (Jost 2003). According to the General Accounting Office (GAO), malpractice premiums rose 45 percent from 1982 to 1984. Furthermore, malpractice premiums had risen to 9 percent of physicians' total costs (U.S. General Accounting Office 1986), whereas they had represented only 1 percent of physicians' total costs in the 1950s (Sloan, Bovbjerg, and Githens 1991). According to the same GAO report, medical malpractice insurance costs increased, but also varied among physicians and hospitals. In 1988, internists experienced a 22 percent increase in their premiums. This was followed by general surgeons (20.5 percent) and pediatricians (20.2 percent). The percentage of orthopedic surgeons paying out $200,000 or more in premiums jumped from 30 to 45 percent, and for internists it jumped from 3 to 8 percent (Paxton 1998).

In Virginia, the largest insurer of medical malpractice in the United States, the St. Paul Fire and Marine Insurance Company, raised the premiums of obstetricians from a national average of $12,481 in 1982 to $51,240 in 1987, an increase of 311 percent. By 1986, of the states' 600 obstetricians, 140 were without medical liability insurance coverage. Another major insurance carrier—Pennsylvania Hospital Insurance Company— left the Virginia market altogether in 1986. About 25 percent of the state's obstetricians could not get an insurance policy at any price (Gallup 1989). When physicians in Florida went on strike to protest spiraling malpractice costs, some emergency rooms were forced to close down, while others had to manage with meager staffs. The situation was described as the "Beirut of American health care," (Korcok 1988).

Malpractice lawsuits also vary regionally. Texas has one of the highest incidence rates of malpractice suits. One out of every seven physicians in Texas becomes a malpractice defendant every year. The percentage of doctors with claims filed against them rose from 10.8 percent in 1988 to about 15 percent in 1992, almost double the national average. The number of claims filed each year against the state's doctors jumped from 1,745 to 5,000 within a decade after 1983 (Rice 1995).

Despite this predominant perception of crisis in medical malpractice insurance, some have argued that no such crisis existed during the 1970s and 1980s. For example, some researchers have expressed concern that medical malpractice insurance companies are obsessed with making a huge profit (M.R. Schwartz 1987). The argument is that the high premiums charged to physicians generate the perception of crisis, when in fact, no crisis exists (Hassan 1991). Some analysts have suggested that data from 1978 to 1986 show that medical malpractice insurance ranked only medium in underwriting profitability compared with other lines of insurance. In fact, during the 1985–86 period, it was the least profitable insurance business (Hassan 1991). Others have argued that the perception of a crisis was based on the misleading notion that there were sudden and dramatic increases in malpractice liability of physicians from the 1960s to the 1980s. Historical data demonstrate that, contrary to the common perception, recent increases in physician liability were neither sudden nor dramatic, and that the growth rates in physician liability between 1960 and 1980 are comparable to growth rates prior to the 1950s (Olsen 1996).

The Twenty-First Century

The Medical Malpractice Crisis of the 2000s

According to many people, the United States is again experiencing a medical malpractice crisis. The current crisis is characterized by both dramatically rising insurance premiums and a reduction in the number of companies offering insurance coverage (Thorpe 2004). The St. Paul Group of Companies, the largest commercial insurer, stopped writing new policies during 2002, and many other companies exited the market (Thorpe 2004). According to many newspaper accounts, the soaring cost of medical malpractice insurance has led many doctors to quit, retire, or relocate and has led hospitals to cut services. However, according to the August 8, 2003, report of the GAO, reports of physicians relocating to other states, retiring, or closing practices were not accurate, or involved relatively few physicians. A review of Medicare claims data also did not identify any major reduction in use of high-risk services (U.S. General Accounting Office 2003). In 2004, the name of the General Accounting Office was changed to Government Accountability Office.

According to the American Medical Association, 24 percent of specialists have stopped providing some high-risk services, such as delivering babies. According to a survey by the American College of Obstetricians and Gynecologists, 73 percent of ob/gyn specialists had been forced to retire, relocate, or modify their services (Adrianson 2003). The premiums for some obstetricians in Florida are as high as $210,000 per year. Some obstetricians in Nevada pay as much as $141,760 per year (Berntsen 2005). In 2003, the median increase in malpractice premiums ranged from 15 to 30 percent, depending on specialty and state, while rate increases in states such as Pennsylvania ranged from 26 to 73 percent (Thorpe 2004). In 2002 alone, the total medical malpractice premiums earned by malpractice insurance carriers increased by 22 percent (Thorpe 2004). Florida and Nevada are not the only states that have experienced dramatic increases in malpractice premiums. States such as Arizona, Illinois, Massachusetts, Mississippi, New York, Ohio, Pennsylvania, Texas and West Virginia have also been hard hit by significant premium increases. The "severity" of the crisis varies across states. The American Medical Association has classified states into three categories: in crisis, showing problem signs, and currently not facing crisis. Figure 7.1 below shows which states fall into one of these categories.

One of the interesting questions is, what accounts for the dramatic increases in malpractice insurance premiums? One explanation is that changes in the investment climate influence insurance premiums. Since insurers price their policies not only on the cost they expect to incur in offering coverage but also on the income they expect to earn through investment of premiums, malpractice insurance premiums are connected to the investment climate. In the malpractice insurance market there is generally a lag of four years between the incident that leads to a claim and the settling of a claim. This lag is the insurer's opportunity to earn investment income (Adrianson 2003). Since 1998, the net investment income of malpractice insurance companies has declined to 6 percent, from the 8 percent rate of 1998. Higher investment income offsets the need to increase premiums, while a decline in investment income leads to higher premiums (Thorpe 2004). Thus, the dramatic increases in malpractice premiums in the early 2000s are attributable to the negative investment climate faced by malpractice insurers.

Figure 7.1 **Medical Malpractice Crisis of 2000s and States**

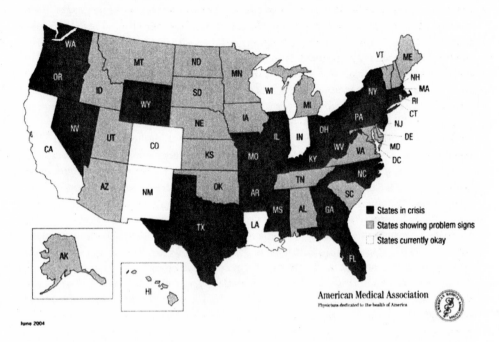

Source: "AMA Adds Massachusetts to Medical Liability Crisis List," *Medical Liability Monitor*, vol. 29, no. 7, July 2004, p. 3.

A second explanation for the increase in malpractice insurance premiums is the increased cost of malpractice litigation. Since 1975, the per-doctor cost has gone up 47 percent. Adjusted for inflation, the per-doctor cost of malpractice litigation has increased 14 percent since 1991 (Adrianson 2003).

The third explanation, cited most frequently by health care professionals, is the increase in the size of jury awards in malpractice cases. The median amount of damages awarded in malpractice jury trials increased from $253,000 in 1992 to $431,000 in 2001 ("Medical Malpractice Awards Soar" 2004). According to data from Jury Verdict Research (a private research firm), jury awards in medical malpractice claims increased 7 percent in 1999. The median malpractice jury award increased from $750,000 in 1998 to $800,000 in 1999. The number of jury awards in excess of $1 million increased from thirty-nine in 1997–98 to forty-five in 1998–99 (Albert 2001). By 2001, the median malpractice jury award had reached $1 million (Adrianson 2003).

However, government data (from the National Practitioner Data Bank [NPDB]) show that medical malpractice awards have increased at a much slower rate than claimed by Jury Verdict Research. The reason for the difference is that Jury Verdict Research data reflect only jury verdict information supplied by attorneys, court clerks, and stringers.

The NPDB data include both verdicts and settlements. Almost 96 percent of all medical malpractice cases are settled, as opposed to decided by juries, and settlements are much lower than jury awards ("Medical Malpractice Award Trends" 2003). The NPDB also reflects reduction of jury awards by judges (Adrianson 2003). According to the NPDB, the average malpractice payment actually fell from $268,605 in 2003 to $262,486 in 2004, and the number of total payments over the same period dropped from 18,996 to 17,696. The prices for medical malpractice coverage, while not falling, increased less steeply in 2004 (Treaster and Brinkley 2005). What this suggests is the need for caution in analysis of data collected from different sources using different methodologies.

The perceived crisis in the medical malpractice insurance market of the 1970s, 1980s, and the 2000s has raised a great deal of concern and criticism about the current system of tort, and has generated much debate and discussion about tort reform at the federal and state level. Rising insurance premiums have led physicians to demand tort reform. Physicians have engaged in protests and work stoppages in states such as Florida, New Jersey, West Virginia, and Mississippi to dramatize their plight (Jost 2003).

In the next section we briefly examine how the current tort system operates. This is followed by a discussion of the criticisms or perceived weaknesses of the present tort system. Next, we analyze a variety of reforms espoused by advocates of tort reform. Then we examine reforms undertaken at the federal and state levels. Finally, we examine new issues and concerns raised about medical liability by the rapid increase of managed care organizations such as HMOs.

The Current Tort System

Medical malpractice can be defined in a broad sense as "any unjustified act or failure to act on the part of a doctor or other health care professional that results in harm to the patient" (Stauch 1996, 247). Within the legal framework of medical injury, negligence is a conduct that fails to achieve accepted standards of professional health care, and malpractice is negligent conduct that does harm to a patient. Negligence is treated as a civil wrong (tort), not a crime or breach of contract (Mullis 1995). In order for a patient (plaintiff) to win a malpractice case in a court, it must be reasonably demonstrated that (1) the health care provider deviated from generally accepted medical practice, and (2) the medical injury/harm caused to the patient was the result of the health care provider's action or failure to act. It must be shown that the patient's injury resulted from negligence and not other causes such as the normal risk of medical treatment or the patient's prior health condition. If this is demonstrated with a preponderance of evidence, then the patient is entitled to recover compensatory damages for both economic and noneconomic losses (e.g., medical expenses, lost and projected earnings, and pain and suffering). Punitive damages can also be awarded in cases where the health care provider's conduct is viewed as willful and wanton (Fielding 1995). According to Eastburn (1999), for malpractice litigation to be successful, the plaintiff and his or her attorney must prove four things: (1) the physician owes the patient a duty to act within established norms or standards established by the medical profession, (2) the physician failed in his or her duty by not practicing within the applicable standard of care, (3) the physician's negligence or omission had a causal link with the injury suffered, and (4) the physician's breach of duty led to actual loss or damage to the patient.

In malpractice action, recovery against the physician is allowed only if one can demonstrate that there was an understanding between the physician and the patient (express or implied) that the physician would treat the patient with appropriate professional care, and that the patient would pay for such care, and that there was breach of professional duty to the patient. The breach of professional duty means that the doctor did something contrary to the recognized standard of medical practice in the community. There must be additional proof that the conduct of the doctor caused injury to the patient and the patient suffered damages. Finally, contributory negligence is another element in malpractice litigation. This involves breach of duty on the doctor's part to use ordinary care that a reasonable prudent person would use and which legally contributed to the injury of the patient (Sloan 1992).

In the context of medical malpractice it is generally not difficult to establish the existence of a duty of care. To establish that the doctor has breached the duty of care is more difficult. Furthermore, to demonstrate causation sufficient to establish a link between the breach of duty and the injury or harm suffered by the patient is even more complex and difficult. With respect to determining reasonable medical care, the courts have generally looked to the customary practice of the medical profession as the benchmark of acceptable behavior (Siliciano and Henderson 1994). The courts have further accepted the notion that the level of skill expected of physicians is ordinary skill and not extraordinary skill, and that physicians are expected to use reasonable and ordinary care in their application of knowledge and skill. Furthermore, the courts have also established that a physician's standard of skill should be judged by local circumstances.

Farber and White have outlined three stages of the litigation process in medical malpractice lawsuits (Farber and White 1991). The first stage of the litigation process generally involves the plaintiff filing a lawsuit against the physician. Often, the filing of lawsuits is preceded by communication in which the plaintiff attempts to extract a settlement offer without filing a suit. In medical malpractice cases the plaintiff's lawyers are paid on a contingency basis, that is, they receive a proportion (usually one-third) of the settlement amount if the case settles or of the damage award if the plaintiff wins at the trial. If the plaintiff drops the case or loses it, the lawyer receives nothing. This gives a potential lawyer incentive to screen cases carefully.

The second stage of the litigation involves pretrial discovery. This involves exchange of information, that is, evidence, between the plaintiff and the defendant. This includes many things. For example, the hospital provides the plaintiff with his or her medical records, while the hospital has a physician it names examine the patient (plaintiff) to verify damage claims. Each side in the case also deposes the other side's expert witnesses. The plaintiff's lawyer also deposes the medical personnel involved in the incident.

The third stage involves the actual trial itself. If the case goes to a local court, either side has the right to demand a trial by jury. Plaintiffs, in general, often demand a jury trial. Jury trials are not available in state courts. The judge or the jury decides whether the defendant is liable as well as the amount of damage to award if the defendant is found liable.

Very few cases actually go to trial. Most malpractice cases are either dropped by the plaintiff or settled out of court during the discovery period. Also, occasionally the judge may dismiss a case; this may be done for a variety of technical reasons at any stage of the litigation process (Jasper 1996).

Medical practice and injuries are governed by well-established principles of the common law tort system. They include the following: if a plaintiff is injured as a result of wrongful (i.e., negligent) behavior by a health care practitioner, the plaintiff is entitled to recover all losses, both financial and nonfinancial, caused by the fault of the medical practitioner. In the absence of negligent behavior, a medical practitioner is not legally responsible for injuries suffered by his or her patient; disputes over whether the medical practitioner was at fault and what injuries the patient suffered are resolved in a civil trial, often before a jury. Finally, if legal fault and liability are established through this process, compensation will be paid to the victim, generally by the liability insurer for the defendant or the institution that employed the doctor (Weiler et al. 1993).

The defenders of the present fault-based system argue that the system promotes two important values. One is the value of fairness, because the party at fault is punished and the victim is able to recover for damages. The second value that the current fault-based system promotes is deterrence, because the prospect of being sued and having to pay for losses deters physicians from providing substandard care. The financial and emotional incentives under this system are directed at the physician to provide careful treatment (Weiler et al. 1993).

Some have argued that a major problem is the fact that the current malpractice system operates on too many accepted presuppositions about medicine that need to be changed. One is the notion that medicine can cure anything and everything, Medicine should be viewed as a cooperative venture with nature. Medicine may not be able to do much if the patient's body lacks the wherewithal to heal or recover. Second, the role of the patient in health care is as important as the role of the doctor. This includes the patient's cooperation, attitude, will, and ability to adapt to new circumstances, among other things. Third, modern medicine does not possess all the forms of expertise that are needed for contemporary health care to be successful. Finally, there is the need to distinguish between three sets of circumstances—medical intervention that leads to a bad outcome but no one's bad work is involved; medical intervention that leads to a bad outcome which results from a physician's bad work that is minor in nature and the recognition that all human beings are fallible; medical intervention that leads to a bad outcome resulting from physician's bad work that is gross and continual, that is, work that does great harm or happens repeatedly so as to suggest that there is a significant risk that the physician will produce a similar bad outcome in the future (Ozar 1994). Many presuppositions about medicine are factually not very sound, and thus hinder our understanding of the concept of justice regarding medical care (Ozar 1994).

Criticisms of the Current Tort System

One of the major criticisms of the current fault-based tort system is that it fails with respect to promoting values of fairness and corrective justice (by compensating victims for injuries suffered and by making the health care provider liable for injuries they cause) and deterrence (the potential threat of medical malpractice lawsuits that prevent doctors from providing substandard care). The system fails to produce fairness because only a very small percentage of negligent behavior actually generates claims, and of the claims that are filed, only 50 percent have any chance of success resulting in compensation for the victim (Weiler 1991). The Harvard Medical Practice Study, based on randomly selected records of 30,000 patients from fifty-one hospitals in New York in 1990, estimated that eight times as many patients suffered an injury from negligence as filed a malpractice claim in the state of New York ("Incidence of Adverse Events . . ." 1991). Patricia Danzon has estimated that only one out of ten victims of medical negligence ever files a claim (Danzon 1985). Another study was based on a fifteen-year evaluation of medical negligence cases in the state of New Jersey. This study, after examining 8,231 cases involving 12,829 physicians, concluded that physicians usually win cases in which physician care was perceived as meeting community standards. Furthermore, severity of injury had very little bearing on whether a physician lost a case. Also, in only 6 percent of all cases reviewed did the settlement or jury award exceed $200,000 (Taragin et al. 1992).

Physicians often cite the fear of medical malpractice suits as the reason for the need to practice defensive medicine. To some, much of this is pure nonsense (Monteleone 1994). In Ohio, physicians prevail in 80 to 95 percent of all cases that go to verdict; that is, 80 percent of all cases are closed without any payment. However, to the defenders of the current system this does not suggest that plaintiffs are treated unfairly. Rather, it simply means that lawyers often file many frivolous lawsuits—that is, malpractice cases that have no merit (Ludwig 1994).

Others have argued that the current system fails to compensate sensibly because no matter how passionately judges may want to compensate victims, they are constrained by the administrative structure of the tort law and the rules of damages. The current tort system leaves too many victims of medical malpractice uncompensated or undercompensated (Sugarman 1985). Sloan et al., in their study of a sample of 187 cases, found that when compensation is awarded, it tends to fall far short of the cost of injuries. Only about one-fifth of the claimants recovered more than economic loss. Punitive damages were not paid explicitly in any of the 187 cases included in the sample (Sloan et al. 1993). There is a fundamental mismatch between claims and injuries, and compensation tends to be inappropriate or unequal (Danzon 1994).

In medical malpractice, punitive damages are seen as moderating abuses of power. Courts themselves have often indicated that punitive damages serve the important social function of punishment and deterrence. The policy underlying punitive damages is to teach both the actual and potential wrongdoer that "tort does not pay." Punitive damages are also seen as a useful tool for augmenting the work of state licensing boards (Rustad and Koenig 1995). Critics also argue that the current tort system fails to act as a deterrent to physicians for a variety of reasons. One reason is that, as we discussed earlier, very few victims of medical injury actually file a lawsuit, and of those that do, only about half have any chance of success. If malpractice litigation were effective in deterring physicians from providing substandard care, one would expect the incidence of substandard care to fall in response to increases in frequency or amount of claims. The empirical data do not support this. Despite increases in the frequency and amount of awards, there has not been any significant decline in incidents of medical malpractice (Starr 1991). Second, punitive damages are more likely to be effective in deterring an institution than a solo practitioner who may flee jurisdiction. The isolated nature of a solo practice also does not subject a deviant physician to peer review, common in institutional settings (Rustad and Koenig 1995). Third, the medical profession does a poor job of self-policing. Physicians often fail to report negligent behavior by fellow physicians, and state licensing boards are notorious for their inaction rather than action when negligent behavior does get reported. In 1985 only 2,108 of the 552,716 licensed physicians in the United States received any disciplinary action. Of the 2,108 who did receive disciplinary action, in only 641 cases were physicians' licenses to practice suspended or revoked (Rake and Thrasher 1996). A study of licensing boards in Florida found that even when licensing boards take disciplinary action, they are more likely to discipline older physicians and noncertified practitioners (Fournier and Mcinnes 1997). Finally, physicians often are ignorant of the common law of tort, and often seem to have an incomplete or incorrect understanding of the legal definition of negligence (Liang 1996).

Most of the medical malpractice lawsuits that end up in courts are tried before a jury. Juries make factual determinations and apply relevant laws to the facts to arrive at a verdict. The philosophy behind the jury system is that an impartial group of citizens can make decisions that reflect their common experiences and community values. For many years, jurors were seen as knowledgeable persons who had some specialized knowledge or expertise about the case that would help them resolve the dispute at hand. Today, however, jurors are seen as persons who have very little advanced knowledge about the case and, thus, have no preconceived ideas or opinions regarding the dispute involved. The emphasis is on having laypersons as jurors (Menon 1995).

The use of juries in medical malpractice cases has come under heavy criticism for a variety of reasons. Some have argued that jurors selected, at least in part, for their ignorance of the case are incompetent to decide issues involving complex scientific and medical evidence (Huber 1988, 1991; Struve 2004; Sugarman 1990). The heavy use of expert witnesses in medical malpractice cases poses a special problem for jurors when each side provides expert witnesses who testify in support of their respective position. It is argued that under this circumstance, jurors are left to determine which expert's testimony to believe since they themselves lack clear understanding of the testimony itself. They can be easily misled by expert witnesses. Jurors are also susceptible to emotional ploys and irrelevant legal arguments (Bovbjerg et al. 1991). A report by the American Medical Association's Specialty Society Medical Liability Project in 1988 argued that juries are not optimally suited to decide complicated issues of causation and duty of care, that jurors cannot independently evaluate testimony of experts, and that jurors cannot be very effective in deciding medical liability cases because their own experience and exposure to medical issues is very limited (Vidmar 1994). Critics also argue that juries are biased and unpredictable in their verdicts. Juries are further criticized for awarding extremely high awards to plaintiffs. Critics claim that this has become a "lottery" system rather than a rational system (Bowen 1987; O'Connell and Kelly 1987). For example, Howard (Brennan and Howard 2004; Howard 1996, 2002, 2003) has argued that the current tort system encourages "extortion lottery" because of the ability of individual plaintiffs to specify the amount of damages they are seeking.

Defenders of the jury system disagree with most of these criticisms. They argue that many of the criticisms of the jury system are based on anecdotal information rather than any hard scientific data. In fact, many empirical researchers have demonstrated that most medical malpractice lawsuits end without payments and that a substantial majority of juries find in favor of the physician defendant (Hyman and Silver 2004). For example, after examining 24,625 civil jury verdicts from state trial courts of general jurisdiction in forty-six counties in eleven states, Stephen Daniels cautions about the danger of making sweeping generalizations about national trends or patterns. This research demonstrates the importance of local context, especially since local socioeconomic and environmental factors provide a primary explanation for variations in jury awards (Daniels 1989, 1990). The findings raise doubts about the notion advanced by critics that the jury system has run amok. It has also been argued that some of the work criticizing the competence of juries is frequently based on misrepresentation of facts (Chesebro 1993).

Are jury decisions biased in favor of the plaintiffs? After examining many studies conducted over a decade in which data on rates at which plaintiffs won were collected, Neil Vidmar concluded that the win rates for the plaintiffs ranged from a low of 13.5 percent to a high of 53 percent. However, the median win rate for all studies was 29.2 percent. In other words, plaintiffs won in only three out of every ten cases (Vidmar 1994). This questions the notion that juries tend to be biased in favor of the plaintiffs. He concludes that the data raise some doubts about extravagant claims of jury bias (Vidmar 1994).

Defenders of the present tort system also challenge the notion that jurors are incompetent and incapable of understanding complex arguments. Some research demonstrates that jurors tend to correct each other during the deliberation process when an individual juror draws an inaccurate factual conclusion. Similarly, an individual juror's failure to recall some fact or instruction is overcome by the collective memory of all jurors (Cecil et al. 1991). Studies show that juries generally take their role very seriously and want to make the best judgment (Bovbjerg et al. 1991). Defenders of the jury system argue that the notions that jurors are incompetent, and that juries award outrageous damage awards, are simply myths with no basis in reality (Vidmar 1995).

Another criticism that has been raised about the current tort system is the use of the expert witness in trials. Aside from the issue of whether jurors can understand the complex testimony of the expert witness, critics charge that the current system invites many forms of abuse. Many expert witnesses are motivated by money, power, or ego. As a result, they are willing to become partisan advocates of any opinion for the client who promises the most gratification (Levitats 1991). Even well-meaning expert witnesses can end up being manipulated by skillful attorneys (Levitats 1991). Defenders of the use of the medical expert argue that medical experts are given a bad rap and unfairly portrayed as "hired guns" or marginally qualified whores willing to travel the country and say anything needed to win (Harway 1992).

The current tort system is also criticized for contributing to rising health care costs. Critics point to the costs of high premiums and the practice of defensive medicine (Brennan and Howard 2004; Howard 1996, 2002, 2003) as two major factors that contribute to rising health care costs. As we discussed earlier in the chapter, it is true that medical malpractice premiums increased dramatically, particularly for high-risk specialties, during the malpractice insurance crises of the 1970s, 1980s, and 2000s. Average annual malpractice premiums for all physicians increased from $6,900 in 1983 to $14,500 in 1990. This figure is much higher for high-risk specialties. In 1988 an average annual premium was $38,200 for orthopedic surgeons, $35,000 for obstetricians and gynecologists, and $25,600 for anesthesiologists (Paxton 1998; Thomas, Pol, and Sehnert 1993). The amount of the premium continues to depend on the health care practitioner's specialty, location, and type of practice (Paxton 1989).

Defensive medicine refers to physicians who, in order to protect themselves from potential malpractice lawsuits, overtreat a patient. Physicians often overprescribe diagnostic and treatment procedures as a defense against possible malpractice lawsuits. Research seems to confirm the presence of defensive medicine, especially in the field of obstetrics. Exposure to malpractice suits seems to increase use of electronic fetal monitors (EFMs), use of the label of fetal distress, and C-section rates (Tussing and Wojtowcycz 1997). According to a report published in 1994 by the U.S. Office of Technology Assessment, fewer than 8 percent of all diagnostic tests were performed by physicians, primarily because of fear of malpractice (Congressional Budget Office 1994). A survey conducted by the American Medical Association in 1986 found that 78 percent of physicians claimed that they practiced defensive medicine (Abramson 1989–90). According to a study by the National Medical Liability Reform Coalition, malpractice insurance, unnecessary tests and procedures, and other measures to guard against malpractice suits cost $9.9 billion in 1991 (McCormick 1993). The American Medical Association's study concluded that the current malpractice system adds almost $21 billion a year to the cost of health care—$15.1 billion in defensive medicine and $5.6 billion in malpractice premiums (Stevens 1991). According to Robert J. Rubin, president of Lewin-VHI Inc., a research firm, Americans could save $35 billion in medical bills over a five-year period by limiting malpractice awards and curbing defensive medicine (Brostoff 1993). A more recent figure cited by critics of defensive medicine is expenditures in excess of $100 billion (Howard 2003). However, the $100 billion figure is very problematic (Hyman and Silver 2004).

Defenders of the current system argue that claims about high premiums and the cost of defensive medicine contributing to spiraling health care costs are highly exaggerated. In 1985, the malpractice premium costs of $4.7 billion accounted for only 1 percent of the $425 billion national health costs. Furthermore, generally a small percentage of physicians account for most of the paid claims (Schmidt, Heckert, and Mercer 1991). Medical malpractice insurance ranks only medium in underwriting profitability compared with other lines of insurance, discrediting the notion that the insurance companies are obsessed with making huge profits (Hassan 1991). Critics of the tort system also argue that many of the medical malpractice lawsuits that are filed are frivolous and lack merit. They suggest that the proliferation of lawyers results in lower income and increases their willingness to accept marginal medical malpractice claims (Southwick and Young 1992).

Critics further argue that the current tort system impairs doctor-patient relationships, and lowers job satisfaction among physicians (McQuade 1991). According to critics, the emotional and psychological costs of medical malpractice litigation is very high. For many physicians, being sued for medical malpractice is a major stress factor in their lives. It often leads to depression and anxiety and has led to retirement and suicide (Hutkins 1989–90). Research is scant with respect to the motivations that lead victims of medical injury to sue their physicians. Research does show that many of the noneconomic motives for suing stem from actual or perceived inadequate communication between the physician and the patient and his or her family (Clayton et al. 1993). Other hidden costs of the current system include a decrease in availability of medical malpractice insurance, reduced availability of services in certain specialties and geographic areas, and fear of new technologies and techniques (Hutkins 1989–90).

Recent surveys of health care professionals do lend some credence to the argument that fear of medical liability lawsuits leads to the practice of defensive medicine, impairs the doctor–patient relationship, and lowers job satisfaction among doctors. In a nationwide Harris Interactive survey of 300 practicing physicians, 100 hospital administrators, and 100 nurses, health professionals said that fear of malpractice leads to defensive medicine and lack of openness in discussing medical errors, and has had a negative impact on their practice. A majority of physicians (94 percent), hospital administrators (84 percent), and nurses (66 percent) believed that unnecessary or excessive care is provided to patients because of fear of malpractice lawsuits. The survey also found that 43 percent of doctors in active practice had considered leaving medicine because of the malpractice liability system. Fifty-nine percent of doctors indicated that liability concerns were a significant factor in discouraging medical professionals from openly discussing and thinking about ways to reduce medical errors and in discouraging hospitals from sharing the results of inquiring into patient injury cases ("Doctors and Other Health Professionals Report . . ." 2003).

A study based on a sample of 824 physician specialists most affected by the malpractice insurance crisis (emergency surgery, general surgery, neurosurgery, obstetrics/gynecology, orthopedic surgery, and radiology) concluded that the malpractice crisis in Pennsylvania has led to a decrease in specialist physicians' satisfaction with their own medical practice in ways that may affect quality of care (Mello et al. 2004).

The criticisms of the current tort system have generated a great deal of debate about the reform of the current system and/or alternatives to the current system. In the next section, we briefly examine a variety of reforms and alternatives advocated by the critics of the current system.

Reforms and Alternatives

Legislative Reforms

Placing Caps on Noneconomic Damages

Legislative (tort) reform is one of the most frequently proposed solutions to the problems of the medical malpractice crisis. One of the proposals is to place a reasonable cap on jury awards for noneconomic damages such as pain and suffering (Berger 1990). At the federal level, President Bush and the Republicans have pushed for such a reform. However, the Congress has failed to pass such legislation because of strong objections by Democrats in the Senate who have successfully used filibusters to block such a measure. Several states have placed a cap on noneconomic damages. Proponents of caps on noneconomic damages argue that such damages are difficult to measure and placing a cap will eliminate the lottery aspect of the current tort system and help reduce health care costs. Critics charge that caps are morally repugnant and unacceptable because they try to put a price on a patient's life, and because they fail to address issues of the patient's emotional vindication and deterrence (Greene 1996). Furthermore, critics argue that damage caps defeat one of the most important purposes of malpractice litigation—compensation for injuries suffered by the plaintiff (Sage 2003).

Accelerated and Fair Compensation

This reform would create a liability system that would compensate for medical injury rapidly and provide for fair compensation without the need to prove negligence. The problem with this approach is the difficulty in defining what an appropriate compensable event is. More recently, the term used is accelerated compensable event (ACE). ACEs are classes of medical injuries that are easily identifiable (Cantor and Wadlington 1994). Some have argued that use of an industrial model of patient safety, which emphasizes reducing medical errors to an acceptable level and provides fair compensation for avoidable injury, will go a long way toward moderating the accusatory tone of malpractice lawsuits and reducing the costs of resolving them. An administrative system that includes an effective patient-safety review mechanism would be able to identify and compensate for medical errors more rapidly than the current system. Such a system could cap damages, but it would be based on a rational schedule and not a one-size-fits-all limit (Sage 2003).

Collateral Offset

Another legislative proposal is to offset payments received by the plaintiff from collateral sources. Under the traditional collateral source rule, if a plaintiff receives compensation from a source independent of the tort, the payment cannot be deducted from the damages assessed against the defendant. Proponents argue that this is necessary to avoid double recovery from both a collateral source and the defendant. Some states have adopted mandatory and discretionary offsets under which the amount of award received by the plaintiff is reduced by the amount the plaintiff received from other sources, such as health insurance. Some states allow information on collateral sources to be entered as evidence before an award is determined (Thorpe 2004). Opponents claim that such limits violate patients' right to due process and the equal protection clause of the Constitution (Greene 1996).

Shortening the Statute of Limitations

Shortening the statute of limitations for filing claims is another solution advocated by reformers. Proponents argue that a shortened time frame for filing claims will reduce the number of cases and discourage lawsuits filed as an afterthought after a long period of time. Opponents argue that often a medical injury may not manifest itself for a long period of time, and shortening the statute of limitations will be unfair to such patients (McMillen 1996).

Limiting Attorneys' Contingency Fees

Other legislative reforms proposed include limiting attorneys' contingency fees (Thorpe 2004). Proponents argue that attorneys who get about one-third of the jury award as their fee have an incentive to seek larger and larger awards. Limiting attorneys' contingency fees would discourage lawyers from filing frivolous lawsuits. Finally, reformers have also advocated reform designed to allow large jury awards to be paid over a period of time rather than in one lump sum as a way of reducing the financial burden imposed by too large an award.

Expert Panels—Special Courts

Some national reform organizations, such as Common Good, have proposed the creation of a special court to hear medical liability claims on the ground that judges on such a court would be expert and can help set precedents to govern the standard of care. Proponents argue that such a specialized court would address criticisms of the jury system that jurors are not competent to judge complex medical cases. However, critics argue that a specialized court would be subject to and susceptible to political pressures from plaintiffs, lawyers, doctors, and malpractice insurers to influence their decisions. Such pressures are less evident in the general court system because of many judges and the different kinds of cases they hear (Struve 2004).

Making the Current System More Transparent

Some have argued that the current tort system encourages hiding of medical errors. The only way to address this problem is to make the tort system more transparent. This could be accomplished by doing several things: (1) requiring providers by law to explain adverse outcomes to patients (or a designated representative) because, under the current system, disclosure remains the exception rather than the rule; (2) outlawing confidentiality agreements that help hide health system failures; (3) replacing the NPDB with a requirement that every medical liability claim trigger a report and at least a cursory investigation by the agency responsible for licensing the organization and defendant names in the suit; and (4) establishing a national body with the authority to monitor medical injury risks (Hatlie and Sheridan 2003).

Alternate Dispute Resolution Methods

A variety of alternate dispute resolution (ADR) methods have been proposed as a way of addressing many of the perceived shortcomings of the present tort system (Cantor and Wadlington 1994). ADR methods and their variations are too numerous to discuss here. Some alternate dispute resolution proposals are moderate in nature and attempt to address problems of the current system, while others are more dramatic, designed to fundamentally change or replace the current system of tort.

In order to avoid and/or address the problems of the present tort system, one of the reforms advocated is the development of *medical practice guidelines.* Practice guidelines generally consist of systematically developed statements designed to help physicians in their health care decisions about patients and the appropriate health care for specific clinical circumstances. Practice guidelines may be developed by federal or state governments, professional medical societies, insurance companies, peer review organizations, and managed care organizations such as HMOs. Medical practice guidelines are viewed as providing a more direct link between quality of care issues and medical malpractice. Such well-established medical practice guidelines may help moderate exaggerated claims by expert witnesses and may provide some guidance to the courts (Hyams, Shapiro, and Brennan 1996). Proponents of practice guidelines argue that predetermined prescriptive standards of care will provide clear legal standards for the practicing physician. Second, guidelines would help lower litigation costs because they would simplify trials, and some trial outcomes would become more predictable. Third, clear and precise practice guidelines may discourage and thus reduce frivolous lawsuits. Fourth, practice guidelines can help make malpractice legal proceedings shorter, simpler, and less costly. Potential problems with such practice guidelines include conflicts that can be created when more than one guideline has been developed for a specific medical condition or procedure. Moreover, if guidelines are very broad and unclear, difficulty could arise in applying such broad guidelines to resolve specific cases (Rinella 1995).

Summary jury is another ADR method. In such a system, lawyers for both sides are given a limited number of hours (e.g., four to five) to call witnesses and make their arguments. Both parties may agree ahead of time to minimum and maximum damages if the jury decides the case in plaintiff's favor. This is designed to rule out jackpot awards ("Can Malpractice be Kept Out of Court?" 1994).

Another ADR method is to use a *neutral evaluator.* A disinterested third party looks at the evidence and provides an evaluation. The idea behind this concept is that if the assessment by a third-party evaluator shows that the plaintiff has a weak case he or she may decide not to pursue a costly court battle. By the same token, a physician who sees the evidence going against him or her, may decide to settle and award damages to the victim of medical injury ("Can Malpractice be Kept Out of Court?" 1994).

Mediation is often defined as a voluntary process in which a neutral third party helps participants reach their own agreement for resolving a dispute. Mediation is an informal, private, voluntary, and confidential process (Liebman and Hyman 2004). However, the third party lacks the authority to impose a solution. The mediation process can take a variety of forms. In a pure mediation, parties communicate with one another in a joint attempt to reach a solution. Proponents of mediation claim that this has several advantages over the current tort system. Advantages claimed include: greater potential for improving the relationship between parties to a dispute through direct communication; enhancing the values of trust, caring, and respect; flexibility; low cost and speedy service; and the fact that the mediation process does not get bogged down by procedural and substantive rules (McMullen 1990). However, some of the available empirical evidence suggests that mediation is not very effective in disposing of medical malpractice cases (Simmons 1996).

Another ADR method is what is referred to as *pretrial screening panels* (Macchiaroli 1990). There are two types of review panels. One type is the medical quality review panel that is commonly found in a hospital. The second type of panel is created by agreement between bar associations and medical societies. The idea is to screen the cases for merit and promote early settlement, thereby reducing the number of cases that go to trial. Typical pretrial screening panels consist of physicians and lawyers, and the panels may occasionally also include laypersons. These panels review medical records and relevant evidence, consult with medical experts, and determine whether the patient's injury was caused by medical malpractice. If such is the case, it encourages settlement. If the panel finds that medical malpractice did not cause medical injury, it encourages dismissal of the claim by the victim. If the case does go to trial, the panel can provide experts who document its findings at the trial (Hutkins 1989–90).

Proponents view pretrial screening panels as potentially reducing tort cost by encouraging early settlement and by reducing the number of cases that end up in court. However, critics argue that a great deal of time and money is wasted if the case is not settled during the pretrial hearings. It has also been argued that review panels tend to favor the physicians since most panels have a physician on the panel. Finally, critics argue that pretrial screening panels are not very successful because their decisions are not binding and they do not have the power to discipline doctors (Hutkins 1989–90).

One of the most widely debated and discussed ADR methods is *arbitration.* In arbitration, parties to a dispute voluntarily agree to refer a dispute to one or more impartial arbitrators for a final decision. The arbitrators are often selected by the parties to the dispute. The arbitrator's decision may or may not be binding. However, even when an arbitrator's decision is not binding, the arbitrator's opinion can exert a great deal of influence on the party against whom the judgment is rendered, to settle the case. Arbitration takes on several different forms and variations. It can be grouped into three broad categories (Mitchell and McDiarmid 1988). In *traditional arbitration*, parties to a dispute, through agreement, create a private forum for the resolution of their disputes. Parties negotiate a set of rules for resolving their disputes and agree to be bound by the results. In a *facilitated arbitration*, the rules and procedures are specified by the state rather than being negotiated and agreed upon by the parties to the dispute. *Mandatory arbitration* is imposed by a state through the law. This form of arbitration often takes on the appearance of a screening panel for the court, since submission of the dispute to the arbitration is mandatory before parties can proceed to the court (Mitchell and McDiarmid 1988).

Proponents of arbitration argue that it relieves overburdened courts of cases that might end up being litigated, saves time spent on resolving claims, and also reduces overall transaction costs and the average size of the awards (Greene 1996). Criticisms of arbitration include the fact that arbitration agreements themselves are of questionable validity—that is, questions can be raised as to when the agreement was signed, and whether the patient or his or her agent was fully informed of all the implications and was in a position to exercise free choice. Furthermore, physicians are often reluctant to ask patients to sign documents that discuss the consequences should something go wrong in treatment. Also, arbitration may not decrease the overall cost of malpractice claims. The final criticism of arbitration is that it does not give parties to the dispute an opportunity to reconcile their differences (Hutkins 1989–90).

In 1988, the American Medical Association proposed an alternative to the current tort system to reduce medical malpractice claims. The proposal has been referred to as the *fault-based administrative system.* The proposal calls for replacing the current court and jury system with an administrative claims tribunal. Under this system, medical malpractice claims would be adjudicated before an expert administrative agency. The proposal would create a state medical board as part of the state government. Its leadership would be appointed by the state governor. Claim adjustors would review claims submitted by patients. Claims with significant questions would be evaluated by a board medical specialist. This specialist would help the claimant evaluate settlement offers by the defendant. In a case that could not be settled, the board's general counsel would provide an attorney for the patient. An administrative judge or hearing examiner would supervise discovery and evaluate expert testimony. The judge could call his or her own witnesses. The judge would issue an opinion within ninety days. A medical board would also provide an appellate review. Appeals could be taken from the medical board's decision to an intermediate appellate court with a very high threshold designed to reduce the number of cases going to court. The state medical board would also handle credentialing and disciplinary functions and act as a clearinghouse for all information about individual providers and disciplinary actions. Overall, the AMA proposal retains the fault-based aspect of the current system (Bovbjerg 1990; Brennan 1995; Ferrari 1990; Johnson et al. 1990).

There are several advantages claimed for such a system. One is that it provides for an inexpensive screening mechanism. Second, it will provide a final resolution much quicker than is the case under the current system. Third, specialization of adjudicators will help streamline the process of presenting evidence, and expert adjudicators will perform the task of determining "standard of care," which is at the heart of most medical malpractice cases, much more efficiently than a jury of lay persons (Baily 1990). A potential major problem with such a system is financing. Would the system be adequately funded? It is almost impossible to estimate the cost of such a new system and it might end up costing more than the current system. Without sufficient resources and adequate manpower, the system might not be able to resolve claims quickly (Baily 1990). Finally, critics charge that such a system might be quick and efficient, but it ignores patients' interests and resolves disputes in a problematic fashion (Hutkins 1989–90).

Enterprise Liability

The concept of enterprise liability moves the focus from individual practitioner liability to institutional liability. This system would allow injured patients to sue either the hospital where they were treated or the health plan (such as an HMO) to which the provider subscribes. Such a system would immunize physicians from malpractice lawsuits. Instead of suing the physician, the injured patient would sue the enterprise in which a physician worked. The enterprise would defend the physician against a lawsuit. An argument in favor of enterprise liability is that it provides incentives to hospitals to improve their quality of care as well as to engage in risk management. It could also decrease administrative costs (Brennan 1995; Cantor and Wadlington 1994; Greene 1996). This proposal, to some, makes sense because, of all the medical malpractice allegations, 60.6 percent occur in hospital settings, while 37 percent occur in physician offices or clinics, and the remainder in other settings (Eastburn 1999).

Channeling

A variation of the enterprise liability reform is referred to as channeling. The idea is to remove the burden of malpractice liability from individual physicians to groups or institutions. Under one method of channeling, patients would be required to provide their own malpractice insurance. This would free physicians from malpractice liability. The problems with this approach are that poor persons may not be able to afford such insurance; that it provides very little incentive to physicians, medical institutions, or health plans to provide higher quality of care; and that it is likely to create greater distrust between physician and patient. Under another method of channeling, hospitals and medical institutions would be required to provide insurance for both hospitals and physicians against any claim resulting from treatment received at the hospital (Hutkins 1989–90).

No-Fault Compensation System

One alternative advocated by the critics of the current fault-based system is what is often referred to as a no-fault system for compensation of medical injury (Havighurst and Tancredi 1974; Horwitz and Brennan 1995; King 1992; O'Connell 1975; Weiler 1991). In contrast to negligence or a fault-based tort system, a pure no-fault system would compensate patients for any injury arising out of medical care, regardless of whether it was caused by negligence of the physician or whether it was an unavoidable risk of normal care. The criterion used for compensation is not based on negligence but rather on medical causation. Thus, the issue of who is to be blamed or whose fault it is becomes irrelevant. Patients are compensated for medical injuries regardless of fault.

A wide range of options and alternatives are available in how one structures a no-fault compensation system. Latz (1989) has provided one of the most comprehensive and excellent analyses of the various options available under the no-fault system. According to him, options fall under three main categories: (1) neo-no-fault early compensation system, (2) pure no-fault system, and (3) limited no-fault system.

Under the *neo-no-fault early compensation system*, following any iatrogenic injury the provider has the option, within a limited time, to foreclose any actual or potential claim by offering the victim compensation for the full net economic loss (medical expenses and wage loss minus any payment from collateral sources) suffered and reasonable legal fees. The provider assesses his or her own liability and determines whether compensation is deserved. Once a provider extends a compensation offer, the injured patient has a limited time to accept or reject the offer but has no tort claim alternative. If the provider does not offer economic compensation, the victim has the full right to proceed in tort. The main reason behind this system is to preempt the tort system without abandoning the fault basis of liability (Latz 1989).

Under a *pure no-fault system* the victim receives compensation for any injury resulting from medical care without assigning fault; that is, compensation is awarded regardless of whether the injury resulted due to negligence or a risk of normal care. Compensation comes from either the provider or the mandatory third-party insurer of the provider, or from the injured party's mandatory first-party insurer. In a *limited no-fault system with specified events*, patients who have suffered negative outcomes that are specifically predetermined to be compensable are automatically compensated. What constitutes compensable outcomes is determined by law or by contract. The criteria used for deciding compensable outcomes are relative avoidability, or the likelihood of the outcomes having arisen as a result of medical error. For outcomes not included in the list of predetermined compensable events, the tort system would remain in place (Latz 1989).

Two statutory variations under a limited no-fault system include the designated compensable events and the catastrophic no-fault schemes. Under the designated compensable events scheme, health care providers would purchase from private insurers a policy of medical adversity insurance (MAI) to automatically indemnify a patient suffering from a designated compensable event (DCE). A statutory board of medical experts and consumer representatives would determine the list of compensable events. Providers would pay premiums rated for claims experience. Patients would be compensated for all medical and hospital expenses and for loss of wages up to a predetermined maximum. A floor would also be imposed on the wage loss compensation (Danzon 1985; Havighurst 1975; Havighurst and Tancredi 1974). Under the second scheme, the law would create a compensation fund to cover participating physicians and hospitals for catastrophic injuries, such as severe brain and spinal cord injuries resulting from obstetrical care. The law would exclude common law tort remedies for qualifying cases. Virginia and Florida opted for such a scheme in 1987 and 1988, respectively. Other forms of limited no-fault designated compensable events schemes include elective no-fault and contractual neo-no-fault systems. The elective no-fault plan rests on elective contractual relations between patients and providers. It is meant for private implementation by health care providers as opposed to public-sector implementation. Health care providers would define all the negative outcomes for which fault-based claims would be foreclosed by automatic compensation. In a contractual neo-no-fault system, the provider obligates itself to offer economic compensation within ninety days of the occurrence of any adverse outcome specified in the patient-provider contract. The victim has the option of accepting the offer of compensation or pursuing the claim in court.

Advantages of a No-Fault System. Proponents claim that under a no-fault system removing the tort issue of whether a physician was at fault or not would remove a major source of litigation. Disputes would focus on technical questions of the exact source and extent of a patient's injury instead of on assigning blame. The system would also reduce expenditures on litigations. In addition, it would not place a doctor and a patient in an adversarial context, thus saving both sides the emotional and financial costs of such a context (Weiler et al. 1993). The money saved would free up funds to finance coverage for all victims of medical injury. It would also save time by avoiding a lengthy court battle, and victims would be compensated in a more timely fashion. Thus a no-fault system would be more efficient, both financially and administratively, than the current tort system. Another advantage claimed for a no-fault system compared to a fault-based system is that it would be more fair, equitable, and rational. It would also remove the "lottery" aspect of the current tort system, in which only a few get large jury awards while others are undercompensated, and a large majority of victims are never compensated because they do not file a claim. In contrast, a no-fault system would compensate all victims of medical injury in a fair and equitable manner. Since a no-fault system guarantees coverage for all economic loss arising from covered or designated events, it would make compensation more predictable and rational by relating compensation to the loss incurred (Latz 1989).

Proponents also argue that if insurance premiums in a no-fault system are not experience-rated, it would remove one of the major factors responsible for defensive medicine, that is, fear of malpractice lawsuits (Danzon 1985). This would eliminate a great deal of the costs of defensive medicine.

Disadvantages of a No-Fault System. Opponents of the no-fault system see many problems with it. They argue that a no-fault system would not deter negligent behavior on the part of health care providers, or at least it would deter such behavior less effectively than the tort system, for two reasons. First, because a no-fault system does not assign blame for specific negligent acts, there is no legal disincentive for the physician to correct his or her behavior. Second, a no-fault system would not provide any information to the medical community about which practices are considered unreasonable (Phillips and Kalb 1991).

Defenders of the no-fault system respond by arguing that of all cases involving medical injury, in a very small percentage of the cases medical injury is caused by negligent or incompetent behavior by the physician. Many medical injuries result from normal risks associated with medical procedures. Moreover, the current tort system does a very poor job of deterring negligent or incompetent behavior. For example, Danzon reported that even though 1,500 individuals were paid malpractice claims in California in 1976, only six disciplinary actions were taken against physicians for incompetence or gross negligence in that year (Danzon 1984). A more recent study of Florida physicians concluded that none of the physicians with the most adverse claims experiences had their licenses suspended or revoked by the state medical board, and fewer than 10 percent of these physicians were disciplined in any manner (Sloan et al. 1989). However, this may not be a fair criticism, since existing disciplinary procedures in the medical profession are not designed to function as a shadow to the tort system (Trebilcock, Dewees, and Duff 1990).

Another major criticism is that a no-fault system would encourage more claims to be filed by injured patients, thereby actually increasing the cost. The increased number of claims would more likely offset or exceed any savings a no-fault system might produce (Hutkins 1989–90; Kapp 1989). Furthermore, since the no-fault system makes causation rather than negligence the test for compensation, it might increase rather than reduce the administrative burden. Such a system would also abolish the notion of patient assumption of risk for possible adverse effects of adequate medical care. Any recovery that is less than perfect might become potentially compensable if there is any chance for alternative judgment, possible omission, or better treatment regardless of the cost (Danzon 1985).

Another controversial aspect of the no-fault system is the fact that most no-fault plans would eliminate compensation for things such as pain, suffering, and the loss of enjoyment of life. In common law they are regarded as compensation for losses. They are also the traditional source of attorneys' fees. This would make it more difficult for patients to sue for medical injuries (Latz 1989). Another problem cited with the no-fault specified or designated event compensation plans is that the occurrence of compensable events is much easier to identify in cases of automobile and work-related accidents, but this is not true with the incidence of iatrogenic injury. Medical malpractice cases involve a variety of injuries, and it would be difficult to define a large number of comprehensible events with enough clarity. This could lead to extensive litigation over whether a particular case falls within a no-fault or a tort system (Danzon 1985).

The general theme running through these criticisms is the notion that a no-fault system would be obtrusive and impersonal. It would focus only on the financial responsibility aspect of the health care provider, and would ignore assigning blame and holding individual health care providers accountable for their behavior and actions (Weiler et al. 1993).

Medical Liability: Federal Government Policy and Reforms

The federal role in the area of medical liability has been a limited one. Product liability provides a strong argument for uniform treatment, and thus a case can be made for federal rules governing product liability. However, medical treatment decisions generally occur and have impact within a state. This is not to say that there are no spillover effects on service providers and consumers. Nonetheless, it is difficult to make a case for a strong federal role in the area of medical liability unless a strong need for national uniformity can be established or it can be demonstrated that there are overriding national interests involved (Blumstein 1996).

It is important to point out that the tradition of state tort law is a uniquely American tradition. In almost every other country, tort law is a national responsibility. In many other federal systems similar to the United States, such as India and Switzerland, tort law is all national law. In Canada and Australia, tort doctrines are developed by the judiciary in provinces or states, but disagreements are resolved by the national supreme court. In the United States, the tradition of state tort law in American society has held up quite well. In general, Congress has respected tort law as a state prerogative (Schwartz 1996). This is not to suggest that the national government has never intervened in this area. In fact, in the twentieth century the national government had assumed an increasing number of responsibilities, and in the process had displaced state lawmaking authority. For example, at the turn of the century a large number of claims were brought by employees against their employers, especially employees against the railroads. In 1908, Congress intervened and passed the Federal Employees Liability Act (FELA). This federal legislation preempted state tort law and governed the liability claims brought by employees against the railroads operating in interstate commerce (Schwartz 1996).

A largely unanticipated event, which later had a profound effect on American health care, was the passage of the Employee Retirement Income Security Act (ERISA) in 1974. ERISA's primary effect in the health care field was to preempt state laws that relate to any employee health benefit plans (Havighurst 2000). ERISA, its interpretation by the courts, and its impact are discussed in detail later in this chapter.

Under the doctrine of sovereign immunity, a government is not liable for the tortuous acts of its employees. However, the Federal Tort Claims Act (FTCA) provided a limited waiver of the federal government's sovereign immunity. It exposes the federal government to tort liability only to the extent that Congress has affirmatively waived sovereign immunity. Under FTCA, Congress gave plaintiffs the option of suing the government rather than the federal employee. However, plaintiffs were not barred from suing a federal employee. Over the years, Congress has given special protection to federal employees, especially medical personnel, who, because of the nature of their work, are at greater risk of being sued for tort committed within the scope of their job (Hart 1990).

In 1985, Congress passed the Medical Malpractice Immunity Act (MMIA). The purpose of the law was to protect medical personnel from any liability arising out of performance of their official medical duties. The MMIA removes a plaintiff's option to sue the physician individually. The law is also intended to provide adequate compensation for legitimate malpractice claims. The law allows the attorney general to remove lawsuits from state to federal courts and to substitute the United States as defendant if he or she certifies that defendants were acting within the scope of their employment (Hart 1990).

Congress had also become concerned that state licensing boards were not adequately weeding out incompetent or unprofessional physicians and that it was too easy for a physician to move to another state (i.e., jurisdiction), and start their practice again. With this in mind, Congress in 1986 passed the Health Care Quality Improvement Act. This law restricted the ability of an incompetent physician to move from state to state without disclosure or discovery of his or her previous incompetent or damaging performance. To prevent such jurisdictional hopping, the law also created the National Practitioner Data Bank. The data bank stores information about physicians and other health care providers who have been defendants in malpractice cases and who, directly or through an insurance carrier, paid damages to claimant by settlement or by verdict after September 1990. The data bank is required to pass this information on to hospitals whenever a physician seeks appointment or reappointment to a medical staff. Information is also sometimes supplied to agencies such as HMOs. However, the information in the data bank is not available to the general public. Information is available upon request by physicians or state licensing boards. Attorneys may get the information only if a malpractice lawsuit has been filed against a physician and it is alleged that the hospital failed to inquire of the data bank about the physician being sued (Atkinson 1994).

The George H.W. Bush Administration

The perceived medical malpractice crisis of the 1970s and 1980s, combined with criticisms of the current tort system, led to significant discussion and debate about medical liability reforms at the federal level. President George H.W. Bush argued that the skyrocketing costs of defensive medicine and malpractice litigation were threatening to make health care unaffordable for many Americans.

Congress made an attempt to develop practice guidelines when, in 1989, it amended the Public Health Service Act by enacting the Omnibus Budget Reconciliation Act. The law created the Agency for Health Care Policy and Research (AHCPR), with a primary mission of conducting or commissioning studies that focus on actual outcomes and effectiveness of various medical treatments. The law also established the Forum for Quality and Effectiveness in Health Care. The forum is a separate office of AHCPR and is responsible for appointing panels of physicians, experts, and consumer representatives to research and develop practice guidelines (Rinella 1995).

In 1991, the Bush administration proposed a plan that would have given states three years to enact a set of very specific malpractice reforms. Under the plan, the federal government would have used financial incentives to compel states to adopt a series of reforms. Those states that failed to enact reforms would be fined 2 percent of their federal Medicaid administrative budgets and 1 percent of the annual increase in the operating cost portion of Medicare payments to hospitals. States that implemented these reforms would be paid bonuses from this money. The specific reform measures the administration wanted included the following: eliminating joint and several liability for noneconomic damages; placing a cap on noneconomic damage awards; requiring structured payments instead of a lump-sum payment for medical malpractice awards; promoting pretrial alternative dispute resolution methods; and eliminating the collateral source rule, among others (Editorial 1991; Geisel 1991; Locke 1991; Stevens 1991). It is important to emphasize that the Bush administration's basic approach was not to enact medical liability legislation at the federal level, but rather to encourage states to adopt reforms at the state level. However, the Bush plan did not get very far, and these initiatives came to an end with his defeat in the 1992 presidential elections.

The Clinton Administration

President Bill Clinton came into the office with a promise to overhaul the U.S. health care system. He had campaigned on the theme of establishing a national health care system that would make health care affordable and accessible to all Americans. After a very lengthy discussion and deliberation by the national task force on health care reform chaired by the First Lady, Hillary Clinton, the Clinton administration came up with a major reform proposal. The Clinton plan to overhaul the U.S. health care system was contained in the proposed Health Security Act of 1993, which was formally sent to Congress in November 1993. The detailed provisions of the Health Security

Act and other major competing plans that emerged in the Congress are presented and discussed in chapter 9 on health care reform. Here, we highlight only those elements of the Health Security Act that dealt with the issue of medical liability for medical malpractice.

President Clinton's proposed plan included several medical malpractice reforms. First, the plan advocated the creation of an alternative dispute resolution mechanism. Second, it required a certificate of merit as a prerequisite for filing a medical malpractice lawsuit. Third, it proposed placing a limit on attorneys' contingency fees. Fourth, it would have required malpractice awards to be paid in installments rather than one lump sum. Fifth, it would have provided the general public with increased access to information about repeat offenders. Finally, one of the cornerstones of the Clinton health care reform package was an attempt to relieve physicians of the burden of medical liability lawsuits by advocating enterprise liability instead of individual liability (Berg 1994).

The Clinton administration believed that one of the most glaring problems with the current tort system is that it leaves individual doctors on the hook for malpractice. Under enterprise liability, malpractice risk would be transferred from individual physicians to institutions such as hospitals, insurance companies, and HMOs. Transfer of liability to managed care networks, also called Accountable Health Plans (AHPs), would help ensure that they would not skimp on needed services in a very competitive environment. Instead of paying malpractice premiums, physicians would pay a negotiated surcharge to their AHP. Proponents of enterprise liability argued that it had several benefits. One, it would remove doctors from the tug-of-war between payers. Second, physicians could end up spending a third less for malpractice coverage. Third, there would be a decrease in the practice of defensive medicine. Supporters also argued that enterprise liability would help improve health care quality. Needless to say, the insurance companies and HMOs that would have inherited malpractice risks strongly opposed this idea (Sage, Hastings, and Berenson 1994; Stevens 1993).

Many other competing health care reform bills that emerged in Congress in response to President Clinton's Health Security Act also contained some provisions dealing with medical liability (Kapp 1994). However, as discussed in chapter 9 on health care reform, for a variety of reasons no reform bill was able to garner majority support in Congress, and by the late summer of 1994, health care reform was declared dead. None of the bills even came up for a vote in Congress.

In 1995, Congress passed the Federally Supported Health Centers Assistance Act (FSHCA). The law extends coverage under the FTCA to community health centers that receive federal funding under a program sponsored by the Department of Health and Human Services. It was implemented as a three-year experiment in 1992 and reauthorized permanently in 1995. The FTCA claims are first handled as administrative claims. If a claim is not settled within six months, the claimant can file a civil suit in federal court. FTCA cases are heard by a judge and not a jury. Attorney fees are limited to 20 percent of administrative claims and 25 percent on settlement of lawsuits (McNay and Gentry 1997).

Congress, in April 1996, passed a broad tort reform bill titled the Common Sense Product Liability Legal Reform Act of 1996. The law would have restricted the amount of punitive damages that can be awarded in a civil action not to exceed three times the amount of damages awarded to the claimant for economic loss, or $250,000, whichever is greater. In the health care liability action, noneconomic damages in excess of $250,000 would be reduced to $250,000 before entry of judgment or by amendment of the judge after entry. On May 3, 1996, President Clinton vetoed the bill, complaining that it would intrude on state authority. Anthony Lewis, after reviewing congressional tort reform, concluded that tort law has been state law for 200 years and stated that "substantive tort law should be left to state courts and legislatures." Similarly, Joan Claybrook, president of Public Citizen, condemned the proposed law for infringing upon state sovereignty. Pamela Liapakis, then president-elect of the American Trial Lawyers Association, used similar language in disapproving federal action in the tort area. The spokesperson of the American Bar Association called federal action unwise and an unnecessary intrusion on the longstanding authority of the states to promulgate tort law (Schwartz 1996).

President Clinton, did however, on June 18, 1997, sign into law the Volunteer Protection Act of 1997. This law protects America's volunteers from meritless, costly, and time-consuming lawsuits. The law protects softball coaches, playground monitors, and emergency service providers, among others. The law establishes uniform rules and creates immunity from litigation for those volunteers who act within the boundaries of their responsibilities, who are properly licensed or certified when necessary, and who do not cause any harm intentionally.

In 1997, President Clinton established the Advisory Commission on Consumer Protection and Quality in the Health Care Industry (also known as the Quality Commission). The Quality Commission released two major reports focusing on patient protections and quality improvement. Following these two reports, President Clinton established the Quality Interagency Coordination Task Force (QuIC). In February 2000, the QuIC Task Force (2000) produced a report in which it endorsed all of the recommendations made by the Institute of Medicine (2000) report, *To Err Is Human.*

The George W. Bush Administration

The issues of a patients' bill of rights and tort reform were pushed off the national agenda during George W. Bush's first term in office following the 9/11 terrorist attack in 2001. However, in 2002, President Bush called for putting a cap of $250,000 on noneconomic damages in medical malpractice suits as part of his tort reform proposal. President Bush and the proponents of caps blamed frivolous malpractice lawsuits and large jury awards, that is, the legal system, for the medical malpractice crisis. Lawyers and consumer group disagreed with President Bush's diagnosis of the problem and his prescription (Jost 2003). The House of Representatives, in both

2003 and 2004, passed legislation advocated by President Bush that places a cap on jury awards. However, the Senate failed to pass similar legislation in 2003 and 2004 due to strong opposition from the Democrats (Heil, Smallen, and Mitchell 2004; Serafini 2004).

President Bush made tort reform an important part of his reelection campaign. He touted his proposal for curbing medical malpractice lawsuits by limiting jury awards and argued that too many frivolous lawsuits was one of the main reasons for rising health care costs (Cohn 2004). According to a national survey conducted by Harris Interactive, 61 percent of respondents blamed medical malpractice and insurance costs for increases in their own health care costs ("Higher Health Care Costs Blamed on . . ." 2002). Another national poll showed that more than half (58 percent) of adult Americans favor new legislation to limit the costs of medical liability and reduce the costs of medical malpractice insurance. The same poll also showed that 62 percent favor medical malpractice cases tried in special courts presided over by medical professionals and other experts, while another 48 percent favored a cap of $250,000 on jury awards for punitive damages and pain and suffering ("National Survey Shows that . . ." 2003).

With the reelection of George W. Bush to a second term in November 2004, coupled with an increased Republican majority in both the House and the Senate, the likelihood that Congress would pass damage cap legislation seemed to increase. Given the strong opposition from Democrats in the Senate, it remains to be seen whether such legislation will become a reality. Democrats have countered the push to cap damage awards by introducing legislation aimed at lowering physicians' malpractice premiums by targeting the insurance industry. A bill introduced by Senators Patrick Leahy (D-VT) and Edward Kennedy (D-MA) would partly remove the antitrust exemption that applied to insurers. The bill would ban price fixing, bid rigging, and market allocations in providing malpractice insurance ("Senate Dems Offer Alternative Approach to Malpractice" 2005).

Sage (2004) has argued for two avenues of federal action with respect to medical liability reform: (1) the federal government should support state-based malpractice reforms designed to replace litigation with a more rational system for reducing injury and compensating the victims; (2) the federal government should engage in a comprehensive restructuring of malpractice claims involving Medicare and Medicaid patients. Medicare-led reform would be especially advantageous, because the program already has an established system of administrative adjudication. According to Sage (2004), this would help malpractice reform on the national policy agenda and it could set the standard for the rest of the health care system.

Medical Liability Reforms at the State Level

Most of the action in the area of medical liability reform has been at the state level. Reforms have ranged from alternative liability systems, such as no-fault, to legislative reforms designed to improve the performance of the current fault-based system.

No-Fault Liability Systems: Florida and Virginia

The states of Virginia and Florida in the late 1980s established a no-fault compensation system for birth-related injuries. The Virginia law, called the Birth-Related Neurological Injury Compensation Act, went into effect on January 1, 1988. The Florida law, which went into effect on January 1, 1989, is also called the Birth-Related Neurological Injury Compensation Act (NICA). Both laws provide for compensation for severe birth-related neurological injuries caused by medical care, regardless of fault or negligence of the health care provider. Both laws allow physicians to choose whether they want to participate in the no-fault plan. In Florida, hospitals are required to participate. Part of the funding for the program comes from levies on physicians and hospitals and assessment on insurers writing other lines of insurance in the state (Danzon 1991). Doctors in Florida challenged the fees placed on them in the court in February 1992; however, the court ruled that the fees did not violate doctors' constitutional rights. In Virginia, the Virginia Medical Society was successful in getting the State Assembly to pass a bill that requires the state to suspend physician assessment any time the compensation fund is adequately funded for birth-related injuries (Larkin 1990; Meyer 1991a, b).

The two laws are similar in many respects. A claimant files a petition with a commission. A medical advisory board composed of physicians evaluates the merits of the claims and files a response within thirty days (in Virginia) or forty-five days (in Florida). The commission is required to hold a hearing within 120 days from the time of the filing of the petition. The commission determines whether the injury is a birth-related neurological injury. The infant is awarded compensation if the commission concludes that the injury suffered by the infant falls within the law. Any amount received from the collateral source is deducted from the compensation award. The commission's decision is final.

Very few states have adopted a no-fault system of compensation for very specific types of medical injuries, as Florida and Virginia have. The usefulness of such a no-fault system of compensation based on available evidence in these two states is questionable. In Florida, the law did help alleviate the crisis of lack of availability of malpractice insurance. For example, 90 percent of all obstetricians in Florida were participating in the program in 1993, and the medical malpractice premium rates for obstetricians had also declined significantly (Bilodeau 1991; Dickenson 1994). In Virginia, the number of obstetricians participating in the no-fault compensation plan had jumped to 96 percent by September 1992. On the negative side, both states have experienced many difficulties with their plans. In Virginia, injury definition is so narrow that very few birth-related injuries fall within the definition, making very few victims eligible to file a claim under such a plan. For example, between 1988 and 1994, a total of only eight claims were filed. Of the eight claims, six were accepted for compensation. In Florida by February 1994 only eighty-nine claims were filed, of which twenty-seven were accepted and paid. However, it is important to remember that since the statute of limitations is seven years, final numbers may be different

(Patel 1995). Another analysis of the Florida NICA program, after it was in operation for five years, gave it passing, if not exemplary, marks and concluded that the evidence from Florida was inconclusive as to whether a broad no-fault-based system is a good replacement for the current fault-based system (Horwitz and Brennan 1995).

Medical Practice Guidelines

Several states, including Maine, Florida, and Maryland, passed health care legislation that included provisions mandating the development of medical practice guidelines in certain specialty areas. Maine has incorporated into state law twenty practice guidelines in four specialties: anesthesiology, emergency medicine, obstetrics, and gynecology. Florida's legislation requires the state agency for health care administration to develop practice guidelines that are intended to reduce unnecessary variations in the delivery of medical treatment and to improve the quality of care. Maryland's legislation calls for a fifteen-member advisory committee to propose practice guidelines for medical specialties. The State Human Resources Planning Commission makes final determination on which guidelines to adopt (Rinella 1995).

Other Legislative Reforms

In response to the medical malpractice "crisis" of the 1970s, 1980s, and the 2000s, many state governments passed a variety of reforms. It is impossible to discuss each and every action taken by a variety of state governments with all types of subtle variations and differences. Thus, we will discuss only some of the major actions taken by a significant number of states and whether these actions have been effective or not. The American Tort Reform Association has provided data on tort reforms enacted by state governments since 1986 (see Table 7.1). According to the National Association of Mutual Insurance Companies (NAMIC), the majority of tort reform laws passed address five areas of tort reform: joint and several liability reform, collateral source rule, product liability, punitive damages, and noneconomic damages ("NAMIC Report Details State Reform Efforts . . ." 2004).

Most of the reforms adopted by state governments are legislative reforms designed to address specific problems or criticisms of the current tort system. For example, by December 31, 2004, thirty-one states had placed a cap on punitive damage awards, thirty-nine states had passed joint and several liability reforms, while eighteen states had placed a cap on noneconomic damage awards (see Table 7.1).

According to the National Conference of State Legislatures (NCSL), thirty-nine states have introduced over 300 bills to address the medical liability insurance situation. In 2005, Maryland and Ohio completed work on medical malpractice reforms enacted in special legislative sessions in December 2004. In February 2005, Georgia passed a comprehensive reform. Similarly, in March 2005, Missouri passed a medical malpractice reform that puts a limit of $350,000 on noneconomic damages in medical liability cases ("Medical Malpractice Tort Reform:

Table 7.1

Tort Reforms Adopted by States Since 1986 (as of December 31, 2004)

Nature of reform	Number of states that have adopted such have reforms
Joint and several liability reform	39
Punitive damage reform	31
Reform of collateral source rule	23
Noneconomic damage reform	18
Product liability reform	15
Prejudgment interest	14
Class action reform	8
Jury service reform	7
Attorney retention sunshine reform	5
Appeal bond reform	31

Source: American Tort Reform Association. Online at www.atra.org.

Background" 2005). Punitive damages are limited to the greater of $500,000 or five times the net amount of the judgment awarded to the plaintiff against the defendant. Finally, under the reform, joint and several liability applies only to defendants 51 percent or more at fault in all cases (O'Dell 2005). In 2004, the Mississippi legislature passed comprehensive tort reform legislation that is considered by many to be a model for the nation. The law caps general business/tort action at $1 million, caps noneconomic damages in medical/health-related actions at $500,000, caps punitive damages to a sliding net-worth scale, and eliminates joint and several liability by replacing it with a pure several liability standard under which a defendant only pays for his share of a fault (Ross 2004). New Jersey, Ohio, and Oklahoma also passed reform measures tightening expert witness requirements and creating funds to help offset rising medical malpractice insurance premiums (Albert 2004). The appendix provides major provisions of current state medical malpractice liability laws.

Effectiveness of Tort Reforms

How effective have these state tort reforms been? Of course, it is too early to evaluate the success or failure of most recent tort reforms passed during the early 2000s. However, the available evidence regarding reforms passed during the 1970s and 1980s points to mixed results. With respect to practice guidelines, the jury is still out.

Practice Guidelines

Practice guidelines are generally developed to assist health care providers, especially physicians, in making clinical decisions regarding treatment choices, appropriate use of tests, and so on. How successful practice guidelines become ultimately depends on how courts use and interpret them. For medical practice guidelines to be admitted in a medical negligence case against a physician, the general standard of care required of a physician in a given clinical setting must be an issue. Furthermore, the proponents of the guidelines are required to establish that the guidelines are probative of a fact of consequence. This generally requires expert medical testimony. Once the guidelines have been admitted into evidence, they do not constitute a predetermined standard of care that a court is forced to apply. The court is free to consider other evidence regarding what the standard of care should be. Furthermore, studies also show that physicians often do not comply with the guidelines, and the compliance rate is estimated to be slightly over 50 percent. Medical practice guidelines have not been in existence for a long period of time and as a result there currently is not a great deal of information available on how courts use these guidelines. More experience with medical practice guidelines is needed before one can make any judgment about their effectiveness (Hyams, Shapiro, and Brennan 1996; Rinella 1995).

Caps on Jury Awards

With regard to the effectiveness of many of the legislative reforms, the results are again mixed. On the positive side, limits on noneconomic damages showed some promise in reducing the number of claims filed as well as severity of claims. For example, in the state of Ohio, payment of medical malpractice claims declined from 3.7 percent prior to the enactment of a cap to 2.9 percent after the adoption of a cap on noneconomic damages. Similarly, Patricia Danzon found that a cap on noneconomic damages reduced claim severity 23 percent on average over the decade in which she studied claims (Danzon 1991).

California was one of the earliest states to impose a ceiling of $250,000 for noneconomic damages through the California Medical Injury Compensation Reform Act of 1975. Technically a jury can award more, but after the verdict the judge limits the award. The law also capped attorneys' fees on a sliding scale. According to recent analysis, California's tort reform has reduced awards in malpractice trials by an average of 30 percent, while the payments to plaintiffs' lawyers have dropped 60 percent ("Medical Malpractice Law Gets Results in Calif." 2004).

However, another study found strong evidence that the impact of the cap was distributed inequitably across different types of injuries, raising fundamental questions about the fairness of imposing fixed caps on jury awards (Studdert, Yang, and Mello 2004).

Some recent evidence seems to suggest that the insurance crisis is less acute in states that have carried out tort reforms. States with realistic limits on noneconomic damages are faring much better compared to states that have not placed any limits on jury awards. For example, combined average premium increases have been in the range of 12 to 15 percent in states with limits of $250,000 or $350,000 on noneconomic damages, compared to 44 percent in states without caps (U.S. Department of Health and Human Services 2002). Another study also found that caps on awards adopted by several states were associated with lower insurance premiums. Premiums in states with a cap on awards were 17.1 percent lower compared to states without caps on jury awards (Thorpe 2004).

However, another study that examined the insurance data in Texas between 1988 and 2002 found no link between rising medical malpractice insurance premium rates and the frequency of claims paid or the amount of jury awards. Texas implemented a $250,000 cap on noneconomic damages in malpractice lawsuits in 2003. The study found that the median jury award for plaintiffs who won malpractice lawsuits in 2002 was about $300,593—about the same as the median jury award in the 1990s ("Study Doubting Link Between Malpractice Premium Rates . . ." 2005). An analysis of comprehensive datasets of jury verdicts of 1992, 1996, and 2001 in counties in twenty-two states also found that an imposition of caps on noneconomic damages had no statistically significant effect on overall compensatory damages in medical malpractice jury verdicts or trial court judgments (Sharkey 2005).

Caps on noneconomic damages have also faced legal hurdles. They were declared unconstitutional under state constitutions in Alabama, Florida, New Hampshire, Ohio, North Dakota, and Texas, and have been challenged in other state courts (Health Coalition on Liability and Access 1997a, b; Magleby 1995).

Similarly, punitive damage caps were declared unconstitutional under the state constitution in Alabama and have faced challenges in other courts. Periodic payment schedules were declared unconstitutional in Arizona, New Hampshire, and Ohio. Statutes of limitations were declared unconstitutional in Arizona and New Hampshire. The modification of the collateral source rule and the establishment of a contingency fee schedule for lawyers were declared unconstitutional under the state constitution in New Hampshire (Depperschmidt 1992; Health Coalition on Liability and Access 1997a, b; Ross 1997; Wall 1997). Most of the court challenges have been raised with respect to individual rights, right to a jury trial, and due process, among other issues. More court challenges are likely to follow.

Review of the empirical literature suggests that tort reforms have encouraged plaintiffs to drop more of the claims filed. Yet, only limiting contingency fees and modifying the collateral source rule increases the likelihood of settlement. Thus, limiting contingency fees and modifying collateral source rules are two promising reforms to reduce litigation costs (Hughes and Snyder 1989). On the other hand, some studies have concluded that efforts to reform medical malpractice laws have not resulted in reduced medical costs or improved care. Even when cost savings are realized, they are not passed on to consumers (Wencl and Brizzolara 1996).

In summary, medical malpractice reforms were undertaken during the malpractice insurance crises of the 1970s, 1980s, and, more recently, the early 2000s. However, evidence regarding the effectiveness of these reforms remains inconclusive due to varying and often contradictory empirical findings. Despite high hopes and good intentions, these reforms have often failed to produce long-lasting positive results. As Hyman (2002, 1654) has suggested, "Medical malpractice reform has long been a graveyard for high hopes and good intentions."

Medical Liability, Managed Care, Enterprise Liability, and ERISA

There has been a dramatic increase in the number of persons enrolled in managed care organizations (MCOs), such as HMOs and PPOs, in the last twenty years (see chapters 3, 4, and 9). Dramatic increases in health care costs to the government, consumers, and businesses have forced them to look for alternative methods for delivering health care as compared to the traditional methods. The competitive environment of managed care has forced hospitals and MCOs to become economically more efficient. This shift from traditional fee-for-service plans to prepaid group health plans has raised some troubling questions and concerns about medical practice and medical liability.

One of the most important issues has to do with how managed care is changing the nature of medical practice and what impact it has on medical liability. As a result of managed care, more and more physicians are losing their professional autonomy and finding themselves working for a hospital or a managed care entity such as an HMO or a PPO. Many doctors are now employees of MCOs or of group practices. MCOs control patients' access to health care by requiring referrals to specialists, which are made only through primary care physicians, who act as "gatekeepers."

Increasingly, medical malpractice lawsuits are being filed against MCOs or hospitals rather than individual physicians (Brienza 1997). The emergence of managed care and capitation has created additional grounds for shifting physician liability for medical malpractice to institutions such as hospitals and MCOs. This has led some to argue in favor of establishment of an enterprise liability. For example, Mello and Brennan (2002) propose that hospitals should voluntarily adopt a system of no-fault enterprise liability for care provided by hospitals and affiliated physicians. The idea of enterprise liability was also included as part of President Clinton's health reform plan in 1993. Similarly, Kilcullen (1996) has argued that individual physicians and the HMOs that dictate the parameters of medical practice are part of a single enterprise that affects patient care. Thus, enterprise liability should be an essential component of any form of managed care liability. Traditional tort law holds the individual physician liable, while enterprise liability shifts the liability burden to MCOs for malpractice. MCO strategies are often directed at the behavior of physicians and MCO oversight influences the clinical behavior of physicians (Studdert and Brennan 1997).

Liability of MCOs for negligence generally falls into two categories. *Direct liability* involves claims that seek to hold MCOs directly liable for negligence and generally center around two aspects of the MCO's work—utilization review and plan design. In such cases, the plaintiff sues on the grounds of negligent utilization review or on the grounds of general features of the health plan itself. Under vicarious liability, an individual or an entity is held to be legally liable for the acts of another if it can be shown that a special relationship existed between the two—for example, a relationship between a physician and an HMO (Studdert and Brennan 1997). In short, direct liability applies when an MCO is the primary wrongdoer, while vicarious liability holds MCOs secondarily liable for errors made primarily by treating physicians (Hall and Agrawal 2003).

Wrongful denial of care or access is an increasingly common tort allegation aimed at health care organizations. Claims have also been made under the theories of vicarious liability for treatment exclusion or for denial of access or coverage. Sacrifice of quality medical care for cost savings can also result in liability (Penhallegon 1997; Robinson 1997).

One of the major hurdles in establishment of enterprise liability is ERISA, which was enacted by Congress in 1974 and designed to standardize the regulation of pension and benefit plans. In general, ERISA preempts the application of state law to employee benefit plans (Studdert and Brennan 1997). At the time of its passage ERISA preemption was a non-issue for health care provisions. However, the rise of managed care and MCOs put payers potentially within the reach of state laws governing medical care provisions (Bloche and Studdert 2004). ERISA's principal effect in the health care field has been to preempt state laws as they relate to any employee health benefit plans. Limiting states' abilities to deal with health plans was an unintended consequence of ERISA. One of the main effects of ERISA was to induce nearly all large employees to self-insure their health benefit plans (Havighurst 2000). The MCOs have tried to shield themselves from liability by invoking the protection of ERISA. The direct liability claims against MCOs that target plan design or utilization review activities must overcome a distinction between an MCO's administrative activities and the actual clinical care that caused the injury. Overall, such claims are more difficult to prove. Malpractice lawsuits that seek to hold MCOs indirectly (vicariously) liable are more common and have had more success in courts (Studdert and Brennan 1997).

According to Studdert and Brennan (1997), the courts have used three approaches in dealing with cases involving negligence claims against MCOs and ERISA preemption. In the first approach, courts have relied on the use of a distinction between the administrative role of the MCO and clinical autonomy of the physician with whom it contracts in deciding whether a MCO can be held liable for a claim of negligence. Under a second approach, courts have denied vicarious liability claims against HMOs on the ground that the MCO did not control the actions of physicians it contracted, that is, the relationship between the two was not one of control. Under the third approach, courts have preempted malpractice claims against MCOs completely by invoking the protections of ERISA.

During the early 1990s, federal courts tended to rule against state authority and favored a deregulatory approach to managed care. Accordingly, several district courts ruled that ERISA immunized workplace-based health plans against tort and contract action on grounds of wrongfully withholding or delaying authorization of care (Bloche and Studdert 2004). This led to the struggle over a patients' bill of rights at the federal level. This is discussed in the next section.

However, by 1995 the thinking of federal courts on the subject was beginning to shift. In the 1995 case of *New York State Conference of Blue Cross and Blue Shield Plans v. Travelers Ins. Co.*, the U.S. Supreme Court signaled a retreat from expansive ERISA protection by ruling that nothing in the language of ERISA suggested that

Congress intended to displace general health care, which historically has been a function of local governments (Bloche and Studdert 2004). Since then, federal courts seems to have shown an interest in vicarious liability as a viable approach for holding MCOs accountable for malpractice. In three federal court decisions in 1995 *(Dukes v. U.S. Health Care, Rice v. Panchal,* and *Pacificare v. Burrage)*, courts ruled that ERISA may not completely preempt vicarious liability claims against MCOs for the negligence of an affiliated physician (Studdert and Brennan 1997). In the 2002 case of *Rush Prudential HMO v. Moran* the U.S. Supreme Court ruled that states can allow patients to seek an independent ruling when their HMOs deny them surgeries or other treatment. This was a major boost for state reforms designed to protect patients from overzealous cost-cutting efforts by MCOs (Appleby and Biskupic 2002; Bloche and Studdert 2004).

Since the 1990s, forty-seven states have enacted some versions of a patients' bill of rights that have attempted to protect patients against managed care abuses. Since 1997, ten states have enacted some form of legislation that imposes liability on MCOs, out of concern that MCOs are not sufficiently held accountable for personal injuries caused by their wrongful actions or inactions (Hall and Agrawal 2003). It is clear that ERISA preemption has been considerably eroded or diluted due to various federal court decisions (Hall and Agrawal 2003).

However, the U.S. Supreme Court, in its decision in the 2004 case of *Aetna v. Davila,* seems to reverse this trend. Juan Davila had sued his HMO in state court because it had refused to cover certain medical services in violation of its duty to "exercise ordinary care" under the Texas Health Care Liability Act (THCLA) and this refusal had led him to suffer certain injuries. The HMO (Aetna) asked that the case be removed to the federal court, arguing that the case should be governed under ERISA rather than the Texas law because ERISA takes precedence over any state law dealing with the same subject matter. The case was removed to the federal court. The federal district court ruled against Davila. However, the fifth circuit Court of Appeals reversed the district court ruling. The case was appealed by Aetna to the U.S. Supreme Court. The U.S. Supreme Court ruled unanimously that Congress intended ERISA to provide a uniform system for regulating retirement plans and benefits and, if a state law conflicts with ERISA, ERISA takes precedence over state law. Thus, Davila could not sue his HMO Aetna in state court because Davila's state law claims were preempted by ERISA.

Federal Patients' Bill of Rights

We noted in an earlier work (Patel and Rushefsky 2002) that during one of the presidential debates between Vice President Al Gore (the Democratic candidate) and Texas Governor George W. Bush (the Republican candidate), Bush was asked whether he supported a patients' bill of rights. He equivocated, noting that Texas has such a law on the books (Bloche 2004; Patel and Rushefsky 2002). However, when the law was challenged, in *Aetna v. Davila,* in the Supreme Court, the Bush administration argued that the law should be overturned and the ERISA preemption maintained. As mentioned above, the Court ruled that the ERISA exemption remains and employer managed care plans cannot be sued (Jost 2004).

While the states have acted to protect the rights of patients in MCOs, they have been, as discussed above, limited by ERISA. Only the federal government could regulate such plans. Beginning in 1997, a small number of patients' rights bills were introduced in Congress. Senator Edward Kennedy (D-MA) and Congressman John Dingell (D-MI) offered the first bill. President Clinton established a commission that same year and it made its recommendations in 1998 (Patel and Rushefsky 2002).

Advocacy groups such as Families USA supported patients' bill of rights laws, while groups such as the American Association of Health Plans (AAHP) opposed it. AAHP offered an alternative, called "Putting Patients First," that was to be a voluntary alternative to legislation on the part of MCOs (Patel and Rushefsky 2002).

Patients' bill of rights laws passed the House and the Senate in 1998–2000, though the versions differed significantly. A 2001 Senate version of the bill, known as the Kennedy-McCain-Edwards bill, was stymied by a filibuster. The House bill was weakened at the request of President George W. Bush and no subsequent legislation has appeared.

Conclusion

This chapter has examined the complex but very important issue of medical liability and malpractice in the American health care system. We have traced the origins of the concept of tort from early history to its development and refinement in Great Britain. British common law concepts and practices were adopted in America's legal system with very few modifications.

One point that should be emphasized is that whereas, in almost all federal systems in the world, tort is a federal responsibility and is covered under federal law, the United States remains one of the few exceptions. In the United States it is accepted that tort is a state responsibility. Even though occasionally the federal government has passed federal laws dealing with some aspect of medical liability, a 200-year history has established state sovereignty over the subject matter.

The crisis in the health insurance market of the 1970s, 1980s, and 2000s, accompanied by many criticisms of the current tort system, stimulated a nationwide debate and discussion of reform of the current tort medical liability system. Attempts at fundamental and comprehensive reform of the U.S. health care system, including medical liability reform, have met with little success at the federal level since the 1980s. However, during the same period a considerable number of reform measures have been adopted at the state level. These legislative reforms have produced mixed results. Their record in controlling medical malpractice costs and malpractice insurance premium costs, in reducing the number of malpractice claims filed, and so on, is very weak, suggesting only minor successes. Furthermore, some of these reforms have been declared unconstitutional under the state constitutions in many states. We are unlikely to know the overall success or failure of these reforms until a considerable amount of time has passed and many of the constitutional conflicts surrounding these reforms have been settled. The dramatic increase in the number of persons enrolled in managed care health plans is significantly changing the nature of medical practice and raising questions about the future of medical liability. The concept of enterprise liability, holding health care organizations liable for the negligent behavior or incompetence of their physicians, rather than holding individual physicians liable, remains a viable alternative to current system.

References

Abramson, Elliot M. 1989–90. "The Medical Malpractice Imbroglio: A Non-Adversarial Suggestion." *Kentucky Law Review* 78: 293–310.

Adrianson, Alex. 2003. "Why Doctors are Quitting Medical Practice." *Consumers' Research Magazine* 86, no. 6 (June): 10–15.

Albert, Tanya. 2001. "Malpractice Awards Pushing Insurance Premiums Higher." March 5. American Medical Association. Online at www.ama-assn.org/amednews/site/access.htm

———. 2004. "3 States Pass Tort Reform: Others Still Waiting." June 14. Online at www .ama-assn.org/amednews.

"AMA Adds Massachusetts to Medical Liability Crisis List." 2004. *Medical Liability Monitor* 29, no. 7 (July): 3.

American College of Legal Medicine. 1988. *Legal Medicine: Legal Dynamics of Medical Encounters*. St. Louis, Mo.: C.V. Mosby.

Andrews, L.B. 1993. "Medical Error and Patient Claiming in a Hospital Setting." *Working Paper 9316*, American Bar Association.

Appleby, Julie, and Joan Biskupic. 2002. "Supreme Court Rules Against HMOs: Court Affirms States' Right to Review Coverage Decisions." *USA Today*, June 21.

Aspden, Philip; Janet M. Corrigan; Jullie Wolcott; Shari M. Erickson, eds. 2004. *Patient Safety: Achieving a New Standard for Care*. Washington, D.C.: National Academy Press.

Atkinson, Nolan R., Jr. 1994. "How the National Practitioner Data Bank Affects Medical Malpractice Clients." *The Practical Litigator,* no. 1, January.

Baily, Mary A. 1990. "The Administrative Approach to Medical Malpractice Disputes." *Courts, Health Science and the Law* 1, no. 1: 29–34.

Banja, John D. 2005. *Medical Errors and Medical Narcissism*. Sudbury, Mass.: Jones and Bartlett Publishers.

Berg, Robert N. 1994. "Malpractice Reform Under President Clinton: Through the Looking Glass." *The Journal of the Medical Association of Georgia* 83, no. 6: 364–66.

Berger, Mitchell S. 1990. "Following the Doctor's Orders—Caps on Non-Economic Damages in Medical Malpractice Cases." *Rutgers Law Review* 23, no. 1: 173–98.

Berntsen, Karin J. 2005. "Looking Beyond Tort Reform Toward Safer Healthcare Systems." *Journal of Nursing Care Quality* 20, no. 1 (January–March): 9–12.

Bilodeau, A. 1991. "Jury Still Out on Plan That Pays for Infants Injured at Birth." *South Florida Business Journal* 11, no. 43: 3.

Blackman, N.S., and C.P. Bailey. 1990. *Liability in Medical Malpractice: A Reference for Physicians*. New York: Harwood Academic Publishers.

Bloche, Gregg M. 2004. Back to the '90s—The Supreme Court Immunizes Managed Care." *New England Journal of Medicine* 351, no. 13 (September 23): 1277–1279.

Bloche, Gregg M., and David M. Studdert. 2004. "A Quiet Revolution: Law as an Agent of Health System Change." *Health Affairs* 23, no. 2 (March–April): 29–42.

Blumstein, James F. 1996. "A Perspective on Federalism and Medical Malpractice." *Yale Journal on Regulation*, (Supplemental Issue): 411–28.

Bovbjerg, Randall R. 1990. "Reforming a Proposed Tort Reform: Improving on the American Medical Association's Proposed Administrative Tribunal for Medical Malpractice." *Courts, Health Science and the Law* 1, no. 1: 19–28.

Bovbjerg, Randall R. et al. 1991. "Juries and Justice: Are Malpractice and Other Personal Injuries Created Equal?" *Law and Contemporary Problems* 54, no. 1–2 (Winter–Spring): 5–42.

Bowen, Otis. 1987. "Congressional Testimony on Senate Bill S.1804." *Journal of the American Medical Association* 257: 816.

Brennan, Troyen A. 1995. "Medical Malpractice Reform: The Current Proposals." *Journal of General Internal Medicine* 10, no. 4 (April 1): 211–18.

Brennan, Troyen A., and Philip K. Howard. 2004. "Health the Law, Then Health Care." *Washington Post*, January 25.

Brienza, Julie. 1997. "Changes Ahead for Lawyers Who Handle Medical Malpractice, Insurers Study Says." *Trial* 33, no. 10: 84.

Britton: Homicide. 1864. Ed. and trans. by F.M. Nichols. London: Macmillan.

Brostoff, Steve. 1993. "Eliminate Defensive Medicine, Save $36B: Study." *National Underwriter Life and Health-Financial Services Edition* 6 (February 8): 5.

Burns, Chester R. 1969. "Malpractice Suits in American Medicine before the Civil War." *Bulletin of the History of Medicine* 43: 41–56.

"Can Malpractice Be Kept Out of the Court?" 1994. *Medical Economics* 71, no. 16 (August 22): 111.

Cantor, Joel C., and Walter J. Wadlington. 1994. "Addressing the Malpractice Problem: The Robert Wood Johnson Foundation's Programs." *Health Affairs* 13, no. 5 (Winter): 229–40.

Cecil, Joe S. et al. 1991. "Citizen Comprehension of Difficult Issues: Lessons from Civil Jury Trials." *American University Law Review* 40: 727, 749.

Chesebro, Kenneth I. 1993. "Galileo's Retort: Peter Huber's Junk Scholarship." *American University Law Review* 42, no. 5: 1637–1726.

Clayton, Ellen W.; Gerald B. Hickson; Penny B. Githens; and Frank A. Sloan. 1993. "Doctor-Patient Relationships." In *Suing for Medical Malpractice*, ed. Frank A. Sloan, Penny B. Githens, Ellen Wright Clayton, David F. Partlett, Gerald B. Hickson, and Stephen S. van Wert, 50–71. Chicago: University of Chicago Press.

Cohn, Jonathan. 2004. "Trial and Error." *New Republic* 231, no. 3 (July 19): 14–15.

Congressional Budget Office. 1994. Office of Technology Assessment, U.S. Congress. *Defensive Medicine and Medical Malpractice*. Publication OTA-H-602. Washington, D.C.: U.S. Government Printing Office.

Daniels, Stephen. 1989. "Verdicts in Medical Malpractice Cases: Shedding Light on the Issues." *Trial* 25, no. 5 (May 1): 23–30.

———. 1990. "Tracing the Shadow of the Law: Jury Verdicts in Medical Malpractice Cases." *Justice System Journal* 14, no. 1: 4–39.

Danzon, Patricia M. 1984. "The Frequency and Severity of Medical Malpractice Claims." *Journal of Law and Economics* 27 (1984): 115–48.

———. 1985. *Medical Malpractice: Theory, Evidence, and Public Policy.* Cambridge, Mass.: Harvard University Press.

———. 1990. "The 'Crisis' in Medical Malpractice: A Comparison of Trends in the United States, Canada, the United Kingdom and Australia." *Law, Medicine and Health Care* 18, no. 1–2 (Spring/Summer): 48–58.

———. 1991. "Liability for Medical Malpractice." *Journal of Economic Perspective* 5, no. 3 (Summer): 51–69.

———. 1994. "Tort Reform: The Case of Medical Malpractice." *Oxford Review of Economic Policy* 10, no. 1 (Spring): 84–98.

De Ville, Kenneth A. 1990. *Medical Malpractice in Nineteenth Century America: Origins and Legacy*. New York: New York University Press.

Depperschmidt, Thomas O. 1992. "The Legality of State Limitations on Medical Malpractice Tort Damage Awards." *Hospital and Health Services Administration* 37, no. 3: 417–26.

Derbyshire, Robert C. 1969. *Medical Licensure and Discipline in the United States*. Westport, Conn.: Greenwood Press.

Dickenson, L.B. 1994. *Update on the Florida Birth-Related Neurological Injury Compensation Association: Internal Report*. Tallahassee, Fla.: Neurological Injury Compensation Association.

"Doctors and Other Health Professionals Report that Fear of Malpractice has a Big, and Mostly Negative, Impact on Medical Practice, Unnecessary Defensive Medicine, and Openness in Discussing Medical Errors." 2003. *Health Care News* 3, no. 2 (February 7): 1–5. Online at www.kff.org/kaiserpolls.

Eastburn, Larry. 1999. "Medical Malpractice Update." *Modern Medicine* 67, no. 7 (July): 58–62.

Editorial. 1991. "Bush Plans a Good First Step on Tort Reform." *American Medical News* 34, no. 9 (March 4): 19.

Farber, Henry S., and Michelle J. White. 1991. "Medical Malpractice: An Empirical Examination of the Litigation Process." *RAND Journal of Economics* 22, no. 2 (Summer): 199–217.

Ferrari, Herbert A. 1990. "Suing for Restitution: The Medical Malpractice Crisis." *USA Today*, January 1.

Fielding, Stephen L. 1995. "Changing Medical Practice and Medical Malpractice Claims." *Social Problems* 42, no. 1 (February 1): 38–55.

Findlay, Steven, ed. 2000. *Reducing Medical Errors and Improving Patient Safety: Success Stories from the Front Lines of Medicine*. The National Coalition on Health Care and the Institute for Healthcare Improvement. Online at www.ihi.org/ihi/uploads/medical_errorsACT.pdf.

Flexner, A. 1910. *Medical Education in the United States and Canada*, Bulletin No. 4. New York: The Carnegie Foundation for the Advancement of Teaching.

Fournier, Gary M., and Melayne M. Mcinnes. 1997. "Medical Board Regulation of Physician Licensure: Is Excessive Malpractice Sanctioned?" *Journal of Regulatory Economics* 12, no. 2: 113–26.

Gadd, Cyril J. 1965. *Hammurabi and the End of His Dynasty*, rev. ed. (*Ancient History*, vol. 2, chap. 5). New York: Cambridge University Press.

Gallup, Cynthia L. 1989. "Can No-Fault Compensation of Impaired Infants Alleviate the Malpractice Crisis in Obstetrics?" *Journal of Health Politics, Policy and Law* 14, no. 4 (Winter): 691–718.

Gearon, Christopher J. 2001. "Your Health: Unmasking Unsafe Doctors." *AARP Bulletin Online*. Online at www.aarp.org/bulletin/yourhealth/articles/a2003-08-07-unmasking.html.

Geisel, Jerry. 1991. "Bush Budget Proposes Malpractice Reform." *Business Insurance* 25, no. 6 (February 11): 1, 26.

Gibson, Rosemary, and Janardan Prasad Singh 2003. *Wall of Silence: The Untold Story of the Medical Mistakes that Kill and Injure Millions of Americans*. Washington, D.C.: LifeLine Press.

Gordon, V.M. 1970. "The Origin, Basis and Nature of Medical Malpractice Liability." *Connecticut Medicine* 35: 73–77.

Greene, Risa B. 1996. "Federal Legislative Proposals for Medical Malpractice Reform: Treating the Symptom or Effecting a Cure?" *Cornell Journal of Law and Public Policy* 4, no. 2: 563–607.

Hall, Mark A., and Gail Agrawal. 2003. "The Impact of State Managed Care Liability Statutes: Despite Some Erosion, ERISA Preemption Remains a Hill that Plaintiffs Must Climb." *Health Affairs* 22, no. 5 (September–October): 138–45.

Hart, Bruce G., Jr., 1990. "Medical Malpractice Protection under the Federal Tort Claims Act: Protecting Both Physicians and Claimants." *Fordham Law Review* vol. 58, no. 5: 1107–20.

Harvard Medical Practice Study. 1990. *Patients, Doctors, and Lawyers: Medical Injury, Malpractice Litigation, and Patient Compensation in New York.* Cambridge, Mass.: Harvard University Press.

Harway, Robert A. 1992. "'Hired Guns' Isn't a Synonym for 'Medical Whore,'" *Medical Economics* 69, no. 6 (March 16): 41–45.

Hassan, Mahmud. 1991. "How Profitable is Medical Malpractice Insurance?" *Inquiry* 28, no. 1 (Spring): 74–80.

Hatlie, Martin J., and Susan E. Sheridan. 2003. "The Medical Liability Crisis of 2003: Must We Squander the Chance to Put Patients First?" *Health Affairs* 22, no. 4 (July–August): 37–40.

Havighurst, Clark C. 1975. "Medical Adversity Insurance: Has Its Time Come?" *Duke Law Journal* 1975, no. 6: 1233–1280.

———. 2000. "American Health Care and the Law—We Need to Talk." *Health Affairs* 19, no. 4 (July–August): 84–106.

Havighurst, Clark C., and Tancredi, Laurence R. 1974. "'Medical Adversity Insurance'—A No-Fault Approach to Medical Malpractice and Quality Insurance." *Insurance Law Journal,* no. 613: 69–100.

Health Coalition on Liability and Access. 1997a. *HCLA Fact Sheet: Non-Economic Damage Cap.* Online at www.hcla.org.

———. 1997b. *HCLA Fact Sheet: State Constitutional Impediments.* Online at www.hcla.org.

Heil, Emily; Jill Smallen; and Cherlie Mitchell. 2004. "Malpractice Lawsuit Curbs Blocked Again." *National Journal* 36, no. 15 (April 10): 1117.

"Higher Health Care Costs Blamed on Prescription Drugs, Medical Malpractice and Increased Hospital Costs." 2002. *Health Care Poll* 1, no. 4 (December 26): 1–3. Online at www.kff.org.

Horwitz, Jill, and Troyen A. Brennan. 1995. "No Fault Compensation for Medical Injury: A Case Study." *Health Affairs* 14, no. 4 (Winter): 164–79.

Howard, Philip K. 1996. *The Death of Common Sense: How Law Is Suffocating America.* New York: Warner Books.

———. 2002. *The Collapse of the Common Good: How America's Lawsuit Culture Undermines Our Freedom.* New York: Ballantine Books.

———. 2003. "Legal Malpractice." *Wall Street Journal,* January 27.

Huber, Peter W. 1988. *The Legal Revolution and Its Consequences.* New York: Basic Books.

———. 1991. *Galileo's Revenge: Junk Science in the Courtroom.* New York: Basic Books.

Hughes, James W., and Edward A. Snyder. 1989. "Evaluating Medical Malpractice Reforms." *Contemporary Policy Issues* 7, no. 2: 83–98.

Hutkins, Allen K. 1989–90. "Resolving the Medical Malpractice Crisis: Alternatives to Litigation." *Journal of Law and Health* 4, no. 1: 21–55.

Hyams, Andrew L.; David D. Shapiro; and Troyen A. Brennan. 1996. "Medical Practice Guidelines in Malpractice Litigation: An Early Retrospective." *Journal of Health Politics, Policy and Law* 21, no. 2: 289–313.

Hyman, David A. 2002. "Medical Malpractice and the Tort System: What Do We Know and What (If Anything) Should We Do About It?" *Texas Law Review* 80, no. 7 (June): 1639–55.

Hyman, David A., and Charles Silver. 2004. "Believing Six Impossible Things: Medical Malpractice and Legal Fear." *Harvard Journal of Law and Public Policy* 28, no. 1 (Fall): 107–18.

"Incidence of Adverse Events and Negligence in Hospitalized Patients." (Parts I and II). 1991. *New England Journal of Medicine* 324, no. 5 (February 7): 370–84.

Institute of Medicine. 2000. *To Err Is Human: Building a Safer Health System.* Washington, D.C.: National Academy Press.

Jasper, Margaret C. 1996. *The Law of Medical Malpractice.* Dobbs Ferry, N.Y.: Oceana Publications.

Johnson, Kirk B.; Carter G. Phillips; David Orentlicher; and Martin J. Hatlie. 1990. "The American Medical Association/Specialty Society Tort Reform Proposal: A Fault Based Administrative System." *Courts, Health Science and the Law* 1, no. 1: 6–18.

Jost, Kenneth. 2003. "Doctors Paying the Price for Progress." *Congressional Quarterly Weekly* 61, no. 11 (March 15): 648–49.

Jost, Timothy S. 2004. "The Supreme Court Limits Lawsuits Against Managed Care Organizations." *Health Affairs Web Exclusive*, August 11, W4-417–W4-426.

Kaiser Family Foundation, Agency for Healthcare Research and Quality, and Harvard School of Public Health. 2004. *National Survey of Consumers' Experiences with Patient Safety and Quality Information.* Publication # 7210. Online at www.kff.org.

Kapp, Marshall B. 1989. "Solving the Medical Malpractice Problem: Difficulties in Defining What Works." *Law, Medicine, and Health Care* 17, no. 2: 156–65.

———. 1994. "Medical Malpractice Reform as Part of Health Care Reform: 1994 Version." *The Florida Bar Journal* 68, no. 5: 28–34.

Kilcullen, Jack K. 1996. "Groping for the Reins: ERISA, HMO Malpractice, and Enterprise Liability." *American Journal of Law and Medicine* 22, no. 1: 7–51.

King, Josephine Y. 1992. "No-Fault Compensation for Medical Injuries." *Journal of Contemporary Health Law and Policy* 8, no. 201: 227–36.

Korcok, A. 1988. "I Will See You in Court: US Still Looking for Malpractice Cure." *Canadian Medical Association Journal* 138, no. 9: 846–47.

Landrigan, Christopher P; Jeffrey M. Rothchild; John W. Cronin; Rainu Kaushal; Elisabeth Burdick; Joel Katz; Craig M. Lilly; Peter H. Stone; Steven W. Lockley; David W. Bates; and Charles A. Czeisler. 2004. "Effect of Reducing Interns' Work Hours on Serious Medical Errors in Intensive Care Units." *New England Journal of Medicine* 351, no. 18 (October 28): 1838–48.

Larkin, Howard. 1990. "Firm to Offer Insurance with No-Fault Features." *American Medical News* 33, no. 24: 9–10.

Latz, Ronald S. 1989. "No-Fault Liability and Medical Malpractice: A Viability Analysis." *Journal of Legal Medicine* 10, no. 3: 479–525.

Levitats, Meron J. 1991. "How to Get Rid of the Hired Guns." *Medical Economics* 68, no. 4 (March 4): 21–28.

Liang, Bryan A. 1996. "Medical Malpractice: Do Physicians Have Knowledge of Legal Standards and Assess Cases as Juries Do?" *Roundtable* 3: 59–111.

Lieberman, Trudy. 2004. "Your Health: Fatal Mistakes." *AARP Bulletin Online.* Online at www.aarp.org/bulletin/yourhealth/Articles/a2004-10-27-fatal_mistakes.html.

Liebman, Carol B., and Chris Stern Hyman. 2004. "A Medication Skill Model to Manage Disclosure of Errors and Adverse Events to Patients." *Health Affairs* 23, no. 4 (July–August): 22–32.

Locke, Adrienne C. 1991. "Bush Unveils Malpractice Reform Proposal." *Business Insurance* 25, no. 20 (May 20): 3–4.

Lockley, Steven W; John W. Cronin; Erin E. Evans; Brian E. Cade; Clark, J. Lee; Christopher P. Landrigan; Jeffrey M. Rothschild; Joel T. Katz; Craig M. Lilly; Peter H. Stone; Daniel Aeschbach; and Charles A. Czeisler. 2004. "Effect of Reducing Interns' Weekly Work Hours on Sleep and Attentional Failures." *New England Journal of Medicine* 351, no. 18 (October 28): 1829–37.

Ludwig, William C. 1994. "The Medical Profession and the 'Health Care Crisis.'" *Ohio Lawyer* 8, no. 5 (September/October): 25–35.

Macchiaroli, Jean A. 1990. "Medical Malpractice Screening Panels: Proposed Model Legislation to Cure Judicial Ills." *George Washington Law Review* 58, no. 2: 181–260.

Magleby, James E. 1995. "The Constitutionality of Utah's Medical Malpractice Damages Cap under the Utah Constitution." *Journal of Contemporary Law* 21, no. 2: 217–58.

McCormick, Brian. 1993. "Study: Defensive Medicine Costs Nearly $10 Billion." *American Medical News* 36, no. 7 (February 15): 4–5.

McMillen, Scott R. 1996. "The Medical Malpractice Statute of Limitations: Some Answers and Some Questions." *Trial Lawyers Forum* 70, no. 2: 44–47.

McMullen, Andrew. 1990. "Comment: Mediation and Medical Malpractice Disputes: Potential Obstacles in the Traditional Lawyer's Perspective." *Journal of Dispute Resolution* 1990, no. 2: 371–86.

McNay, Don, and Thomas L. Gentry. 1997. "Structured Settlements and the Federally Supported Health Centers Assistance Act of 1995." *Trial Diplomacy Journal* 20, no. 3: 173–75.

McQuade, J.S. 1991. "The Medical Malpractice Crisis—Reflections on the Alleged Causes and Proposed Cures: Discussion Paper." *Journal of Royal Society of Medicine* 84 (July): 408–11.

"Medical Malpractice Awards Soar." 2004. *USA Today*, August 4.

"Medical Malpractice Award Trends: Believe Government Sources, Not Doctors." 2003. *Public Citizen*, January 14. Online at www.citizenorg.

"Medical Malpractice Law Gets Results in Calif." 2004. *Modern Health Care* 34, no. 29 (July 19): 33.

"Medical Malpractice Tort Reform: Background." 2005. August 31, National Conference of State Legislatures. Online at www.ncsl.org.

Mello, Michelle M., and Troyen A. Brennan. 2002. "Deterrence of Medical Errors: Theory and Evidence for Malpractice Reform." *Texas Law Review* 80, no.7 (June): 1628–31.

Mello, Michelle M.; David M. Studdert; Catherine M. DesRoches; Jordan Peugh; Kinga Zapert; Troyen A. Brennan; and William M. Sage. 2004. "Caring for Patients in a Malpractice Crisis: Physician Satisfaction and Quality of Care." *Health Affairs* 23, no. 4 (July–August): 42–53.

Menon, Jody W. 1995. "Adversarial Medical and Scientific Testimony and Lay Jurors: A Proposal for Medical Malpractice Reform." *American Journal of Law and Medicine* 21, nos. 2, 3: 281–300.

Meyer, Harris A. 1991a. "Doctors Fight Fees for No-Fault Patient Compensation." *American Medical News* 34, no. 46: 4.

———. 1991b. "Doctor Fee for No-Fault Patient Compensation Upheld." *American Medical News* 34, no. 46: 7.

Mitchell, Chester N., and Shona McDiarmid. 1988. "Medical Malpractice: A Challenge to Alternative Dispute Resolution." *CJLS/RCDS* 3: 227–45.

Monteleone, Michael J. 1994. "Trial Lawyers and the Health Care Crisis." *Ohio Lawyer* 8, no. 5 (September–October): 25–33.

Mullis, Jeffrey. 1995. "Medical Malpractice, Social Structure, and Social Control." *Sociological Forum* 10, no. 1 (March 1): 135–63.

"NAMIC Report Details State Tort Reform Effort." 2004. *Insurance Journal*, January 9. Online at www.insurancejournal.com.

"National Survey Shows That More Than Half of Adult Americans Support Medical Malpractice Reform." 2003. *Health Care Poll* 2, no. 2 (March 6): 1–4. Online at www.kff.org/kaiserpolls/.

O'Connell, Jeffrey. 1975. "No-Fault Insurance for Injuries Arising from Medical Treatment: A Proposal for Elective Coverage." *Emory Law Journal* 24, no. 1: 21–42.

O'Connell, Jeffrey, and C. Brian Kelly. 1987. *The Blame Game*. New York: Lexington.

O'Dell, Kathleen. 2005. "Blunt Signs Malpractice Litigation Reform." *Springfield News-Leader* (Missouri), March 29.

Olsen, Reed N. 1996. "The Reform of Medical Malpractice Law: Historical Perspectives." *American Journal of Economics and Sociology* 55, no. 3 (July): 257–75.

Ozar, David T. 1994."Malpractice and Presupposition of Medical Practice." *Annals of Health Law* 3, no. 1: 139–52.

Patel, Kant. 1995. "No-Fault Medical Liabililty in Virginia and Florida: A Preliminary Evaluation." *Evaluation and the Health Professions* 18, no. 2 (1995): 137–51.

Patel, Kant, and Mark Rushefsky. 2002. *Health Care Policy in an Age of New Technologies.* Armonk, N.Y.: M.E. Sharpe.

Paxton, Harry T. 1989. "Just How Heavy Is the Burden of Malpractice Premiums?" *Medical Economics* 66, no. 2 (January 16): 168–83.

———. 1998. "Which Practice Expenses Are Out of Control?" *Medical Economics* 75, no. 22 (November 6): 91–117.

Penhallegon, John R. 1997. "Emerging Physician and Organization Liability under Managed Health Care." *Defense Counsel Journal* 64, no. 3: 347–56.

Phillips, Carter G., and Paul E. Kalb. 1991. "Replacing the Tort System for Medical Malpractice." *Stanford Law and Policy Review* 91, no. 3 (Fall): 210–15.

"Politics Keeps Real Remedies for Medical Errors Off Radar." 2004. *USA Today*, September 14.

Quality Interagency Coordination Task Force. 2000. *Doing What Counts for Patient Safety: Federal Actions to Reduce Medical Errors and Their Impacts.* Washington, D.C.: Government Printing Office.

Rake, Buddy, and Bobby Thrasher. 1996. "Medical Malpractice Myths, Truths and Solutions." *Arizona Attorney* 32, no. 7: 21–27.

Rice, Berkeley. 1995. "Where Doctors Get Sued the Most." *Medical Economics* 72, no. 4 (February 27): 98–108.

Rinella, Lore. 1995. "The Use of Medical Practice Guidelines in Medical Malpractice Litigation—Should Practice Guidelines Define the Standard of Care?" *University of Missouri Kansas City Law Review* 64, no. 2: 337–55.

Robinson, Glen. 1991. "Rethinking the Allocation of Medical Malpractice Risks between Patients and Providers." *Law and Contemporary Problems*, 49, no. 2: 173–99.

Robinson, William T. 1997. "New Deep Pocket: Managed Care Entity Liable for Alleged Improper Denial of Access." *Defense Counsel Journal* 64, no. 3: 357–63.

Rosenthal, Marilyn M., and Kathleen M. Sutcliffe, eds. 2002. *Medical Error: What Do We Know? What Do We Do?* San Francisco: Jossey-Bass.

Ross, Charles. 2004. "Winning the Tort War in Mississippi: Keys for Success in Other States." American Tort Reform Association. Online at www.atra.org.

Ross, Jacqueline. 1997. "Will States Protect Us, Equally, from Damage Caps in Medical Malpractice Legislation?" *Indiana Law Review* 30, no. 2: 575–60.

Rustad, Michael, and Thomas Koenig. 1995. "Reconceptualizing Punitive Damages in Medical Malpractice: Targeting Amoral Corporations, Not 'Moral Monsters.'" *Rutgers Law Review* 47, no. 3 (Spring): 975–1083.

Sage, William M. 2003. "Medical Liability and Patient Safety." *Health Affairs* 22, no. 4 (July–August): 26–36.

———. 2004. "The Forgotten Third: Liability Insurance and the Medical Malpractice Crisis. *Health Affairs* 23, no. 4 (July–August): 10–21.

Sage, William M.; Kathleen E. Hastings; and Robert A. Berenson. 1994. "Enterprise Liability for Medical Malpractice and Health Care Quality Improvement." *American Journal of Law and Medicine* 20, nos. 1, 2: 1–28.

Schmidt, Winsor C.; D. Alex Heckert; and Alice A. Mercer. 1991. "Factors Associated with Medical Malpractice: Results from a Pilot Study." *Journal of Contemporary Health, Law and Policy* 7, no. 157: 157–82.

Schwartz, Gary T. 1996. "Considering the Proper Federal Role in American Tort Law." *Arizona Law Review* 38, no. 3: 917–51.

Schwartz, M.R. 1987. "Liability Crisis: The Physician's Viewpoint." In *Medical Malpractice: Tort Reform*, ed. J.E. Hammer and B.R. Jennings, 15–28. Memphis: University of Tennessee Press.

"Senate Dems Offer Alternative Approach to Malpractice." 2005. *CongressDaily*, January 13: 11.

Serafini, Marilyn W. 2004. "Sill Counting Votes on Malpractice Caps." *CongressDaily*, November 13: 25.

Sharkey, Catherine M. 2005. "Unintended Consequences of Medical Malpractice Damage Caps." *New York University Law Review* 80, no. 2 (May): 391–512.

Shindell, S. 1965. "A Survey of the Law of Medical Practice." *Journal of the American Medical Association*, 193: 601–7.

Siliciano, John A., and James A. Henderson, Jr. 1994. "Universal Health Care and the Continued Reliance on Custom in Determining Medical Malpractice." *Cornell Law Review* 79, no. 6 (September): 1382–1405.

Simmons, Walter O. 1996. "An Economic Analysis of Mandatory Mediation and the Disposition of Medical Malpractice Claims." *Journal of Legal Economics* 6, no. 2 (Fall): 41–74.

Sloan, Frank A.; P. M. Mergenhagen; and W.B. Burfield. 1989. "Medical Malpractice Experience of Physicians: Predictable or Haphazard?" *Journal of the American Medical Association* 262, no. 23 (December 15): 3291–97.

Sloan, Frank A.; Randall R. Bovbjerg; and Penny B. Githens. 1991. *Insuring Medical Malpractice*. New York: Oxford University Press.

Sloan, Frank A.; Penny B. Githens; Gerald B. Hickson; and Stephen S. van Wert. 1993. "Compensation." In *Suing for Medical Malpractice*, ed. Frank A. Sloan, Penny B. Githens, Ellen Wright Clayton, David F. Partlett, Gerald B. Hickson, and Stephen S. van Wert, 187–210. Chicago: University of Chicago Press.

Sloan, Irving J. 1992. *Professional Malpractice*. Dobbs Ferry, N.Y.: Oceana Publications.

Smith, Hubert W. 1941. "Legal Responsibility for Medical Malpractice." *Journal of the American Medical Association* 116 (June 14): 2672–73.

Southwick, Lawrence, and Gary J. Young. 1992. "Lawyers and Medical Torts: Medical Malpractice Litigation as a Residual Option." *Applied Economics* 24, no. 9 (September 1): 989–98.

Spiegel, Allen D., and Florence Kavaler. 1997. "America's First Medical Malpractice Crisis: 1835–1865." *Journal of Community Health* 22, no. 4: 283–308.

Starr, David S. 1991. "Does Malpractice Litigation Deter Substandard Care?" *Medical Trial Technique Quarterly* 37, no. 3 (Spring): 360–84.

Stauch, Marc S. 1996. "Causation Issues in Medical Malpractice: A United Kingdom Perspective." *Annals of Health Law* 5: 247–58.

Stevens, Carol. 1991. "Is George Bush the White Knight of Malpractice Reform?" *Medical Economics* 68, no. 17 (September 2): 87–91.

———. 1993. "Will the Clinton Plan End Your Malpractice Woes?" *Medical Economics* 70, no. 11 (June 14): 24–49.

Struve, Catherine T. 2004. "Improving the Medical Malpractice Litigation Process." *Health Affairs* 23, no. 4 (July–August): 33–41.

Studdert, David M., and Troyen A. Brennan. 1997. "Deterrence in a Divided World: Emerging Problems for Malpractice Law in an Era of Managed Care." *Behavioral Science and the Law* 15, no. 1 (Winter): 21–49.

Studdert, David M; Y. Tony Yang; and Michelle M. Mello. 2004. "Are Damage Caps Regressive? A Study of Malpractice Jury Verdicts in California." *Health Affairs* 23, no. 4 (July–August): 54–67.

"Study Doubting Malpractice Premium Rates, Jury Awards Receives Criticism at AEI Forum." 2005. *Kaiser Daily Health Policy Report*. April 1. Online at www.kaisernetwork.org/daily_reports/rep_hpolicy.cfm/#29073.

Sugarman, Stephen D. 1985. "Doing Away with Tort Law." *California Law Review* 73: 555–664.

———. 1990. "The Need to Reform Personal Injury Law Leaving Scientific Disputes to Scientists." *Science* 248: 823.

Taragin, M.I. et al. 1992. "The Influence of Standard of Care and Severity of Injury on the Resolution of Medical Malpractice Claims." *Annals of Internal Medicine* 117: 780–84.

Thomas, Richard K.; Louis Pol; and William F. Sehnert, Jr. 1993. *Health Care Book of Lists*. Winter Park, Fla.: PMD Publishers Group.

Thompson, Cheryl W. 2005a. "Medical Boards Let Physicians Practice Despite Drug Abuse." *Washington Post*, April 10: A01.

———. 2005b. "Poor Performance Records are Easily Outdistanced." *Washington Post*, April 12: A01.

Thorpe, Kenneth E. 2004. "The Medical Malpractice 'Crisis': Recent Trends and the Impact of State Tort Reforms." *Health Affairs*, Web Exclusive W-4 (January–June): 20–30.

Treaster, Joseph B., and Joel Brinkley. 2005. "Behind those Medical Malpractice Rates." *New York Times*, February 22.

Trebilcock, Michael J.; Donald N. Dewees; and David G. Duff. 1990. "The Medical Malpractice Explosion: An Empirical Assessment of Trends, Determinants and Impacts." *Melbourne University Law Review* 17, no. 4: 539–65.

Tussing, Dale A., and Martha A. Wojtowcycz. 1997. "Malpractice, Defensive Medicine, and Obstetric Behavior." *Medical Care* 35, no. 2: 172–91.

U.S. Department of Health and Human Services. 2002. *Confronting the New Health Care Crisis: Improving Health Care Quality and Lowering Costs by Fixing Our Medical Liability System*. Paper prepared by the Office of Disability, Aging, and Long-term Care Policy. Online at aspe.hhs.gov/daltcp/reports/litrefm.htm.

U.S. General Accounting Office. 1986. *Medical Malpractice Insurance Costs Increased but Varied among Physicians and Hospitals*. Washington, D.C.: General Accounting Office.

———. 2003. *Medical Malpractice: Implications of Rising Premiums on Access to Health Care*. Washington, D.C: Government Printing Office.

"U.S. Trails Other English Countries in Use of Electronic Medical Records and Electronic Prescribing." 2001. *Health Care News* 1, no. 28 (October 1). Online at www.Kaiser.org.

Vidmar, Neil. 1994. "Are Juries Competent to Decide Liability in Tort Cases Involving Scientific/Medical Issues? Some Data from Medical Malpractice." *Emory Law Journal* 43, no. 3 (Summer): 883–911.

———. 1995. *Medical Malpractice and the American Jury: Confronting the Myths about Jury Incompetence, Deep Pockets, and Outrageous Damage Awards*. Ann Arbor: University of Michigan Press.

Wachter, Robert M., and Kaveh G. Shojania. 2004. *Internal Bleeding: The Truth Behind America's Terrifying Epidemic of Medical Mistakes*. New York: RuggedLand.

Wall, Brett M. 1997. "Sympathy for the Devil: How the Ohio Tort Reform Act Creates a Flawed System of Punitive Damages." *Ohio State Law Journal* 58, no. 3: 1023–54.

Weigel, Charles J., II. 1974. "Medical Malpractice in America's Middle Years," *Texas Reports on Biology and Medicine* 32 (Spring): 203.

Weiler, Paul C. 1991. *Medical Malpractice on Trial*. Cambridge, Mass.: Harvard University Press.

Weiler, Paul C.; Howard H. Hiatt; Joseph P. Newhouse; William G. Johnson; Troyen A. Brennan; and Lucian I. Leape. 1993. *A Measure of Malpractice: Medical Injury, Malpractice Litigation and Patient Compensation*. Cambridge, Mass.: Harvard University Press.

Wencl, Annette, and Margaret Brizzolara. 1996. "Survey of States." *Trial* 32, no. 5: 20–26.

Wetch, C.H. 1977. "Legal Medicine: An Historical Review and Future Perspectives." *New York Law School Law Review* 22: 873–903.

White, Michelle J. 1994. "The Value of Liability in Medical Malpractice." *Health Affairs* 13, no. 4 (Fall): 76–87.

Wood, Cece L. 1993. "Historical Perspectives on Law, Medical Practice and the Concept of Negligence." *Emergency Medicine Clinic of North America*, 11, no. 4: 819–32.

8

Health Care Technology

Health care technology was mentioned in chapter 6 as one of several factors that have contributed to spiraling health care costs. This chapter focuses on the role of technology in the U.S. health care system. Technological developments in the past twenty years have dramatically changed the methods for diagnosing illnesses and the delivery of health care services in the United States. These medical technologies have created high levels of expectations on the part of health care providers as well as consumers and have opened up diagnostic and treatment avenues once unimaginable. These technological advancements encompass not just diagnoses and treatment abilities but also patient monitoring. For example, patient monitoring systems are making increased use of computer technology for data display and retrieval.

The past twenty-five years have seen significant developments in physics, electronics, computer science, and biotechnology, which are increasingly felt in the field of health care (Hill 1991). This in turn has raised questions about the factors that have contributed to the growth of medical technologies, the cost and effectiveness of such technologies, and the ethical dilemmas they raise. If technology is to be used effectively and efficiently, we must understand not only the technological tools used by modern medicine but also the ethical dilemmas involved, and must learn to make decisions that are individually and socially correct (Bronzino, Smith, and Wade 1990). In this chapter we address these issues. First, we examine the growth of medical technology and the factors that have contributed to this growth. Second, we analyze the cost of the medical technology and its relation to overall health care costs. Third, we address the issue of the assessment of medical technology. Fourth, we examine the potential implications of managed care on medical technology. Finally, we examine the ethical concerns and dilemmas raised by medical technology by analyzing some specific cases.

The Growth and Diffusion of Medical Technology

Before we discuss the growth of medical technology and the factors that have contributed to its growth, it will be helpful to define medical technology. *Medical technology* can be defined simply as drugs, devices, and medical or surgical procedures used in medical care (Kalb 1990). More recent medical technology has been defined by some to include medical techniques, equipment, and pharmaceuticals (Kosterlitz 1993). Examples of medical technology under these definitions include pharmaceutical drugs such as azidothymidine (AZT), medical devices such as computerized tomography (CT) scanners, and organ transplants (Kalb 1990). "High-tech medicine" is the term often used to refer to developments in the field of medical technology in the past twenty or so years. *High-tech medicine* has been defined as the "sum of all the advances in medical knowledge and techniques that have been translated into improved diagnostic, therapeutic, and rehabilitative procedures during the last several decades" (Ginzberg 1990, 1820).

The transformation of medicine is associated with the Renaissance, when different applications of scientific methods were introduced. Disciplined observation of the empirical symptoms of illness was brought about by the influence of Francis Bacon (1561–1626) and Thomas Sydenham (1624–1689). During the seventeenth century, there was a significant increase not only in the ability to understand illnesses but also to classify them. By the nineteenth and twentieth centuries, medicine had progressed to the point where it was capable of healing illnesses and preventing illnesses from starting (Wildes 1994).

The use of medical technology emerged in the late 1800s as an outgrowth of scientific advances that created a need for clinical pathology laboratories. Before the 1890s, physicians were expected to perform and interpret almost all laboratory tests themselves. By the early 1900s, interns in larger hospitals had begun to perform laboratory tests as part of their responsibilities. The years 1890 to 1928 marked the emergence of clinical laboratory practice as an occupation separate from medicine and nursing. Pathology became established as a recognized specialty after World War I. Laboratory testing and interpretation of results became the responsibility of the pathologist (Lotlarz 1991).

The professionalization of medical technology occurred between the 1920s and 1930s. In 1928 the American Society of Clinical Pathologists set up the national Board of Registry for clinical laboratory technicians. For the first time, educational and training standards for students were established. The Board of Registry also assumed responsibility for accreditation of schools of medical technology and for certification of clinical laboratory technicians. The professionalization of medical technology was also reflected in the establishment and publication of professional journals: the *Bulletin of the American Society of Clinical Laboratory Technicians* in 1933 and the *American Journal of Medical Technology* in 1935. The latter journal was renamed the *Journal of Medical Technology* in 1984, and in 1988 it came to be called *Clinical Laboratory Science* (Lotlarz 1991).

Some of the major advances in medical technology during the first fifty years of the twentieth century included X-rays for diagnoses (1901); insulin (1921); the first sulfa drug (1937); penicillin (1943); dichlorodiphenyl; trichloroethane (DDT) (1944); renal dialysis (1945); streptomycin, the first antituberculosis drug (1948);

and tetracycline, the first broad-spectrum antibiotic (1949) (Berlinger 1987). These early developments, particularly antisepsis techniques and anesthesiology, made a critical contribution to the advancement of medicine and the health of human beings.

In the sixty years since the end of World War II, dramatic developments in medical technology have revolutionized the American health care system. Almost all of today's disease diagnosis and treatment devices and techniques were unknown fifty to sixty years ago. The role of the physician was mainly that of diagnostician, limited to identification of illness, prediction of likely outcome, and the provision of guidance to the patient and his or her family while the illness ran its course. All this has changed dramatically. Today the scope of medical intervention includes kidney dialysis, organ transplantation, laser surgery, arthroscopic surgical techniques, computerized tomography scanners, nuclear magnetic resonators, and much more.

The rate of medical technological change has been very rapid since the end of World War II. This is related to the dramatic growth in federal funding for biomedical research and medical education. The research budget of the National Institutes of Health (NIH) grew from about $26 million in 1945 to around $7 billion in 1990 (both in 1988 inflation-adjusted dollars). The NIH had the largest basic research budget across all sectors (Gelijns and Rosenberg 1994). However, in recent years, there has been some shift in the funding pattern, with more funding coming from private-sector coffers. The share of total health research and development (R&D) conducted within private-sector industries increased from 42 percent in FY 1986 to 52 percent in FY 1995. During the same period, the government's share of total spending on health research fell from 53.2 percent in FY 1986 to 44.2 percent in FY 1995 (Neumann and Sandberg 1998). In 2000, in the the United States, all sectors combined spent $264 billion on R&D. The federal government supported more than two-thirds of R&D efforts in 1964. In 2001, it supported only a quarter (Zinner 2001).

In the future, this trend toward increased private-sector funding may accelerate, due to increased R&D spending by the pharmaceutical industry and the growth of biotechnology companies (Neumann and Sandberg 1998). Along with government, academe, and industry, equity markets have become an important fourth player in medical R&D. Government funding is largely devoted to basic or applied research. Small biotech companies need funding to help develop new ideas and keep them operating until they can accumulate enough data to market their product or to partner with larger firms. Public offerings have become the single largest source of support for biotech firms. Despite the fact that most small biotech companies have very little or no earnings, the prospect of future revenues allows them to offer equity positions to the public to fund their research (Zinner 2001). It is also important to remember that a high percentage of new medical devices have emerged not out of biomedical research but through transfer of technologies developed in other fields, such as lasers, ultrasounds, and magnetic resonance spectroscopy, among others (Gelijns and Rosenberg 1994).

Not too long ago, except for X-rays, the only way a doctor could see inside a patient's body was through exploratory surgery. Today a variety of medical technologies are available that are nonintrusive to the patient. One such technique is the CT scan, or computerized tomography. A CT scan provides a detailed X-ray of the entire body and converts a two-dimensional picture into three-dimensional images. Magnetic resonance imaging (MRI) uses a combination of radio waves, a computer, and a magnetic coil that allows a doctor to see tissues hidden or surrounded by bone. This is not possible to do with a simple X-ray. MRI scans are used by doctors to diagnose tumors, arthritis, and problems associated with tissues and organs. Magnetic resonance spectroscopy uses a similar technology to gather information about body chemistry, while magnetoencephalography (MEG) allows the doctor to measure brain activity. Another imaging technique—PET scan, or position emission tomography—uses a low-level radioactive chemical that travels through the body. PET scans are used to diagnose strokes, epilepsy, schizophrenia, and Parkinson's disease (Kambert 1990).

As diagnostic abilities have improved, so have the treatment options available to doctors. For example, surgeons have been using lasers instead of scalpels since the 1970s to cut skin, remove growths, and unclog blood vessels. The new free-electron laser has made possible photodynamic therapy that makes it possible to kill viruses in the blood (Kambert 1990). Surgical techniques have also undergone dramatic changes in the past forty to fifty years. Organ transplants have become increasingly common, especially with respect to the heart, liver, and kidney. Replacement of human body parts with artificial parts is also becoming a reality. Today it is possible to replace a human arm or hand with a realistic artificial arm or hand that can perform almost the same functions. Soon it may be possible to replace eyes, ears, bones, and other vital organs.

Biomedical research in general and surgical innovations in particular have revolutionized surgical practices. Surgeons are engaged in high-tech/low-tech enterprises that include laser devices, flexible fiber-optic scopes, tissue-specimen retrieval capabilities, high-resolution operative microscopes, and surgical instruments that allow surgeons to operate through tiny incisions, making many surgeries minimally invasive (Detmer 1993). New frontiers of surgery include high-tech gynecologic procedures, such as fallopian tube dilation, which may restore female fertility. In vitro fertilization and gamete intrafallopian transfer techniques can circumvent infertility and allow women who were previously unable to do so, the ability to bear their own children (Detmer 1993).

New miracle drugs are being marketed each year. About 35 percent of the 200 largest-selling prescription drugs each year are new (Weisbrod 1991, 1994). In 1990 alone, 5,000 new devices were introduced in the United States (Gelijns and Rosenberg 1994). As a result of the enactment of the Prescription Drug Use Fee Act of 1992, which required user fees from the pharmaceutical industry to be used to finance additional Food and Drug Administration (FDA) review staff, average approval time for new molecular entities (NMEs) dropped from 30.6 months in the 1987–92 period to 19.2 months in the 1993–97 period (Neumann and Sandberg 1998). Progress in genetic science has created the potential to customize pharmacotherapy: for example, genetic tests could be routinely given to patients and a drug therapy tailored to a patient's drug-response profile. Pharmacogenetics will raise a host of legal, ethical, and policy challenges for major actors in the health care system (Patel and Rushefsky 2002; Robertson et al. 2002).

Three emerging technologies—personalized medicine (genetic diagnostics and genetic profiling for targeting drugs), regenerative medicine (culturing and grafting human cells and stem cell research), and remote patient monitoring (monitoring at-risk patients from a remote distance because of advances in sensor and wireless broadband technology and computerized intelligent clinical information systems with decision support tools)—will significantly alter the role of hospitals in the health care delivery system (Goldsmith 2004). In addition, the practice of online medicine, because of advances in communications and information technologies, will require a new regulatory regime to ensure accountability and acceptable standards of medical practice (Miller and Derse 2002). Computerized physician order entry systems (physicians can prescribe medications on computer) will have the potential to reduce medical errors in hospitals (Doolan and Bates 2002). President George W. Bush, in his January 2004 State of the Union address, called for a transformation of electronic health records within the next ten years (Abrahamsen 2005). His plan also called for the appointment of a national health-technology coordinator (McGee and Clayburn 2004).

One of the problems faced by hospitals in their decisions about adoption of information technology is figuring out the costs and benefits of such technologies in the midst of varying claims made by hundreds of competing information technology vendors. Three groups hope to address this issue. The Healthcare Information and Management Systems Society (Chicago) has launched a Web site (www.himss.org/ASP/index.asp) that provides comparative information about vendors and their products. The Center for Information Technology Leadership (Boston) has begun research on the worth of new technologies. The third group, The Health Technology Center (San Francisco) examines emerging embryonic medical technologies, including information technology (Morrissey 2002).

Most of the developments in the field of medical technology can be classified as one of two types (Wildes 1994). One is replacement technology, which replaces an old procedure with a new one. Replacement technology enables doctors to do more efficiently and effectively what they have already been doing. An example is diagnostic tests such as the CT scanner, which replaces intrusive exploratory surgery. A second development is what might be called "new technologies." These allow doctors to do things that were not being done or that were not possible to do before. Some examples include organ transplants, reproductive technologies, and life-extending and life-sustaining technologies. Both types of technology are developing rapidly.

Lewis Thomas provides another useful way of classifying technology in medicine (Thomas 1975). "Nontechnology" is offered to patients with diseases that are not well understood. It mainly involves reassuring patients and providing nursing and hospital care, but offers little hope for recovery. Nontechnology is applied in cases such as intractable cancer, multiple sclerosis, and stroke. The second level of technology is called "halfway technology." This represents the "kinds of things that must be done after the fact, as efforts to compensate for the incapacitating effects of certain diseases whose course one is unable to do very much about. It is a technology designed to make up for disease, or to postpone death" (Thomas 1975, 37). Examples include organ transplants and the use of artificial organs. Halfway technology for chronic kidney failure means dialysis or kidney transplant. For heart disease, the halfway technology can mean open heart surgery, a pacemaker, a transplant, or an artificial heart. Such halfway technologies are generally very expensive (Morris 1984). John Cooper, president of the American Association of Medical Colleges, in 1973 congressional testimony, described halfway technology as not "really evidence of success in dealing with disease," but rather "confessions of failure, of a lack of understanding to prevent disease before clinical signs and symptoms appear. They are the consequence of partial understanding" (Morris 1984, 198). The final level of technology, "high technology," is exemplified by immunization, antibiotics for bacterial infections, and prevention of nutritional disorders. High technology "comes as a result of genuine understanding of disease mechanisms, and when it becomes available it is relatively inexpensive to deliver" (Thomas 1975, 40).

In recent years, most of the growth in medical technology has been in the area of halfway technologies, which is the most expensive ("Health Care Dollars" 1992). What accounts for the growth of medical technology in general and halfway technologies in particular?

Factors Responsible for the Growth of Medical Technologies

Many factors have influenced the dramatic growth in medical technologies in the United States. In this section we discuss some of the major influences on the growth of medical technologies. These factors are not discussed in any particular order. Thus we do not suggest the relative contribution of each factor to the overall growth in medical technologies.

The Public and Private Sectors

Vannevar Bush, science adviser to President Franklin Roosevelt, in his 1945 report, *Science: The Endless Frontier*, recommended a significantly enlarged federal government role in support of science. The federal government not only dramatically increased its funding for biomedical research but made large amounts of federal funds available to outlying communities for construction of hospitals. During the 1960s, the federal government played a role in expanding physician supply (heavily weighted toward specialists) through funding of medical schools and medical students. It also created Medicare and Medicaid, enlarging federal funding. One of the results of the massive flow of federal dollars into the health care system was the rapid development of academic health centers. Given the availability of a large amount of federal dollars, leading medical schools changed their focal interest from the training of medical students to biomedical research. This, combined with the increasing supply of medical specialists, set the stage for rapid growth in medical technologies (Ginzberg 1990). Modern hospitals became repositories of high-tech medical equipment. Similarly, private-sector spending in R&D has exploded. At present (2004), the industry invests 7 to 13 percent of its annual gross profit in R&D.

All parties in health care—hospitals, clinics, physicians, consumers, and manufacturers of medical devices—have a stake in the development and diffusion of medical technology (Rutten and Bonsel 1992). From World War II to the early 1970s, health care financing in most countries was very generous, based on retrospective pricing. The result was the emergence of very expensive halfway technologies such as organ transplants, MRI, and high-priced drugs with marginal value. Such financing also contributed to the development of such "high-technology" items as new antibiotics and vaccines that were cost effective (Rutten and Bonsel 1992).

The Health Insurance/Finance System

The usual method for limiting demand in the marketplace is to raise prices. The third-party payment system has made such a mechanism largely irrelevant in the health care market. The third-party payment system insulates the consumer from the high cost of the treatment. Consumers have little incentive to question expensive care since the third party (the insurance company) is going to pay most or all of the entire bill (Freed 1994). The reimbursement system used by the insurance companies—retrospective payment, which pays a provider on the basis of costs incurred—stimulated demand for medical technology by encouraging any innovation that promises some benefit, regardless of the cost. Victor Fuchs has claimed that hospitals operate under a technological imperative that drives them to adopt the latest technology, regardless of the cost. The incentive system helps explain the rapid and indiscriminate adoption of medical innovations (Fuchs 1986; Gelijns and Rosenberg 1994). The retrospective payment mechanism also sends a clear message to research and development. The message is to develop new technologies that enhance the quality of care, regardless of the cost. Examples of high-cost medical innovations made possible by a retrospective payment system might include natural organ transplants and artificial organs (Weisbrod 1994).

The new prospective payment finance mechanism, which pays health care providers sums that are independent of the costs incurred, sends a different signal to the R&D sector. The message here is to develop new technologies that reduce costs as long as quality does not suffer too much. The shift to this new system under Medicare, while not resulting in decreased use of intensive-care units, does seem to have helped decrease the use of diagnostic procedures such as chest X-rays (Weisbrod 1994). But the long-term effect of the Prospective Payment System (PPS) on Medicare is far from conclusive.

In most industries, before a new cost-increasing technology is adopted it must satisfy two criteria: it must represent advancement beyond what we currently have, and there must be a market for it. Unfortunately, in the health care market, whether a technological change occurs or not is largely determined by the first criterion. The presence of a third-party-payer system makes the second criterion irrelevant. Insurance leads to technological change, and more costly technological change increases demand for insurance, since most patients cannot pay for costly technology out of their own pockets (Nyman 1991). Some of the evidence gathered thus far suggests that insurance coverage largely determines whether or not a new technology is developed, manufactured, and used (Kane and Manoukian 1989).

The Hospitals

Aside from the influence of a retrospective insurance payment system, hospitals have other reasons for the acquisition of the latest medical technology (Anderson and Steinberg 1994; Griner 1992). By stocking hospitals with the latest medical technologies, hospitals hope to recruit physicians and attract patients. From the physician's perspective, a hospital with the latest technology and empty beds promises little delay in admitting and treating his or her patients. Hospitals also hope to attract patients by portraying themselves as state-of-the-art facilities. The result is a medical arms race between hospitals as each hospital tries to maximize its own status, prestige, and profits. The result often is a tremendous duplication of very expensive medical technologies among many hospitals within the same community. This is helped by the fact that there is a lack of incentives for hospitals to cooperate and coordinate efficient use of medical technology (Freed 1994). The acquisition of diagnostic imaging technologies (CT scan, MRI, etc.) by hospitals requires a significant initial capital investment and a high level of operating costs. To avoid the financial risks involved and generate profit requires a high volume of use of such technologies. Thus, once a hospital buys an expensive new technology, there is pressure to use it more frequently to produce sufficient demand to cover the operating costs and increase profit margins (Sussman 1991). This has often led to excesses and overuse of medical technology in the United States.

Physicians

According to Eric Cassell, five human characteristics help explain physicians' enchantment with medical technology. One is wonderment about something new that can do fantastic or inexplicable things. This causes physicians to use and overuse medical technology. It also helps solve the problem of boredom and loss of motivation. A second reason for physicians' attraction to technology is that technology tells them directly what it means in immediate terms. For example, computer-generated electrocardiogram (EKG) interpretations provide immediate information and answers. The third reason for technology's hold on physicians is that virtually all technology is characterized by unambiguous values. Lack of ambiguity is generally considered essential for a good science of medicine. Thus, technological values and medical values reinforce each other because both are intolerant of ambiguities. A fourth and related factor has to do with the fact that one of the main problems physicians confront is uncertainty. This is caused by shortcomings in the individual physician's knowledge and/or the inadequacies of the profession's knowledge. Technology helps physicians reduce some uncertainty. A medical problem is often redefined in terms of a technological answer. The final reason why technology lures physicians is the power it confers on them. Every therapeutic and diagnostic test is a demonstration of a physician's efficacy and thus of his or her power (Cassell 1993).

According to David Freed (1994), physicians have capitulated to the growth of medical technology at both the structural and the applied level. At the structural level, medical education has emphasized the scientific basis of medicine and downplayed its role as a healing "art." Physicians and the science community's compulsion about avoiding uncertainty have stimulated excessive dependence on clinical tests and treatments of marginal value in pursuit of certainty. Another structural factor is a strong tradition of professional autonomy in the medical profession. Physicians are the key decision makers with respect to the use of medical technology, and as long as physicians believe that a new technology might benefit a patient, they are likely to use it. At an applied level, physicians are trained to be advocates for their patients. They are also comfortable doing what they learned to do in their training. There are no general decision-making models that all physicians can apply with respect to the use of technology, and thus decisions are made at an individual level, resulting in a wide variance in physician practice.

Others have argued that physicians play an important role in the choice of technologies they use. Factors that influence physician thinking and behavior regarding adoption of new technologies include advanced professional training, increased specialization, scientific orientation, close ties with medical organizations, desire for professional advancement, enhanced reputation for providing high-quality care, and financial gain (Bozic, Pierce, and Herndon 2004).

A mail survey of 225 leading general internists measured their opinions regarding the relative importance to patients of thirty medical innovations. The survey revealed that general internists ranked diagnostic and surgical innovations much higher compared to innovations that take the form of medications. When innovations were clustered by disease groups, those that are used to treat cardiovascular diseases were ranked much higher than any other disease group. The rankings of a few innovations were related to physician age, but the greatest variability in responses was related to the physicians' patient mix (Fuchs and Sox 2001). Finally, the fear of malpractice lawsuits and medical liability risks has also encouraged tremendous growth of expensive diagnostic imaging technologies (Freed 1994; Phelps and Parente 1990). How physicians will respond to the new era of economic constraints and the changing health policy environment and market forces—managed care, managed competition, HMOs—remains to be seen (Fendrick and Schwartz 1994; Hillman 1992).

The Health Policymaking Environment

The diffusion of medical technology has taken place in the United States in an environment of both regulation and free enterprise. Attempts at regulating the diffusion of CT scanners through certificate-of-need (CON) programs were not very successful. By the 1980s, the use of CT scanners had become widespread, and CON agencies were either abandoned in some states or had become liberal in their requirements. Supporters of the marketplace model (i.e., the free-enterprise system) argue that the health care delivery system should operate according to the principle of supply and demand. Thus the diffusion of medical technology in the United States has taken place between the two competing models—the regulation model and the free-enterprise, marketplace model. Health care providers have manipulated each, to some extent. Overall, the market model has continued to operate in the medical technology area, despite some attempts at regulation (James et al. 1991).

Societal Culture and Values: American Consumers

American society places a great deal of emphasis on individual autonomy, self-determination, personal privacy, and shared belief in justice and equality. This is reflected in the health care field by a belief held by many that health care is a right to which everyone is entitled. Access to the latest medical technology is also viewed as a right, and demand for it has increased because of greater public awareness of the latest technological innovation. Compared to many other countries, the American public is more aware of the latest technological advances in medicine because of considerable coverage in the mass media. The public demands the newest and the best in medical technology, even though it continues to express dissatisfaction with high cost and low efficacy (Freed 1994).

A multicountry survey of public views and expectations about medical innovations and technologies revealed that Americans and Canadians express more interest in new medical discoveries than do citizens in twelve European countries. U.S. seniors are more likely to express interest in new medical discoveries than seniors in most other industrialized countries. Americans, in general, are also more likely than Europeans to consider themselves knowledgeable about medical discoveries. Americans also have much higher expectations for medicine than do Europeans (Kim, Blendon, and Benson 2001). These findings suggest that policymakers in American society will continue to face political pressure to spend more on new medical research and technologies. Also, the combination of high interest and high political participation rates among U.S. elderly will make it more difficult to control future Medicare expenditures for new medical technologies (Kim, Blendon, and Benson 2001).

The process by which the public's expectations are met is often referred to as technology transfer. Technology transfer is "the sharing and dissemination of scientific knowledge between researchers and research organizations and those who can make practical use of the information, including physicians, health care providers, and industry" (Campbell et al. 2004, 64–65). The United States has the highest rate of use of sophisticated medical procedures of any other country in the world (Campbell et al. 2004).

In addition to a significant emphasis on individual autonomy, rights, and self-determination, American culture is heavily predisposed toward progress through technological means and faith in scientific progress. Our culture equates reduction of uncertainty and gaining control over ambiguities with progress. This has often led to an unrealistic dependence on technology to fix problems of the health care system and exclusion of nontechnological solutions. We have come to equate sophisticated medical procedures with better health care (Blank 1988).

We are a culture that believes that "we can have it all." We want the latest, the most sophisticated medical technology, and we want to use it indiscriminately for the very young, the very old, and the hopelessly ill. We want the physician to do everything possible for the patient even when there is little or no hope for survival. We want the best, yet we want to pay the least. We admire countries that place limits and global budgets on health care and want to adopt their health care systems, but we do not want to accept any limits (Melski 1992).

In view of the above discussion, it is not too surprising that we have witnessed a rampant growth in medical technology in the United States, and such a growth is likely to continue in the future. The biotechnology industry has seen revenues more than quadruple, from $8 billion in 1992 to $33.6 billion in 2002. It employed 713,000 workers in 2002. Biotechnology-related R&D expenditures amounted to $16.4 billion in 2001, about 10 percent of all U.S. industry R&D that year ("Biotechnology: High Growth Industry Profile" 2004). The availability of large-scale technology has been much greater in the United States than in Western European countries. The concentration of medical equipment in the United States is far greater than in other countries that have good-quality health care systems (Atkins and Bauer 1992). For example, the United States had 11.2 MRI units per million population in 1992 compared to 1.1 units per million in Canada and 3.7 units per million in Germany. Similarly, in 1992, the United States had 3.7 installed open-heart surgery units per million population compared to 1.3 units per million in Canada and 0.8 units per million in Germany (Rublee 1994).

The rapid proliferation of health care technologies has raised concerns in many quarters about the costs of such technologies and the strain they put on the nation's resources. It also raises issues about the cost-effectiveness of such technologies.

Health Care Technology and Costs

A great deal of modern technology—medical equipment, medical techniques, and pharmaceuticals—is very expensive. New medical technology and the overuse of such technologies helps drive health care costs upward (McClellan 1996; Nitzkin 1996). One of the most significant advances in medical technology, and one of the most costly, is the spread and increased use of such diagnostic tools as MRI and CT scans. Since such new diagnostic therapies are simpler and safer than exploratory surgery, they are used at a much higher rate, adding to health care costs. MRI equipment costs between $2 million and $3 million, and the cost of one MRI scan ranges from $600 to $800. In fact, MRI equipment has proved to be so popular that today it is available not only in hospitals and doctors' offices but in roadside facilities and shopping centers (Kosterlitz 1993). Many critics of CT scans had initially voiced concern that this technology was proliferating more rapidly than it should (Fineberg 1977).

The field of neonatology is another example of how technology has allowed us to save lives at increased cost. Due to numerous medical breakthroughs—incubators, intravenous feeding, advances in caesarean section, controls for infection—that were made during the 1950s and 1960s, doctors have succeeded in saving the lives of babies with increasingly lower birth weights. However, the cost has been very high. In 1984 constant dollars, the cost per survival of an infant born weighing between 750 and 1,000 grams is estimated to be about $125,000, while the cost for an infant born weighing less than 750 grams is about $175,000 (Rhodes 1992). Many economists argue that we would be better off providing intensive care for babies over 1,000 grams than spending resources on children with birth weights of less than 800 grams. They justify such arguments on the ground that we could actually reduce suffering by targeting only those newborns who are most likely to benefit from medical intervention (Rhodes 1992). This example demonstrates the complexity as well as the difficult nature of the problems created by medical technology.

Technological change has been seen as a prime culprit for increases in health care spending over time (Baker et al. 2003; Cutler and McClellan 2001). Most health care economists seem to agree that new health care technology is the largest factor driving up annual health care cost growth in the United States (Aaron 1991; Fuchs 1993; Newhouse 1992; Schwartz 1987; Weisbrod 1991). They believe that technology accounts for as much as 50 percent of the growth in health care cost beyond overall inflation (Kosterlitz 1993). Furthermore, the diffusion of these technologies has outpaced our ability to evaluate their need and their cost-effectiveness. Despite regulatory and competitive strategies to control diffusion of technology, excessive supply exists (Bryce and Cline 1998). Most analysts believe that advances in medical technology have been largely responsible for a 4 to 5 percent annual rate of growth in the industrialized nations' health care costs (Collins 1993). According to Henry Aaron, medical technologies that did not exist thirty to forty years ago account for most of the rise in health care spending in the United States (Aaron 1991). He argues that developments in medical technology affect outlays in two ways: new technology adds new treatments, and because of its less intrusive nature, many more patients benefit from it, resulting in increased use and costs (Aaron 1991). Cutler and McClellan (2001) have argued that medical technology affects the health care system in different ways. Some technologies often substitute for older technologies in therapy of established patients, which is called the treatment substitution effect. Such new technologies often bring health improvements and are valued highly.

New technologies also lead more people to be treated for diseases. This is called the treatment expansion effect. A study that examined the relationship between the supply of new technologies and health care utilization and spending related to diagnostic imaging and cardiac, cancer, and newborn care technologies concluded that more availability of medical technology is associated with higher use and more spending (Baker et al. 2003).

The hospital is the major center of high-tech medicine, and hospital care constitutes the single largest component of our health care spending, about 40 percent. The most important factor stimulating hospital cost increases is the rapid adoption of new medical technology, according to a report by the General Accounting Office (GAO). Competition among hospitals combined with a third-party reimbursement system provides incentives for rapid advancement of medical technologies in hospitals. Since hospitals do not compete for patients on the basis of price, hospitals try to gain market advantage by offering the most up-to-date services, and the cost of these technologies is passed on to the third-party payers—insurance companies (General Accounting Office 1992).

Efforts aimed at health care cost containment produce conflict with the nation's commitment to medical innovation, which receives widespread support from both elites and the general public (Rettig 1994). Furthermore, attempts to control costs associated with medical technology immediately produce confrontation between two powerful interests in the health care system: insurance companies and manufacturers of medical devices. Medical device manufacturers argue that they are unfairly singled out and that many new inventions provide less costly alternatives for diagnosis and treatment. They argue that any technology that allows us to produce existing goods or services at a lower cost while maintaining or increasing quality, is to be welcomed. Nevertheless, rapid cost escalation related to wasteful technologies deserves scrutiny.

Insurance companies generally try to limit coverage to care that is "reasonably necessary" or "medically necessary." These terms are generally interpreted broadly to cover any nonexperimental technology accepted by the medical community that is not considered unsafe or ineffective. Courts have often expanded the scope of insurance coverage by relying on the notion that all ambiguities should be interpreted against the insurer and in favor of the beneficiary. Courts have often forced insurance companies to cover technologies and treatments still considered to be in an experimental stage. Extra insurance rights established through the courts are often called "judge-made insurance" (Kalb 1990).

Gelijns and Rosenberg (1994) have argued that there are two critical characteristics of innovation in medicine. One is the fact that new technologies retain a high degree of uncertainty long after their initial adoption. Second is the closer interaction between developers of medical innovations and the users. Development of new medical interventions is influenced not only by advances in scientific knowledge but also by the potential demand for particular medical innovations. In the past, developers viewed physicians acting as the agents for their patients as the primary users of medical technologies. However, many other groups, such as hospital administrators, patients, payers, and regulatory groups also influence the demand for new technologies (Gelijns and Rosenberg 1994). The United States leads the world both in demand for health care advances and also in R&D that produces these advances (Weisbrod and LaMay 1999).

The relationship between health care technology and health care costs is a complex one because technology affects costs in many different ways. Part of the difficulty in determining the precise relationship between medical technology and health care costs lies in the many ambiguities surrounding such a discussion. Sometimes it is clear whether a new technology reduces the cost of treating a particular illness (e.g., polio vaccines). However, the impact of a new innovation on health care cost is often not clear. In addition, it is not easy to measure whether a new technology is reducing costs or increasing them. Also, defining what constitutes a health care cost is difficult (Weisbrod and LaMay 1999).

Of course, not all technology is completely good or bad. On the positive side, technology can play a significant role in supporting the provision of adequate care in the areas of prevention and rehabilitation. Mobile health care units can help overcome the challenge of geographic maldistribution by helping extend service areas and making medical service distribution more equitable (Jaros and Boonzaier 1993). On the negative side, technology can be unsafe, ineffective, and inefficient. Just because technological change may contribute to growth in health care spending, it does not follow that such change is bad, because it can bring benefits in addition to costs. Thus, the real question is this: Are the benefits derived from new technological innovation worth the costs?, that is, Do the benefits far outweigh the costs? If so, technological change is good, despite the fact that it brings increased costs. Similarly, if the costs far outweigh the few marginal benefits produced by a new technology, one can argue that the cost of new technology is not worthwhile. Cutler and McClellan (2001) analyzed technological change in five medical conditions—heart attacks, low-birth-weight infants, depression, cataracts, and breast cancer. They concluded that in four of the five conditions examined—heart attacks, low-birth-weight infants, depression, and cataracts—the estimated benefits of technological change were far greater than the costs. In the fifth condition, breast cancer, costs and benefits were about equal in magnitude. Thus, they argued that medical spending as a whole is worth the increased cost of care.

Some technologies can increase costs considerably through introduction of new diagnostic or treatment therapy but result in improved health. In other words, some technologies are both high cost and high benefit. Some technologies may decrease costs by allowing care to be given in a lower-cost setting, replacing expensive procedures, keeping people healthier, reducing hospital stay and recovery time, and returning people to work sooner. Such technologies may be both low cost and high benefit. In contrast, some technologies may be very costly but produce only marginal benefits. It is these technologies—the high-cost and low-benefit technologies—that raise serious concerns among critics of the U.S. health care system. Some technologies are unsafe, while others are ineffective. Some technologies are medically effective, but are not cost effective. Technologies that are unsafe, ineffective, or not cost effective are called "wasteful technologies" (Kalb 1990).

Examples of wasteful technologies abound. An estimated 50 percent of all U.S. births are electronically monitored. Eight controlled studies have found that electronic monitoring has no advantage over a stethoscope placed on the mother's stomach, even in high-risk pregnancies. Yet electronic monitoring is growing at a cost of $1 billion a year (Cowley 1993). U.S. doctors perform about 600,000 hysterectomies a year at a cost of $5 billion. Almost a third of women undergo the operation by the time they are sixty. Yet it is not clear how many of these women gain anything from it (Cowley 1993). In recent years, late-stage breast cancer victims have turned to a treatment known as autologous bone marrow transplant. The procedure is considered risky and costly, costing about $100,000 a patient; however, there is no solid evidence that it works better than less expensive treatments (Kosterlitz 1993). Every year, about 400,000 patients undergo heart bypass surgery at a cost of about $12 billion. Studies show that it is no better than drug treatment for less dire conditions. About 300,000 Americans receive angioplasties a year at a cost of $10,000 a procedure. Drug treatment generally yields similar benefits at a fraction of the cost. The procedure has not been shown to prevent heart attacks (Cowley 1993).

Neither procompetitive policies nor regulation have dealt effectively with the oversupply of technology services. Regulatory loopholes have allowed hospitals to escape CON reviews before expanding capacity. Market-based incentives to rationally distribute health care services also seem to have failed, because hospitals have competed to attract and retain physicians and patients by acquiring new technologies. Furthermore, cost-based reimbursement and cost shifting by providers often mitigate potential financial losses associated with oversupply of technology (Bryce and Cline 1998). Currently in the United States, most drugs and medical devices are assessed for safety and efficacy only and not for cost-effectiveness. Most medical and surgical procedures are not formally evaluated at all. It is clear that what is needed is a systematic assessment of medical technologies that would allow us to weed out wasteful technologies.

Medical Technology Assessment

The rate of diffusion of high-cost technology varies between countries. In mainly public, government-funded, and planned nonmarket health care delivery systems, such as those in Great Britain and Scandinavia, there are generally more built-in constraints that limit the introduction of new technologies. In the United States, market forces are the most influential with respect to diffusion of high-cost technologies, often resulting in a medical arms race (Rutten and Bonsel 1992).

According to M. Roy Schwartz, senior vice president of medical education and science with the American Medical Association (AMA), most of America's economic growth comes from technology, specifically biotechnology, and technological development pays off in the long run ("Cost/Benefits of High-Tech Medicine" 1992). New insights into molecular and cell biology and developments in other scientific disciplines will only accelerate the pace of medical advances (Schwartz 1994). Consumer demand will play a major role in driving new technological developments (Goldsmith 1994).

Nevertheless, the country is facing some tough decisions about access, funding, distribution of health care resources, and cost containment. Evaluating health technology is one of the most important challenges facing policymakers and researchers alike. Improving the process of technology diffusion requires continuous monitoring of technological development, identifying technologies for assessment, and conducting early assessment before technology is marketed (Banta and Vondeling 1994). With more availability of outcome data, employers, insurers, and researchers are beginning to question the value of certain high-cost technology (Taylor 1993).

History of Technology Assessment in the United States

The Federal Government

The history of technology assessment in the United States is a very brief one. The dramatic growth in medical technologies in the 1970s raised some concerns about technology.

The Office of Technology Assessment: 1972–95. In 1972, the Office of Technology Assessment (OTA), a congressional staff agency, was established through passage of the Technology Assessment Act (Public Law 92-484) to help Congress in the identification and probable impacts of technological application. The office provided analytical resources to balance the resources of the executive branch. It became a important resource for members of Congress in crafting public policies dealing with technological issues. The 104th Congress opted not to fund the agency's work and the OTA was shut down in September 1995.

Government Accountability Office. Another congressional agency, the Government Accountability Office (GAO), formerly known as the General Accounting Office (it was created in 1921 and its name was changed on July 7, 2004), often analyzes the role of technology in its health reports. However, the GAO is primarily concerned with evaluation of ongoing programs. GAO is often called the watchdog of Congress. It is an independent, nonpartisan agency that evaluates federal programs and also conducts audits of program expenditures.

Agency for Health Care Research and Quality. In 1978, the National Center for Health Care Technology (NCHCT) was established by law; it was responsible for examining the cost-effectiveness of new technologies. Although the agency was reauthorized in 1981 at the urging of the medical device industry, the Reagan administration did not seek any funding for the agency in its 1982 budget. No funds were appropriated, and the agency went out of existence in 1982 (Rettig 1994). At the urging of the Reagan administration, Congress also cut off funds for state health planning agencies that required hospitals to seek approval of large capital investment in technology.

Skyrocketing health care costs and evidence of inappropriate use of technological devices and procedures led both Congress and President George H.W. Bush to revisit the issue of health care technology assessment in the late 1980s. The result was the establishment in 1989 of the Office of Health Technology Assessment (OHTA) in the National Center for Health Services Research (NCHSR). The NCHCT's function of advising Medicare on coverage decisions was delegated to OHTA (Rettig 1994).

In 1989, the Agency for Health Care Policy and Research (AHCPR) was also created within the NCHSR, to develop guidelines on the appropriate treatment of common illnesses and to evaluate the effectiveness and cost of specific technologies related to federal health programs (Pillar 1990).

The 1999 Healthcare Research and Quality Act reauthorized the AHCPR but changed its name to the Agency for Healthcare Research and Quality (AHRQ) to reaffirm that AHRQ is a scientific research agency. The law also eliminated a require-ment that the agency support the development of practice guidelines, and the agency ended its clinical practice guideline program in 1996. The agency's technology as-sessment program provides technology assessment for the Centers for Medicare and Medicaid Services (CMS). The CMS uses this information to make its national cov-erage decisions for the Medicare program. Technology assessment may be done in-house by AHRQ staff or in collaboration with one of the agency's Evidence-Based Practice Centers ("Agency for Healthcare Research and Quality: Reauthorization Fact Sheet" 2005; "Technology Assessments" 2005).

Food and Drug Administration. Another agency, the Food and Drug Administration (FDA), is responsible for regulating the safety and efficacy of drugs and medical devices, but not their cost-effectiveness. The FDA's role in the regulation of drugs has been shaped by the 1906 Food and Drug Act; the 1938 Federal Food, Drug and Cos-metic Act; and the 1962 amendments. The drug companies are required to get ad-vance permission from the FDA for every important step in testing, production, and marketing new drugs. The 1938 Federal Food, Drug and Cosmetic Act gave the FDA jurisdiction over medical devices for the first time.

The FDA's authority for evaluating safety and effectiveness of drugs and biologics was extended to medical devices under the Medical Devices Amendments of 1976 (Banta and Thacker 1979; Rettig 1994). The 1990 Safe Medical Devices Act also strengthened the FDA by controlling the entry of new products and monitoring the use of marketed products (Merrill 1994). Today, the FDA's Center for Drug Evalua-tion and Research evaluates all new drugs before they are sold. Nevertheless, it is important to emphasize again that the FDA is mainly concerned with the safety and efficacy of drugs and medical devices, and it is not heavily involved in assessing cost-effectiveness. Furthermore, the FDA evaluates the safety and efficacy of investiga-tional pharmaceuticals, biotechnologies, and medical devices based on scientific evidence supplied primarily by sponsoring companies (Goodman 1997).

The FDA's Center for Devices and Radiological Health (CDRH) regulates all medical devices. High-risk devices or new technologies that the FDA has not previously evaluated must be submitted through the premarket approval (PMA) process. Simple devices are generally exempted from this process. They are governed by manufacturing practice regulations (GMP). A large majority of medical devices are approved through 510(k) submissions. Under this process, the manufacturer demonstrates substantial equivalence to an already marketed product. Such devices do not require controlled clinical evaluations (Kessler et al. 2004). Most medical/surgical procedures are not evaluated at all in the United States.

The FDA's Center for Biologics Evaluation and Research regulates biological products for disease prevention and treatment such as blood and blood products, plasma, vaccines, and allergenic products. Its scientists also evaluate the safety and effectiveness of products resulting from biomedical research.

The National Institutes of Health. The National Institutes of Health's (NIH) Office of Medical Application of Research (OMAR) uses consensus development as a primary assessment methodology. NIH's recognition of the lack of well-validated information about many medical technologies led to the development of a consensus mechanism (Banta and Thacker 1979). It relies on a panel of experts, who review the evidence from a clinical condition, drug, or device and respond to key questions on the topic raised by a planning group. It holds several consensus development conferences during the year to seek consensus on the safety, efficacy, and appropriate conditions for the use of medical technologies (Bozic, Pierce, and Herndon 2004; Pillar 1990).

The Centers for Disease Control and Prevention (CDC). CDC analyzes the public health benefits of new technologies.

State Governments

State governments, which historically have not played a significant role in the assessment of medical technologies, began to reevaluate their role when faced with increased pressure to control escalating health care costs during the 1980s. State governments are now more involved in medical technology assessment than in the past (Mendelson, Abramson, and Rubin 1995). Most of the state government medical technology assessment activities fall into four categories: (1) creation of a specific program charged with responsibility for evaluating and making recommendations on emerging technologies, (2) development and dissemination of practice guidelines, (3) regulatory oversight of medical technology through state certificate-of-need programs, and (4) collection and dissemination of data (Mendelson, Abramson, and Rubin 1995).

Overall, just like the federal government, technology assessment activities at the state level are highly fragmented and suffer from overlap and lack of coordination.

The Private Sector

The private sector's record in technology assessment has also been uneven. The Council on Health Care Technology of the Institute of Medicine, created in 1986, operated for four years and became defunct in 1990 (Rettig 1994). Several specialty groups and associations have established medical technology assessment programs. The AMA has a Diagnostic and Therapeutic Technology Assessment Program (DATTA) that provides about ten assessments per year. However, groups that their medical technology assessed must subscribe to this service. The Blue Cross and Blue Shield Association also has a Center for Quality Healthcare, which includes a technology assessment program. The Health Industry Association of America has a Medical Practice Assessment Unit. The American Hospital Association (AHA) publishes the *Hospital Technology Series*, a group of publications that provides guidelines on technologies and updates and reviews of new technologies. The American College of Physicians has a Clinical Effectiveness Assessment Program (CEAP) that performs ten to twelve assessments per year that are published in the *Annals of Internal Medicine* (Pillar 1990).

In a survey of 150 hospitals, the consensus was that hospital-based technology assessment programs could provide many benefits. The presumed benefits included a comprehensive review of all significant issues of a potential technology; helping hospital administrators and medical professionals balance competing values of cost containment, access, and quality; connecting the scientific and technical research world (theoretical) with the world of decision making (applied); helping provide clinicians with supportive data for proven technologies; saving financial resources; and guiding hospitals' technology acquisition decisions; among others (Rogers 2002).

Current Status of Health Care Technology Assessment

Rettig (1994) has argued that there are several problems with the state of health technology assessment in the United States. One is that federal responsibilities are decentralized and spread over several agencies. Second, the federal government has failed to develop the capacity to assess medical and surgical procedures. Third, both the public and private sectors have failed to create strong mechanisms for reviewing new technology for coverage and reimbursement decisions. Fourth, the federal government spends relatively little money on supporting research designed to assess the effects of medical technology and innovations. Fifth, there is a lack of connection between technology assessment and decision making regarding health care expenditures.

What is clear is that the efforts at technology assessment in the United States have been uncoordinated and poorly funded. Furthermore, there is a lack of coordination between public- and private-sector groups to address issues of diffusion of medical technology and its impact for quality of care and resource distribution (Bozic, Pierce, and Herndon 2004). The Office of Technology Assessment once estimated that less than 20 percent of all existing medical technology has been subjected to systematic study via controlled clinical trials (Kilpatrick, Dhir, and Sanders 1991). Spiraling health care costs in the 1980s revived interest in technology assessment. Technology assessment raises a number of questions: What constitutes health care technology? What is technology assessment? How is it conducted? Who should conduct technology assessment?

Goodwin (1998) argues that health care technology includes six things: (1) drugs; (2) biologics such as vaccines and blood products; (3) equipment devices and supplies such as CT scanners, cardiac pacemakers, diagnostic test kits, surgical gloves, and so forth; (4) medical and surgical procedures; (5) support systems that include patient record systems, blood banks, and the like; and (6) organizational and managerial systems such as prospective-payment systems, clinical pathways, and computer-based drug utilization review systems.

Traditionally, technology assessment concerned itself with evaluating the safety and efficacy of drugs and medical devices. In recent years, there has been a broadening of the perspective in defining technology assessment. Proponents of technology assessment argue that it should go beyond the traditional concerns of safety and efficacy to include evaluation of the cost-effectiveness of various technologies, including therapeutic and surgical procedures (Littell and Strongin 1996).

David Banta and Stephen Thacker have argued that "technology assessment is a comprehensive form of policy research that examines short- and long-term social (e.g., clinical, societal, economic, ethical, and legal) consequences of the applications of technology" (1990, 235). As the perspective on technology assessment has changed, so has the nature of researchers who engage in that assessment and the methods of assessment. In the past, mainly scientists and physicians carried out technology assessments.

As a result of an emphasis on cost and quality-of-life concerns, among others, the approach to technology assessment has become more interdisciplinary, requiring more collaborative effort on the part of researchers trained in economics, epidemiology, operations research, ethics, and other social sciences (Fuchs 1990). Americans, on the one hand, demand more and more technology. On the other hand, they are reluctant to pay for it and believe they are not getting good returns (benefits) for their money. Given this, one of the tasks of technology assessment is to connect the costs of medical service to the value attached to it (Eddy 1990).

In traditional technology assessment, where safety and efficacy were the two main concerns, the most important methodological tool was clinical testing or randomized clinical trials. The new perspective on technology assessment, with its emphasis on cost-effectiveness and medical, social, and ethical results, requires the use of many different methodological tools. Today, technology assessment relies on a variety of methods. They include randomized clinical trials, case series and cohort studies, epidemiological and surveillance studies, and quantitative syntheses such as meta-analysis. Health economic evaluations have included cost-minimization, cost-effectiveness, cost-utility, and cost-benefit analyses (Bozic et al. 2004). A highly developed set of rules and conventions governs sampling, random selection, reliability, and validity. Statistical analysis has contributed to technology assessment with techniques of sample designs, proper testing methods, and the use of confidence intervals. In short, methodologies for technology assessment have become more varied and more sophisticated (Muller 1991). However, it is important to remember that despite better and more sophisticated methodologies, technology assessment is still not a perfect science and subjective factors may influence the assessment itself or the interpretation of results (Muller 1991).

Another relevant question about technology assessment is who should do the assessment. Medical device manufacturers and professionals who perform high-tech procedures have fought government efforts to assess health care technology on the ground that it would lead to a small number of people deciding whether Americans have access to new technologies. They also argue that government involvement would lead to cost controls and national spending limits, which would have a detrimental effect on technological innovation. Critics of the medical device industry argue that the industry opposes the government's role in technology assessment for purely selfish reasons—out of the fear that technology assessment by the government will lead to useless products and procedures being weeded out of the marketplace, cutting into industry's profit. Given the huge economic self-interest involved on the part of the medical device industry, we cannot leave the task of technology assessment to the manufacturers and marketers of new medical products and procedures (Kosterlitz 1993).

Insurers and health plans argue that they are not in a position to assess new technologies because of the scarcity of information about new products and lack of resources to develop the information base. When individual health or insurance plans do engage in assessment, the results are kept in-house for competitive reasons. Even if individual insurers or health plans conduct their own assessment, they may reach different conclusions about the value of various technologies because of differences in methodologies used or differences in interpretations (Kosterlitz 1993).

Governments play a more prominent role in health care technology assessment in many Western European countries than in the United States. Given the fragmented nature of technology assessment in the private sector and the economic and profit motives at work, it seems to us that the federal government needs to play a more active role in technology assessment. The federal government can influence the diffusion of technology in two ways. First, the government could issue regulations or directives. These could include premarket controls, pricing decisions, reimbursement methods, licensing of advanced medical facilities, and generating and distributing information about the cost-effectiveness of medical devices and procedures. Second, the government could use economic incentives. These could include changing the financing or fee system, requiring cost sharing, or inducing competition in the marketplace. This second approach has gained momentum (Rutten and Bonsel 1992).

Technology assessment can add a great deal of information that can help policymakers make decisions about the allocation of scarce resources. It can inject rationality and scientific knowledge into the policymaking process. Nevertheless, it is important to remember that technology assessment is not a miracle cure that will solve all problems. There is a limit to how much policymaking can be guided strictly by scientific knowledge and rational processes. Policymaking is a very complex process that attempts to integrate a variety of economic, social, political, and ideological values and belief systems (Battista 1992). Policymaking often involves the "science of muddling through" (Lindblom 1959). Even good cost-effectiveness analysis may have only a limited impact on policymaking (Van Rossum 1991). Technology assessment may tell us something about cost-effectiveness; however, it cannot tell us how much we should be willing to pay for a given health effect. This involves making explicit value judgments, something that both the old and the new technology assessment abhors (Fuchs 1990).

While health care technology assessment has come to be viewed as an important component in policymaking, the social, political, and ethical aspects of health care technology are still not integrated in health care technology assessment. What is required is a more interdisciplinary approach (Lehoux and Blume 2000). While the rise of evidence-based medicine has added more analytical rigor and made technology policy decisions better grounded, this evidence-based analytical enterprise still has many limitations because often the evidence is lacking, is incomplete or it is difficult to establish clear cause-effect relationships (Atkins, Siegel, and Slutsky 2005; Claxton, Cohen, and Neumann 2005; Fox 2005; Gelijns et al. 2005; Mendelson and Carino 2005; and Steinberg and Luce 2005).

Despite these weaknesses, health care technology assessment can play an important role in societal decision making about the allocation of scarce resources and the acceptance or rejection of new technologies. Technology assessment raises two issues. One has to do with the value of economic efficiency, that is, whether the new technology is cost effective. This involves making societal judgments about whether to accept or reject new technology. The other issue has to do with the value of equity. This involves making societal judgments about relationships between needs and demands, distribution of health care spending, and access to high-cost technology for different groups in society. These issues have ethical implications. Ethical issues become more prominent when values of efficiency and equity come in conflict (Rutten and Bonsel 1992).

The ethical implications of and concerns raised by biomedical technology have created a new field of bioethics (Capron 1991; d'Oronzio 1994; Harris 1992; Mabie 1993). At present, there is an ambivalent relationship between medical technology assessment and ethics. The current method of technology assessment treats ethics itself as just another problem-solving technology. Ethics needs to play a more critical role in technology assessment by better understanding the complex relationship between society, medicine, and technology and by recasting how problems are defined (Have 1995).

Before we turn to the discussion of health care technology and ethics, let us briefly examine how the health care marketplace has changed because of the managed care revolution and whether managed care can contain the growth of medical technology and, thus, health care costs.

Managed Care and Health Care Technology

Earlier we cited two contributions to growth in medical technology and, thus, to health care costs: the third-party payment system, which insulates the consumer from the cost of health care, and the cost-based reimbursement system, which allows hospitals to acquire and stock medical technology without fear of financial losses. The managed care revolution with its capitation system changed many economic incentives as the country moved from a traditional fee-for-service health care system to capitated payment under a managed care system (see chapter 10). Under capitation, providers have contracts from insurance companies that call for them to provide care for a fixed per capita annual payment regardless of what the provision of certain services costs. Under such a system payments to providers are drastically reduced. This gives health service providers economic incentives to reduce their costs by adopting cost-cutting strategies (Tabbush and Swanson 1996).

Managed care organizations (MCOs), insurance companies, and the employers that ultimately pay the bills have resorted to the capitation method of payment. In all managed care programs, the primary care physician plays the role of a technology gatekeeper who controls patients' access to hospitals and specialists (Spencer 1995).

Considerable evidence supports the idea that managed care health plans, specifically health maintenance organizations (HMOs) reduce expenditures on health care services, as compared to traditional fee-for-service health plans. However, the evidence is mixed with regard to HMOs' ability to moderate growth in health care costs (Chernew, Fendrick, and Hirth 1997). Furthermore, despite the fact that considerable evidence suggests that the development, adoption, and diffusion of new medical technology increases health care expenditures, very little is known about how HMOs control the diffusion of new medical technology. A significant challenge for an HMO is to control the use of medical technology for which there is a strong patient demand but the value of which is questionable (Chernew, Fendrick, and Hirth 1997).

Today, hospitals find themselves saddled with large and expensive excess capacity of hospital beds and sophisticated medical equipment. In a new era of managed care such excess capacity has become unaffordable. Yet, surprisingly, relatively little of the excess inpatient capacity has been closed. Consequently, insurance companies and other purchasers of health care such as HMOs have begun to join together to demand deep discounts, as large as 40 percent. The rate paid for heart bypass surgery has dropped from as much as $45,000 under indemnity insurance to $15,000 under a managed care plan (Tabbush and Swanson 1996).

Despite such examples, it is unclear whether managed care plans will succeed in restraining the growth of medical technology. A recent study analyzed how cholecystectomy (surgical removal of the gallbladder) rates in different types of health delivery systems (health plans) changed following the introduction of an important new surgical technique, laparoscopic cholecystectomy. The study found no systematic difference between HMOs and the traditional fee-for-service population in the rate of growth in utilization following the introduction of this new technology (Chernew, Fendrick, and

Hirth 1997). Another study found that the market share of managed care plans and the concentration of enrollment had no relationship to hospitals' decisions to offer expensive health care technologies such as neonatal intensive care. The decision as to whether to offer such a service was influenced more by a hospital's teaching status, the proportion of infants in the market area with documented high risk, and the market concentration of major competition (Friedman et al. 2002).

The health care provider culture may have greater impact on cost growth than managed care health plans' cost-containment strategies because adoption of new technologies is driven primarily by external factors outside of the control of health care plans. These external factors include the clinical benefits of new technology, professional competition among physicians, consumer demand, and manufacturers who have a direct incentive to encourage utilization. In addition, factors internal to managed-care health plans such as care management (guiding treatment in specific clinical situations), environment management (creating incentives to influence practice patterns), and coverage policy (whether a plan should cover specific services) play a very limited role in influencing the diffusion of medical technology (Chernew et al. 2004). Reasons for this include reluctance to alienate physicians, consumers, and employers; difficulty in monitoring health plans through micromanaging care and limiting access to new technologies; lack of definitive evidence to restrict use of new technologies, that is, difficulty in justifying restriction; and the willingness on the part of health plans to keep cost growth trends within same range of the overall trend line (meaning there is less pressure to reduce costs if costs are also rising in competing plans) (Chernew et al. 2004).

However, it is important to point out that very few studies have systematically examined how managed care plans have dealt with adoption and diffusion of new medical technology. Until this is done, it is premature to come to any conclusion regarding the implications of managed care and capitation systems with regard to development, adoption, and diffusion of new medical technology. As the system for health care delivery continues to undergo further changes in the coming years, it becomes all the more important that the federal government improve the measurement of the costs and benefits of health care research so that it can make informed decisions about federal funding for health care research and recognize the tradeoffs among alternative policies for promoting innovation in health care (Garber and Romer 1996).

The capitated method of payment under managed care requires cost assessment and rationing with respect to new medical technology. Physicians and other health care providers under the financial pressures imposed by capitation face increased ethical dilemmas as they try to ration health care services. Physicians' single-minded devotion to patients' medical interests without concern for cost comes into direct conflict with financial pressures to contain costs (Malinowski 1996).

Medical Technologies: Law, Politics, Religion, and Ethics

Technology assessment has been highly fragmented and sporadic in the United States. As a society, we have failed to make systematic decisions about research and development of medical technologies, such as: Who should determine whether a particular technology should be developed and funded? On what basis should individuals be provided access once a technology is available in the marketplace? What level of technological intervention is appropriate for a specific medical problem, and what is the total impact of the rapid spread of high-cost medical technologies on society in general and on the U.S. health care system in particular? (Blank 1989).

The rapid proliferation of halfway technologies and spiraling health care costs raises many ethical concerns and dilemmas that we as a society must confront and address through public policies related to health care. The term "dilemma" in a popular sense is understood to mean a difficult choice between two or more alternatives. An ethical dilemma refers to a situation in which all the alternatives are morally problematic, that is, each alternative seems to involve a wrong act or action (Van DeVeer 1987).

Advancements in medical technology and ethical concerns raised by such technologies have given rise to the field of bioethics. "Bioethics is the application of ethical analysis to issues of health care" (Pillar 1992, 419). Debates about ethical issues raised by medical technology start during the developmental stage and continue through the experimental and implementation stages. Arthur Caplan (1989) has argued that society's obligation to provide health care exists if four conditions are present. One is that the person is in clear need of help. The second condition is that help exists and is available. Third, the person in need wants help and our obligation to help is stronger if such a help does not harm others. Finally, there is a reasonable chance of actually providing some help, that is, doing some good.

Any discussion of the ethical uses of medical technology must also take into consideration special concerns about respecting the patient's dignity. Threats to a patient's dignity can arise from a variety of sources, such as substandard conditions of treatment (inadequate space, equipment, etc.), health care providers' decisions and behaviors, and from the clash of new innovative technology with traditional standards (Pillar 1992).

Unfortunately, the use of many new medical technologies raises a complex set of political, legal, and ethical issues that are not easily resolved. The discussion about medical technology is never purely a matter of science. Political beliefs and ideologies, along with religious values, constantly enter into debates about reproductive and life-sustaining technologies because they raise some fundamental questions about what is life, what is quality of life, when does life begin, and do individuals have the right to refuse the use of life-sustaining technologies to prolong their lives? Can religious beliefs and health care needs or necessities coexist? The current health care market has seen an unprecedented growth in the size and influence of religious health systems, which can impact access to reproductive health services and end-of-life decisions. Religious hospitals are the fastest-growing type of hospital systems in the United States. Five of the ten largest health care systems in the United States are Catholic. There has also been a recent expansion of religiously affiliated managed care plans (Fogel and Rivera 2003).

Religiously sponsored managed care plans often do not provide certain services, such as contraceptive services. Refusal clauses, such as the 1973 Church amendment, allow health care providers to opt out of providing abortion or sterilization services (Fogel and Rivera 2003).

In the following pages, we discuss some of the ethical dilemmas raised by medical technology at two levels. First, we discuss the ethical dilemmas raised by specific medical technologies such as reproductive technologies and life-sustaining technologies. Second, we end this section with a broad discussion of the issue of health care rationing and the ethical concerns it raises.

The Beginning of Life: Assisted Reproductive Technologies

The growth of assisted reproductive technologies (ARTs) has raised a host of legal and ethical issues regarding decision making and the use of such technologies. ARTs are noncoital methods of conception involving manipulation of both eggs and sperm. Such technologies challenge people's basic values and create intense controversy. "Reproductive technologies include drugs, devices, and medical interventions that control reproduction and/or prevent sexually transmitted infections (STIs), such as contraceptives and products used to enhance fertility, as well as techniques for in vitro and in vivo fertilization" (Woodsong and Severy 2005, 194). In other words, reproductive technologies include technologies designed to prevent unwanted pregnancies and births as well as those aimed at enabling a couple to conceive and bear children (Beckman and Harvey 2005).

Of the about 60 million women of reproductive age in 1995 in the United States, about 1.2 million, or 2 percent, had an infertility-related medical appointment in the previous year, and another 13 percent had received infertility services (tests to diagnose infertility, medical advice, and treatments to help become pregnant) at some point in their lives. In 2002, use of ARTs resulted in 33,141 live births (delivery of one or more living infants) and 45,751 babies (Centers for Disease Control and Prevention 2004).

According to the Centers for Disease Control and Prevention (2004), ARTs include all fertility treatments in which both eggs and sperm are manipulated. In general, ART procedures involve surgically removing eggs from a woman's ovary, combining them with sperm in the laboratory, and returning them to a woman's body or donating them to another woman. The three types of ARTs are: (1) in vitro fertilization (IVF), (2) gamete intrafallopian transfer (GIFT), and (3) zygote intrafallopian transfer (ZIFT). In an IVF procedure, eggs are removed from the ovary and fertilized with semen in a laboratory. The resulting embryos are transferred back into the woman's uterus through the cervix. GIFT uses a fiber-optic instrument called a laparoscope to guide the transfer of fertilized eggs and sperm (gametes) to the woman's fallopian tubes through a small incision. ZIFT involves fertilizing a woman's eggs in the laboratory and then using a laparoscope to guide the transfer of the fertilized eggs (zygotes) to the woman's fallopian tubes.

Procedures that involve only the use of fertility drugs or intrauterine insemination (IUI), generally known as artificial insemination (AI), are not considered ARTs. In this procedure a woman takes medicine to stimulate egg production without the intention of having the eggs retrieved. Both IVF and IUI allow a couple to contract with a third-party woman (a surrogate) who carries the child. The child is genetically linked to one or both partners (a couple). The third-party woman relinquishes the child to the couple after the child is born (Beckman and Harvey 2005).

Since the birth of the first test-tube baby, about a million children have been conceived with high-tech help. Some studies have suggested that babies born through ARTs might be at higher risk of birth defects and genetic disorders. However, a comparative study of the health of ART babies and naturally conceived babies by a panel of experts from Johns Hopkins University, the American Society for Reproductive Medicine, and the American Academy of Pediatrics, found that ART babies do not have a greater risk of birth defects, cancer, or problems with growth or psychological development (Stenson 2005).

It is important to understand the role of consent and contract with respect to ARTs. In the context of ARTs, consent forms serve a dual purpose. One, the consent form serves the purpose of providing information about the medical risks, benefits, and alternatives. Second, it provides for selection of options regarding the disposition of any excess embryos that may be created. It is this duality and the enforceability of the terms of the consent that have often led to legal disputes between divorcing couples who no longer agree about the disposition of excess embryos remaining after the fertility treatment. In most cases, courts have viewed such consent agreements as contracts between both members of the couple (Elster 2005).

In contractual parenting (surrogacy), the intended parents (couple) contracts with a woman to carry a child for them and to relinquish that child after birth. In traditional surrogacy, the surrogate is impregnated with the sperm of the male partner of the intended parents through artificial insemination. This is also called IA surrogacy. In this situation, the impregnated woman is both the genetic and birth mother and the intended father is also the genetic father. Gestational surrogacy is used when the female partner of the intended parents has viable eggs but is unable to successfully carry a pregnancy to term. Here, the intended mother's eggs are fertilized with her male partner's sperm in a laboratory using IVF and the embryo is then implanted into the surrogate mother's uterus. In this case, the surrogate has no genetic connection to the child and the intended parents are the genetic parents (Ciccarelli and Ciccarelli 2005).

ARTs have created many challenges to traditional notions of family building and the legal construction of parenthood. ARTs produce many legal and ethical dilemmas. Medical technology in this area has advanced much more rapidly than the law's ability to address questions of rights and responsibilities that arise between the parties. It raises questions such as who should control stored embryos when the couple who created them no longer agree on their disposition? Who should be recognized as a child's legal parent or parents when donated gametes or a surrogate are involved in the child's conception? How do we define motherhood when one woman provides an egg to be gestated by another woman once it has been fertilized? Can an intended parent escape liability for child support where a child has been conceived through third-party assisted reproduction and the couple eventually gets a divorce? Who has the right to determine if preserved embryos will be used to create a baby where a couple has divorced after the embryos have been frozen but before they have been implanted (Ciccarelli and Ciccarelli 2005; Elster 2005)?

ARTs and Courts

Courts have tended to support the premise that intent, as reflected in consent forms or contracts, should define the relationships created through collaborative reproductive arrangements. In the case of *Davis v. Davis* in 1992 in Tennessee, where the issue involved was who should have control over stored embryos in the case of a divorcing couple, the court determined that the party seeking to avoid procreation (in this case the husband) should prevail. *Kass v. Kass*, a 1998 New York case, involved a situation in which seven embryos remained frozen when a couple divorced. The wife wanted control over the embryos so she could continue her attempts to have a child but the husband objected on the ground that he did not want to have a child with his ex-wife. The appellate court enforced a written directive signed by the couple at the time the embryos were created that specified that the embryos should be donated for scientific research. However, in the 2000 case of *A.Z. v. B.Z.* in Massachusetts, the court refused to enforce a prior written disposition agreement arguing that the consent form did not state that the husband and wife intended the consent form to act as a binding agreement. In a 2001 New Jersey case, *J.B. v. M.B.*, where a husband in a divorce case wanted to exercise control over the stored embryos over the wife's objection, the court concluded that that the party choosing not to become a biological parent should prevail (Daar 2001; Elster 2005).

With respect to contract and surrogacy, one of the most well-known cases is that of Baby M in 1988. This case involved a surrogacy arrangement in which the surrogate not only gestated the child but was also the genetic contributor. The surrogate, Mrs. Whitehead, turned over the baby to the intended parents (Mr. and Mrs. Stern). However, the very next day, she changed her mind. Fearing she might commit suicide, the intended parents gave the child back to Mrs. Whitehead. Four months later, the baby was forcibly taken by the police from a home where Mrs. Whitehead was hiding the baby. Mr. Stern filed a complaint seeking possession and custody of the child and enforcement of the terms of the surrogacy contract. The trial court found that the surrogacy contract was valid and granted sole custody to Mr. Stern. The appellate court argued that the surrogacy contract was equal to baby selling and found the contract to be void and unenforceable. However, the court also concluded that the surrogate was the mother of the child. The court granted custody of the child to Mr. Stern but remanded the case back to the lower court for determination of the nature and extent of Mrs. Whitehead's visitation rights (Ciccarelli and Ciccarelli 2005; Foote, Reibstein, and Figueroa 1998).

In the 1989 case of *In re Marriage of Buzzanca*, a couple—John and LuAnne Buzzanca—had selected an egg donor and a sperm donor and contracted with a gestational surrogate party to carry the resultant embryo. The couple was divorced before the child was born and the husband argued that he had no child support obligation. The trial court ruled that the child had no legal parents since neither John nor LuAnne had any genetic or biological link to the child nor had they adopted the child. The appellate court, however, reversed the decision on the ground that the child would never have been born without the actions undertaken by the Buzzancas and thus determined that they were the legal parents (Elster 2005).

ARTs and Politics

About thirty-five states have laws regarding artificial insemination by donor. These laws, in general, consider the husband or male partner, with his consent to the insemination, to be the legal father of any child born of the arrangement. However, only eight states specifically address the issue of egg donation by women. These statutes recognize the recipient couple as the legal parents of any child born through such an arrangement but do not confer parental rights or obligations upon the donor of the eggs (Elster 2005). Fourteen states have amended their constitutions to prevent gay couples from having the right to marry. However, hundreds of gay couples are finding ways to create families with or without marriage through surrogates.

In addition to technologies that help overcome infertility problems, a host of technologies make it possible for a woman to prevent unwanted pregnancies and limit unwanted births. These include female hormones delivered via injection or pill, mechanical devices placed in the uterus, and surgical procedures (Beckman and Harvey 2005). These technologies are not high-tech like the ones that help conceive children. Of course, the 1973 *Roe v. Wade* decision helped to legalize abortion in the United States.

Religious groups are active in influencing the public regarding issues such as procreation, infertility treatments, and abortion (Schenker 2005). Technologies designed to control birth such as contraceptives and abortions have been very controversial on religious grounds. Some religious groups view many of these technologies as unacceptable. For example, the Catholic church characterizes abortion and contraception as immoral (Beckman and Harvey 2005).

Reproductive technologies have received a great deal of public attention and debate because politics and religious belief systems have become intertwined in public policymaking. This is reflected in a very mobilized and well-funded pro-life movement that has advocated that legal personhood be conferred at conception (Solinger 1998). Social conservatives have also pushed for more restrictive policies with respect to fertility treatments as well as stem cell research (which we discussed in chapter 2). The fact that these new technologies are often viewed by some as "playing God" brings religious interests to the policy debate (Russo and Denious 2005). Pro-life advocates have lobbied for defunding organizations such as family planning clinics that provide abortions and have pushed for extending the gag rule. Even appointments to scientific advisory panels have become political and there has been unprecedented interference by politicians, policymakers, and ideological groups with the peer-review process used by government agencies such as NIH, combined with attempts to distort, misrepresent, and/or suppress scientific findings that run counter to the conservative social agenda (Russo and Denious 2005). The politics of reproductive technologies is characterized by conservative religious groups promoting policies that attempt to limit women's access to these technologies. On the other side of the political spectrum, advocates for women's rights have lobbied for public policies designed to increase access to reproductive technologies (Beckman and Harvey 2005).

In the field of bioethics, a philosophical consensus was developed in 1970 which was to keep a close eye on scientific innovations and their social implications, and to apply the brakes now and then through regulations and guidelines. This was called the Great Bioethics Compromise (Moreno 2005). The President's Council on Bioethics was founded in November 2001. As science became politicized, there was a breakdown of the consensus known as the "great bioethics compromise" on the President's Council on Bioethics (Moreno 2005). This is reflected in several of the council's recent reports on cloning, stem cell research, and reproductive technologies, in which it has taken a much more conservative position. The council's report on reproductive technologies recommends that Congress impose unspecified penalties on clinics for not reporting assisted reproduction as required under federal statute. It urges professional societies to create unspecified enforcement mechanisms to force compliance with ethics and practice guidelines. Furthermore, it recommends that Congress enact eight prohibitions on practice and research related to assisted reproduction. The council calls for a temporary moratorium on practices and research related to assisted reproduction, but ironically proposes no time limit or sunset provisions (President's Council on Bioethics 2004). In effect, the indefinite duration of these prohibitions makes them functionally close to a permanent ban. However, the council fails to provide any meaningful analysis for its recommendations and the report fails to address important ethical and policy questions (Wolf 2004). The council's work reflects a shift in balance toward using law to ban and penalize and away from a more moderate and rights-oriented approach (Wolf 2004).

ARTs and Ethics

Aside from the legal and political issues, ARTs also raise a host of ethical issues. This is reflected in a plethora of literature on this topic (Baruch, D'Adamo, and Seager 1988; Bayles 1984; Beck and Cowley 1994; Cohen 1996; Cohen and Taub 1989; Devine 2004; Garrett, Baillie, and Garrett 1989; Henifin 1993; Hoffman, D'Adamo, and Seager 1988; Kolata 1994; Nichols 1993; Raymond 1993; Robertson 1994; Ryan 2001; Shannon 2004; Strathern 1992).

The ethical and legal issues are likely to get only more complicated in the future because of several new trends. First, there is a growing movement of surrogate mothers who are choosing to carry children for gay couples over traditional families. Second, many surrogates, whether for heterosexual or gay couples, work as gestational carriers, meaning that they bring children to term, but not with their own genetic material (Bellafante 2005). Finally, there is a growing trend of harvesting sperm from cadavers. Such a practice is becoming more common nationwide. Ethicists seem to be in agreement that whatever is done should reflect what the dead person would have wanted. When a wife makes the request to extract sperm from the deceased husband because she wants to conceive a child it raises few questions. But, even in such a case, the issue can get very complex, as demonstrated by an example that arose in Florida. In this case, two weeks after marriage, the husband was killed in an automobile accident. At the request of the widow and her mother, physicians extracted a sperm sample from the deceased husband. Soon after, the wife met someone new and she decided not to use her husband's sperm to conceive. However, her mother wanted to carry the child herself, that is, she wanted to give birth to her own grandchild! The sperm bank refused to release the sample (Bauman 1997).

Ethical issues of fertility and reproduction can be examined from two perspectives—from the perspective of the infertile individual who wants to have a child and from the perspective of a community—and these two perspectives do not always coincide. ARTs raise not only issues of autonomy and personal choice but also issues of nonmalfeasance and justice (Baird 1996). Some of the ethical issues raised by ARTs are the following.

In U.S. society, private marketplaces play a major role. One of the important issues is how to control and balance private commercial activity to protect vulnerable consumer interests, since commercial organizations, who are solely interested in making money, have no reason or incentives to balance conflicting interests. What role should government play in protecting consumer interests through regulations and a system of accountability? How should collective resources be allocated in a society? Is there a danger of devaluing human dignity if the process of having children and creating families becomes commercialized? Are ARTs luxury items, or services that should be underwritten by a society? How do we ensure that everyone in society has equal access to ARTs (Baird 1996; Shanner and Nisker 2001)?

Other ethical questions raised by ARTs include: What constitutes informed consent, specifically, when it is applied to posthumous assisted reproduction? Is it ethical to retrieve spermatozoa from patients who are in a coma? What is the best way to respect the wishes of the deceased donor and to protect the interests of the unborn child? Could gametes be considered property, and what is the definition of paternity in cases of children born in such circumstances (Bahadur 2004; Benagiano 2003)? Are embryos persons, property, objects, or a unique category (Shanner and Nisker 2001)?

Since, in some of the ARTs, as many a five adults may play a parenting role (genetic mother and father—ovum and sperm provider; the gestational mother; and the intended social parents) and are all operating in his or her best interest, how do we protect the offspring, since they could not consent to an arrangement that may significantly shape their developing identities? In such arrangements, donor anonymity protects the privacy of donors and recipients, but what about the rights of the off-spring with regard to having access to his or her genetic medical history (Shanner and Nisker 2001)?

Finally, one of the most important issues is ensuring equal access to medically necessary and appropriate ARTs and avoiding overuse, both at the micro and macro level. At the macro level, issues of accountability, cost-effectiveness, and justice become important in distribution of resources. At the micro level, issues of autonomy, personal choice, and responsibility play an important role.

Advocates for ARTs argue that many factors, such as lack of uniform laws governing surrogacy, lack of health insurance coverage for expensive infertility treatment, lack of information about available options, and the like restrict women's access to ARTs. Furthermore, acceptability of ARTs is influenced by factors such as culture, social class, ethnicity, age, and sexual preference. Some analyses suggest that only a group of well-off non-Hispanic white women have access to many of the available options, and not disadvantaged women, thus creating differential access to ARTs (Beckman and Harvey 2005).

The End of Life: Life-Sustaining Technologies and the Right to Die

Today's life-support technologies are capable of keeping patients alive for a long time, even when they have no chance of regaining consciousness. Mechanical ventilators can keep patients breathing and artificial nutrition and hydration can sustain severely debilitated and dying individuals for many years. This raises the specter of individuals being kept alive in a vegetative, helpless state, sustained by a host of tubes and machines (Cantor 1993). The questions of who shall live, who shall die, and who shall decide raise difficult ethical and legal issues (Buckley 1990). Some well-publicized court cases help illustrate the complexities involved in such situations.

The Karen Quinlan Case

One of the early cases to highlight the ethical and legal dilemmas involved a New Jersey woman named Karen Quinlan who, at the age of twenty-one, slipped into a deep coma. She was hooked up to a respirator in a hospital. Her doctor informed her parents that their daughter was never going to come out of her coma because her brain was severely damaged. She might not necessarily die and, kept on a life-support system, might live for many years. Quinlan's parents asked the doctor to turn off the respirator. The doctor refused, and they went to court. The judge in the lower court disagreed with the parents. They then appealed the decision to the N.J. Supreme Court and, on March 31, 1976, the parents won the right to have the respirator turned off. The state supreme court ruled that Karen had a constitutional right of privacy, which her guardian could assert on her behalf (Peters 1990). Ironically, Karen Quinlan was able to breathe on her own. She was moved from a hospital to a nursing home, where she died in June 1985.

The Elizabeth Bouvia Case

A different dilemma was presented in the case of twenty-six-year-old Elizabeth Bouvia, who in September 1983 admitted herself to the psychiatric unit of California's Riverside General Hospital. She had had a very difficult life and was almost totally paralyzed from cerebral palsy. Once admitted, she asked for assistance in starving herself to death. What was unique about this case is that Ms. Bouvia was not terminally ill, but wanted the hospital staff to provide her with pain-killing drugs and hygienic care while she waited to die. The hospital refused. Elizabeth Bouvia went to court and lost; the court ordered that she be force fed. On April 7, 1984, she left the hospital. The hospital bill for 217 days, excluding physicians' fees, was more than $56,000; it was paid by the hospital and the state of California. After repeated court appeals, the California Court of Appeals found in her favor. The court said that she could refuse life-sustaining medical treatment. The court ruled that the right of a competent adult patient to refuse treatment is a constitutionally guaranteed right. After her victory, Ms. Bouvia changed her mind and did not kill herself (Pence 1995; Shreve and Kailes 1990).

The Nancy Cruzan Case

Another case involved thirty-two-year-old Nancy Cruzan of Missouri. She had been in a persistent vegetative state for seven years since a car accident. Her prognosis was hopeless. Her cerebral cortex had atrophied, but she was not dead, and she could have lived in such a vegetative state for many more years. The cost of her medical treatment was about $130,000 a year, paid by the state. In 1987 her parents requested that Nancy's feeding tube be removed so she could die. A lower court granted the request in July 1988, but the state supreme court in November 1988 reversed the decision, agreeing with the state's argument that the state of Missouri had an "unqualified" interest in preserving life. According to the court, the state's interest was not in the "quality" of life; the state's interest was in "life" (Angell 1990). Nancy's parents appealed the decision to the U.S. Supreme Court. In June 1990, the Court, in a five-to-four decision, agreed with the decision of the Missouri Supreme Court. The Court found that a competent person has a constitutionally protected right to refuse life-saving hydration and nutrition. If the person is incompetent, the Court ruled, the state is entitled to require rigorous proof that this person, when competent, would have requested removal of a feeding tube in the event of his or her future incompetence. According to the Court, the state of Missouri was entitled to require clear and convincing proof that a surrogate decision maker was choosing what Ms. Cruzan herself, when competent, desired (Meilaender 1990). It is interesting to note that the Court based its ruling, not on the ground of a fundamental privacy right, as was the case with Quinlan, but on the ground of a liberty interest. The court argued that the state's interests must be balanced against the interests of the patient (McCormick 1990; Peters 1990). On December 14, 1990, the Circuit Court of Jasper County, Missouri, declared that there was clear and convincing evidence that if Nancy Cruzan was mentally able, she would want to terminate her nutrition and hydration, and she would not want to continue her present existence. Her parents were authorized to remove the nutrition and hydration tube. After the removal of the feeding tube, Nancy Cruzan died on December 26, 1990.

On the other side of the ledger was a case in Minnesota in which a public hospital sought permission to remove a respirator from an eighty-seven-year-old woman who was in a persistent vegetative state. The hospital argued that continuing treatment was not in the woman's best medical or personal interest; however, the family of the woman opposed the request. The family won, and the woman died a year later (Kamisar 1991).

The Barbara Howe Case

The case of Barbara Howe, who suffered from Lou Gehrig's disease, reflects the complexities involved in such cases. She was admitted to Massachusetts General Hospital on November 1999. She had told her daughter, doctors, and nurses to do whatever was necessary to keep her alive as long as she could appreciate her family. Over the years, Barbara Howe continued to lose control of her body. A ventilator breathed for her and a feeding tube nourished her. She was no longer able to communicate with her caregivers what she wanted. Blue Cross and Blue Shield of Massachusetts had stopped covering her hospital stay in 2003. Howe's longtime doctor and nurses believed that she was in pain and that keeping her alive was tantamount to torture. However, Barbara Howe's oldest daughter, Carol Carvitt, who was her health care proxy, disagreed. Barbara Howe had become stuck in a limbo that no one foresaw. Howe's doctors and nurses wanted to withdraw life support, but the Probate and Family Court in February 2005 found that there was no sufficient cause to overturn Carol Carvitt as her mother's health care proxy (Kowalczyk 2005a). However, the judge urged Carvitt to think about her mother's best interest. Finally, in March 2005, Carol Carvitt agreed to terminate life support to her mother by June 30, 2005 (Belluck 2005). Barbara Howe passed away on Saturday, June 4, twenty-six days before a court settlement that would have allowed the hospital to turn off her life support (Kowalczyk 2005b).

One subtle change that has occurred in right-to-die cases is that most of the earlier cases involved a conflict between family members and hospitals in which the families pressed to let their loved ones die, while the hospitals tried to keep the patient alive. However, in the past decade or so, in instances when family members and hospitals have clashed, it is often the family members who want to continue life support and aggressive medical treatment while the doctors believe it is time to stop. This is the case partly because extraordinary medical advances have given hope to families. Patients and families are often skeptical or suspicious of doctors' and hospitals' intentions and believe that a life-support system may be terminated for economic reasons (Belluck 2005). The technology of artificial hydration and nutrition (AHN) that helps prolong life has become common practice. The question has become who decides when technology actually stops benefiting and becomes harmful to the patient. Drs. Jeffrey Ponsky and Michael Gauderer, who created the current techniques for inserting feeding tubes into patients in 1979, recently stated that the procedure has gone too far, because the feeding tubes are often used for patients who do not have any potential for recovery. They never imagined that their procedure would lead to such a massive ethical dilemma. Today, feeding tubes are used 250,000 times a year and have become a routine part of end-of-life care (Milicia 2005).

The Terri Schiavo Case

No right-to-die case has received more national attention, media publicity, and generated more political maneuvering than the tragic case of Terri Schiavo in Florida. On February 25, 1990, she suffered a cardiac arrest, apparently caused by a potassium imbalance. Her heart stopped temporarily, cutting off oxygen to her brain and causing brain damage. In June of 1990, a court appointed Terri's husband, Michael Schiavo, her guardian. Terri's parents, the Schindlers, did not object, because, according to all the reports, Michael and the Schindlers got along splendidly. In November of 1992, Michael Schiavo won a malpractice case against one of Terri's doctors for misdiagnosing Terri's medical condition. He was awarded $750,000 for Terri's care and $300,000 for himself.

It is at this point that the relationship between Michael Schiavo and his in-laws, the Schindlers, started to turn sour and they began to have disagreements over the use of this money and Terri's treatment. In 1993, the Schindlers attempted to remove Michael as Terri's legal guardian, but the state district court refused. On March 1994, a court-appointed guardian said that Michael Schiavo had acted appropriately and attentively toward his wife. In May 1998, Michael Schiavo filed a petition to remove Terri Schiavo's feeding tube. The Schindlers were strongly opposed to the removal. A second court-appointed guardian, in December 1998, reported that Terri Schiavo was in a persistent vegetative state with no chance for improvement. However, he also indicated that Michael Schiavo's decision making might be influenced by the potential to inherit the remainder of Terri's estate. The court trial began on January 20, 2000. Terri Schiavo had not left a living will. Her husband Michael testified that in their past conversations, Terri had indicated that she would not want to live her life this way. Based on the testimony of her husband and two other individuals, Judge George Greer, on February 11, 2000, ruled that Terri would have chosen to have her feeding tube removed. He ordered the removal of the feeding tube but later stayed his order to give the Schindlers an opportunity to appeal. On January 24, 2001, the Second District Court of Appeals upheld Judge Greer's ruling permitting removal of Terri's feeding tube. On April 18, 2001, the Florida Supreme Court elected not to review the decision of the Second District Court of Appeals (Cerminara and Goodman 2005; "Indepth: Terri Schiavo, Schiavo Timeline" 2005; "Key Dates in Schiavo Right-to-Die Case" 2005; "Terri Schiavo Timeline" 2005).

For the next several years, the struggle between Michael Schiavo and the Schindlers continued, as appeals after appeals were filed by the two sides. After many appeals, Judge Greer ordered the removal of the feeding tube to take place on October 15, 2003. On October 7, 2003, Florida Governor Jeb Bush filed a brief in federal district court supporting the Schindlers' efforts to stop the removal of the feeding tube. On October 10, 2003, a federal judge ruled that he lacked jurisdiction to hear the case. Terri Schiavo's feeding tube was removed on October 15, 2003 (Cerminara and Goodman 2005).

It was at this point that politics took over. As the Schindlers' legal options dwindled, Catholic, evangelical, and anti-abortion groups seized on their cause, helping to publicize it and fund it. In fact, starting in 2001, the anti-abortion Life Legal Defense Foundation paid for the Schindlers' legal costs. All this helped get the attention of politicians eager to show off their pro-life credentials (Campo-Flores 2005).

Within days of the feeding tube removal, the Florida legislature passed a special law, referred to as "Terri's Law," that gave Governor Jeb Bush the power to issue a "one-time stay" in certain cases ("Can States Intervene in Medical Decisions?" 2004). On October 21, 2003, Governor Bush issued an executive order to reinstate the feeding tube, which was done. On October 29, 2003, Michael Schiavo, joined by the American Civil Liberties Union, filed a lawsuit in state court arguing that "Terri's Law" was unconstitutional. In September 2004, a unanimous Florida Supreme Court declared "Terri's Law" unconstitutional on the grounds that it violated the principle of separation of powers between the executive, legislative, and judicial branches of government (Hallifax 2004, Sutton 2004). Governor Bush filed a petition seeking U.S. Supreme Court review of the Florida Supreme Court's decision. On January 24, 2005, the U.S. Supreme Court refused to grant such a review (Roig-Franzia 2005).

At this point, conservatives decided to nationalize the issue. Representative Dave Weldon (R-FL) and Senator Mel Martinez (R-FL) pushed for Congress to pass a broadly worded law aimed at due process law for disabled people like Terri. House Majority Leader Tom DeLay (R-TX) and Senate Majority Leader Bill Frist (R-TN) provided the leadership. The U.S. Senate wanted a narrowly worded bill specifically addressing Terri Schiavo's situation. After compromises, on March 21, 2005, the Congress of the United States passed a narrowly crafted law that applied only to Terri Schiavo. The law, called "An Act of the Relief of the Parents of Theresa Marie Schiavo," gave the U.S. District Court for the Middle District of Florida jurisdiction to hear and review the Schiavo case. President Bush signed it into law the same day (Hulse 2005). This set in motion a series of lawsuits filed by the Schindlers in federal district courts and appeals to U.S. Court of Appeals and the U.S. Supreme Court in an effort to have the feeding tube reinserted in Terri Schiavo. The federal courts consistently rejected the Schindlers' various constitutional claims and refused to reinstate the feeding tube. The U.S. Court of Appeals and the U.S. Supreme Court similarly denied such requests on several appeals (Goodnough 2005a, b; Goodnough and Liptak 2005a, b; Long 2005).

The feeding tube was removed on March 18, 2005. The parents of Terri Schiavo appealed to Governor Bush to intervene further in the case (Lyman 2005). Responding to political pressure from the conservatives, Governor Bush asked the Florida Department of Children and Families (FDCF) to obtain custody of Terri Schiavo in light of allegations of spousal abuse brought against Michael Schiavo. After holding a hearing, Judge Greer on March 24, 2005, issued a restraining order prohibiting the FDCF from removing Terri Schiavo from the hospice or reinstating the feeding tube. The Schindlers decided to end their federal appeals (Associated Press 2005). Terri Schiavo died on March 31, 2005. President Bush called upon the nation to build a culture of life. The Vatican issued a statement calling Ms. Schiavo's death a violation of the sacred nature of life that shocked the conscience (Goodnough 2005c).

An autopsy of Terri Schiavo backed her husband's contention that she was in a persistent vegetative state. The medical examiner's office stated that Terri Schiavo had suffered massive and irreversible brain damage and was blind. It also found no evidence that she was strangled or otherwise abused as had been alleged by her parents and others ("Schiavo Autopsy Finds No Sign of Trauma" 2005; "Schiavo Autopsy Shows Irreversible Brain Damage" 2005). Senator Mel Martinez (R–FL), who had pressed Terri Schiavo's case in Congress the most, stated that he had since had second thoughts about Congress's involvement in the case. Senate Majority Leader Bill Frist, an M.D., on March 17, 2005, on the Senate floor had voiced his opinion, after viewing videotape of Ms. Schiavo, that it was clear to him that she was responsive. Democrats cited the autopsy results as proof that Ms. Schiavo's husband and critics of federal government intervention in the case had been vindicated. Dr. Frist angrily stated that he had never made a formal diagnosis and had nothing to retract and did not respond to questions about the autopsy findings (Kornblut 2005b).

For the social conservatives who argue that sanctity of life trumps everything else, Terri Schiavo's case came along at the right time—their ascendancy in U.S. politics. The election of November 2004 had resulted in the reelection of George W. Bush to the presidency and strengthened Republican control of both houses of Congress (Stolberg 2005a). They did not the like the outcome in Schiavo's case. Pat Robertson called the removal of the feeding tube "judicial murder," while Tom DeLay called it "an act of medical terrorism" (Eisenberg 2005). DeLay threatened retribution against judges who had refused to intercede in the case (Hulse and Kirkpatrick 2005). It is ironic that, in the fall 1988, when his own father Charles Ray DeLay was in a coma and kept alive by intravenous lines and oxygen equipment, Tom DeLay had joined his family in a difficult decision to let his father die (Roche and Verhovek 2005). It is also interesting to note that President Bush, who flew into the nation's capital from a vacation in Crawford, Texas, to sign the law that allowed federal review of the Terri Schiavo case, had signed a law in 1999, while he was governor of Texas, that allowed attending physicians, in consultation with a hospital bioethics committee, to discontinue life-support efforts when a patient's condition was hopeless. In fact, only about two weeks prior to Terri Schiavo's death, a hospital in Houston, Texas, acting under this law, with the concurrence of a judge, disconnected a critically ill baby from life support over his mother's objections. According to medical ethicists, this was the first such case in the United States (Nichols 2005).

Representative Christopher Shays (R-CT), one of the only five Republicans in the House who had voted against Congress's emergency legislation throwing the Terri Schiavo case into the federal courts, declared that "this Republican Party of Lincoln has become a party of theocracy" (Eisenberg 2005, 23).

Public Opinion and the Right to Die

The tragic case of Terri Schiavo that captivated national attention also resonated with the public, as they found themselves contemplating difficult philosophical issues and matters of trust, such as what constitutes a life worth living? To whom should I delegate my own end-of-life decisions? How should I face death (Mehren and Verhovek 2005)? A number of polls have suggested that Americans had strong feelings about the Terri Schiavo case and that social conservatives had miscalculated public opinion. In a CBS poll of a nationwide random sample of 737 adults who were interviewed by telephone between March 21 and 22, 2005, 66 percent said that the feeding tube should not be reinserted into Terri Schiavo. Sixty-one percent said that the case should not be heard by the U.S. Supreme Court. A larger number, 82 percent, indicated that Congress and the president should not be involved in the Schiavo matter. Seventy-two percent said that Congress members got involved to advance their own political agenda and not because they really cared about Terri Schiavo. Only 34 percent said that they approved of Congress's job performance—the lowest rating Congress had received since December 1997. A strong majority of 75 percent said that the government should stay out of deciding life-support cases ("Poll: Keep Feeding Tube Out." 2005).

What is even more interesting is that, according to a telephone poll conducted by *Time* magazine between March 22 and 24, 2005, most Americans, including those who call themselves born-again or evangelical Christians, supported the decision to remove Terri Schiavo's feeding tube. Overall, 59 percent of all respondents and 53 percent of those who called themselves evangelical Christians supported removal of the feeding tube. Seventy-five percent said that it was wrong for Congress to get involved while 70 percent said that it was wrong for President Bush to get involved. Sixty-five percent said that the president and Congress's involvement in the case had more to do with politics than values. In fact, 51 percent indicated that they were more likely to vote against their representative/senator if he/she had voted in favor of moving the case to the federal courts (*"Time* Poll: The Schiavo Case" 2005). Of course, for the Senate that would mean voting against all incumbent Senators, since the Senate had passed the measure with unanimous consent!

The Legacy of Terri Schiavo

Terri Schiavo's case has spurred debate in statehouses across the country and many states are taking a new look at end-of-life legislation. All fifty states already have laws that allow people to write advance directives or a living will that allows them to specify their health care preferences if they are incapacitated or designates a health care proxy to make decisions for them. The new proposed legislations are designed to address situations like Terri Schiavo's, in which the incapacitated person has not left a living will or designated a health care proxy. End-of-life legislation has been introduced in at least ten states (Dewan 2005). A new coalition of disability rights activists and right-to-life individuals has emerged to push new laws in the area of right-to-die (Tanner 2005).

Thus, the broader legal battle over the laws that govern when and how a person dies has restarted as states consider measures that will change standards for letting patients die (Kornblut 2005a). The forces of politics, religion, and medicine are on a collusion course (Goodnough 2005b). The outcome is uncertain because, depending on the nature of politics and the coalition of these forces, different states may craft different policies. For example, Alabama is considering a law that would forbid the removal of feeding tubes without express written instructions from the patient, while a Democratic legislator in Michigan is writing a bill that would bar adulterers (Terri Schiavo's husband Michael, while still married to Terri, was living with another woman and had two children with this woman) from making decisions for an incapacitated person (Dewan 2005; Eisenberg 2005). In Kansas, a measure that would have given courts a greater chance to review decisions to end life-sustaining care and a lesser role to guardians or doctors stalled in the state senate (Tanner 2005). A Georgia state senator has authored legislation that would prohibit the removal of feeding tubes from patients who are able to breathe on their own unless they left a living will specifying otherwise (Eisenberg 2005).

Spurred by right-to-life sentiments or by advocates of the disabled, even the U.S. Congress, undeterred by public opinion that opposed intervention by Congress and the president in the Schiavo case, is taking a fresh look at end-of-life issues (Feldman and Richey 2005). The Schiavo case has also created a tension between social and economic conservatives within the Republican Party. High-profile economic conservatives such as Grover Norquist and Stephen Moore who have generally supported President Bush and the congressional Republican leadership were very critical of them for turning what would normally be considered a state issue over to the federal courts (Feldman and Richey 2005). How many states actually pass new laws, once the emotions over Terri Schiavo's case have subsided, remains to be seen.

The Right-to-Die Movement

The cases discussed above illustrate the legal and ethical complexities created by today's life-sustaining technologies. Who should live and who should die? Who decides? When is life worth preserving? Who determines what is quality of life? How does one measure a person's quality of life? Should the courts be involved in making such decisions? Does a patient have a right to demand unending medical treatment in a hopeless case? Does a patient have a right to seek assistance of a physician to help end his or her own life? Can euthanasia ethically be justified? What should be the ethical role of the physician and other caregivers? Is every life precious no matter how disabled? Do human beings have the right to self-determination and to decide when life has value? These are the ultimate questions that have been debated throughout the history of Western thought. The answers depend on our understanding of what makes us human beings. Aristotle argued that existence itself is inviolable. Thus, the plea to continue feeding Terri Schiavo against the wishes of her husband or the courts' determination of her expressed inclination is consistent with Aristotle's teaching. On the other side, René Descartes, an enlightenment philosopher, defined human life not as biological existence (an inviolable gift of life from God) but as consciousness about which people can make judgments. The argument in favor of removing the feeding tube on the ground that Terri Schiavo's quality of life had deteriorated to such an extent that it was not worth living would be consistent with Descartes's thinking (Leland 2005).

Two recent Oscar-winning films, *Million Dollar Baby* and *The Sea Inside,* which provided sympathetic views of people seeking to end their own lives, have brought issues of assisted suicide once again to center stage. Lawmakers in California and Vermont are debating assisted-suicide legislation (Costello 2005).

Approximately 10,000 patients live in a vegetative state in the United States. The complexities created by the life-sustaining technologies have given rise to the "right-to-die" movement across the country. Proponents of the right to die argue that individuals have a right to die with dignity and to determine when to end their lives. Proponents argue that passive as well as active euthanasia is justified. Passive euthanasia refers to a situation in which death results from omitting or terminating treatment. Active euthanasia—that is, actively assisted suicide—refers to a situation in which the health care provider gives the patient a means to kill himself or herself, or assists in the administration of the means. The publicity surrounding pathologist Jack Kevorkian of Michigan, who assisted numerous terminally ill patients in killing themselves, has heightened the debate over the issue of the right to die. In fact, it has led the state legislature to pass a law making it a crime to assist someone in euthanasia.

Opposition to the right-to-die movement has come from many sources, including the right-to-life movement. These opponents argue that suicide is wrong on religious and theological grounds, as well as being harmful to the community and the common good, and that it produces harmful consequences for other individuals in society (Garrett, Baillie, and Garrett 1989). Others have argued that no human being has a right to decide, for himself or herself or for others, when life is no longer worth living. They argue that there is a danger that such decisions may be based on wrong or ulterior motives. An example would be an agreement to end the life of a patient whose continual stay in the hospital was a financial burden to his or her family, or of a patient whose family members stood to benefit financially by inheritance. It can be argued that, once a society agrees that at some stage a life is not worth sustaining, the society is on a "slippery slope." Once passive euthanasia becomes acceptable, the next step will be active euthanasia, which in turn can easily lead to forced or involuntary euthanasia. Another worry is that if active euthanasia became a common practice, it could undermine the role of doctors as healers and caregivers (Gibbs and Sachs 1990).

Public sentiment seems to favor the right-to-die movement. A poll conducted in 1990 for Time/CNN by Yankelovich Clancy Shulman revealed that 80 percent of those surveyed said that decisions about ending the lives of terminally ill patients should be made by their families and doctors and not by lawmakers. Eighty-one percent believed that if a patient is terminally ill and unconscious but has left instructions in a living will, the doctor should be allowed to withdraw life-sustaining treatment—passive euthanasia. Fifty-seven percent went even further and said that in such cases it is all right for a doctor to administer a lethal injection or provide a lethal pill—active euthanasia (Gibbs and Sachs 1990). A more recent poll suggests that Americans' views have not changed on the subject. In a 2004 Gallup poll, 65 percent agreed that a doctor should be allowed to assist a suicide when a person has a disease that cannot be cured and that person is living in pain, while 41 percent opposed physician-assisted suicide on moral or religious grounds. The support for physician-assisted suicide in this 2004 survey actually went up from 52 percent who supported physician-assisted suicide in a 1996 survey (Schwartz 2005). In a survey by *Time* magazine in March 2005, 52 percent of Americans said that they agreed with Oregon's physician-assisted-suicide law, while 41 percent disagreed (Eisenberg 2005).

Washington state's "death-with-dignity" initiative, also known as Initiative 119 on the state ballot in a 1991 election, failed to garner a majority vote and lost by a margin of 54 percent to 46 percent. The initiative was supported by a large majority of voters for much of the campaign, but it lost support in the last few weeks before the election. A similar initiative in California in 1992 was defeated by the same margin as in Washington state ("Oregon's Assisted-Suicide Law. . ." 1995). In 1999, opponents in California successfully defeated assisted-suicide legislation. Legislative committees in California and Vermont are scheduled to vote in the near future on whether to adopt an Oregon-style law. According to a Field poll conducted in April 2005, 70 percent of Californians agreed that incurably ill patients should have the right to ask for and get life-ending medication (Eisenberg 2005).

Oregon's Death with Dignity Act

On November 8, 1994, Oregon voters approved the Death with Dignity Act by a margin of 52 percent to 48 percent. Known as Ballot Measure 16, the act allows physicians in the state to write lethal drug prescriptions for terminally ill patients who are expected to die within six months (International Anti-Euthanasia Task Force n.d.). Opponents of the law took the issue to the federal courts and lost. The Ninth U.S. Circuit Court of Appeals rejected the argument that depressed terminally ill adults would be prevented under the law from making informed decisions. The court stated that the specter of involuntary suicides was merely speculative. The U.S. Supreme Court, in October 1997, refused to hear the challenge and without comment issued an order letting the ruling of the Ninth U.S. Circuit Court of Appeals decision stand

(Biskupic 1997; "Challenge to Oregon's Assisted-Suicide Law . . ." 1997). On June 9, 1997, the Oregon legislature, declining to either amend or repeal the act, placed it on the ballot for a second vote. In the November 4, 1997, election 60 percent of voters voted against repeal of the law, while 40 percent voted in favor of repeal ("Oregon's Right to Die Movement" 1995). According to the Oregon Department of Health and Human Services, in the seven years from the 1997 enactment and implementation of the law to 2004, 208 individuals took lethal overdose prescriptions out of 64,706 Oregonians who died of the same diseases (Eisenberg 2005). Thus, contrary to opponents' fears, only a handful of terminally ill patients have requested and received assistance in ending their lives. It should be noted that the U.S. Supreme Court in March 2005 agreed to hear the George W. Bush administration's challenge to Oregon's law. The Bush administration wanted to revoke the license of doctors who prescribe a lethal prescription on the ground that federal drug laws trump states' rights to regulate medical practice (Eisenberg 2005). Thus, it remains to be seen whether Oregon's law survives and what impact the outcome of the case might have on other states.

Individual health care providers and society have tried to address some of the problems arising out of life-sustaining technologies in a variety of ways. Many hospitals have established ethics committees to help with ethical and related issues arising out of treatment of terminally ill patients. They often perform the functions of educating the hospital staff, developing policies in problem areas, and acting as advisory consultants to health care providers and occasionally to family members. Some have expressed concerns that the committees' decisions, instead of being advisory, may turn into de facto binding decisions, diminishing the role and rights of patients, family members, and health care providers (Garrett, Baillie, and Garrett 1989).

Living Wills and Durable Power of Attorney

There has also been a significant interest in "living wills" and "durable power of attorney." A living will is signed by a competent person in good health and gives permission to his or her doctor to turn off life-support systems in the case of terminal illness or a permanent coma. Thus the living will gives the person some control over his or her last few days or weeks of life. Because both the National Conference of Commissioners of Uniform State Laws and the American Bar Association have given their stamp of approval to the Uniform Rights of the Terminally Ill Act, the number of persons signing living wills is expected to increase. The national attention given to the Schiavo case could also increase interest in living wills. To prevent abuse, state laws in the area of living wills often stipulate specific conditions that must be met. For example, some states require that at least two physicians certify that the patient's illness is terminal. Some states require that the living will be witnessed by people who are not health care providers or beneficiaries of the person's last will.

An alternative to a living will is for an individual to assign a permanent power of attorney to another person. In this scheme, another person (for example a spouse, a family member, or a friend) is designated as a surrogate health care decision maker in case a person is unable or incompetent to make decisions for herself or himself due to serious illness.

Health Care Rationing

The state of Oregon adopted a rationing plan for Medicaid to contain rising health care costs. The Oregon plan has been praised by some and criticized by others (Strosberg et al. 1992). We discussed the plan in chapter 3 on Medicaid and in chapter 6 on cost containment. Here, our discussion focuses on health care rationing in general.

As past efforts at cost containment have failed, and as health care costs have continued to escalate, the debate over health care rationing has intensified. How much can we afford, and for how many people? Should everyone or every group have equal access to high-cost technology? If not, what criteria do we use to allow access to some and deny access to others? Do patients have a right to receive the best technology available, regardless of their ability to pay? Should patients be denied medical treatments when social costs outweigh individual benefits? Should patients' medical needs or economic status (i.e., ability to pay) determine the treatment they receive? Given limited resources, what is the best and the most efficient way of allocating scarce resources? How do we limit access and allocate resources in a way that is acceptable to society (Johnsson 1991; Kruse 1989; Wright 1993)?

The term "rationing" can be used in two different ways. One way in which rationing occurs is when market economies deny goods or services to those who cannot afford them. Like many other goods, health care is certainly rationed in this manner, especially for the poor and the uninsured, who cannot afford a variety of expensive health care services (see chapter 5). This type of rationing affects only about 15 percent of the population.

The current debate about health care rationing focuses on the second type of rationing. The question is: Should certain health care goods and services (e.g., halfway technologies) be denied or their availability limited even to those who can afford to pay? This type of rationing raises intense debate, since it would cover about 85 percent of the population—those who have access to health insurance (Aaron and Schwartz 1990). Such rationing is not common in the United States, but it has been practiced in other countries, such as Great Britain, for a long time. For example, virtually every patient suffering from chronic kidney failure is treated in the United States; in Britain, most are not treated. British society is much more willing to deny treatment for chronic kidney failure to older patients. Similarly, in Britain, patients over the age of sixty are generally not considered suitable for kidney transplants. Limited resources and age are two factors that act as a basis for a great deal of rationing in Britain. Consequently, the rate and the cost of treatment for certain health services are much lower in Britain than in the United States (Aaron and Schwartz 1984).

In the United States, Medicare provides major funding for acute health care of persons over sixty-five and for the permanently disabled between the ages of fifty-five and sixty-five. But there is no comparable source of funding for the young, except through Medicaid, which provides limited support. Some people feel that it is unethical for a society to devote so much of its resources to the care of the elderly and to spend so little on the young. They argue that this imbalance is more the result of the political clout of the elderly, who are organized and vote in large numbers, than of a rational allocation of resources (Ginzberg 1989). Some find the use of age as a criterion in allocating resources unjustifiable (Kilner 1988). Still others express concern over keeping extremely low-weight babies alive even when there is a high probability that they will be confined to a life of severe and permanent disability, and when many of them will require continuing institutional or specialized care for the remainder of their lives.

Some observers have argued that if the U.S. government is serious about containing health care costs, it needs to seriously consider rationing. One of the prominent proponents of health care rationing is Daniel Callahan. Callahan (1990) argues that in the United States, from the beginning, bioethics has gravitated toward an emphasis on individual autonomy and integrity, because it fits very well with the dominant ideology and values of American society. According to Callahan, this has led to ignoring the value of the common good or public interest. What is needed, he argues, is a communitarian ethic—a blending of cultural judgment and personal judgment (Callahan 1994). In his book *Setting Limits: Medical Goals in an Aging Society*, Callahan addresses the question of how much health care the aged should have (Callahan 1987). In a more recent book, he addresses the question of how much health care Americans are entitled to have. Callahan argues that individual demand for health care is limitless, and he blames the "liberal society" for not curbing individual desires and needs (Callahan 1995). John Kilner challenges the popular myth that Americans have enough resources to treat every terminal disease and argues for rationing (Kilner 1991, 1992). Others have also argued for rationing health care in the United States (Menzel 1990). Critics of health care rationing argue that any attempt to justify rationing using principles such as social worth, ability to pay, or age leaves enormous potential for mischief. Furthermore, arriving at any societal consensus about these principles would be very complex and problematic at best.

Conclusion: Medical Technology, Ethics, and Public Policy

The discussion of reproductive and life-sustaining technologies in this chapter exemplifies the complexities of legal and ethical issues raised by modern medical technology. Similar complex issues are raised by health care technology in areas such as organ transplants (Garrett, Baillie, and Garrett 1989; General Accounting Office 1989; Shaw et al. 1991). Organ transplants raise many ethical issues for donors, recipients, health care providers, and society as a whole. When is it ethical to donate organs? What criteria should be used in deciding who gets an organ transplant and who does not? Is it ethical to sell organs? Since it is reasonable to assume that there will always be more demand for than supply of available organs, would allowing the selling of organs produce an economic market for organs, in which organs would be bought and sold as other goods and services are? What are the ethical issues related to the living donor versus the living but terminal donor? Is it ethical to end the life of a terminal patient in order to make an organ available?

Health care technology has also produced a revolution in reproductive processes that raises many difficult ethical problems. Ethical objections to artificial insemination are often raised on religious or theological grounds. Objections are also raised on the ground that artificial insemination produces harmful consequences for society when the woman is not married, when the donor is not screened, or when the identity of the donor is concealed. Similar ethical concerns are raised with in vitro fertilization (i.e., test-tube fertilization), surrogate parenthood, embryo transfers, and the use of frozen embryos and sperm banks.

End-of-life technologies have produced many legal and ethical concerns as reflected in the right-to-die cases discussed in this chapter. The case of Terri Schiavo also highlights the clash of science, religion, and politics when it comes to policymaking.

Health care technology is developing at a rapid pace, while our capacity and our ability to comprehend and deal with the legal and ethical issues raised by medical technology are lagging behind. Now that we have entered the twenty-first century, policymakers will be increasingly confronted with the challenge of formulating public policies that require an understanding of the legal and ethical implications of rapidly emerging new technologies. Developments in the United States can be best characterized as a patchwork approach to bioethics. Most initiatives have tended to be private rather than government-sponsored. This has the advantage of producing multiple or pluralistic approaches that foster diversity. Private bodies also are under less political pressure (Cohen and McCloskey 1994). But such approaches often lack the necessary authority to produce meaningful and timely responses. Kathi E. Hanna, Robert M. Cook-Deegan, and Robyn Y. Nishimi (1993) have advocated that the United States adopt a new approach to addressing issues of bioethics. They have called for the establishment of a centralized national forum, along the lines of a presidential commission, which would conduct research, hold hearings, and address issues of broad public interest dealing with, for example, assisted-suicide and life-sustaining and reproductive technologies. They have also recommended creation of an entity within the Department of Health and Human Services to establish protocols for federally funded biomedical experiments and research (Hanna, Cook-Deegan, and Nishimi 1993). Such proposals have come under criticism from some quarters. For example, Ira H. Carmen argues that "good" biomedicine or "ethical" biomedicine cannot be defined in the abstract. According to Carmen, our constitutional and political order requires a delicate weighing and balancing of competing interests by policymakers. The Madisonian model that underlies our political system requires that the people's representatives, not some presidential commission, work through the political branches to formulate national policies (Carmen 1994). Whether the Congress of the United States is up to the task remains to be seen.

References

Aaron, Henry J. 1991. *Serious and Unstable Condition: Financing America's Health Care*. Washington, D.C.: Brookings Institution.

Aaron, Henry J., and William B. Schwartz. 1984. *The Painful Prescription: Rationing Hospital Care*. Washington, D.C.: Brookings Institution.

————. 1990. "Rationing Health Care: The Choice before Us." *Science* 247, no. 4941 (January 26): 418–22.

Abrahamsen, Cathie. 2005. "Washington Taps into Healthcare Technology." *Nursing Management* 36, no 3: 52–55.

"Agency for Healthcare Research and Quality: Reauthorization Fact Sheet." 2005. Online at www.ahrq.gov/about/ahrqfact.htm.

Anderson, Gerald F., and Earl P. Steinberg. 1994. "Role of the Hospital in the Acquisition of Technology." In *Adopting New Medical Technology*, ed. Annetine C. Gelijns and Holly V. Dawkins, 61–70. Washington, D.C.: National Academy Press.

Angell, Marcia. 1990. "Prisoners of Technology: The Case of Nancy Cruzan." Editorial. *New England Journal of Medicine* 322, no. 17 (April 26): 1226–28.

Associated Press. 2005. "Schiavo's Parents Give Up Their Federal Appeal." *New York Times*, March 27.

Atkins, David; Joanna Siegel; and Jean Slutsky. 2005. "Making Policy When Evidence Is In Dispute." *Health Affairs* 24, no. 1 (January–February): 102–13.

Atkins, G. Lawrence, and John L. Bauer. 1992. "Taming Health Care Costs Now." *Issues in Science and Technology* 9, no. 2 (Winter): 54–60.

Bahadur, G. 2004. "Ethical Challenges in Reproductive Medicine: Posthumous Reproduction." *International Congress Series* 1266 (April): 295–302.

Baird, P. A. 1996. " Ethical Issues of Fertility and Reproduction." *Annual Review of Medicine* 47, no. 1: 107–116.

Baker, Laurence; Howard Birnbaum; Jeffrey Geppert; David Mishol; and Erick Moyneur. 2003. "The Relationship Between Technology Availability and Health Care Spending." *Health Affairs*, Web Exclusive (November 5): W3-537–W3-551.

Banta, David H., and Stephen B. Thacker. 1979. "Policies Toward Medical Technology: The Case of Electronic Fetal Monitoring." *American Journal of Public Health* 69, no. 9 (September): 931–35.

————. 1990. "The Case for Reassessment of Health Care Technology: Once Is Not Enough." *Journal of the American Medical Association* 265, no. 2 (July 11): 235–40.

Banta, David H., and Hindrik Vondeling. 1994. "Strategies for Successful Evaluation and Policy-Making toward Health Care Technology on the Move: The Case of Medical Lasers." *Social Science and Medicine* 38, no. 12: 1663–74.

Baruch, Elaine H.: Amadeo F. D'Adamo, Jr.; and Joni Seager, eds. 1988. *Embryos, Ethics, and Women's Rights: Exploring the New Reproductive Technologies*. New York: Haworth Press.

Battista, Renaldo N. 1992. "Health Care Technology Assessment: Linking Science and Policy Making." *Canadian Medical Association Journal* 146, no. 4 (February 15): 461–62.

Bauman, Norman. 1997. "Dead Men Conceiving: Trend Raises Ethical, Legal Questions." *Urology Times* 25, no. 2 (February): 4–5.

Bayles, Michael D. 1984. *Reproductive Ethics*. Englewood Cliffs, N.J.: Prentice Hall.

Beck, Melinda, and Geoffrey Cowley. . 1994. "Mother Nature?" *Newsweek*, January 17.

Beckman, Linda J., and S. Marie Harvey. 2005. "Current Reproductive Technologies: Increased Access and Choice?" *Journal of Social Issues* 61, no. 1 (March): 1–20.

Bellafante, Ginia. 2005. "Surrogate Mothers' New Niche: Bearing Children for Gay Couples." *New York Times*, May 27.

Belluck, Pam. 2005. "Tide Has Turned When Hospitals, Families Clash Over Patient Care." *San Diego Union Tribune*, March 27.

Benagiano, G. 2003. "Public Health and Infertility." *Reproductive Medicine Online* 7, no. 6 (December): 606–14.

Berlinger, Howard S. 1987. *Strategic Factors in U.S. Healthcare: Human Resources, Capital, and Technology*. Boulder, Colo.: Westview Press.

"Biotechnology: High Growth Industry Profile." 2004. U.S. Department of Labor, Employment and Training Administration, Business Relations Group. Online at www.careervoyages.gov/pdf/biotech-profile-504.pdf.

Biskupic, Joan. 1997. "Oregon's Assisted Suicide Law Lives On." *Washington Post*, October 15, A03.

Blank, Robert H. 1988. *Rationing Medicine*. New York: Columbia University Press.

———. 1989. "Introduction." In *Biomedical Technology and Public Policy*, ed. Robert H. Blank and Miriam K. Mills, vii–xv. New York: Greenwood Press.

Bozic, Kevin J; Read G. Pierce; and James H. Herndon. 2004. "Health Care Technology Assessment." *Journal of Bone and Joint Surgery* 86, no. 6 (June): 1305–14.

Bronzino, Joseph D.; Vincent H. Smith; and Maurice L. Wade. 1990. *Medical Technology and Society: An Interdisciplinary Perspective*. Cambridge, Mass.: Massachusetts Institute of Technology Press.

Bryce, Cindy L., and Kathryn Ellen Cline. 1998. "The Supply and Use of Selected Technologies." *Health Affairs* 17, no. 1 (January/February): 213–24.

Buckley, Jerry. 1990. "How Doctors Decide Who Shall Live, Who Shall Die." *U.S. News and World Report*, January 11.

Callahan, Daniel. 1987. *Setting Limits: Medical Goals in an Aging Society*. New York: Simon and Schuster.

———. 1990. "Why We Must Set Limits," in "A Good Old Age?" In *The Paradox of Setting Limits*, ed. Paul Homer and Martha Holstein, 23–43. New York: Simon and Schuster.

———. 1994. "Bioethics: Private Choice and Common Good." *Hastings Center Report* 24, no. 3 (May 1): 28–31.

———. 1995. *What Kind of Life: The Limits of Medical Progress*. Washington, D.C.: Georgetown University Press.

Campbell, Eric G; Joshua B. Powers; David Blumenthal; and Brian Biles. 2004. "Inside the Triple Helix: Technology Transfer and Commercialization in the Life Sciences." *Health Affairs* 23, no. 1 (January–February): 64–76.

Campo-Flores, Arian. 2005. "The Legacy of Terri Schiavo." *Newsweek*, April 4.

"Can States Intervene in Medical Decisions?" 2004. *Christian Science Monitor*, August 3.

Cantor, Norman L. 1993. *Advance Directives and the Pursuit of Death with Dignity*. Indianapolis: Indiana University Press.

Caplan, Arthur. 1989. "Heard Data on Efficacy: The Prerequisite to Hard Choices in Health Care." *The Mount Sinai Journal of Medicine* 56, no. 3: 185–90.

Capron, Alexander Morgan. 1991. "Biomedical Technology and Health Care: Transforming Our World." *Southern California Law Review* 65, no. 1 (November 1): 1–10.

Carmen, Ira H. 1994. "Bioethics, Public Policy and Political Science." *Politics and Life Sciences* 13, no. 1 (February 1): 79–81.

Cassell, Eric J. 1993. "The Sorcerer's Broom: Medicine's Rampant Technology." *Hastings Center Report* 23 (November/December): 32–39.

Centers for Disease Control and Prevention. 2004. *Assisted Reproductive Technology Success Rates: National Summary and Fertility Clinic Report 2002*. Online at www.cdc.gov/reproductivehealth/ART02/index.htm.

Cerminara, Kathy, and Kenneth Goodman. 2005. "Key Events in the Case of Theresa Marie Schiavo." Joint Project of the University of Miami Ethics Programs and the Shepard Broad

Law Center at Nova Southeastern University. Online at www.miami.edu/ethics2/schiavo/timeline.htm.

"Challenge to Oregon's Assisted-Suicide Law Dies in Appeals Court." 1997. Associated Press, February 28. Online at www.wcinet.com.

Chernew, Michael, E.; A. Mark Fendrick; and Richard A. Hirth. 1997. "Managed Care and Medical Technology: Implications for Cost Growth." *Health Affairs* 16, no. 2 (March/April): 196–206.

Chernew, Michael E; Peter D. Jacobson; Timothy P. Hofer; Keith D. Aaronson; and A. Mark Fendrick. 2004. "Barriers to Constraining Health Care Cost Growth." *Health Affairs* 23, no. 6 (November–December): 122–28.

Ciccarelli, John K., and Janice C. Ciccarelli. 2005. "The Legal Aspects of Parental Rights in Assisted Reproductive Technology." *Journal of Social Issues* 61, no. 1 (March): 127–37.

Claxton, Karl; Joshua T. Cohen; and Peter J. Neumann. 2005. "When Is Evidence Sufficient?" *Health Affairs* 24, no. 1 (January–February): 93–101.

Cohen, Cynthia B., ed. 1996. *New Ways of Making Babies: The Case of Egg Donation.* Bloomington: Indiana University Press.

Cohen, Cynthia B., and Elizabeth L. McCloskey. 1994. "Private Bioethics Forums: Counterpoint to Government Bodies." *Kennedy Institute of Ethics Journal* 4, no. 2 (September 1): 283–89.

Cohen, Sherrill, and Nadine Taub, eds. 1989. *Reproductive Laws for the 1990s.* Clifton, N.J.: Humana Press.

Collins, Sara. 1993. "Saving Lives Isn't Cheap." *U.S. News and World Report,* June 7.

"Cost/Benefits of High-Tech Medicine." 1992. *Health Systems Review* 25, no. 1 (January 1): 16–18.

Costello, Daniel. 2005. "Assisted Suicide at Center Stage Once Again." *Los Angeles Times,* March 7.

Cowley, Geoffrey. 1993. "What High Tech Can't Accomplish." *Newsweek,* October 4.

Cutler, David M., and Mark McClellan. 2001. "Is Technological Change in Medicine Worth It? *Health Affairs* 20, no. 5 (September–October): 11–29.

Daar, Judith F. 2001. "Frozen Embryo Disputes Revisited: A Trilogy of Procreation-Avoidance Approaches." *Journal of Law, Medicine, and Ethics* 29, no. 2 (Summer): 197–202.

Detmer, Don E. 1993. "Adhesive Tape and Red Tape: The Strangling of Surgical Innovation in America." *USA Today* 121, no. 2572 (January): 56–59.

Devine, Richard J. 2004. *Good Care, Painful Choices: Medical Ethics for Ordinary People.* New York: Paulist Press.

Dewan, Shaila. 2005. "States Taking a New Look at End-of-Life Legislation." *New York Times,* March 31.

Doolan, David F., and David W. Bates. 2002. "Computerized Physician Order Entry System in Hospitals: Mandates and Incentives." *Health Affairs* 21, no. 4 (July–August): 180–88.

d'Oronzio, Joseph C. 1994. "Bioethics and the Body Politic." *Cambridge Quarterly of Health Care Ethics* 3, no. 2: 300–1.

Eddy, David M. 1990. "Connecting Value and Costs: Whom Do We Ask, and What Do We Ask Them?" *Journal of the American Medical Association* 254, no. 13 (October 3): 1737–39.

Eisenberg, Daniel. 2005. "Lessons of the Schiavo Battle." *Time,* April 4: 22–30.

Elster, Nanette R. 2005. "Assisted Reproductive Technologies: Contracts, Consents, and Controversies." *American Journal of Family Law* 18, no. 4 (Winter): 193–99.

Feldman, Linda., and Warren Richey. 2005. "The Terri Schiavo Legacy." *The Christian Science Monitor,* April 1.

Fendrick, A. Mark, and J. Sanford Schwartz. 1994. "Physicians' Decisions Regarding the Acquisition of Technology." In *Adopting New Medical Technology,* ed. Annetine C. Gelijns and Holly V. Dawkins, 71–84. Washington, D.C.: National Academy Press.

Fineberg, H.V. 1977. "Computerized Tomography: Dilemma of Health Care Technology." *Pediatrics* 59, no. 2 (February): 147–49.

Fogel, Susan B., and Lourdes A. Rivera. 2003. "Religious Beliefs and Healthcare Necessities." *Human Rights: Journal of the Section of Individual Rights and Responsibilities* 30, no. 2 (Spring): 8–11.

Foote, Donna; Larry Reibstein; and Ana Figueroa. 1998. "And Baby Makes One." *Newsweek* 131, no. 5 (February 2): 68–69.

Fox, Daniel M. 2005. "Evidence of Evidence-Based Health Policy: The Politics of Systematic Reviews in Coverage Decisions." *Health Affairs* 24, no. 1 (January–February): 114–27.

Freed, David H. 1994. "Toward Redefining Expectations About Medical Technology." *Trends in Health Care, Law and Ethics* 9, no. 2 (Spring): 21–28.

Friedman, Bernard; Kelly J. Devers; Claudia A. Steiner; and Steven Fox. 2002. "The Use of Expensive Health Technologies in the Era of Managed Care: The Remarkable Case of Neonatal Intensive Care." *Journal of Health Politics, Policy and Law* 27, no. 3 (June): 441–64.

Fuchs, Victor R. 1986. *The Health Economy*. Cambridge, Mass.: Harvard University Press.

———. 1990. "The New Technology Assessment." *New England Journal of Medicine* 323, no. 19 (September 6): 673–77.

———. 1993. *The Future of Health Care Policy*. Cambridge, Mass.: Harvard University Press.

Fuchs, Victor R., and Harold C. Sox, Jr. 2001. "Physicians' Views of the Relative Importance of Thirty Medical Innovations." *Health Affairs* 20, no. 5 (September–October): 30–42.

Garber, Alan M., and Paul M. Romer. 1996. "Evaluating the Federal Role in Financing Health-Related Research." *Proceedings of the National Academy of Sciences* 93, no. 23 (November 12): 12717–25.

Garrett, Thomas M.; Harold W. Baillie; and Rosellen M. Garrett. 1989. *Health Care Ethics: Principles and Problems*. Englewood Cliffs, N.J.: Prentice Hall.

Gelijns, Annetine C., and Nathan Rosenberg. 1994. "The Dynamics of Technological Change in Medicine." *Health Affairs* 13, no. 3 (Summer): 28–46.

Gelijns, Annetine C; Lawrence D. Brown; Corey Magnell; Elettra Ronchi; and Alan J. Moskowitz. 2005. "Evidence, Politics, and Technological Change." *Health Affairs* 24, no. 1 (January–February): 29–40.

General Accounting Office. 1989. *Heart Transplants: Concerns about Cost, Access, and Availability of Donor Organs*. Washington, D.C.: Government Printing Office.

———. 1992. *Hospital Costs: Adoption of Technologies Drives Cost Growth*. Washington, D.C.: Government Printing Office.

Gibbs, Nancy, and Andrea Sachs. 1990. "Love and Let Die: In an Era of Medical Technology, How Are Patients and Families to Decide Whether to Halt Treatment—or Even to Help Death Along?" *Time*, March 19.

Ginzberg, Eli. 1989. "Balancing Dollars and Quality." *Midwest Medical Ethics* 5, no. 4 (Fall): 1–5.

———. 1990. "High-Tech Medicine and Rising Health Care Costs." *Journal of the American Medical Association* 263, no. 13 (April 4): 1820–22.

Goldsmith, Jeff. 1994. "Perspective: The Impact of New Technology on Health Costs." *Health Affairs* 13, no. 3 (Summer): 80–81.

———. 2004. "Technology and the Boundaries of the Hospital: Three Emerging Technologies." *Health Affairs* 23, no. 6 (November–December): 149–56.

Goodman, Clifford S. 1997. "Closer Inspection: The Recent Evolution of Technology Assessment." *Health Systems Review* 30, no. 2 (March–April): 38–42.

Goodnough, Abby. 2005a. "Appeals Court Refuses to Order Schiavo's Feeding Reinstated." *New York Times*, March 23.

———. 2005b. "Few Options for Schiavo's Parents as U.S. Judge Denies Request." *New York Times*, March 25.

————. 2005c. "Schiavo Dies, Ending Bitter Case Over Feeding Tube." *New York Times*, April 1.

Goodnough, Abby, and Adam Liptak. 2005a. "Schiavo's Parents Appeal to the Supreme Court on Feeding Tube." *New York Times*, March 24.

————. 2005b. "Supreme Court Rejects Request to Reinsert Feeding Tube." *New York Times*, March 24.

Goodwin, C S. 1998. Health Care Technology Assessment: Methodology, Frameworks, and Role in Policy Making." *American Journal of Managed Care* (special issue), 4: 200–216.

Griner, Paul F. 1992. "New Technology Adoption in the Hospital." In *Technology and Health Care in an Era of Limits*, ed. Annetine C. Gelijns, 123–32. Washington, D.C.: National Academy Press.

Hallifax, Jackie. 2004. "Fla. Court Nixes Law Keeping Woman Alive." Associated Press, September 23. Online at story.news.yahoo.com.

Hanna, Kathi E.; Robert M. Cook-Deegan; and Robyn Y. Nishimi. 1993. "Finding a Forum for Bioethics in U.S. Public Policy." *Politics and Life Sciences* 12): 205–19.

Harris, John. 1992. *Wonderwoman and Superman: The Ethics of Human Biotechnology.* New York: Oxford University Press.

Have, Henk A.M.J. ten. 1995. "Medical Technology Assessment and Ethics: Ambivalent Relations." *Hastings Center Report* 25, no. 5 (September/October): 13–20.

"Health Care Dollars." 1992. *Consumer Reports*, July: 435–48.

Henifin, Mary S. 1993. "New Reproductive Technologies: Equity and Access to Reproductive Health Care." *Journal of Social Issues* 49, no. 2 (Summer): 61–74.

Hill, D.W. 1991. "25 Years of Medical Technology." *British Journal of Hospital Medicine* 46, no. 4 (October): 242–43.

Hillman, Bruce J. 1992. "Physicians' Acquisition and Use of New Technology in an Era of Economic Constraints." In *Technology and Health Care in an Era of Limits*, ed. Annetine C. Gelijns, 133–49. Washington, D.C.: National Academy Press.

Hoffman, Elaine; Amadeo F. D'Adamo; and Joni Seager, eds. 1988. *Embryos, Ethics, and Women's Rights: Exploring the New Reproductive Technologies.* New York: Harrington Park Press.

Hulse, Carl. 2005. "Congress Passes and Bush Signs Legislation on Schiavo Case." *New York Times*, March 21.

Hulse, Carl, and David D. Kirkpatrick. 2005. "Even Death Does not Quiet Harsh Political Fight." *New York Times*, April 1.

"Indepth: Terri Schiavo, Schiavo Timeline." 2005. *CBC Online News*, March 31. Online at www.cbc.ca.

International Anti-Euthanasia Task Force. n.d. "The Facts about the Oregon 'Death with Dignity Act' Initiative." Online at www.iaetf.org.

James, Everette A., Jr., et al. 1991. "The Diffusion of Medical Technology: Free Enterprise and Regulatory Models in the USA." *Journal of Medical Ethics* 17: 150–55.

Jaros, G.G., and D.A. Boonzaier. 1993. "Cost Escalation in Health-Care Technology—Possible Solutions." *South African Medical Journal* 83, no. 6 (June 1): 420–22.

Johnsson, Julie. 1991. "High-Tech Health Care: How Much Can We Afford?" *Hospitals* 65, no. 16 (August 20): 80.

Kalb, Paul E. 1990. "Controlling Health Care Costs by Controlling Technology: A Private Contractual Approach." *Yale Law Journal* 99, no. 4 (March): 1109–26.

Kambert, Mary-Lan. 1990. "High-Tech Health Care: Medical Devices and Treatments for the Future—and Present." *Current Health* 16, no. 8 (April 2): 4–9.

Kamisar, Yale. 1991. "Who Should Live—or Die? Who Should Decide?" An Interview with Professor Kamisar at the University of Michigan Law School. *Trial* 27, no. 12 (December 1): 20–26.

Kane, N., and P. Manoukian. 1989. "The Effect of the Medicare Prospective Payment System on the Adoption of New Technology: The Case of Cochlear Implants." *New England Journal of Medicine* 321: 1378–83.

Kessler, Larry; Scott D. Ramsey; Sean Tunis; and Sean D. Sullivan. 2004. "Clinical Use of Medical Devices in the 'Bermuda Triangle.'" *Health Affairs* 23, no. 1 (January–February): 200–207.

"Key Dates in Schiavo Right-to-Die Case." 2005. Associated Press, May 23. Online at news.yahoo.com.

Kilner, John F. 1988. "Age as a Basis for Allocating Lifesaving Medical Resources: An Ethical Analysis." *Journal of Health Politics, Policy and Law* 13, no. 3 (Fall): 405–23.

———. 1991. *Who Lives? Who Dies? Ethical Criteria in Patient Selection.* New Haven, Conn.: Yale University Press.

———. 1992. *Life on the Line: Ethics, Aging, Ending Patients' Lives, and Allocating Vital Resources.* Grand Rapids, Mich.: W.B. Eerdmans.

Kilpatrick, Anne O.; Krishna S. Dhir; and John M. Sanders. 1991. "Health Care Technology Assessment: A Policy Planning Tool." *International Journal of Public Administration* 14, no. 1: 59–82.

Kim, Ninah; Robert J. Blendon; and John M. Benson. 2001. "How Interested Are Americans in New Medical Technologies? A Multicountry Comparison." *Health Affairs* 20, no. 5 (September–October): 194–201.

Kolata, Gina. 1994. "Reproductive Revolution is Jolting Old Views." *New York Times*, January 11.

Kornblut, Anne E. 2005a. "A Next Step: Making Rules to Die By." *New York Times*, April 1.

———. 2005b. "Schiavo Autopsy Renews Debate on G.O.P. Actions." *New York Times*, June 16.

Kosterlitz, Julie. 1993. "Paying for Miracles." *National Journal* 25, no. 32 (August 7): 1967–71.

Kowalczyk, Liz. 2005a. "Hospital, Family Spar Over End-of-Life Care." *Boston Globe*, March 11.

———. 2005b. "Woman Dies At MHG After Battle Over care." *Boston Globe*. June 8.

Kruse, Lowell C. 1989. "Some Thoughts about Resource Allocation in Health Care." *Midwest Medical Ethics* 5, no. 4 (Fall): 15–16.

Lauritzen, Paul. 1993. *Pursuing Parenthood: Ethical Issues in Assisted Reproduction.* Bloomington: Indiana University Press.

Lehoux, Pascala, and Stuart Blume. 2000. "Technology Assessment and the Sociopolitics of Health Technologies." *Journal of Health Politics, Policy and Law* 25, no. 6 (December): 1083–1120.

Leland, John. 2005. "Did Descartes Doom Terri Schiavo?" *New York Times*, March 27.

Lindblom, Charles E. 1959. "The Science of Muddling Through." *Public Administration Review* 19 (Spring): 79–88.

Littell, Candace L., and Robin J. Strongin. 1996. "The Truth About Technology and Health Care Costs." *IEEE Technology and Society Magazine* 15, no. 3 (Fall):10–15.

Long, Mark. 2005. "Federal Judge Nixes Schiavo's Feeding Tube." Associated Press, March 25. Online at news.yahoo.com.

Lotlarz, Virginia. 1991. "History of Medical Technology in the United States." *Clinical Laboratory Science* 4, no. 4 (July/August): 233–36.

Lyman, Rick. 2005. "Governor is Pressed on Schiavo as Legal Moves Dwindle." *New York Times*, March 27.

Mabie, Margot C.J. 1993. *Bioethics and the New Medical Technology.* New York: Atheneum.

Malinowski, Michael J. 1996. "Capitation, Advances in Medical Technology, and the Advent of a New Era in Medical Ethics." *American Journal of Law and Medicine* 22, no. 2–3 (Summer/Fall): 331–60.

McClellan, Mark. 1996. "Are the Returns to Technological Change in Health Care Declining?" *Proceedings of the National Academy of Sciences of the United States* 93, no. 23 (November 12): 12701–709.

McCormick, Richard A. 1990. "Clear and Convincing Evidence: The Case of Nancy Cruzan." *Midwest Medical Ethics* 6, no. 4 (Fall): 10–12.

McGee, Marianne K., and Thomas Clayburn. 2004. "High-Tech Cure." *Information Week* no. 987 (May 3): 22–25.

Mehren, Elizabeth, and Sam H. Verhovek. 2005. "The Death of Terri Schiavo: A Very Private Issue Resonates with Public." *Los Angeles Times*, April 1.

Meilaender, Gilbert. 1990. "The Cruzan Decision: 9.5 Theses for Discussion." *Midwest Medical Ethics* 6, no. 4 (Fall): 3–5.

Melski, John W. 1992. "Price of Technology: A Blind Spot." *Journal of the American Medical Association* 267, no. 11 (March 18): 1516–18.

Mendelson, Dan, and Tanisha V. Carino. 2005. "Evidence-Based Medicine in the United States— De Rigueur or Dream Deferred?" *Health Affairs* 24, no. 1 (January–February): 133–36.

Mendelson, Daniel N.; Richard G. Abramson; and Robert J. Rubin. 1995. "State Involvement in Medical Technology Assessment." *Health Affairs* 14, no. 2 (Summer): 83–98.

Menzel, Paul T. 1990. *Strong Medicine: The Ethical Rationing of Health Care*. New York: Oxford University Press.

Merrill, Richard A. 1994. "Regulation of Drugs and Devices: An Evolution." *Health Affairs* 13, no. 3 (Summer): 47–69.

Milicia, Joe. 2005. "Doctors: Feeding Tube Goes Beyond Purpose." Associated Press, March 26. Online at news.yahoo.com.

Miller, Tracy E., and Arthur R. Derse. 2002. "Between Strangers: The Practice of Medicine Online." *Health Affairs* 21, no. 4 (July–August): 168–79.

Moreno, Jonathan D. 2005. "The End of the Great Bioethics Compromise." *Hastings Center Report* 35, no. 1 (January–February): 14–15.

Morris, Jonas. 1984. *Searching for a Cure: National Health Policy Considered*. New York: Pica Press.

Morrissey, John. 2002. "Making IT Compute." *Modern Healthcare* 32, no. 37 (September 16): 37–42.

Muller, Charlotte. 1991. "Objective Health Care Technology Evaluation—It Isn't Easy." *Social Work in Health Care* 16, no. 1: 119–32.

Neumann, Peter, and Eileen A. Sandberg. 1998. "Trends in Health Care R&D and Technology Innovation." *Health Affairs* 17, no. 6 (November–December): 111–19.

Newhouse, Joseph P. 1992. "Medical Care Costs: How Much Welfare Loss?" *Journal of Economic Perspectives* 6, no. 3: 3–21.

Nichols, Bruce. 2005. "Hospital Ends Life Support of Baby." *Dallas Morning News*, March 15.

Nichols, Mark. 1993. "Tinkering with Mother Nature: A Controversial Report on Reproductive Technologies." *Maclean's* 106, no. 48 (November 29): 38–40.

Nitzkin, Joel L. 1996. "Technology and Health Care—Driving Costs Up, Not Down." *IEEE Technology and Society Magazine* 15, no. 3 (Fall): 40–46.

Nyman, John. 1991. "Costs, Technology, and Insurance in the Health Care Sector." *Journal of Policy Analysis and Management* 10, no. 1 (Winter): 106–11.

"Oregon's Assisted Suicide Law Stokes the Fires of Controversy." 1995. *State Health Notes* (February 20): 1–3.

"Oregon's Right to Die Movement." 1995. Denver, Colo.: The Hemlock Society, USA. Online at www.endoflifechoices.org/learn/index.jsp

Patel, Kant, and Mark Rushefsky. 2002. *Health Care Policy in an Age of New Technologies*. New York: M.E. Sharpe.

Pence, Gregory E. 1995. *Classic Cases in Medical Ethics*, 2d ed. New York: McGraw Hill.

Peters, Philip G., Jr. 1990. "The Constitution and the Right to Die." *Midwest Medical Ethics* 6, no. 4 (Fall): 13–16.

Phelps, Charles E., and Stephen T. Parente. 1990. "Priority Setting in Medical Technology and Medical Practice Assessment." *Medical Care* 28, no. 8 (August): 703–23.

Pillar, Barbara. 1990. "Nursing and Technology." *Nursing Economics* 8, no. 3 (May–June): 199–200.

———. 1992. "Bioethical Issues in the Use of Technology." *Nursing Economics* 10, no. 6 (November–December): 419–22.

"Poll: Keep Feeding Tube Out." 2005. March 21. Online at www.cbsnews.com/stories/2005/03/23/opinion/polls/main682674.shtml.

President's Council on Bioethics. 2004. Reproduction and Responsibility: The Regulation of New Biotechnologies. A Report of the President's Council on Bieoethics. Washington, D.C. Online at www.bioethics.gov.

Raymond, Janice G. 1993. *Women as Wombs: Reproductive Technologies and the Battle over Women's Freedom*. San Francisco: Harper.

Rettig, Richard A. 1994. "Medical Innovation Duels Cost Containment." *Health Affairs* 13, no. 3 (Summer): 7–27.

Rhodes, Robert P. 1992. *Health Care: Politics, Policy and Distributive Justice: The Ironic Triumph*. New York: State University of New York Press.

Robertson, John A. 1994. *Children of Choice: Freedom and the New Reproductive Technologies*. Princeton, N.J.: Princeton University Press.

Robertson, John A; Baruch Brody; Allen Buchanan; Jeffrey Kahn; and Elizabeth McPherson. 2002. "Pharmacogenetic Challenges for the Health Care System." *Health Affairs* 21, no. 4 (July–August): 155–67.

Roche, Walter F., Jr., and Sam H. Verhovek. 2005. "DeLay's Own Tragic Crossroads." *Los Angeles Times*, March 27.

Rogers, Lynn T., Jr. 2002. "Hospital-Based Technology Assessment." *Journal of Clinical Engineering* 27, no. 4 (Fall): 276–79.

Roig-Franzia, Manuel. 2005. "Court Lets Right-To-Die Ruling Stand." *Washington Post*, January 25.

Rublee, Dale A. 1994. "Medical Technology in Canada, Germany, and the United States: An Update." *Health Affairs* 13, no. 4 (Fall): 113–17.

Russo, Nancy F., and Jean E. Denious. 2005. "Controlling Birth: Science, Politics, and Public Policy." *Journal of Social Issues* 61, no. 1 (March): 181–91.

Rutten, Frans F.H., and Gouke J. Bonsel. 1992. "High Cost Technology in Health Care: A Benefit or a Burden?" *Social Science and Medicine* 35, no. 4: 567–77.

Ryan, Maura A. 2001. *Ethics and Economics of Assisted Reproduction: The Cost of Longing*. Washington, D.C.: Georgetown University Press.

Schenker, Joseph G. 2005. "Assisted Reproductive Practice: Religious Perspectives." *Reproductive BioMedicine Online* 10, no. 3 (March): 310–19.

"Schiavo Autopsy Finds No Sign of Trauma." 2005. (June 15). Online at www.cnn.com.

"Schiavo Autopsy Shows Irreversible Brain Damage." 2005. Associated Press, June 15. Online at www.msnbc.msn.com.

Schwartz, John. 2005. "New Openness in Deciding When and How to Die." *New York Times*. March 21.

Schwartz, William B. 1987. "The Inevitable Failure of Current Cost-Containment Strategies: Why They Can Provide only Temporary Relief." *Journal of the American Medical Association* 257, no. 2 (Janaury 9): 220–24.

———. 1994. "In the Pipeline: A Wave of Valuable Medical Technology." *Health Affairs* 13, no. 3 (Summer): 70–79.

Shanner, Laura, and Jeffrey Nisker. 2001. "Bioethics for Clinicians: 26. Assisted Reproductive Technologies." *Canadian Medical Association Journal* 164, no. 11 (May 29): 1589–94.

Shannon, Thomas A., ed. 2004. *Reproductive Technologies: A Reader*. Lanham, Md.: Rowan & Littlefield Publishers.

Shaw, Linda R., et al. 1991. "Ethics of Lung Transplantation with Live Donors." *Lancet* 338, no. 8768 (September 14): 678–81.

Shreve, Maggie, and June Isaacson Kailes. 1990. "The Right to Die or the Right to Community Support." *Midwest Medical Ethics* 6, no. 2, 3 (Spring/Summer): 11–15.

Solinger, Rickie, ed. 1998. *Abortion Wars: A Half Century of Struggle, 1950–2000.* Berkeley: University of California Press.

Spencer, Peter L. 1995. "Technology Gatekeepers." *Consumers' Research Magazine* 78, no. 7 (July): 43.

Steinberg, Earl P., and Bryan R. Luce. 2005. "Evidence Based? Caveat Emptor!" *Health Affairs* 24, no. 1 (January–February): 80–92.

Stenson, Jacqueline. 2005. "Viva in Vitro." *Health* 19, no. 2 (March): 77.

Stolberg, Sheryl G. 2005a. "A Cacophony of Epitaphs." *New York Times*, March 31.

———. 2005b. "Schiavo's Case May Reshape American Law." *New York Times*, April 2.

Strathern, Marilyn. 1992. *Reproducing the Future: Essays on Anthropology, Kinship and the New Reproductive Technologies.* New York: Routledge, Chapman and Hall.

Strosberg, Martin A.; Joshua M. Wiener; Robert Baker; and I. Alan Fein, eds. 1992. *Rationing America's Medical Care: The Oregon Plan and Beyond.* Washington, D.C.: Brookings Institution.

Sussman, Jason H. 1991. "Financial Considerations in Technology Assessment." *Topics in Health Care Financing* 17, no. 3 (Spring): 30–41.

Sutton, Jane. 2004. "Florida Court Strikes Down Law in Right-To-Die Case." Reuters News, September 23. Online at news.yahoo.com.

Tabbush, Victor, and Gerald Swanson. 1996. "Changing Paradigms in Medical Payment." *Archives of Internal Medicine* 156, no. 4 (February 26): 357–61.

Tanner, Robert. 2005. "Schiavo Case Spurring Statehouse Debate." Associated Press, April 4. Online at news.yahoo.com.

Taylor, Kathryn S. 1993. "Technology's Next Test: Regional Systems Laying Groundwork for Post-Reform Technology Planning." *Hospitals and Health Networks* 67, no. 11 (June 5): 42–44.

"Technology Assessments." 2005. Online at www.ahrq.gov/clinic/techix.htm.

"Terri Schiavo Timeline." 2005. CBS News, April 1. Online at www.cbs4.com/moreinfo/local_story_053154624.html.

Thomas, Lewis. 1975. *The Lives of a Cell.* New York: Bantam Books.

"*Time* Poll: The Schiavo Case." 2005. *Time*, April 4: 26–27.

Van DeVeer, Donald. 1987. "Introduction." In *Health Care Ethics: An Introduction*, ed. Donald Van DeVeer and Tom Regan, 3–57. Philadelphia: Temple University Press.

Van Rossum, Wouter. 1991. "Decision-Making and Medical Technology Assessment: Three Dutch Cases." *Knowledge in Society* 4, no. 1, 2 (September): 107–24.

Vicini, James. 2005. "Supreme Court to Decide Appeal on Suicide Law." Reuters News, February 22. Online at news.yahoo.com.

Weisbrod, Burton A. 1991. The Health Care Quadrilemma: An Essay on Technological Change, Insurance, Quality of Care, and Cost Containment." *Journal of Economic Literature* 29 (June): 523–55.

———. 1994. "The Nature of Technological Change: Incentives Do Matter!" In *Adopting New Medical Technology: Medical Innovation at the Crossroads*, ed. Annetine C. Gelijns and Holly V. Dawkins, 8–48. Washington, D.C.: National Academy Press.

Weisbrod, Burton A., and LaMay, C. L. 1999. "Mixed Signals: Public Policy and the Future of Health Care R&D." *Health Affairs* 18, no. 2 (March–April): 112–25.

Wildes, Kevin W. 1994. "Health Reform and the Seduction of Technology." *America* 170, no. 12 (April 9): 30.

Wolf, Susan M. 2004. "Law and Bioethics: From Values to Violence." *Journal of Law, Medicine & Ethics* 32, no. 2 (Summer): 293–306.

Woodsong, Cynthia, and Lawrence J. Severy. 2005. "Generation of Knowledge for Reproductive Health Technologies: Constraints on Social and Behavioral Research." *Journal of Social Issues* 61, no. 1 (March): 193–205.

Wright, Robert. 1993. "The Technology Time Bomb." *New Republic* 208, no. 13 (March 29): 25–30.

Zinner, Darren. 2001. "Medical R&D at the Turn of the Millennium: Medical Innovation Is Becoming More Dispersed Over a Larger Set of Players." *Health Affairs* 20, no. 5 (September–October): 202–9.

9

Reforming the System

*Politics is how society manages conflicts about values and interests.
The United States, a large, heterogeneous society with complex cross-
cutting divisions by race, ethnicity, class, region, and more, naturally
presents many such conflicts to manage. Health care, an arena of high
popular expectations, settled professional prerogative, and expenses
that now total nearly $1 trillion per year, piles on further problems of
its own. The conflict management that is politics, therefore, is not some
nonrational and inefficient sideshow that threatens the reformist visions
of the best and the brightest but rather a challenge central to making
health reform come out for the better—indeed, come out at all. And no
issues trigger battles over values and interests more quickly and acutely
than do the source and use of money in health reform proposals.*
—Lawrence D. Brown (1994, 175)

As Brown (1994) states, reforming the health care system presents a huge challenge.
Previous chapters have concentrated on specific aspects of health care. Chapters 1
and 2 presented some background material for understanding the context of health
care policymaking in the United States. Chapter 1 discussed the politics of health care
and chapter 2 presented a history of health policy in the United States. Chapter 3
looked at Medicaid and chapter 4 examined Medicare. Chapter 5 examined the problems of the disadvantaged. Chapter 6 focused on cost control, chapter 7 on medical
liability issues, and chapter 8 on technology. But none of these chapters provided a
systematic examination of the health care system as a whole. That is the purpose of
this chapter.

We begin by looking at some of the problems of the health care system, in a sense
bringing together much of the material of the previous chapters. We then look at
economic critiques of the health care system, which suggest major reform. Following
that, we present some policy history of attempts to inject competitive reforms into the
health care system. In particular, we examine the development of ideas that eventually

became known as "managed care" and "managed competition." Using this as a focus, we look at the attempt to reform health care in the early and mid-1990s and why that attempt failed. We also examine the role of the states and the private sector in the transformation of the American health care system.

Systemic Problems

Various problems of the health care system have been dealt with at length in this book. The underlying problem is one of finance. From an individual perspective, medical care is expensive. For those with adequate and secure sources of health insurance, medical costs are ameliorated. Even then, premiums for health insurance continue to rise. For those with no health insurance, public or private, cost is a key barrier (though not the only one) to obtaining care. Medicaid covers fewer than half the people whose incomes are below the poverty line. A growing number of people find that their health insurance is either inadequate or insecure.

Cost is also a problem for the business sector. Smaller firms are less likely to provide health insurance for their employees than are larger firms, again primarily because of cost. Larger firms do provide health insurance, but the cost of providing that insurance has risen markedly. Firms have sought to manage those costs by cutting back, shifting more costs to employees, and moving their employees toward managed care plans. In recent years, fewer of even the larger firms are providing health insurance to their employees, employees' families, or retirees.

For governments, health care costs are barely controllable. On the state level, Medicaid is one of the fastest-growing budgetary items. At the federal level, Medicare costs have grown faster than either the growth of the overall economy or government budgets. The new Medicare law exacerbates the cost problem. Governments have sought to control costs through reimbursement policies in both Medicaid and Medicare (diagnosis-related groups, or DRGs, and physician fee schedules), with some success. But the result has been either some cost shifting or fewer physicians participating in the programs (especially Medicaid).

Other problems exist. For residents of inner cities and rural areas, there is an insufficient supply of providers. Medicaid eligibility does not guarantee service if few doctors are willing to accept Medicaid patients. Certain sectors of society, the poor and minorities, have less access to care and thus higher rates of health problems than the population at large. And over 15 percent of the population is not covered by health insurance.

From the systemic perspective, the United States spends more on health care (absolutely and relatively) than any other country. Health care is the largest sector of the American economy. Yet, by many health indicators (such as infant mortality rates), the population is not necessarily healthier. Medical technology is most developed in this country, yet that same technology presents problems. It is one of the reasons for the cost problem, and it creates ethical problems surrounding the issue of quality of life. Much of the technology is "halfway" technology, which does not cure "but requires months or years of extremely expensive life-prolonging therapies" (Stone 1993, 111).

Furthermore, and paradoxically, the United States has both the most complex regulatory control over health care and the least control over the system. Because of numerous decisions that have largely left medical care in the hands of providers, insurers, and pharmaceutical and medical technology companies, government response has been at best reactive and piecemeal. Medicare and Medicaid (as well as other programs of the 1960s) reinforced the predominant "values and interests," to use Lawrence Brown's term in the book's epigraph, of health providers and insurers. The federal tax code aided in the development of private insurance but never challenged the medical establishment (see Krause 1977; Leyerle 1994; and Starr 1982).

In various chapters we have looked at attempts to overhaul the system through national health insurance. Some six tries have failed, most recently in 1993–94. But alongside those attempts at nationalizing health care were critiques of the system and of government's role, based on an economic analysis of health care, which led to calls for reform. These critiques would eventually become married to some form of national health insurance, relying on competition strategies and peaking in the 1990s.

The Economic Critique

The economic critique begins with a consideration of some classic works in economics. The "bible" of economics is Adam Smith's *The Wealth of Nations*, published in 1776.[1] Smith argued that unfettered markets, free from government or monopoly interference, would produce the greatest benefits for humankind. Such markets were the most efficient, producing precisely the amounts of a good or service that producers want to sell and that consumers want to buy through the price mechanism. Anything that impeded the price mechanism would lower efficiency.

Smith's work formed the basis for classical (and neoclassical) economics and remains an important part of American ideology. The American bias has always been toward free markets and away from government control, though, as we see below, in health care (as in other areas) the viability of free, competitive markets is questionable.

Frederick Hayek (1944), writing just at the end of World War II, warned the country of moving toward more government control. Most influential was Milton Friedman's (1962) *Capitalism and Freedom*. Friedman argued that economic freedom supported political freedom. He discussed a number of policy issues showing how free markets would work better than government intervention or control.

So what is the economic critique of the health care system that dates back to Adam Smith? The critique is that the incentive structure of health care moves the system toward inefficiencies. It does this in several ways. Consider the traditional *fee-for-service, third-party payment system.*[2]

There are four parts to the transaction: the patient with health insurance seeks a service; the patient sees a doctor, who provides that service; the doctor's charges depend on the amount of services provided; the more services, the higher the charge (that is why it is called fee-for-service). The doctor knows that the patient is covered by health insurance provided by the employer through an insurance company. The patient pays the bill and then files a claim with the insurance company for reimbursement. In some instances, the health insurance policy is so generous that the patient does not have to pay anything. In other cases, the doctor's office files the claim and bills the patient for the balance after the claim is paid. Depending on the policy, the patient may have met the deductible (the amount the patient has to pay before the insurance pays) for the year and may have limited copayments (the percentage of the remaining part of the bill, after the deductible, that the patient pays). The insurance company processes the claim and either pays the doctor or reimburses the patient. The employer may pay the premiums on the employee's health insurance and may also (if the policy is especially generous) pay premiums for dependents. If not, then the employee pays the premiums, but at a group rate.

Who is concerned about the cost of care and the quality and efficiency of care (whether a particular test or treatment is really necessary) under such a system? If the doctor and the patient both know that third-party insurance will cover the cost, they have little concern. As long as the premiums cover the reimbursements (plus a profit), the insurer does not care. As long as premium costs are reasonable, and the federal government allows a business tax deduction for premiums (an incentive to cover or continue coverage), the employer does not care. The same situation is true for hospital care.

That is exactly the point that economic reformers seek to make. Under this kind of situation, typical up through most of the 1980s, the cost and the price of service are irrelevant. Economists argue that in the absence of paying the true cost of care, consumers will demand more health care than they really need, a problem labeled *moral hazard* (Pauly 1971).

Health care suffers from another problem that impedes the operation of free, competitive markets: *imperfect information*. Providers have considerable information and expertise (though not complete information) and are in a power position compared to other actors, especially consumers, or patients. Thus additional treatments are not the result of consumer demand for them, but of provider requests. In that sense health care is provider driven, rather than consumer driven. Furthermore, consumers do not shop around comparing service and price at critical times (e.g., during a heart attack). Imperfect information, power asymmetries, and lack of a clear price mechanism work together to create market failures in health care (for a discussion of asymmetries in health care, see Arrow 1963). The question is how to solve these problems.

Market Reforms

The simplest way to reform health care markets is to focus on the consumer and insurance. The more generous the insurance policy, the less likely it is that costs are a consideration. The obvious solution would be to make health insurance less generous. Insurance may have what is known as *first-dollar coverage*, beginning coverage with the smallest illnesses. Rather than cover everything, a *catastrophic health insurance policy* might be substituted. Such a policy would go into effect after a rather high deductible was met, perhaps as a percentage of family income.

A typical health insurance policy might have a $300 deductible (some have no deductibles). After the first $300 of medical expenses, 80 percent or more of further medical expenses might be covered by insurance. But what if the policy were changed so that the deductible were $2,000, or 10 percent of a family's income? Then the consumer, or patient, would have to bear the expenses of further care and might not go to the doctor for every cold or sniffle. Only truly needed care would be undertaken. Further, the family would be protected from very high medical expenses (such as a cancer operation and treatment) after the deductible was met. Moreover, as we know with automobile insurance, the higher the deductible, the lower the premium to the worker and/or the employer.

There is an element of simplicity to such plans, which were proposed in the late 1970s and early 1980s and have reappeared in the 2000s under the guise of consumer-driven health care (see chapter 10). Such analysis largely underlies the advocacy of *medical savings accounts* (MSAs), as they were originally known, and, more recently, *health savings accounts* (HSAs). These policies were first included in Medicare in 1996 on an experimental basis and then in the larger population, also on an experimental basis in 1997. MSAs were replaced by HSAs as a result of the 2003 Medicare legislation discussed in chapter 4. Chapter 10 discusses HSAs in more detail. Consumers preferred first-dollar coverage, and the MSAs never went anywhere.

Such catastrophic plans concentrated on what could be called the *demand side* of health care, the consumer, but most reform plans focused on the *supply side* of health care, the provider.[3] This would mean changing the incentives built into the traditional system and trying to create more competitive markets.

The first attempt at a supply-side, market-reform solution came in the 1960s and 1970s. This was the *health maintenance strategy* mentioned in chapters 2 and 6. The strategy, the brainchild of Dr. Paul Ellwood, was an elegant idea (Bauman 1976; Falkson 1980). Based on already-existing *prepaid group plans* (PGPs), the idea was to limit the money available to providers through a *capitation* system. The health maintenance organization (HMO) enrolls subscribers, who pay a monthly premium. The premiums constitute the total budget for the HMO. Providing more services does not produce more revenues. So the incentive was not to overtreat, as market reformers argue is done in the fee-for-service system, but to treat only as necessary. The HMO became the prototype of a *managed care organization* (in 1990s language), one that would review services and try to eliminate unnecessary care.

There was a further hope behind the HMO strategy: HMOs would create competitive pressures on the fee-for-service system so that all providers and insurers would begin to look at costs. As HMOs penetrated a market, competitive pressures would increase. This idea was embodied in the 1973 Health Maintenance Organization Act to promote, with federal assistance, the development of HMOs. Into the 1980s, at least, the competitive impact of the strategy was questionable.

The second stage came in the late 1970s and early 1980s. Alain Enthoven (1978a, b; 1980) took the competitive strategy a step further by suggesting a complete reorganization of the health care system, in essence national health insurance. Originally writing in the 1970s in the *New England Journal of Medicine* (and other journals) and then in his book *Health Plan*, Enthoven wanted to eliminate the employment-insurance connection.

The *Consumer-Choice Health Plan* (CCHP) was a form of national health insurance that would work as follows (Rushefsky 1981): Providers and insurers would organize into competitive health care plans. Each plan would then determine what its premiums would be. The federal government would estimate the average cost of care in various geographical areas and pay a percentage of that average cost through tax credits or 100 percent of the average cost for the poor via vouchers. CCHP featured an open-enrollment period, community rating (see chapter 5), and a limit on out-of-pocket costs. Consumers would then choose among the competing plans, which could include a traditional fee-for-service plan, an HMO, a plan with a very high deductible, and so forth. Each plan would charge a different premium, but the federal government would pay the same amount regardless of the plan chosen. Thus, consumers would face the decision of what plan to choose depending on the financial consequences for them. The newly regained place of price signals plus open enrollments would create the competition among the plans and (it was hoped) restrain costs. Thus health care would be consumer driven rather than cost driven.

A somewhat less ambitious version of CCHP built on the employment-based insurance system already in place. For those with work-based insurance, the employer would pay the same premium for each employee regardless of which plan was chosen. Employees would have a choice of plans, with similar features, as mentioned above. For the poor or those without employment-based insurance, vouchers from the federal government could be used.

Competition plans created a great deal of interest in the late 1970s and early 1980s (Demkovich 1979; Wehr 1979). Congressmen Richard Schweiker (R-PA) and David Stockman (R-MI) offered bills based on the CCHP. In 1981 Schweiker became the secretary of the Department of Health and Human Services (HHS) and Stockman became director of the Office of Management and Budget (OMB) in the Reagan administration. A task force within HHS was created to investigate competitive ideas; however, nothing further came of the effort, perhaps because CCHP or a variant was essentially a form of national health insurance at a time when the Reagan administration was seeking to reduce the federal government's role.

In addition, several practical developments began to move toward competitive plans. One was a focus on deregulating the health care industry but engaging in vigorous anticompetitive regulation (Havighurst 1982). For example, the American Medical Association (AMA) had for a long time opposed the group practice of medicine, arguing that it trespassed on the traditional autonomy of the individual practitioner. Over time, this opposition lessened, though the AMA still has some problems with managed care organizations.

Two developments among public employers provided some experience with choosing among competitive plans. The Federal Employees Health Benefits Program (FEHBP) allows federal employees to choose among competing plans, while the federal government provides level premium contributions. A similar program established in California, the California Public Employees' Retirement System (CalPERS), enrolls nearly a million public employees at all levels of government. CalPERS is a purchasing cooperative that negotiates with a number of different plans, such as HMOs, *preferred provider organizations* (PPOs), and traditional fee-for-service plans.

In the late 1980s and early 1990s, Ellwood, who had moved from Minnesota to Jackson Hole, Wyoming, formed a working group to develop a strategy for change based on the idea of managed competition. The work group and guests "included academics, public officials and leaders of the insurance and health industries" (Reinhold 1993; see also Enthoven 1993).

Enthoven, perhaps the chief theorist of the Jackson Hole group, began advocating *managed competition* in the late 1980s and continued into the 1990s (see Enthoven 1991; Enthoven and Kronick 1989a, b; 1992). Managed competition is an attempt to marry several different ideas—national health insurance, insurance reform, managed care, organization of providers and purchasers, and choice for consumers—while building on the present system.

Managed Competition

The managed competition proposal was designed, according to Enthoven and Kronick (1989a, 31), to meet two major goals: "to provide financial protection from health care expenses for all . . . and to promote the development of economical financing and delivery arrangements." This would be done by enabling those not already in Medicare or Medicaid to purchase health insurance either through their employer or through a public sponsor organized by the states. The purpose of aggregating purchasers of insurance, either through employment or through sponsors (*health care alliances*), would be to allow them to bargain and contract with provider organizations, such as HMOs, PPOs, or the traditional fee-for-service system (or some other of the many possibilities).

Employers would pay a specific amount for full-time employees and dependents, and would pay a payroll tax for those not covered.[4] An employer's contribution would be 80 percent of an average of the price of plans offered (a *defined contribution* regardless of the plan chosen); subscribers would pay the difference. The tax laws would be changed to limit contributions by employers beyond the specified amount. Those not covered by an employer plan, such as the self-employed, would pay into the public sponsor plans, up to an income ceiling. The program would also include subsidies to pay for the premiums of the poor (not covered by Medicaid) and for small businesses.

Employers and sponsors would then negotiate with qualified health plans, made up of some combination of providers and insurers, who would offer a variety of plans.

Subscribers would elect a plan each year. The federal government would collect the funds and make determinations about average costs of plans. The program could be run entirely by the federal government or by both the states and the federal government. Medicaid and Medicare would be left alone, at least at first, though recipients would be encouraged to join HMOs.

Like the earlier CCHP, the intent is to promote efficient organization of health providers and provide competition among those organizations. The major difference between the earlier and later plans is that purchasers would also be aggregated and would be in a position to bargain with providers, not at the time of the occurrence of an illness, but at the point of purchasing coverage.[5] While the plan does not attempt radical surgery on the health care system, the hope is that forces put into place will in fact create significant changes, cover virtually the entire population, and cost less than the present system.

Moving toward Reform

The push for managed competition was one of the forces that led to a renewed focus on health care in the 1990s. The problems of the health care system were also creating a momentum toward change. The increasing costs of heath care to business and government and the associated rise in the cost of premiums were major problems (see chapter 6). There were other difficulties as well, many created by cost problems. Fewer workers found themselves covered by employer-based health insurance. The number of uninsured kept rising, with about 14 percent of the population lacking health insurance (see chapter 5). The problem of the uninsured was compounded by growing economic insecurity. Even those with health insurance were fearful that if they or their dependents became sick, their health insurance would be inadequate. Changing jobs might result in losing coverage for a preexisting problem. Medicaid seemed to cover smaller and smaller proportions of families with incomes below the poverty rate. All of this was exacerbated by the recession of 1990–91 and the reengineering of corporations to become more efficient and more competitive (i.e., more productive with the same or fewer workers).

One response to the growing problems was the report of the *Pepper Commission*, originally known as the U.S. Bipartisan Commission on Comprehensive Health Care. Created in 1988, the report called for coverage for long-term care and for universal coverage for those under the age of sixty-five. Medicare would be retained, but Medicaid would be phased out. The report proposed the elimination of experience rating among insurance companies (Rockefeller 1990). While there was more consensus on long-term coverage than on universal coverage, there was no agreement on financing. Nevertheless, the Pepper Commission report was another factor in moving toward consideration of change.

Perhaps the most important factor was political.[6] The political aspect was set off by an unusual off-year senatorial election in Pennsylvania. Republican Senator John Heinz[7] died in a plane crash in 1991, and Democratic Governor Bob Casey appointed

Harris Wofford to the seat. Wofford would have to run in a special November 1991 election to see who would fill the remainder of Heinz's term (which was up in 1994). Wofford's Republican opponent was one of the most popular politicians in Pennsylvania, Richard Thornburgh. Thornburgh, at the time attorney general of the United States in the George H.W. Bush administration, had previously been governor of the state. He resigned his position and was widely expected to win against the little-known Wofford.

To the surprise of everyone, Wofford won. In his campaign, Wofford played up the economic insecurity issue, focusing on health care. His memorable campaign sound bite was that if we had the right to a lawyer, we should have the right to health insurance. Wofford's call for national health insurance resonated well among the voters and was widely considered to be one of the major factors in his victory.

The Pennsylvania off-year election demonstrated that health care could be a powerful campaign tool. In December 1991 Democrats began holding "town meetings" to discuss health care. Potential Democratic presidential candidates met on television to discuss health care. A group of touring Democratic senators held hearings and news conferences around the country. A majority of House Democrats held a simultaneous town meeting in January 1992 (Clymer 1991).

In February 1992 President Bush announced a health care initiative that would cost an additional $100 billion over a five-year period, to be paid for by limits on Medicare and Medicaid. The plan was based on tax credits and vouchers. Tax credits of up to $3,750 per year would go to families with incomes ranging up to $70,000 (and phased out as incomes rose). For poor families, a voucher equal to that amount would be issued. For the self-employed, there would be a tax deduction equal to the size of the premiums. Small business would be given tax inducements to band together and spread risk. There would also be some mild insurance reform (Wines 1992). The plan was a limited one and vague in detail, especially concerning cost control. Further, the plan did not address long-term care and was administratively complex. Finally, the value of the tax credits, deductions, and vouchers would erode over time. This was true because their value would be indexed to the consumer price index (CPI), but the cost of insurance premiums generally climbs faster than the CPI. Thus the amount of insurance the voucher or tax incentives could buy would decrease over time. Nevertheless, the Bush plan was an important piece in moving health care reform forward (Pear 1992a).

Even at this early stage of the health care reform debate, the outlook for change was troubling. This reflected the presence of interest groups representing the major financial stakes in health care. They included the American Medical Association and its specialty groups; the American Hospital Association; specialty hospital groups such as those representing the for-profit or proprietary sector; insurance groups such as the Health Insurance Association of America; a group representing the five largest insurers such as Aetna; and business groups of all sizes. While larger employers supported employer mandates, small businesses did not. The American College of Physicians came out in favor of a cap on spending and a managed competition plan (Pear 1992f).

The lobbyists and lawyers for these groups continued their efforts into 1994, and their impact was largely one of impeding change or, to put it another way, of protecting their interests. According to one observer of the health policy scene:

> On the whole, health-care lobbyists have had the effect of retarding change and blocking it. That's because most of the effort has come from smart, well-financed groups that have a vested interest in the status quo. They do a good job of pointing out the potential risks and costs of change, but there is little information about the broader public interest in the benefits of change. (Jack A. Meyer quoted in Pear 1992b.)

Meyer's comment is an example of a pervasive problem of American politics and government. As government, especially at the federal level, has sought to do more, additional groups with stakes in the outcome of government deliberations have risen. Each program that government undertakes, whether a subsidy, a tax credit, or services, has interest groups to protect it. In 1979 there were about 117 national health care interest groups; by 1992 that number had increased to 741, an increase of over 500 percent (Pear 1992b).

The more general problem is one that has been labeled *demosclerosis*. As Rauch (1994, 1999; see also Olson 1965, 1983) describes it, demosclerosis is analogous to hardening of the arteries, or arteriosclerosis. As the numbers of interest groups increase, and as the numbers of their lawyers, lobbyists, and consultants increase, government is less likely to cut unneeded programs or to make needed changes that might adversely affect an interest.[8] This early stage of the health care reform debate started ominously.

The motivation for the Bush plan was clearly the coming presidential elections (as well as the 1991 Pennsylvania senatorial elections). Arkansas Governor Bill Clinton promised that he would offer a health care plan. To support Clinton, Democratic leaders in the House of Representatives offered a health plan in June 1992 similar to one that Clinton was discussing. The plan would extend coverage to most, but not all, of the uninsured, and it contained provisions to control costs (price controls). The politics of the situation was clear: the Democrats offered a plan knowing that President George H.W. Bush would veto it, thus giving them a campaign issue (Krauss 1992). In a preview of the split among congressional Democrats in 1993–94, conservative Democrats in the House offered a plan, sponsored by Jim Cooper (D-TN), based on managed competition but with spending limitations ("Conservative Democrats" 1992).

By October 1992, both President Bush and Governor Clinton had endorsed managed competition as the centerpiece of their health care plans.[9] The difference between the two proposals was that the Bush plan relied on tax incentives, while the Clinton proposal also had mandates and spending limitations. Both proposals would, at least in the short run, increase health care expenditures (see "Editorial: The Bush-Clinton Health Reform" 1992; Pear 1992f). With Clinton's election in November 1992, health care reform was placed solidly on the governmental agenda.

Health Care Reform on the Front Burner

It appeared that after all the previously failed attempts in this century, health care reform and national health insurance had finally arrived. Most thought that change would take place, and many sought to benefit from it. The insurance industry, long an opponent of federal regulation, began to advocate universal health insurance. The major interest group, the Health Insurance Association of America (HIAA), advocated tax incentives, an individual mandate to purchase insurance (and possibly an employer mandate), and insurance reform. Part of the reasoning behind the insurance industry move was to become a player in reform. The industry also felt that it would benefit substantially from reform because more people would be buying insurance (Kerr 1992; Pear 1992g).

Further, early public opinion polls supported President Clinton's efforts. A strong majority of the public, which included supporters of President Bush, felt that the president would be successful in extending health insurance coverage (Clymer 1993a). A poll several months later found that support for change remained, but that it was in some cases shaky. There was backing for change and even for paying additional taxes, under some circumstances. Typically, most Americans expressed dissatisfaction with the health care system as a whole, but satisfaction with their own coverage and their own doctors. But the results of the poll also showed what would eventually become a problem for the Clinton plan: "the political conundrum that some analysts see at the heart of the health-care debate: The public wants the current quality of care, at a lower cost and with the assurance that they will never lose it" (Toner 1993a).[10] Other poll results showed that physicians favored universal health coverage and supported managed competition. This was true even though managed competition would likely reduce physician income (Morin 1993).

To develop a health care reform plan, Clinton set up a series of task forces, composed of some 500 people, headed by First Lady Hillary Rodham Clinton and Ira Magaziner. The task forces, composed of people in government and the private sector, met in secret over a period of months. Details of the plan leaked out, with the major roadblock being how to finance the plan. The alleged secretness of the task force meetings became a point of controversy. According to one account, Clinton and his aides had decided on the overall health care reform plan prior to the inauguration in January 1993 (Wessel and Seib 1993). The outlines of what became the Clinton plan were mentioned during the campaign with the slogan "competition within a budget," and a proposal and rationale for such a plan were published in book form in 1992 (Fallows 1995).[11] Some charged that the meetings violated the Federal Advisory Committee Act because private-sector people were involved. Others, especially industry representatives, complained that they were left out of the deliberations, though members of the task force met with outside groups as well as members of Congress and their staffs.[12]

The president's plan was presented to the nation in September 1993 and a bill was sent to Congress the next month. The proposal, entitled the Health Security Act, had several fundamental value premises. One, captured by the title of the bill, was security. The bill provided for universal coverage through an employer mandate and through subsidies for poor people and workers without health insurance. The Clinton motto was "health care that's always there" (Clymer 1993b). There would be a minimum benefits package covering the following services: hospital, emergency, physician, clinical preventive, mental health and substance abuse, family planning, pregnancy-related matters, hospice care, home health care, extended care, ambulance, outpatient laboratory and diagnostic service, outpatient prescription and biologicals, outpatient rehabilitation, durable medical equipment, vision and hearing, preventive dental services for children, and health education classes (White House Domestic Policy Council 1993). There were, of course, limitations on the services. For example, the extended-care services were limited to 100 days a year.

The plan was based on the concept of managed competition.[13] All individuals would belong to a health alliance, a purchasing cooperative, that would be set up by the states. Large corporations (those with 5,000 or more workers) could set up their own health alliances. Similarly, insurers and providers would establish plans. The alliances and plans would negotiate and subscribers would be offered a minimum of three plans. One would be a health maintenance organization providing all services to subscribers. A second would be the traditional fee-for-service system, the most expensive plan in terms of premiums and copayments. The third alternative was a hybrid or combination plan. This might be a preferred provider organization, where subscribers would get discounts for providers on the approved list.

The plan also specified how people would pay for health care. For example, self-employed workers would pay their own health premiums up to a point ($1,800 for individuals and $4,200 for families), and all premiums would be fully tax deductible. In the case of employees, employers would pay 80 percent of the premiums and workers the remainder. Small employers (those with fewer than fifty workers) would receive government subsidies. The unemployed would receive government subsidies for premiums. Medicaid would be eliminated, but the federal and state governments would pay the premiums for the poor (though only for the low-cost plans). Medicare would remain and the federal government would pay the bills. For retired people under the age of sixty-five, the federal government would pay the premiums.

The plan continually mentioned that employers would pay 80 percent of the premiums. The reference was to 80 percent of the average cost of premiums for the alliances (a defined contribution). Subscribers would pay the additional amount. This, as mentioned earlier, was an essential component of consumer choice: give the consumer a financial stake in the decision of which plan to choose. The alliances would also work toward insurance reform, so that experience rating would not be allowed, but some premium adjustments based on risk could be granted.[14]

The Clinton proposal also discussed financing. Part of the financing would come from employers and subscribers. While mid-size and large businesses paid for health insurance under the current system, small employers were less likely to (see chapter 5). Through the employer mandate, they would now be brought into the system. Even those who were uninsured would be contributing. Thus about 75 percent of the financing for health care under the Health Security Act would come from the private sector (Rivlin, Cutler, and Nichols 1994). A second source of funds was savings from Medicaid and Medicare. Medicaid would be eliminated entirely, and there would be savings in Medicare. The plan was less specific about new sources of financing. After considering a number of options, a tax on tobacco was the most politically feasible one.

The Health Security Act also focused on cost control. Both managed competition and managed care would help restrain cost increases. Analysts believed that a sizable portion of the population would choose an HMO or another managed care option. This would, as explained above and in chapters 2 and 6, change the incentive structure of medical care toward more efficient care and away from cost-increasing, dubious services. The competition-inducing effect, based on experience with the federal employees program, the system in use in California, and other programs, would also lower costs and change the system toward more integrated care. Finally, supporters of the plan argued that the Health Security Act would reduce administrative complexity. All these things, it was hoped, would eventually result in lowered costs (Zelman 1994). The Clinton administration recognized that costs would rise in the near future because more of the population would have health insurance.

But what if managed competition and managed care did not restrain cost increases? The Clinton plan contained a set of backup regulatory provisions. This "second line of defense" was a cap or ceiling on growth of insurance premiums (Starr 1994a, 101). Paul Starr describes how the premium caps would work:

> Under the Clinton plan, the caps apply not to the premiums of individual health plans but to an alliance's weight-average premium (the average of all premiums weighted according to the share of enrollment in the various plans). Federal legislation would set a growth rate for premiums for covered benefits for the country as a whole, and the National Health Board would adjust that rate for specific alliances depending on demographic changes and other factors. Alliances could meet their targets without any enforcement of caps as competition held down premium increases of individual plans or as consumers switched out of high-cost plans, thereby dragging down the average. If, however, health plans' bids threatened to push an alliance's average over the allowable growth, the federal government would deny full rate increases to the plans seeking the biggest jumps and require the plans to pass on these rate reductions to their providers. (Starr 1994a, 102)

As can be seen from this brief description, the Clinton proposal was complex. It was also over 1,300 pages in length. It was a combination of ideas. It contained an employer mandate (and to some extent an individual mandate for the unemployed) combined with subsidies for both businesses and individuals. It promised universal coverage. It allowed for the possibility of a single-payer system, by permitting states to establish such a system if they wished. Most important, it sought to reform the health care system through a set of health care purchasing cooperative alliances and incentives for providers to integrate into more efficient units. It sought to marry competition with regulation.

The Clinton plan was therefore not a pure plan. While it provided for universal coverage, insurance, and administrative reforms, it did not adopt a single-payer system. Such a system is simpler than either the present system or the one envisioned under the Clinton plan. A single-payer system was not viewed as politically feasible, however, and the Clinton plan sought to build on the present employer-based insurance system. It was also designed to meet the needs of various constituencies (Pearlstein and Priest 1993).

Insurance companies in general would benefit in two ways. First, a larger proportion of the population would be covered. Second, insurers could be major forces behind the provider plans. This would be truer for large insurance companies such as Aetna and Prudential.

Business would also benefit from the plan in several ways. It was true that there would be an employer mandate. This was good from the standpoint of large businesses, because with everyone covered and more paying, cost shifting would effectively be ended. For small businesses, there were subsidies and limitations on their contributions. Further, the Health Security Act would cover early retirees (those under sixty-five and therefore not yet eligible for Medicare), a growing cost burden for larger employers (see chapter 6).

Thus there appeared to be something for everyone. States had an important role, managed competition would be tried, everyone would be covered. The plan, as originally estimated, would reduce the budget deficit in the long run, as health care costs were restrained.

The early reaction to the Clinton plan was positive. Initially, public opinion seemed to support the proposal, though there was some concern about the complexity of the plan and the additional layers of bureaucracy and government regulation that the plan proposed. In this early stage, both interest groups and Republicans supported the plan to remain part of the action (Schneider 1993). Some, however, argued that the public did not support the proposal so much as they supported recognition of the problems with the health care system and a desire to do something about them (see, for example, Bowman 1994).

It should be further noted that, despite the complexity of the plan and the effort that went into the formulation stage, the Clinton administration never saw the plan as written in stone. Policymakers knew the plan would be modified in Congress; this was the opening move (Cohen 1993). Indeed, some of the provisions, such as a generous benefits package, high employer cost sharing, and strict limitations on the growth of insurance premiums, were designed to allow some negotiating room (Fallows 1995).

It was also clear that despite the administration's attempt to meet the needs of various constituencies, there would still be those who won and lost by the Clinton plan. Younger people would be asked to pay more, as would those in rural areas. Working couples would also be losers under the Clinton plan because both would have to pay for health insurance, rather than rely on one job for insurance. Couples with self-employed spouses, who currently paid nothing, would also be dramatic losers (Kosterlitz 1993b).

Similar estimates could be made among providers and insurers. Primary-care physicians would be winners, and specialists would be losers. This is true because under managed care arrangements, especially HMOs, primary-care physicians would act as "gatekeepers," deciding when additional services would be necessary. Specialists, therefore, would be more limited in their ability to offer services. Doctors who joined health care plans would be both winners and losers. They would be winners in that they would be guaranteed access to patients and losers in that they would lose some autonomy and perhaps some income. Doctors who did not join plans would likely be losers because they would not be able to hold onto their patients. Large insurers would be able to organize health care plans, whereas small- and medium-size insurers would not (Broder 1994; Freudenheim 1993).

The Legislative Stage

Deliberations over the health care reform plan did not begin until 1994, an election year. One of the key aspects of the legislative process is that a complex plan such as the Health Security Act is generally shared among a number of congressional committees. The bill was divided among six committees in the House and five in the Senate (Cohen 1993). To pass health care legislation would take strong leadership on the part of the majority Democrats. Only one committee in Congress, the Senate Labor and Education Committee, under the guidance of its chairman, the long-time national health insurance advocate Edward M. Kennedy (D-MA), approved even a modified version of the president's proposal.

One problem was financing. A study by Lewin-VHI, a health care consulting firm, found the cost estimates optimistic. The original estimate of the additional costs of the program was $286 billion over a five-year period. The Lewin study estimated that the program would cost about $78 billion more than the administration estimated over the same period. So, rather than reduce the budget deficit by $103 billion, it would decrease it by about $25 billion (Pear 1993b; see also Sheils and Lewin 1994). During the deliberations of the task force in 1993, economists in the Treasury Department argued that the cost figures were not reliable (Pear 1993a; see also Greenhouse 1993). The Congressional Budget Office (CBO), which scores legislation (estimates how much bills would cost if enacted), came up with the estimate of the near-term negative impact of the Health Security Act on the budget deficit. It also made several rulings that decreased support for the plan, for example, that mandated premiums should be considered as part of the federal budgets and that the health alliances should be considered as federal agencies (Rubin 1994). On the other hand, no one, including the CBO, knew what the plan would actually cost if enacted (see Bilheimer and Reischauer 1995).

Doubts were also expressed about various aspects of the health plan. For example, an early 1994 report by the Congressional Budget Office said that the regional alliances were being asked to do numerous complex tasks in a very short period of time. The tasks included "the functions of purchasing agents, contract negotiators, welfare agencies, financial intermediaries, collectors of premiums, developers and managers of information systems, and coordinators of the flow of information about themselves and other alliances" (quoted in Allen 1994, 23).

Even those whose support should have easily been forthcoming criticized the Clinton plan. The Jackson Hole group opposed the plan on a number of grounds. Enthoven wrote that the plan promised too much (covering everyone, restraining costs) and would likely not result in cuts in Medicare. He opposed the employer mandate. The group also did not like the price controls that were an important part of the plan. More important, Enthoven stated that the Clinton plan had taken the idea of health care cooperatives of a limited size and changed them into monstrous alliances (Enthoven 1994). Enthoven favored a bill by Congressman Jim Cooper (see below).

In response, Paul Starr, a member of the Clinton health care reform task force and one of its leading advocates, argued that in some respects the Clinton plan was quite close to what Enthoven had previously written. For example, Starr pointed out that Enthoven had once favored an employer mandate but no longer did so. Further, Starr noted that Enthoven took a strong antigovernment position about the Clinton plan, yet the Jackson Hole proposals would require significant government involvement to help restructure markets (Starr 1994b).

The Clinton plan was not the only one put before Congress. Some six alternative plans were proposed, some by Democrats, others by Republicans.[15] The Clinton plan had 100 co-sponsors in the House and 31 in the Senate. Co-sponsorship is an indicator of support for a proposal. The Democratic proposals were divided among two widely disparate proposals. On the left, the bill by Senator Paul Wellstone (D-MN) and Congressman Jim McDermott (D-WA) called for a single-payer approach to be administered by the states. That bill had ninety-two co-sponsors in the House and five in the Senate. On the right, Congressman Jim Cooper (D-TN) and Senator John Breaux (D-LA) sponsored a bill that was sometimes referred to as "Clinton-lite." Their bill would expand access to insurance through voluntary cooperatives, subsidies for low-income people, and insurance reform. The Cooper bill had fifty-seven co-sponsors in the House and four in the Senate.

Republicans offered three different plans. One bill, offered by House Minority Leader Robert Michel (R-IL) and Senator Trent Lott (R-MS), expanded access to insurance but contained no mandate. It was a voluntary program that expanded Medicaid and provided for insurance reforms. Employers had to offer their employees health insurance, though they did not have to pay for it. The bill had 139 co-sponsors in the House and ten in the Senate. A second Republican bill was offered by Congressman Cliff Stearns (R-FL) and Senator Don Nickles (R-OK). The bill was a voluntary program but had penalties for individuals not purchasing catastrophic insurance. There would be tax changes regarding the deductibility of health costs and expansion of Medicaid. The bill had eighteen co-sponsors in the House and twenty-five in the Senate. The final bill was the one offered by Congressman William Thomas (R-CA) and Senator John Chafee (R-RI). The bill was basically an individual mandate to purchase insurance and enroll in a plan (either government, employer, or purchasing cooperative). Employers had to offer coverage but did not have to pay for it. Those not purchasing insurance would be penalized. The bill also called for an individual mandate to purchase long-term care insurance. The Thomas-Chafee bill had four co-sponsors in the House and twenty in the Senate.

The abundance of plans did not necessarily translate into support for health care reform. There seemed to be a consensus that some change would take place, given the Democratic majority in Congress and the priority placed on reform by the Clinton administration. But the motives of those proposing and supporting the other plans varied. Some wanted to show that they were involved and wanted to have a say in the final outcome. Others had particular features they wanted included in a health care reform bill. Some wanted to demonstrate their concern about the issue (Clymer 1993c).

As the debate over health care reform moved closer to congressional deliberation, however, support for the plan began to diminish. Interest groups began to attack individual portions of the plan. Perhaps the strongest opposition came from the National Federation of Independent Businesses (NFIB), the association of small businesses. NFIB opposed the employer mandate and lobbied against the Clinton plan from the beginning.

Another major opponent was the Health Insurance Association of America (HIAA). A trade association composed of most of the nation's insurance companies, its members felt that they were left out of the plan. Unlike the largest insurance companies, they would not be able to sponsor or work with alliances and so would be forced out of business. They, therefore, opposed alliances; they also argued that the Clinton plan reduced patients' choice of doctors. The insurance industry was not of one mind, however. The five largest insurance companies (Aetna, Cigna, Metlife, Prudential, and Travelers) formed the Alliance for Managed Competition and sponsored ads promoting managed competition and managed care. This did not, nevertheless, translate into support for the Clinton plan.[16]

This is not to say that no interest groups supported the Clinton plan. The Democratic National Committee was given a major role in sending out mail to contributors and potential contributors for their campaign in support of health care reform. The liberal group Families USA also engaged in direct-mail campaigns. Conservative groups likewise utilized direct mail (Kosterlitz 1993a). Interest groups (about 650 of them) and lobbyists on both sides flooded key congressmen and senators with campaign contributions. For example, from January 1, 1993, to May 31, 1994, the AMA political action committee gave almost $1 million in contributions (Lewis 1993; Seelye 1994b).

Interest groups on both sides also turned toward the grass roots, trying to mobilize supporters for their positions in the districts. Some of the grassroots support was genuine, especially on the part of employees of tobacco firms, who argued against additional taxes on tobacco products, and small business owners, who argued against employer mandates (Krauss 1993). Other support was manufactured (sometimes known as "AstroTurf" lobbying):

Pharmaceutical companies, for instance, are writing to their shareholders warning them that profits could suffer if price controls impede new drug research. Planned Parenthood is encouraging its members to deluge Congress with a post-card campaign demanding that abortion services, prenatal care and estrogen replacement therapy are covered under a proposed insurance blanket. (Krauss 1993)

A portion of the health care reform debate was fought through advertising, both print and electronic. The most famous of the television ad campaigns were the "Harry and Louise" and "Libby and Louise" ads by the Health Insurance Association of America. HIAA's major problems with the Clinton health care plan were threefold: HIAA opposed the ceiling or cap on insurance premiums; it opposed the requirement that people join the regional cooperatives (because smaller and midsize insurance companies would not be large enough to participate and would be forced out of the business); and it opposed community rating. As an example of the kind of pitch made in the HIAA ads, consider the following:

Harry:	I'm glad the President's doing something about health care reform.
Louise:	He's right, We need it.
Harry:	Some of these details—
Louise:	Like a limit on health care?
Harry:	Really.
Louise:	The Government caps how much the country can spend on health care and says, "That's it!"
Harry:	So, what if our health plan runs out of money?
Louise:	There's got to be a better way. (Kolbert 1993).

A related HIAA ad saw Louise and her business partner, Libby, discussing the Clinton plan:

Libby:	I want Congress to pass health care reform . . .
Louise:	Make sure everyone is covered.
Libby:	. . . but not force us to buy our insurance from these mandatory government "health alliances."
Louise:	So we couldn't choose a plan that's not on their list even if we think it's better for our employees and their families.
Libby:	Not according to this. (Holds up president's health plan.)
Louise:	But Congress can fix that—cover everyone and let us pick the plan we want.
Libby:	And they will, if we send them that message.
Announcer:	For the facts you need to send a message, call today. (Toner 1994b)

Opponents of the Clinton plan used ads to attack various aspects of the proposal. Some, such as the Project for the Republican Future, argued that the greatest jeopardy to health care security was in fact the Clinton plan. Others, such as HIAA, attacked the plan as being bureaucratic and as restricting choice. Still others argued that the plan would cost more for people who currently had coverage (Toner 1994b; for a critique of the HIAA campaign, see Kosterlitz 1995).

The ads were often incorrect or misleading. Some suggested that the Clinton plan would reduce choice of doctors. The reality is that the Clinton plan might in fact have increased choice for certain segments of the population. One could argue that the changes produced in the health care system by the advent of managed care reduced choice more than the Clinton plan would have, had it gone into effect (see chapter 10). Other ads attacked health care alliances long after that idea had been dropped by Congress (Waldman and Cohn 1994).

Supporters of the program were also active. The Democratic National Committee (DNC) ran a series of ads that counterattacked and parodied the "Harry and Louise" ads. In the DNC version, the couple get injured and lose their health insurance, and Harry loses his job. Louise turns to Harry and says: "You said universal coverage was too complicated. You said you'd never lose your job, so we'd always be covered. You said, what would we do when the government runs out of money? Well who's out of money now, Harry?" The ad closed with the tag line, "There is a better way. Tell Congress you want what they already have: the security of affordable, universal health care" ("Spin Doctors" 1994). A coalition of consumer, labor, civic, professional, and other groups ran a newspaper and radio campaign touting the benefits of health care reform (Toner 1994a). Pro-choice and pro-life groups ran ads on whether health reform should include or exclude abortion provisions ("Muddling Through the Message" 1993). Another parody of the "Harry and Louise" ads came from those sponsoring a single-payer system, with the tag line delivered by comedienne Anne Meara, "Harry and Louise, there is a better way." Of course the money raised by those supporting the single-payer plan was dwarfed by other interests (Toner 1994c).

The ads may have made a bigger impact on the Clinton administration and on the media than on the public. The Clinton administration attacked the ads and, as noted, the Democratic National Committee ran ads parodying them. News media focused on the ads and the attacks on them and attributed to them more power than perhaps they had. A study testing the effectiveness of the "Harry and Louise" ads found little retention of the content of the ads and showed little effect of the ads on attitudes (Jamieson 1994).

Another way that opponents of health care reform had of attacking the plan was to suggest that while the country's health care problems were serious, they were not critical, requiring radical surgery. For example, Senate Minority Leader Robert Dole (R-KS) stated in January 1994 that there was no crisis in health care; Senate Finance Committee Chairman Daniel Patrick Moynihan (D-NY) made a similar point (Clymer 1994a). Public opinion polls gave ambiguous signs about whether the public saw a crisis. When asked to name the country's most important problems, only 7 percent listed health care (considerably behind the economy and crime). On the other hand, when asked whether the country faced a health care crisis, a problem, or no crisis, 57 percent said it had a crisis and 42 percent said a problem. Further, most people were satisfied with the quality of health care they received and with their health insurance. At the same time, a sizable majority favored universal health insurance (Morin 1994b). To some extent, the idea of a crisis in health care in the early 1990s that could fuel an upset victory by Harris Wofford was caused by the economic conditions of that time. The recession of 1990–91, the continued increase in health care costs, and the diminishment of health insurance coverage among workers also contributed to the feeling of a crisis. But as the economy recovered from the recession and began to expand, and as health care cost increases moderated, the atmosphere of crisis diminished. Between the lessened crisis atmosphere, heavy lobbying, and advertising on the part of opponents, public support for the Clinton plan dwindled (Schneider 1994).

Public Opinion and the Health Care Reform Debate

Early public opinion polls showed some support for the Clinton plan, though on a partisan basis. In a New York Times/CBS News poll, 61 percent said they would be willing to pay higher taxes so that universal coverage could be achieved. Forty-five percent felt that the president would be able to bring about reform, 41 percent said that the plan would being about needed changes, 40 percent said that it would be fair, and 46 percent said that it would make health care better. Republicans and independents expressed greater skepticism and much lower levels of support for change. The poll, like most others, showed the public's dissatisfaction with the system as a whole, though satisfaction with their care. A majority would support a limitation on choice of doctors and increased waiting for noncritical appointments if it meant that more could be covered. Only 36 percent, however, supported rationing (limiting coverage for expensive treatments with limited effectiveness). The poll showed majority support for employer mandates and for several ways to finance universal coverage: increased taxes on alcohol and tobacco and limitations on charges by doctors and hospitals through the Medicare program (Toner 1993b; see also Toner 1993a).

A study of public opinion polls commissioned by the House of Representatives Ways and Means Committee found limited and declining support for increased taxes, though an increase in the number of people who felt that the country was spending too much on health care. The report concluded that "most Americans would rather see the scope of the Clinton reform plan scaled back than pay new taxes. In addition, the public is strongly opposed to increasing the deficit in order to pay for health reform" (Robert J. Blendon, quoted in Morin 1994a).

By March 1994, public support for the Clinton plan was declining precipitously. While there was support for the goals of the plan, more people disapproved of the proposal than approved of it. Part of the problem was that the complex plan was difficult to understand. Another part was the criticisms leveled at the proposal through ad campaigns. There was fear that the quality of care would decline, that rationing would occur, and that the middle class would be hurt by the proposal. A slim majority hoped that either nothing changed or that Congress would make changes in the plan. Nevertheless, the public still supported employer mandates and controls on premiums. Further, the public gave Clinton credit for trying to change the system (Broder and Morin 1994).

Two findings about public opinion were especially interesting. One was that while the public thought that the government could guarantee security of insurance coverage, there was doubt that the government could control costs. This was one reason the administration deemphasized cost control and emphasized security (Fallows 1995). A second finding came from a March 1994 focus group presented with the Clinton plan without stating that it was the Clinton plan. The group preferred that plan to other alternatives. When the group was told that it was the Clinton plan, support dropped dramatically (Fallows 1995).

It should be pointed out that part of the problem with public opinion polling is that slight differences in question wording can affect the results. When asked whether the Clinton plan was better or worse than the present system, a majority (52 percent) said better. When the phrase "or don't you know enough about the plan to say" was added, only 21 percent said it was better. The percentage of those who felt that the Clinton plan was worse declined to 27 percent from 34 percent. Thus a substantial portion of those polled (52 percent) admitted ignorance of the plan (Morin 1994c).[17]

As the struggle over health care reform continued in Congress, public support for change decreased. By September 1994, only about 40 percent approved of the way President Clinton was handling the health care issue. But the opinion of other players in the health care reform debate also diminished. Robert Dole's unfavorability ratings had increased by ten points over the previous year. Strong support remained for universal coverage and the idea that the health care system was in crisis. The major targets for blame included the opposition to the Clinton plan and the high level of government regulation in the plan (Toner 1994f).

Health Care Reform Defeated

While several committees in the House of Representatives passed a version of the Clinton health care reform bill, there was never a vote on the floor of the House. House Democrats, despite the crafting of a bill by House Majority Leader Richard Gephardt (D-MO) calling for universal coverage by 1999, never united behind a single plan (Seelye 1994a; Toner 1994e). By early August, House leaders decided that between Republican opposition and the hesitancy of a number of Democrats, they would let the Senate take the lead (Clymer 1994b).

One of the interesting things that happened during deliberations over health care reform was how little of the original plan remained. President Clinton said his major concern was universal coverage. Then the question raised was: What did universal mean? Was it 100 percent or would some lesser figure, such as 95 or 90 percent, be acceptable? The president agreed to a lesser figure. Lost in the debate was another major concern: controlling the cost of care (Pear 1994a). But Senate Democrats were also not united. Senate Finance Committee Chairman Moynihan stated that he saw no crisis in health care that warranted emergency surgery. Several Republicans and Democrats on the Finance Committee proposed a plan that had an individual rather than an employer mandate (Clymer 1994c). The feeling of some of those on the committee was that even though the individual mandate was not desirable, it would help get a bill reported to the floor of the Senate. But a group of civic, consumer, and labor groups, known as the Health Care Reform Project, opposed the proposal. They wanted an employer mandate; they felt that the individual mandate would not achieve universal coverage and that middle-income families without insurance would still have financial problems (Clymer 1994d; Toner 1994c). At the same time, Senate Minority Leader Bob Dole moved away from his previous advocacy of universal coverage toward a much less ambitious goal of assisting the poor in purchasing insurance and prohibiting insurance companies from denying coverage to those with previous medical conditions (Clymer 1994e).

It also became clear that Republicans in both the House and the Senate were opposing reform with an eye on the forthcoming November 1994 elections, a strategy that would ultimately be successful. House Minority Whip Newt Gingrich (R-GA) told Republicans on the Ways and Means Committee not to support any amendments that would improve the chances of a committee bill passing. Further, Gingrich told Republicans that, if they supported a tax increase, one portion of the bill the Ways and Means Committee was considering, such support could be used against them by Democrats in the elections. To a small extent, the Republican strategy backfired. Democrats on the committee who had previously been divided on a bill came together to support one in a show of party unity (Clymer 1994b). Overall, the Republicans were emboldened in their opposition, as support for the Clinton plan eroded and House Democrats showed little unity (Kosterlitz 1994).

In early August, Senate Majority Leader George Mitchell (D-ME) made one last try at a bill (Clymer 1994f). The Mitchell bill relied on individual mandates, with the goal of 95 percent coverage by the end of the century. The president supported the Mitchell bill (Wines 1994). A few days later, Mitchell agreed to compromise with a bill being prepared by Senator Chafee (Clymer 1994h). After debate began on the Mitchell bill, Senate Republicans began a filibuster to prevent a vote on the floor of the Senate. Mitchell was unable to get enough votes to end debate and at one point threatened to keep the Senate in an around-the-clock session to break the filibuster (Clymer 1994i). Mitchell's efforts would eventually fail, and health care reform was doomed. Moderate Republicans and Democrats, in what became known as the Mainstream Group, attempted to fashion a compromise bill but got little support beyond their group (Pear 1994b).

By the end of August, it became clear that health care reform could not be passed in any version. Republicans were not only opposing any reform in both the Senate and the House but were threatening to drop support for the trade agreement, the General Agreement on Tariffs and Trade (GATT), which would be debated later in the year (Clymer 1994j; Purdum 1994).

The November elections brought a historic Republican victory. Health care was not an important issue in the campaigns, and the Republicans gained control of both houses of Congress for the first time in forty years (Clymer 1994l). Perhaps most symbolic were losses by two Democrats. Jim Cooper, the author of a major alternative to the Clinton health plan in the House, lost his bid for senator from Tennessee. Harris Wofford, whose unexpected victory in the special senatorial election in Pennsylvania in 1991 sparked the political movement toward health care reform, lost his effort to serve a complete term.

The Failure of Health Care Reform

> After hundreds of town hall meetings, months of congressional hearings and markups by five committees, days of Senate consideration and an unprecedented lobbying campaign by special interest groups, neither the House nor the Senate ever did vote on a health care bill. As the 103d Congress adjourned, its unwillingness to act on what President Clinton described as his most important domestic priority stood as the most conspicuous symbol of Clinton's failure to implement the ambitious reform agenda. (Priest and Weisskopf 1994b)

Why did health care reform fail to win approval in 1994?[18] A number of reasons have been put forth to explain the failure. One was the inability of the president to maintain public support, either for himself or for his reform proposal. While the initial returns from the president's September 1993 speech were quite positive, opinion polls always showed that support was tenuous. The public wanted change but was also satisfied with its care. It wanted security but feared government bureaucracy (Morin 1994d).

This last point is an important one. The Clinton plan, rightly or wrongly, was characterized by opponents, such as the Health Insurance Association of America and congressional Republicans, as big government. This ran into the traditional American distrust of government, particularly at a time (1994) when government was under attack.[19]

The president's own approval ratings also were a problem. Bill Clinton won the 1992 election but captured only 43 percent of the popular vote. During his first two years in office, his approval ratings hovered in that area, only periodically exceeding 50 percent. Questions about his character and finances (Whitewater) also affected Clinton's approval ratings. Further, during the 1992 elections, he had run behind virtually all the congressmen and senators who ran that year. He clearly had no coattails that one could cling to in 1994 (Dewar 1994).[20]

The process by which the Health Security Act was formulated also may have contributed to its defeat. The 500-person task force headed by First Lady Hillary Rodham Clinton and Ira Magaziner focused on technical issues and not political feasibility (Fallows 1995; Priest and Weisskopf 1994a). It was conducted in secret and created antagonism from the beginning. The bill produced was very complex, and its complexity and length (more than 1,300 pages) did not help win it public support (Butler 1993; Waldman 1994). The administration was urged by moderates within the White House to come up with a general set of principles and goals and to let Congress work out the details. Instead, the detailed, highly complex plan became a target for those opposed either to reform or to portions of it. One could argue that the health care system envisioned by the Clinton plan was no more and perhaps less complex than the current system. That assertion was never made by the Clinton forces or its allies.

The administration did not respond well to attacks by interest groups, particularly via television advertisements. Nor was the administration able to portray its flexibility and willingness to negotiate (Clymer 1994k; Dionne 1994).

Time was also a problem (Clymer, Pear, and Toner 1994). The proceedings of the task force were lengthy, and a bill promised in April 1993 was not unveiled until September 1993. Even then, the bill was not delivered to Congress until the next month. The anticipation and buildup that accompanied the early stages of policy formulation dissipated with delay.

Other administration priorities blocked the way (Fallows 1995). In 1993, this included the big deficit-cutting budget bill and the North American Free Trade Agreement (NAFTA). In 1994, the administration's crime bill got in the way. To a certain extent, Republicans' opposition to the crime bill in the House was designed to impede passage of health care reform.

Another thing that hurt the Clinton plan was the economy. While the 1990–91 recession was over by the time of the 1992 elections, the effects of the recession were still being felt because the recovery was slow. By 1994, things had changed. The economy was growing at a good clip and inflation was low. Further, medical inflation was relatively low in 1994. Thus, Senator Dole could with some reason claim that there was no health care crisis. The slowdown in health care inflation has been attributed to the reduction in overall inflation and to changes in the health care system as it moved toward managed care. The more cynical could argue that providers and insurers kept cost increases low as a means of deflating the drive for reform (Hilzenrath 1993/1994).[21]

Of course, a major portion of the failure is attributable to opposition on the part of interest groups, most prominently the National Federation of Independent Businesses (NFIB) and the Health Insurance Association of America. The financial resources devoted to the campaign for advertising, lobbying, and grassroots activity towered over those of supporters. One estimate is that interest groups spent about $300 million to oppose the Clinton plan (Waldman and Cohn 1994).

These groups, especially NFIB, were able to mobilize their members to contact their congressmen. NFIB was also able to convince groups that originally supported reform to come out in opposition to the Clinton plan. The AMA and the Chamber of Commerce are cases in point. Small businesses began to quit the chamber because of its support for the Health Security Act. The chamber reversed its position. Other groups that originally supported the plan, such as the Business Roundtable, eventually came out against it (Waldman and Cohn 1994).

Partisanship was also a problem. Democrats in both the House and Senate were divided. This was in contrast to the considerable unity among Republicans in opposition to the Clinton plan. As the Republicans saw that public support was low and that the outlook for a successful election in 1994 grew, they became less inclined to negotiate and see the passage of a bill (Fallows 1995).

There was also division among policy experts as to what course of action to take. One study conducted shortly after the demise of comprehensive reform in 1994 found that while policy elites were pretty much agreed on the nature of the problems with the health care system (though disagreeing with the general public about what those problems were), there was no consensus about what to do (Patel and Rushefsky 1998).

There was one last factor, an institutional one. The institutional perspective takes note of the structure of the American political system (discussed in chapter 1), such as checks and balances, separation of powers, and federalism, and sees how that structure affects policy debate. The system devised by the delegates to the Constitutional Convention of 1787 was designed for two purposes. The first was to create a government that could act. The second was to create barriers to precipitous action by what the Founding Fathers called "factions" (what we would call interest groups and political parties). The Founding Fathers were distrustful of democracy and sought ways to limit the power of factions and of government that could be controlled by them.

The history of attempts at health care reform and national health insurance in the twentieth century bears witness to the power of the Founding Fathers' vision of limited government. And so while other Western industrialized countries moved toward some form of national health insurance and universal coverage, the United States did not (see Blake and Adolino 2001). The barriers created, especially in Congress, provided the access points for interest groups opposed to reform and made the development of broad majorities at several different points of the legislative process very difficult.

After reviewing the institutionalist argument and the history of health care reform attempts in the United States, two political scientists, Sven Steinmo and Jon Watts, predicted eight months before the Health Security Act was presented to Congress that comprehensive health care reform would fail:

> America cannot pass major comprehensive health care reform that will control costs and offer complete coverage to all Americans because her political institutions are designed to prevent this kind of reform. To truly pass meaningful reform would require imposing costs on certain groups (factions). Clearly the majority (faction) both want and would benefit from such a reform. But the fragmentation of authority designed into the U.S. Constitution makes it virtually impossible for the majority's will to supersede the minority—at least when that minority is well financed and well organized. To overcome the opposition of the minority faction, the majority must buy off their opposition. The effect (in the case of health care reform at least) is to throw fat onto the inflationary fire. (Steinmo and Watts 1995)[22]

The States and Comprehensive Health Care Reform

Although the federal government considered health care reform in 1992–94, little was actually accomplished. Some major pieces of legislation were passed in the ensuing years, such as the 1996 Health Insurance and Portability Accounting Act, the 1997 Balanced Budget Act, and the 2003 Medicare Modernization Act. In the years following the demise of the Clinton plan, some states sought to take action on comprehensive health care reform. Those efforts waned for various reasons. Certainly, the fiscal problems the states experienced (because of increases in Medicaid spending, the 2001 recession and the slow recovery that followed it, and the federal tax cuts in the early 2000s) made cost control the major concern. Yet the states remain important actors in health care. Even attempts at comprehensive care reappeared in the 2000s.

There are several rationales for state action. One is flexibility. States differ along many dimensions—size, economic base, urbanization, and so forth. From this perspective, a single plan from the federal government would not be appropriate for all states (Nelson 1994). A second rationale is that states already have important roles in health care: insurance and hospital regulation, rate regulation, licensing, delivery of public services, and education and training (National Commission on the State and Local Public Service 1993; see also the Web site of the National Conference of State Legislatures: www.ncsl.org).

A third rationale for looking at states (and local governments) is that even under a national plan, the states would have an important administrative role. This is typical of other domestic policy areas, such as welfare. Medicaid, building on the welfare system, is a joint federal-state program. Under the Clinton plan, states would have had an important role in designing and overseeing regional health alliances (DiIulio and Nathan 1994). Even with the demise of comprehensive reform at the national level, states undertook new programs, encouraged by the Clinton administration's waivers from Medicaid regulations (Holahan and Nichols 1996).

A fourth rationale was the pressure that health care costs, especially Medicaid, was placing on state budgets. It was hoped that some changes, such as Medicaid reform, would alleviate that pressure (Boyd 2003; Gold 1996; and Oberlander 2003).

The earliest state health reform effort was in Hawaii in 1974. Hawaii has an employer mandate, even covering part-time workers. For low-income people, there is an insurance premium subsidy. The Hawaii program, including Medicaid, covers about 93 percent of the state's population (Nelson 1994; Neubauer 1993). As with other states, Hawaii has experienced budget difficulties and has moved more toward market reforms and cost control.

Some thirteen states engaged in attempts at comprehensive health care reform (in some cases predating the federal effort), designed to cover more of the population as well as restraining Medicare costs. Some of the most far-reaching reforms were in Florida, Massachusetts, Minnesota, Oregon, Vermont, and Washington (Brown and Sparer 2001; Fox and Iglehart 1994; Holahan and Nichols 1996; Oliver and Paul-Shaheen 1997; and Paul-Shaheen 1998).

One of the more interesting attempts at reform came when Oregon, beginning in 1989, sought to impose an explicit rationing program within Medicaid (Leichter 1997). It did this by ranking some 709 medical procedures and then setting a line of what would be and would not be funded by the state. For example, medical therapy for AIDS patients was allowed, unless they were in the last six months of life. Liver transplants would be allowed for those suffering from cirrhosis of the liver unless it was related to alcohol consumption (Pear 1992c). Oregon argued that this rationing scheme could cover up to 400,000 more people with the same amount of money.

The Oregon plan required a Medicaid waiver from the federal government, but the Bush administration rejected it. There were several reasons for the rejection. One was that the plan was too inflexible given the variety of medical conditions physicians are presented with. A second reason was that explicit rationing affected only Medicaid recipients. Thus the least politically powerful would bear the brunt of rationing. Third, if health care costs rose more than expected after rationing went into effect, the cutoff point would have to be drawn higher (Pear 1992d).

Perhaps the most important reason was that advocacy groups and others felt that the rationing plan would discriminate against disabled persons and therefore violate the 1990 Americans with Disabilities Act. Those making this claim included pro-life groups, the liberal Children's Defense Fund, the Catholic Church, and the 1992 Democratic vice-presidential candidate, Al Gore (Pear 1992d).

Oregon's governor, Barbara Roberts, argued that the plan was well thought out, that it had the participation of a wide variety of interests, and that disability groups in Oregon supported it. Further, she asserted that neither the General Accounting Office nor the Office of Technology Assessment (both staff arms of Congress) had raised the disabilities issue. Finally, Governor Roberts said that the Justice Department had not said how the Oregon plan might violate the act (Roberts 1992). After changing the plan to meet some of the objections, the Clinton administration approved the Medicaid waiver in March 1993 (Iglehart 1994). A second waiver and an exception from the Employee Retirement Income Security Act (ERISA) were not granted and the employer mandate was rescinded (Oliver and Paul-Shaheen 1997).

The Florida reforms began with some insurance revisions and agency consolidation in 1992. In 1993, Florida passed legislation designed to bring managed competition to the state (mimicking some of the elements of the Clinton Health Security Act). Attempts to increase the use of managed care for Medicaid recipients and extend coverage to more working families failed. The state did modestly expand coverage for children and enrolled a small number of people in the health alliances program (Oliver and Paul-Shaheen 1997).

By early 1994, eight states had enacted health care reform plans, some successfully, some not so successfully. Some states focused on insurance reform. One important failure was the insurance reforms enacted in New York. The combination of community rating and limitations on preexisting conditions restrictions induced healthier and younger residents to drop insurance coverage. A second failure was in Massachusetts. The state passed a comprehensive universal health care law in 1988, based on the "play-or-pay" formula, under Democratic Governor Michael Dukakis, the Democratic presidential candidate in that year. But economic problems, some opposition, and the political destruction of Dukakis after his unsuccessful campaign as the Democratic nominee for president against George Bush in 1988 led to delay in implementation of the plan until 1995. The Republican governor, William Weld, supported repeal of the law, despite popular support for it (Iglehart 1994). Implementation of the law was delayed by the state legislature three times, and the employer mandate was finally repealed in 1996. Massachusetts then turned to extending Medicaid to more children and to long-term unemployed families and adults with incomes just above the federal poverty line (Oliver and Paul-Shaheen 1997).

More encompassing health care reform programs were adopted, for a time, in Florida, Minnesota, and Washington. These programs generally sought to employ both managed competition and regulation, a goal of the Clinton Health Security Act. The Florida law provided for a basic benefits package and created eleven regional alliances similar to those in the Clinton plan (Iglehart 1994; Nelson 1994). The Washington law had both an individual and an employer mandate. It also had controls over insurance premiums, organized provider delivery systems, and purchasing cooperatives (Crittenden 1993).

Brown and Sparer (2001) point out that state health care reforms went through three phases in the 1990s. The first is what they call the "learning curve" phase (51) and focused on comprehensive changes to the health care system. This phase included the Oregon, Massachusetts, Washington, and Florida plans mentioned above. It also included the reaction to the defeat of the Clinton plan, such as the repeal of the Washington law that had been passed two years prior. The same kind of politics that led to the defeat of the Clinton plan affected state action.

The second phase of health care reform was the focus on insurance reform (Brown and Sparer 2001). The idea was to cover, through changes such as requiring community rating, more of the population. Purchasing alliances, such as in California, were also part of this stage (Quinn 1994). The data on increases in the number of those without health insurance suggest that this phase was not very successful.

The third and final phase of state health care reform in the 1990s was what Brown and Sparer (2001) call the "home-court" advantage. Rather than fight business and insurance companies, states focused on public programs, largely Medicaid (see chapter 3). Some states, such as California and New York, began increasing their coverage of children even prior to the passage of the federal State Children's Health Insurance Program in 1997. As is typical of state programs, there was considerable variation in coverage among the states. The 1996 welfare reform bill eliminated the automatic enrollment of welfare recipients into Medicaid. This also hurt coverage of poor families (Brown and Sparer 2001). Perhaps more important, the fiscal crisis of the states led to cutbacks in the programs that became even more evident in the 2000s.

The 2000s saw some modest, halting moves toward comprehensive reform. In 2003, Maine adopted legislation focusing on the three major areas of health care reform: quality, access, and cost (Greenblatt 2003). The plan is to cover, in a variety of ways, all of the state's uninsured residents by 2009. This will be done by expanding Medicaid, requiring small businesses to pay as much as 60 percent of the costs of premiums, and finding private insurers to cover those currently uninsured. Some of the costs of the program will come from an assessment of insurance companies. Minnesota is looking at a purchasing cooperative as a way of controlling costs and expanding care to the uninsured (Broder 2004). The purchasing cooperative includes private-sector employers and has been expanded to public-sector employees. But Maine and Minnesota are unusual. Most states are seeking ways to limit their costs. Tennessee, Missouri, Mississippi, and Oregon are trying to shrink their Medicaid rolls (Tanner 2004). On the other hand, in 2004, California voters approved some state health initiatives and defeated some others (Lemov 2005). Lemov (2005) writes:

> California voters had the option of giving thumbs up or down to an expansion of mental health services, renovation of children's hospitals, a mandate for "play or pay" employer-based health insurance and a plan to cover uncompensated care provided by emergency health workers.
> All totaled, the five health initiatives represented a broad approach to health care reform—from new therapies to expanded services to broader access to care for everyone. But the initiatives weren't, in fact, a package. Each program had to stand on its own, and in the end, voters went for three of them. Those that won voter approval—stem-cell research, mental health services and children's hospitals—were relatively narrow programs targeting a single, self-contained issue. The broadest of the initiatives—the health insurance mandate—went down to defeat.

Lemov draws three lessons from the 2004 California initiative votes. First, health care is an important issue. Second, voters are willing to pay for some solutions. Third, if policymakers do not work with stakeholders (i.e., insurance companies, employers), voters will look toward incremental, piecemeal changes. But these do not address the issues of cost, quality, and access (2005).

There is at least one other proposal that seeks comprehensive health care reform. This is a proposal that calls for federal/state cooperation. It has been crafted by two health policy analysts. One is Stuart Butler from the conservative Heritage Foundation. The other is Henry Aaron of the liberal-centrist Brookings Institution (Butler and Aaron 2003). Their proposal has four parts.

First, it calls for Congress to set goals for a new health care policy, including reducing the number of uninsured and providing benefits equal to what Medicaid requires. Second, the proposal calls for creating a "toolkit" of policies that states could choose from. These include tax credits, expansion of public programs such as Medicaid, individual mandates, focusing on those close to retirement or children, association plans (which allow small businesses to join in cooperative purchasing of health insurance for their employees, see chapter 10), and allowing nonfederal workers to buy into the Federal Employees Health Benefits Plan. Third, states would propose a plan subject to federal approval. The fourth element would be federal grants for participating states. The idea behind the proposal is to take advantage of the federal system and meld liberal and conservative approaches.

Conclusion

Comprehensive health care reform (i.e., national health insurance) found its way onto the policy agenda in the early and mid-1990s, fueled by economic distress and corporate restructuring, by political events such as the 1991 Pennsylvania special senatorial election and the 1992 presidential election, and by budget and fiscal issues. This was not, as we have seen in chapter 2, the first effort to enact national health insurance. This effort was different from the previous attempts in some ways but similar in one important way.

One difference was that a bill actually went further in Congress than any previous legislation. The most important difference was the incorporation of marketlike mechanisms (managed care and managed competition) as part of the proposal.

The important similarity was that this effort, like all previous ones, also failed. A number of reasons have been offered to explain failure at the federal level: the structure of Congress, the opposition of interest groups, lack of public support, a weak president, disagreement among policy elites, political calculations by political opponents, and so forth.

If the federal government could not act, might the states? Here the message was mixed. A number of states enacted insurance reforms; some sought comprehensive coverage; others looked toward market reform. Many laws were, in fact, enacted. The Clinton administration aided this effort through the generous granting of Medicaid waivers. Yet this effort by the laboratories of democracy[23] was ultimately unsatisfactory. Ambitious attempts were followed by retrenchment. The retrenchment, with a few exceptions, continued into the 2000s.

That comprehensive efforts to change the health care delivery system in the United States and to ensure coverage for all citizens failed is not surprising. The political fallout from that failure, the Republican congressional victories in 1994, seemed to spell doom to the possibility for anything but cutbacks. But as the doomed attempt at national health insurance in 1948 eventually led to the establishment of Medicare and Medicaid, so too did the 1993–94 effort eventually lead to change at both the state and the federal level. Medicare and Medicaid became the focus of activity in the 1995–96 period. What emerged from that debate were new programs directed at managed care, insurance coverage, and extension of insurance coverage to children. In the 2000s, proposals sought marketlike mechanisms that focused on the individual as a way of solving the problems of the U.S. health care system. This incremental movement, typical of public policy making in the United States, is the subject of chapter 10.

Notes

1. It is an extraordinary coincidence that Adam Smith's *The Wealth of Nations*, which extolled the virtues of free, unfettered markets, appeared in the same year as the Declaration of Independence, which declared humanity's freedom.

2. This traditional structure is becoming less prominent, largely because of the press of cost increases and the development of managed care.

3. It might be more correct to argue that providers were both the demand and the supply sides.

4. This is a variation of the play-or-pay rule and contains an employer mandate.

5. The managed competition plan has some resemblance to the German system, whereby Sickness Funds negotiate with organizations of providers. See Graig (1993), White (1995).

6. Kingdon argues that the political and problem streams are the most important in placing an item on the governmental agenda. See Kingdon (1984), Rushefsky and Patel (1998), and Skocpol (1996).

7. Heinz was the heir to to the Heinz fortune, based on food products. His widow, Teresa, later married Senator John Kerry, a Democrat from Massachusetts and the 2004 Democratic candidate for president.

8. For a discussion of interest groups in the health policy debates of the 1990s, see Rushefsky and Patel (1998), chapter 5.

9. For a discussion of the acceptance of managed competition by many policy elites and decision makers during this time, see Hacker (1997).

10. For a discussion of public opinion polls and health care reform, see Rushefsky and Patel (1998, chapter 7). See also Blendon, Brodie, and Benson (1995); and Jacobs and Shapiro (1995; 2000).

11. The book was the first edition of Paul Starr's (1994a) *The Logic of Health Care Reform*.

12. This was mostly a political complaint. Whatever plan the president proposed would have had to be approved by Congress, where the deliberations were relatively open. This is the opposite of the situation during both the Reagan and George H.W. Bush administrations (when secret meetings with industry were held that affected regulations and would not be subject to open meetings or congressional oversight at a later time). On this point see Nathan (1983) and Tiefer (1994). On the openness of the task force to outside review, see Fallows (1995), Hacker (1997), and Skocpol (1996). A similar issue arose in 2001, when Vice President Dick Cheney put together an energy task force that consumer and environmental groups asserted was loaded with industry representatives. In 2005, a federal appeals court ruled that records of the meetings could remain secret. See Leonnig and Vandehei (2005).

13. The following description is based on Hacker (1997).

14. As we shall see in chapter 10, some of these provisions become part of the consumer-driven approach to health care reform.

15. The following two paragraphs are based on Kaiser Commission (1994).

16. For a discussion of interest groups and health care reform proposals, see Rushefsky and Patel (1998) and Johnson and Broder (1996).

17. This lack of information about policy issues is a fairly common finding. On the importance of looking at questions to get a real sense of changes in public mood, see Stimson (1991).

18. For a discussion of the failure of health care reform on the part of sympathetic observers, see Fallows (1995) and Starr (1995). See also Skocpol (1996), Johnson and Broder (1996), and Rushefsky and Patel (1998).

19. For a discussion of trust in government, see Craig (1993) and Nye, Zelikow, and King (1997).

20. For a discussion of President Clinton's approval ratings, see Rushefsky and Patel (1998), chapters 3 and 7.

21. There is some precedent for this, both before and after the Clinton proposals. In the late 1970s, President Jimmy Carter proposed legislation that would result in some federal controls over hospitals. The health care sector promised to restrain inflation through what became known as the Voluntary Effort. While Carter was president, medical inflation was constrained. With Carter's defeat in 1980, the Voluntary Effort was dropped. For a graphic discussion of the ups and downs of medical care cost increases and public policy, see chapter 6 and Altman and Levitt (2003).

22. This is essentially the argument made by journalists Haynes Johnson and David Broder, who wrote that "the system" itself was broken. See Johnson and Broder (1996).

23. The phrase is from Supreme Court Justice Louis B. Brandeis. See the discussion in Oliver and Paul-Shaheen (1997).

References

Allen, Jodie T. 1994. "New Blue Smoke and Mirrors." *Washington Post National Weekly Edition* (February 21–17): 23.

Altman, Drew E., and Larry Levitt. 2003. "The Sad History of Health Care Cost Containment as Told in One Chart." *Health Affairs* (October 25): W83–W84.

Arrow, Kenneth J. 1963. "Uncertainty and the Welfare Economics of Medical Care." *American Economic Review* LIII, no. 5 (December): 851–83.

Bauman, Patricia. 1976. "The Formulation and Evolution of the Health Maintenance Organization Policy, 1970–1973." *Social Science and Medicine* 10 (March–April): 129–42.

Bilheimer, Linda T., and Robert D. Reischauer. 1995. "Confessions of the Estimators: Numbers and Health Reform." *Health Affairs* 14, no. 1 (Spring): 37–55.

Blake, Charles H., and Jessica R. Adolino. 2001. "The Enactment of National Health Insurance: A Boolean Analysis of Twenty Advanced Industrial Countries." *Journal of Health Politics, Policy and Law* 26, no. 4 (August): 679–708.

Blendon, Robert J.; Mollyann Brodie; and John Benson. 1995. "What Happened to Americans' Support for the Clinton Plan?" *Health Affairs* 14, no. 2 (Summer): 7–23.

Bowman, Karlyn H. 1994. *The 1993–1994 Debate on Health Care Reform: Did the Polls Mislead the Policy Makers?* Washington, D.C.: AEI Press.

Boyd, Donald J. 2003. "The Bursting State Fiscal Bubble and State Medicaid Budgets." *Health Affairs* 22, no. 1 (January/February): 46–61.

Broder, David S. 1994. "Of Gored Oxen and Health Care." *Washington Post National Weekly Edition* (January 17–23): 4.

———. 2004. "Minnesota's Health Care Gamble." *Washington Post,* December 9.

Broder, David S., and Richard Morin. 1994. "Clinton's Health Plan: A Turn for the Worse." *Washington Post National Weekly Edition* (March 7–13): 15.

Brown, Lawrence D. 1994. "Politics, Money, and Health Care Reform." *Health Affairs* 13, no. 2 (Spring): 175–84.

Brown, Lawrence D., and Michael S. Sparer. 2001. "Window Shopping: State Health Reform Politics in the 1990s." *Health Affairs* 20, no. 1 (January/February): 50–67.

Butler, Stuart S. 1993. "Rube Goldberg, Call Your Office." *New York Times,* September 28.

Butler, Stuart S., and Henry J. Aaron. 2003. "Four Steps to Better Health Care." *Washington Post,* July 6.

Clymer, Adam. 1991. "Democrats Call Town Meetings on Health Care." *New York Times,* December 22.

———. 1993a. "Americans Have High Hopes for Clinton, Poll Finds." *New York Times,* January 19.

———. 1993b. "Clinton Asks Backing for Sweeping Change in Health System." *New York Times,* September 23.

———. 1993c. "Many Health Plans, One Political Goal." *New York Times,* October 17.

———. 1994a. "Debate on Health Care May Depend on Crisis." *New York Times,* January 17.

———. 1994b. "G.O.P. in the House Trying to Block Health Care Bill." *New York Times,* June 17.

———. 1994c. "Centrists on Senate Panel Near Compromise on Health Care Bill." *New York Times,* June 23.

———. 1994d. "Blind Eye Now, Eyeing Victory Later." *New York Times,* June 24.

———. 1994e. "Dole Gathering Broad Backing for a G.O.P. Health Care Plan." *New York Times,* June 30.

———. 1994f. "Senate Leader Unveils His Plan for Health Care." *New York Times,* August 3.

———. 1994g. "House Is Letting Senate Go First on Health Care." *New York Times,* August 5.

———. 1994h. "Mitchell Sees Room for Dealing on Rival Health Care Proposals." *New York Times,* August 13.

————. 1994i. "Mitchell Announces Plan to End G.O.P. Filibuster." *New York Times,* August 16.

————. 1994j. "Clinton Is Urged to Abandon Fight Over Health Bill." *New York Times,* September 21.

————. 1994k. "Hillary Clinton Says Administration Was Misunderstood on Health Care." *New York Times,* October 3.

————. 1994l. "Defying Omens, Health Care Drops from Campaign Stage." *New York Times,* October 22.

Clymer, Adam; Robert Pear; and Robin Toner. 1994. "For Health Care, Time Was a Killer." *New York Times,* August 29.

Cohen, Richard E. 1993. "Ready, Aim, Reform." *National Journal* 25, no. 44 (October 30): 2581–86.

"Conservative Democrats Offer Health-Care Plan." 1992. *Springfield News-Leader,* September 17.

Craig, Stephen C. 1993. *The Malevolent Leaders: Popular Discontent in America.* Boulder, Colo.: Westview Press.

Crittenden, Robert. 1993. "Managed Competition and Premium Caps in Washington State." *Health Affairs* 12, no. 2 (Summer): 82–88.

Demkovich, Linda E. 1979. "Adding Competition to the Health Industry." *National Journal* 11 (October 27): 1796–1800.

Dewar, Helen. 1994. "Health Care's Real Issue: November." *Washington Post National Weekly Edition* (July 11–17): 12–13.

DiIulio, John J., Jr., and Richard P. Nathan, eds. 1994. *Making Health Reform Work: The View from the States.* Washington, D.C.: Brookings Institution.

Dionne, E.J., Jr. 1994. "Clinton's Health Care Crisis." *Washington Post National Weekly Edition* (March 14–20): 29.

"Editorial: The Bush-Clinton Health Reform." 1992. *New York Times,* October 10.

Enthoven, Alain C. 1978a. "Consumer Choice Health Plans" (first of two parts). *New England Journal of Medicine* 298 (March 23): 650–58.

————. 1978b. "Consumer Choice Health Plans" (second of two parts). *New England Journal of Medicine* 298 (March 30): 709–20.

————. 1980. *Health Plan: The Only Practical Solution to the Soaring Cost of Medicare Care.* Reading, Mass.: Addison-Wesley.

————. 1991. "Universal Health Insurance through Incentives Reform." *Journal of the American Medical Association* 265, no. 19 (May 15): 2532–36.

————. 1993. "The History and Principles of Managed Competition." *Health Affairs* 12 (Supplement 1993): 24–48.

————. 1994. "Why Not the Clinton Health Plan?" *Inquiry* 31, no. 2 (Summer): 129–35.

Enthoven, Alain C., and Richard Kronick. 1989a. "A Consumer-Choice Health Plan for the 1990s: Universal Health Insurance in a System Designed to Promote Quality and Economy" (first of two parts). *New England Journal of Medicine* 320, no. 1 (January): 29–37.

————. 1989b. "A Consumer-Choice Health Plan for the 1990s: Universal Health Insurance in a System Designed to Promote Quality and Economy" (second of two parts). *New England Journal of Medicine* 320, no. 2 (January 12): 94–101.

————. 1992. "Will Managed Competition Work? Better Care at Lower Cost." *New York Times,* January 25.

Falkson, Joseph L. 1980. *HMOs and the Politics of Health Service Reform.* Chicago: American Hospital Association and Robert J. Brady.

Fallows, James. 1995. "A Triumph of Misinformation," *Atlantic Monthly* 275, no. 1 (January): 26–37.

Fox, Daniel M., and John K. Iglehart, eds. 1994. *Five States That Could Not Wait: Lessons for Health Reform from Florida, Hawaii, Minnesota, Oregon, and Vermont.* Cambridge, Mass.: Blackwell Publishers.

Freudenheim, Milt. 1993. "Changing the Fortunes of the Medical Business." *New York Times,* September 19.

Friedman, Milton. 1962. *Capitalism and Freedom.* Chicago: University of Chicago Press.

Gold, Steven D. 1996. "Health Care and the Fiscal Crisis of the States." In *Health Policy, Federalism, and the American States,* ed. Robert F. Rich and William D. White, 97–125. Washington, D.C.: Urban Institute.

Graig, Laurence A. 1993. *Health of Nations: An International Perspective on U.S. Health Care Reform.* Washington, D.C.: CQ Press.

Greenblatt, Alan. 2003. "Maine Embarks on a Bold and Broad Health Plan." *Governing* (August). Online at www.governing.com.

Greenhouse, Steven. 1993. "Many Experts Say Health Plan Would Fall Far Short on Savings." *New York,* September 21.

Hacker, Jacob S. 1997. *The Road to Nowhere: The Genesis of President Clinton's Plan for Health Security.* Princeton, N.J.: Princeton University Press.

Havighurst, Clark C. 1982. *Deregulating the Health Care Industry.* Cambridge, Mass.: Ballinger.

Hayek, Frederick. 1944 *The Road to Serfdom.* Chicago: University of Chicago Press.

Hilzenrath, David S. 1993/1994. "Health Care Costs' Double-Edged Sword." *Washington Post National Weekly Edition* (December 27–January 2): 22.

Holahan, John, and Len Nichols. 1996. "State Health Policy in the 1990s." In *Health Policy, Federalism, and the American States,* ed. Robert F. Rich and William D. White, 39–70. Washington, D.C.: Urban Institute.

Iglehart, John K. 1994. "Health Care Reform: The States." *New England Journal of Medicine* 330, no. 1 (January 6): 75–79.

Jacobs, Lawrence R., and Robert Y. Shapiro. 1995. "Don't Blame the Public for Failed Health Care Reform." *Journal of Health Politics, Policy and Law* 20, no. 2 (Summer): 411–23.

———. 2000. *Politicians Don't Pander: Political Manipulation and the Loss of Democratic Responsiveness.* Chicago: University of Chicago Press.

Jamieson, Kathleen Hall. 1994. "When Harry Met Louise." *Washington Post National Weekly Edition* (August 22–28): 29.

Johnson, Haynes; and David S. Broder. 1996. *The System: The American Way of Politics at the Breaking Point.* Boston: Little, Brown.

Kaiser Commission on the Future of Medicaid. 1994. *Health Reform Legislation: A Comparison of Major Proposals.* Washington, D.C.: Henry J. Kaiser Family Foundation.

Kerr, Peter. 1992. "Insurers Stand to Profit Big from a Health Care Overhaul." *New York Times,* December 4.

Kingdon, John W. 1984. *Agendas, Alternatives, and Public Policies.* Boston: Little, Brown.

Kolbert, Elizabeth. 1993. "Health Plan Foes Try Campaign-Style Ads." *New York Times,* October 21.

Kosterlitz, Julie 1993a. "Health Lobby Cranks Up Its Postage Meter." *National Journal* 25, no. 42 (October 16). Online at nationaljournal.com.

———. 1993b. "Winners and Losers." *National Journal* 25, no. 50 (December 11).

———. 1994. "Brinksmanship." *National Journal* 26, no. 28 (July 9): 1648.

———. 1995. "Harry, Louise and Doublespeak." *National Journal* 26, no. 26 (June 25): 1542.

Krause, Elliott A. 1977. *Power and Illness: The Political Sociology of Health and Medical Care.* New York: Elsevier.

Krauss, Clifford. 1992. "Democrats Offer a Health-Care Plan." *New York Times,* June 26.

———. 1993. "Lobbyists of Every Stripe on Health Care Proposals." *New York Times,* September 24.

Leichter, Howard M. 1997. "Rationing of Health Care in Oregon: Making the Implicit Explicit." In *Health Policy Reform in America: Innovations from the States,* 2d ed., ed. Howard M. Leichter, 138–62. Armonk, N.Y.: M.E. Sharpe.

Lemov, Penelope. 2005. "California Dreamin.'" *Governing* (January). Online at www.governing.com.

Leonnig, Carol D., and Jim Vandehei. 2005. "Cheney Wins Court Ruling on Energy Panel Records." *Washington Post*, May 11.

Lewis, Neil A. 1993. "Medical Industry Showers Congress with Lobby Money." *New York Times*, December 13.

Leyerle, Betty. 1994. *The Private Regulation of American Health Care*. Armonk, N.Y.: M.E. Sharpe.

Morin, Richard. 1993. "Even Doctors Are on the Health Reform Bandwagon." *Washington Post National Weekly Edition* (April 19–25): 37.

———. 1994a. "Health Care Reform, Yes, but Not at Any Price." *Washington Post National Weekly Edition* (January 10–16): 37.

———. 1994b. "Is There a Health Care Crisis? Yes and No." *Washington Post National Weekly Edition* (February 21–27): 37.

———. 1994c. "Don't Know Much About Health Care Reform." *Washington Post National Weekly Edition* (March 14–20): 37.

———. 1994d. "A Health Care Reform Post-Mortem." *Washington Post National Weekly Edition* (September 12–18): 37.

"Muddling Through the Message." 1993. *Newsweek* (October 11): 44.

Nathan, Richard. 1983. *The Administrative Presidency*. New York: Wiley.

National Commission on the State and Local Public Service. 1993. *Frustrated Federalism: Rx for State and Local Health Care Reform*. Albany, N.Y.: Nelson A. Rockefeller Institute of Government.

Nelson, Harry. 1994. *Federalism in Health Reform: Views from the States That Could Not Wait*. New York: Milbank Memorial Fund.

Neubauer, Deane. 1993. "Hawaii: A Pioneer in Health System Reform." *Health Affairs* 12, no. 12 (Spring): 3–39.

Nye, Joseph S. Jr.; Philip D. Zelikow; and David C. King, eds. 1997. *Why People Don't Trust Government*. Cambridge, Mass.: Harvard University Press.

Oberlander, Jonathan. 2003. "The Politics of Health Reform: Why Bad Things Happen to Good Plans." *Health Affairs* (August 27): W3-391–W3-404.

Oliver, Thomas R., and Pamela Paul-Shaheen. 1997. "Translating Ideas into Actions: Entrepreneurial Leadership in State Health Care Reforms." *Journal of Health Politics, Policy and Law* 22, no. 3 (June): 721–88.

Olson, Mancur. 1965. *The Logic of Collective Action: Public Goods and the Theory of Groups*. Cambridge, Mass.: Harvard University Press.

———. 1983. *The Rise and Decline of Nations: Economic Growth, Stagflation, and Social Rigidities*. New Haven, Conn.: Yale University Press.

Patel, Kant, and Mark Rushefsky. 1998. "Health Care Elites and Health Care Reform." *Health: An Interdisciplinary Journal of the Social Study of Health, Illness and Medicine* 2, no. 4 (October): 459–84.

Paul-Shaheen, Pamela A. 1998. "The States and Health Care Reform: The Road Traveled and Lessons Learned from Seven That Took the Lead." *Journal of Health Politics, Policy and Law* 23, no. 2 (April): 319–90.

Pauly, Mark V. 1971. *Medical Care at Public Expense: A Study in Applied Welfare Economics*. New York: Praeger.

Pear, Robert. 1992a. "President Leaves Many Areas Gray." *New York Times*, February 7.

———. 1992b. "Conflicting Aims in Health Lobby Stall Legislation." *New York Times*, March 18.

———. 1992c. "Plan to Ration Health Care Is Rejected by Government." *New York Times*, August 4.

———. 1992d. "Too-Bitter Medicine." *New York Times*, August 5.

————. 1992e. "Doctors' Group Offers Plan to Curb Health-Care Costs." *New York Times,* September 15.

————. 1992f. "Bush and Clinton Aren't Saying It, but Health-Care Taxes Are Likely." *New York Times,* October 18.

————. 1992g. "In Shift, Insurers Ask U.S. to Require Coverage for All." *New York Times,* December 3.

————. 1993a. "Early Doubts on Health, Papers show." *New York Times,* September 8.

————. 1993b. "Analysis Says Cost of Health Care is Underestimated." *New York Times,* December 9.

————. 1994a. "Cost is Obscured in Health Debate." *New York Times,* August 7.

————. 1994b. "Diverse Elements Criticize 'Mainstream' Senate Plan." *New York Times,* August 21.

Pearlstein, Steven, and Dana Priest. 1993. "Some Spoonfuls of Sugar Help the Medicine Go Down with Special Interests." *Washington Post National Weekly Edition* (September 27–October 3): 7.

Priest, Dana, and Michael Weisskopf. 1994a. "Death from a Thousand Cuts." *Washington Post National Weekly Edition* (October 17–23): 9.

————. 1994b. "Health Care Reform: The Collapse of a Quest." *Washington Post,* October 11.

Purdum, Todd S. 1994. "Clinton's Allies on Health Concede that Broad Plan is All But Dead This Year." *New York Times,* August 27.

Quinn, Michelle. 1994. "California's Health Pool: Limits, but Lower Rates." *New York Times,* June 11.

Rauch, Jonathan. 1994. *Demosclerosis: The Silent Killer of American Government.* New York: Times Books.

————. 1999. *Government's End: Why Washington Stopped Working.* New York: Public Affairs.

Reinhold, Robert. 1993. "A Health-Care Theory Hatched in Fireside Chats." *New York Times,* February 10.

Rivlin, Alice M.; David M. Cutler; and Len M. Nichols. 1994. "Financing, Estimation, and Estimation Effects." *Health Affairs* 13, no. 1 (Spring): 30–49.

Roberts, Barbara. 1992. "Bush Blows It on Health Care." *New York Times,* August 11.

Rockefeller, John D., IV. 1990. "The Pepper Commission Report on Comprehensive Health Care." *New England Journal of Medicine* 323, no. 14 (October 4): 1005–7.

Rubin, Alissa J. 1994. "CBO Turns Budget Spotlight on Health-Care Overhaul." *Congressional Quarterly Weekly Report* 52, no. 6 (February 12): 290–91.

Rushefsky, Mark E. 1981. "A Critique of Market Reform in Health Care: The 'Consumer-Choice Health Plan.'" *Journal of Health Politics, Policy and Law* 5, no. 4 (Winter): 720–41.

Rushefsky, Mark E., and Kant Patel. 1998. *Politics, Power and Policy Making: The Case of Health Care Reform in the 1990s.* Armonk, N.Y.: M.E. Sharpe.

Schneider, William. 1993. "Health Care Reform: What Went Right." *National Journal* 25, no. 40 (October 2): 2404.

————. 1994. "Health Care: So Where's the Crisis?" *National Journal* 26, no. 24 (June 11): 1378.

Seelye, Katharine Q. 1994a. "Some House Democrats Like Plan but Not Political Risks." *New York Times,* July 30.

————. 1994b. "Lobbyists Are the Loudest in the Health Care Debate." *New York Times,* August 16.

Sheils, John F., and Lawrence S. Lewin. 1994. "Perspective: Alternative Estimate: No Pain, No Gain." *Health Affairs* 13, no. 1 (Spring): 50–55.

Skocpol, Theda. 1996. *Boomerang: Clinton's Health Security Effort and the Turn against Government in U.S. Politics.* New York: Norton.

"Spin Doctors Wreck Harry and Louise." 1994. *New York Times,* July 8.

Starr, Paul. 1982. *The Social Transformation of American Medicine*. New York: Basic Books.
———. 1994a. *The Logic of Health Care Reform: Why and How the President's Plan Will Work*. New York: Penguin Books.
———. 1994b. "Why the Clinton Plan Is Not the Enthoven Plan." *Inquiry* 31, no. 2 (Summer): 136–40.
———. 1995. "What Happened to Health Care Reform?" *American Prospect*, no. 20 (Winter): 20–31.
Steinmo, Sven, and Jon Watts. 1995. "It's the Institutions, Stupid! Why Comprehensive National Health Insurance Always Fails in America." *Journal of Health Politics, Policy and Law* 20, no. 2 (Summer): 329–72.
Stimson, James A. 1991. *Public Opinion in America: Moods, Cycles, and Swings*. Boulder, Colo.: Westview Press.
Stone, Deborah A. 1993. "When Patients Go to Market: The Workings of Managed Competition." *American Prospect* 13 (Spring): 109–15.
Tanner, Robert 2004. "States Starting to Tackle Health Care." *Newsday*, November 23.
Tiefer, Charles. 1994. *The Semi-Sovereign Presidency: The Bush Administration's Strategy for Governing without Congress*. Boulder, Colo.: Westview Press.
Toner, Robin. 1993a. "Support Is Found for Broad Change in Health Policy." *New York Times*, April 6.
———. 1993b. "Poll on Changes in Health Care Find Support amid Skepticism." *New York Times*, September 22.
———. 1994a. "Ads Are Potent Weapon in Health Care Struggle." *New York Times*, February 1.
———. 1994b. "Highlighting Fears about the Clinton Plan." *New York Times*, February 1.
———. 1994c. "Ad Drive Opens for Canadian-Style Health Care." *New York Times*, May 3.
———. 1994d. "Health Coalition Strongly Opposes Compromise Plan." *New York Times*, June 24.
———. 1994e. "House Democrats Unveil Proposal for Health Bill." *New York Times*, July 30.
———. 1994f. "Health Impasse Sours Voters, New Poll Finds." *New York Times*, September 13.
Waldman, Steven. 1994. "How Clinton Blew It." *Newsweek* (June 27).
Waldman, Steven, and Bob Cohn. 1994. "Health Care Reform: The Lost Chance." *Newsweek* (September 19): 32.
Wehr, Elizabeth. 1979. "Competition in Health Care: Would It Bring Costs Down?" *Congressional Quarterly* 37, no. 31 (August 4): 1587–95.
Wessel, David, and Gerald F. Seib. 1993. "Clinton Had Devised His Health Package before the Inaugural." *Wall Street Journal*, September 22.
White House Domestic Policy Council. 1993. *The President's Health Security Act: The Clinton Blueprint*. New York: Times Books.
White, Joseph. 1995. *Competing Solutions: American Health Care Proposals and International Experience*. Washington, D.C.: Brookings Institution.
Wines, Michael. 1992. "Bush Announces Health Plan, Filling Gap in Re-Election Bid." *New York Times*, February 7.
———. 1994. "Clinton Puts Onus for Health Care on Republicans." *New York Times*, August 4.
Zelman, Walter A. 1994. "The Rationale behind the Clinton Health Reform Plan." *Health Affairs* 13, no. 1 (Spring): 9–29.

—— 10 ——

The Triumph of Incrementalism

From Managed Care to Consumer-Driven Health Care

The demise of comprehensive health care reform, as represented by the Clinton administration's Health Security Act, did not end policy debates or action on health care. It is pretty much a given within political science and the policy studies field that the dominant style of decision making in the United States is *incrementalism*, defined as making small changes over a period of time (see Jones 1978; Lindblom 1959; and Lindblom and Woodhouse 1993). *Comprehensive reform* is an attempt to change the whole system at one time.

This is not to say that comprehensive reform is impossible. The passage of welfare reform legislation in the summer of 1996 is an excellent example of such change. But health care affects far more people (everybody!), than welfare, and the structure of the political system, the political system's values, and interest group activity make radical reform highly unlikely.

Just because policymaking is gradual, that does not mean that it is uncontroversial or unproductive. The mid- to late 1990s saw health care policy reform attempts become, in some ways, even more important than the Clinton attempt. It helped lead to two shutdowns of government and was an important issue in the 1996 and 1998 elections. Health care policy, as the United States approached the twenty-first century, saw dizzying change, revolution, and reaction. Incremental or not, the pace of change was astonishing.

We begin this chapter by considering the fallout from the 1993–94 debates: the Republican congressional victories in 1994, the Republican agenda as set forth in the Contract with America, the big budget battles, and the role of Medicare and Medicaid in those battles. We look at health care policies that emerged from that struggle. We then turn to the "armistice" in that battle, the 1997 budget agreement and the changes it wrought. Our attention next focuses on the managed care revolution, concentrating on the private sector (though considering Medicare and Medicaid as well) and tracing the tremendous increase in managed care. This is followed by a look at the reaction to managed care. We then look at newer forms of health care reform, based on market views and focusing on the consumer.

Retrenchment

Prologue: The Republican Congressional Triumph

The Republicans enjoyed a double triumph, killing reform and then watching jurors find the president guilty. It was the political equivalent of the perfect crime. (Starr 1995)

Congressional Republicans, especially in the House of Representatives, saw health care as a wonderful opportunity to reclaim control of Congress. President Bill Clinton and congressional Democrats could be blamed both for their failure to fulfill the Democratic campaign promise to reform the health care system and for proposing a system that would mean, as Republicans depicted it, more bureaucracy, more taxes, and more government intrusion.

To separate themselves from the Democrats, who seemingly did not have a coherent program, House Republicans under the leadership of minority whip Newt Gingrich (R-GA) produced the Contract with America. The contract, in its various versions, promised change. The Republicans would pass (or at least vote on) term limits for office, a balanced budget constitutional amendment, welfare reform, a rollback of government regulations, and so forth. Health care was not mentioned in any version of the contract. Most House Republican candidates signed on to the Contract in a September 1994 ceremony in front of the Capitol building.

The Republican triumphs in the 1994 elections were of historic proportions. They picked up nine seats in the Senate, recapturing that body for the first time since 1986. More impressive were the gains in the House. Republicans picked up forty-two seats, ending the virtual Democratic lock on the House and gaining control of both bodies for the first time since 1954, control that the Republicans have retained, with a brief exception in the Senate, into the early twenty-first century.

The Republican Agenda

The Republican agenda was originally focused on reducing government. Though all the proposals that the Contract promised to consider in the first one hundred days of the 104th Congress were in fact voted upon in the House, a major defeat was the balanced budget amendment, which failed to get the required two-thirds vote in the Senate by one vote, with Republican Mark Hatfield (Oregon) voting against the measure.[1] With the failure of the balanced budget measure, Congress turned to the regular budget process to balance the budget. The goal was a balanced budget by fiscal year (FY) 2002.

President Clinton's FY 1996 budget proposal did not call for a balanced budget. The president's reasoning was that if the Republicans wanted to balance the budget, they should set out the plan to do so. In June 1995, Congress passed a budget resolution calling for $983 billion in total spending through 2002, including $270 billion in Medicare cuts and $180 billion in Medicaid cuts. The proposal also called for $245 billion in tax cuts (Hager and Rubin 1995). Republicans, especially in the House, also proposed a series of rollbacks in consumer and environmental regulation. Clinton eventually agreed to the 2002 balanced budget goal, but opposed virtually the entire Republican set of proposals.

The proposals to cut Medicare (and, to a lesser extent, Medicaid) gave Democrats an opening to counterattack the Republicans. Democrats charged that Republicans were trying to cut a program that was immensely popular. Republicans replied that they were trying to save or strengthen the program, bolstered by the Social Security and Medicare trustees report that Medicare Part A would go bankrupt by 2001, though only about a third of the proposed cuts would have addressed the bankruptcy issue (see chapter 4). Democrats used the Republican proposals to mount a series of campaign attacks and continually employed the mantra of protecting Medicare, Medicaid, education, and the environment from Republican hands.

The budget battles led to a congressional-presidential standoff or, perhaps more appropriately, a train wreck. Clinton vetoed appropriations bills, and Congress refused to pass a new debt ceiling bill that would permit the federal government to borrow money and meet its obligations. The result was two government shutdowns, one in November 1995 and another in December 1995–January 1996.

Clinton's popularity rose as the confrontation tightened, and Republicans' approval ratings, especially those of the architect of the Republican revolution, Speaker of the House Newt Gingrich, fell. By spring 1996, congressional Republicans and the president had agreed on a budget, though provisions concerning Medicare and Medicaid were not dealt with.

The FY 1997 proposals by both Clinton and the Congress for the two huge public programs were considerably smaller than those under discussion (and rejected by Clinton). The most revolutionary proposal concerned Medicaid. Republicans, with the backing of the governors, wanted to transform Medicaid into a block grant, essentially eliminating the program as an entitlement. This was the same proposal that recommended welfare reform, and the two programs were thus linked together. Opposition to the Medicaid block proposal led to its being dropped. Welfare reform passed (in the Personal Responsibility and Work Opportunity Act of 1996) with some linkage to Medicaid eligibility (see chapter 3). Medicare reform would have to wait one year.

Health Care Legislation in the 104th Congress

While Medicare and Medicaid were an integral target of the budget battles during this period, other health legislation, with some difficulty, was enacted. The new legislation moved the federal government into somewhat new ground—insurance reform.

One of the findings of public opinion surveys taken as early as 1991 was that a sizable number of Americans were concerned about what became known as "job lock" (Eckholm 1991). People were concerned about losing insurance when they changed or lost jobs (e.g., through downsizing). This was especially true for those with preexisting medical conditions.

A bill to address these issues was introduced in the Senate in 1995. Commonly known as the Kassebaum-Kennedy bill, after its co-sponsors Nancy Landon Kassebaum (R-KS) and Edward M. Kennedy (D-MA), it became the focus of attention in 1996.

Senate Majority Leader Robert Dole (R-KS) delayed the bill, partly to ensure that medical savings accounts (MSAs) would be included (others, such as House Speaker Newt Gingrich, also wanted MSAs included), and partly because he saw delay as helping his presidential aspirations (Atchinson and Fox 1997; Rushefsky and Patel 1998). While the Senate passed a "clean" version of the bill, one that included only the portability issues, the House passed legislation that included the MSA program as well as health insurance tax deductions. The conference committee to reconcile the differences between the two branches of Congress was delayed by Dole to get senators favorable to MSAs on the committee. Passage of the bill was facilitated when Dole resigned his Senate seat to concentrate on what became his ill-fated presidential quest. The conference committee agreed on a number of compromises, including the MSAs, and Congress overwhelming passed the legislation in the summer of 1996. President Clinton signed the bill in August.

The Health Insurance Portability and Accountability Act (HIPAA) built on previous federal–state relations regarding health insurance. In general, the states have the primary responsibility for regulating health insurance. Actions by the U.S. Supreme Court and Congress dating back to the mid-1940s carved out the relationship (Ladenheim 1997; Nichols and Blumberg 1998). A 1944 Supreme Court decision, *United States v. South-Eastern Underwriters Association*, 322 U.S. 533, held that insurance companies were engaged in interstate commerce and therefore covered by federal antitrust law. In 1945, Congress passed the McCarran-Ferguson Act, which excused insurance companies from such regulations if the states were regulating. The 1973 Health Maintenance Organizations Act attempted to foster the growth of health maintenance organizations (HMOs) through subsidies, overriding prohibitions to group practices and requiring employers to offer HMO plans to their employees under certain conditions (Nichols and Blumberg 1998).

A critical law in this brief history is the Employment Retirement Income Security Act (ERISA) of 1974. The law was originally designed to protect employee pension funds, but it has been interpreted to also prohibit states from regulating health insurance plans financed and administered by employers (self-insured firms). This turned out to be a critical exemption, because almost half of those covered by job-related insurance are in self-insurance firms (Ladenheim 1997). The final federal foray into insurance reform prior to HIPAA was the 1990 legislation regulating and standardizing private medigap policies (see chapter 4).

The major purpose of HIPAA is to eliminate health status from health insurance consideration. That is, for the small employer and individual insurance markets, the focus of reform, preexisting conditions cannot be considered by insurance companies when a person changes jobs. This is especially true for those who are "eligible individuals": those who

> have had eighteen months of continuous prior coverage (no coverage gap lasting longer than sixty-two days), most recently group coverage; have exhausted any Consolidated Omnibus [Budget] Reconciliation Act (COBRA) benefits to which they are entitled and have no current access to group insurance or a public program; and are eligible for some type of guaranteed issue coverage in the individual market. (Nichols and Blumberg 1998, 33)

In the spring of 1997, the three federal departments with responsibility for implementing HIPAA (the Treasury, Labor, and Health and Human Services) issued implementing regulations. The regulations required employers to certify that someone leaving a job had health insurance (and eventually whether dependents were covered). The Clinton administration estimated that twelve million out of twenty million people changed jobs every year (along with seven million dependents). It predicted that businesses would have to pay about $500 million a year in new administrative costs and higher premiums (Pear 1997a).

There are two interrelated ways of looking at the implementation of HIPAA: what states are doing and what private insurers are doing. The purpose of HIPAA, again, was to affect risk pooling, that is, that ability of insurers to segment or separate high-risk from low-risk (sick from healthy) clients. HIPAA constrains insurers from eliminating patients with the preexisting restrictions and guarantees renewal for eligible individuals and small groups. It does not, however, guarantee affordable prices. This issue remains, as well as the associated risk segmentation (Patel and Pauly 2002). HIPAA also led to new regulations concerning the use of health information and privacy of health records (see Patel and Rushefsky 2002). Concern has been raised that the enhanced emphasis on privacy has hurt patient care. For example, required written authorizations for emergency care have slowed the delivery of services. Further, HIPAA adds about $17 billion in compliance costs over a ten-year period (Lewis 2004). HIPAA is also in the forefront of efforts to put medical records in electronic form (see "Medical Paper-Pushers" 2004).

Two other actions were taken by Congress in 1996. The first was to include mental health coverage on an equal basis with physical health. The second was to mandate minimum hospital stays of two days for regular births and four days for caesarean births.

Covering Children

If, in the 1960s, the incremental strategy for health insurance focused on the elderly as the deserving group that should be covered, in the late 1990s, it was children. We have noted, in previous chapters, gaps in insurance coverage. Coverage by employers, in terms of percentage of population, was decreasing. Even with the changes in Medicaid discussed in chapter 3, many children were still uncovered. According to the General Accounting Office (now the Government Accountability Office), about one-third of Medicaid-eligible children were not covered by Medicaid, due to either ignorance of the program or application difficulties. Most of the uninsured children were in working families who had too much income even for the expanded Medicaid eligibility and who worked for firms that did not provide such coverage. The Medicaid expansions of the 1980s and 1990s (see chapter 3) did begin to cover some children from working families who were not eligible for Medicaid, but there still was a large gap, about three million children in 1996 (General Accounting Office 1995; Summer, Parrott, and Mann 1996). All told, some ten million children lacked insurance in 1996 (Rosenbaum et al. 1998).

As discussed in chapter 5, insurance coverage is important because it can lead, other things being equal, to better access to health services. A General Accounting Office review of the literature found that children with health insurance had better access to a wide variety of health care services than children without such coverage (General Accounting Office 1997; see also Weinick, Weigers, and Cohen 1998).

The issue of children's health insurance became intertwined with two unrelated policy issues at the federal level. The first was the federal budget. The 1995–96 policy debates revolved around the issue of federal budget deficits. Indeed, the fiscal constraint of the budget deficits has affected politics and policy at the federal level since the start of the Reagan administration. The conflict between President Clinton and the Republican-controlled Congress over the deficit and related issues (Medicare and Medicaid, as well as other issues) led to two partial government shutdowns and a shrinking of the Republican House majority. The budget politics of 1997 would play to a different beat.

Thanks to the 1990 and 1993 budget agreements and a good economy, 1997 (really FY 1998) looked more promising. Where once there were budget deficits as far as the eye could see, suddenly the word "surplus" appeared. By mid-1998, the Congressional Budget Office was predicting budget surpluses of over a trillion dollars for the next ten years. One question that was raised with this apparent turnaround of budget politics was what to do with the surplus. It could be used to pay off the multi-trillion-dollar federal deficit; to ensure the financial viability of Social Security; to reduce taxes; or to expand programs, such as health insurance for children.

The other element in this mixture was tobacco. In 1997, the tobacco industry and most of the state attorneys general reached an unprecedented agreement to deal with the issue of the health effects of tobacco. The agreement had to be ratified by the federal government. The Clinton administration and congressional Democrats proposed a large tax increase on the price of a package of cigarettes (over $1 a pack), the revenues from which could be used for a children's health insurance program. It was also felt that the large price increase would reduce demand for cigarettes on the part of young people. Republicans balked at the proposal and it was dropped. Indeed, the whole tobacco agreement went up in smoke as the industry and its supporters successfully portrayed the issue not as a health one, but as a large tax increase, particularly on the lower and working classes.

Children's health insurance did become part of the Balanced Budget Act of 1997, which we discussed in connection with Medicaid in chapter 3 and Medicare in chapter 4. The State Children's Health Insurance Program (SCHIP), a grant program to the states, became Title XXI of the Social Security Act.

In the move to extend coverage to uninsured children, states led federal action. By May 1997, more than fourteen states had passed legislation to extend coverage to uninsured children (Navarro 1997).

The federal government was faced with several questions, based on the experience of the states, about covering uninsured children. One question was whether to offer coverage through Medicaid or through a program created by the states. Another question was financing: Should tobacco taxes cover some, all, or none of the costs? A third question was whether the federal government should give the states a block grant (a set amount of money) and let states take full responsibility for designing and running the program (a position favored by the governors and echoing policy debates over welfare reform in 1996), or whether a categorical program should be used, leaving more control with the federal government (Pear 1997b).

The final proposal included in the 1997 Balanced Budget Act (BBA) was cosponsored by Senator Kennedy and Senator Orrin Hatch (R-UT). They provided the rationale for the legislation:

> If the act succeeds, working families that do not earn enough to purchase health insurance on their own will no longer have to make heartbreaking decisions among spending scarce resources on groceries, rent or medical bills for their children.
>
> Investing in children's health yields high returns. Preventive health care early in life is extremely cost-effective in avoiding large long-run costs of disease and disability. The hospital emergency room should not be a child's family doctor.
>
> Health care pays dividends in education, too. Basic vision care and hearing care can make all the difference for many children in school. Children who have difficulty seeing the blackboard or hearing the teaching also have difficulty learning. No young mind should be lost for want of an eye test or hearing exam.
>
> The Balanced Budget Act removes any excuse for the world's strongest industrial nation to deny health insurance to any child. (Kennedy and Hatch 1997)

The State Children's Health Insurance Program was a block grant of $20 billion over a five-year period beginning FY 1998 (October 1, 1997). The purposes of the new law were to provide health insurance for uninsured children and to coordinate with other children's health programs.

SCHIP gives states two implementation options, combining the two approaches mentioned above. States can either extend Medicaid to eligible uninsured children, or they can create or extend their own programs (such as Florida's Healthy Kids). In either case, the state must pay some of the costs of the program, a matching requirement (which they would have to do under Medicaid anyway). Eligibility for a separate state program must be no lower than state children Medicaid eligibility levels as of June 1, 1997 (Mann and Guyer 1997).

If a state chooses the Medicaid route, benefits are the standard Medicaid benefits. For state-initiated programs, the benefits package is more complicated. Such a state can choose among four options:

1. *Federal Employees Health Benefits Program Equivalent Coverage*—A state may offer health benefits coverage equivalent to the benefits offered under the standard Blue Cross/Blue Shield preferred provider option service plan offered to federal employees.

2. *State Employee Coverage*—A state may offer health benefits coverage equivalent to the benefits provided under a health plan that is offered and generally available to a state's public employees.

3. *HMO Coverage*—A state may offer health benefits coverage equivalent to the benefits offered by the HMO within the state that has the highest commercial enrollment (excluding Medicaid enrollment).

4. *Benchmark Equivalent Coverage*—A state can choose one of the three plans listed above to serve as a "benchmark" for an alternative package of benefits. The alternative must meet three criteria: (1) it must have an "aggregate actuarial value" equivalent to the benchmark plan selected by the state; (2) it must offer hospital, physician, lab and X-ray, and well-baby and well-child care (although the state can determine the scope of the coverage offered in each of these categories); and (3) *if* the state's benchmark offers coverage for prescription drugs, mental health, vision, or hearing benefits, the children's benefit package must offer some coverage in each of these areas. (Specifically, the coverage must have an actuarial value that is equal to at least 75 percent of the actuarial value of the coverage under the benchmark plan.) (Mann and Guyer 1997, 7)

An early evaluation of state implementation of SCHIP by the Children's Defense Fund (CDF) found some areas of concern, though most states were positively implementing the new program (Children's Defense Fund 1998). On the positive side, the CDF found that most states proposed income eligibility standards covering children in families up to 185–200 percent of the poverty line. About two-thirds of states that had made a decision about benefits were using the Medicaid benefits package. Nine states chose to create or expand their own programs without using Medicaid.

On the other hand, the CDF report noted that implementation of the program has been slow, with most states not beginning the program until July 1998. Some states, such as Wyoming and Washington State, have decided not to participate in the program, whereas others—Alabama, Mississippi, and Texas—stop income eligibility at 100 percent of poverty level. The latter three states are simply speeding up coverage that is required under present law.

SCHIP certainly has had an impact. By the first quarter of fiscal year 2005, almost 3.9 million children were enrolled, with about 40 percent enrolled in separate SCHIP state programs and the remainder in extended Medicaid programs (calculated from Centers for Medicare and Medicaid Services n.d.). Further, both Medicaid and the SCHIP programs picked up some of the slack of the increase in the number of those uninsured during the 2000–2003 period (Ku, Broaddus, and Wachino 2005). SCHIP remains subject to budget issues and there is some evidence of substitution of SCHIP coverage for private-sector coverage. SCHIP is also a good (or bad) example of incremental expansion of health insurance coverage. It has created its own set of inequities among the states (which have different programs and eligibility requirements) (for a discussion of the successes and weaknesses of SCHIP, see Kenney and Chang 2004).

Managed Care

> By managed care, we mean forms of coverage that integrate financing and delivery, as well as the organizations that provide this coverage—health maintenance organizations (HMOs), preferred provider organizations (PPOs), and point-of-service (POS) plans (Gold and Hurley 1997, p. 29).

> The bottom line is that the American public doesn't want to give too much power to *any bureaucrats*. It doesn't matter whether they work for the federal government or for the insurance industry. (Schneider 1998)

Definitions

One important and confusing aspect of policy debates and experiences with managed care is definitional. In this section, we offer some definitions so that we will all know what we are talking about.

We define *managed care* broadly as any health insurance plan that seeks to restrain the use of health care services. Such restraint can be as simple as requiring preauthorization for a nonemergency hospital stay (Weinder and de Lissovoy 1993; for a discussion of the symbolic significance of definitions, particularly in regard to managed care, see Hacker and Marmor 1999). Plans can also encompass more organized forms of provider delivery.

The classic type of managed care organization is the *health maintenance organization* (HMO). An HMO is an organization whose providers, generally primary care physicians, are prepaid through monthly subscriber premiums (known as *capitation*) to deliver a comprehensive set of services. The HMO assumes the financial risk of providing those services. The original label for such an organization was prepaid group plan (PGP). PGPs were developed to provide health care services to employees in areas where medical services were thin. Kaiser-Permanente is typical of such plans.

To complicate the situation, HMOs come in various forms. A *staff-model HMO* is one in which the physicians are on a salary and members obtain services primarily from the HMO. In a *group-model HMO*, a multispecialty group of doctors works primarily for the HMO's members. There are hybrid versions of these HMOs.

A looser type of HMO is an *independent practice association* (IPA). In this case, physicians contract to work for the HMO. A physician in an IPA can work on a fee-for-service basis or a capitation basis (so much money per patient). HMOs of any type can be nonprofit or profit.

Another type of managed care organization is the *preferred provider organization* (PPO). Here the employer or insurer contracts with physicians for discount rates on services. Consumers can use providers outside the PPO but must pay higher copayments.

As physicians have been losing power and autonomy to managed care plans, they have sometimes sought to sponsor their own plans, known as *provider-sponsored organizations* (PSOs). One last type of managed care plan, which was incorporated in the Balanced Budget Act of 1997 with Medicare, is the *point-of-service* (POS) plan. Here the consumer chooses the provider at the time the service is needed.

The Development of Managed Care

While managed care has been increasingly a part of the public health care programs Medicaid, and to a lesser extent, Medicare, the push in the 1980s and 1990s came from the private sector, particularly large employers. The impetus was partly the drastically increasing cost of health insurance and partly decreases in corporate profits and a weak economy (Bodenheimer and Sullivan 1998a; Leyerle 1994). For example, the cost of employee health care for General Motors in the mid-1980s was twice the cost of steel, a problem that remains, twenty years later, for the giant corporation (Brink and Shute 1997; Lazarus 2005).

The first significant move by a large employer into managed care came in 1988, when Allied-Signal canceled its health care plans and transferred its employees into Cigna's HMO (Bodenheimer and Sullivan 1998a; see also Anders 1996). Other large companies soon followed. The trend toward managed care can be easily shown (see Table 10.1). Table 10.1 presents some data concerning growth of HMOs. First, there has been a sizable increase in enrollment, from just over nine million people in 1980, to thirty-three million in 1990, to almost eighty-one million by 2000. Second, most of this growth has come from the private sector. HMO growth in Medicare and Medicaid is much lower as a percentage of the appropriate population, with Medicaid HMO enrollments much higher than for Medicare.

Third, the dominant type of HMO has become the independent practice association, closely followed by the mixed type. The classic HMO, the group model, has become less important. For this classic HMO, both the number of plans and enrollment has significantly declined, reflecting a backlash against HMOs (see below) as well as withdrawals of some HMOs from Medicare participation in the late 1990s and early 2000s.

Table 10.1

HMO Growth, Plans and Enrollment, and Percentage of the Population, 1980–2003

	1980	1985	1990	1995	2000	2003
Plans (number of plans)						
All plans	235	487	572	562	568	454
Model type						
Individual practice association	97	244	360	332	278	203
Group	138	234	212	108	101	105
Mixed				122	188	146
Enrollment (in millions of people)						
All plans	9.1	21.0	33.0	50.9	80.9	71.8
Model type						
Individual practice association	1.7	6.4	13.7	20.1	33.4	28.0
Group	7.4	14.6	19.3	13.3	15.2	16.1
Mixed				17.6	32.3	27.7
Federal program						
Medicaid	0.3	0.6	1.2	3.5	10.8	14.5
Medicare	0.4	1.1	1.8	2.9	6.6	4.9
Percent of population enrolled						
in HMOs	2.8	4.0	13.4	19.4	30.0	24.6

Sources: National Center for Health Statistics 1998 (Table 135), 2004 (Table 134).

The private sector has seen the most change with regard to managed care (see Table 10.2). In 1988, 73 percent of covered workers were in conventional fee-for-service plans. By 2002, that number had dropped dramatically, to just 4 percent. HMO enrollment went from 16 percent of covered workers to a high of 29 percent in 2000, and has shrunk a bit since then. The major increase has been in PPOs, a much looser form of managed care. By 2002, PPOs accounted for more than half of all covered private-sector workers. POS plans also became more important, peaking in 2001 (Kaiser Family Foundation 2004).

One other change needs to be mentioned regarding HMOs. They have increasingly become for-profit. In 1988, 88 percent of HMO enrollees were in nonprofit HMOs. By 1997, that number had decreased to about 37 percent, with the enrollment percentage remaining near that level since (Kaiser Family Foundation n.d.).

Employees are often given no choice among plans; they use the chosen HMO (or other type of plan). Bodenheimer and Sullivan report that about 47 percent of employees in large companies have no choice of plans, while about 91 percent of employees in small firms have no choice (Bodenheimer and Sullivan 1998a). The significance of this, apart from the lack of choice of provider that will be discussed below, is that competition among health plans, which managed competition sees as an important mechanism for ensuring both high quality of care and cost control, is missing.

Table 10.2

Health Plan Enrollment for Covered Workers by Plan Type, 1988–2004 (percentage)

	Conventional plan	HMO	PPO	POS
1988	73	16	11	
1993	46	21	26	7
1996	27	31	28	14
1998	14	27	35	24
1999	10	28	39	24
2000	8	29	42	21
2001	7	24	46	23
2002	4	27	52	18
2003	5	24	54	17
2004	5	25	55	15

Source: Kaiser Family Foundation 2004, Chart #7.

Rather, firms rely more on negotiating with plans and providers than on managed competition. Maxwell and Temin (2002, 25) refer to this as "industrial purchasing":

> Instead of acting as managed competition sponsors, the majority of Fortune 500 companies purchase health coverage as they would the inputs to their production processes. Their purchasing practices rely on bidding and vendor management techniques with which they are familiar. By formulating and implementing these strategies, companies seek to achieve a number of different corporate objectives, including holding down increases in health care premiums and recruiting and training a healthy workforce.[2]

Still, a large number of employees do have a choice of plans. In that case, the driving concept is "'pay more for higher-cost health plan'" (Bodenheimer and Sullivan 1998a, 1004). With this method, the employer pays the same amount of premiums for each employee, regardless of the cost of the plan. When the yearly open enrollment period comes around, employees can change plans, but there are financial considerations attached to those changes. This is an idea that Alain Enthoven (1978) has championed, going back to the 1970s, and which is still being advocated (see below). Additionally, large employers use their clout (large numbers of potential subscribers) to directly contract with a health plan and negotiate rates (Bodenheimer and Sullivan 1998a, b).

An important trend in managed care is for such organizations to offer more than one type of plan or product. The products referred to are traditional HMO, open-ended HMO, PPO with and without a primary gatekeeper, exclusive provider organization, and POS plans. Seventy-one percent of the plans in one survey offered more than one product, with the group or staff model the least likely to offer more than one product. The reason for offering multiple products is twofold: "to expand choice in response to customer interest or to ease transition to more traditional managed care arrangements" (Gold and Hurley 1997, 31; see also Gabel 1997).

Another important, critical managed care trend is the growth of national managed care companies and the related trend of the growth and dominance of for-profit companies. By 1994, a majority of managed care enrollees were in national plans, and most of these plans were for-profit (Corrigan et al. 1997). Corrigan et al. (1997, 12) describe the significance of this trend:

> Although it is often said that "health care, like politics, is local," it is likely the emergence of national managed care companies and national provider organizations will have some impact on how care is delivered in local communities. To the extent that national companies benefit from greater access to capital markets and economies of scale, there is the potential for these companies to improve quality and efficiency through investment in technology (e.g., clinical information systems), enhanced management systems (e.g., financial accounting systems, marketing), and access to specialized clinical and managerial expertise.
>
> But concerns have been voiced that national companies, almost all of which are for-profit, may seek returns on investment at the expense of access and quality. There are worries that these firms may be less responsive to community needs, such as care of the uninsured and provision of public health services, the benefits of which accrue to society at large. There is also the concern that over time, national companies may engage in predatory pricing to drive out competition, leaving consumers with few choices.

As we saw above, for-profit HMOs have become more dominant.

Gabel (1997) asks why for-profits grew so much. One explanation is that for-profits were more aggressive in seeking growth. A second explanation is their better access to capital (Wall Street), and this is why many HMOs converted their status. A third explanation is that nonprofits tended to prefer the group model that required expensive infrastructure, whereas for-profits favored IPAs, or networks. It is these latter forms of managed care organizations that have grown the fastest.

Another change caused by the managed care revolution concerns the types of organizational situations in which doctors practice. In 1988, 61 percent of physicians had at least one managed care contract and these contracts provided about 23 percent of their revenue. By 1999, 91 percent of physicians had at least one managed care contract and these contracts provided almost half of their revenue. The numbers for 2001 are slightly lower, reflecting a managed care backlash (Kaiser Family Foundation n.d.).

The Successes of Managed Care

As the data indicate, there has been a dramatic move of consumers, or patients, from conventional fee-for-service indemnity plans into various kinds of managed care arrangements. The sustained movement suggests that managed care has had some successes, and that is in fact the case. As Easterbrook puts it, their successes have been in "restraining costs, avoiding unneeded surgeries, promoting prevention" (1997).

The major accomplishment of managed care has to do with costs. After all, the major reason the public and private sectors turned to managed care was to save money.

Table 10.3

Annual Percentage Increases in Employee Health Insurance Premiums, 1990–2003

	Overall	FEHBP	CalPERS
1990	14.0		
1993	8.5	8.6	6.0
1996	0.8	−0.2	−4.0
1999	5.3	9.4	6.1
2000	8.2	9.2	9.0
2001	10.9	11.0	11.8
2002	12.9	13.3	9.6
2003	13.9	11.4	24.1

Source: Kaiser Family Foundation n.d., Exhibit 3.6.
Note: FEHBP is the Federal Employees Health Benefits Program. CalPERS is the California Public Employees' Retirement System.

If managed care did not save money, given all the problems discussed below, there would be no point to it.

The data are clear. In 1990, depending on the source of the data, the cost of employment-based health insurance increased by 14 percent. For two large public employee groups, the 1993 increase was between 6 and 9 percent (see Table 10.3). Table 10.3 shows that there was a dramatic decline in the increases from the early 1990s and even some declines.

One reason, as we have seen, was the increasing shift of employees from conventional fee-for-service plans to managed care and the competition among insurance plans for business. Table 10.3 shows the change in health insurance premiums for two large public employers, both of whom employed variations of managed competition plans. However, average insurance premium increases for different types of plans over the 1996–2004 period were fairly close. For all plans, the annual average increase was 8.5 percent. For conventional plans, the increase was 8 percent; for HMOs, 8.4 percent; for PPOs, 8.5 percent; and for POS plans, 7.7 percent (Kaiser Family Foundation n.d.).

Another reason for the decline in cost increases was the dramatic decline in overall inflation. In 1990, inflation was around 5.4 percent, and by 1996 it had declined to around 2 percent, where it has pretty much remained through 2004 (Kaiser Family Foundation n.d.).

Managed care was been able to control spending so quickly through a number of mechanisms. Managed care organizations changed the incentives facing physicians and the way doctors practice medicine. The move toward capitation and away from fee-for-service alone changed the incentives. This is probably the most important change. Under fee-for-service, physicians (and other providers) get more money for each service provided. Under capitation, providers get no more money for more services. Indeed, the pressure may be to underserve rather than to overserve.

In a sense, managed care turns all the incentives around. Defenders of managed care, such as Susan Love (1998), argued that the fee-for-service system was flawed. Because of third-party payments, neither the patient nor the doctor was concerned about the costs of care, and overtreatment occurred (it may also have been spurred on by the medical malpractice issue, discussed in chapter 7). Additionally, under fee-for-service or indemnity insurance, preventive treatments and services such as mammograms, physicals, well-baby checkups, and immunizations were not necessarily covered. A good managed care organization will provide these services, usually at no extra cost, because they save money in the long run.

Managed care can also save money by limiting medications to a list of approved drugs, known as a formulary. Related to this is that managed care organizations negotiate fees with suppliers (medical supply companies, pharmaceutical companies, clinical laboratories) as well as providers (doctors, hospitals, nursing homes, home health companies).

The use of standardized procedures for disease treatment, along with monitoring the treatment practices of doctors, also produces savings. Utilization review panels and preauthorizations also help, as does the use of primary care physicians as gatekeepers. Additionally, managed care saves money by paying only for actual services (as opposed to charges) and by enrolling healthier and younger people (Brink 1998).

The effectiveness of these techniques is clear. A study by the Lewin Group found that over the 1990–96 period, managed care saved between $116 and $180 billion. In 1996, employers saved about 11 percent of what they would have spent under the fee-for-service system (Brink 1998).

The successes of managed care are not just cost-related. Managed care organizations appeared to detect some kinds of cancers earlier than under the fee-for-service arrangement, largely, again, because of preventive screening. There is also some evidence that dying patients were less likely to be given futile but painful treatments and thus suffered less. Open-heart surgery managed care patients in California were directed to high-volume, high-quality facilities (Brink 1998).

Quality

In some ways, the underlying issue surrounding managed care is quality of care. All the anecdotal stories that depict the horrors of managed care concern denial of service or refusal to pay for services.

Quality is an important concern of managed care, though whether it outweighs cost concerns is questionable. There is an industry committee, the National Committee for Quality Assurance (NCQA), with its own set of standards. The American Association of Health Plans (AAHP) has its Patients' First program. There is an industrywide effort at data gathering, known as HEDIS—Health Plan Employer Data and Information Set. Employers have started using accreditation from the National Committee for Quality Assurance and collecting data on performance through HEDIS, which "measures preventive services such as immunizations, access to medical providers and services, and the medical outcomes of specific illnesses" (Serafini 1997, 1035–36). The HEDIS data set includes clinical measures (such as childhood immunizations, first trimester prenatal care, breast and cervical cancer screening and caesarean section rates) as well as measures of patient satisfaction (including referrals to specialists, choice of physicians, and waiting times) (Thompson et al. 1998). There is debate about how well these kinds of measures actually capture the quality of care in a managed care organization (see, for example Lohr 1997; Wilensky 1997).

Three studies, however, suggest that information about quality is not critical in evaluating HMOs. One study, a survey of large employers, found that employers (purchasers) did not make much use of the available clinical outcomes data. The authors of the study described a decision process characterized by multiple factors and multiple goals. Given this complex decision-making situation, decision makers look to simplify the decision and avoid the overload of information (Hibbard et al. 1997).

Two studies funded by the Commonwealth Fund support this finding. One study of firms with over 200 employees found that 99 percent of employers did not provide data on health quality to their employees, 91 percent did not require NCQA mandatory accreditation for plans, and 94 percent did not use HEDIS data to select plans. The second study of employers found the overwhelming majority of them (65 percent) were not even familiar with HEDIS or NCQA accreditation (Commonwealth Fund 1998).

A third study came up with a similar result. This time it looked at HMOs in the south Florida market and found that they did not channel their coronary artery bypass graft surgery to either low-mortality or high-quality hospitals. Low-quality hospitals offered lower prices. The implications the authors drew is that cost considerations may outweigh quality considerations (Escarce, Shea, and Chen 1997).

A study by Sullivan (2000) found that claims of efficiency gains from managed care over more conventional plans were problematic. He points out what he calls two errors in evaluating managed care. The first error is concluding that lower medical costs in managed care plans mean that total costs are lower. Sullivan argues that total costs include medical plus administrative costs as well as any profit. The second error, according to Sullivan, is asserting that because premiums are lower for managed care plans (see above for a comparison of plan premiums), managed care plans must be more efficient than conventional plans. Sullivan argues instead that managed care plans have very high administrative costs and have shifted costs to others. He then argues that the slowdown in health care spending and inflation (see chapter 5) was due to factors other than the rise of managed care (such as the changes in provider reimbursements wrought by the 1997 Balanced Budget Act and the insurance underwriting cycle).

A review of the literature on HMO performance found a mixed bag of results (Luft and Miller 2002). The authors found that quality of care was pretty much the same for HMOs and more conventional plans. They also found more studies showing access-to-care problems for HMOs than the more conventional plans. A very consistent finding was less satisfaction with HMOs than the conventional plans, including quality issues and communications with providers. HMOs were very strong, according to the literature, in offering preventive services. In terms of use of services, HMOs appeared to use less resources for hospitals than conventional plans.

Luft and Miller (2002, 77) also found significant impacts on communities where the managed care market share was higher:

> Higher HMO or HMO/PPO penetration rates are associated with less access; more prevention; less use of expensive resources; and lower employer health plan premiums, Medicare FFS [fee-for-service] expenditures, and hospital cost growth.

While the successes are undeniable, especially concerning costs, the same techniques that control costs have led to a managed care backlash. It is to this that we now turn.

Managed Care Backlash

We begin this section by first pointing out that the arguments against managed care come generally under the name of consumer protection or patients' rights (Annas 1998). Another point we want to make is that to a great extent, the issue is one of power, trust, and accountability.

It is an issue of *power* because managed care organizations gained control over patients or consumers, and providers. Providers, physicians especially, lost the professional dominance that had characterized the medical profession for decades (Starr 1982).[3] For many years, the medical profession opposed both the group practice of medicine and corporate control of medicine. Both group practice and corporate control now characterize the practice of medicine. More and more, doctors see themselves as employees; the cottage industry of medicine has given way to corporate rationalization and industrialization. Thus some of the backlash comes from doctors. Managed care impinged upon doctors' incomes and their sovereignty. The review panels and practice guidelines, combined with the financial incentives, limited what managed care doctors can do. Some physicians reasoned that, if they are no longer professionals with complete autonomy over their medical decisions, they should act like employees. In response to managed care, they began considering unions as a countervailing power (see Greenhouse 1996; Kilborn 1996).

Power is also important to the patients, consumers, or subscribers. Patients are generally assigned a primary care physician and restricted from using some services without the authorization of the physician and the plan. For example, consumers may be prohibited from seeing a specialist without a referral from the primary care physician (gatekeeper). The use of certain hospitals or treatment centers may be restricted because managed care organizations contract with specific facilities and negotiate fees.

The second important concept is *trust* (Gray 1997; Mechanic 1996, 1998; New-comer 1997). Patients place their health and lives, and those of their loved ones, in the hands of a provider. There is certainly an asymmetry of power, because patients generally lack information and providers possess it (Arrow 1963). The assumption is that doctors and other providers will furnish all the necessary services; this is a fiduciary or trust-based relationship (Annas 1998). Under the fee-for-service plans, some unneeded services were provided. Under managed care, many have argued, all the incentives, for the provider and the organization, are to underserve. Sub-scribers who are satisfied with managed care, in general, are those who are healthy and do not need much. The conflicts arise when care, emergency or chronic, is needed. Can patients trust that providers have only their interests at heart, or are they influenced by other factors? Related to trust is the issue of quality of care versus cost of care.

In addition, managed care, according to Annas (1998), has sought to change the patient into a consumer. We will see this usage of language later in this chapter, in the section concerning consumer-driven health care. This makes the relationship with the organization and its providers a business transaction, with the assumption that con-sumers can make choices based on "cost, coverage, and quality" (Annas 1998, 696)

The third major concept at issue in the managed care backlash is *accountability*. Because managed care organizations make decisions about the provision of care, and their decisions are sometimes different from what a doctor might want, they should also be responsible, many have argued, for the outcomes of that care. Holding a man-aged care organization accountable for medical decisions is known as *enterprise liability* (Daniels and Sabin 1998; Emanuel 1997; Gosfield 1996).

Public Opinion

One way of looking at the backlash is to ask whether in fact there was one. That is, what is the public position on managed care? Newspapers, magazines, and journals are filled with anecdotal information. Survey research can tell us how the public as a whole feels. Public support, or lack of support, was critical in the eventual outcome of the Clinton Health Security Act (Rushefsky and Patel 1998). There was evidence to suggest that public support for action has motivated both Republicans and Democrats (Alvarez 1998).

A Kaiser Family Foundation/Harvard University study found that most people are satisfied with their health insurance plans (Blendon et al. 1998). But the survey also found considerable support for consumer protection regulation, even if costs were increased (a point often made by those opposed to patients' rights bills). A sizable portion of those surveyed believe that managed care is hurting the quality of health care being received and will do so in the future. Blendon et al. note that those in managed care plans show less satisfaction about quality of care than those in fee-for-service plans and also show more concern about obtaining care; but they also note that public perceptions of managed care programs, which affect only a relatively small number of people, are based on both personal experience and reporting of problems with managed care. They conclude:

> Public concerns about the need for increased regulation of managed care are likely to be with us for the long term. Experience in other industries suggests that Americans have limits on how far they will allow marketplace decisions to put them at individual risk. As with airline safety and banking, public support for regulation is being driven in part by the anxiety the public feels relating to the occurrence of visible events questioning the behavior of managed care plans, as well as the problems people experience in their own lives. As a result, debate about regulation of the managed care industry is likely to be a permanent fixture on the health care agenda for years to come. (Blendon et al. 1998, 91–92)

An August 1997 Louis Harris survey found growing dissatisfaction with managed care: 54 percent of those polled saw managed care as detrimental to their health care, compared to 43 percent the year before (Kilborn 1997).

A more recent survey (Kaiser Family Foundation 2001) found continued public concern about managed care, though evidence of some change in views is apparent. In 1997, 34 percent of those surveyed thought that managed care plans were doing a good job in serving health care consumers; 21 percent thought they were doing a bad job. By 2000, the numbers had reversed: only 24 percent thought that they were doing a good job, while 39 percent thought they were doing a bad job. Four years later (2001) 39 percent of those surveyed thought managed care plans were doing a bad job, but 32 percent thought they were doing a good job.

Ladd argues, however, in an article entitled "Health Care Hysteria, Part II," that most people are satisfied with their health insurance, even those who had episodes of serious illnesses (Ladd 1998). While most people would like regulation of managed care plans, only about one-quarter of those polled preferred government regulation over other choices. When the possible additional cost of such regulation is inquired about, support for government regulation drops substantially (see also Kaiser Family Foundation 2001).

The Case against Managed Care

There appear to be three basic concerns that have fueled the managed care backlash (Moran 1997). The first, and most important, is *access to care. Quality of care* is another phrase that expresses this concern. Managed care organizations grew because of their promise of control of costs. The question is whether control of costs has come at the expense of access and quality of care. There has been, some have asserted, this very tradeoff.

The incentives that physicians face, the capitation fees, is one part of this concern. Easterbrook describes the impact of capitation on physicians and therefore on patient care:

> Consider what happens when an HMO member walks into a doctor's office. Many plans pay physicians a fixed fee per registered member, regardless of how much treatment

each patient needs [capitation]. Primary-care doctors for HMOs that pay this way currently receive a median of about $150 per patient annually. If a patient is healthy or needs only incidental care, the physician keeps the $150 and comes out ahead. But if the patient becomes ill, that $150 can be wiped out fast—and if the patient needs extensive attention, the doctor may end up paying from his or her own pocket. (Easterbrook 1997, 64)

A different type of financial incentive, bonuses to physicians based on how much they have limited care, essentially a quota system, also plays a role.

An interesting managed care practice is the use of formularies, medications that are on an approved list. Physicians in managed care organizations are usually limited to the listed drugs. Problems arise when plan doctors order a particular prescription drug and the plan's pharmacy on its own substitutes a less costly generic equivalent. Sometimes the generic equivalent can cause severe side-effects that the original prescription would have avoided. Apart from this, the use of formularies is seen by physicians and pharmacists as an interference in patient care. The formularies may be based on deals between plans and pharmaceutical firms (Freudenheim 1996; Herbert 1996).

As the cost of drugs has continued to rise, one response on the part of HMOs was to put doctors on a monthly drug budget. That is, they were not supposed to prescribe more than the budgeted amount, a specific amount per patient per month. This is another way that doctors were losing autonomy and weakening their roles as patient advocates. Patients may not know about the drug budget (Johannes 1997).

Other managed care practices play a role. Limiting access to specialists, who are more expensive than primary care physicians, is another way that managed care organizations saved money. Limitations placed on emergency care visits—for example, requirements for prior authorization or contracting with some emergency clinics rather than others—have been among the most contentious issues. Out-of-area coverage has raised similar concerns. In the case of emergency care, hospitals are required to treat all those who need care, regardless of their ability to pay. When managed care organizations such as HMOs refused to pay for such care, it created conflict over reimbursement (Pear 1995).

Managed care organizations also made use of standardized protocols on how to treat patients and utilization committees to see if providers were within those standards. For example, surgical procedures such as bone marrow transplants for women with advanced breast cancer have been disapproved as experimental (Anders 1996). This helps explain public opinion surveys that showed that most people, even in managed care organizations, were satisfied with their health coverage. Most people are healthy and thus do not need a great deal of care.

However, those who are severely or chronically ill, the kinds of cases that are most expensive, are the ones who have the most concern about managed care. These people represent losses, not profits, to managed care organizations. This helps explain why a number of HMOs left the Medicare+Choice program in the late 1990s and early 2000s (see, for example, Kilborn 1998a).

Another concern raised about access to care and HMOs was whether the list of providers in the plan was accurate or up to date. People may join an HMO because of a particular practitioner who may later leave. One California HMO advertised some doctors who were dead. Even if a provider's name is on the list it does not mean he or she is still a participant in the plan. Some employer plans contracted with only a portion of the plan's providers, a limited-provider network. So even if a physician is part of an HMO, he or she may not be covered by a particular employee's plan (Crooper 1996).

Another issue that raised questions about access to care is the limitations managed care organizations have placed on what physicians can tell patients, such as the financial arrangements mentioned above. While most of these so-called gag clauses are no longer around, largely because of state legislation that has restricted them, as well as actions taken by HMOs and other types of managed care organizations in response to concern, the use of gag clauses does relate to the trust issue discussed above. The *New York Times* provided excerpts from some physician and HMO contracts to illustrate the gag clauses:

> Do not discuss proposed treatment with Kaiser Permanente members prior to receiving authorizations.
>
> Do not discuss the H.R.M. [Health Risk Management, the company that issued the set of practice guidelines used by Kaiser Permanente] process with members.
>
> Do not give out H.R.M. phone numbers to members.
>
> This agreement and the terms and conditions herein shall be treated by the parties as strictly confidential. Accordingly, the parties agree not to directly or indirectly disclose this agreement or the terms and conditions therein, including but not limited to all schedules and financial terms, to any third party.
>
> The provider expressly waives provider's rights to contact plan members in any way about the termination of this agreement, and expressly agrees not to communicate in any form or manner with such members concerning the termination; the options such members may have to join other health care service plans (including H.M.O.'s) or to switch to other providers as a result of the termination; or the fact that the provider will no longer be the member's health care provider. (Pear 1996a)

This relates to the trust issue discussed above.

The third concern was that managed care organizations may engage in what is known as *risk selection*, or marketing to healthy people. That is, some have argued that managed care plans reduce costs not just by limiting services (rationing) but by seeking to enroll healthier subscribers.

Risk selection (also known as "creaming" or "cherry picking") makes a certain amount of economic sense. Because managed care plans work on a largely capitated basis, such plans and their providers make money by limiting the provision of services. If their subscribers are generally healthy, they will use fewer services and covering them will be more profitable for the plans.

There are a couple of factors that lessen the fear of risk selection. First, Medicare-eligible managed care plans are not allowed to reject Medicare recipients. Second, employers, especially large ones, do not allow plans to risk-select.

Nevertheless, there are ways for HMOs and other managed care plans to engage in risk selection. One of the most prominent ways to engage in risk selection was through advertising campaigns designed to get more subscribers. Neuman et al. (1998) found that HMOs did market in such a way that healthier Medicare recipients were attracted to them. HMOs advertised their lower costs (compared to traditional Medicare plus medigap policies) and the additional benefits they provided compared to traditional medigap policies.

The analysis of HMO television and newspaper marketing ads by Neuman et al. (1998) indicated that most ads showed healthy seniors engaging in hobbies and physically demanding activities. None showed HMO beneficiaries in a hospital or a wheelchair, or using a walker, and almost none mentioned that Medicare recipients seeking to enroll in an HMO cannot be refused because of their health status. Neuman et al. (1998) also noted that many of the seminars at which HMOs made presentations to potential subscribers were not accessible to people confined to wheelchairs. Nor did HMOs seem to market to the under-sixty-five group, or to the disabled. Television and newspaper ads either did not note limitations, such as those on pharmaceuticals, or did so only in fine print.

Another set of charges made about managed care is related to its profit status (Bartlett and Steele 2004). As we saw in an earlier section of this chapter, much of the growth in managed care plans and managed care enrollment came from for-profit plans. For-profits can take advantage of equity financing and have proved to be profitable on the stock market.

But the profits, some have feared, have come from cutting costs. Kuttner (1998a, b), for example, distinguishes between socially oriented and market-oriented HMOs. Socially oriented HMOs attempt to be efficient in three ways: prevention and patient education, a lack of monetary incentive to undertreat, and educating providers about the best practices, based on monitoring.

Market-oriented HMOs may require physicians to assume some of the financial risks of providing care, to use primary care physicians as gatekeepers, to select healthier patients, to underserve, and to use outside contractors for utilization review and preapprovals (Kuttner 1998a).

The basic question that Kuttner raises is whether the bad HMOs (market-oriented) are driving out the good ones (socially oriented), or at least forcing the good ones to change. He notes that nonprofit HMOs "tend to score better on many objective indicators and in surveys of consumers" (Kuttner 1998a, 1562). For example, an analysis of National Committee for Quality Assurance data found that nonprofits composed 89 percent of the top thirty-seven HMOs.

Easterbrook argues that the entry of for-profit managed care organizations may be very disruptive:

> For-profit health care firms can engage in private extravagance unknown to the old system. J.T. Sebastianelli, for example, president of Aetna U.S. Healthcare, took home $4.9 million last year. And the firms may claim a fiduciary obligation to shift funds from patient care to stockholder dividends. (Easterbrook 1997, 67)

Marketing expenses and compensation for chief executive officers (though not limited to for-profits) have also become part of national health care expenditures (Brink and Shute 1997; Easterbrook 1997).

Another concern raised by managed care, and especially the for-profit version, is that to reduce costs managed care has also reduced some important cross-subsidies. A portion of fees charged by physicians and hospitals has gone to charitable care, that is, care for those who are uninsured and cannot afford to pay their bills. This is especially true for emergency visits to hospitals. In negotiating low rates with doctors and hospitals, managed care organizations effectively squeezed out such charitable care. This is extremely short-sighted, because emergency care is costly and needed care is delayed (Kilborn 1998c). Declining reimbursements by Medicare and Medicaid have a similar effect. Managed care is also putting pressure on research and teaching hospitals, which have also benefited in the past from cross-subsidies.

The Role of the Media

One could argue that the case against managed care was heavily overstated and largely a function of the mass media's search for stories that will catch the public's eye. Certainly cases about mismanaged care would meet that criterion. The media did pay increasing attention to managed care, as judged by the number of articles in newspapers. Another indicator, for instance, was that the movie *As Good As It Gets* contains a scene in which the character played by Helen Hunt denounces HMOs for not providing sufficient care and coverage for her child. The HBO movie *Damaged Care* focused on one managed care organization (Humana) and how it was more interested in profits than patients.

A careful study of newspaper and television coverage of managed care found that, over the 1990–97 time period, media coverage became more critical or negative in tone. Most of the stories on managed care were neutral, but of those stories that had a tone, negative stories dominated positive stories by about seven to one. Such stories made heavy use of anecdotes, drama, and villains, and increasingly, managed care organizations were the villains (Brodie, Brady, and Altman 1998).

Brodie, Brady, and Altman (1998, 22) wrote that "the vast majority of media coverage is neutral, but the most visible media sources—broadcast and special series —are more negative and focus on more graphic examples of problems people have had." This is important because, as the authors pointed out, people tend to generalize from the anecdotal stories that typify news reporting. On the other hand, the authors also cited survey data that indicated most people thought that media coverage of managed care was fair and that their opinions were largely based on personal experience or the experience of others that they know (Brodie, Brady, and Altman 1998).

Karen Ignagni (1998), chief executive officer of the American Association of Health Plans, responded that the media were unduly negative in their coverage and often used inaccurate reports. Ignagni provided three examples of poor media coverage that undermines public confidence: physician "gag" rules, "drive-through" deliveries, and outpatient mastectomies. As a result of inaccurate reporting, using the gag rule as an example, some thirty-two states have outlawed a problem she says is nonexistent. What managed care plans had to do was communicate better, demonstrate improvement, and provide comparisons, especially with fee-for-service plans. Additionally, managed care plans have to make the case that the development of managed care is ongoing. Ignagni gave the example of providing consumers with more choice of physicians.

Kuttner, however, points out that the GAO report referred to by Ignagni was issued in the summer of 1997. There were gag rules in effect in 1995 and 1996. They had been removed by 1997, according to Kuttner, because of media pressure and legislation that Ignagni decried (Kuttner 1998b).

The Response to Managed Care Problems

Assuming the problems with managed care are real, the question then is: What do we do about it? Moran (1997) suggests three sets of policy tools for dealing with the problems of managed care. The first he calls "information utilities." These could include a requirement that plans disclose important information, such as financial incentives facing physicians. There could also be regulation of the form of disclosure so that the information is understandable.

A second type of tool is what Moran (1997) calls "private enforcement." This would use the judicial system to take legal action against plans because of their medical decisions. Moran calls this "enterprise liability," and it was at the heart of the debate over federal patient protection legislation.

The third type of tool is economic regulation of various aspects of managed care plans. This has been the providence of states, which have been concerned about the financial viability of plans and their structure at licensure time as well as enforcing a variety of consumer protection plans. Such economic regulation includes contracts, liability, property rights, and antitrust regulation (Enthoven and Singer 1997).

"Putting Patients First"

The response of the managed care industry, largely through the American Association of Health Plans, was to adopt an industrywide set of standards known as "Putting Patients First." AAHP responded to issues that are usually publicly driven. Jones says that this is not cynical if it is responsive to public concern (Jones 1997).

Putting Patients First addressed a number of public issues, including allegations of drive-through maternity care and outpatient mastectomies. Jones (1997) argued that drive-through maternity care was really an issue of the need for authorization. As for outpatient mastectomies (apart from what Jones said was a confusion between lumpectomies and mastectomies), AAHP issued a policy statement saying that outpatient mastectomies were not required and that physicians and patients together should determine whether a mastectomy should be outpatient or inpatient. The voluntary policy also called for more communication between patients and providers about what was covered and what was not and what the appeals processes were. Another area of concern addressed by the policy was emergency care. Putting Patients First called for making sure that emergency care was provided as necessary and that the patient be stabilized. It also called for notifying the primary care physician as soon as possible (Jones 1997).

The AAHP policy was not without its critics. Peter Lee (1997), a consumer advocate, criticized Putting Patients First on two grounds: it assumed that there were no real problems with managed care, just bad publicity or "anti-managed care misinformation." Further, Lee argued that just letting plans be accountable is not enough. He suggested that an important problem with managed care was the incentives it offered physicians to refrain from giving care. Also, as managed care plans became increasingly for-profit, there was the tension, which Jones does not mention, of profits versus patients.

Lee also discussed the weaknesses of self-regulation. First, he found, in a national survey, that 59 percent of respondents said they could not trust their health plans. He also noted that AAHP did not review health plans for compliance with standards and that there were few if any penalties for violating the standards. Some parts of the standards had already been enacted into state laws (Lee 1997).

Clark Havighurst (1997), a long-time advocate of legal changes that affect the health care industry, such as antitrust action, argued that the AAHP's Putting Patients First as described by Jones was essentially a "benign cartel theme" (Havighurst 1997, 123). Jones's article, according to Havighurst, contains themes of "collective action and collective responsibility" (Havighurst 1997, 123). The result of such a policy would be increasing centralization of power in the health care industry, a result he thought worked against the interests of society.

The Public-Sector Response to Managed Care

State Action

Much of the public-sector action on managed care has been at the state level. According to a report by Families USA (1996b), the 104th Congress (1995–96, the Congress especially known for its battles with President Clinton) passed three pieces of health legislation. One was welfare reform (the Personal Responsibility and Job Opportunity Act), which had features that dealt with Medicaid eligibility. The second was the Health Insurance Portability and Accountability Act. The third piece of health legislation dealt with consumer protections: maternity stays and mental health parity. In 1996, state legislatures passed laws on health insurance in more than eight categories, from purchasing to maternity stays, gag clauses, access to providers, and so forth (Families USA 1996b). More than 1,000 pieces of legislation were proposed in state legislatures and thirty-three states took action (Families USA 1996a).

The major concern of both patients/consumers and providers was the impact of the financial incentives on care (Families USA 1996a). The states varied dramatically in their consumer protection bills. Vermont passed the most protections, eleven of thirteen types, while South Dakota was the only state that passed no protections. Further, the Employment Retirement and Income Security Act of 1974 (ERISA) denied some protections to consumers in managed care plans, such as remedies for delay or denial of services. That is why a Families USA (1998) report was entitled *Hit and Miss*.

The Federal Government

The federal government began addressing managed care issues in 1996. Legislation was passed, as mentioned earlier, to require minimum stays for deliveries. In 1997 and 1998 Congress and President Clinton debated managed care bills. One reason for considering federal action even in the light of state initiatives was the impact of ERISA. That act, passed in 1974 to protect employee pension funds, has been interpreted as prohibiting state regulation of employer self-insured health plans. HMOs have claimed immunity from enterprise liability in employer-sponsored health plans under ERISA (Pear 1996b). Because so many people were in plans that have ERISA protection, states are limited in what they can do. Some examples will illustrate the problem:

1. A federal appeals court in New Orleans ruled that an insurance company could not be sued for damages by a mother-to-be when her fetus died after her company refused hospitalization for her high-risk pregnancy.
2. A Denver appellate court judge said that a husband could not sue his HMO after his wife died when the HMO refused to approve a bone marrow transplant.
3. In St. Louis, an HMO was protected by ERISA after it refused to approve a heart surgery recommended by a patient's doctor. The patient died.
4. In Cincinnati, a utilization review company was protected after it refused approval of psychiatric treatment for a man who eventually committed suicide. (Pear 1998a)

One action that President Clinton took in 1997 was to create by executive order the Advisory Commission on Consumer Protection and Quality in the Health Care Industry. The commission drafted a Consumer Bill of Rights and Responsibilities, covering eight areas: information disclosure, choice of providers and plans, access to emergency services, participation in treatment decisions, respect and nondiscrimination, confidentiality of health information, complaints and appeals, and consumer responsibilities (Advisory Commission on Consumer Protection 1998). In his 1998 State of the Union message, President Clinton called for the passage of consumer-protection legislation.

Between 1998 and 2002, a number of patients' rights bills were proposed in Congress by both Republicans and Democrats, with the Democratic bills tending to be more encompassing and protective of patient rights.

For example, one contrast concerned access to emergency medical services. The problem here was that some managed care plans would not pay for such services unless previously authorized. The Democratic bill in the House would require the plan, such as an HMO, to cover the emergency medical service without prior authorization using the "prudent layperson" standard. Essentially, this standard says that if the average person thinks that the absence of the emergency medical service would result in immediate and serious harm, the plan would have to pay.

The Republican House bill was more complicated. In stage one, the plan used the prudent layperson standard for initial screening in an emergency ward. For further treatment in the emergency room, a "prudent emergency medical professional" standard would be used to judge whether treatment was necessary and then "the need for such services must be certified in writing by 'an appropriate physician'" (Pear 1998c). One doctor said that this new standard was "'invented out of thin air'" (quoted in Pear 1998c).

Interest groups became active in the debate over patients' rights. The controversy altered somewhat the alliance of interest groups from what it was during the 1993–94 period. Then, consumer groups supported the plan, while business groups such as the Chamber of Commerce and the National Federation of Independent Businesses opposed it. Provider groups, especially the American Medical Association, were undecided. As an example, both the American Trial Lawyers Association and the American Medical Association supported patients' rights, though for different reasons. Doctors wanted to protect themselves against the restrictions that managed care organizations place on them, while trial lawyers wanted to be able to sue managed care organizations for bad decisions. The coalition supporting patients' rights, the National Partnership for Women and Families, also included labor unions, consumer groups, midwives, and chiropractors. Business groups, such as the Health Benefits Coalition, contained both large and small employers, and they agreed on some issues, disagreed on others. Some HMOs were more supportive (Pear 1998b), and some of the larger insurers quit the Health Insurance Association of America to better represent their own interests (Kilborn 1998b).

The House passed a patients' rights bill in July 1998 that was crafted by an ad hoc committee. The Senate has never acted.

The George W. Bush administration came out against patients' rights legislation (see Patel and Rushefsky 2002). As governor of Texas, Bush allowed such legislation to pass without his approval. In 2002, he convinced Representative Charles Norwood (R-NC) to abandon his own bill, which had considerable support in the House of Representatives. The administration also argued before the Supreme Court to continue the ERISA immunities of managed care plans, an argument that seemingly went against the Texas legislation. In 2004, as we saw in chapter 7, the Court did sustain the ERISA immunity (Bloche 2004; Jost 2004). The issue has not come up since then.

The response to the backlash was a loosening of some of the restrictions of managed care as well as a move to less restrictive forms of managed care, from HMOs to PPOs, for example (see Cunningham and Sherlock 2002; Draper et al. 2002; Hurley,

Strunk, and White 2004). Of course, the impact of restraint on managed care was, in part, more rapid increases in health care costs.

And that has led to a managed care rebound or resurgence (Mays, Claxton, and White 2004). Mays, Claxton, and White conducted a tracking study of twelve communities, which included Boston; Indianapolis; Phoenix; and Orange County, California, and found a reemergence of managed care cost control techniques. One set of techniques was utilization management. This included requiring prior authorizations, such as referrals to specialists and outpatient procedures. The researchers point out that the new utilization management techniques were more lax than during the 1990s and focused on services that appeared to be of little benefit. Reviews of services and provider profiling were other tools used here. Again, the researchers point out that plans in the subject cities did not impose gatekeeping requirements.

Other techniques included disease and case management. For example, some plans concentrated on high-risk patients, providing them with immediate services rather than delaying them. A third technique was developing fairly restrictive provider networks (Mays, Claxton, and White 2004).

Back to the Market

Managed care has proven not to be the solution, at least by itself, to the problems of the health care system. Analysts, policymakers, interest groups, think tanks, and others continue the search for a way to reform the system.

One solution would be to build on Medicare, which up to 2003, at least, was the U.S. example of a universal, single-payer system (see chapter 4). But given the financial problems that Medicare faces, compounded by the Medicare Modernization Act enacted in 2003, this is unlikely. Rather, pressures will increase to control costs. Medicaid is another possibility. It has proven to be a more adaptable program than originally thought (see Brown and Sparer 2003). But the fiscal problems that the states faced in the early twenty-first century and the increased costs of the program to the states have led to cutbacks.

A third possibility is to build on the current employer-based system. But the continued increases in health care costs and efforts by employers to shift costs suggest continuing in this direction is not the answer. Indeed, Enthoven (2003) has argued that the employer-based system of health insurance itself exacerbates the problem; he calls it a failed system.

Relman (2005; see also Krugman 2005) argues that the market-based system has failed and needs to be replaced. His proposal is essentially a single-payer system. His proposal has four major parts. The first is a national budget to pay for a national plan, funded by employer taxes. Under this proposal, there would be no billing for services and thus considerable administrative costs would be saved. Second, services should be given by "not-for-profit, prepaid multi-specialty groups of physicians [who] should provide all necessary care on the approved list of insured services" (Relman 2005, 28). The physicians would be salaried.

Third, Relman proposes that patients be free to choose among plans, with switching allowed, with everyone belonging to a plan. Additionally, doctors could join any plan they wish and change plans but, intriguingly, would not be able to provide services covered by the plan outside the plan. Fourth, a National Health Care Agency should be established to oversee the system. The model for such a board is the Federal Reserve System (see also Emanuel and Fuchs 2005).

Bartlett and Steele (2004) conclude their biting critique of the U.S. health care system (and particularly its reliance on the profit-oriented private sector) with a call for a single-payer plan. They see the health care system as highly fragmented with

> thousands of individual entities heading off in many directions on missions that frequently conflict. It's really no system at all. Rather, it's a stunningly fragmented collection of businesses, government agencies, health care facilities, educational institutions, and other special interests wasting tens of billions of dollars and turning the treatment of disease and sickness into a lottery where some losers pay with their lives. (Bartlett and Steele 2004, 235–36)

For them, a single-payer plan would rid the system of weaknesses, corruption, complexity, and gaps.

Politically, such a change as Bartlett and Steele and Relman propose is highly unlikely. The twentieth century was full of failures to enact comprehensive change, the most recent being the attempt by the Clinton administration.

Consumer-Driven Health Care

It can be argued, however, that change is coming, partly by design and partly by momentum. The momentum is the decline in employer-based health insurance, coupled with cost-shifting. That is, employers are looking for ways to alleviate their health care costs and the most popular way is to shift costs to employees. Employees are being asked to pay higher premiums, combined with higher deductibles and copayments. Even managed care plans have been moving in this direction. Consumers have become more responsible for their own health care and for financing it.

This has led to the development of what has been called consumer-driven health care (CDHC) (Bachman 2004; Gabel, Lo Sasso, and Rice 2002; Patterson 2004; see also Gupta 2003). The basic principle behind CDHC is that the consumer will behave one way if he or she is confronted with the costs of a product or a service and another way if there is no cost. This is essentially the idea of "moral hazard" that we mentioned in chapter 6 (see Pauly 1978). People will consume more of a good or service if it is free than if they have to pay for it. This was confirmed by the RAND Corporation health insurance experiment that occurred during the 1970s and 1980s. The researchers found that consumers did consume less when there was some cost to them (Newhouse 2004). Such cost-sharing is becoming more evident even in programs such as Medicaid (see Ku 2005). Consumer-driven health care plans allow consumers to choose the type of coverage they want, through such things as tiered hospital coverage. By 2002, about 1.5 million people were enrolled in such plans (Gabel, Lo Sasso, and Rice 2002). By 2006, according to one survey, a projected 72 percent of employers may be offering such plans (Reden and Anders, Ltd. 2005).

One of the most enthusiastic advocates of market- and consumer-driven health care is Regina Herzlinger (1997, 2004), a professor at the Harvard Business School. Herzlinger (2004, 249) describes the virtues of such a system:

> Just what would a consumer be in the context of health care? Real consumers are people who weigh the price of a product against its quality. If the quality isn't good enough for the money, they don't buy it. Producers quickly get the message. They then madly innovate to provide consumers with the quality they want at the price they are willing to pay for it. The winners do well; the losers go out of business. In a real market cost control does not come about because producers limit goods or services; it comes about because producers innovate—they develop new ways to give consumers what they want. Although advocates of government-controlled health care systems rail against competition, it is key to the success of virtually every sector of our economy.

The idea of consumer-driven health plans is very much a part of what President George W. Bush has called the "ownership society" (see, for example, Calmes 2005; Vieth 2004). The phrase "ownership society" was introduced during Bush's 2004 reelection campaign and briefly mentioned during his 2005 State of the Union address.

The ownership society, as President Bush describes it, would mean that each of us would take more responsibility for education, retirement, health care, home ownership, and so forth. For example, Bush (and others) have advocated private or personal savings accounts as an alternative to Social Security (Calmes 2005). Under such a system, a portion of the money that goes into the Social Security trust fund would be diverted into those accounts. Eventually, such accounts would replace Social Security. The money would be invested in bonds and stocks (depending on the plan), with benefits depending on how much is invested, how well it was invested, and how the markets do. For education, vouchers for private (and possibly public schools, again depending on the plan) would be the policy of choice. Parents would choose schools based on how well they met the needs of their children, and schools, like other producers of goods and services, would have to respond, as Herzlinger describes in the quote above (see Rushefsky 2002).

The ownership society also means that more responsibility, more risk, is placed on employees, retired people, patients, and so forth, and less on employers or government (Hacker 2005). One could argue that the ownership society means that you are on your own!

Two interesting examples show consumer-driven health care at perhaps its most extreme, including the notion that consumers/patients are on their own. In one case (Fuhrmans 2005), Sandra Hughes had to negotiate the costs of the birth of her third child herself. Hughes's first two births were via caesarean procedures and her husband was self-employed. Because of the two C-sections, she could not obtain health insurance. So Hughes went shopping. She negotiated with a physician to lower his fee from \$3,000 to \$1,900. Her negotiations with the hospital were less successful, but she did at least save some money. Fuhrmans, the author of the article, said that this is a good example of consumer-driven health care, because there is a substantial period of time between conception and delivery and so prospective parents have time to negotiate. This would not work quite so well, obviously, with a stroke or heart attack victim.

The second example is, in some ways, more interesting. Howard Staab outsourced his critical surgery by flying to New Delhi, India, for his heart-valve replacement surgery. The total costs, which included the travel expenses, were about \$10,000. This included a trip to visit the Taj Mahal. Similar surgery in the United States would have cost about \$200,000 and Staab had no health insurance (Dentzer 2004). Dentzer, taking her theme from Staab's story, observes that if we outsourced health care for the uninsured to India, we could save billions of dollars. But as with Sandra Hughes, Staab's surgery, while vital, was not immediate, and so he could shop around. Some HMOs in California have taken to sending their subscribers for nonemergency care to Mexico, because the costs are so much lower (Geis 2005).

The health care equivalent is some form of health savings accounts. A small bit of history is necessary at this point. In 1997, Congress passed the Health Insurance Portability and Accountability Act (HIPAA) (see Rushefsky and Patel 1998). Like much legislation at the federal (and state) level, HIPAA had several different provisions. The one that was the most discussed during the process leading to enactment was portability of health insurance, that is, the ability of covered workers to change jobs and be able to get health insurance from the new employer (if the employer provided the benefit). A second important set of provisions focused on privacy of health records (and transforming the written records into electronic forms). The privacy provisions and the regulations implementing them overtook the portability ones in importance (see Patel and Rushefsky 2002).

It is the third set of HIPAA provisions that concerns us here. HIPAA created, on an experimental basis, medical savings accounts (MSAs), which were expanded a year later under the Balanced Budget Act of 1997. The idea behind MSAs is that consumers/employees would put aside, on a monthly basis, money from their salary into a tax-free savings account, similar to an individual retirement account (IRA). That money would then be used for medical expenses. So consumers would be responsible for paying the first part of their medical expenses and, thus, presumably, would not seek unneeded services because they would be paying for them. Consumers would also buy a high-deductible (or catastrophic) health insurance plan to cover expenses beyond what was put in the tax accounts. Because the deductibles are so high (as high as \$5,000), the premiums are low.

MSAs were limited in several senses. First, there was a limit on the number of such MSAs that could be set up around the country, about 700,000. Second, the money could only be used for health care expenses; any other use and they would be subject to taxation. Third, the funds in the account did not roll over from one year to the next.

In 2003, major changes were made to the idea of tax-free accounts. This came about via the 2003 Medicare Prescription Drug Improvement and Modernization Act (Medicare Modernization Act, or MMA). While most of the act dealt with Medicare, as is obvious from the title of the legislation (see chapter 4), the act also created health savings accounts (HSAs) to replace the MSA program. The new HSA program vastly expanded the program. There was no limit on the number of such accounts. Money that was left over at year's end could be rolled over into the next year and funds could be used even for nonhealth-related activities and remain tax free (if the person was over 65). More and more companies are resorting to high-deductible plans accompanied by HSAs (see Alonso-Zaldivar 2005b). By September 2004, over 400,000 had signed up for the plans (Alonso-Zaldivar 2005a). Indeed, one reporter (Alonso-Zaldivar 2005a) writes that this trend is leading to significant changes in the health care system (see also Higgins 2005). One observer (Rubenstein 2005) argued that HSAs can be a mechanism for building wealth, because the money is tax free as it enters the account *and* as it is spent (if spent), even if not on health care (if over 65). Of course, this depends on the health of the owner of the account.

Trude and Conwell (2004) found, however, in a survey they conducted, reluctance on the part of employers to pursue CDHC plans for their employees. First, there was some skepticism that such plans would save money or control costs. Because workers tend to be healthier than the general population, such plans might encourage more use. A second finding, which we discuss below, was that case management through such plans was no better at producing savings than managed care plans. This was because most people do not make much use of the health care system, but there are a small number that make great use, and that is where the cost issues arise. The biggest savings for employers was from a fixed contribution to health care (a defined-benefit program, see below).

Another issue the survey found was the effort it would take to educate employees to be wise consumers of health care services. There was also concern that the plan would be too complicated for many workers (Trude and Conwell 2004).

HSAs and a consumer-driven health care approach have not gone without criticism. As Davis (2004) points out, a presumption underlying CDHC is that there is too much consumption of health care services, and that putting the costs up front will reduce utilization. There are several problems with this presumption. First, much of the spending on health care is concentrated among a small portion of the population (Enthoven 2003). Berk and Monheit (2001) found that, using 1996 data, the top 1 percent of the population accounted for 27 percent of payments, the top 2 percent accounted for 38 percent of payments, and the top 5 percent accounted for 55 percent of payments. Given this concentration of expenditures, the focus should be on those whose health conditions produce the most expenditures. This is what Trude and Conwell (2004) found in their survey of employers. A second problem is that once the high deductible limit is reached, then we are back to the problem of health insurance coverage that market advocates decry (Trude and Conwell 2004). Further, Davis (2004) notes that the RAND health insurance experiments discussed above found that those who had low incomes and were at high risk of needing care (i.e., those with chronic conditions such as hypertension) were less likely to use health care services when deductibles and copayments were charged. Thus, Davis suggests that we need to examine whether such plans result in poor outcomes. It should not be surprising that healthier people choose the HSA or high-deductible option and sicker people choose the more conventional plans (Davis 2004). This is known as adverse selection. Again, these plans are fairly new and the research on their impacts is still very tentative.

Davis, Doty, and Ho (2005) argue that plans such as HSAs, those having high deductibles, erode the foundations of insurance. Those foundations include providing security from financial hardship and making it easier to attain necessary medical services (see also Hacker 2005).

There is another variant of market-driven or consumer-driven care, health care vouchers. Emanuel and Fuchs (2005) propose such a program, coming from the liberal spectrum. They suggest seven tests that any comprehensive reform should be evaluated against:

> First, it should cover every American, no exceptions.
> Second, it should pay for covering those who are currently uninsured by cutting waste, not by increasing the total amount our country spends on health care.
> Third, it should hold down the rate of increase of future health-care costs.
> Fourth, it should give Americans more choice of health plans, not less.
> Fifth, it should make our economy more productive, not less.
> Sixth, it should reduce, not expand, government bureaucracy.
> Finally, to get anywhere, a comprehensive reform plan must be politically viable by offering advantages to more (and more powerful) interest groups than those it upsets, while cohering with American values so that it can draw a broad base of support. (Emanuel and Fuchs 2005, 21)

Emanuel and Fuchs call their plan Universal Health Vouchers (UHVs). Everybody gets a voucher, adjusted for health conditions, with which they purchase a health plan that provides a basic set of services. Those currently on Medicare will stay on Medicare. Employer-based health insurance will end (see Enthoven 2003). This would benefit employers who would become more competitive because they would no longer have to pay for their employees' health care costs. Medicaid would be eliminated and there would be an oversight board, modeled after the Federal Reserve. Those who wanted benefits beyond the basic package would be able to have them, but they would have to pay for them themselves. Emanuel and Fuchs also argue that a value-added tax earmarked for the voucher program should be instituted. They offer the UHVs as an alternative to either the present system or the conservative market-based system that leaves consumer/patients on their own.

Of course, even plans like the voucher system are market-based, or private-sector based. Some, such as Bartlett and Steele (2004) and Relman (2005), argue that health care is not the same as other goods and services, such as groceries or automobiles. Therefore, they require more public-sector involvement.

Conclusion

The 1990s saw an almost a breathless amount of activity in both the public and the private sector. The federal government considered and then rejected comprehensive health care. It then turned to an incremental strategy, focusing on a specific range of problems: portability of health insurance, hospital maternity stays, and expanding coverage for uninsured children. In addition to the SCHIP program, Congress also passed new Medicare legislation, via the 1997 Balanced Budget Act. Congress and the president also considered legislation that would effectively establish a patients' bill of rights. But work on the patients' rights bill was stalled because of many of the same factors that led to the failure of the Health Security Act. In the 2000s, cost control came to dominate the scene, particularly at the state level. At the federal level, the major change was enactment of yet more new Medicare legislation that provided both a new prescription drug benefit but also sought to change the health care system (via HSAs).

Many of the changes that took place in health care took place in the private sector. Led by big business's desire to curb employee health expenditures, a revolution in health care organization and financing took place, the managed care revolution. By 1998, the vast majority of people with employer-based health insurance were in some type of managed care organization. States were moving Medicaid recipients into managed care, and increasing, though small, numbers of Medicare recipients were making the same choices.

Along with this change came distress. Physicians found that they had lost a great deal of their power and autonomy. Provider reimbursement was squeezed. Members of managed care organizations (i.e., consumers) found that they faced limits on the choice of provider and plan, and that their faith that physicians had patients' best interests in mind, rather than various kinds of incentives to limit care, was lowered.

This is not to say that managed care has had only deleterious effects. Managed care helped dramatically to reduce cost increases for a while. While the debate over the quality of care is inconclusive, there are certainly some areas where managed care excels. For those who are not disabled, or seriously or chronically ill, managed care has provided high-quality care. The focus on well-baby care, immunizations, and screening for breast and prostate cancer has been helpful. But for those who need more than ordinary care, managed care has been shown to be, in too many cases, a maze worthy of Franz Kafka.

One of the major complaints about the Clinton Health Security Act was that it was too bureaucratic and would involve too much government intervention in medical care. Schneider argues that the managed care backlash in 1996–98 was really a striking out at bureaucratic rationing. While most people were happy with their managed care plan, it was the basic concept "that a bureaucrat can control you health care" that created the anxiety and the backlash (Schneider 1998, 1714).

The major change that has come in the health care system is a shifting of costs and responsibilities onto patients, or as market advocates prefer to call them, consumers.

Those who had employer-based health insurance found that their premiums rose, their deductibles rose, and their copayments rose. The concepts of consumer-driven health care and the ownership society reflected these changes. Managed care was not the answer, managed competition has not been tried enough to know if it will work. The health care system continues to grow and cost more. While there are any number of proposals to change the system, from all ideological perspectives, it is likely that change will be only piecemeal, incremental, and driven by the problem of costs.

Notes

1. Term limitations were voted on in the House, but failed.
2. For commentary on Maxwell and Temin (2002), see Aaron (2002) and Enthoven (2002).
3. For a retrospective discussion of Starr's book, see the August/October 2004 issue of the *Journal of Health Policy, Politics and Law.*

References

Aaron, Henry J. 2002. "Commentary—A Funny Thing Happened on the Way to Managed Competition." *Journal of Health Policy, Politics and Law* 27, no. 1 (February): 31–36.

Advisory Commission on Consumer Protection and Quality in the Health Care Industry. 1998. *Quality First: Better Health Care for All Americans.* Online at www.hcqualitycommission.gov/final/.

Alonso-Zaldivar, Ricardo. 2005a. "Healthcare Overhaul Is Quietly Underway." *Los Angeles Times,* January 31.

———. 2005b. "Insurance Option has Workers Pay More." *Los Angeles Times,* May 23.

Alvarez, Lizette. 1998. "After Polling, G.O.P. Offers a Patients' Bill." *New York Times,* July 16.

Anders, George. 1996. *Health against Wealth: HMOs and the Breakdown of Medical Trust.* Boston: Houghton Mifflin.

Annas, George J. 1998. "A National Bill of Patients' Rights." *New England Journal of Medicine* 338, no. 10 (March 5): 695–99.

Arrow, Kenneth J. 1963. "Uncertainty and the Welfare Economics of Medical Care." *American Economic Review* LIII, no. 5 (December): 851–83.

Atchinson, Brian K., and Daniel M. Fox. 1997. "The Politics of the Health Insurance Portability and Accountability Act." *Health Affairs* 16, no. 3 (May/June): 146–50.

Bachman, Ronald E. 2004. "Consumer-Driven Health Care: The Future Is Now." *Benefits Quarterly* 20, no. 2 (second quarter): 15–22.

Bartlett, Donald L., and James B. Steele. 2004. *Critical Condition: How Health Care in America Became Big Business & Bad Medicine.* New York: Doubleday.

Berk, Marc L., and Alan C. Monheit. 2001. "The Concentration of Health Care Expenditures, Revisited." *Health Affairs* 20, no. 2 (March/April): 9–18.

Blendon, Robert J.; Mollyann Brodie; John W. Benson; Drew E. Altman; Larry Levitt; Tina Hoff; and Larry Hugwick. 1998. "Understanding the Managed Care Backlash." *Health Affairs* 17, no. 4 (July/August): 80–94.

Bloche, M. Gregg. 2004. "Back to the '90s—The Supreme Court Immunizes Managed Care." *New England Journal of Medicine* 351, no. 13 (September 23): 1277–79.

Bodenheimer, Thomas, and Kip Sullivan. 1998a. "How Large Employers Are Shaping the Health Care Marketplace" (first of two parts). *New England Journal of Medicine* 338, no. 14 (April 2): 1003–7.

———. 1998b. "How Large Employers Are Shaping the Health Care Marketplace" (second of two parts). *New England Journal of Medicine* 338, no. 14 (April 9): 1084–87.

Brink, Susan. 1998. "HMOs Were the Right Rx: America Got Lower Medical Costs—But Also More Worries." *U.S. News and World Report* 124, no. 9 (March 9): 47–50.

Brink, Susan, and Nancy Shute. 1997. "Are HMOs the Right Prescription?" *U.S. News and World Report* 123, no. 14 (October 13): 60–64.

Brodie, Mollyann; Lee Ann Brady; and Drew E. Altman. 1998. "Media Coverage of Managed Care: Is There a Negative Bias?" *Health Affairs* 17, no. 1 (January/February): 9–25.

Brown, Lawrence D., and Michael S. Sparer. 2003. "Poor Program's Progress: The Unanticipated Politics of Medicaid Policy." *Health Affairs* 22, no. 1 (January/February): 31–44.

Calmes, Jackie. 2005. "In Bush's 'Ownership Society,' Citizens Would Take More Risks." *Wall Street Journal,* February 28.

Centers for Medicare and Medicaid Services. n.d. "SCHIP Enrollment Reports." Washington, D.C.: Centers for Medicare and Medicaid Services. Online at www.cms.hhs.gov/schip/enrollment.

Children's Defense Fund. 1998. *CHIP Checkup: A Health Start for Children.* Washington, D.C.: Children's Defense Fund. Online at www.childrensdefense.org.

Clymer, Adam. 1997. "Cigarette Tax Rise Pays for Child Health Plan." *New York Times,* February 28.

Commonwealth Fund. 1998. "Majority of Employers Do Not Consider Reports on HMO Quality When Choosing Employee Health Plans." (September 15). Online at www.cmwf.org/media/gabel293-0915.html.

Corrigan, Janet M.; Jill S. Eden; Marsha R. Gold; and Jeremy D. Pickreign. 1997. "Trends toward a National Health Care Marketplace." *Inquiry* 34, no. 1 (Spring): 11–28.

Crooper, Carol Marie. 1996. "The H.M.O. Says the Doctor Is In. Is He Really?" *New York Times,* November 10.

Cunningham, Robert, and Douglas B. Sherlock. 2002. "Bounceback: Blues Thrive as Markets Cool toward HMOs." *Health Affairs* 21, no. 1 (January/February): 24–38.

Daniels, Norman, and James Sabin. 1998. "The Ethics of Accountability in Managed Care Reform." *Health Affairs* 17, no. 5 (September/October): 50–64.

Davis, Karen. 2004. "Consumer-Directed Health Care: Will It Improve Health System Performance?" *Health Services Research* 39, no. 4, Part II (August): 1219–33.

Davis, Karen; Michelle M. Doty; and Alice Ho. 2005. "How High Is Too High? Implications of High-Deductible Plans." Report No. 816. New York: Commonwealth Fund.

Dentzer, Susan. 2004. "It's the Taj Mahal of Health Insurance Schemes." *Washington Post,* October 31.

Draper, Debra A., and Gary Claxton. 2004. "Managed Care Redux: Health Plans Shift Responsibilities to Consumers." Issue Brief No. 79 (March). Washington, D.C.: Center for Studying Health System Change. Online at www.hschange.com.

Draper, Debra A.; Robert E. Hurley; Cara S. Lesser; and Bradley C. Strunk. 2002. "The Changing Face of Managed Care." *Health Affairs* 21, no. 1 (January/February): 11–23.

Easterbrook, Gregg. 1997. "Healing the Great Divide: How Come Patients and Doctors Ended Up on Opposite Sides?" *U.S. News and World Report* 123, no. 14 (October 13): 64–67.

Eckholm, Erik. 1991. "Health Benefits Found to Deter Job Switching." *New York Times,* September 26.

Emanuel, Ezekiel, and Victor R. Fuchs. 2005. "Solved." *Washington Monthly* 37, no. 6 (June): 20–24.

Emanuel, Linda L. 1997. "Professional Standards in Health Care: Calling All Parties to Account." *Health Affairs* 16, no. 1 (January/February): 52–54.

Enthoven, Alain C. 1978. "Consumer Choice Health Plans" (first of two parts). *New England Journal of Medicine* 298 (March 23): 650–58.

———. 2002. "Commentary—The Fortune 500 Model for Health Care: Is Now the Time to Change?" *Journal of Health Policy, Politics and Law* 27, no. 1 (February): 37–48.

————. 2003. "Employer-Based Health Insurance Is Failing: Now What?" *Health Affairs* (May 28): W3-237–W3-249.

Enthoven, Alain C., and Sara J. Singer. 1997. "Markets and Collective Action in Regulating Managed Care." *Health Affairs* 16, no. 6 (November/December): 26–32.

Escarce, Jose J.; Judy A. Shea; and Wei Chen. 1997. "Segmentation of Hospital Markets: Where Do HMO Enrollees Get Care?" *Health Affairs* 16, no. 6 (November/December): 181–92.

Families USA. 1996a. "HMO Consumers at Risk: States to the Rescue." Washington, D.C.: Families USA

————. 1996b. "Health Legislation Enacted by the 104th Congress." Washington, D.C.: Families USA.

———— 1988. *Hit and Miss: State Managed Care Laws.* Washington, D.C.: Families USA.

Freudenheim, Milt. 1996. "Not Quite What the Doctor Ordered." *New York Times,* October 8.

Fuhrmans, Vanessa. 2005. "Childbirth for Bargain-Hunters." *Wall Street Journal,* April 5.

Gabel, Jon R. 1997. "Ten Ways HMOs Have Changed during the 1990s." *Health Affairs* 16, no. 3 (May/June): 134–45.

Gabel, Jon R.; Anthony T. Lo Sasso; and Thomas Rice. 2002. "Consumer-Driven Health Plans: Are They More Than Talk Now?" *Health Affairs* (November 20): W395–W407.

Geis, Sonya. 2005. "Passport to Health Care at Lower Cost to Patient." *Washington Post* (November 6).

General Accounting Office. 1995. *Insurance for Children: Many Remain Uninsured Despite Medicaid Expansion.* Washington, D.C.: General Accounting Office.

————. 1997. *Health Insurance: Coverage Leads to Increased Health Care Access for Children.* Washington, D.C.: General Accounting Office.

Gold, Marsha, and Robert Hurley. 1997. "The Role of Managed Care 'Products' in Managed Care Plans." *Inquiry* 34, no. 1 (Spring): 29–37.

Gosfield, Alice G. 1996. "Who Is Holding Whom Accountable for Quality?" *Health Affairs* 16, no. 3 (May/June): 26–40.

Gray, Bradford H. 1997. "Trust and Trustworthy Care in the Managed Care Era." *Health Affairs* 16, no. 1 (January/February): 34–49.

Greenhouse, Steven. 1996. "Podiatrists to Form Nationwide Union; a Reply to H.M.O.'s." *New York Times,* October 25.

Gupta, Amit K. 2003. "The Arrival of Consumer-Centric Healthcare." *Managed Care Quarterly* 11, no. 1 (Winter): 20–23.

Hacker, Jacob S. 2005. "Insurance Policy: Reviving the Social Safety Net." *The New Republic* 4,720, no. 233 (July 4): 18–21.

Hacker, Jacob S., and Theodore R. Marmor. 1999. "The Misleading Language of Managed Care." *Journal of Health Politics, Policy and Law* 24, no. 5 (October): 1033–43.

Hager, George, and Alissa J. Rubin. 1995. "Last-Minute Maneuvers Forge a Conference Agreement." *Congressional Quarterly Weekly Report* 53, no. 25 (June 24): 1814–19.

Havighurst, Clark C. 1997. "'Putting Patients First': Promise or Smoke Screen?" *Health Affairs* 16, no. 6 (November/December): 123–25.

Herbert, Bob. 1996. "Prescription Switches." *New York Times,* December 27.

Herzlinger, Regina. 1997. *Market Driven Health Care: Who Wins, Who Loses in the Transformation of America's Largest Service Industry.* Cambridge, Mass.: Perseus Books.

————, ed. 2004. *Consumer-Driven Health Care: Implications for Providers, Payers, and Policymakers.* San Francisco: Jossey-Bass.

Hibbard, Judith H.; Jacquelyn J. Jewett; Mark W. Legnini; and Martin Tusler. 1997. "Choosing a Health Plan: Do Large Employers Use the Data?" *Health Affairs* 16, no. 6 (November/December): 172–80.

Higgins, Marguerite. 2005. "Health Savings Accounts Booming." *Washington Times,* May 5.

Hurley, Robert E.; Bradley C. Strunk; and Justin S. White. 2004. "The Puzzling Popularity of the PPO." *Health Affairs* 23, no. 2 (March/April): 56–68.

Ignagni, Karen. 1998. "Covering a Breaking Revolution: The Media and Managed Care." *Health Affairs* 17, no. 1 (January/February): 26–34.

Johannes, Laura. 1997. "Some HMOs Now Put Doctors on a Budget for Prescription Drugs." *Wall Street Journal*, May 22.

Jones, Charles O. 1978. *An Introduction to the Study of Public Policy.* North Scituate, Mass.: Duxbury Press.

Jones, David A. 1997. "'Putting Patients First': A Philosophy in Practice." *Health Affairs* 16, no. 6 (November/December): 115–20.

Jost, Timothy Stoltzfus. 2004. "The Supreme Court Limits Lawsuits Against Managed Care Organizations." *Health Affairs* (August 11): W4-417–W4-426.

Kaiser Family Foundation. n.d. "Trends and Indicators in the Changing Health Care Marketplace." Menlo Park: Calif.: Henry J. Kaiser Family Foundation.

———. 2001. "The Public, Managed Care, and Consumer Protections." Menlo Park, Calif.: Henry J. Kaiser Family Foundation.

———. 2004. "Employer Health Benefits 2004 Survey." Menlo Park: Calif.: Henry J. Kaiser Family Foundation.

Kennedy, Edward M., and Orrin Hatch. 1997. "Health Insurance for Every Child." *Washington Post National Weekly Edition* 14, no. 42 (August 25): 26.

Kenney, Genevieve, and Debbie I. Chang. 2004. "The State Children's Health Insurance Program: Successes, Shortcomings, and Challenges." *Health Affairs* 23, no. 5 (September/October): 51–62.

Kilborn, Peter T. 1996. "Devalued by the Growth of H.M.O.'s, Some Doctors Seek Union Banner." *New York Times*, May 30.

———. 1997. "Dissatisfaction Is Growing with Managed Care Plans." *New York Times*, September 28.

———. 1998a. "Largest H.M.O.'s Cutting the Poor and the Elderly." *New York Times*, July 6.

———. 1998b. "Patients' Rights Debate Engenders Unlikeliest of Alliances." *New York Times*, July 21.

———. 1998c. "The Uninsured Find Fewer Doctors in the House." *New York Times*, August 30.

Krugman, Paul. 2005. "Health Economics 101." *The New York Times*, November 14.

Ku, Leighton. 2005. "The Effect of Increased Cost-Sharing in Medicaid: A Summary of Research Findings." Washington, D. C.: Center for Budget and Policy Priorities.

Ku, Leighton; Matt Broaddus; and Victoria Wachino. 2005. "Medicaid and SCHIP Protected Insurance Coverage for Millions of Low-Income Americans." Washington, D.C.: Center for Budget and Policy Priorities.

Kuttner, Robert. 1998a. "Must Good HMOs Go Bad?" (first of two parts). *New England Journal of Medicine* 338, no. 21 (May 21): 1558–63.

———. 1998b. "Must Good HMOs Go Bad?" (second of two parts). *New England Journal of Medicine* 338, no. 22 (May 28): 1635–39.

Ladd, Everett C. 1998. "Health Care Hysteria, Part II." *New York Times*, July 23.

Ladenheim, Kala. 1997. "Health Insurance in Transition: The Health Insurance Portability and Accountability Act of 1996." *Publius* 27, no. 2 (Spring): 33–51.

Lazarus, David. 2005. "Costs of Health Care Drag America Down." *San Francisco Chronicle*, June 8.

Lee, Peter V. 1997. "The True Test of Whether Health Plans Put Patients First." *Health Affairs* 16, no. 6 (November/December): 129–32.

Lewis, Shawn D. 2004. "Patient Care Suffers Under Privacy Law." *Detroit News*, March 29.

Leyerle, Betty. 1994. *The Private Regulation of American Health Care*. Armonk, N.Y.: M.E. Sharpe.

Lindblom, Charles E. 1959. "The Science of Muddling Through." *Public Administration Review* 19, no. 1 (Spring): 79–88.

Lindblom, Charles E., and Edward J. Woodhouse. 1993. *The Policy-Making Process.* Englewood Cliffs, N.J.: Prentice-Hall.

Lohr, Kathleen N. 1997. "How Do We Measure Quality?" *Health Affairs* 16, no. 3 (May/June): 22–25.

Love, Susan. 1998. "H.M.O.'s Could Save Your Life." *New York Times,* June 7.

Luft, Harold S., and Robert H. Miller. 2002. "HMO Performance Update: An Analysis of the Literature, 1997–2001." *Health Affairs* 21, no. 4 (July/August): 63–86.

Mann, Cindy, and Jocelyn Guyer. 1997. "Overview of the New Child Health Block Grant." Washington, D.C.: Center for Budget and Policy Priorities.

Maxwell, James, and Peter Temin. 2002. "Managed Competition versus Industrial Purchasing of Health Care among the Fortune 500." *Journal of Health Politics, Policy and Law* 27, no. 1 (February): 5–30.

Mays, Glen P.; Gary Claxton; and Justin White. 2004. "Managed Care Rebound? Recent Changes in Health Plans' Cost Containment Strategies." *Health Affairs* (August 11): W4-427–W4-436.

Mechanic, David. 1996. "Changing Medical Organization and the Erosion of Trust." *Milbank Quarterly* 74, no. 2 (June): 171–89.

———. 1998. "The Functions and Limitations of Trust in the Provision of Medical Care." *Journal of Health Politics, Policy and Law* 23, No. 4 (August): 661–86.

"Medical Paper-Pushers Resist Opportunity to Improve Care." 2004. *USA Today,* May 12.

Moran, Donald W. 1997. "Federal Regulation of Managed Care: An Impulse in Search of a Theory?" *Health Affairs* 16, no. 6 (November/December): 7–21.

National Center for Health Statistics. 1998. *Health US, 1998.* Washington, D.C.: Department of Health and Human Services.

———. 2004. *Health US, 2004.* Washington, D.C.: Department of Health and Human Services.

Navarro, Mireya. 1997. "Group Plan Gives Florida Children Access to Affordable Health Care." *New York Times,* May 23.

Neuman, Patricia; Ed Maibach; Katharine Dusenbury; Michelle Kitchman; and Pam Zupp. 1998. "Marketing HMOs to Medicare Beneficiaries." *Health Affairs* 17, no. 4 (July/August): 132–39.

Newcomer, Lee N. 1997. "Measures of Trust in Health Care." *Health Affairs* 16, no. 1 (January/February): 50–51.

Newhouse, Joseph P. 2004. "Consumer-Directed Health Plans and the RAND Health Insurance Experiment." *Health Affairs* 23, no. 6 (November/December): 107–13.

Nichols, Len M., and Linda J. Blumberg. 1998. "A Different Kind of 'New Federalism'? The Health Insurance Portability and Accountability Act of 1996." *Health Affairs* 17, no. 3 (May/June): 25–42.

Patel, Kant, and Mark E. Rushefsky. 2002. *Health Care Policy in an Age of New Technologies.* Armonk, N.Y.: M.E. Sharpe.

Patel, Vip, and Mark V. Pauly. 2002. "Guaranteed Renewability and the Problem of Risk Variation in Individual Health Insurance Markets." *Health Affairs* (August 28): W280–W289.

Patterson, Martha Priddy. 2004. "Defined Contribution Health Plan to Consumer Driven Health Benefits: Evolution and Experience." *Benefits Quarterly* 20, no. 2 (second quarter): 49–59.

Pauly, Mark V. 1978. "Is Medical Care Different?" In *Competition in the Health Care Sector: Past, Present and Future,* ed. Bureau of Economics, U.S. Federal Trade Commission, 19–48. Washington, D.C.: Government Printing Office.

Pear, Robert. 1995. "H.M.O.'s Refusing Emergency Claims, Hospitals Assert." *New York Times,* July 9.

———. 1996a. "The Tricky Business of Keeping Doctors Quiet." *New York Times,* September 22.

————. 1996b. "H.M.O.'s Asserting Immunity in Suits over Malpractice." *New York Times,* November 17.

————. 1997a. "New Health Insurance Rules Spell Out Rights of Workers." *New York Times,* April 2.

————. 1997b. "Capitol in Discord Over Plan to Aid Uninsured Youths." *New York Times,* June 17.

————. 1998a. "Hands Tied, Judges Rue Law That Limits H.M.O. Liability." *New York Times,* July 11.

————. 1998b. "H.M.O. Group Backs Controls G.O.P. Rejects." *New York Times,* July 14.

————. 1998c. "Common Ground on Patient Rights Hides a Chasm." *New York Times,* August 4.

Reden and Anders, Ltd. 2005. "Consumer Directed Insurance Products: Survey Results." (April). San Francisco: Reden and Anders, Ltd. Online at fahs.com/publications.

Relman, Arnold S. 2005. "The Health of Nations: Medicine and the Free Market." *The New Republic* 232, no. 4,703 (March 7): 23–30.

Rosenbaum, Sara H.; Kay Johnson; Colleen Sonosky; Anne Markus; and Chris DeGraw. 1998. "The Children's Hour: The State Children's Health Insurance Program." *Health Affairs* 17, no. 1 (January/February): 75–89.

Rubenstein, Sarah. 2005. "For Some, HSAs Can Be Attractive Wealth Builders." *Wall Street Journal,* March 2.

Rushefsky, Mark E. 2002. *Public Policy in the United States: At the Dawn of the Twenty-First Century,* 3rd ed. Armonk, N.Y.: M.E. Sharpe.

Rushefsky, Mark E., and Kant Patel. 1998. *Politics, Power and Policy Making: The Case of Health Care Reform in the 1990s.* Armonk, N.Y.: M.E. Sharpe.

Schneider, William. 1998. "Fear of Bureaucrats Strikes Again." *National Journal* 30, no. 29 (July 18): 1714.

Serafini, Marilyn Werber. 1997. "Quality Time." *National Journal* 29, no. 1 (May 24): 1035–37.

Starr, Paul. 1982. *The Social Transformation of American Medicine.* New York: Basic Books.

————. 1995. "What Happened to Health Care Reform?" *American Prospect,* no. 20 (Winter): 20–31.

Sullivan, Kip. 2000. "On the 'Efficiency' of Managed Care Plans." *Health Affairs* 19, no. 4 (July/August): 139–48.

Summer, Laura; Sharon Parrott; and Cindy Mann. 1996. *Millions of Uninsured and Underinsured Children Are Eligible for Medicaid.* Washington, D.C.: Center for Budget and Policy Priorities. Online at www.cbpp.org/mcaidprt.htm.

Thompson, Joseph W.; James Bost; Faruque Ahmed; Carrie E. Ingalls; and Caly Sennett. 1998. "The NCQA's Quality Compass: Evaluating Managed Care in the United States." *Health Affairs* 17, no. 1 (January/February): 152–58.

Trude, Sally, and Leslie Jackson Conwell. 2004. "Rhetoric vs. Reality: Employer Views on Consumer-Driven Health Care." Issue Brief no. 86. Washington, D.C.: Center for Studying Health System Change.

Vieth, Warren. 2004. "Bush Makes His Pitch for 'Ownership Society.'" *Los Angeles Times,* September 5.

Weinder, Jonathan P., and Gregory de Lissovoy. 1993. "Razing a Tower of Babel: A Taxonomy for Managed Care and Health Insurance Plans." *Journal of Health Politics, Policy and Law* 18, no. 1 (Spring): 75–103.

Weinick, Robin M.; Margaret E. Weigers; and Joel W. Cohen. 1998. "Children's Health Insurance, Access to Care, and Health Status: New Findings." *Health Affairs* 17, no. 2 (March/April): 127–36.

Wilensky, Gail R. 1997. "Promoting Quality: A Public Policy View." *Health Affairs* 16, no. 3 (May/June): 77–81.

—— 11 ——

Conclusion

Health Care Policy at the Dawn
of the Twenty-First Century

In these final pages, we would like to summarize the discussion of the text, focusing on the features that help explain the course of health care policy in the United States. Based on this review, we end by making some reasonably educated guesses about the future of health care policy.

We began this text by examining various factors that affect the policymaking process, whether in health care or some other policy area. Policymaking and the policies that result from that process are profoundly affected by the constitutional structure of government. In the United States, that constitutional structure creates a bias against major changes. The system of separation of powers and checks and balances creates separate institutions that share power. Chief among them is the separation between executive and legislative powers. In a parliamentary system, such as in England, the party with a majority in the legislature would be able to enact its program (party discipline is important here too). In the United States, even under conditions of party control of both Congress and the presidency (i.e., 2003–2005), the passage of programs is hardly assured. Separation of powers creates institutional jealousies that are difficult to overcome. When there is divided control (i.e., 1995–2000), the institutional jealousies may be reinforced.[1] This is not to say that major changes cannot take place, only that they occur under constitutionally difficult circumstances.[2] And all three branches of government—executive, legislative, and judicial—are brought into policymaking. At the beginning of the twenty-first century, the federal government experienced unified control, with Republicans in charge of both the executive and legislative branches (and influencing the makeup of the judicial branch). Even here, while much as accomplished, such as tax cuts, program changes such as Social Security reform proved difficult.

A further constitutional feature is federalism, the division of powers between different levels of government. States (and local governments) are independent actors, and policy made at the federal level must consider its impact on states. The result of federalism and separation of powers (as in a system of checks and balances) is the deliberate fragmentation of power, vertically and horizontally. It would be little exaggeration to say that no other country faces as difficult a set of constitutional barriers as the United States. Additionally, some states have shown great initiative in trying to control the costs of Medicaid and helping their citizens afford prescription medications.

A second key set of factors is the political environment, which is shaped by constitutional structure and the institutional environment. Fragmentation of power requires that policies be adopted as a result of consensus building, especially in legislatures. It also means that rather than adopt major reforms or new ways of doing things, we in the United States tend to adopt smaller changes, tinkering as we go along. This incremental style of decision making characterizes policymaking in health care. Numerous attempts at comprehensive change in the twentieth century have failed, most recently in 1994 (see chapter 9).

Our political philosophy or ideology has a strong promarket, antigovernment bias. Those who seek positive government action have the burden of justifying new programs and then maintaining political support for them. This antigovernment bias, among other factors, helps explain why the public sector's role in health care is limited in the United States, as compared to other countries.[3] Even in other countries, some have argued that markets have become predominant (Yergin and Stanislaw 1998). As chapter 10 shows, the private sector has taken the lead in effecting change in the health care system and consumers/patients are being asked to bear more of the burden of paying for their health care.

The same political philosophy, along with the same constitutional and institutional factors, allows for another important feature of our political environment: the presence of interest groups. The right to assemble, the rights of free speech and press, the right of association, and the right to petition government create a constitutional basis for interest groups. Fragmentation in government, where there are multiple sources of power at different levels of government, invites interest groups to try to influence those sources of power. Recall the definition of politics offered by Lawrence Brown in the opening epigraph to chapter 9: politics involves the resolution of conflicts of values and interests. For every program, a set of interests is affected by it. Interest groups seek either to defend programs that benefit them or to get rid of programs that adversely affect them. They are also prepared to defend themselves against policy proposals that would hurt them. We certainly saw the mobilization of interests in chapters 9 and 10, but this occurs in other ways as well. Medicaid, Medicare, and the planning programs of the 1960s all contained provisions in their original legislation that effectively said that the program could not interfere with the practice of medicine. The Medicare Modernization Act of 2003 contains several provisions highly favorable to the pharmaceutical industry. The danger of interest-group activity is that once programs are enacted and entrenched, their interest-group defenders man the barricades against change. The result is what Rauch (1994) calls demosclerosis.

All these factors help explain the peculiar nature of the health care system in the United States. It is a combination of mostly private-sector coverage with substantial public programs and public regulation. If we were to develop a health care system from scratch, we would likely never produce the system we currently have.

This system has problems. Costs remain a problem, which affects governments, businesses, insurers, individuals, and providers. At the same time that the health care sector has grown to be the largest sector (about one-seventh of the economy), a sizable and increasing number of people (over 15 percent of the population) have inadequate access to quality care, largely but not entirely because of lack of health insurance. This is compounded by developments in biomedical technology that present ethical questions, such as What is life? Is there a right to die?, that we have not yet and may never resolve.

Given these political features, problems, and policy failures (as in 1994), what is the future of health care policy in the United States? It is always hazardous to go out on a limb and make projections, but certain trends seem obvious, based on our analysis in the previous ten chapters.

First, whatever change is likely to take place will be incremental. Public health care programs, Medicaid and Medicare, have been tinkered with as a means of controlling costs and expanding access. Of the two, Medicare is perhaps the better example of incremental policymaking that can, over a period of time, result in significant change.

Consider the Balanced Budget Act (BBA) of 1997. Without altering some of the basic fundamentals of the program, potentially significant change were enacted. Prospective payment, imposed first on hospitals and then on doctors, has been extended to other providers, such as home health care and nursing homes. Some commentators have argued that the policy consensus underlying Medicare has eroded, particularly with the passage of the 2003 Medicare legislation (Oberlander 2003; Oliver, Lee, and Lipton 2004).

A further change that was part of the BBA was expansion of health insurance to children in families lacking health insurance. This is the State Children's Health Insurance Program (SCHIP), in which, with federal grants and state matching funds, states can either extend Medicaid to children or create new programs to cover children's health care.

Another incremental, but critical, policy initiative includes laws regulating managed care and patients' rights bills. The federal government passed some legislation in 1996 (affecting maternity care and portability of insurance) and discussed patients' rights bills in 1998. Meanwhile, over thirty states enacted some version of managed care regulation. By the early twenty-first century, thanks to a new administration and court decisions, the patients' rights momentum had stalled.

Problems remain in specific policy areas. In the case of Medicaid, there has been considerable change, though the basic elements remain the same. Decentralization of authority to the states during the Reagan and Clinton administrations was accompanied by liberalization of eligibility so that more people, primarily children, could be covered. At the same time, states have taken steps to control costs, such as moving Medicaid recipients into managed care, limiting services, and restricting provider reimbursements. As we concluded in chapter 3, the states by themselves are unable to solve the problems with the program. The federal government still has a significant role to play. And certainly the demographic impact of an aging population will continue to place strains on the federal-state program.

The same demographic problem affects Medicare (chapter 4). Medicare remains a popular program and has, in a sense, weathered the storms of attacks upon it in 1995–96. The cost problems remain, especially as the population ages. The issue of the long-term financial viability of Medicare Part A (the hospital trust) remains. Changes enacted in 1997 and 2003 portend a dramatically different future for the program.

Related to Medicare and Medicaid is the issue of long-term care. It is one of the fastest-growing areas of health care spending, again a result, largely, of the aging of the population. Nursing home care is extremely expensive, and the long-term care insurance market is small and growing at a slow rate. Further, both nursing homes and home health agencies have been cited for fraudulent billing. No easy solution appears for an area where the private sector, including individuals and families, remains the largest provider and payer of services.

Equally discouraging, in some respects, is the issue of the disadvantaged, those who do not have the financial resources to afford health insurance and adequate health care. If there is one demonstrable finding in the health care literature, it is that lack of access to health care leads to poor health outcomes. There are ways to cover more people, as we mentioned in chapter 5. Medicare and Medicaid could be expanded; tax credits for purchase of health insurance would help. Medical savings accounts or the newer health savings accounts could provide insurance coverage to the uninsured who are working, especially the self-employed, though few people to date have opted for these programs. National health insurance would, of course, largely end the lack of insurance problem, but as we have seen, it is the least likely policy to be enacted.

Even these programs could prove inadequate if providers are not available. Inner cities and rural areas suffer from an insufficient number of doctors. The literature also shows that minorities are more likely to lack access to services and insurance than whites.

While access to services has been a perennial issue, the issue that drives change in the health care system remains cost containment (chapter 6). The initial efforts at cost containment were regulatory in nature. At the state level, this involved hospital price regulation (which met with some success) and certificate-of-need (CON) regulation (which met with much less success). At the federal level, planning was tried (again with limited success) and then rate setting in Medicare (prospective payment first for hospitals, then for doctors, and eventually for other providers, such as home health care services). The Prospective Payment System (PPS) met with some success and has become an integral part of Medicare. Managed care has produced cost savings, at least in the short run. Cost-shifting seems to be the preferred policy.

Medical technology, the subject of chapter 8, raises a whole range of questions, apart from its impact on costs. Technology has enhanced what medicine can do and in the process has raised troubling ethical questions. These include issues such as how organs ought to be made available to those who need transplants and the ethics of ending life for terminally ill patients (either to end suffering or to make organs available). Developments in reproductive technology make it possible for people to have children under circumstances that had not even been thought of two decades before. Right-to-die movements, a reaction to life-sustaining technologies, confront those who object on religious grounds. How well the U.S. political system is equipped to deal with these complex, difficult issues is an important question. Some, such as right to die, have been the object of voter initiatives (e.g., Oregon). The Terry Schiavo case brought together many of the political and value-laden elements that we have discussed. Are initiatives, with all the trappings of political campaigns, the best forum for deciding these kinds of issues? Will genetic testing lead to some people being unable to obtain health insurance?

Regulation as a means of cost control has largely been eliminated (a few states like Maryland retain their programs). The private sector's attempt to control employees' health care costs has led to significant change. The increasing costs of premiums has led some employers to reduce or eliminate coverage, or to shift more costs to employees. And the move to managed care has faltered somewhat, though it has recovered a bit (chapter 10).

Managed care was successful, at least in the short run. Double-digit inflation in premiums in the late 1980s and early 1990s changed to low-single-digit inflation and, in some cases, to decreases in premium costs in the middle and late 1990s. But increasing costs and premiums returned in the late 1990s and early 2000s, thanks in part to the backlash against managed care.

If there is one trend that is most noticeable in the middle of the first decade of the twenty-first century, it is that more of us are being asked to pay for more of our health care costs. The private sector is leading the way with consumer-driven health care.

Concluding Thoughts

Some commentators have argued that, as long as the basic issue is one of trying to deal with the tradeoffs among the three values of cost, access, and quality, the problems with health care in this country may never be solved:

> If you want an end to the health-care debate—don't hold your breath. It won't happen now. It won't happen 50 years from now. This is not because our politicians are incompetent, although they often are. Nor is it because doctors, hospitals, drug companies and insurers try to manipulate the system, although they do. The real reason is that we Americans want contradictory things from the health-care system: We want unlimited medical care without unlimited spending. Because this is impossible—and because our politicians reinforce our unrealistic demands—we are doomed to complain forever about the health system's defects. (Samuelson 1998; see also Ginzberg 1977)

Notes

1. However, Mayhew (1991) argues that, even under conditions of divided government, significant policy initiatives can be enacted. Freedman (1995) finds that the Reagan and Nixon administrations, periods of divided government, were especially good times for health care legislation.

2. For a discussion of how major changes can occur, see Baumgartner and Jones (1993) and Kingdon (1984).

3. For a discussion of markets and health care that focuses on the twenty-first century, see the special issue of *Journal of Health Politics, Policy and Law* 22, no. 2 (April 1997).

References

Baumgartner, Frank R., and Bryan D. Jones. 1993. *Agendas and Instability in American Politics*. Chicago: University of Chicago Press.

Freedman, Grace Roegner. 1995. "Toward a Macro Theory for Health Care Policymaking: Lessons from the Enactment of Health Care Legislation 1945–1992." Paper prepared for delivery at the annual meeting of the American Political Science Association, August 31–September 3, Chicago.

Ginzberg, Eli. 1977. *The Limits of Health Reform: The Search for Realism*. New York: Basic Books.

Kingdon, John F. 1984. *Agendas, Alternatives, and Public Policies*. Boston: Little, Brown.

Mayhew, David R. 1991. *Divided we Govern: Party Control, Lawmaking, and Investigations*. New Haven, Conn.: Yale University Press.

Oberlander, Jonathan. 2003. *The Political Life of Medicare*. Chicago: University of Chicago Press.

Oliver, Thomas R.; Philip R. Lee; and Helene L. Lipton. 2004. "A Political History of Medicare and Prescription Drug Coverage." Paper presented at the annual meeting of the American Political Science Association, September 2–5, Chicago.

Rauch, Jonathan. 1994. *Demosclerosis: The Silent Killer of American Government*. New York: Times Books.

Samuelson, Robert J. 1998. "Having It All." *Newsweek* (September 28): 71.

Yergin, Daniel, and Joseph Stanislaw. 1998. *The Commanding Heights: The Battle between Government and the Marketplace That Is Remaking the Modern World*. New York: Simon and Schuster.

Appendix
State Medical Liability Laws, Section 1

States	Limits on Damage Awards	Statutes of Limitation	Joint and Several Liability	Limits on Attorney Fees	Patient Compensation or Stabilization Fund
Alabama	No limitations. Limits declared unconstitutional by State Supreme Court.	§6.5.482. 2 years from date of injury or 6 months from discovery. No suit may be brought 4 years after date of injury. Minors under 4 by age 8 if statute would have otherwise expired by that time.	No separation of joint and several liability.	No limitations.	None provided.
Alaska	Enacted 2005: §09.55.549. Noneconomic damages limited to $250,000; limited to $400,000 for wrongful death or injury over 70% disabling; limits not applicable to intentional or reckless acts or omissions. §9.17.020. Punitive damages limited to $500,000 or 3 times compensatory damages.	§09.10.070. 2 years from discovery of injury.	§09.17.080. Defendants are proportionally liable for damages awarded according to percentage of fault.	No limitations.	None provided.

(continued)

Appendix *(continued)*
State Medical Liability Laws, Section 1

States	Limits on Damage Awards	Statutes of Limitation	Joint and Several Liability	Limits on Attorney Fees	Patient Compensation or Stabilization Fund
Arizona	No limitations. Limits constitutionally prohibited.	§12–542. 2 years after cause of action, not afterward for personal injury and wrongful death.	§12–2506. Defendants are proportionally liable for damages awarded according to percentage of fault, unless defendant acted in concert with another person.	§12–568. Not limited, but court may review reasonableness of fees upon request of either party.	None provided.
Arkansas	§16–55–205–209. Punitive damages limited to $250,000 per plaintiff or 3 times amount of economic damages. Not to exceed $1 million. Limits adjusted for inflation at 3-year intervals beginning in 2006. Contingent on proof of recklessness or intentional malice.	§16–114–203. 2 years from date of injury. Foreign objects: 1 year from discovery. Minors: before age 9, until age 11.	§16–55–201. Defendants are proportionally liable for damages awarded according to percentage of fault.	No limitations.	None provided.
California	Civil Code §3333.2. $250,000 limit for noneconomic damages.	Civil Procedure §340.5. 3 years after injury or 1 year after discovery, whichever is first. No more than 3 years after injury unless caused by fraud, concealment, or foreign object. Minor under age 6: 3 years or before age 8, whichever is longer.	Civil Code §1431.2. Defendants are proportionally liable for noneconomic damages according to percentage of fault, but jointly and severally liable for economic damages.	**Business and Professions §6146.** Sliding scale, not to exceed 40% of first $50,000, 33 1/3% of next $50,000, 25% of next $500,000, and 15% of damages exceeding $600,000.	None provided.

State					
Colorado	§13-64-302. $1 million total limit on all damages; $300,000 noneconomic limitation.	§13-80-102.5. 2 years from date of injury, no more than 3 years from act. Foreign objects: 2 years from discovery. Minors under age 6: before age 8.	§13-21-111(5). Defendants are proportionally liable for damages awarded according to percentage of fault, unless act proved deliberate.	No limitations.	§10-4-901-913. Stabilization Reserve Fund fully outlined and enacted; **however, provisions never funded and implemented.**
Connecticut	No limitations.	§52-584. 2 years from date of injury, but no later than 3 years of the act or omission.	§52-572h. Defendants are proportionally liable according to percentage of fault for damages awarded.	§52-251c. Sliding scale, not to exceed 1/3 of first $300,000; 25% of next $300,000; 20% of next $300,000; 15% of next $300,000; and 10% of damages exceeding $1.2 million.	None provided.
Delaware	§18.6855. Punitive damages may be awarded only on finding of malicious intent to injure or willful or wanton misconduct. No mandated limit.	§18.6856. 2 years from injury; 3 years from discovery if latent injury. Minor: age 6 or same as adult.	No separation of joint and several liability.	§18.6865. Sliding scale, not to exceed 35% of first $100,000; 25% of next $100,000; and 10% of all damages exceeding $200,000.	§18.6833. Stabilization Reserve Fund created.

(continued)

Appendix *(continued)*

State Medical Liability Laws, Section 1

States	Limits on Damage Awards	Statutes of Limitation	Joint and Several Liability	Limits on Attorney Fees	Patient Compensation or Stabilization Fund
Florida	**§766.118.** Noneconomic damages limited to $500,000 per claimant. Death or permanent vegetative state, noneconomic damages not to exceed $1 million. **§768.73.** Punitive damages limited to the greater of 3 times amount of economic damages or $500,000. If deliberate intent to harm, no limit on punitive damages.	**§95.11.** 2 years from injury or discovery, no more than 4 years from injury. Minors: age 8. If fraud, concealment of injury or intentional misrepresentation prevented discovery within 4-year period, 2 year limit from discovery, not to exceed 7 years after the act.	**§768.81.** Defendants are proportionally liable according to percentage of fault for damages awarded, monetary limits in liability according to percentage as level of fault increases.	**Adopted 2004: Florida Constitution, Article I, Section 26.** Limits attorney fees in malpractice lawsuits to 30% of first $250,000; 10% of any award over $250,000.	**§766.102.** Patient Compensation Fund and Birth-Related Neurological Compensation Fund fully outlined and enacted; **however, provisions never implemented.**
Georgia	**Enacted 2005: §51–13–1.** Noneconomic damages in medical malpractice actions limited to $350,000 against physicians regardless of number of defendants. Noneconomic damages limited to $350,000 against single medical facility; $700,000 against multiple facilities. Aggregate amount of noneconomic damages limited to $1.05 million.	**§9–3–71, 72, 73.** 2 years from injury or death; in no event longer than 5 years from act or death. Foreign object: 1 year from discovery. Minors: 2 years from age 5 if action arose before 5th birthday.	**Enacted 2005: §51–12–33.** Multiple defendants liable for apportioned damages according to percentage of fault of each person. Damages reduced by court in proportion to percentage of fault if plaintiff is found partially responsible for injury. Plaintiff not entitled to receive any damages if found 50% or more responsible for injury.	No limitations.	**§33–20–13 (c).** Health care corporation regulations require insurers to establish and maintain reserve funds for unpaid claims and other known liabilities.

Hawaii	**§663.8.5, 8.7.** $375,000 limit for pain and suffering damages.	**§657.7.3.** 2 years from discovery, not to exceed 6 years from act. Minors: age 10 or within 6 years, whichever is longer. **§671.18.** Arbitration tolls statute until 60 days after panel's decision is delivered.	**§663.10.9.** When negligence is less than 25%, noneconomic damages awarded in proportion according to degree of fault.	**§607.15.5.** Attorney fees must be approved by court.	None provided.
Idaho	**§6.1603–4.** $250,000 limit on noneconomic damages, adjusted annually according to state's average annual wage. Punitive damages limited to $250,000 or amount 3 times of compensatory damages.	**§5.219.** 2 years from injury. Foreign object: 1 year from reasonable discovery or 2 years from injury, whichever is later.	**§6.803.** Defendants are proportionally liable according to percentage of fault for damages awarded, except in cases of intentional act.	No limitations.	None provided.
Illinois	**Enacted 2005: §735 5/2–1706.5.** Noneconomic damages limited to $500,000 against individual physician, $1 million against hospital. **§735 5/2–1115.** Punitive damages not recoverable in medical malpractice cases.	**§735 5/13–212.** 2 years from discovery but not more than 4 years from act. Minors: 8 years after act but not after age 22. **§740 180/2.** Wrongful death: 2 years if limitation on personal injury still valid at time of death.	**§735 5/2–1117.** No separation of joint and several liability.	**§735 5/2–1114.** Sliding scale, not to exceed 1/3 of first $150,000; 25% of $150,000 to $1 million; 20% of damages over $1 million.	None provided.

(continued)

Appendix *(continued)*
State Medical Liability Laws, Section 1

States	Limits on Damage Awards	Statutes of Limitation	Joint and Several Liability	Limits on Attorney Fees	Patient Compensation or Stabilization Fund
Indiana	**$34–18–4–3.** $1,250,000 total limit. Liability limited to $250,000 per health care provider. Any award beyond limits covered by Patient Compensation Fund.	**$34–18–7–1.** 2 years from act, omission, or neglect. Minors: under age 6 until age 8.	No separation of joint and several liability.	**$34–18–18–1.** Plaintiff's attorney fees may not exceed 15% of any award made from Patient Compensation Fund.	**$34–18–6.** Patient Compensation Fund pays awards over $250,000 up to $1,250,000.
Iowa	No limitations.	**§614.1.** 2 years from reasonable discovery but not more than 6 years from injury unless foreign object. Minors under age 8: until age 10 or same as adults, whichever is later. Mentally ill: extends to 1 year from removal of disability.	**§668.4.** Defendants are proportionally liable according to percentage of fault. Several liability not granted for economic damages when defendant is found more than 50% at fault.	**§147.138.** Court to review plaintiff attorney fees in any personal injury or wrongful death action against specified health care providers or hospitals.	None provided.
Kansas	**$60.19a02.** $250,000 limit on noneconomic damages recoverable by each party from all defendants. **$60.3702.** Punitive damages limited to lesser of defendant's highest gross income for prior 5 years or $5 million.	**$60.513.** 2 years from act or reasonable discovery, but can be up to 10 years after reasonable discovery.	No separation of joint and several liability.	**$7.121b.** Attorney fees must be approved by court.	**$40.3403.** Health Care Stabilization Fund pays claims over $200,000, maximum payout of $300,000 per year on claim. Mandatory participation by medical professionals.

Kentucky	No limitations.	**§413.140.** 1 year from act or reasonable discovery, but not more than 5 years after act.	**§411.182.** When court apportions percentage of fault, defendant is only liable for comparable share of damages.	No limitations.	None provided.
Louisiana	**RS §40:1299.42.** $500,000 limit for total recovery. Health care provider liability limited to $100,000. Any award in excess of all liable providers paid from Patient's Compensation Fund.	**RS §9:5628.** 1 year from act or date of discovery, but no later than 3 years from date of injury. **CC §2315.2.** Wrongful death: 1 year from death.	**CC §2324.** Defendants are liable only for percentage of fault unless conspiracy of intentional or willful act.	No limitations.	**RS §40:1299.44.** Patient Compensation Fund pays claims over $100,000 up to $500,000. Physicians levied surcharge directly into fund for purpose of paying malpractice claims.
Maine	**Enacted 2005: §24.2907.** Noneconomic damages in medical liability actions limited to $250,000; punitive damages limited to $75,000. **§18A.2.804.** Noneconomic damages in wrongful death cases limited to $400,000, punitive damages limited to $75,000.	**§24.2902.** 3 years from cause of action. Minors: 6 years after accrual or within 3 years of minority, whichever is first. Foreign objects: accrue from reasonable discovery.	**Enacted 2005: §14.156-A.** In action involving multiple defendants, damage liability if several only for amount of damages in proportion to percentage of fault. Joint liability for defendants in case of acting in concert.	**§24.2961.** Sliding scale, not to exceed 1/3 of first $100,000; 25% of next $100,000; and 20% of damages exceeding $200,000.	None provided.

(continued)

Appendix *(continued)*
State Medical Liability Laws, Section 1

States	Limits on Damage Awards	Statutes of Limitation	Joint and Several Liability	Limits on Attorney Fees	Patient Compensation or Stabilization Fund
Maryland	**§3–2A–09(A).** Noneconomic damages limited to $650,000 from 2005 to 2008, thereafter increasing by $15,000 per year beginning on January 1 of applicable year.	**§5–109.** 5 years from act or 3 years from discovery.	No separation of joint and several liability.	No limitations.	**§6–101-104, 6–301.** Premium 2% tax exemption repealed, tax assessed on HMOs and MCOs to offset medical liability premium rates.
Massachusetts	**§231.60H.** $500,000 limit for noneconomic damages, some exceptions released from limitations.	**§260.4.** 3 years from injury and no more than 7 years, unless foreign object discovered. **§231.60D.** Minors: before age 6 until age 9, no longer than 7 years from injury.	No separation of joint and several liability.	**§231.601.** Sliding scale, not to exceed 40% of first $150,000; 33.33% of next $150,000; 30% of next $200,000 and 25% of award over $500,000.	None provided.
Michigan	**§600.1483.** $280,000 limit on noneconomic damages; $500,000 limit on noneconomic damages applies to certain other circumstance. Limit adjusted annually by state treasurer according to consumer price index.	**§600.5805.** 2 years from injury. **§600.5838a.** 6 months from reasonable discovery. No more than 6 years from injury. **§600.5851.** Minors under age 8: the latter of 6 years or age 10. Reproductive injuries until age 13.	**§600.2925a.** Defendants are proportionally liable according to percentage of fault for damages awarded, except when uncollectible shares are reallocated among solvent defendants.	**Court Rules 8.121(b).** Maximum contingency fee for personal injury action is third of amount recovered.	None provided.

Minnesota	**§549.20.** No limitation for punitive damages but are only allowed if defendant proven to have deliberate disregard to safety. Award subject to judicial review.	**§541.076.** 4 years from injury or termination of treatment. **§541.15.** Disability extends limitation to 7 years.	**§604.02.** Defendants are proportionally liable according to percentage of fault for damages awarded, except when defendant is assessed greater than 50% of fault, or proven to have intentional malice.	No limitations.	None provided.
Mississippi	**§11.1.60.** $500,000 limit on noneconomic damages. **§11.1.65.** Punitive damages only awarded if willful malice or gross negligence proved. Court determines if award granted and amount. Damages limited based on defendant's net worth.	**§15.1.36.** 2 years from act or reasonable discovery, no more than 7 years.	**§85.5.7.** Defendants are proportionally liable according to percentage of fault for damages awarded, except when defendant is proven to have intentional malice.	No limitations.	None provided.
Missouri	**Amended 2005: §538.210.** Noneconomic damages limited to $350,000 regardless of number of defendants. (Inflation index repealed.) **Enacted 2005: §510.265.** Punitive damages limited to $500,000 or 5 times net amount of judgment.	**§516.105.** 2 years from act. Foreign object: 2 years from discovery. **Amended 2005:** Minor under 8: until age 20, or 2 years from 18th birthday. In no event longer than 10 years from injury.	**Amended 2005: §537.067.** Defendants are proportionally liable according to percentage of fault for damages awarded; jointly liable if found more than 51% at fault.	No limitations.	Tort Victim's Compensation Fund does *not* apply in actions of improper health care.

(continued)

Appendix *(continued)*
State Medical Liability Laws, Section 1

States	Limits on Damage Awards	Statutes of Limitation	Joint and Several Liability	Limits on Attorney Fees	Patient Compensation or Stabilization Fund
Montana	§25.9.411. $250,000 limit on noneconomic damages. §27.1.221. Liability for punitive damages determined by court, defendant must have been proven guilty of deliberate malice. Enacted 2005: §27.6.103. Damages for negligence awarded based on "reduced chance of recovery."	§27.2.205. 3 years from injury or discovery, no more than 5 years from act. Minors under age 4: age 11 or death, whichever occurs first.	§27.1.703. Defendants are proportionally liable according to percentage of fault for damages awarded, except when defendant is assessed greater than 50% of fault.	No limitations.	Enacted 2005: §33.23. Insurance Commissioner to perform study of medical liability insurance market; create market assistance plan, joint underwriting association, or stabilization reserve fund based on findings.
Nebraska	§44.2825. Total damages limited to $1,750,000. Health care provider liability limited to $500,000. Any excess of total liability of all health care providers paid from Excess Liability Fund.	§44.2828. 2 years from injury or 1 year from reasonable discovery; in no event longer than 10 years from injury.	§25.21,185.10. Defendants are proportionally liable according to percentage of fault for noneconomic damages awarded, and jointly liable for economic damages.	§44.2834. No limitations, but court can review for reasonableness at request of prevailing party.	§44.2829–2831. Excess Liability Fund participation required and surcharge assessed to physicians. Pays claims over $500,000 per defendant up to $1,750,000.

Nevada	**§41A.035.** $350,000 limit on noneconomic damages, no exceptions. **§42.005.** Punitive damages limited to $300,000 or 3 times compensatory damages; only awarded by court for fraud, oppression, or malice.	**§41A.097.** 4 years from injury or 2 years from reasonable discovery if injury or wrongful death prior to Oct. 1, 2002. If after Oct. 1, 2002, 3 years from injury or 1 year from discovery.	**§41A.045.** Defendants proportionally liable according to percentage of fault for economic and noneconomic damages awarded.	**§7.095.** Sliding scale for attorney fees, not to exceed 40% of first $50,000; 33 1/3% of next $50,000; 25% of next $500,000; 15% of any amount over $600,000.	**§686B.180.** State insurance commissioner may create insurance coverage through regulation if access to essential insurance in voluntary market is limited.
New Hampshire	No limitations. Limits declared unconstitutional by State Supreme Court.	**§507-C:4.** 2 years from injury or 2 years from discovery. Minors under age 8: until age 10.	**§507:7-d.** Defendants are proportionally liable according to percentage of fault for damages awarded.	**§507-C:8.** Sliding scale, not to exceed 50% of first $1000; 40% of next $2000; 1/3 of next $97,000; 20% of excess of $100,000. If settled out of court, fee limited to 25% of up to $50,000.	None provided.
New Jersey	**§2A:15–5.14.** $350,000 limit on punitive damages, or 5 times compensatory damages, whichever is greater.	**§2A:14–2.** 2 years from accrual of claim or discovery. Minor from birth: until age 13.	**§2A:15–5.2.** Defendants only responsible for share of fault if less than 60%. Defendants found more than 60% at fault subject to modified rule.	**Court Rules §1:2107.** Sliding scale, not to exceed 1/3 of first $500,000; 30% of next $500,000; 25% of third $500,000; and 20% of fourth $500,000. 25% limit for minor or incompetent plaintiff.	None provided.

(continued)

Appendix *(continued)*
State Medical Liability Laws, Section 1

States	Limits on Damage Awards	Statutes of Limitation	Joint and Several Liability	Limits on Attorney Fees	Patient Compensation or Stabilization Fund
New Mexico	**§41.5.6–7.** $600,000 total limit on all damages. Health care providers not liable for any amount over $200,000; any judgment in excess paid from Patient's Compensation Fund.	**§41.5.13.** 3 years from injury.	**§41.3A.1.** Defendants are proportionally liable according to percentage of fault for damages awarded, except when defendant is proven to have intentional malice.	No limitations.	**§41.5.25–29.** Patient's Compensation Fund only expended for purposes provided in authorizing act. Superintendent has authority to purchase insurance for fund and its obligations.
New York	No limitations.	**§214.A.** 2 1/2 years from injury, 1 year from discovery. **§208.** Minors: statute tolled until disability ceases, not to exceed 10 years.	**§16–1601.** Defendants are proportionally liable according to percentage of fault for noneconomic damages awarded, unless found more than 50% at fault. Defendants can be held jointly liable for economic damages.	**Jud. §474-A.** Sliding scale, not to exceed 30% of first $250,000; 25% of second $250,000; 20% of next $500,000; 15% of next $250,000; 10% over $1.25 million.	None provided.
North Carolina	**§1D-25.** $250,000 limit on punitive damages, or 3 times economic damages, whichever is greater.	**§1–15.17.** 3 years from act or 1 year from reasonable discovery, not more than 4 years after injury. Foreign object: 1 year from discovery but not more than 10 years. Minors: until age 19.	**§1B-7.** No separation of joint and several liability.	No limitations.	None provided.

North Dakota	§32.42.02. $500,000 limit on noneconomic damages. §32.03.2.08. Economic damage awards in excess of $250,000 subject to court review.	§28.01.18. 2 years from act or reasonable discovery but not more than 6 years after act unless concealed by fraud. §28.01.25. Minors: 12 years	§32.03.2.02. Defendants are proportionally liable according to percentage of fault for damages awarded, except when defendant is proven to have intentional malice.	No limitations.	§26.1.14.01–09. Reserve fund enacted but not implemented unless majority of doctors in state have difficulty securing malpractice insurance.
Ohio	§2315.18. $250,000 limit on noneconomic damages or three times plaintiff's economic loss, determined by court. Maximum noneconomic damages $350,000 per plaintiff or $500,000 per occurrence. No limit for permanent injury that prevents victim from independently caring for self. §2315.21. Punitive damages limited to twice amount of economic damages or percentage of defendant's net worth. No limit where defendant acted knowingly.	§2305.11–13. 1 year from act, no more than 4 years for discovery. Foreign object: 1 year from discovery. Minors: 4 years from act.	§2307.22. Defendants are proportionally liable for economic damages according to percentage of fault for damages awarded, unless found more than 50% at fault. Severally liable only for noneconomic damages.	§2323.43 (F). No limitations but court must approve if fees exceed limits on damage award.	None provided.

(continued)

Appendix *(continued)*
State Medical Liability Laws, Section 1

States	Limits on Damage Awards	Statutes of Limitation	Joint and Several Liability	Limits on Attorney Fees	Patient Compensation or Stabilization Fund
Oklahoma	**§63–1-1708.1F.** $300,000 limit on noneconomic damages; also specific to obstetric and emergency room care. No limits for negligence or wrongful death. **§23–9.1.** Punitive damages based on misconduct.	**§76–18.** 2 years from reasonable discovery. **§12–96.** Minors under 12: 7 years. Minors over 12: 1 year after attaining majority but in no event less than 2 years from injury.	**§23–15.** Defendants are proportionally liable according to percentage of fault for damages awarded, unless found more than 50% at fault or guilty of willful misconduct or reckless disregard.	**§5–7.** Fee may not exceed 50% of net judgment.	**§76–22.** State Insurance Fund authorized to offer malpractice insurance and/or reinsurance based on claims and loss ratio. State Board for Property and Casualty Rates must approve prior to release.
Oregon	No limitations. Limits declared unconstitutional by State Supreme Court; 2004 ballot measure to institute noneconomic damage limits rejected by voters. **§31.740.** Punitive damages not awarded if physician is found acting in scope of duties without malice.	**§12.110.** 2 years from injury or reasonable discovery, not more than 5 years from act.	**§31.610.** Defendants are proportionally liable according to percentage of fault for damages awarded.	**§31.735.** No more than 20% of punitive damages to attorney, no limitation of percentage of economic damages.	**§752.035.** Professional Liability Fund established to pay sums as provided that members are legally obligated to as result of malpractice. Maintained by Director of Department of Consumer and Business Services.

Pennsylvania	No limitations. Constitutionally prohibited. **§40.1301.812-A.** Punitive damages granted only if defendant found guilty of willful misconduct or reckless disregard.	**§42.5524.** 2 years from injury or discovery. **§42.5533.** Minor: 2 years after age of majority.	**July 2005:** Commonwealth Court declared separation of joint and several liability unconstitutional based on germane standard of legislation enacted in 2002. (Statute **§42.71.7102.**)	No limitations.	**§971.165.** Medical Professional Liability Catastrophe Loss Fund to provide up to $700,000 per occurrence. Participating physicians pay annual surcharge.
Rhode Island	No limitations. **§9.19.34.1.** Collateral source rule requires jury to reduce award for damages by sum equal to difference between total benefits received and total amount paid to secure benefits by plaintiff.	**§9.1.14.1.** 3 years from injury, death or reasonable discovery. **§10.7.2.** Minors and incompetents: 3 years from removal of disability.	No separation of joint and several liability.	No limitations.	None provided.
South Carolina	**Enacted 2005: §15-32-220.** Noneconomic damages limited to $350,000 against single health care provider or facility; limit of $1.05 million for multiple defendants. Limits increased or decreased annually based on Consumer Price Index. No limits on noneconomic or punitive damages for cases of willful negligence or misconduct.	**§15-3-545.** 3 years from act or omission, or 3 years from discovery, not to exceed 6 years. Foreign object: 2 years from discovery. Minors: tolled for up to 7 years while a minor.	**§15-38-10.** No separation of joint and several liability.	No limitations.	**§38-79-420.** Patients' Compensation Fund to pay portion of malpractice claim, settlement or judgment over $200,000 for each incident or over $600,000 in aggregate for one year.

(continued)

Appendix *(continued)*
State Medical Liability Laws, Section 1

States	Limits on Damage Awards	Statutes of Limitation	Joint and Several Liability	Limits on Attorney Fees	Patient Compensation or Stabilization Fund
South Dakota	**§21–3-11.** $500,000 limit on noneconomic damages. No limit on special damages.	**§15–2-14.1.** 2 years from act or omission.	**§15–8-15.1.** Defendants are proportionally liable according to percentage of fault; defendants found less than 50% liable not jointly liable for more than twice percentage of fault allocated.	No limitations.	None provided.
Tennessee	No limitations.	**§29.26.116.** 1 year from injury or discovery, no more than 3 years from act unless foreign object.	Joint and several liability provisions in statute, declared unconstitutional by State Supreme Court.	**§29.26.120.** Fees limited to 1/3 of award to plaintiff.	None provided.
Texas	**Civil Practice §74.301.** $250,000 limit per claimant for noneconomic damages. $500,000 limit per claimant for noneconomic damages in judgments against health care institutions.	**Civil Practice §74.251.** 2 years from occurrence, no more than 10 years. Minors under 12: until age 14.	**Civil Practice §33.013.** Defendants are proportionally liable according to percentage of fault for damages awarded, unless found more than 50% at fault.	No limitations.	None provided.
Utah	**§78.14.7.1.** $400,000 limit on noneconomic damages for actions arising after July 1, 2002. Adjusted annually by Administrative Office of Courts.	**§78.14.4.** 2 years from discovery but not more than 4 years from act; foreign object or fraud: 1 year from discovery, applies to all persons regardless of minority or disability.	**§78.27.40.** Defendants are proportionally liable according to percentage of fault for damages awarded.	**§78.14.7.5.** Contingency fee not to exceed 1/3 of award.	None provided.

State					
Vermont	No limitations.	**§12.521.** 3 years from incident or 2 years from discovery, whichever is later. No later than 7 years. Fraud: no statute of limitations. Foreign object: 2 years from discovery.	No separation of joint and several liability.	No limitations.	None provided.
Virginia	**§8.01–581.15.** $1.5 million limit on recovery damages. Increased by $50,000 each year from 2001 to 2006. Increased by $75,000 each year in 2007 and 2008.	**§8.01–243.** 2 years from occurrence, no more than 10 years unless under disability. Foreign object: 1 year from discovery.	No separation of joint and several liability.	No limitations.	**§38.2–5000–5020.** Birth-Related Neurological Injury Compensation Fund to provide compensation for infant sustaining brain damage during birth delivery. Physicians pay annual assessment.
Washington	**§4.56.250.** No specific limits on damage awards. Judgment for noneconomic damages cannot exceed formulation of average annual wage and life expectancy of injured.	**§4.16.350.** 3 years from injury or 1 year from discovery, whichever is later. No more than 8 years after act.	**§4.22.070.** Defendants are proportionally liable according to percentage of fault for damages awarded, unless found to be deliberately acting in concert with others.	**§7.70.070.** Court to determine reasonableness of each party's attorney fees.	None provided.

(continued)

Appendix *(continued)*
State Medical Liability Laws, Section 1

States	Limits on Damage Awards	Statutes of Limitation	Joint and Several Liability	Limits on Attorney Fees	Patient Compensation or Stabilization Fund
West Virginia	§55.7B.8. $250,000 limit for noneconomic damages. $500,000 limit for compensatory damages, limit goes up beginning in 2004 according to inflation index. Physicians must carry at least $1 million malpractice insurance to qualify for limits.	§55.7B.4. 2 years from injury or reasonable discovery, no longer than 10 years after injury. Minors under 10: 2 years from injury or age 12, whichever is longer.	§55.7B.9. Defendants are proportionally liable according to percentage of fault for damages awarded.	No limitations.	§29.12B.1–14. Medical Liability Fund to assist in making malpractice insurance more readily available to specific health care providers.
Wisconsin	**July 2005:** State Supreme Court declared noneconomic damages in medical injury cases unconstitutional, *Ferndon v. Wisconsin.* (Statute §893.55(4)(d).)	§893.55. 3 years from injury or 1 year from discovery, not more than 5 years from act. Foreign object: 1 year from discovery or 3 years from act, whichever is later. Minors: by age 10 or standard provision, whichever is later.	§895.045.(2). Defendants are proportionally liable according to percentage of fault for damages awarded, unless found to be deliberately acting in concert with others or found more than 50% at fault.	§655.013. Sliding scale, not to exceed 1/3 of first $1 million, or 25% of first $1 million recovered if liability is stipulated within time limits, 20% of any amount exceeding $1 million.	§655.27. Injured Patients and Families Compensation Fund pays amounts in excess of statutorily prescribed future damages awards. Health care providers required to pay into fund annually.
Wyoming	§97.3.027. Limits prohibited. 2004 ballot measure to adopt constitutional amendment allowing noneconomic damage limits rejected by voters.	§1.3.107. 2 years from injury or reasonable discovery. Minors: until age 18 or within 2 years, whichever is later. Legal disability: 1 year from removal.	§1.1.109. Defendants are proportionally liable according to percentage of fault for damages awarded.	Ct. Rules, R. 5. Recovery $1 million or less: 1/3 if claim settled prior to 60 days after filing; 40% if settled after 60 days or judgment; 30% over $1 million.	§26.33.105. Medical Liability Compensation Fund to provide malpractice insurance coverage in event of cause of action. Participating physicians pay surcharge.

Source: National Conference of State Legislators, www.ncsl.org

State Medical Liability Laws, Section 2

States	Doctor Apologies	Pretrial Alternative Dispute Resolution	Affidavits or Certificates of Merit	Expert Witness Standards	Medical or Peer Review Panels for Malpractice
Alabama	No provision.	**§6.5.485.** Voluntary arbitration, agreed to in writing.	**§6.5.551.** Medical liability complaint filing to include detailed specification and factual description of act or omission alleged; failure to include is grounds for dismissal.	**§6.5.548.** Expert witness must be licensed in same specialty as defendant and must have practiced within previous year.	**§34.24.56–60.** Board of Medical Examiners to receive annual reports from physicians of any final judgment or settlement rendered resulting from claim or action for damages. Board to review record of and determine disciplinary action against any licensee who has 2 or more judgments or settlements over $100,000 within 3 years preceding or 4 or more final judgments or settlements within 3-year period.
Alaska	No provision.	**§09.55.535.** Voluntary arbitration, cannot be a prerequisite to receiving care or treatment. **§09.55.536.** Expert advisory panel used after lawsuit is filed. Must issue report within 30 days of selection on the facts of the case. Report is admissible evidence in trial.	No provision.	**§09.20.185.** Expert witness must be trained and licensed in defendant's discipline and certified by a board recognized by state.	**§08.64.130.** State Medical Board to maintain records concerning outcome of malpractice actions and claims, subject to periodic review. **§08.64.326.** Grounds for disciplinary sanctions include intentional or negligent care even if the patient was not injured or repeated negligent conduct.

(continued)

Appendix *(continued)*
State Medical Liability Laws, Section 2

States	Doctor Apologies	Pretrial Alternative Dispute Resolution	Affidavits or Certificates of Merit	Expert Witness Standards	Medical or Peer Review Panels for Malpractice
Arizona	**Enacted 2005:** **§12–2605.** Any statement or conduct expressing apology, responsibility or sympathy made by health care provider to patient or patient's relative relating to injury is inadmissible as evidence of admission of liability or against interest.	**§12–583.** Good cause hearing determines if basis exists to go to trial.	**§12–2603.** Claimant or nonparty at fault must certify in written statement if expert opinion will be necessary to prove standard of care or liability in claim. If expert testimony is required, preliminary expert opinion affidavit must be filed.	**Enacted 2005:** **§12–2604.** Expert witness must be medical care provider of same type of specialty as defendant, must be practicing or teaching medicine the year preceding the malpractice action.	**§32–1451.** Board of Medical Examiners to investigate any evidence indicating a doctor may be medically incompetent or guilty of unprofessional conduct in the practice of medicine; done on written request of complainant. Definitions of grounds for revoking medical license.
Arkansas	No provision.	**§16–108–102.** Voluntary arbitration and dispute resolution. **§16–7-101.** Permits courts to set mediation and/or arbitration to encourage their use to promote settlement of cases.	No provision.	**§16–114–206.** Expert witness must be medical care provider of same type of specialty as defendant.	**§17–80–106.** Department of Health inspectors with authorization from applicable licensing board to investigate alleged misconduct by medical licensees.
California	No provision.	**Civil Procedure §1295.** Voluntary arbitration contract. Entering contract removes option for trial and is binding.	No provision.	**Business and Professions §2220.08.** Expert witnesses to have pertinent education and training to evaluate specifics to claim and case.	**Business and Professions §2220.** Medical Board of California to investigate and prosecute charges of negligence and/or misconduct. Complaints to be evaluated by panel prior to referral to courts. Only board with authority to extend disciplinary action.

Colorado	§13–25–135. Statements or conduct by health care provider expressing apology, sympathy or fault to victim or relative of victim relating to suffering or injury inadmissible as evidence of admission of liability or against interest.	§13–22–311. Court may refer case to mediation. §13–22–201–223. Voluntary arbitration.	No provision.	§13–64–401. Expert witness must be licensed physician and substantially familiar with standard of care on date of injury.	§12–36.5–104. Professional review panels to investigate qualifications of physician, quality of patient care, or professional conduct. Findings and recommendations forwarded to Board of Medical Examiners to take action, held confidential.
Connecticut	**Enacted 2005: §52–195–8.** Any statements or conduct expressing apology, sympathy or fault made by health care provider to victim or relative of victim relating to pain or injury inadmissible as evidence of admission of liability or against interest.	§38a-32 and 33. Medical Screening Panel selected when all parties agree. Proceedings confidential.	**Enacted 2005: §52–190a-2.** Claimant to obtain written and signed opinion of similar health care provider that evidence shows medical negligence, must include detailed basis for the formation of such opinion.	§52–184c. Expert witness must be similar health care provider or have sufficient training and experience in related field of medicine.	§20–8. Medical Examining Board to create hearing panels to hear evidence and make recommendations to Board. **Enacted 2005: §20–13b-20.** Commissioner of Public Health to establish guidelines for screening and investigating medical liability complaints. **Enacted 2005: §38a-25–17.** Department of Public Health and Medical Examining Board to establish guidelines for use in the disciplinary process.

(continued)

Appendix *(continued)*
State Medical Liability Laws, Section 2

States	Doctor Apologies	Pretrial Alternative Dispute Resolution	Affidavits or Certificates of Merit	Expert Witness Standards	Medical or Peer Review Panels for Malpractice
Delaware	No provision.	**§18.6803–6812.** Medical negligence review panel part of court review; panel's findings admissible as evidence at trial.	**§18.6853.** All health care negligence lawsuits filed must be accompanied by affidavit of merit signed by expert witness stating reasonable grounds to be negligence has been committed by defendant.	**§18.6853–6854.** Expert witness required to establish applicable standard of care unless panel found negligence to have caused injury; expert's knowledge of similar field to testify.	**Enacted 2005:** **§24.1730–1739.** Board to receive written reports of misconduct or incompetence, investigate, conduct hearing. All applicable medical records admitted to Board. Board documents subject to Freedom of Information Act. Liability insurance carriers to report malpractice judgments or settlements.
Florida	**§90.4026.** Statements or gestures expressing sympathy relating to the pain or death of person involved in an accident to person or family member inadmissible as evidence in civil action; statement of fault admissible. In general evidence rules, not solely for medical liability actions.	**§766.106–108.** Pre-suit investigation and informal discovery conducted by defendant's insurer prior to submission to courts. Court may require submission of claim to arbitration, non-binding, limits on what is admissible at trial. Mandatory mediation and mandatory settlement conference held prior to trial if no binding arbitration agreed to. **§766.207.** Guidelines for binding voluntary arbitration.	**§766.203.** Pre-suit investigation conducted by claimant must include verified written medical expert opinion to corroborate grounds to support claim of medical negligence.	**§766.102.** Expert testimony by licensed physician in same practice or practicing for 3 years before claim filed.	**Adopted 2004: Florida Constitution, Article X, Section 25.** Patient's Right to Know includes patient access to records of health care facility or provider relating to adverse medical incidents. **Enacted 2005: §456.50.** Repeated medical malpractice defined as 3 or more findings of negligence; party may not receive or renew medical license in state.

Georgia	Enacted 2005: §24-3-37.1. In any medical malpractice civil action, any statements or conduct expressing apology, sympathy, mistake or error made by a health care provider to the patient or relative or representative of the patient is inadmissible as evidence of admission of liability or against interest.	§9-9-61, 62, 63. Voluntary arbitration subject to court review; binding if prior agreement to make it so.	Enacted 2005: §9-11-9.1. Complaint must contain affidavit of expert stating that facts justify a claim of negligence; must include at least one specific negligent act or omission to justify claim.	Enacted 2005: §24-9-67.1. Experts in medical liability cases must have professional knowledge and experience in same medical specialty as opinion is to be given; practicing or teaching in same specialty for at least 3 of previous 5 years; member of same profession or field of medicine as defendant.	Enacted 2005: §43-34-37. Medical Board to investigate health care provider's fitness to practice medicine if Board receives notice of judgment or settlement over $100,000; if physician has received 2 or more judgments or settlements. Assessment conducted of fitness to practice if disciplinary action has been taken 3 times in last 10 years for malpractice; Board may take any action deemed necessary including revoking or limiting medical license.
Hawaii	No provision.	§601.20. Mandatory nonbonding arbitration for all cases involving $150,000 or less. §671.11-20. Mandatory submission to medical claim conciliation panel; results not admissible at trial.	No provision.	No provisions.	§663-1.7. Peer review committee of medical organization or facility to report every adverse decision made to Department of Commerce and Consumer Affairs. Quality assurance committee to report patient care not meeting standards of care and resulting in disciplinary action.

(continued)

Appendix *(continued)*
State Medical Liability Laws, Section 2

States	Doctor Apologies	Pretrial Alternative Dispute Resolution	Affidavits or Certificates of Merit	Expert Witness Standards	Medical or Peer Review Panels for Malpractice
Idaho	No provision.	§6.1001–1011. Mandatory submission of claim to pre-trial hearing panel; results non-binding and not admissible at trial.	No provision.	§6.1013. Expert witness must have professional expertise, practical knowledge of community standards, be in a similarly trained field as defendant.	§54–1806A. Committee on Professional Discipline part of Board of Medicine; investigate misconduct or unprofessional behavior, make disciplinary recommendations to Board. Proceedings open to public.
Illinois	Enacted 2005: §735 5/8–1901. Any expression of apology or explanation provided by health care provider to patient, family or legal representative about inadequate or unanticipated outcome provided within 72 hours of provider's knowledge of potential cause not be admissible as evidence in any action of any kind.	§735 5/2-1001A. Arbitration may be court ordered for cases totaling less than $50,000.	§735 5/2-622. In medical liability actions, plaintiff must file affidavit of merit declaring consultation with health care professional on merits on claim. Amended 2005: Medical professional certifying affidavit must meet same standards as expert witnesses.	Enacted 2005: §735 5/8-2501. Expert witness licensed and certified in same medical specialty as defendant, same class of license, majority of professional time in practice or teaching of medicine within previous 5 years.	§225 60/5–7. Internal peer review encouraged for health care providers and facilities. Complaint Committee of state Medical Disciplinary Board to conduct investigations. Amended 2005: Increased disciplinary fines, extended statute of limitation for complaint, Board restructured.

Indiana	No provision.	§34–18–10. Claim must be filed with medical review panel prior to filing lawsuit unless all parties agree to dispense with review panel. Panel provides expert opinion admissible at trial and panelists may testify in trial.	No provision.	§34–18–10–22. Medical Review Panel findings and testimony qualify as expert testimony.	§25–22.5–6–4. Licensing board may sue physician accused of malpractice and going through disciplinary hearings to prevent continued practice of medicine considered harmful to public until decision has been rendered.
Iowa	No provision.	§679A.1. Written arbitration agreement not mandatory, but binding once entered into.	No provision.	§147.139. Qualifications of expert must relate directly to medical problem or type of treatment at issue.	§147.135. Peer review committees to investigate relating to discipline or professional competence of physicians. Records of committee confidential, not admissible as evidence in court or any proceeding but may be released to licensing body.
Kansas	No provision.	§65.4901, §60.3502. Voluntary submission to medical screening panel upon request of party; panelists must include medical professional of same specialty as defendant. Report is admissible in court and panelists may testify.	No provision.	§60.3412. 50% of the expert's professional time over preceding 2 years must have been devoted to clinical practice.	§65.4915. Peer review committees to determine that services rendered are professional and in compliance with standard of care, evaluate qualifications, competence, performance of health care providers. Proceedings and records not admissible in court, held confidential unless requested by state licensing or disciplinary board.

(continued)

Appendix *(continued)*
State Medical Liability Laws, Section 2

States	Doctor Apologies	Pretrial Alternative Dispute Resolution	Affidavits or Certificates of Merit	Expert Witness Standards	Medical or Peer Review Panels for Malpractice
Kentucky	No provision.	**§417.050.** Written arbitration agreements voluntary, once entered are considered enforceable and irrevocable. **§454.011.** Courts encouraged to make referrals to mediation prior to trials.	No provision.	No provisions.	**§311.591.** Inquiry panel to receive grievances, conduct inquiry. If evidence exists of violation of medical care, administrative hearing conducted. Proceedings open to public; information confidential but may be released to licensing boards.
Louisiana	**Enacted 2005: RS §13:3715.5.** Any communication or conduct by health care provider expressing apology or regret, made to patient or patient's relative inadmissible as admission of liability or against interest. Statement of fault is admissible.	**RS §9.4231.** Voluntary arbitration, binding once entered. **RS §40:1299.47.** Review panel established for all claims not submitted to arbitration. Reports considered expert opinion and admissible as evidence in trial. Panelists can be called as witnesses.	No provision.	**RS §9.2794.** Expert witness must be licensed physician trained in specialty at question, practicing when claim arose, possess knowledge of accepted standards of care and treatment.	**RS §13:3715.3.** Peer review records confidential and not admissible as evidence in court, exceptions specified.

State					
Maine	Enacted 2005: §24.2908. Any statement or conduct by health care practitioner expressing apology, regret or fault made to patient or relative inadmissible as admission of liability or against interest.	§24.2851–59. Mandatory pre-litigation screening and mediation panel, findings confidential except under certain provisions. **Amended** 2005: panel to designate division of fault among multiple defendants.	No provision.	No provisions.	§24.2501 - 2511. Professional Competence Committees enact and enforce standards of professional qualification, competence, conduct or performance.
Maryland	§10–920. Any expression by health care provider expressing apology or regret inadmissible as admission of liability or against interest. Statement of liability or fault is admissible.	§3–2A–06-C. Mandatory dispute resolution or mediation within 30 days of filing defendant's answer or defendant's certificate of qualified expert, whichever is later. No mandatory mediation if all parties file agreement not to participate.	§3–2A–04. A certificate of a qualified expert must be submitted by the plaintiff; certificate of expert must be also filed by defendant to dispute claim.	§3–2A–02. Expert witness must have clinical experience, provided consultation relating to clinical practice, or taught in defendant's specialty or a related field within previous five years. Can't spend more than 20% of time testifying in personal injury cases.	§14–201. State Board of Physicians established. §4–401. Malpractice claims must be reported to the State Board of Physicians.
Massachusetts	§233.23D. Statements or gestures expressing sympathy relating to pain or death of person involved in accident made to person or family inadmissible as evidence of admission of liability. Not exclusive to medical profession.	§231.60B. Mandatory submission of claims to medical malpractice court tribunal, decision admissible at trial.	No provision.	No provisions.	Board of Registration in Medicine investigates complaints about medical negligence or unprofessional conduct. Division of Administrative Law Appeals conducts hearings, Board imposes disciplinary sanctions.

(continued)

Appendix *(continued)*
State Medical Liability Laws, Section 2

States	Doctor Apologies	Pretrial Alternative Dispute Resolution	Affidavits or Certificates of Merit	Expert Witness Standards	Medical or Peer Review Panels for Malpractice
Michigan	No provision.	§600.4903–4919. Mandatory review by mediation panel, findings not admissible at trial. §600.2912g. Voluntary arbitration binding if total damages claimed less than $75,000.	§600.4911. Plaintiff and defendant must each submit brief to mediation on party's factual or legal position within action.	§600.2169. Expert must be licensed and board certified health professional in practice of similar specialty, in active practice or education during year preceding action.	§338.22. Director of board of department to investigate any complaints against or alleged violations by any licensee; inform board of investigations; final determination of complaint decided by roll call vote of board.
Minnesota	No provision.	§484.76 Alternative dispute resolution program.	§145.682. Plaintiff must consult with expert prior to trial to determine validity of claims asserted.	§145.682. Claimant must file affidavit stating that expert has been consulted.	§214.104. Health-related licensing board to make determinations about disciplinary action because of substantiated maltreatment.
Mississippi	No provision.	§11.15.1. Voluntary arbitration must be agreed to in writing.	§11.1.58. Certificate of consultation required in medical malpractice actions declaring that plaintiff's attorney has consulted with at least one expert as to standard of care and basis for commencement of action.	§11.1.61. Expert witness must be licensed physician.	§73.25.83–95. State Board of Medical Licensure granted authority to investigate professional competence and conduct.

Missouri	**Enacted 2005: §538.229.** Statements or gestures expressing sympathy by health care provider relating to pain or suffering made to person or family inadmissible as admission of liability. Statement of fault admissible.	No provisions.	**§538.225.** Plaintiff required to file affidavit with court with written opinion by health care provider stating defendant failed to meet standard of care. **Amended 2005:** Time frame to submit statement, information to be included.	No provisions.	**§537.035.** Peer review committees function through authority of health care licensing board; proceedings and findings are privileged and not admissible into evidence in judicial malpractice action.
Montana	**Enacted 2005: §26.1.1.** Any statement or conduct expressing apology or sympathy relating to pain or death of a person made to person, family or friend, not admissible for any purpose in medical malpractice action.	**§27.6.101–704.** All malpractice claims submitted to Medical Legal Panel for review unless voluntary arbitration agreed to. Findings not admissible into court evidence.	No provision.	**Enacted 2005: §27.6.103.** Expert witness must be licensed as health care provider, treats diagnosis or provides treatment at question in malpractice claim within previous 5 years; or teaches within previous 5 years; same specialty as defendant.	**Enacted 2005: §37.4.201.** Medical board to establish a screening panel for disciplinary matters and to oversee any rehabilitation program. **§27.6.704.** Decision and basis of peer review not admissible as evidence in court; panel members not allowed to testify.
Nebraska	No provision.	**§44.2840–2847.** Mandatory review of malpractice claims by medical review panel. Proceedings of panel confidential, but panelists may testify as expert witnesses at trial.	No provision.	No provisions.	**§71.7901–7903.** Peer review committees to maintain high standard of medical care; all communications remain confidential.

(continued)

Appendix *(continued)*
State Medical Liability Laws, Section 2

States	Doctor Apologies	Pretrial Alternative Dispute Resolution	Affidavits or Certificates of Merit	Expert Witness Standards	Medical or Peer Review Panels for Malpractice
Nevada	No provisions.	§41A.081. All parties, insurers and attorneys required to participate in settlement conference before district judge other than trial judge.	§41A.071. Affidavit must be filed by medical expert practicing in area similar to defendant; failure to submit results in dismissal of claim.	No provisions.	§630.130. Medical Board hears disciplinary actions. **Enacted 2005: §630.2–3.** Physicians applying for medical license in the state must undergo a criminal background check by the FBI.
New Hampshire	**Enacted 2005: §507-E:4.** Any statement or action expressing sympathy or commiseration relating to pain or death of individual made to individual or family is inadmissible as admission of liability. Does not apply to statement of fault or negligence.	**Enacted 2005: §519-B:1–12.** Screening panels for medical injury claims to identify meritorious claims and encourage early resolution. Hearings only made public if all parties agree. Proceedings and records inadmissible in court action, panelists may not testify.	No provision.	§507-C:3. Expert witness must be competent and duly qualified to render or supervise equivalent care to defendant's specialty.	§329:17. Medical board to investigate any health care licensee with 3 claims, complaints or actions within 5 years. Hearings are public, decisions not made public until released to parties in complaint.
New Jersey	No provision.	§2A:23A-20. Mandatory arbitration of medical claims under $20,000; voluntary if over $20,000. §2A:53A-39. Presiding judge may refer malpractice action to complementary dispute resolution mechanism.	No provision.	§2A:53A-41. Expert witness must be licensed and practicing physician in same specialty as defendant, authorized to administer treatment in question.	**Enacted 2005: §C.45:1–29.** All health care professionals must undergo criminal background check at FBI to acquire or renew medical license in state.

New Mexico	No provision.	No provision.	§41.5.14–20. Mandatory submission of malpractice claims to hearing panel; panel report not admissible as court evidence.	$41–5–23. Expert witness must be physician qualified in field of medicine involved in complaint.	$41–5–14. Medical Review Commission reviews all malpractice claims.
New York	No provision.	§3045. When liability is conceded, either party may call for arbitration of damages amount.	§3012. Certificate of consultation of expert submitted within 90 days of filing complaint.	No provisions.	§230. Board for Professional Medical Conduct to investigate complaints and hold disciplinary proceedings; held confidential; panelist may not testify in court.
North Carolina	§8C-4.413. Statements by health care provider to apologize for treatment not admissible to prove negligence or culpable conduct.	§7A-38.1. Mandatory pre-trial, mediated settlement conference for all civil actions filed in Superior Court.	No provision.	§90–21.12. Expert witness must testify as to standard of care used in community. Must be licensed physician.	§90–21.22. Medical Board, state and local Medical Societies, and Academy of Physician Assistants may coordinate peer review and quality assurance activities. Includes investigation, review, and evaluation of complaints, litigation and other information. Proceedings confidential.
North Dakota	No provision.	§32.42.03. Attorneys must disclose alternative dispute resolutions; good faith effort to resolve dispute required.	**Enacted 2005:** §28–01–46. Affidavit of expert opinion required to maintain medical malpractice action, or complaint dismissed.	No provisions.	§43–17–07.1. Required self-reporting by applicant or licensee of any information the board determines may indicate possible deficiencies in practice, performance, fitness, or qualifications.

(continued)

Appendix *(continued)*
State Medical Liability Laws, Section 2

States	Doctor Apologies	Pretrial Alternative Dispute Resolution	Affidavits or Certificates of Merit	Expert Witness Standards	Medical or Peer Review Panels for Malpractice
Ohio	§2317.43. Any statements or conduct expressing apology or sympathy made by health care provider to alleged victim or relative relating to injury or death inadmissible as admission of liability or against interest.	§2711.01. Voluntary arbitration, decision not admissible as court evidence.	No provision.	§2743.43. Expert testimony limited to licensed physician or surgeon who devotes 3/4 time to active clinical practice or teaching.	§4731.22. Medical board by vote may take disciplinary action for failure to maintain standard of care, negligence.
Oklahoma	§63–1-1708.1H. Expression of apology or sympathy by health care provider not admissible as admission of liability.	No provisions.	§63–1-1708.1E. Affidavit to be submitted by plaintiff stating consultation with qualified expert; includes written opinion from expert that act or omission constituted professional negligence and claim is meritorious.	§63–1-1708.1I. Expert witness must be licensed to practice medicine or have other substantial training and experience in area of health care relevant to claim; actively practicing or retired from services relevant to claim.	§59–509.1. State Board of Medical Licensure and Supervision may impose disciplinary actions. §76–17. Medical malpractice claims against individual health practitioner or facility required to be reported to licensing board.
Oregon	§677.082. Any expression of regret or apology made by person licensed by Board of Medical Examiners does not constitute admission of liability in civil action.	§31.250. All parties and attorneys to participate in some form of dispute resolution unless case is settled or all parties voluntarily waive in writing.	No provision.	No provisions.	§676.175. Health professions regulatory board investigates all complaints made against health professionals and health care institutions.

State				
Pennsylvania	No provision.	**§40.1301.825-A.** Mandatory conciliation hearing, which may be a settlement conference or mediation as the parties prefer.	No provision.	**§40.1301.821-A.** Attorney's signature on complaint certifies that attorney has consulted expert who will attest to position.	**§49.16.51–54.** Hearing examiners and medical consultants review and investigate complaints of medical negligence and issue recommendations to Board.
Rhode Island	No provision.	**§10.3.1.** Arbitration Act requires request for arbitration be in writing. Voluntary.	No provision.	**§9.19.41.** Expert witness qualifications are training/education levels. **§9.19.30.** Statements in published material, if found by court to be relevant are admissible as evidence.	**§5–37–1.3.** Board of medical licensure and discipline investigates all complaints and charges of unprofessional conduct, holds hearings to determine if charges are substantiated.
South Carolina	No provision.	**Enacted 2005: 15–79–120, 125.** All medical malpractice complaints required to submit to mediation prior to filing for trial. Parties may also agree to participate in binding arbitration.	**Enacted 2005: §15–36–100 (C).** Affidavit must be filed from expert witness and specify at least one negligent act or omission claimed factual basis for claim based on available evidence.	**Enacted 2005: §15–36–100 (A).** Expert witness must be licensed and board certified in area of practice in question; been teaching area of practice for at least half of professional time or regularly practicing, at least 3 of previous 5 years.	**§40–47–200.** State Medical Board can suspend or revoke licenses for physician misconduct. **Amended 2005:** Notification requirements of suspension or revocation of medical license to any place individual has license to practice medicine.

(continued)

Appendix *(continued)*
State Medical Liability Laws, Section 2

States	Doctor Apologies	Pretrial Alternative Dispute Resolution	Affidavits or Certificates of Merit	Expert Witness Standards	Medical or Peer Review Panels for Malpractice
South Dakota	**Enacted 2005: HB 1148.** No apology, offer of corrective treatment, or gratuitous act of assistance made by health care provider is admissible to prove negligence. Statement constituting admission against interest is admissible.	**§21–25–B.1.** Voluntary arbitration between hospitals or physicians and patients.	No provision.	No provisions.	**§36–4–43.** Peer review done internally within medical organization, includes review of qualifications, competency, conduct, or performance of any health professional.
Tennessee	No provision.	**§29.5.101.** Voluntary arbitration.	No provision.	**§29.26.115.** Expert witness must be licensed in state or contiguous state and practice in corresponding specialty for one year preceding date of injury.	**§63.6.219.** Peer review to evaluate and review professional conduct and competence to practice medicine; documents and testimony furnished to peer review committee are held confidential.
Texas	No provision.	**Civil Practice §74.451.** Voluntary arbitration.	**Civil Practice §74.351.** Expert reports to be submitted to defendant and defendant's attorney within 120 days of filing claim.	**Civil Practice §74.401.** Expert witness must be licensed physician practicing medicine and/or with knowledge of accepted standards of practice.	**Occupations §164.001– 061.** Medical review panel for disciplinary action; hearings conducted; authority to suspend or revoke medical license; proceedings and documents not subject to discovery or evidence in any associated trial.

Utah	No provision.	§78.14.12–17. Voluntary pre-litigation panel may be requested. Upon written agreement by all parties, proceedings may be considered a binding arbitration hearing.	No provision.	No provisions.	§58.67.401–503. Physicians Licensing Board has authority to conduct disciplinary proceedings, suspend or revoke medical license or assess other penalties.
Vermont	No provision.	§12.7002. Voluntary arbitration, panel consists of judicial referee selected by court administrator, layman and member of same profession as defendant.	No provision.	No provisions.	§26.1441-1443. Peer review committees to evaluate and improve quality of health care rendered, or determine that services rendered were in compliance with applicable standard of care. Proceedings and records not admissible in trial but may be used for disciplinary action.
Virginia	**Enacted 2005: §8.01–581.20:1.** Any statement, writing or conduct made by health care provider to patient or relative or representative of patient inadmissible as evidence of admission of liability or against interest. Statement of fault admissible.	§8.01–581.2-8. Review by pre-trial panel by request of either party. Findings admissible in court but not considered conclusive. §8.01–581.12. Voluntary arbitration, decision binding.	**Enacted 2005: §8.01–20.1 AND §16.1–83.1.** Certification of expert witness opinion required when complaint filed in medical malpractice action. Not required when expert testimony unnecessary due to alleged act of negligence.	§8.01–581.20. Expert witness must be licensed and have active clinical practice in defendant's field or related specialty.	**Enacted 2005: §54.1–2912.3.** Board of Medicine to assess competency of physicians with three medical liability payments within ten-year period. Annual reports from Board to Legislature of number of assessments conducted.

(continued)

Appendix *(continued)*

State Medical Liability Laws, Section 2

States	Doctor Apologies	Pretrial Alternative Dispute Resolution	Affidavits or Certificates of Merit	Expert Witness Standards	Medical or Peer Review Panels for Malpractice
Washington	No provision.	**§7.70.100.** Mandatory pre-trial mediation. Panel members shall have expertise related specialty or action in question, and be a member of state bar association for minimum of 5 years or is a retired judge.	No provision.	No provisions.	**§18.130.** Uniform Disciplinary Act authorizes licensing board to investigate complaints of unprofessional conduct, conduct adjudicative proceedings; issue penalties. **§18.71.350.** Reports to Commission of 3 or more awards or settlements during 5-year time period.
West Virginia	**Enacted 2005: §55.7.11.** Any statement or conduct of healthcare provider expressing apology or condolence to patient, or relative or representative of patient relating to pain, injury or death of patient is inadmissible as evidence of admission of liability or against interest.	**§55.10.1.** Voluntary arbitration, agreement entered in court record. **§55.7B.6 (f).** Health care provider may demand pre-litigation mediation with claimant.	**§55.7B.6.** Plaintiff must file notice of lawsuit with certificate of merit stating expert's familiarity with standards, qualifications, opinion of breach of standard of care.	**§55.7B.7.** Expert witness must be currently trained and licensed to practice in same or similar specialty as defendant, must devote at least 60% of professional time to clinical practice or teaching at accredited university.	**§30.3.4.** Medical peer review committees within professional medical societies or health care facilities; evaluate medical and health care services.

(continued)

Wisconsin	No provision.	§655.42-4. Voluntary. Mediation request must be made prior to court action and tolls statute of limitations until 30 days after the last day of mediation period.	No provision.	No provisions.	§655.275. Injured Patients and Families Compensation Fund Peer Review Council reviews claims and issues recommendations.
Wyoming	§1.1.130. Any statement or conduct expressing apology or sympathy made by health care provider to alleged victim, or relative or representative of alleged victim relating to pain, injury or death is inadmissible as evidence of admission of liability or against interest.	**Enacted 2005:** §9.2.1517. Medical Review Panel to review all malpractice claims and render decision prior to claim being submitted to court.	No provision.	No provisions.	§33-26-202. State medical board empowered to investigate misconduct, hold disciplinary proceedings, restrict or suspend or revoke medical licenses. Annual reviews for any health care provider with restricted or conditional medical license.

Source: www.ncsl.org

Index

Kant Patel (Ph.D., University of Houston, 1976) is professor of political science at Missouri State University. He teaches health policy, policy analysis, and intergovernmental relations. He has published articles in journals such as *Evaluation and Health Profession*, *Health Policy and Education*, *Political Methodology*, *Journal of Political Science*, *International Journal of Policy Analysis and Information Systems*, and *Journal of Health and Social Policy*, among others. He is co-author (with Mark E. Rushefsky) of *Politics, Power, and Policy Making: The Case of Health Care Reform in the 1900s* (M.E. Sharpe, 1998); *Health Care Policy in an Age of New Technologies* (M.E. Sharpe, 2002); and *The Politics of Public Health in the United States* (M.E. Sharpe, 2005).

Mark E. Rushefsky (Ph.D., State University of New York at Binghamton, 1977) is professor of political science at Missouri State University. He teaches and writes on public policy and public administration. He is the author of *Making Cancer Policy* (SUNY Press, 1986); *Public Policy in the United States: At the Dawn of the Twenty-First Century*, 3rd ed. (M.E. Sharpe, 2002); as well as articles and chapters on health care and the environment. He is co-author (with Kant Patel) of *Politics, Power, and Policy Making: The Case of Health Care Reform in the 1990s* (M.E. Sharpe, 1998); *Health Care Policy in an Age of New Technologies* (M.E. Sharpe, 2002); and *The Politics of Public Health in the United States* (M.E. Sharpe, 2005).